Praise for *Print the Legend*

"For those of us who consider John Ford to be the greatest of all American directors, *Print the Legend* is cause for celebration—a thorough, honest, empathetic biography that examines both the man and his towering achievements."

—Leonard Maltin

"Eyman has emerged as one of the most distinguished and reliable of popular film historians. *Print the Legend* displays his broad knowledge, his tact, his willingness to credit other writers, his capacity to avoid sensationalism but not to flinch from difficult truths."

—Robert Sklar, *Washington Post Book World*

"The indispensable *Print the Legend* gives us a vivid, comprehensive portrait of John Ford, an infuriating but admirable man completely devoted to making motion pictures."

—Kevin Brownlow

"Scott Eyman, Ford's latest and best biographer, has his work cut out sorting through the blarney Ford left strewn in his wake. But what a wake . . . Everything about this model biography is a pleasure."

—Malcolm Jones, *Newsweek*

"I thought I knew everything there was to know about the life of the great John Ford. *Print the Legend* proved me wrong. Reading it is a very rewarding experience."

—Harry Carey, Jr.

"*Print the Legend* makes all previous books on Ford, and most books on any other filmmaker, seem undernourished. Eyman . . . has given us a 600-plus-page book without an ounce of fat."

—Allen Barra, *Los Angeles Times Book Review*

"One of the greatest strengths of this excellent book is that Eyman finally unravels the skeins of legend to reveal the truth about Ford's background. . . . As definitive a biography as we are likely to get of one of America's greatest filmmakers."

—*Kirkus Reviews*

"A quietly magnificent biography of an American original who shaped our perception of movies as a serious art . . . Eyman's study serves up a big, gorgeous chunk of Hollywood history, chock-full of priceless anecdotes."

—*Publishers Weekly* (starred review)

ALSO BY SCOTT EYMAN

John Wayne: The Life and Legend

Empire of Dreams: The Epic Life of Cecil B. DeMille

Lion of Hollywood: The Life and Legend of Louis B. Mayer

John Ford: The Complete Films, 1894–1973 [ed.]

Ernst Lubitsch: Laughter in Paradise

The Speed of Sound: Hollywood and the Talkie Revolution, 1926–1930

Mary Pickford: America's Sweetheart

Five American Cinematographers

WITH LOUIS GIANNETTI

Flashback: A Brief History of Film

WITH ROBERT WAGNER

You Must Remember This: Life and Style in Hollywood's Golden Age

Pieces of My Heart: A Life

PRINT THE LEGEND

THE LIFE AND TIMES OF JOHN FORD

Scott Eyman

Simon & Schuster Paperbacks

New York   London   Toronto   Sydney   New Delhi

SIMON & SCHUSTER PAPERBACKS
An Imprint of Simon & Schuster, Inc.
Rockefeller Center
1230 Avenue of the Americas
New York, N.Y. 10020

First Simon & Schuster paperback edition April 2015

Simon & Schuster Paperbacks and colophon are registered
trademarks of Simon & Schuster, Inc.

Designed by Jeanette Olender

Manufactured in the United States of America

1   3   5   7   9   10   8   6   4   2

The Library of Congress has cataloged the hardcover edition as follows:
Eyman, Scott, date.
   Print the legend : the life and times of John Ford / Scott Eyman.
     p.   cm.
   "John Ford filmography" : p.
   Includes bibliographical references and index.
   1. Ford, John, 1894–1973.   2. Motion picture producers and directors—
United States Biography.   I. Title.
PN1998.3.F65E96   1999
791.78'0233'092—dc21
[B]   99-37046 CIP

ISBN 0-684-81161-8
ISBN 978-1-4767-9772-4 (pbk)
ISBN 978-1-4516-8511-4 (ebook)

IN MEMORY OF

Lindsay Anderson and Darcy O'Brien

"Lest We Forget . . ."

CONTENTS

The United States themselves are essentially the greatest poem . . . the genius of the United States is not best or most in its executives or legislatures, not in its ambassadors or authors or colleges or churches or parlors, nor even in its newspapers or inventors . . . but always most in the common people. Their manners speech dress friendships—the freshness and candor of their physiognomy—the picturesque looseness of their carriage . . . their deathless attachment to freedom—their aversion to anything indecorous or soft or mean . . . the fierceness of their roused resentment—their curiosity and welcome of novelty—their self-esteem and wonderful sympathy—their susceptibility to a slight—the air they have of persons who never knew how it felt to stand in the presence of their superiors—the fluency of their speech—their delight in music, the sure symptom of manly tenderness and native elegance of soul . . . their good temper and open-handedness . . . these too are unrhymed poetry. It awaits the gigantic and generous treatment worthy of them.

FROM THE INTRODUCTION TO WALT WHITMAN'S
"LEAVES OF GRASS"

Half of an Irishman's lies are true

ANONYMOUS

PRINT THE LEGEND

PROLOGUE

The old man was in rare form, and he had picked a fine place for it.

The Lido is a tree-covered island about eight miles long and a few hundred yards wide that forms the eastern boundary of the Venice lagoon. In the first week of September 1971, John Ford came to the Lido, to the arabesque Excelsior Hotel, to be honored by the Venice Film Festival.

He was a frail, seventy-seven-year-old man in poor health who invariably contrived to give the entirely correct impression that he was not to be trifled with. On the boat from the airport, he had been plagued by a fussy attendant in the private vaporetto. "Water a bit choppy, sir?" the attendant had inquired. "Fancy saying that to an admiral in the Navy," he shot back.

And now there was a critic at the door of his hotel room, come for his scheduled interview. Barbara Ford, her father's traveling companion and handler, politely told the critic that the interview might not be possible; Daddy was being inconvenienced by some sudden stomach trouble. "Come in, come in," yelled Ford from the lavatory. "I can deal with two shits at once."

The critic soon disposed of, a couple of people from the British Film Institute arrived to talk to him about the upcoming season devoted to his films. He hadn't wanted to do any more talking, but Barbara said that she'd "go ask Daddy." She came back quickly. "Daddy said he would give you three minutes."

Ford was in bed now, looking rough and ready. Ken Wlaschin, the director of the BFI, told him that they were looking for 35mm prints of some of his rarer films. It was a subject of no interest to Ford. "Where do you come from?" he asked Wlaschin.

"Uh, Nebraska."

"Yes, I can understand what you say. And where do you come from?" Ford said, turning to John Gillett.

"London."

"I can't understand a goddamn thing you say."

Being put on the defensive was the customary surcharge for the pleasure of Ford's company, and your reaction to the tough, unhelpful persona he had perfected would determine whether or not you were worthy to endure more of it. Gillett made a quick mental calculation that capitulation would be fatal.

"In that case," he said, "I'll move a little closer."

"What's happening tonight?"

Gillett explained that a number of artists were going to be given awards and declared Maestros of Cinema.

"Who?"

"Well, Marcel Carné . . ."

"Never heard of him."

"And Bergman."

"Ingrid?"

"Ingmar."

"Oh. He called me one of his favorites . . ."

An hour past their allotted three minutes, it was time for Wlaschin and Gillett to leave. John Ford had to get ready for the ceremony.

One of the two closing-night films of that year's festival was *Directed by John Ford*, a documentary by Peter Bogdanovich that traced Ford's career from his first directorial efforts in 1917. It was narrated by Orson Welles and contained excerpts from twenty-six of Ford's more than 130 films, interviews with John Wayne, Henry Fonda, and James Stewart, and some hilariously cursory, unhelpful comments from Ford himself.

It was a rich tapestry that effectively communicated the bounty of Ford's career, as well as his deceptive range. Here was *The Iron Horse*, the first Western epic, there the passionate sympathy for the dispossessed of *The Grapes of Wrath*; here the moody fatalism of sailors fighting a losing campaign in *They Were Expendable*, there the romantic idyll of *The Quiet Man*; here the unleashed misanthropic savagery of Ethan Edwards in *The Searchers*, there the gloomy resignation of *The Man Who Shot Liberty Valance*; here the glowing humanity of *How Green Was My Valley*, there the lean, laconic gravity of *My Darling Clementine*—a tapestry of film cumulatively creating a vision of humanity that defined a nation and influenced the world.

The film also gave a good sense of Ford's perverse personality. Six Academy Awards, more than any other director has ever won, had been presented to a man who resolutely refused to talk seriously about movies—his own or anybody else's. Ford was so skilled at playing the part of a crusty but simple working stiff with an uncanny way of blundering into masterpieces, that there were those who believed he had been staggeringly lucky for nearly eighty years.

On the night of September 5, *Directed by John Ford* was screened at the Lido Cinema Palace. After it was over, everybody traveled to the Doge's Palace for the awards ceremony. On St. Mark's Square, there were trumpeters and drums and banners waving in the gentle Venetian night. Ford, wearing a dinner jacket covered with his military medals, made his entrance being pushed in a wheelchair. The Moors in the clocktower struck midnight and the old man slowly rose and had yet another honor pinned to his jacket.

With the superb command of dramatic understatement that would never leave him, John Ford brushed away a tear as the audience stood and cheered.

"The first thing that happened when you got an assignment with Ford is that everybody told you legendary stories about him," remembered the screenwriter Winston Miller. It would often be the famous one about a producer telling him he was five pages behind schedule, whereupon Ford ripped five pages out of the script, handed them to the crestfallen producer, and snapped, "Now we're back on schedule."

Or it could be lesser known but similar tales, such as the one concerning the producer who discovered that Ford had missed an angle in a scene. Against everybody's advice, the producer went down to the set and told Ford that the rushes were excellent, but that there was a shot missing and, maybe, perhaps, Ford might be able to pick it up?

"You really think we need it?" Ford asked. The producer said yes. Rising from his chair, Ford said, "You shoot it," walked off the set, off the lot, and onto his boat.

"Everybody in town knew these stories," said Winston Miller, "and [everybody thought] they were true."

If all the stories about John Ford weren't absolutely true, it's because a lot of them were spread by him. He loved to tell stories; whether they were true or false didn't really matter. He would tell people the most outrageous falsehoods with a perfectly straight face. He would assert that his father had come to America to fight in the Civil War, when his father hadn't arrived in America until seven years after Appomattox.

Sometimes he would admit to having acted in his early days in Hollywood, other times he would snap, "I deny it. I just doubled for my brother." Several times he told people he had worked as a cowboy in Arizona, which raised the question of why he was such a bad rider.

"I was born in a pub in Ireland," he would say, and then this man who had been born and raised in Maine would engage in a lengthy discussion of the glories of pub life.

"He told so many straight lies," said Robert Parrish, who did time with Ford as an actor, editor, and a member of Ford's unit during World War II. "The thing of it was, he wasn't telling the lies to get anything important. He was the most secretive man I ever knew. He could be talkative and friendly one day, another day abusive. There was no hard rule. He was not the most reliable man; he'd say one thing and do another."

Ford was a man who told stories for the sake of telling stories—to amuse his audience, of course, but mostly to amuse himself. He would mention in passing that he knew Wyatt Earp—quite true—that Earp told him all about the gunfight at the O.K. Corral, and that the way Ford reproduced it in *My Darling Clementine* was "exactly the way it had been"—utterly false. He told screenwriter Joel Sayre that he rode with Pancho Villa, neatly appropriating an adventure director Raoul Walsh claimed for himself. (Actually, Walsh only directed location footage of Villa in 1914.)

Mostly, Ford laid down these thickets of stories so that he could give the impression of a physically rambunctious, horny-handed son of the soil. It was all part of the vast, comprehensive smoke screen that was part and parcel of John Ford.

Such flights of fancy are hardly grievous character flaws; Ford was, after all, a professional storyteller. That some of the stories turn out to be true in no way detracts from their deceptive purposes. He was a product of the age of Teddy Roosevelt—self-reliance and a sense of adventure were vital qualities for a man who made movies about and associated with men of action. Ford tried hard to live up to the legend he created for himself.

John Ford delighted in pretending to be a roughneck, but his films show that he was deeply tender and sensitive. He tested people relentlessly, tested their abilities, their temperament, their fears, and above all their loyalty, mostly by abusing them. If they remained loyal despite his taunts, Ford would reciprocate forever. If they failed, or were even perceived to have failed, he "closed the iron door on them." It would not do to sentimentalize this man; although Ford's bark was worse than his bite, he could draw blood, and often did.

As nearly as can be determined, he never gave himself completely to anyone.

• • •

The primary quandary of the director in Hollywood has always been how to make the movie you want while using other people's money. To come on like an artist was invariably fatal, as Sternberg and Welles, among others, would find out. No, the best way to get your way was to adopt the pose of a hardworking commercial carpenter who just happened to work in the movie business.

Ford perfected that persona and added other things to it—fear, mostly. He was fast and good, rebellious and caustic, irascible and witty and contradictory. With Ford, everything had an edge. Very quickly, word got out that he could make a successful picture on time and on budget, but it would have to be made his way. That he was a terrible-tempered man who summed himself up in the phrase, "Give me the script and leave me alone." Oh yes, one other thing: on occasion, he would drink.

Other directors, even good ones, photographed scripts, used actors and words. At his best, John Ford gave the impression he was bypassing all that and was photographing pure story, the essence of narrative.

"I've never known anybody [in Hollywood] that commanded such respect," said Robert Parrish. "Willy Wyler made wonderful pictures, but he would shoot an awful lot of film. Ford would shoot very little; often it was only one take. The casts and crew had all worked with him for quite a while. They knew what it meant if he raised his hand or shook his head or lit his pipe. They were a company, like a play that had been on the road for three years. Everybody knew what everybody else was doing."

What John Ford brought to movies was a sense of the turning of the earth, the easy rhythm of life as experienced by people who have a bond with the land. Fueling this was his fascination with people.

"He knows the birthplace and blood of the waiter that brings dinner to his room," was the way one reporter phrased it. "He interviews the interviewer. . . . Once or twice he . . . stopped a stray passer-by for directions—a couple hurrying home, an unshaven man who lifted his hand to point and revealed that three fingers were missing, a slightly puzzled newcomer who was lost too. Each time Mr. Ford saluted politely and went on. But each time his eyes hesitated for an unnecessary moment on the face of his guide as if he would like to stop for a few moments swapping stories and talk under a street lamp."

In his heart, he would always remain nostalgic, romantic, and, socially speaking, innately conservative, which makes his lifelong adherence to liberal principles even more startling. Deeply shy, he loved the physical act of making movies because it was the only thing that enabled him to come out of himself. Terrified of being found out to be a sensitive man and artist, he constructed a rocklike carapace, a character that he could play. He would be curmudgeonly, old-before-his-time Jack Ford, the man who made Westerns—half contrary, bloody-minded Irishman, half flinty New Englander, 100 percent anarchic individualist.

If you told him you liked Roosevelt, he'd claim allegiance to Alf Landon; encountering a Republican, he would claim to be a diehard New Dealer. Once a man asked him if it was true that he had given a tank to Franco's army in Spain. "That's right," he said, "but don't worry about it. I gave one to the good side too."

Claimed as one of their own by conservatives, accused of treating Indians badly and blacks with a patriarch's affectionate condescension, three of his last films were serious movies about blacks (*Sergeant Rutledge*), Indians (*Cheyenne Autumn*), and women (*7 Women*).

The point was to never let anybody know who the real John Ford was. He wanted nothing, *nothing*, known of his thought processes, his motives, goals, or inner needs. It was a front he maintained with more than due diligence, dropping it only when drunk, when he would get sloppy and sentimental. Yet, actors knew that he was one of them, at least as far as sensitivity was concerned, knew that, as one put it, "He cried more than he roared."

The roots of his extraordinary talent remained elusive. His childhood had nominal creative input, his adolescence only slightly more so. His sole aspirations were vague longings for a career in the Navy, which wasn't pursued until middle age.

Yet it was John Ford, more than any director since D. W. Griffith, who instinctively understood the potential of film, who knew how to utilize all the devices intrinsic to the medium. He understood pacing, framing, angles, lighting, composition. He understood characters and reality, understood the value of myth, understood people and understood time.

He had a long list of dislikes, which included actors who acted like actors, almost all producers, most critics, and certain family members. Like all men capable of great cruelty, he was an expert psychologist, with an unerring sense of another's weak spot.

Because his personal list of pet peeves was so long, he didn't have much time for the prejudices of society at large. He was not, for instance, homophobic, although, having been born in the last decade of the nineteenth century, and brought up Roman Catholic, it might have been expected. He regularly employed a wardrobe man who was well known as a homosexual. Ford knew it and wouldn't allow any of his stock company, some of whom were, shall we say, less than sensitive in these matters, to taunt the man.

In his work, Ford's Irish melancholy manifested itself in a sense of loss—for a vanished innocence, for a lost love, for a community, for a home. Many of Ford's films are large-scale, even epic, yet they contain the same warmth, domestic detail, and intimacy of his small movies. He had humor, of course, but he also had an intense and sustained gravity and feeling for the dramatic—in landscape, and in people. His sense of rapport with the men and women of his movies was remarkable; it is a world of genial humanity—not of cardinal sins, but of venial, hedonistic ones.

Ford's deepest moments concern memory and loss—Ma Joad burning her letters and keepsakes before leaving for California; Frank Skeffington walking home alone while the winner's parade moves in the opposite direction; Abe Lincoln at the grave of Anne Rutledge; Hallie Stoddard remaining in love all her life with the man who really shot Liberty Valance; Ethan Edwards exiling himself from his family and society. Ford's vision moved from one of inclusion—the climaxes of *Stagecoach* and *My Darling Clementine*—to exclusion, where the dances and burials and civilization itself are regarded with the wary eye of the outcast.

A good case can be made that America's sense of itself, as far as the movies are concerned, derives from two people: Frank Capra and John Ford. Of these two men, it was John Ford who told the truth.

For all of Capra's supposed respect for the common man, the films that made his reputation are largely repetitions of one single plot trope—ruthless businessman finds it childishly easy to manipulate the public against the simple, lanky man of the people, the incarnation of the mob for which Capra pretended to have such respect. Capra's morality tales say that all that stands in the way of human happiness is one nasty banker or politician. Once they are vanquished, usually through public abasement, the world returns to its natural state.

Ford's social vision was every bit as intense, but far more nuanced and mature. America's humane idealism gave him his themes, and his best films are energized by his recognition of his country's internal conflicts; as Geoffrey O'Brien wrote, "Behind every assertion of God and Motherhood, and Country, a covert blasphemy peeps fitfully out; the suspicion that it might all be a sham."

Ford insisted that doing the right thing can and probably will get you killed, that defeat may be man's natural state, but that honor can and must be earned. His men are not leaders so much as loners, and their greatest acts are renunciations. It's no accident that, when Ford made a movie about World War II, he made one about a campaign America lost. Ford's films can be seen as one cumulative epic of America's national mythology as told by its foot soldiers, an elegiac, driving history that Ford saw as part nostalgic fantasy, part hardshell objective reality.

Although Ford had an affecting faith in both the idea and the people of America, he was never blind to the ongoing presence of bigotry and racism, whether against his own people (*Mother Machree*), the Okies (*The Grapes of Wrath*), Indians (*Fort Apache*), or blacks (*Sergeant Rutledge*). While most of his films are about, to use the title of a 1930 Ford film, *Men Without Women*, in the trilogy of films Ford made with John Wayne and Maureen O'Hara, he evoked very nearly every phase of mature heterosexual romance—courtship, raw sexual need, the compromises of marriage, the difficult rearing of children, catastrophic misalliance, and bitter estrangement.

And of course there are the Westerns. Ford's Westerns have the feeling of life as well as the aura of legend. You can hear the timber creak as he combines the theme of the odyssey with his abiding sense of unkempt humanity. Ford's Westerns fulfill the essential requirement of anything lasting about America—they are about promise and, sometimes, its betrayal.

John Ford brought the art form to what still seems an ultimate synthesis of character and landscape—pictures superseding words, meanings too deep to be explained, yearnings that must remain unspoken. Most movies are all plot—what happens next?—but Ford's movies are less about what the main character will do than they are about the mysterious question of what he actually is.

Any artist's work takes precedence over his life, but, to an unusual degree, Ford's work was his life; his own history and beliefs are scattered like seed through his films, and ripened into vast statements in both his middle and late periods.

I have tried to record John Ford's life, what he said and did and thought. I have attempted to resist the oppressive moral vanity of our age, in which biographers adopt the role of prosecutor and profess disappointment over human failings that occur nearly as frequently among biographers as they do among artists.

To be a serious artist is to have a single-minded mania for control, the precise quality that makes it extremely difficult to be a loving husband and father. To spend hundreds of pages primly documenting every instance of ill temper or alcoholic outburst strikes me as pointless as writing about fish and reporting with outrage that they are cold and wet.

Any artist who arouses clean, uncomplicated feelings will almost certainly turn out to be unworthy of serious attention. Human beings are not clean and uncomplicated, and John Ford was a very human being.

The great epigram of Ford's career is, of course, "When the legend becomes fact, print the legend," from *The Man Who Shot Liberty Valance*. With all due respect for the amber hue of myth, this book concerns itself with how the facts of John Martin Feeney led to the legend of John Ford.

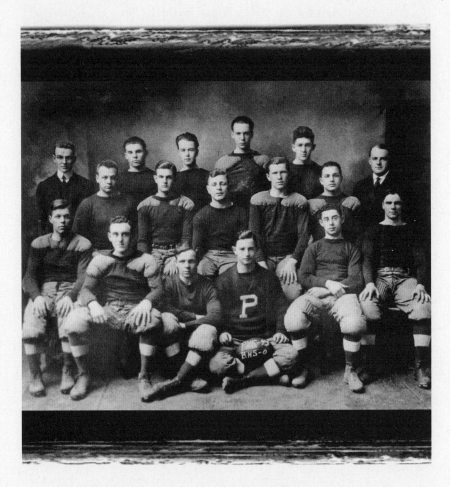

Young Jack Feeney (back row, right) along with the rest of the state championship Portland High football team in 1913.
BFI FILMS: STILLS, POSTERS AND DESIGNS

PART ONE

FROM MAINE TO HOLLYWOOD

"His father was a lobsterman. He was a wonderful old man. Jack looked more like his father than his mother . . . [He had] a brogue you could cut with a knife."

OLIVE CAREY

CHAPTER ONE

Today, western Ireland is a sparsely populated landscape, but in the early nineteenth century it was filled with people. John Feeney, the father of John Ford, was just one of four million people who abandoned Ireland in the long aftermath of the potato famine of 1846, when three-fourths of the potato crop was blighted and much of the western part of the country was threatened with starvation.

By 1851, Ireland had already lost about 2.4 million people, 1.1 million to death by starvation, 1.3 million to emigration. As the Irish dispersed to other lands, they took their country with them. Ireland has a very specific spiritual temper—irreverent, socially conservative, with a booziness of almost manic proportions, and an authentic contempt for demagogues and politicians. The guile of the Irish fails to stem their self-destructiveness, the nihilistic alcoholism that often accompanies song, entertaining persiflage, historical reminiscence. The Irish know how to maneuver; they're a nation of factionalists and operators.

As a country that has been occupied for most of its history, the only power the Irish were allowed was over their families, their only self-expression dance, music, literature, and conversation. So Ireland became a land of indirection and duplicity, with a people wary of betrayal. The concept of victory in defeat, and the hero as stylish victim—Parnell, Wilde—are as ingrained in the Irish character as eloquence, and would come to their finely polished perfection in the work of John Ford.

John Feeney was born June 16, 1854, in Galway, the son of Patrick Feeney and Mary Curran. Spiddal, the town in which John grew up, was a little farming community. It was a time when, as one Galway man remarked, a local Catholic "would *gladly* embrace any pecuniary assistance that would take them *anywhere* they could make a living." That assistance came in the form of a visit from an uncle named Mike Connelly (some accounts spell it Connolly) who had gone to America more than a decade before, and done very well for himself.

At eighteen, John Feeney was a large, strong young man, not without intellect, not without ambition. The only opportunity to be had in Spiddal was eking out a living by farming on somebody else's land. He could see there was more opportunity someplace else. Someplace like America.

There was, in the western part of Ireland at that time, a tradition called an "American wake" that John Feeney might well have been accorded. It was a farewell party for the departing native—food and drink and dancing to a vigorous fiddle into the wee hours, and then little or no sleep into the morning, when it would be time to make the rounds and say farewell. It was the kind of social ritual—outwardly exuberant but with an underlying touch of valedictory sadness—that John Feeney's son would portray better than anybody.

John Feeney arrived in America on June 8, 1872. The town was Boston, the ship a Cunard vessel he had boarded in Queenstown. The year John Feeney arrived in America, about 72,000 other Irish did as well.

Feeney was typical in every sense, for the immigrants of Feeney's time were predominantly young, predominantly Catholic, predominantly from poor rural or western districts. They were laborers and farmers who had little capital—a couple of pounds at most. But they didn't need a great deal of capital to make the voyage. Because of the volume of traffic, and the rise of steamships that could carry a thousand or so people in steerage, the fares were surprisingly affordable—an Irishman could travel to America for as little as $8.75.

The great majority of the Irish sailed to either New York or Boston. The dangers on the long voyage were typhus and cholera from overcrowding; the dangers upon landing were only marginally less—gangs of "runners," Irish hustlers who stole baggage and cheated countrymen trying to make their way from the port. Confused and broke, many Irish immigrants got no farther than the tenements of their landfall city.

John Feeney was made of sturdier stuff. There was no work in Boston? Very well, he'd go someplace else, someplace where there was family, a cousin or two, and plenty of work to be had—Maine. John Feeney, like his youngest son, had a knack for finding his way.

If the famine was the defining event of the nineteenth century in Ireland, it turned out to be one of the defining events of America as well. The influx of the Irish in various Northern cities strengthened institutions—the Democratic Party, Tammany Hall—but it also traumatized immigrants like Feeney. No matter where they settled, they remained more intimately connected to their native land than many other European immigrants, who were only too glad to come to America. For the Irish, it was a forced march, and their ambivalence would infect their children.

As soon as John Feeney emigrated, he followed in the emotional footsteps of millions of his countrymen. The harshness, the dourness, the malice of his native country was forgotten, and all that was remembered was the beauty, the whimsy. Ireland became a green place where joyous people had an endless party and uttered memorable aphorisms. The inherited Ireland, the Ireland of the imagination, became far more important than the often disillusioning reality.

In time, John Feeney's son would come to know and like Joseph Kennedy and support Jack Kennedy in his political rise, but that family's carefully constructed country club fantasy held no charms for him. John Ford's Irish were and would always remain hard-drinking peasants—raffish, tough sons of bitches—as well as generous, funny, curiously honest, and complex people.

Despite the success to be found by so many of the Irish in America, many Irish-Americans never overcame deep-seated feelings of inferiority and insecurity; emotional conflicts were often internalized, and resulted in self-destructive behavior—overwork, apostasy, alcoholism.

In 1875, three years after John Feeney came to America, he married Barbara Curran, who would be known to family and friends as Abby. Barbara had been born in the town of Kilronan on the island of Inishmore, one of the ferociously hostile Aran Islands, a limestone reef at the mouth of Galway Bay, unreclaimable rock separated by a profusion of crude stone walls. For Abby, life in Maine would have been a year-round Christmas compared to the insular hardships of Kilronan.

The year after they were married, the children began arriving, eleven of them—Mary Agnes in 1876, Della in 1878, Patrick in 1879, Francis in 1881, Bridget in 1883, Barbara in 1888, Edward in 1889, Josephine in 1891, Joanna in 1892, John in 1894, and Daniel in 1898.

Of these children, five died in infancy, leaving Mary Agnes (known as Maime), Patrick, Francis, Edward, Josephine, and John—six brothers and sisters. Despite the dreadful infant mortality, which couldn't have been much of an improvement over Spiddal, America seemed to suit the Feeneys; eight years after his arrival in America, on September 11, 1880, John Feeney became an American citizen.

John Ford always claimed to have been born Sean Aloysius O'Fearna—or some small variant—on February 1, 1895. For ninety-odd years, he was taken at his word. But the registry of births for Cape Elizabeth, Maine, clearly records the birth of John Martin Feeney on February 1, 1894. That is the date on his birth registration, on his school records at

Portland High School, and on his death certificate. When young John—family and friends always called him Jack—was born in Cape Elizabeth, an agrarian community a few miles outside of Portland, his father was working as a farmer.

The subtraction of a year from Jack's age stemmed from a childhood bout with diphtheria that caused him to lose a year at school. His reasons for Gaelicizing his name were almost certainly because it made him feel more Irish, more authentic. O'Fearna is indeed the Gaelic equivalent of Feeney, but there are no O'Fearnas in Spiddal, and if you inquire about that family, you will get the response, "No, Feeney."

From his Irish roots, his New England environment, and from what he observed around the dinner table, young Jack's character was formed. Ford rarely spoke in specifics about his parents, but it's probable that his father's nature was a combination of the loving but stern fathers that Donald Crisp would play in his films, crossed with the transparent braggadocio of Victor McLaglen's Sergeant Quincannon. John Feeney was many things, for he had a large family to feed. He would be a fisherman, a farmer, a saloonkeeper, an unofficial alderman around Portland's Munjoy Hill. He would be whatever he needed to be.

In old age, John Feeney looked like a potential hard case—tall, with big shoulders, long arms, and huge, gnarled hands—but the testimony of his children and the people who knew him is of a benign, engaging character. When the spirit moved him, he could tear off a prodigious Irish jig. He loved horse races, and he loved to gamble.

"He would tell about the great things he'd done as a young man," Ford would say of his father, "such as the time he lifted a heavy boulder up out of the water, or how he swam Galway Bay. Of course, he was a damn liar, but he would entertain us as kids. He was always stopping runaway horses—in fact it was his great yen; it was all horses and buggies in those days and, like a bullfighter, he stopped a horse and grabbed it—he was a big, powerful man—and yanked this horse to its knees."

There would be a persistent legend in the Feeney family that they believed explained their doggedly contrarian natures. It seemed that John Feeney's uncle Mike Connelly—or Connolly—had emigrated to America early in 1862. As he descended the gangplank, he was asked by a smiling stranger if he would like to be a streetcar conductor. Mike thought that was a very fine idea indeed, so he was given a uniform which he found entitled him only to fight in the battle of Shiloh. He took this duplicity amiss and promptly deserted to the Confederacy, serving with great distinction in that cause.

Ford was always to claim a kinship with Uncle Mike. The story is probably apocryphal—there was a Michael Connolly who served as a volunteer in the Maine Infantry, but he never deserted, entering and departing the service as a private, while, on the Confederate side, there were numerous Michael Connollys, Connellys, or Conleys, but none of them were from Maine. More importantly, the idea of a man without a clear allegiance to any political interests besides his own would always have a metaphorical resonance for Ford.

P ortland, Maine, is a peninsula jutting into Casco Bay. It is three miles long by about three-fourths of a mile wide, and its shape resembles that of a Viking ship, with the area called Munjoy Hill at the prow. The French and English fought over the land, and the English won, building the town they called Falmouth. White pines from nearby forests provided masts for the Royal Navy, but the English failed to have any sense of gratitude; during the Revolution, they opened fire on the town from the harbor and destroyed it. On July 4, 1786, Falmouth was renamed Portland, so as to obliterate the hated English patrimony.

By the mid–nineteenth century, Portland was a lively maritime town, the second largest molasses port in America after New York. The city was only partially derailed by a great fire that swept through its heart in 1866. By 1872, sixty-five trains stopped in Portland every day, and that was before the Boston & Maine Railroad came into town, or, in 1875, the Portland & Rochester. By 1880, the population was 33,810.

Portland was no backwater. There was a B. F. Keith vaudeville house, and the Jefferson Theater opened in 1897. The Feeneys could have seen Bernhardt in *Camille* and Maude Adams in *Peter Pan*. As far as the nascent nickelodeons were concerned, Preble Street was the site of the Nickel, which was one of the few theaters in America to show an early talking picture system called Cameraphone. Portland had clean, wide, tree-lined streets of cobblestone and dirt, with streetcars and a few broughams. The only famous person to emerge from Portland in the nineteenth century was Henry Wadsworth Longfellow, whose statue has occupied a place of honor in the heart of town since before Jack Feeney was born.

Jack's world was small but rich. In the long New England summers of this time that would later be enshrined as the Gilded Age, the wealthy families of Portland would head for Bar Harbor, while the middle class would settle for a twenty-minute ferry ride to Peaks Island, picturesquely located in Casco Bay, with magnificent views of the ocean, the harbor, and the mountains eighty miles away. On Peaks Island, people could amuse themselves with a band concert, a play from the repertory theater, a trip to Greenwood Amusement Park, and a climactic clambake, followed by the trip back to Portland. It was an idyllic setting, with bowling alleys, swings, and old apple trees.

The Gem Theater was adjacent to one of the boat landings on the island, and offered movies and dancing at the same time. You could dance with your girl in the darkness while watching a movie over her shoulder. The Union House, the oldest hotel on the island, was particularly favored for its fish chowder. Although the year-round population of Peaks Island was only about 370, in summer the population would swell to around 1,300, not counting day-trippers.

A few miles from downtown Portland is Portland Head Light, which has been there since 1791, the first lighthouse erected on the Atlantic Coast. It's a beautiful white pillar erupting 101 feet from the rocky shoreline. In a storm, the waves break and the spray scatters as high as the lighthouse itself. Young Jack Feeney learned of the awesome power of a Maine storm as soon as he was old enough to listen to the foghorn moaning its warnings to the ships offshore.

In those days, if you wanted to call somebody a bad name, you called him an Irishman, so Jack quickly learned to adopt an air of don't-mess-with-me truculence. The rapid population growth of the 1890s made Munjoy Hill a village unto itself. Most of the Irish population of Portland were laborers on the waterfront, the railroad, or the auto works at the base of the Hill.

Maine enacted prohibition in the mid–nineteenth century, but there was a good deal of back-and-forth on the issue. The temperance movement was at least partially stimulated by the nearly universal drunkenness of the time. Every grocery store had casks of rum and gin, and rum breaks at 11:00 and 4:00 occurred every working day.

In 1880, the year he was naturalized, John Feeney and his family were living at 53 Center Street and he was working for the gas company. The year after Jack was born, John Feeney quit farming and went into a new business. "Mr. Feeney had a barroom," remembered Portland native Mary Corcoran, whose father worked for Feeney.

John Feeney came by his calling honestly: he married into it. Several of Abby Feeney's sisters had bars. As Don MacWilliams, the local historian of Munjoy Hill, says, "They couldn't always read and write [English], but they could count money." The farm on Cape Elizabeth may have been purchased as a buffer against the periodic spasms of prohibition, and there was a family legend to the effect that the only reason the farm was sold was because the children were growing older and needed the higher quality schools in Portland.

Feeney's bar was located near the apex of a five-corner meeting place called Gorham's Corner, which, until World War II, was the heart of Munjoy Hill. (Today, the site of Feeney's Saloon is a vacant lot.) By 1900, the census listed John Feeney's occupation as "restaurant," a pleasant euphemism. Five of the six surviving children were living at home at 48 Danforth Street. (Also renting at that address was one Edward Feeney and family, presumably John's brother or cousin.) Pat was working at the "restaurant" with his father; the mercurial Francis, newly returned from the Spanish-American War, was working as a tailor; and Eddie, Josie, and young Jack were all at school.

The Portland city directories tell the tale of the extended Feeney clan. In 1898, half the thirty-nine Feeneys in the city were laborers; by 1915, there were seventy-eight Feeneys, four-fifths of them tradesmen. America was working for John Feeney's family; by the turn of the century, their long climb up the ladder was well under way.

CHAPTER TWO

Nearly every Munjoy Hill street had a blend of Yankees, Jews, Irish, Scandinavians, Scots, Canadians, and blacks. As late as World War II, Gaelic would be commonly heard. When the occasional fist-fight broke out, Russian and Polish Jews would side with the Italians and Irish against the Protestants. It was the New England equivalent of a Hell's Kitchen melting pot, except less dangerous. Doors were almost never locked, if only because any intruder was certain to receive a serious beating for his troubles.

John and Abby Feeney earned a reputation for relatively quiet, businesslike behavior. Mr. Feeney was interested in making a living, bringing up his children, and attending church on Sunday. Munjoy Hill was a distinct, self-contained little village, with its own haunted house (the Carleton mansion), the Cathedral of the Immaculate Conception for the Catholics, three synagogues for the Jews, and the Green Memorial African Methodist Episcopal Zion Church for blacks.

The modest amounts of domestic bickering in the Feeney home seemed to derive from the fact that John Feeney spoke a different dialect than his wife, and they had constant spats over pronunciation. As a result, the Feeneys only spoke Gaelic occasionally, although Mary McPhillips, the daughter of Ford's brother Patrick, recalled that when the odd expression of the Ould Sod came out, "Uncle Jack tried to learn it, but my father didn't."

While Jack was growing up, John Feeney never owned a home in Portland proper. Instead, he preferred to rent for around $15 to $20 a month. The houses were all similar: three- or four-story tenement flats on narrow but deep lots. Many of the tenements had yards that were big enough for a good-sized vegetable garden or a game of three-way catch, although the houses where Ford spent his adolescence had no yards at all.

The owner of the building lived in one flat, usually the ground-level one, and rented out the other two. Each apartment had its own porch. A passerby could tell when tenants were home on a warm summer's evening by the rhythmic creak of a hammock swinging on its chains, or the odor of burning citronella wafting down to the street.

For a real estate investment, John Feeney bought a simple frame house on Peaks Island for about $800. The modest but comfortable house still stands, on 1st Street, the open front porch now enclosed, the living room fireplace still needed even in the summer. The house is situated on a rise, with the yard sloping down to the bay. The house on 1st Street remained in the family until after World War II.

There, John Feeney established a large vegetable garden and became known for his strawberries. "Abby, what would you like tonight for vegetables?" he would ask his wife, and after she made her choices, he would gather them from his garden. "We grew everything," remembered John Ford, "we dragged seaweed up from the shore to use as fertilizer."

As with most of the working-class kids young Jack grew up with, sports were an outlet for the animal energies. While he was attending kindergarten through eighth grade at Emerson School in Munjoy Hill, he was a regular attendee at one of the Hill's four baseball diamonds. Pickup football games were common at Wills Playground and Water District Park, in spite of the fact that the ground was rock-hard and the kids had almost no protective equipment.

The bumptious good health of youth was interrupted only once, when Jack was twelve and came down with diphtheria. He had to lie in bed for months while his throat was swabbed with alcohol and he ate ice. His sister Maime read to him—*Treasure Island, Tom Sawyer, Huckleberry Finn, A Connecticut Yankee in King Arthur's Court*. The stories opened wondrous vistas before Jack; he fell in love with narrative, with drama, the mind's ability to visualize adventure. The boy developed a ferocious appetite for reading. He would replicate the experience of an ill, fragile child with matchless delicacy in *How Green Was My Valley*. His illness held him back a year at school, so he had to work all the harder to make up for lost time.

Even as a child, Jack tended to hide the most thoughtful part of himself. "He seemed about as unintellectual a person as you could imagine," said Robert Albion, a classmate who became a Harvard professor. "In one class Jack was told he had no imagination. But at our fiftieth reunion in 1964 he surprised us all by saying he had always had a love affair with Eleanor of Aquitaine."

Others, however, knew that young Feeney was an avid reader. "Every time you'd see him he'd have a book in his hand, Shakespeare or something," remembered a classmate named Oscar Vanier. "He'd fight at the drop of a hat, but he had a great mind and a great sense of humor. Someone would tell him a funny story, and the next day [he] would retell it, adding all kinds of new touches to it."

He was even then a combination of pagan and poet, although he preferred to emphasize the former. "At the school proms I was a washout," he claimed. "With my two left feet I could never keep time to 'Dardanella.' " He would tell his grandson Dan Ford that he had a very happy childhood, and he remembered his mother saying, "When he was growing up, all he did was play football and read books."

Intellectually, Ford was stimulated by the attention he received from a Yankee schoolteacher named William B. Jack, whom he remembered as the first person to tell him he could do something with his life. Academically, young Jack was what would now be termed an underachiever. His report card from the Emerson School for 1905–06 shows Reading (next to filmmaking, the great passion of his life) vacillating from Fair to Good, Arithmetic ping-ponging from Poor to Good, Geography going from Poor to Excellent. Even at twelve, he could do anything he set his mind to, but academic excellence was not a priority.

With some justification, Ford claimed extenuating circumstances. "I was a good student," he said in a conversation with his grandson Dan and Katharine Hepburn. "I never took a book home because I had to work in the morning, sprint all the way to school, go to school and then go out on the athletic field, then at night I worked in the theater."

Although many working-class Portland families moved every year or so, the Feeneys tended to stay put, a pattern that would be repeated by Jack when he grew up—as an adult, in fifty-odd years he lived in only three houses. In 1897, and for the next four years, the family lived at 48 Danforth Street; in 1902, they moved to 65 Monument Street; in 1906, to 21 Sheridan Street (sharing the house with the families of Michael Myers and Patrick Mahone, plumbers). The year after that, they moved next door to 23 Sheridan, accompanied once again by the Myers clan.

Jack usually shared a room with his brother Pat, while the loner Eddie often had a room to himself. From the window of the third-floor apartment at 23 Sheridan Street, Jack had a spectacular view of the town. To the east were the ships, loaded with coal and grain, crammed into the wharves on Portland Harbor. To the south were the wagons and horses that were the heart of the bustling commercial town.

It was a thriving, attractive place, but there was a downside: the Irish of Portland could make a living, they could improve their lot, but they could never quite be accepted by the town's WASP ruling class. Ford was never ashamed of his humble beginnings. "I am of the proletariat," he stated with quiet dignity in 1964. "My people were peasants. They came here, were educated. They served this country well. I love America."

Jack's contemporaries remembered that his first taste of the theater came at the Jefferson. Jack got a job as an usher, and would tell Portland friends that everybody went on strike the very first night he reported for work. When De Wolf Hopper came through in a play, Jack was delegated the vital job of buying Hopper his bottle of ale, for which he gave Jack a dollar. (We can safely assume that Ford kept it in the family and purchased the ale at his father's saloon.)

Another favored memory was arising at 5:30 A.M. and serving the 6:00 A.M. Mass, which offered him a memorably detailed glimpse of a great star in some private distress. "A woman was sitting halfway back," he remembered in 1962. "She wore a beautiful fur coat; the sun came through a window and touched down on it and made it shine. She had on an Alice blue cloche with a veil; when she came to the rail to receive communion she lifted the veil, there were tears in her eyes. I recognized her because I'd seen her when ushering in the theater, but I never knew what made her so sad at that time." The woman was Ethel Barrymore.

Because of his omnipresence around the Jefferson, John was chosen to do a walk-on in a play starring Sidney Toler. He was supposed to make an entrance and hand a telegram to Toler.

"What's this?" Toler asked.

"A telegram, sir," said a terrified Ford.

"A telegram. You mean a wire, don't you?" Toler was ad-libbing and cruelly playing with the young boy.

"A wire, yes sir, a wire, sir," said John.

"What does it say?"

"I don't know."

"Well, why don't you know?"

"Because I haven't read it."

"Why haven't you read it?"

"Well, I . . ."

Toler eventually let the young boy offstage.

Ford was enthralled by show business. He told Katharine Hepburn that after the second performance of any play in Portland, he'd begin repeating the lines. Even more than the theater, however, he was attracted by movies. "Whenever I got a nickel, I went to the nickelodeon. At that time, the things I loved the most were westerns." For a boy in provincial Maine, the movies, and California, the place where some of the movies were being made, seemed impossibly glamorous, a place of golden sunshine and boundless opportunity.

Jack seems to have been, in most respects, typical for his place and time. He was shy of girls but developed a crush on one of his school-teachers, a Mrs. Sills. He and his friends formed a loose confederation called the Sheridan Streeters that, as he remembered, "formed a Portland High bulwark in the four major sports every year." In the manner of an old soldier spinning yarns about his glorious adventures in combat, he claimed to have had his nose broken in three places in his first high school football game.

In a 1950 letter to a Portland friend, Ford waxed sardonically nostalgic about the Portland summers, when, "as a reward for virtue, Tim Dona-hue, one of Portland High's famous captains and erstwhile Dock Master of Peaks Island, let us—as a special priviledge [sic]—move all the heavy baggage from the Casco Bay steamers. By heavy stuff I only mean things like safes, pianos, 50 foot lengths of steel cables, telegraph poles, cement blocks and railroad engines. The important stuff like ladies' handbags and mail was personally taken care of by Timmy himself. During leisure hours we retrieved punts and forward passes thrown by Timmy."

By the time he was fifteen, Jack had developed a sense of responsibility; he took out an insurance policy with Prudential that paid $500 in the event of his death and made his mother the beneficiary.

Ford respected and enjoyed his father, but he adored his mother. "My God, what a marvelous cook," he remembered. "I still practically live on baked beans. . . . I don't know what her secret was, but she could make baked beans that would make your mouth water. . . . She could make a codfish taste like chicken. She made her favorite dish, boiled brisket of beef—she never cooked it with cabbage. She always cooked the cabbage separately. Oh, God, it was delicious." Years later, Ford cast Sara Allgood as the unprepossessing but dominant mother in *How Green Was My Valley* largely because she reminded him of Abby Feeney. "She looked like my mother and I made her act like my mother."

As with most Irish Catholic households of the time, rituals were con-trived to give a form and shape to the daily minutiae. Every night before dinner, John Feeney would take two belts of Irish whiskey—no more, no less. "It never had any effect on him that you could see," remembered his son. "He'd always say a blessing before his drink. So it was a religious ceremony."

Drink was not the problem for all the Feeneys that it would be for Jack. Francis would be a good man with a bottle, as was Eddie, but Pat was a teetotaler, and didn't smoke either. Abby Feeney didn't drink, and had a hostility toward alcohol. She wouldn't allow Jack near her husband's cache of liquor, and Ford always claimed he wasn't even sure where it was kept.

Abby was the dominant disciplinary force in the house. "One word from her and that was it," said her daughter Josephine. Although it has been reported that Abby never learned to read and write English, that would seem to be incorrect. There survives at least one postcard from her to Jack; unless it was written by a third party, Abby obviously had a working knowledge of written English.

Jack would come to be known for a waggish humor that would peek out in random moments, and it was already evident during adolescence. Once, Portland High's baseball team was challenged by an outfit calling itself the Bloodmer Girls, a barnstorming team of women passing through town. On the day of the game, a crowd was assembled at Bayside Park, waiting, along with the Portland High team, for the appearance of this fearsome feminist vision. At last, from the cellar of a house across the street, came the girls in bloomers, actually a group of neighborhood boys in drag, one of whom bore the unmistakable Irish features of Jack Feeney.

Joseph McDonnell, a friend of Jack's, witnessed the appearance of the Bloodmer Girls and remembered Jack Feeney as "a wit and a brilliant boy, who never discovered himself in high school. . . . He wrote a parody of our new school song [in 1913] and was a natural born artist who made us all look ridiculous in his caricatures."

Jack seems to have been popular, probably because of his athletic accomplishments. Although he entered Portland High in September 1910, he didn't show up on the football team until 1912, as the second-string fullback. He played well enough to earn a letter, and was the starting fullback on the team that won eight, lost three, and won the state championship in 1913. He must have been a bruiser; he soon won the nickname of Bull Feeney, "because he could hit the line and was hard to stop," according to one Portland old-timer. A few months later, on June 18, 1914, Jack graduated from Portland High.

As with his experience at the Emerson School, he hadn't covered himself with academic glory. His overall grade average was 84.9, just missing a B. He had earned three football letters and twice won Honorable Mention on the Maine all-state team. Jack's classmates named him toastmaster for their class. The diary of a girl named Bessie Dawson reports that, "At the end [of the senior prom] 'Bull' Feeney . . . asked Ralph Mahoney to give one [toast] but he wouldn't."

Jack would probably have preferred to be known as a jock, but he was more than that. Lucien Libby, an English literature teacher who began teaching at Portland High in 1901 (Libby later became an administrator, retiring in 1947), was a particular favorite of Jack's, opening his mind to new ideas and—ironically for a man who would spend nearly a half-century teaching in a small New England town—the idea of new places.

Bull Feeney would never forget a real kindness or an imagined cruelty; more than thirty years after he left Portland, he honored Libby by naming one of the ships in *They Were Expendable* the *Lucien Libby*.

Jack remained tied to Portland and Portland High all his life. One of his closest friends on the football team was Joe McDonnell, who would turn around after college and spend the rest of his career teaching English at Portland High. When it came time for McDonnell's retirement ceremony in 1963, it had to be interrupted so the teacher could take a congratulatory phone call from his old friend Bull.

Among the Feeney children, the randy black sheep was Francis, or, as he was generally known, Frank. Born on August 14, 1881, Frank dropped out of high school at seventeen and went into the Army. After serving in the Maine infantry during the Spanish-American War, he was mustered out, met a woman named Dell Cole in Portland, and promptly got her pregnant. There was a shotgun wedding that narrowly preceded the birth of Frank's son, Philip. The marriage broke up; Dell took her son and left for Boston, while Frank, in some disgrace, left Portland.

Frank led a raffish existence for the next couple of years, working in vaudeville. Supposedly, he was cleaning gas lamps on the streets of New York in 1907 when someone from the Centaur Film Company in Bayonne, New Jersey, spotted him, liked his sharp, dramatic profile, and got him into the movies. Frank became a journeyman actor, working for early companies headed by David Horsley and Al Christie. He kept moving, to Edison, then to the American branch of Georges Méliès's Star Films.

To avoid bringing any more shame on the family, Frank had early on adopted the name Ford, from, he said, the automobile. (Jack had a slightly different explanation: that Frank substituted for a drunken actor named Francis Ford and was credited as such in the program, getting stuck with the name. Given the unlikely coincidence of subbing for an actor with the same first name, it seems safe to place more credence in Frank's version.)

The Méliès company was located first in New Jersey, later near San Antonio, where Frank developed a special affinity for Westerns. After a couple of years with Méliès, Frank joined Thomas Ince in the latter part of 1911. It was a step up, as Ince was one of the most vigorous, innovative talents in American film. Frank seems to have been hired only as an actor, but he had been doing some light production duties at Méliès. San Antonio papers talk of him scouting locations and placing the camera, although they are careful to assign actual directorial credit to someone else.

Frank was working as an assistant director or production manager, and had been working in Texas and the Southwest. He knew as much about the West as Ince, a native of Newport, Rhode Island, and that bit of knowledge would become increasingly important.

Ince's studio was called Bison, and it was headquartered at the mouth of Santa Ynez Canyon, above Santa Monica, where the studio leased eighteen thousand acres and the Miller Brothers 101 Ranch Wild West Show for $2,500 a week. There, Ince had everything he needed to make Westerns. Extras who played Indians and cowboys lived in the canyon in tents and cabins; second leads took a bus from Venice, a few miles away; lead actors were chauffeured the twenty-five miles from Los Angeles. Working at Inceville was like stepping back about forty years into a small, orderly town somewhere on the Plains. There was lots of dust, lots of authentic cowboys, lots of authentic Indians.

In February 1912, Ince made a two-reel Western entitled *War on the Plains* that the *Moving Picture World* praised for its "historical accuracy, correct costuming, perfect photography. . . . Some of the scenes are sublime in their grandeur; others are impressive in the number of people employed; others are startling in realism, and prolific in incident. . . . [The] impression that it all leaves is that here we have looked upon a presentation of Western life that is real and that is true to life."

War on the Plains launched Ince on a series of Westerns that proved so popular he needed to expand production. For the first six months of 1912, Ince directed everything himself, but in June he divided his company in half and put Frank in charge of the new unit.

Because Frank and his crew were ranging over the hills of Santa Ynez Canyon, Ince devised a method of supervising his employee: a complete shooting script, with each shot carefully described in terms of action and camera position. After Frank shot his film, Ince would view the daily rushes and personally edit the negative. The approved style was intensely pictorial; the subject was invariably the epic of the American frontier.

B ack home in Portland, Jack was watching movies, and learning to like Ince's work. "Ince had a great influence on films, for he tried to make them move," he said. Ince also had a good eye for talent—he made Frank Borzage a director and turned Sessue Hayakawa into one of the more unlikely stars of the early American cinema.

Ince's main drawback, other than the regimentation his exhaustively detailed scripts imposed, was his ego; he was an inveterate credit-hog. Two of the major Bison releases were *The Invaders* (November 1912) and *Custer's Last Fight* (October 1912), the latter possibly directed by Ince, the former almost certainly directed by Frank, although Ince took the credit for both.* *Custer's Last Fight* is particularly impressive, with long shots that have a real epic sweep. The film is so good it was reissued as late as 1924, a far more sophisticated filmmaking era than 1914.

Even if Frank hadn't been of an independent—Ince preferred the term "choleric"—nature, he would have resented Ince's high-handed behavior.

The Struggle was released in January 1913, with Frank billed as "Associate Director." It features realistic costumes, a lot of dust, silhouetted riders, evocative landscapes, consistent depth of focus, and a plot that involves the hero looking for the man who killed his father, whom he can identify by a scar on his face. With the minor alteration of a missing finger for the scar, it's the identical plot of *The Iron Horse*. When Indians launch an attack, the camera furiously tracks with the stagecoach being pursued. The acting is ordinary, as are the interiors, but Frank's exteriors are superb, the full equal of the work his brother, not to mention William S. Hart, would be doing in a few years.

Another Ince/Ford production, *Blazing the Trail*, features a remarkably beautiful final shot: a grave in the foreground, with riders and mourners walking away from the grave and the camera, then making a 90-degree turn right into a diagonal on the horizon as the screen fades to black.

As Kevin Brownlow would note, these one- and two-reelers were authentic, often sympathetic to the Indian, often concerned with the details of military life on the frontier. Sound familiar?

Some of Francis's films for Ince were so good that D. W. Griffith followed dutifully in their footsteps. Griffith's *The Massacre* is closely patterned after Frank's work in this period, and Frank's 1912 *Blazing the Trail* contains plot elements and compositions that Jack would use as late as *The Searchers*.

For all the often unhealthy competitiveness that would mark their relationship, Jack would be a true younger brother, following Frank's lead in all sorts of ways. A trade paper noted that "When you first meet him, Francis Ford . . . strikes you as being rather a dreadful man. He's gruff and has eyes that look right through you and muss up everything that you were going to say. After a while, you become conscious that you like him a lot."

In a 1915 article in *Motion Picture Magazine*, readers were told that "It

*Ince's partisans point to the credits; Ford's partisans point to the films Ince directed at Imp, just before he started up the Bison label. As Robert Birchard says, "The Imps show no sense of directorial talent whatever. And we're supposed to believe he was suddenly liberated in the wilds of Santa Monica?" Ince's credit-hogging got so extreme that in one of the pictures Frank directed he prominently inscribed "F.T.F.," his initials, on the back wall of a set as both an act of defiance and assertion of authorship.

takes a man who knows Francis Ford to write of him, otherwise, all one gets is the story of his shoveling snow in boyhood, his lack of beauty and his failures and tummy aches. He delights in leading writers astray, and if his friends point out that they do not think it wisdom, he will laugh and say, 'It will look awfully funny in print.' "

Within a few years, Frank would use his own money to establish a club room for members of his company, where they could read and rest when not working—just like the Field Photo Farm that Jack would establish after World War II. And, like Jack, Frank had a yen for far-off places and ocean voyages; in May 1923, he took off for the South Seas, accompanied only by a movie camera with which he planned to take some scenes of natives and animals for later, vaguely defined use in some films.

On the set, Frank worked brusqely, often using sarcasm: "Now, boys, remember you are not in a drawing room," he would instruct his cowboys. "Don't bow to each other or apologize if you take a piece of skin from the man you are fighting. This is to be the real thing. Go to it. Who will roll down that bank? Who will fall off a horse? I don't believe one of you will dare—Huh! You will?—and you will? Good! I thought there might be one or two who did not want a cushion to fall on. . . . Listen boys, a dollar for a bloody nose and two for a black eye."

Richard Willis, in *Motion Picture Magazine*, wrote of Frank that "under the quiet, almost sarcastic manner, there is deep seriousness, and below the veil of indifference there is one of the warmest hearts imaginable . . . he gives a wrong impression to those who do not know him well."

Either the two brothers shared an identical emotional perversity, or Jack consciously modeled much of his behavior on Frank.

An actress named Grace Cunard, christened by Carl Laemmle after the shipping line he habitually used for his trips home to Laupheim, Germany, arrived at the Ince studio and quickly began an affair with Frank. Unfortunately for all concerned, Frank had remarried, to a woman named Elsie Van Name. Cunard began nudging her lover to assert his independence, so Frank got word to Carl Laemmle that he, not Ince, was responsible for the recent surge in quality Westerns coming out of Bison. Frank's last film for Ince, *Texas Kelly at Bay*, was released in March 1913. Frank and Grace Cunard both went to work at Laemmle's Universal.

Married to Elsie, carrying on a serious affair with Grace Cunard, and with a growing reputation as a talented actor and director, Frank had his hands full, and for a time he was up to it all. His first film at Universal, a Civil War story entitled *The Coward's Atonement*, was hailed by *Moving Picture World* for the "director's masterly handling of battle scenes. He has closely followed Griffith and Ince in giving swift military action in the foreground with equally intense action in the far reaching landscapes of great beauty and has held up to view some stirring conflicts in both large and small scope."

While much of this was going on, the family hadn't heard from Frank. One day some of the men went to a movie in town, and there was Frank on the screen, being heroic. Abby went, then dragged her husband to the movie. Tracing Frank to California, they asked him to come home for a visit—all was forgiven. Frank visited in fine style, wearing expensive, tailor-made clothes. By 1913, the Feeneys were familiar with Frank's success, but they didn't broadcast it. "You'd never even have known that [Jack's] brother was in the movies," remembered his friend Oscar Vanier. "He never mentioned it."

At Universal, from 1913 to 1916, Frank produced and directed around eighty films of one to four reels, plus four serials. Beginning in April 1914, with the release of the first chapters of *Lucille Love, Girl of Mystery*, Ford and Cunard became, along with Pearl White, the leading serial stars of the period. (A Ford-Cunard serial called *The Broken Coin* had to be expanded from fifteen chapters to twenty-two to meet public demand, and 1,500 newspapers carried the serialization of the weekly chapter.)

Enthralled by the movies, with an older brother who was a movie star and a talented director, Jack's future was fairly obvious. In later life, Jack often claimed he had attended the University of Maine, although the extent of his higher education varied in the telling. He told a story about having to rise at 5:30 in order to wait on tables for money and slugging someone who made an anti-Irish slur, but the fact of the matter is that the university has no record of John Martin Feeney ever registering.

There is a slim chance that Jack registered but never actually showed up for classes, resulting in his entrance papers being discarded. But, since he graduated from high school in June of 1914, and college registration didn't begin until August, when Jack was already in Hollywood—he had a small part in *The Mysterious Rose*, one of his brother's movies, filmed in the second week of August—it's highly probable that he never showed up in Orono at all.

Jack would always remain uneasy about his lack of higher education. But going out to Hollywood to, as he later put it, "bum a couple of weeks free board" from his brother proved to be the right move at the right time. In a few years, the railroad would pull out of Portland, precipitating a depression in that town that the 1929 stock market crash only amplified.

Some of the Feeney children—Eddie, Maime—would eventually follow Frank and Jack to California; others would stay in Portland. Pat Feeney, who seems to have been Jack's favorite brother—Ford would name his son after him—married a woman named Kate Devine. Their family home was on Sheridan Street as well, but at the opposite end of the street from the Feeney house. Pat went into the fish business, and was known as a pleasant, well-adjusted man with no desire to emulate his brothers. In years to come, whenever Jack would visit Portland, he would first go to his parents' house, then travel down Sheridan to Pat's house. "He remembered his family and friends," asserted Mary Corcoran.

Jack would always emphasize his Irishness, so commentators and critics followed his lead. But he was also that staunchest of New Englanders, a Maine man, with an abiding memory of a New England town, that is to say, an ideal community of enduring values.

From Portland, Jack learned the value of common people, the beauty of the natural world, and the symmetry when the two were joined. He felt the lure of the sea and the unspoken bonds that hold working men together. He saw the wrecks off Portland Head Light, the catastrophe that can result when good men are overwhelmed by fate, and he observed the dignity of the women who quietly waited while their men went down to the sea in ships.

Beyond that, his Maine upbringing had given him a valuable lesson in modesty, for you do not put on airs if you live in Maine; the worst thing a Yankee can be is a snob. He had, in short, learned the emotional dynamic that would inform practically every film he would ever make.

A bare five months after he graduated from high school, in the November 1914 issue of *The Racquet*, Portland High's alumni bulletin, there is this brief notation: "John Feeney is closely connected with the Universal Film Company at Hollywood, California."

For the sake of convenience, and to take advantage of whatever nepotistic connections could be made, Jack adopted the same last name as his brother Frank. Jack "Bull" Feeney was now Jack Ford.

Jack Ford directs Harry Carey in 1919.

PART TWO

LEARNING A CRAFT

Harry wanted to make Westerns.

OLIVE CAREY

CHAPTER THREE

To get to Universal Studios from Hollywood, you picked up a nickel bus at the corner of Hollywood and Cahuenga. Or you could take a jitney cab over the dirt road that was the Cahuenga Pass. In 1914, Universal was a couple of buildings, a single row of dressing rooms and a couple of stages amidst the rolling hills and grass.

Jack Ford arrived at Carl Laemmle's studio long before the March 15, 1915, inauguration of the vastly expanded Universal City, so he was probably one of the ten thousand people who poured through the decorative arch that formed the entrance to the studio. Laemmle purchased the 230-acre lot in 1914 for $165,000. On it he constructed stages, barns, offices, storage vaults, town sets, streets, and buildings, making it by far the most ambitious plant for the manufacture of movies in the world. The guest of honor for the grand opening was Thomas Edison, and as the tiny, five-foot Laemmle walked out to address the throng, the first words out of his mouth were "I hope I didn't make a mistake coming out here."

For entertainment, a group of enterprising employees constructed a sideshow that featured a group of local freaks. Lon Chaney and Lee Moran did a buck-and-wing dance and admission was charged, with the money going to a local children's hospital. Carl Laemmle paid $100 to get in.

The bulk of Laemmle's operation would always be cheap, bread-and-butter movies—Westerns in the 1910s and 1920s, horror films in the 1930s. Among the actors populating Laemmle's Westerns was Henry De-Witt Carey II, born in Harlem in 1878. The son of a White Plains judge, Carey was enraptured by the lurid dime novels that began the legend of the West. He came by his fascination naturally. "He told me one time," remembered his wife, Olive, "that his mother tried to talk Judge Carey into going when they opened up the Cherokee Strip. To go on a land drive. But she couldn't talk him into it. That I think is where the pioneer spirit came from in Harry."

For a time, Carey went to law school at New York University, where he became a good friend of Jimmy Walker, the future mayor of New York City. With an excess of youthful high spirits, Carey once borrowed some long, female underwear from a nearby whorehouse called Madame Moran's and raised them on the university flagpole. He was promptly expelled, and afterward referred to himself as a "premature alumnus" of NYU.

Carey drifted into acting, then wrote a successful play entitled *Montana*. He made his first film in 1908 for D. W. Griffith and Biograph, and by 1915 was at Universal. John Wayne captured Harry Carey's screen appeal as well as anybody. "Harry Carey wore a good hat," he said, "and a good pair of boots, and what he wore in between didn't matter too much. He tried to play it natural."

Carey grew up to be a tough but warm man, and was like his friend Jack Ford in at least one important facet: "It was hard to get him to talk about movies," remembered his son, Harry Carey Jr. "He wouldn't talk about them at all. He'd talk about cattle, horses, sailing, FDR—he was a great admirer of FDR—but movies . . . he never gave them much credence."

John Ford usually asserted that he did no acting whatever in his early days in the movies, but surviving stills clearly show him working as an actor in some of his brother's films, and trade paper reviews prove that he even starred in a couple of now-lost two-reelers.

He would also claim that he was one of the hooded klansmen in *The Birth of a Nation*, but that the hood interfered with his sight and he fell off his horse, knocking himself unconscious. He awoke to find D. W. Griffith bending over him, calling for whiskey. Telling Griffith that he felt okay, the director responded by saying the whiskey was for him.

The story sounds like one of Ford's fancies, but some of his apparently invented stories turn out to be true. Also, Ford was, as everybody who later worked for him knew, a terrible rider. "He looked like a sack of walnuts on a horse," said Ben Johnson.

Ford's Griffith connection was independently confirmed by Mae Marsh. Toward the end of her life, Marsh said that "[We've] known each other for a very long time, all the way back to the early Griffith days, when he was a little extra boy during *The Birth of a Nation*, riding as a clansman in the Ku Klux Klan. In all the other pictures we made, I'd be a blue-eyed Indian and he'd be a cowboy."

Despite Ford's awkwardness on a horse, he must have liked them; in

June of 1916, he bought a bay gelding with a white blaze on his face named Woodrow. He paid $50, slightly more than the monthly rent on his apartment at 1712 Whitley Street.

Around Universal, Jack was a general dogsbody, doing what he was told, working as a propman, assistant director, stuntman, bit actor. He was learning the movie business from the ground up, learning all facets of it as a craft, without which no art can be made.

While Jack might have been a big man in Portland, the Californians took one look at the skinny redhead and came to a cruel but more or less accurate estimation: "hayseed."

"He brought a very strange language into pictures, due, no doubt, to his ignorance of the business," remembered the writer Grover Jones. "When [Francis] Ford would send him to the prop shop to get something, it was his lack of knowledge that made him refer to the thing as a 'Razz-a-ma-tazz,' a 'Thing-a-ma-bob, you-know-what-I-mean,' 'Whatcha-ma-callit,' or a 'Hootenanny.' He had a thousand other expressions but once he pointed to something that resembled the thing he was after and went through a few pantomimic gestures, the experienced man in the prop shop would put two and two together and finally supply him with the necessary article."

Any gift Jack might have had for acting was hampered by the fact that he couldn't see without his glasses, which didn't stop Francis from calling on him for stuntwork. "Yeah, a sissy like you might get hurt," Francis would say to a worried actor. "I'll have my little brother do it for you." At whatever he did, he was "a hell of a smart cookie," as propman Lefty Hough remembered. But his essentially covert personality was already firmly in place. "[He was] a mysterious sort of guy," said Hough. "Nobody ever got close to him. Not even his own brothers, Eddie and Frank."

Jack was young, engaged in a great adventure: the romance of the movies, the birth of an art form. "Those were great days," Ford wrote in 1946. "We rode out in the morning in blue uniforms and army forage caps, while tied to our saddles would be gray blouses and black plumed slouch hats. We would charge as Union soldiers, pull up and change into the gray blouses and charge back as Confederate soldiers. . . . We used very few closeups in those days. Nearly everything was played on horseback. It was all very fast moving. Motion, action, was the keynote of the times."

Jack doubled for his brother and other actors in serials like *Lucille Love*. "I had to drive over bridges, jump over ravines on horseback and things like that. I had just finished school and was fairly sprightly. I did everything."

He attempted to dodge, with indifferent success, rough fraternal humor. Once, he was doubling for his brother in a Civil War picture, when a little bit too much gunpowder was used in a battle scene. The explosion, recalled Lefty Hough, "put him in the hospital for six weeks. He never got over that. He blamed it on me, and I didn't do it, I had nothing to do with it, but he claimed that I was the instigator. [Actually] his brother Francis did it."

Ford woke in the hospital with a broken arm. "That was a close thing," Frank blithely said to his bruised younger brother. "Another second and audiences would have realized I was using a double."

Backing up stories of Francis's lack of brotherly love was a Universal electrician of this period named Munroe, who would assert that Francis often abused his younger brother on the set, verbally and, on occasion, physically.

John Ford was a man who remembered—no, who *nurtured*—a grievance. Nearly twenty years later, during the production of *Judge Priest*, he had Frank play a scene in a wheelbarrow in front of a general store. When Frank was distracted, Ford had an assistant tie a rope from the wheelbarrow to the axle of a prop carriage. As the heroine rode off in the carriage, Frank had his perch yanked out from under him and took a hard fall, swallowing his tobacco.

"That was for the grenade," Ford said shaking his finger under his brother's nose, as if Frank had pulled his stunt the previous week.

Neither of the fratricidal brothers seemed able to stifle the raising of hell for its own sake. Propman Lefty Hough recalled an episode during the making of an Eddie Polo serial in which a circus tent was to be set on fire, then extinguished. Jack, working as an assistant to his brother as well as playing a small part, put gas in all the water barrels. When the gas was thrown on the fire, "all hell broke loose," recalled Hough. "We were all fired the next day, [but] after they sold the film, it was so good, everybody was in such a panic with that damn tent burning down . . . that we all got hired back again."

From the vantage point of 1951, by which time their professional positions had been completely reversed, Francis Ford remembered that "As a prop man he stunk; as an assistant director he was worse, and as an actor—well, such a ham! When I would tell Jack to put a chair in the corner for a scene, Jack would turn and say, 'Joe, get a chair and put it in the corner'; Joe would turn around and holler, 'Dutch, get a chair and put it in the corner'; Dutch would turn around and holler, 'Jake get a chair.' "

Jack Ford learned the motion picture business from the ground up, and inside out. He went to the movies, especially movies by D. W. Griffith, and, in 1928, he would assert that "The showing of those early pictures in the old Philharmonic Auditorium in Los Angeles meant more to the film industry and to the making of Hollywood than all the spectacles of inauguration that Hollywood promotes in these later days and nights."

He learned the mechanics and optics of a camera; he learned to prize the invaluable craftspeople, the unassuming blue-collar backbone of moviemaking. Like them, he was one of the workers and disdained the airs of the actor. He learned how a good director inspires loyalty and devotion. And he was reminded of how mothers worry about their sons.

"Dear Jack," Abby Feeney wrote on July 26, 1916, "I am at old orchard [beach in Maine] and am having a fine time. How is everything? Your dear mother." Ford was, at this point, living at the Virginia Apartments, 6629½ Hollywood Boulevard, and making $35 a week as an assistant director. The Virginia was east of Highland, a two-story building of pink stucco, a fashionable place for young picture people. In the summer of 1917, John and Abby Feeney visited their boy at his apartment. "What's this?" asked Ford's father, uneasily eyeing Jack's sleeping arrangements.

"It's a Murphy Bed," replied his son.

"The hell it is. No Irishman ever built a bed like this."

The success of his two sons meant that John Feeney could afford to retire. By 1920, he owned his own home mortgage-free at 91 Atlantic Street in Portland and was enjoying his leisure, although he and Abby still had four other people under their roof—daughter Josie, a schoolteacher; Maime, a widow; and Maime's daughters, Cecile and Mary McClean.

Although Jack's name was now Ford, he was, in many ways, still truculent Bull Feeney. "Jack Ford was his brother's right hand," remembered Jules White, who was also working at Universal at the time. "He was a carpenter, a cutter, a cameraman's assistant—anything that Francis Ford wanted him to be."

One day, while Frank and Jack were working on a serial called *The Adventures of Peg O' the Ring*, Jack asked White if he wanted to pick up some extra money—$5!—by patching negative on a Sunday. White enthusiastically agreed and spent his day off taking each piece of negative from Ford, splicing the film, taking the next piece, and so on.

The next day, White was told that an enraged Ford was going to kick his teeth in. It seems White had made every splice the wrong way, putting the end of the shot first. Besides that, every splice had come loose. For three days, White ran every time he saw Ford coming toward him or going away from him. His friends figured Ford was big enough and mean enough to break down any door, except one, so they took to locking White in a projection booth.

Finally, White worked up the nerve to confront Ford. "I did the best I could," he explained. "I don't know much about patching."

"Why didn't you tell me?" asked Ford.

"I was afraid I might wreck something."

For the next forty years, every time the two would meet, Ford would tell everyone he had no idea how White (who became head of short subjects at Columbia) could possibly be in the movie business, because he didn't even know how to splice negative.

At this point in his life, Jack appears to have been fairly social and very responsible; in September 1916, he joined the Knights of Columbus, and a month later he took out another insurance policy, paying $18 for $3,000 worth of coverage, again payable to his mother. Under "Occupation," he wrote, "assistant motion picture director, not acrobat or gymnast."

His relationship to Frank didn't insulate him from the vicissitudes of studio life; there were frequent layoffs at Universal, so he had to look elsewhere for work. He preserved a dismissal letter from L-KO, a lowly comedy studio, dated February 3, 1917. Things couldn't have been too grim, for that same month he was purchasing two custom shirts for $10 apiece.

To a great extent, the Jack Ford of this period was the John Ford who would be a world-famous film director in 1940. Even as a young man, he was very obviously Irish, and he had a crusty aura that signaled that he wasn't to be trifled with. "There wasn't any 'Please step over this way,' " remembered Allan Dwan. "It was, 'Come on, you bastards, get in line and shut up.' He was only 20 years old, but there was no doubt about who the boss was. . . . That's why he was a leader, that's why he could handle the men."

Hollywood was full of Irish directors in the silent days—Rex Ingram, Herbert Brenon, William Desmond Taylor, Marshall Neilan, Allan Dwan, Joseph Henabery, William Wellman, Raoul Walsh—but Ford would be the only one to consistently play the professional Irishman, as if he was in the Foreign Legion without a countryman in sight. There was an element of performance in this, but Ford's assertiveness would also be a form of compensation for his insecurity.

There are several variant versions of how Ford made the jump to the ranks of director. Ford's own version, repeated both to Peter Bogdanovich and others, was that he was pressed into service as a prop director, using a camera without film, to impress Carl Laemmle, who had suddenly appeared from New York. "I was just the prop boy . . . [but] I told the cowboys to go down to the end of the street and come back toward the camera riding fast and yelling like hell. Laemmle came up with his entourage and I had the cowboys do their stuff. Lammle seemed to like it."

Ford improvised some more action, even having some of the cowboys fall off their horses on cue. "A little later, they needed a director for a two-reeler and Laemmle said, 'Try Ford. He yells loud.' "

This is a viable scenario, but there is also an alternate version, in which Frank was the pivotal figure. "Harry had done a picture with Fred Kelsey at Universal," remembered Olive Carey, then Harry Carey's soon-to-be wife. "So Francis came to him one day and said, 'My kid brother is here. I understand that Kelsey is no longer to be your director and I think he'd be a hell of a director.' So Harry said, 'Well, bring him around.' So that's how they met and they just clicked."

Either version is possible, if only because in those days Universal was expanding exponentially, and all sorts of people were pressed into service to meet the demand for shorts and features geared to the largely rural market Universal specialized in. Expansion continued until late 1916, when the foreign market dried up completely because of World War I. But Universal cut back far less than the other studios, slicing off only some of the more marginal units being directed by Cleo Madison and Ida May Park. As was his lifelong knack, Ford was in the right place at the right time.

Whoever provided the spark, Carey gazed upon a skinny young man, six feet tall, with lots of deep red hair and glasses that evened out his near-sightedness. "He had a magnificent sense of humor," remembered Olive Carey of the young Ford, "and he was very graceful when he walked. He had a beautiful walk. He was imaginative, didn't miss a trick. A fantastic eye for the camera. He lined up all the shots. He was fascinated with everything, went into great detail about everything. He delved into all sorts of different things."

Harry went to Laemmle and told him he'd like to try out Francis Ford's little brother as his director. Laemmle said it was fine with him. Ford, said Olive Carey, had been getting $45 a week working for his brother, but after Carl Laemmle went back to Germany on one of his frequent trips, Universal's general manager, Isadore Bernstein, cut Ford's salary to $35. Losing $10 a week for the privilege of directing must have appealed to Ford's mordant humor, as well as providing him with a good example of the often Byzantine ways of the movie business.

Although he would always claim to view actors with horror, the fact is that Ford continued to be tempted by Frank's profession. In films that one would give much to be able to see—alas, they're lost—Ford directed and starred in a couple of Universal two-reelers, *The Tornado* in March of

1917, and *The Scrapper* in June. In the first film, Ford played Jack Dayton, a son of old Ireland known as "The No-Gun Man," whose great desire is to get enough money to send for his mother. Dayton goes after a vicious badman unarmed to earn the reward money.

The Scrapper had a fascinating plot, as outlined in *Moving Picture World* of June 4, 1917: "Buck the Scrapper loses his girl, who goes to the city when she is bored with the ranch. There, unemployed, she is innocently thrust into a house of questionable repute. When Buck and his friends bring a cargo of cattle to the city to sell, he is lured by a lady of the streets to the house and finds his girl there as she is being attacked. Buck fights her assailant, and takes the girl back to the West."

This sounds like a rough-and-ready Western, without the moralizing of the William S. Hart pictures that were at the height of their popularity, or the free and easy showmanship of the Tom Mix pictures that were still in their formative stages. Even at this nascent stage, Ford was interested in the reality of humanity.

Either Ford or Laemmle must have had some misgivings about his acting potential, because by the time *The Scrapper* was released, Ford was behind the cameras again, directing his first feature with Harry Carey. On June 9, 1917, the *Moving Picture News* reported that John Ford was now directing at Universal.

The first Ford-Carey collaboration was called *The Soul Herder; Moving Picture World* rated it "an excellent picture in every way." It was the first of more than twenty films that Jack and Harry would make over the next four years.

By this time, Carey had married Olive. The newlyweds and Jack formed a rollicking threesome who lived in Carey's little house in Newhall. Since there was only a kitchen and a living room in the house, the Careys and Ford slept in bedrolls in an alfalfa patch. ("Oh brother, were we Western!" said Olive Carey. "It was fun.") Their bedrolls had little canvas awnings that could be propped up so that when it rained the bedroll itself remained dry.

Carey had a tendency to collect dogs and cowboys, eight or nine of the former, five or six of the latter. Ford loved to sleep and he loved lounging in bed—in his later years, whenever he could get away with it, he'd have story conferences and other meetings take place around his bed—and hated to get up. "In order to get Ford out of the bedroll in the morning," said Ollie Carey, "Harry would turn all the dogs loose and they'd come over and lick Jack's face and wake him up. Then they'd go out and shoot movies around Newhall."

At the studio, Carey and Ford were treated little better than maintenance workers. Carey always insisted that his dressing room "was between Charlie the elephant and Joe the Monk," because his quarters were adjacent to the small zoo that Laemmle kept for jungle pictures.

On days when the Carey unit was working at the studio, Carey would drive into Hollywood, pick up a couple of horses at Otto Meyer's barn, and he and Ollie would ride up through the Cahuenga Pass to Barham Boulevard, "this beautiful valley," and go into the back end of Universal. "We rode to work every morning," Ollie Carey remembered with a sigh. Locations were at Newhall, Placerito Canyon, or the Vasquez Rocks.

"They weren't shoot-em-ups," said Ford of these early pictures, in which Carey usually played a modest, shambling saddle tramp rather than a bold gunfighter. "They were character stories. Carey was a great actor . . . he always wore a dirty blue shirt and an old vest, patched overalls, very seldom carried a gun—and he didn't own a hat. On each picture, the cowboys would line up and he'd go down the line and finally pick one of their hats and wear that; it would please the owner because it meant he worked through all that picture. . . . All this was fifty percent Carey and fifty percent me."

For a time, Jack roomed with a young rodeo cowboy–turned–actor named Hoot Gibson, who would remember his old roommate as "a natural. Only 21 and already close to a genius. He'd make up bits off the cuff, shoot them on the wing as he went along, then afterwards scribble them into the script." Ford was not shy about expressing his temper. Gibson told a story about Ford picking up a piano stool and braining him because he insisted on playing "Dardanella" constantly. Ford helped out Gibson by hiring him to work as Harry Carey's stuntman, which led him to supporting parts, then leads in B Westerns for the next twenty years.

Ford and Carey fell into an easy working rhythm, and Ford watched the older man at work, noted the economy with which he got his effects. "I learned a great deal from Harry," remembered Ford. "He was a slow-moving actor when he was afoot. You could read his mind, peer into his eyes and see him think."

After only a few months, Jack Ford was gaining notice within the industry; he was solicited by a publicity man named Clancy, who offered to place stories about him in the trade papers for $15 a month—payable in advance. And his pictures were being noticed by old friends back in Portland. One, a very coquettish girl named Marie, wrote in August 1917 that one of the two-reelers Jack had starred in as well as directed "nearly caused a riot in this old town. . . . Personally, I thought the picture was very good and thought you did wonderfully to direct it. . . . And did you really write it too? And you yourself, why my dear, you were positively handsome."

George Hively, who was helping to write and edit for Ford and Carey, became close to both men, as did his wife, Georgina, a stuntwoman. The Hivelys would often spend weekends at Carey's ranch at Newhall. "Harry Carey taught me how to swim," reminisced Jack Hively, George Hively's son. "He just threw me in the pool and said, 'Swim, you little son of a bitch.' And I started swimming. See, I'd let all the horses out of the corral just before that, and he didn't like that very much. Of course, if I'd have had some trouble, he would have been right in there after me. He was a warm, warm man. The real Harry Carey? Remember the character he played in *Mr. Smith Goes to Washington?* That was Harry Carey."

Things were about as formal at the studio as they were in Newhall. Ollie Carey always insisted that many of the stories for the Ford-Carey films were dreamed up around the wood stove in the kitchen. Jack and Harry would shoot their film off-the-cuff, then George Hively would write up an after-the-fact script so the front office would be happy.

In off moments, Jack would draw sketches—good ones—of faces on the back of a script page. Around the lot, there was friendship, there was freedom, and there were girls. He was not completely impervious to the good times traditionally enjoyed by young men in Hollywood, as this note, preserved on the back of an old still from the Universal period, attests: "Jack: Joe got the girls & made the date for tonight. 6 p.m. Jimmie." Ollie Carey remembered that a girl named Janet was Jack's first girlfriend.

America got involved in World War I, but Jack seems to have paid little attention. His sister Josie wrote him from Portland that "the old crowd seems pretty much broken up. There was no draft in Portland. The enlistments were so large and above the quota that they took no one. Fat Riley from the West end is in France with Jimmy Walsh and [they] have already been fired on. Bet they wish they were back 'doing' Congress Street."

While the early Ford-Carey two-reelers have disappeared, a few survive in script form. One, provisionally titled *A Dumb Friend* or *Cactus Pal*, has a rather touching story by Ford, about Cheyenne Harry being forced to sell the horse that he loves. The script contains little more than bare-bones outlines of shots: "Foreman rides into scene—gives order gruffly to Harry also to other boys who hasten off to get horses—Harry mounts and rides off with foreman . . ." The film was shot from May 20 to 23, 1917, and released under the title *Cheyenne's Pal* in August.

Across town at the Ince studios, where Westerns were also a mass-produced stock-in-trade, Ince was continuing to hand out incredibly detailed scripts for two-reelers, complete with indications for close-ups and medium shots, and parenthetical instructions to the director. Laemmle's Universal was satisfied with a script that was really just a series of telegraphic impressions. For most directors of series Westerns, this resulted in line-it-up-and-shoot-it hackwork, but the evidence of these years is that Ford had the requisite imagination to fill in the gaps with behavioral or visual grace notes.

Which is not to say that the studio was some sort of laissez-faire haven. Laemmle was concerned not so much with style as with content. A July 16, 1917, memo to all directors spells out lists of things "Wanted and Not Wanted" in Universal pictures. Among the things "Not Wanted" were fake wallops in fight scenes, stories dealing with the ruin of young girls, betrayal of virtue, neglect of children, cruelty to animals, excessive smoking, "cowboy stories which get over the idea that cowboys are either always drunk—getting drunk—fighting—or looking for a fight," "extreme" manifestations of sex, maudlin displays of patriotism, smoking by women, situations likely to instill fear, especially in the minds of young people, insanity, hunchbacks, "sissies," gruesomeness, tough dancing, gunplay, milk bottles to indicate poverty, rats, snakes, kittens, war drama, and, most curiously, "distressing situations."

Among the things deemed desirable were light drama, comedy-drama, amusement, good fights, fine riding, topical stories, domestic drama and little plays of everyday life, mother stories, heart interests, suspense, and "stories based on war conditions but not showing actual war stuff." Universal then, wanted their movies nice and polite, not too intense, with a leisurely sort of charm. They also wanted them cheap; rather than invest in striking prints for editing purposes, the rushes were run in negative.

For the most part, Jack Ford was just their man. He had already defined himself as someone who could do quality work, but would have to be let alone to do it his way, studio protocol be damned, as one memo from Universal studio executive William Sistrom proves: "Every once in a while, I have occasion to get after some of your actors for not being here earlier in the morning. Generally, they come back with the proposition that there is not much use getting here very early because the director usually arrives about 9:30 or 10 o'clock. I wish you would make a point of getting started as early as possible in the morning."

Jack and Harry both wanted to move up to features. Their entreaties met with indifference from the studio, so they elected to chisel their way in. Although they could shoot a feature in nearly the same amount of time they took to make a two-reeler (three to five days), they couldn't do it with the amount of raw film stock Universal doled out for a short. They simply told the purchasing department that the stock they had been issued had fallen in the water and they needed an equivalent amount of footage. That, at least, was Ollie Carey's version, but it does have the right combination of boys-will-be-boys clubbishness and chicanery.

Only two of Ford's early features survive, but they are clearly the work of a man with a future, and a surprisingly mature man at that—the frenetic movement-for-movement's-sake showing off of the young director is, on the basis of the surviving evidence, absent.

Providentially, Ford's first feature is also his earliest surviving complete film, and *Straight Shooting* shows that Ford had already developed components of his great talent, specifically his gift for landscape. The compositions, usually in deep focus, have balance, depth, and spaciousness, and he easily constructs all sorts of natural frames out of a tree and some foreground bushes. Interior sets were built in real locations so authentic exteriors can be glimpsed through windows and doorways.

The actors are easy and natural, with less gesticulation than was normal for the period; there are naturalistic tics scattered through the film, as in Harry Carey's lack of a gun belt; the gun is tucked in his pants.

Like any young man, Ford was influenced by others. There was Griffith, of course, but there was also Frank. After Frank was dead and their long rivalry was over, Ford would pay tribute to his brother. "He was a great cameraman—there's nothing they're doing today—all these things that are supposed to be so new—that he hadn't done; he was really a good artist, a wonderful musician, a hell of a good actor, a good director—[Jack] of all trades—and *master* of all; he just couldn't concentrate on one thing too long."

Sometimes the influences show. The settlers barricading themselves from attack in *Straight Shooting* carry echoes of both Griffith's *The Battle of Elderbush Gulch* and *The Birth of a Nation*. And there's more than a trace of Griffith in other shots—a gun barrel being forced through a slowly opening door—not to mention the gathering of the cattlemen, a pocket version of the gathering of the Klan in *The Birth of a Nation*. A gunfight in the street seems derived from Owen Wister's *The Virginian*; it's well done, but it's the sort of stock scene that Ford would seldom do in his maturity.

Straight Shooting reflects some of the sober austerity of the William S. Hart Westerns that were all the rage, but that was unavoidable because Hart was the only star making major Westerns. (Harry Carey was a star, but of a smaller magnitude, and Universal's production policy meant that his pictures were produced far more casually than Hart's, which usually had elements that elevated them beyond the status of quickie star vehicles.)

Yet, as William K. Everson noted, if the *Shane*-like plot of *Straight*

Shooting—the homesteaders vs. the cattlemen—and general air of realism are clear echoes of Hart, the level of production polish is considerably greater than comparable films from Universal, and certainly greater than you'd expect from a director making his first feature after quickly matriculating in slam-bang two-reelers, where there was no time for characterization, only story.

And there are fascinating foreshadowings of later films. In the end, Cheyenne Harry touches aspects of Tom Doniphon in *The Man Who Shot Liberty Valance*, as he experiences a deep sense of melancholy by helping homesteaders who inevitably will destroy his way of life. Harry's loneliness, his idea of himself as an outsider who can only cross the threshold of a home as a guest, will also be seen in Ethan Edwards in Ford's great, savage *The Searchers*.

Straight Shooting already reflects the sober, uncondescending approach that Ford would bring to Westerns. It looks more like a film from 1922 or 1923 than one from 1917, and, in an art form that moved as torrentially as the movies did in their infancy, that is no small statement.

The studio was upset about Ford and Carey going behind their back and making a feature. Plans were afoot to cut *Straight Shooting* back to a two-reeler, when Carl Laemmle ran the picture and said it was fine as it was. "If I order a suit of clothes," said Laemmle, "and the fellow gives me an extra pair of pants free, what am I going to do—throw them back in his face?"

Ford knew that *Straight Shooting* was a watershed for him; he kept the August 18 issue of the *Universal Weekly* that featured an article about the film and called it "the most wonderful Western picture ever made." (On the opposite page was an ad for a film starring and directed by Frank, *Who Was the Other Man?*)

Movies like *Straight Shooting* clearly set Jack aside as a talent to watch, as did *Hell Bent*, a 1918 vehicle for Carey. The story, by Ford and Carey, is nothing special, but there are some lovely, creative visual touches. At the beginning, a Western author is asked to provide a more realistic hero than the usual dime-novel heroics. He walks over to Frederic Remington's painting *The Misdeal*, a scene of the aftermath of barroom bloodshed, which then comes to life and the story begins. Ford finds visual expression for emotional states; as Cheyenne Harry carries the girl home in the rain, his abandoned friend wanders alone through a darkened saloon.

Trade papers began using phrases about Jack's films that had heretofore been reserved for Frank's: "Thrilling . . . teeming with life and color and action." In the *Motion Picture World*'s review of a Ford film called *Bucking Broadway*, the reviewer said, "Jack Ford again demonstrates his happy faculty for getting all outdoors onto the screen." Another review for another film singled out the "marvellous river location and absolutely incomparable photography."

The *Universal Weekly* wrote that "For a long time people have said, as they heard the name 'Ford' in connection with a picture: 'Ford? Any relation to Francis?' Very soon, unless all indications of the present time fail, they will be saying: 'Ford? Any relation to Jack?' "

CHAPTER FOUR

The Universal flack was on to something, for Frank's career would follow a slow but steady downward path. Frank's films for Universal lacked the authenticity they had reflected at Ince. In April 1916, Frank and Grace Cunard walked out of Universal in the middle of a serial when an efficiency expert named H. O. Davis demanded that Ford reimburse the studio $100 for the tent that Jack had helped burn.

Universal gave in, but it was a preview of coming attractions. Frank's temper burned bridges. When Cunard married someone else, he went on a monumental bender. Frank was forced to reconcile with his wife, and Universal split the co-stars up, only to find that their commercial appeal took a dive when they didn't work together. Soon afterward, Frank left Universal.

In 1919, Frank built his own studio at Sunset and Gower, and made a series of films that he wrote, starred in, and directed. But finding theaters that would play independent films was increasingly difficult as the 1920s wore on, and Frank's experiment ended after about four years. For the rest of the silent era, Frank directed Poverty Row Westerns and melodramas with stars like Texas Guinan, Jack Hoxie, Franklyn Farnum, and Jack Mower. "My father drank," remembered Francis Ford Jr. "He wasn't a drunk, but he enjoyed a party. He was like Jack in that he'd go on binges, then give it up."

Francis Jr.'s childhood memories of his father's home life are of a succession of houses and apartments—nothing settled, nothing permanent. Yet, as Francis Jr. recalled, "People liked my father. I remember walking down Hollywood Boulevard with him when I was a boy. He would constantly be stopped by people, and he was pleasant to everybody."

The conventional wisdom is that Frank's personal and professional capriciousness led him on a downward slide till he became a shameless hack who would turn his hand to anything that paid him a salary. *The Four from Nowhere*, a 1922 film starring and directed by Frank, was described by William K. Everson with open-mouthed admiration for its gall: "Anything really interesting happens out of sight. . . . Francis Ford has to make a 28-mile hike through snow and blizzard—and back again; this he manages within a 24-hour span, and even does some shopping en route, but all we see of the event is him going out of the cabin door—and coming back in again!"

When the characters are snowed in for the winter, all they have to entertain themselves with is a copy of *The Count of Monte Cristo*, which gives Frank the opportunity to kill an entire reel doing tableaus from Dumas. Similarly, Kevin Brownlow wrote that one of Frank's later efforts, *The Lash of Pinto Pete* (1924) was "so embarrassing it would put you off silent films for life."

But a recently discovered fragment of a 1927 Universal film directed by Frank called *Wolf's Trail* proves that he was far from over the hill. Although in cast and budget it's nothing but a B Western, *Wolf's Trail* is very snappily shot and edited, fully up to the high standards of A pictures of the late silent era. Frank frames shots between trees, uses whip pans, tracking shots, and even frames shots through doorways, just like his little brother. It's proof that the judgments of history are dependent on films whose survival is often completely arbitrary.

Jack's relationship with his older brother would always be fraught with unspoken tensions. As Jack's grandson Dan would say, "Francis scattered himself, and Jack Ford focused on one thing. Francis had his shot and he lost it, out of neglect. He took a long trip to the South Pacific—well, you take months and months away from your business, your business is going to be gone. Francis would tell Carl Laemmle to get fucked, and he probably told his brother to get fucked as well. And Jack Ford would remember every time he did."

For most of this period, Jack was flying beneath the publicity radar, which is undoubtedly the way he wanted it. You can look through dozens of issues of the *Universal Weekly* from 1914 to 1920 and find little more than nominal references to Ford—"once again, Harry Carey is directed by Jack Ford, one of the youngest directors in Hollywood."

Likewise, the New York critics couldn't be bothered with anything as déclassé as Westerns; the *New York Times* reviewed no John Ford movies made before 1922, and even after 1922 ignored such major releases—if not major achievements—as *Cameo Kirby*, *Kentucky Pride*, *The Shamrock Handicap*, and *The Blue Eagle*, among others.

There was no reason it should have been otherwise; the pictures that

Ford was making were unpretentious programmers, and, in any case, the movie business sold stars, not directors, unless it happened to be D. W. Griffith or that young but imposing man Cecil B. DeMille, who was putting Famous Players-Lasky on the map.

Ford was cranking them out—seven features in 1918, nine in 1919, plus a few two-reelers thrown in for good measure. Production schedules averaged no more than a week or so for a two-reeler, about two to three weeks for an average five-reel feature.

Despite the rushed schedules, Ford was able to instill some individuality into even the poorest of these sausages; a scene, sometimes just a couple of shots, to indicate someone had taken pains over the picture. Occasionally, people would notice.

For a 1918 feature entitled *Three Mounted Men*, a trade paper proclaimed that "you can always bank on Jack Ford producing a good picture. When you add a good cast to it, then he is bound to produce a knockout." By 1919 and a Harry Carey vehicle called *Rider of the Law*, the *Motion Picture News* was writing that "Mr. Ford's work has long been a source of admiration to those who follow closely the various western plays of the screen. The amount of rapid action he instills into his work and the manner in which he has emphasized the human note establish him as a very capable director." That same year, the *Moving Picture World* proclaimed that a Ford-Carey picture called *Riders of Vengeance* contained "much to please the eye by way of artistically chosen locations."

It was a very good time, not merely for Ford, but for all of Hollywood. The movie business was a bumptious, good-natured adolescent, growing by leaps and bounds amidst a Southern California that was virgin territory.

H. Bruce Humberstone would join Universal in 1920 as a propboy and assistant cameraman, and his first assignment was with Ford. The location was the Vasquez Rocks, north of Hollywood. Ford, Hoot Gibson, and the cameraman traveled on horses, but the lowly Humberstone had to hike with camera over one shoulder while holding a supply of film. Once they reached the top of a plateau, Ford asked him, "Humberstone! What do you think of this location?"

"I think," said the green kid, "that the top of that plateau over there would be better."

"Okay!" snapped Ford. "You heard the kid. Everybody over to the other plateau." Thus did an exhausted Humberstone discover one of the inviolable commandments of the Ford unit: never, but never answer a rhetorical question.

Hoot Gibson was once instructed by Ford to run his horse directly into a river where the water would be chest high on the horse. Gibson was an experienced cowboy, and knew that basic physics would cause the horse to rear up when the water struck his chest—the broadest part of the animal's body. Just before he hit the water, Gibson slowed the horse and rode him in on an angle.

"What's the matter?—You yellow?" screamed Ford. So Ford got on Gibson's horse to show him how easy the stunt was. "Jack jumped on my horse and ran him wide-open head on into the water. The horse exploded, reared up, fell back on top of him. So then I pulled my horse off of him and dragged him out. He didn't say a word."

Ford's theatrically self-effacing personality was evident even in the ads he took out in the trade papers. In *Wid's Daily Year Book for 1919–1920*, the forerunner of the *Motion Picture Daily Year Book*, Ford's ad is on the page across from Harry Carey's. It's a pen-and-ink drawing in a woodcut style. Ford is depicted leaning on a camera, back to the reader, watching Carey go through his paces. "Jack Ford Directing Harry Carey" is the legend on top. "Plain Westerns" is the line on the bottom.

The money was getting steadily better. As of September 1917, he was being paid $125 a week, with a raise to $150 six months later. In July 1919, he was offered a contract to direct an eighteen-episode serial for Universal (*The Adventures of Cavendish*) for $300 a week plus a $100 bonus for each episode completed for less than $4,000. (Ford ultimately did not direct the serial.) In September 1919, Jack traded in his Stutz on a brand-new Jordan that cost $3,155. Accompanying this rising tide of prosperity were great friends, new ones like the boxer James J. Corbett, old ones like Harry and Ollie. "Are you licked?" they wrote Ford from Cheyenne's Frontier Days on February 28, 1919. "Have had a great trip. They are still running *Wild Women* [a Ford-Carey production of the year before], regardless of the fact that 'Cowboys don't go on boats.' "

The bread-and-butter Westerns that Ford and Carey had been making were still the studio's financial backbone, but the films that got the publicity and enraptured the critics were by the studio's eccentric, brilliant young directors Erich von Stroheim and Tod Browning.

While on a trip to Denver, Harry and Olive Carey became friendly with an exhibitor named F. O. Brown, and convinced him to show them his books. They were appalled. Universal was charging Brown $2,500 a week for a Carey-Ford picture, but back at the home office they were only carried as having earned $250. The difference was applied to the large-scale productions on which Universal was spending all their money, to make it look as if they were doing much better business than they actually were.

Both Carey and Ford left Universal around the same time, and neither seemed to regret abandoning the Laemmle operation, a family-run organization in the worst tradition. One day Carl Laemmle was about to run a recently completed Ford picture when his adolescent son, Carl Jr., already known throughout the movie business as Junior, came in with his pet monkey on his shoulder. The senior Laemmle said he wanted his son to see the movie. Ford said he had no objection, but he refused to screen a movie for a monkey.

The monkey properly disposed of, the screening went ahead. When the lights came up, Laemmle asked his son what he thought of the picture. "I think it stinks," he said, whereupon Ford stood up and said, "Throw out the kid and bring back the monkey."

Harry Carey had collaborated on stories, scripts, production, and directing duties. He had given Jack Ford an opportunity, and then he had given him a career. But, with the single exception of *The Prisoner of Shark Island*, nearly twenty years later, the two men would never work together again, although they remained social friends. Something happened to cause a breach. Although neither man would speak of it, Ford's grandson Dan would come to believe that there was a financial element to the conflict between the two men.

"Ford was making $300 a week and Harry was making $2,000, with a very expensive lifestyle. He imported Navajos to live on his ranch in Newhall, where he had a trading post, a Western show. He spent money like a drunken sailor. I think Ford felt he was doing half the work and getting less than equivalent compensation. I think there was a deep-seated resentment about money."

It was time to move. In December of 1920, Jack Ford left Universal and went to work for William Fox.

It was not the only change in his life. That March, Mary McBryde Smith came to California to visit her brother Wingate. She had been born in Laurinburg, North Carolina, and educated at boarding schools, at one of which she had shared a room with the young Dorothy Parker. Mary had trained as a nurse, but her family moved to New Jersey when her father became a member of the New York Stock Exchange.

The Smiths were landed gentry, and Mary's mother, Martha Francis Roper Smith, could trace her ancestry back to the early twelfth century. One of her ancestors, William Roper, had married Margaret More, the daughter of Thomas More. Charles Edward Wingate Smith, Mary's father, made and lost several fortunes on Wall Street. When he died in Paris in 1925, Charles Smith was broke, but in 1920, the family was fairly prosperous.

Hollywood Boulevard was called Pepper Tree Lane when Mary Smith arrived. She found the town of Hollywood "beautiful and generous. . . ."

We only had one restaurant, and that was called The Oasis, and you could tell who was working because that was who the maitre d' would bring the check to at dinner."

Mary and Jack met at a St. Patrick's Day dance thrown by Rex Ingram, the director of *The Four Horseman of the Apocalypse*, at the Hollywood Hotel at Highland and Hollywood Boulevard. Mary had been invited because of her friendship with the wife of the future director William K. Howard. Mary would remember that it wasn't a courtship per se: "We met that night with Rex, and we saw each other every day after, and just naturally got married. Just naturally."

There was a sort of evergreen Confederate pridefulness in the Smith family. Jack sensed it and it made him self-conscious, even as he desired it. Mary had an unflappable calm that the far more volatile Jack sensed he needed for ballast. Jack felt himself to be marrying slightly beyond his station, and there are those who believe that much of his later work in the Navy during World War II was an effort to justify himself to his wife as much as to himself.

Besides the status she embodied, Mary knew nothing about the movie business—a strong point in her favor. "I had never heard about Harry Carey, and he was Jack's close friend," she reminisced. "They couldn't understand that I didn't know who Harry Carey was. It was a different life."

She wasn't threatened by the business either; her upbringing seems to have been more Edwardian than Victorian in that she had a tolerance for male misbehavior. One of her frequently repeated maxims was that if a man didn't have a mistress, it was because he couldn't afford it. Mary would always be an attractive woman, with a serene, self-possessed quality. Her grandson Dan would remember her as "an extraordinary woman, a real lovely lady, at least by Hollywood standards."

The relationship grew quickly. In June 1920, Ford rented a two-bedroom stucco house at 2233 Beechwood Drive; the lease was signed by "Jack and Mary Ford." A month later, on July 3, Jack Ford and Mary were married, but not in the Church because she had been previously married, during the war. Irving Thalberg and William K. Howard stood up for the bride and groom, and Allan Dwan, who knew his man, gave the couple a keg of bonded whiskey as a wedding present.

In October, they moved to a house at 6860 Odin Street in Hollywood that Jack purchased for $14,000. The house was attractive—stone-built, with leaded windows, situated on a hill in back of the Hollywood Bowl. The music from the concerts would waft over the four acres of wild gardens, the site of the Sunday parties that the Fords soon began throwing for their friends. Ford and Mary would live on Odin Street for thirty-four years; rather than move to a larger house, they would occasionally add a room, which lent the house a rambling, homey feel.

Nine months to the day after the wedding, on April 3, 1921, Patrick Michael Roper Ford was born. Little more than a month later, on May 16, 1921, Harry and Ollie Carey welcomed their child, Harry Jr., or, as he would be generally known, Dobe (because his hair was the color of adobe brick). Young Mr. Carey was greeted by Ford and Jimmy Walker, who were in the next room getting drunk on Melwood whiskey. "Melwood" would be Ford's insult name for Dobe, although he would occasionally resort to convention and address him by his preferred nickname.

Shortly after Patrick was born, Jack left on his first trip to Ireland. Mary must have begged off, citing the pressures of the baby, because Jack mentioned in his letters how much he wished she was with him. "Dear Old Fruit," he wrote her. "I am going to keep a sort of diarrhea for you about happenings on board (with the provison of course that I am able)."

The night that the ship left port, Ford wrote that "I am sorry to say, I am slightly drunk. Yes sir! Burned! I also have hiccoughs! Mary How I wish you were with me. Gosh we would have had such a delightful trip. It's really wonderful on the boat. I have spent the entire afternoon in the bar drinking bass ale and feel quite wonderful (except for the hiccoughs). Honey, the first opportunity we get you and I & Pat shall take a sea trip. . . . I think that after [new best friend, drinking companion, and successful director] Emmett [Flynn] and I finish our contracts, I shall persuade him to take Jean + then we all can take a trip around the world. How I wish you were with me."

Jack had already developed the thirst and the religiosity that would, in varying degrees, help define him for the rest of his life. "In the second-class cabins today saw an old friend Wyndham Standing, the actor," he wrote Mary. "He showed me a new drink called 'Bismarck,' a pint of Guinness stout and a pint of [illegible] champagne. Great. I'll show it to you when we get home. . . . I found a couple of Irish priests in the second cabins, and today they will serve Mass at 10:30 A.M. I went and tell [sic] grampa and then with a gulp of joy in his throat went on with the mass. Of course all the tads had tears running down their cheeks and when the prayer . . . came, it sounded like a hymn of heaven, so joyous these old folk were. . . .

"Just as the priest lifted the host, the clouds and fog lifted and three miles away we could see the shores of our beloved fatherland, 'The Emerald Isle' as green and as fresh as dew on the down. Even the priest stopped . . . [and] gazed."

Mary seems to have missed Jack as much as he missed her. In an undated letter that's probably from the trip, Mary addressed her husband as "Jack—My old sweetheart. I've never been so lonesome in my life as I am for you. Truly my dear. It's almost too terrible—I'm positively sick for the sight of you. . . . Really, Jack I have a wild, fiendish, *terrible* crush on you, and I miss you so it hurts awfully. I hope you come home soon sweetheart, I surely do love you more and more every day."

In Galway, Ford rented a touring car and rode on to Spiddal, where he had "a deuce of a time finding Dad's folks. There are so many Feeney's [sic] out there that to find out our part of the family was a problem. At last I found them. Spiddal is all shot to pieces. Most of the houses have been burned down by the Black and Tans"* and all of the young men had been hiding in the hills. As it was during the truce that I was there I was unmolested but as Cousin Martin Feeney (Dad's nephew) had been hiding in the Connemara Mountains with the Thornton boys, I naturally was followed about and watched by the B & T fraternity. Tell Dad that the Thornton house is entirely burned down."

Jack's exposure to the wet, thin soil of the western counties so frequently breached by limestone, the stone walls and small fields, the beautiful rolling hills, caused him to fall in love for the second time in a year.

The trip to Galway lit a fire in Jack that would never flicker. Like an assimilated American Jew transformed into an ardent Zionist after a trip to Israel, the political side of Ford's Irish identity kicked in with a vengeance. Martin Feeney would assert that Jack was questioned and "roughed up" by the Black and Tans, then put back on a boat for England and told not to return to Ireland. If Martin Feeney's story is true, it was an order Ford would disobey with the greatest enthusiasm for the rest of his life.

One of his early biographers, evidently stimulated by some stories of Mary's that undoubtedly derived from stories of Jack's, reported that the trip was, in some vague way, to "help in Ireland's final struggle for independence." While it might be too much to expect a written confirmation of such deliciously dangerous espionage, it's odd that Ford wouldn't write about such things then or later. A sentimental visit home, absolutely; reconnoitering the land of his forefathers, probably; actively engaging in subversion of the English, doubtful.

---

*The Black and Tans were basically a paramilitary militia, mostly veterans of World War I who needed jobs and would not be deterred by the rules that governed the army and conventional police. There were not enough uniforms, so the British usually gave them army tunics and policeman's trousers—a combination of black and tan. "They behaved like the German SS in World War II, and did lasting damage in Ireland which we are still paying for," says Kevin Brownlow.

• • •

After leaving Spiddal, Ford went to London ("Which I didn't like"), Paris, Marseilles, Nice, Monte Carlo, and Italy. "I had quite a wonderful trip but as I say I missed 'my fambly.' " On board the *Olympic*, he got a wire on December 25: "MERRY XMAS DADDY ALL WELL LOVE. PAT AND MARY."

Back in New York, Ford chummed around with writer Carl Harbaugh, who delivered the riding trousers Ford had had made in London for Emmett Flynn. "Tell Emmett to have them washed or cleaned with gasoline & they will soon turn white and nifty ala [cameraman and later director] George Hill's."

Leaving a wife and baby for a pleasure trip to Europe would be strange behavior for most men, but not Ford. There was a clear line of demarcation between those parts of his life that were private and those that could be shared by his family. "He said he only married me because I didn't want to get in pictures," Mary Ford would say. "I never went on the [movie] stage the whole years I was married. Never went near. That was one of the agreements we had. He said, 'If I were a lawyer, you wouldn't sit in my office. If I were a judge, you wouldn't hear my cases. . . . That's where all the trouble starts.' He'd bring scripts home, but he'd never ask me to read them. It was very funny, his work was a closed organization as far as the family was concerned."

While still in New York, Ford directed Mary Carr in a prologue to the film *Silver Wings*. He had been gone from his wife and baby three months and the economic conditions of the movie business in New York made him uncomfortable.

"I sure miss you and Pat. I gaze at his picture (and yours and Nana's) all evening long. I will sure be tickled to get back to Old Calif. Things here are in a terrible state. Nobody working at all it seems. Mary, we must buckle down and save money for this old game is going to be bad for a long while. I pity the poor folks who while they had it, spent it and then when it stopped, they stopped *eating*. We should draw a good lesson from it and do a lot of *economising* [sic]. You never know when you're going to get sick or injured or something else."

Ford had indeed missed his wife; as soon as he returned to the Coast, she became pregnant again. Barbara Nugent "Bobby" Ford arrived on December 16, 1922. Both children would have the best clothes, parties, and schools lavished upon them. Cecile de Prita, Jack's niece, said that Barbara lived the life of a "little princess."

In adulthood, Barbara would remember one incident that summed up the entire rarefied, storybook atmosphere of growing up in the movie colony: Barbara was attending a birthday party for Tom Mix's daughter when the cowboy star rode his horse into the entryway of his Beverly Hills mansion and shot out all the lights in the chandelier, to the utter rapture of the children.

Ford's reasons for signing with Fox were both economic and creative. His salary quickly doubled, from $13,618 in 1921 to $27,891 in 1922. Besides that, the studio was on the brink of a major building program spurred by William Fox's long-standing desire to be on an equivalent footing with Zukor and Paramount.

Ford arrived on a lot whose stars were Buck Jones, Tom Mix, William Farnum, and Annette Kellerman; in just a few years those names would be replaced by Charles Farrell, Janet Gaynor, Victor McLaglen, Edmund Lowe, and George O'Brien—not a roster equal to MGM's perhaps, but leagues ahead of Universal's. And Fox's list of cameramen and contract directors would be second to none—the cinematographers included George Schneiderman, Ernest Palmer, James Wong Howe, and Lee Garmes. Within five years, Ford would be directing pictures alongside F. W. Murnau, Frank Borzage, Raoul Walsh, and Howard Hawks, with a second-string roster that included William K. Howard, William Cameron Menzies, and Harry Lachman. Once again, Ford was in the right place at the right time.

Compared to Paramount, Fox had a small operation—four stages, just about the same size as the lowly Warner Bros. lot on Sunset. "They were producing as many [two-reel] comedies as they were features," remembered stuntman John Weld, who arrived in Hollywood in 1923.

Weld began the circuitous road to becoming a member in good standing of the Ford unit by doing a 136-foot dive off a cliff on Santa Cruz island. He had cards printed up, gave them to every studio casting office, and soon began working as a stuntman. Although only technically trained as a high diver, Weld was soon falling off horses, and turning over cars for Ford and other directors.

The main star on the lot was Tom Mix, "a tasteless kind of fellow," according to Weld. "I thought he was a phony, getting away with murder," specifically giving the impression that he did most, if not all of his stunts, when in fact he was regularly doubled by a long list of stuntmen that included Weld and Harvey Parry.

Bringing up the rear was the second-string cowboy star Buck Jones and a young leading man named John Gilbert. Mix was a showman, but not much of an actor; Jones was a better actor, but lacked the theatrical quality that Mix had in spades; and Gilbert was still a few years away from his apotheosis at MGM. Absent the unassuming authenticity that Harry

Carey brought to his pictures, Ford had to take what he could get, which did not always play to his strengths.

Providentially, Ford's first film for Fox was a good one, and it has survived. *Just Pals* is essentially a Buck Jones vehicle that could have been a Harry Carey vehicle, with the qualities that were already characteristic of Ford—folksy, well-observed characters in a setting rife with Americana—a town on the border between Wyoming and Nebraska—laced with Western-type action.

Bim is the town's good-for-nothing, terminally lazy layabout. "Wanna earn two bits?" he is asked. "I got two bits," he says. A gentle soul who can't bring himself to kill a chicken, he loves the schoolteacher, but from afar. Hooking up with a child hobo, he sends the boy to school, where he peers through the windows like Mae Marsh in *Intolerance*, but with fatherly concern replacing a mother's anguish.

By dint of some melodramatic plot machinations, Bim saves the schoolteacher from an embezzling charge, reunites the young hobo with his parent, and earns a rich reward for his troubles. When last seen, he is walking in the woods with the schoolteacher and the smugly dismissive townspeople have learned the error of their original estimation. Bim's life as an outcast is over.

Narratively, *Just Pals* is of nominal interest, but visually it's fascinating. Already Ford is making the landscape a character; *Just Pals* is full of dappled light and shade, leaves moving softly in the breeze, gently rolling landscapes revealed in quiet pans and tracking shots. *Just Pals* probably gives a good idea of what Ford's films at Universal were like—confident, relaxed, with an understated lyrical touch, a sense of domestic detail, and a protective sense of humanity that only a few men of the period—Griffith, Maurice Tourneur—could match. As Lindsay Anderson would write of the film, "For all the artifice of its plotting, the way people behave is real; feelings are experienced, not just represented, and in this way the stereotypes are brought to life."

Just Pals puts in place one of Ford's primary thematic mainstays: the superiority of people on society's margins to mainstream solid citizens. Take away the melodrama and it's a Will Rogers picture, nearly the equal of *Judge Priest*, fourteen years later.

The critics noticed: "It is the human touches, both of comedy and pathos; the well created atmosphere of the small . . . town; the very natural dialogue; and the picturesque character of 'Bim' that will win favor for this picture. It is well directed throughout."

And William Fox noticed as well. "*Just Pals*," he wrote, "was one of the most artistically done pictures that I have reviewed in years. . . . Ford has proven that if Jones is properly directed he can play any part."

• • •

The West Coast operation of Fox—the studio was at Sunset and Western—was run by a tough character named Sol Wurtzel, who was possessed of a strange facial tic that made him look like he was smiling when he wasn't. Much of the studio's energy derived from Winfield Sheehan, formerly the secretary to Rhinelander Waldo, the police commissioner of New York. Sheehan was a sharp operator who had been one of the three men supervising gambling in Manhattan and allocating protection money. He had been forced to resign in 1914, when the madam of a whorehouse named him as "the Man Higher Up."

William Fox liked a man who liked money and power. Sheehan took a surprisingly personal interest in his actors; in October 1919, he wrote Buck Jones a letter that treated the actor as an idiot teenager: "Please bear in mind that you will give personal, painstaking attention to the following. . . . Your hair in pictures must always be neatly combed unless you are in a fight. You should arrange to have your hair cut and washed and oiled once a week to give it proper appearance and gloss. . . . Your teeth require proper attention with polishing and cleaning by a dentist once every two months and very careful attention several times daily. It should be a practice of yours to open your mouth a little wider when you smile so that your teeth are seen more."

Sheehan also took the initiative when it came to recommending story material. "I am enthusiastic and confident in my recommendation that a production of THE VILLAGE BLACKSMITH based on Henry Wadsworth Longfellow's poem, would be a wonderful box office attraction," Sheehan wrote William Fox on November 15, 1921. "Every man, woman and child who can speak English throughout the world has read THE VILLAGE BLACKSMITH and one out of every three people know the entire poem by heart.

"My idea of the scenario is that it should show the strong, regular, vigorous life the blacksmith leads, how his family, four children, two boys and two girls, progress in the world, in true Christian Spirit, and in contrast to showing the life of the idle rich classes, and the misery endured because they do not live a regular, honorable and religious life."

Having made his case, Sheehan then moved in for the clincher: "I understand THE VILLAGE BLACKSMITH has run out of copyright." Ford was a natural for the project—not only was the homespun Americana of the material up his alley, but Longfellow had been raised in Portland, Maine.

Only a single reel of the film survives, and it's not much, but the complete script exists, and shows that the common idea of Ford being dealt unfamiliar scripts as if they were playing cards was and is erroneous.

Clearly, Ford was intimately involved in the construction of the scenario that was invented from little more than Longfellow's title. Screenwriter Paul Sloane structured the script with an opening in which the characters are all children, followed by a Part II in which they are adults, and his script is full of parenthetical asides deferring to Ford's ideas about staging.

The blacksmith's shop was to be "built as per Mr. Ford's plans"; "above the altar is a large mural painting in which are prominent the figures of a male and female—Mr. Ford understands that this is intended for an effective dissolve at the finish of the picture"; "The addition of further gags and scenes with dogs will be made as per discussion between Mr. Ford and Mr. Sheehan."

In an undated letter from about 1921, Ford wrote to a supervisor at Fox about a script he had read, offering some insight into his taste in material: "Tho it starts out very interesting, it takes a decided flip about the middle. It leads to *nothing*. There is too much uninteresting 'mellerdrama' and not enough of the mystic 'supernatural' about it to make a big feature. It could be made into a fairly interesting story, however, if some of the coincidental sequences were worked over."

But stories with a sufficient amount of mystical qualities were hard to come by at Fox or any other studio, and Ford willingly applied himself to whatever was at hand, including reshoots on other directors' films.

J. Gordon Edwards had shot a spectacle called *Nero* in Europe and turned in his cut early in 1922. Fox felt the climax needed punching up. Ford proposed slightly more than a week of retakes to turn the climax of the film into as close a simulation of a patented Griffithian ride to the rescue as possible: "I propose building several enormous drums to be used by the Roman soldiers for signaling," Ford wrote in a memo to Winfield Sheehan on March 3, 1922. "Upon the beating of these drums show different cuts of Roman soldiers on horseback and in chariots riding towards a gathering place (a la clansmen). During the gathering of these men we could cut several times to the signal drums. Just at the point where the Christian martyrs are seen leaving the dungeon to enter the Roman arena, I think a shot showing the different horsemen entering a great field and getting in line would be very effective."

Ford went on to suggest a sequence where horsemen struggle for a place on a narrow bridge, causing some of them to tumble into the water. "I will shoot this in a place where I know about ten of the leading horsemen will go down with a crash so that I can use a cutback of part of Nero's army composed of archers shooting at them to heighten suspense. . . . By this time the audience, I hope, will be on their feet cheering, praying to God that they get there on time."

Ford appended a note telling Sheehan that riders would cost $7.50 a day, horses, $2.50. Add costumes, and Ford figured that one man would cost about $13 for each day of shooting. Figuring 150 riders for three days of long shots and twenty-five riders for close-up work for six days, Ford estimated the cost for the added scenes would be $7,800. "The picture as it stands is such a tremendous thing that, personally, I think the amount of money I mentioned would be but a drop in the bucket; however, this is a matter for you to decide." Ford was given the go-ahead to make the scenes and they were used in the picture.

Since Ford had directed Universal's main Western star, he was put into harness with Fox's counterpart, Tom Mix, for a couple of the slickly produced, slam-bang melodramas he specialized in.*

Ford continued his ascent at Fox with *Cameo Kirby*, a prestigious adaptation of a play by the popular Booth Tarkington. Except for some atmospheric photography, the dashing John Gilbert, and the first, indistinct appearance of Jean Arthur, *Cameo Kirby* is a film directed on autopilot; Ford would always be helpless when confronted with the conventions of stage melodrama.

Although the only apparent surviving print is in tatters, enough visual glory remains—a horseback chase through the pastures of the South, a pistol duel amidst tall grasses—to boost the viewer over the tedious plotting. Ford's command of exteriors is leagues ahead of the interiors.

It was with *Cameo Kirby* that Ford felt dignity creeping up on him. Although his friends would call him Jack for the rest of his life, for public consumption his billing was no longer Jack Ford. From *Cameo Kirby* on, he was to be professionally known as John Ford.

---

*"Powerful! Written by Destiny, directed by the hands of Fate, enacted by God's select! Thrilling!" went the parodically breathless ad copy for *North of Hudson Bay*, a "Northern" that Ford directed for Mix. The pressbook also claimed that Mix made his own canoe after having been taught construction by "thoroughbred Indians."

CHAPTER FIVE

On July 1, 1862, Abraham Lincoln signed the Pacific Railroad Act, which authorized the construction of a transcontinental railroad connecting the eastern half of America with the West, a feat of engineering that nobody was even sure could be accomplished. The railroad was to be financed by a combination of government loans and land grants; the government agreed to lend the two railroad companies involved $16,000 per mile in the Plains area, and $48,000 per mile for mountain construction.

The Central Pacific, employing thousands of Chinese, began laying track east from Sacramento, going up and over the Sierra Nevadas. The Union Pacific, using mostly Irish and Italian immigrants, worked westward from Omaha. Seven years after construction began, on May 10, 1869, the two railroads met at Promontory Point, Utah, symbolically uniting a nation torn apart by Civil War.

Equally as important, the joining of the rails signaled the closing of the American frontier. As one film historian noted, "When the horse begins to give way to the train, the West is changing," an observation that could have come from any number of John Ford characters.

In 1923, Paramount had an unexpected blockbuster with James Cruze's *The Covered Wagon*. To modern eyes, the film is distinguished only by Karl Brown's superb photography, but the novelty of its story and the scope of the unfamiliar locations provoked an enormous response from audiences and critics alike.

The Covered Wagon was the film that fired the starting gun for the Western epic. William Fox quickly determined to try to top it. If *The Covered Wagon* told of the courage and hardships of the pioneers of the late 1840s, then Fox would make a film about the post–Civil War building of the transcontinental railroad, which rendered such wagon trains obsolete.

Ford campaigned hard for the assignment, and seems to have used the semilegendary Michael Connelly's connection with the transcontinental railroad to get the job. "I had an Uncle Mike who was in the Civil War," he told a panel discussion in 1964. "In fact, I had four uncles in the war. I used to ask my Uncle Mike to tell me about the battle of Gettysburg. All Uncle Mike would say was, 'It was horrible. I went six whole days without a drink.' Uncle Mike was a laborer on the Union Pacific Railroad when it was built. He told me stories about it and taught me the songs they had sung. I was always interested in the railroad and wanted to make a picture about it."

Although still a young man, Ford had amassed a considerable body of experience, and Fox clearly thought he was a comer. When he undertook *The Iron Horse*, he was only thirty-one years old, but he had directed more than a dozen two-reelers and over thirty-five features—far more finished film than any modern director can hope to accomplish in his working life.

George O'Brien was born in April 1899, twenty-nine years after his family emigrated from Ireland; George's father, Dan O'Brien, was the San Francisco chief of police from 1920 to 1928 and was, remembered his grandson Darcy, "a better actor than my parents."

George did odd jobs around the city stables and took his payment in horseback riding. Later, he learned the crafts of roping and bulldogging from a friend of the family who owned a nearby ranch. High school gave him the opportunity to excel as an athlete; the young man earned letters in four sports.

O'Brien didn't want to go to college, but enlisted in the Navy instead, where he became light-heavyweight champion of the Pacific fleet. Upon being discharged in 1919, O'Brien was back in San Francisco, handling police horses when Tom Mix came to the city for a visit. Mix liked the young man's gung ho athleticism and matching personality and offered him a job as an assistant in his unit at Fox.

While lugging cameras, stunting, and doing extra work around the Fox lot, O'Brien tested unsuccessfully for the lead in *Ben-Hur*, as well as a popular series of Universal two-reelers called *The Leather Pushers*. While he had the requisite looks and physique, MGM wanted at least a semi-name for their biblical epic, while Universal told him that they were looking for an actor who could look like a boxer, not the other way around. So it was back to Fox, and sharing a room with a young gag man named Mervyn LeRoy and a young actor named Gary Cooper.

According to O'Brien, Ford had tested fifty-eight actors for the lead of *The Iron Horse* by the time they got around to him. As always, Ford took advantage of the moment, calling out to actress Gertrude Olmstead as she walked across the stage during the test, "George is making a test for the part; would you do a little scene with him?" He proceeded to improvise a five-minute love scene—man pursued, has only five minutes to say goodbye to the girl he loves, etc.

The test went off to New York, while O'Brien continued his catch-as-catch-can life around Hollywood. Ford called him back for another test, this time a fight scene with Fred Kohler, and some action footage with O'Brien vaulting onto a horse. On the last take, the saddle cinch broke, the horse went one way and O'Brien went another. Bouncing up unhurt, O'Brien was ready for more. Ford loved actors who could absorb abuse of all kinds; as far as he was concerned, O'Brien had the part.

For all Ford's conviction that he had found the right man, William Fox remained hesitant about building a major epic on the back of an untried actor. O'Brien was working as one of the galley slaves in *The Sea Hawk* when he finally got the word to report to Fox. There, Ford and Sol Wurtzel read the young man a letter from William Fox himself: ". . . and I caution you again—this is entirely untried, an entirely new man, unknown. You will take the scenes 90 times if necessary." O'Brien must have looked worried, because Ford promptly told him he was sure ninety takes wouldn't be necessary.

O'Brien and Ford would prove a good match; the young actor was a hearty, good-natured man, similar in temperament to the parts he usually played, and, as his performance in Murnau's *Sunrise* proved, a good actor when he had the chance. On the set, O'Brien called Ford "Coach," and appreciated the fact that the older man was totally committed to his work.

"It may be theatrical to say, 'He lived it,' " O'Brien remembered, "but he did and we did. And this is the way he liked it. You'd sit around at nighttime on location and talk over the scenes. He'd pick you up on a Sunday morning after church, go down to the studio and run some film." United by their heritage, their religion, and their love of the sea, the two men became close friends.

The West was only slightly less hazardous for filmmakers of 1924 than it had been for the railroad builders of the 1860s. Indians were no longer a threat, but the elements were, and Ford was determined to venture into the wilderness and build the encampments and towns in which he would be shooting. Because the Old West had not entirely disappeared, Ford opened his film to as much authentic atmosphere as he could find. To make a story about pioneers, Ford insisted that the crew and actors had to live like pioneers.

A skeleton crew under Ford began work in Mexico, traveling down through Douglas, New Mexico, finally reaching their destination 250 miles across the border. There, they photographed scenes with a herd of cattle large enough for the production's requirements. The cattle were fine, but the hotels were nonexistent, so, as cameraman George Schneiderman remembered, "We spent a week shooting from dawn to dusk and sleeping at night under the well-known Mexican skies."

From there, they doubled back to New Mexico, where Schneiderman and the crew had the dubious pleasure of seeing their breakfast slaughtered in front of them. Schneiderman promptly swore off beef for the duration of the New Mexico shoot. And then it was time for the long location in Nevada, where most of the film would be made.

The film's logistics were difficult; they needed railroad track, of course, but they also needed an adjacent spur where railroad cars and equipment could be parked. There were three hundred people in the company, most of whom were living in Pullman cars that Fox rented from the Al G. Barnes circus. The right spur was finally located at Dodge, Nevada.

Before the company moved to Dodge, Ford shot the film's prologue, in which the young George O'Brien—played by Winston Miller—meets Abraham Lincoln. The location was a town called Wadsworth, and Ford remembered that when they got off the train it was 20 below zero. "We went up there prepared for routine Hollywood weather—all sunshine and blue skies," Ford would tell Lindsay Anderson. "We got out of the train . . . and nearly froze to death." It was at this point that it began to snow.

For one of the few times in his career, if not his life, Ford was stunned into immobility. "I said to George Schneiderman, the cameraman, 'What'll we do? We only have four weeks to make it.' George said there must have been snow when they built the railroad so why don't we shoot anyway?" Assistant editor Harold Schuster took a series of snapshots of the early stages of production. Ford is wearing a leather jacket and a ski cap, while George O'Brien is bundled up in a winter coat. When it came time to shoot, O'Brien had to doff the coat and pretend it was summer.

"It was winter, cold as hell," remembered Winston Miller. "Everybody lived on the circus train in the middle of nowhere, except me. My father was up there with me, and they sent me back to Reno every night to a nice warm hotel. The rest of them were freezing!"

For the opening scenes of the picture, Lincoln (played by Charles Edward Bull, a Reno judge) talks to the children who grow up to become O'Brien and Madge Bellamy. In the background appeared a Basque sheepherder with several hundred head of sheep. "We've got to get this in the picture," Ford ordered. "Run out there and stop the sheep herder."

As propman Lefty Hough didn't speak Basque, he had to come up with another alternative. He quickly ran over to his prop box, put on a sheriff's badge, and ordered the sheepherder to halt while they made some shots of the herd. Since the composition of the shot had been radically altered to accommodate the sheep, there was now a seven-foot willow tree in the way. Much scurrying around looking for an ax. Hough finally found one in a track walker's shack. He also found a gallon jug of whiskey. The ax took care of the willow tree, and the jug took care of the crew.

In Dodge, the crew constructed the frontier towns that would figure in the story. George Schneiderman and the other five men in the camera crew slept in the set that was built for the Pony Express office.

The company lived on the train; for a mess hall, they erected a circus tent. Madge Bellamy, the film's efficient, colorless leading lady, was given a berth in the train's observation and sitting room section. Normally, the director would also have taken a berth in that section, but Ford elected to bunk with the extras, sending a very clear message. The general having set the tone, the troops willingly followed.

"People ask me about John Ford's genius," wrote Madge Bellamy near the end of her life. "I don't think it lay in his direction of individual scenes; it lay in his panoramic view of the whole picture—his ability to achieve artistic unity. The timing, the emphasis, his grasp of the whole drama constituted his art."

Back in Hollywood, Sol Wurtzel wired Ford: "Received first day's work of North Platte, street looks splendid snow makes it doubly realistic and attractive—believe after you review scenes on screen you will feel all trouble of present location was worthwhile."

Ford was performing that most difficult of directorial tasks—shooting blind, shipping each day's work to Hollywood; Fox would ship it back days later. By the time he saw a day's work, it could be a week later, making retakes difficult.

The unit rigged up a projection room in one of the boxcars, but it was so cold nobody wanted to go in. "Nobody looked at a foot of the film," asserted Lefty Hough. "I never saw a foot of it, Ford never saw a foot of it, and how the hell it ever went together I'll never know, but it was [all in] this guy's mind."

As the work ground on, tempers began to flare, especially back at the studio. Four weeks came and went, and the picture was nowhere near finished. Ford told a story about Sol Wurtzel coming out on location to see what the hell was going on, and getting so involved in a marathon crap game that he went back to Hollywood without ever pulling the plug. It's more likely that William Fox looked at the rushes and liked what he was seeing. Just as Irving Thalberg did with *The Big Parade*, Fox okayed the expansion of a big picture into an epic.

There was a very high percentage of authentic roughnecks on the picture—"Every man we took up there could ride, could shoot and would do stunts," Lefty Hough told Kevin Brownlow—so things like ketchup bottles had to be removed from the mess hall, lest they come into play during fights. Outhouses were constructed on the back of the town sets. Lefty Hough said that "You could walk in anytime, and you were liable to find an Indian woman sitting in there."

Although no one seems to have been born on the picture, it's probable that several people were conceived, and at least one person died, a young circus steward named Kelly who expired from pneumonia.

Ford seems to have moved steadily forward. He had only one slip from his responsibilities, an alcoholic outburst that lasted a couple of days. *The Iron Horse* and Chaplin's *The Gold Rush* were both shooting in and around Truckee. Ford, as was his habit, endeavored to make sure his own set was dry, but when he heard that Rollie Totheroh, Chaplin's cameraman, was well supplied, he couldn't resist.

"Ford heard I had a couple of bottles of Scotch with me," Totheroh told Timothy Lyons. "He looked all over, he called me 'Rollo, Rollo.' And he came in . . . and tore the toilet off the floor [and] threw it out the window. They raised the devil . . . and then they had their hook shop down there. They wrecked all the hook shops . . . they wrecked everything."

Ford was finally found lying in a drunken sleep with a couple of extras. "That was just Jack," George O'Brien would remember. "Who knows? He needed it."

"Most of the picture was actually shot off the cuff," said Lefty Hough. "It was discussed—they'd had several writers—but Ford had his own conception of how he was going to play it. I don't think there were more than three or four [copies of the] script in the whole troupe. It all came out of Ford's mind, his imagination; whatever he had on paper didn't make any difference. It was the idea of the railroad."

"*The Iron Horse*, as written, wasn't a good scenario," recalled stuntman John Weld, "but he made something out of it. We [stuntmen] didn't play Indians, we *had* Indians. He felt that this was his great opportunity, and he should not try to be funny about it or use fakes of any kind. He went at it wholeheartedly."

Hot water was generally supplied by the tank of the train engine, and the weather was a constant factor. A scene would be begun in a normal street; during the night it would snow, and at dawn the entire company would be out with shovels and brooms, moving the snow out of camera range so they could begin shooting by 9:00 or 9:30.

This communal, off-the-cuff quality of location life would come to be prized by Ford; it was catch-as-catch-can, away from the hated front office. It forced Ford to rely on his instincts, and forced the large, dependent film unit to look to Ford for guidance.

In some cases, it was an extended family in the literal sense—Eddie O'Fearna, Ford's brother, worked for one of the first times as his assistant, and, remembered Lefty Hough, they "were fighting all the time. This goes back to the days in Maine when Eddie and the others ran a saloon and they used to kick Ford out of there and wouldn't let him drink. Ford never got over this. I had to break up the fights." Once, Hough remembered, Eddie went after Jack with a pickhandle.

"[Ford] would have nothing to do with anybody outside his crew," said Lefty Hough. "He hated strangers, didn't want a new man on the crew, and was very difficult. He'd have nothing to do with producers. You see, Ford was . . . a very difficult man to understand, but if he liked you and you knew what you were doing, he never bothered you, never questioned your ability. But if you tried to outsmart him, it was a little different story. I had started with him, I could talk to him, and he would let me make suggestions. He let very few [people] do that."

To encourage the feeling of a community, someone started up a little newspaper called "Fox Folks Junior, Published daily at Camp Ford Nevada," two or three mimeographed pages buttressed by an admirably succinct editorial motto: "It Might Be Worse and It Isn't So Bad." Each issue contained mild jokes ("No, Jack Ford is no relation to Henry but neither is Henry to Jack—so there"), weather forecasts ("Fair enough"), waggish queries ("How [do] Director Jack Ford and his assistant Eddie O'Fearna keep their pipes lighted?"), and news and notes of the production.

"First scenes were shot yesterday by Director Jack Ford on the North Platte Street," announced the edition of January 6, 1924. "Now that the ice has been successfully broken let's hope that nothing happens to interrupt the good work." The publication would muse about racial history: "It is a peculiar twist of fate that these Americans [the Paiute Indians] whose ancestors were driven from their homes during the actual construction of the railroad which serves as a theme of the Ford picture, should now extend a welcoming hand of assistance to the descendants of their forefathers' enemy."

There were bad puns ("There have been some smart arguments on this trip between Jack Ford, Cyril Chadwick and Col. McGee regarding 'berth-right'—but none of them get heated") and even cozy little blind items: "A budding romance seen from the back/The girl's a queen named Frances/And the man's name is Jack."

The newspaper unwittingly preserved the bloodcurdling racial attitudes of the day, as in this proudly documented anecdote from the edition of January 14, 1924: " 'Lefty' Hough, our beloved 'prop-master' had his opportunity one day last week to display his well known 'wise-cracking' ability.

"It seems that 'Lefty' was giving his official once-over to some of the 'prop' graves that had been dug for Mr. Ford's 'pitcher' when a stolid old Indian wandered up to 'Lefty' and asked him what he was looking at (a stupid question, old boy).

" 'Why, that's a grave,' replied the curly-locked 'Lefty.'

" 'Well, bury me there—huh,' said the dark-skinned one.

" 'What for,' came right quick from the demon 'propmaster.' 'You've been dead and buried ever since you have lived in this part of the country.' The redskin evidently saw the reason of 'Lefty's' logic reply—he turned on his heel and walked away. 'Lefty' hasn't seen him since."

Everybody was doubling up. Assistant editor Harold Schuster played eight or nine small parts, Lefty Hough two or three. Even the makeup man was pressed into service before the cameras. In time Ford relaxed his "no booze" rule and allowed the company their own bootlegger ("the worst whiskey of anybody in the world," asserted Lefty Hough. "It must have been 200 proof") and, evidently, their own brothel. "This car stopped and a beautiful woman got out and she beckoned to somebody to come over. We had an English actor by the name of Cyril Chadwick that spoke the King's English and Ford says, 'Cy, you go over and see what the lady wants.' Well, we sent Cyril over, he comes back and says, 'John old boy, this is quite a problem. She wants to bring six prostitutes out here and put up a tent.' A true story."

Ford had about six real Indians, including one called Great White Spear who could ride, shoot, and was a good actor to boot. Ford managed to round up about thirty-five Chinese extras, but he needed more than that for the tracklaying scenes, so some of the Indians were pressed into service to play Chinese laborers.

For battle scenes, Ford hired Pardner Jones, an Old West character who fired live ammunition around George O'Brien's scrambling body. Bullets came through the railroad ties that had been used to construct many of the buildings. "We were scared to death," remembered Hough. "Ford kept on yelling, 'Fire more, to hell with it, just get the hell out of the way. Fire back, fire back.' We kept digging in and getting lower and lower all the time. Sounds funny now, but it wasn't funny then."

Another time, Ford instructed Pardner to shoot a clay pipe out of the mouth of a man named McCluskey without McCluskey knowing about it. "It scared him to death," reported Lefty Hough. "For that matter, his jaw was sore for two weeks. It scared the hell out of him, and everybody else too."

Ford fell in love with the texture of the air when it was filled with dust. There weren't any wind machines on location, so before a take, hay wagons and horses would be run through, churning up just enough dust to lend some atmosphere.

Lefty Hough estimated that *The Iron Horse* company laid about a mile and eight hundred yards of railroad track, and used only two real engines. Since the story called for more than two engines, the crew would alter the position of the smoke stacks and change the numbers on the side. Nobody ever noticed.

Up in Truckee, there was so much snow that the engine froze and couldn't be moved. Since the story involved the constant movement westward of the rails, Ford was on the verge of admitting defeat. They attached fifty head of horses to the locomotive, but it still wouldn't budge. Finally, Ford rigged up a dolly shot and tried to slide the camera past the engine rather than the other way around. The result was rough but successful.

The Iron Horse brought a sense of reality to the screen, and to the people making it. "There was real suffering on that picture," said Lefty Hough. "It was hard, tough, awfully primitive conditions. Christ, it was cold. You'd get out there and have to work on that track, and the wind blew in the snow, and have to mount a horse and the Indians had to go around with no clothes on. It was murder, hard work, a long tough day every day. There were very few parties, not too much drinking, but nothing to extremes, not like a normal picture that goes on location."

As production plodded on, the difficult weather and the roughing-it nature of the production began to wear everybody down. The company newspaper ran an item that needed to be read with a wail: "There's one thing in this wide world/That troubles my poor brain/When will we see dear Los Angeles/Or Hollywood again?"

Ford staged the re-creation of the driving of the Golden Spike, with what William Fox claimed was the original *Jupiter* locomotive, lent by the Central Pacific, and a twin of the original Union Pacific engine. "We stood watching these two ancient engines move slowly toward each other," reported the location newsletter, "and finally touch over the last tie and the golden spike. This ceremony, though only the motion picture revival of the original, took on a greater significance than is usually felt during the filming of scenes that are inspired by a lesser theme."

Ford finally began looking at his film when the unit arrived back in Hollywood. "Every day after work we used to quit about 3:30 or 4 o'clock and we would run some part of the picture," said Lefty Hough. The final negative cost of *The Iron Horse* was about $250,000.

• • •

As the film was cut together in the early summer, William Fox began the publicity drumbeat, indulging in the usual gross exaggerations. Fox claimed ten thousand head of cattle, thirteen thousand buffalo, and a thousand Chinese were used in the production. Every available billboard in New York was plastered with posters and teaser ads; every paved road leading into the city carried huge signs announcing the imminent arrival of *The Iron Horse*. Fox even hired a skywriter (at $1,000 a trip) to spell out T H E I R O N H O R S E in the skies over Manhattan.

The ads certainly created the impression of an epic: "Blazing the Trail of Love and Civilization," said one. "A soul-stirring drama of the building of the first transcontinental railroad, with the dreams, the courage, the sacrifice and suffering, the sin and the songs, and the love and devotion of the good men and women of those days."

Fox wasn't about to miss an angle, so three different ad campaigns were used. Besides the primary message of epic adventure, there was one suggesting a nonexistent romantic triangle ("Woman Against Woman in a Romance of East and West, Blazing the Trail of Love and Civilization") and one building up George O'Brien ("He's Not a Sheik or a Caveman or a Lounge Lizard—He Is a Man's Man and an Idol of Women").

The Iron Horse premiered in New York on August 28, 1924. The reviews were nearly as enthusiastic as the publicity. "It is a big, fine achievement," said the *New York World;* "I stood up—I admit it—and cheered," said the *New York Journal.* And the all-important *Times* noted that "John Ford, the director of this film, has done his share of the work with thoroughness and with pleasing imagination." They called *The Iron Horse* "an instructive and inspiring film, one which should make every American proud." Even *Harrison's Reports,* an exhibitor's trade paper known for its sour criticism, raved: "Today 'The Covered Wagon' stands out as the best western that has ever been turned out. 'The Iron Horse,' is as good. In some respects it is even better."

In Los Angeles, *The Iron Horse* preceded *The Gold Rush* into Grauman's Egyptian in February 1925. As a promotional gambit, the historic brassbound locomotive *Collis P. Huntington* was towed down Hollywood Boulevard. As was the custom in premiere presentations, Sid Grauman mounted a lavish prologue to precede the picture. There was an overture from the orchestra, then Colonel Tim McCoy presented twenty-five Shoshone and Arapahoe Indians complete with squaws and children—"The finest types of Redmen to be found in America today." Next came Chief Yowlachie, singing Indian songs. This went on for another four scenes, climaxed by the arrival onstage of two locomotives, where the Golden Spike was driven. It must have all been very impressive, although it made the film itself a bit redundant.

• • •

*T*he Iron Horse introduced the element of the epic into Ford's work—vast open spaces, characters who are heroic, not just because of what they are, but because of what they do: linking the railroads in the face of Indian attacks and hostile natural elements—all combined with a dramatic story and intimate characterizations.

Ford would play out the theme of *The Iron Horse*—the conflict between wilderness and civilization—many times over the years, up to and including *The Man Who Shot Liberty Valance*. But the youthful Jack Ford allowed only trace elements of somber melancholy to intrude on *The Iron Horse*—it was, after all, about the successful unification of a nation. He did nothing much with the Chinese laborers of the Central Pacific, made more of the Irish and the Italians and their recurring work song, "Drill, Ye Tarriers, Drill." The men are working and singing when the Indians attack. They stop, fight off the Indians, then go back to work and song.

As it happened, "Drill, Ye Tarriers, Drill" wasn't written until 1888, so was completely unknown to the railroad workers. Likewise, Ford had read enough history to know that a brutally cynical capitalism deserved as much credit as Manifest Destiny for the ceremony at Promontory Point, and that there were often homicidal feuds between the Irish and Chinese laborers—each group fired blasts through the mountains meant to injure or kill workers on the other side. But Ford kept his eye on the larger picture, intent on his ultimate goal: to direct a moving historical romance about the country he loved, peopled by those with whom he felt a kinship—the laborer, the mechanic, the engineer, all in the service of visionary American progress.

It is the locations that make *The Iron Horse*, that give the film its air of documentary reality—Manifest Destiny couldn't be captured in a studio. When the two-fingered renegade murders and scalps Davy Brandon's father, the act is joltingly savage; when horses storm into town, their breath and the condensation from their sweating bodies nearly obliterate the figures of the townspeople; when a gambler throws a drink in the face of a dance-hall girl she promptly pulls a derringer and shoots him. The movie has the stink of life, a sense of figures in a landscape beyond any director working at the time, including the declining Griffith.

Towns disappear and appear overnight as the population ceaselessly moves to the head of the track, but as the caravan moves on a woman kneels at her husband's grave in the foreground. Ford bestows a sense of humanity to all in brilliant little bits of directorial shorthand—an Indian is shot in the course of an attack, and a dog (named Foreground by Ford, according to Lefty Hough) comes and lies down on the face of his dead master. It's an unusual film in many ways; Ford is so confident of his story and theme that his handsome, muscular star doesn't make his entrance for more than forty-five minutes of a movie that runs slightly more than two hours.

At the film's end, more than the tracks of the Union Pacific and the Central Pacific are united; an Italian laborer marries Nora Hogan and is congratulated by his Irish boss. One nation, one people. With *The Iron Horse*, Ford found his theme: a people triumphing over sectionalism and parochialism to stand together, not just on May 10, 1869, but for all time.

Lindsay Anderson, Ford's best if not gentlest critic, wrote of the film's "poetic sense of history, its vision of the building of a nation by uniting a continent. The epic theme is brought to life, not by the platitudes of the official record, not by the gestures of melodrama, but by the ever-present sense that the whole massive design is built up out of countless, unique, individual lives."

Lincoln, Buffalo Bill Cody, and Wild Bill Hickok mingle with Ford's fictional characters, but it is the latter we remember, because Ford had discovered his ability to make one person emblematic of the larger community, as in the moment when George O'Brien reflectively straddles the newly joined tracks, then suddenly kneels to feel the rails—". . . union, now and forever, one and inseparable," as Daniel Webster thundered in 1830.

With *The Iron Horse*, Ford created his first masterpiece, and staked out his territory as America's tribal poet.

William Fox sensed *The Iron Horse* would be a success before it was released. On August 1, 1924, just a few weeks before the film premiered, he signed Ford to a new contract that started at $1,500 a week and ended three and a half years later with Ford making $2,250 a week.

Besides accumulating money, Ford was accumulating the components of his legend, and gathering the men and women that would make up his stock company.

Ford auditioned musicians to help the cast of *The Iron Horse* get in the proper mood. Danny Borzage, the brother of Frank, who was also directing on the lot, showed up with his trusty accordion.

"He asked me if I knew 'My Buddy,' " Borzage remembered. " 'Yes, sir, I happen t'know that one.' He stopped me before I was through and I was kinda nervous, thought I didn't have the job. Then he asked m'name. 'Y'any relation to Frank Borzage?' And I said, 'Yes,' an' he said, 'Well, why didn't cha say so?' An' I said, ' 'Cause I don't want the job on his account.' And he said, 'You go over an' tell Frank Borzage his brother has a job.' " Danny Borzage played mood music for John Ford for the next forty-odd years, as well as playing a wide variety of small parts.

• • •

In March 1925, Ford was preparing a picture called *Thank You*, about a preacher. The California Church Federation had other ideas, and demanded a conference with Ford, Will Hays, and John Golden, the producer of the play on which the film was based. The matter seems to have been in some doubt until Ford got up to speak. He told them that his wife was the daughter of a minister who practically starved himself to death in order to serve his parishioners. He told the ministers that he was intimately familiar with and sympathetic to the problems and conditions of the kind of people depicted in the play.

After a few minutes of what was undoubtedly a terse, understated narration that thinly covered a well of deep emotion, the ministers declared that they would be happy to endorse the picture, for they believed that Ford would make the important point that ministers need love and tending just as much as parishioners do. Ford closed by promising to stay in close touch with the ministers, and to seek their advice whenever possible.

His speech, of course, was entirely false, one more roguish bit of notice that Jack Ford would do what he had to do to make his pictures; if it meant lying to ministers, well, it was their own fault for not checking the facts.

Success agreed with him. Personally, "he was slender, no fat on him," remembered John Weld. "I never knew him to have a cold. Six feet tall. In those days, directors would wear puttees, but he just wore gray flannels and sweaters. He was quite independent; he didn't have much friendliness for everybody. He liked us boys.

"Ford had been a stuntman himself. He was very kind to his stuntmen. Almost every time he worked, we worked. There were four or five of us that worked with him all the time, mainly to amuse him. We liked him so much. I never saw him when he wasn't gracious, except when we did something he didn't like. Then he would reprimand us."

A mood of gentle—and sometimes not so gentle—fun was rigorously maintained. Ford delighted in ordering his crew to do things that weren't necessary and weren't in their job description—stuntmen fetching sandwiches, etc. In return, Ford could take a joke.

"One time we were working in the studio," recalled John Weld. "There was a high ceiling, with rafters, and a couple of us climbed up there while we were waiting for a setup to be lit. We took a dummy with us. When Ford was just about ready to call 'Action' [one of us screamed] and we dropped the dummy down. It landed right next to Ford and, My God, they thought it was a real body. There was this horrible pause. But everybody ended up having a nice laugh on it.

"After *The Iron Horse*, he was still the same guy. I was [with him] for three years, and all during that time, he was progressing, getting better and better, getting to know more and more about what he was doing."

As for the traditional directorial *droit de seigneur*, sleeping with the actresses, Ford had little time for such energy-depleting nonsense. "Ford didn't go to bed with any actresses that I know of," said John Weld. "He didn't pay court to *anybody*." (Bessie Love, a veteran of Griffith's glory days, worked with Ford on *The Village Blacksmith*, and observed that Ford wouldn't even allow her to bring her ukelele on the set.)

Although the great success of *The Iron Horse* could have undoubtedly earned Ford a fair amount of autonomy, he elected to keep his head down, directing good stories and bad, good casts and bad. Instead of another big Western, he went back to programmers, sometimes with stars, sometimes with hardly anybody—*Hearts of Oak* featured Hobart Bosworth and Pauline Starke, minor names by that period in film history. Ditto *Hoodman Blind*, with Marc MacDermott—who usually played heavies—and Gladys Hulette. Ford's favorite leading man in this period remained George O'Brien: *The Fighting Heart*, *Thank You* ("How a Slip of a Girl Tamed a Townful of Hypocrites"), and a sea story called *The Blue Eagle*.

He was, in short, creatively erratic. Shortly after *The Iron Horse*, Ford made one of his worst silents, an adaptation of the old Frank Bacon theatrical warhorse *Lightnin'*, starring a charisma-free character actor named Jay Hunt. (Will Rogers would star in the sound remake.) It's an ambling tale about the ironically named title character, a shiftless layabout at a hotel on the California-Nevada border who foils swindlers attempting to take the hotel away from his wife.

Thematically, the film is only interesting for the way in which it demonstrates Ford's early concern and appreciation for the aged—uncharacteristic of such a young man. This quality would later figure in much better movies such as *Pilgrimage*, *Judge Priest*, and *The Grapes of Wrath*.

Beyond that, however, Ford settles for illustrating the action suggested by the titles; entire reels go by without an interesting or creative shot. At one point, he settles for comic reaction shots from a dog. *Lightnin'* is incomprehensible coming from the man who had made *The Iron Horse* the year before. At this point, Ford's artistic personality was still too tentative to be injected into every picture.

And yet his next film, *Kentucky Pride*, was a charming, sweet-natured return to something like form. Featuring the great Henry B. Walthall and the not-so-great Gertrude Astor, *Kentucky Pride* is a horse story told *by* the horse, with subtitled comments about the horse's Rules of Behavior: "You'll never be worth your grass unless you always remember the first Law of the Turf—Run straight and run fast!"

Only owner Henry Walthall and trainer J. Farrell MacDonald appreciate the horse named Virginia's Fortune; the wife and her boyfriend regard him as potential dogfood. When the horse breaks down in a race, Walthall loses his fortune and exiles himself. After some complications involving mistreatment of the horse, Virginia's Fortune foals, and her progeny wins back Walthall's money.

Someone had obviously been reading *Black Beauty* and *Beautiful Joe*, but Ford doesn't shy away from the sentimental heart of his story. Along with a pleasantly unexpected scene featuring the legendary Man O' War, there's an underlying, strongly felt message about the helplessness of animals at the hands of humans. *Kentucky Pride* remains a shameless—and shamelessly effective—film.

William Fox and Ford must have been pleased by *Kentucky Pride*, for six months later there was *The Shamrock Handicap*, another horse story, this time set largely in Ireland, but not half as effective as its predecessor. Another impoverished landowner is reduced to selling his horses—this time they're jumpers. There is one Griffithian subtitle to explain a disgusting custom ("Note: In Ireland, spitting on the palm and shaking hands binds a sale"), and there is a Fordian sense of communal effort, when the characters, now in America, join together to dig ditches for the money needed to enter the horse in the great race, which they regard as a sure thing: "What with a jew jockey, an' an Irish horse—it'll be a killin'." So it's back to Ireland with their American winnings.

The film should work better than it does, but the leads (Janet Gaynor and Leslie Fenton) are so innocuous they barely cast shadows, and there's unfortunate darky humor—at one point, the black stableboy gets a whiff of ether, and Ford sends the camera into slow motion. Still, Ford was increasingly well regarded by the press, for *Variety* said that, "Ford . . . loves anything Irish, and he made the most of the little human interest touches. It is as much Ford's direction as anything else that puts this one over, for he did not have a particularly effective cast and his leads did not seem to get across at all."

Why was Ford wasting his professional time when he could have been capitalizing on his first stab of great success? He was in a contradictory psychological bind; on the one hand, Ford's quixotic, increasingly evasive personality made him afraid to reveal anything about himself. On the other hand, artistry *requires* the expression of an inner personality. It would be years before Ford achieved sufficient self-confidence as a man and artist to make the films he wanted to make, all of the time. Ford may have been billing himself as John, but he remained a Jack of all directorial trades.

Some of these pictures had elements that must have appealed to

Ford—*The Fighting Heart* took place in New England, with O'Brien as a young man whose grandfather is drinking himself to death and ruining the family farm in the process; a 1927 picture called *Upstream* centered on a theatrical boarding house; for *The Blue Eagle*, Ford had some of the Pacific fleet to play with on location in Santa Cruz and San Pedro; *Hearts of Oak* involved an old sea captain in a small New England town who brings up a couple of orphans.

Most of these stories derived from stock magazine fiction of the period and didn't offer much in the way of thematic resonance, but their inherent commerciality gave Ford leeway to explore aspects of character and landscape, or simply to work with the kind of people he liked—unpretentious, salty old character actors like Henry B. Walthall and J. Farrell MacDonald.

The Blue Eagle is a curious picture, part slam-bang melodrama in the approved Fox silent manner, part Irish-Catholic male bonding epic of a sort very particular to Ford. The film posits George O'Brien as a tough but lovable stoker, with William Russell as his opposite number during World War I. The two men come to dislike each other because they're both competing for Janet Gaynor.

"Wars may end, but a soldier of the cross carries on." After the war, Russell becomes a cop fighting drug dealers, while O'Brien's brother gets mixed up with bad company. The brother—played by Phil Ford, Francis's son, who looks spookily like his father—is killed when a submarine that the obviously well-financed drug smugglers are using for transporting their goods submerges with him on it.

The former antagonists unite to fight the bad guys, and eventually blow up the sub, after which they have one last boxing match to settle their feud, with the local parish priest as referee. Ford doesn't play the fight for laughs or camaraderie but for brutality and realism—the two men pound each other to a pulp, refusing to quit until they simply can't fight anymore. Then they open an American Legion post together.

It's not a distinguished picture by any means, but, by God, it *moves*—something is always happening, and Ford makes sure to photograph it artfully. The *Motion Picture News* said of *The Blue Eagle* that "This thriller comes from the Fox organization that boasts, justly, of John Ford as one of its ace directors," but other trade paper critics realized that Ford was coasting.

As Charles Silver has pointed out about this period, the nonintuitive part of Ford hasn't kicked in; even in the good movies, there is only one level of meaning. When Ford isn't exercising his matchless camera eye, when he is obligated to show actors acting, his attention does not seem fully engaged.

Still, compared to the work of almost every other Fox director save Murnau—who only arrived on the lot in 1926—and Frank Borzage, Ford's pictures are clearly superior—tight, dramatically focused, well shot. They pale only when compared to the production polish, elaborate atmospherics, and glowing camerawork that Clarence Brown and King Vidor were bringing to their work at MGM, or Ernst Lubitsch's delicate lacework at Warners and Paramount. Part of that difference was attributable to Fox's less-impressive story department, which existed to serve a more threadbare group of stars than MGM or Paramount.

Latter-day critics have made claims for Ford's *Three Bad Men*, a 1926 film with beautiful locations in Jackson Hole and a great climactic land-rush sequence shot in Victorville. It's the story of a lovable trio—card sharks, horse thieves, drunks (Tom Santschi, J. Farrell MacDonald, and Frank Campeau)—who chase down the man who took advantage of the sister of one of the men.

The writer was a man named John Stone, real name Strumwasser. He had changed it after Sol Wurtzel, yelling that he didn't want anybody named Strumwasser at the studio, fired him. By the time Wurtzel hired him back, Strumwasser had become Stone, so Wurtzel could indeed claim that he never again employed anybody named Strumwasser.

Stone visited the company on location in Victorville about the time of Yom Kippur. Ford dug a pit in the ground to hold the camera for a shot he wanted, and talked Stone into going into the hole with the cameraman. After the shot of wagons and horses rolling overhead was completed, Ford moved on to the next series of setups, leaving Stone and the cameraman in the hole for the entire day. Because the roof had been constructed out of heavy planking, the imprisoned men had to sit there and bake.

Although Stone always liked Ford, enjoyed telling the story, and thought of the practical joke as funny, he misinterpreted Ford's egalitarian sadism and wondered whether he might have acted out of some veiled anti-Semitism.

Fox clearly designed *Three Bad Men* to fit in tandem with Ford's great hit of two years before. "John Ford's Successor to 'The Iron Horse' Looms as One of Biggest Hits on Film Horizon," proclaimed Fox's in-house magazine. "When John Ford set as his mark to eclipse even his achievements in 'The Iron Horse,' he simultaneously set his mind to evolving all sorts of extraordinary directorial touches, which bid fair to distinguish this super-film as in a class to itself."

William K. Everson wrote that the film was originally intended to be a starring vehicle for all three of Fox's Western stars: Tom Mix, Buck Jones, and George O'Brien, under the variant titles *Over the Border* and

End of the Trail. But the film was downgraded and the script fine-tuned; a framing device of a couple of traders was wisely jettisoned.

Such all-star extravaganzas were almost unheard of in those days. From a purely business standpoint, they weren't necessary; a film with Mix, Jones, and O'Brien wouldn't necessarily gross three times more than a film with just Mix. Also, Fox might not have wanted three stars tied up for one picture when he could have gotten three pictures in the same amount of time. In any case, the casting dynamic that Ford ended up with is clearly modeled on *The Covered Wagon*—a straightforward, slightly colorless lead propped up by engagingly hammy character performances.

But, compared to *The Iron Horse,* and to the multitude of Ford films that would come later, the characterizations of *Three Bad Men* seem stock, the emotions superficial. The story *is* stronger than that of the earlier film, and gains stature by being dramatized against the opening of the West—as represented by the Cherokee Strip land rush. Then there is the familiar Ford theme of the nobility of society's outcasts.

The bad men sacrifice themselves for the young people, i.e. the future, the first statement of a theme that Ford would return to again and again—sacrifices made to build a future that will never be as vital as the rough good times that are replaced. In the end, the bad men are ghost riders on the horizon, watching over the young family they died for—the future of the West.

Three Bad Men remains a rich, companionable picture, in which all the girls, including a houseful of whores, are lovely. As Roger Greenspun would write, "even the villain (Lou Tellegen) seems to suffer chiefly from the fault of being too killingly handsome." But to call it the greatest silent Western, as some have done, seems like hyperbolic enthusiasm; there are a half-dozen austere William S. Hart Westerns that are better. They don't have the expansive scale of *Three Bad Men*, but that epic quality only makes the vacuum at the center of the movie more obvious.*

Even *Variety* said that "This feature falls just short of being a terrific knockout," which, over seventy years later, seems an eminently fair assessment.

A certain lack of full emotional investment may not have been Ford's fault. Priscilla Bonner, who was playing the part of the traduced sister, recalled the three-month production period as a comedy of errors. Ford had sold her the part as that of the female lead, with the three bad men spending the picture looking for her, the little sister who had run off with

*Ford integrates some characteristic Hart sequences into the film, notably a violent scene where the bad guys launch flaming wagons down a hill and into a church, where the faithful are gathered. When the minister comes out to beg them to stop, a woman takes the bullet meant for him. It's very *Hell's Hinges.*

Lou Tellegen. "It's very dramatic," he told her, "you're a natural, you're perfect for the part. Yes, there's a love interest, but it's minor. It will be your part and your picture." Ford was overstating the case and must have known it; given the direction of the script, and his own dramatic bent, the focus of the picture was bound to be on the land and the title characters.

Because Bonner wanted to work with Ford, and because of the way he had described the part, she took the job. But things began to break down as soon as the company arrived at Jackson Hole.

"The other girl was played by Olive Borden," Bonner told James Curtis, "and when Olive Borden took a bath in the barrel, that was the end of me. They sent the dailies back down to the studio here, and all of the executives saw it and called Ford up and said, 'We want more of Olive . . .' And Olive smiled and quirked and shook her beautiful head and shook her beautiful curls and dunked herself a little bit more, and the camera went down as far as it dared to, and then it came back up again and the whole picture changed.

"And John Ford said, 'It's not my picture. I didn't even direct that picture. I just watched while she acted up.' He would say this to anybody that would listen. 'I didn't direct *Three Bad Men*. That's not my picture. I can still direct a picture called *Three Bad Men*, and some day I'm gonna make it. It's a hell of a story.' "

Up to that point, Ford had been working smoothly, in his accustomed style. "He was a very quiet director," said Bonner, "not a lot of talking, no shouting, didn't act up. Not personal, not colorful, very quiet and determined. He would chew on his handkerchief, hold it and pull on it, and he knew what he wanted."

But Bonner believed that after the studio began interfering, Ford "gave up. He wasn't very nice to Olive, he was mad at her, he was mad at the executives, he was mad at everybody. He was just irritable about the whole situation. He had failed in making the picture he was trying to make.

"He was furious and there was nothing he could do. I sat most of the time and watched them photograph her. I had one scene, in which Lou Tellegen attacked me with a whip and they cut it out of the picture because they needed space to show some more of Olive Borden. That's the truth! I ended up with a bit and she stole the picture."

As if studio interference wasn't bad enough, dysentery swept through the company. Bonner was rooming with another woman in one of a series of rough cabins that had been built for the cast and crew. In the middle of the night, the bug struck Bonner. It was a cold, windy night, so Bonner threw her heavy robe on to find her way to the outhouse.

"I opened the door of our cabin and the wind was blowing, so I closed the door and locked it from the outside and ran down to the girls' toilets. And [Sol] Wurtzel was already in there. 'Lady, I'm sorry,' he said, 'but I can't help it.' So I ran to the men's outhouse, and there was one man in there but he didn't care and I didn't either."

When Bonner got back to the cabin, she found her roommate straddling a water pitcher, desperate and furious. "She said she was going to report me to the director if I didn't have any more sense than to lock her in the cabin. And she did, she went and talked to Ford! Well, Ford laughed himself half to death, right in her face. 'What would you have her do,' he said, 'leave the door wide open so you could freeze to death?' "

Ten years after he began directing, Ford was earning more than the $1,500 a week paid to Frank Borzage, Raoul Walsh, and Victor Fleming, less than the $2,500 a week brought home by Herbert Brenon and Victor Seastrom. In mid-1928, Ford signed a new two-year deal with Fox that paid him $2,500 a week for the first year and $2,750 for the second. Ford was in the top 10 percent of the industry, but not yet in the same category as eminences such as von Stroheim (who got the amazing fee of $100,000 a picture) or Henry King, James Cruze, and George Fitzmaurice, at $50,000 a picture.

Ford was similar to many directors of the time, who tended to be tough, laconic men, but he didn't shoot film like they did. Ford was already avoiding the accepted industrial style of shooting entire scenes in long master shots, then moving in for medium shots and close-ups and dumping all the footage in the lap of the editor to cut as they saw fit. Rather, he would shoot only those portions of a given shot that he needed for the scene as he had mentally formulated it. This severely limited editing choices, and meant that Ford had to be right the first time.

On a film titled *Upstream* (shot in 1926, released 1927), Ford was working with cameraman Charles G. Clarke, who would remember that "I could see no relationship between the different scenes we would be filming and often wondered when we would settle down and start making the picture. After about three weeks of this sort of casual filmmaking, the unit manager announced, 'The picture is finished, everybody is off salary.'

"The shock of this floored me for I could see no rhyme or reason in what we had been filming. It was such a different directorial style. . . . To my amazement it all went together and was quite a good picture. What I did not realize then was that John Ford edited his picture as he directed it, and that his casual manner was only a cover for the actual planning and thought that lay behind his direction all along."

CHAPTER SIX

Ford remained a good soldier, without a great deal of authorial ego, willing to step in and help out as his employers deemed necessary. Frank Borzage was as skilled an emotional director as anybody in Hollywood, but he was not regarded as being talented with action, so Ford was called in to shoot the scenes of the troop mobilization in *7th Heaven*. Even an experienced action director was at the mercy of circumstance, however, as the powderman on the picture, hearing his cue—notes on a bugle—exploded a church steeple before he was supposed to. As it happened, the bugler was just warming up and the cameras weren't ready. Nobody was killed, but four cars were destroyed. Ford also helped out Raoul Walsh by shooting a sequence of the troops moving to the front in *What Price Glory?*

Beneath Ford's flinty exterior was a man yearning to be thought of as more than he actually was. In 1926, he spun a yarn to *Variety* after a visit to Portland. Hardly anybody in his hometown knew he was in the movie business, said Ford, and those few that did thought he was an actor. From there, things got even wilder. He asserted that an old Portland friend had been his top sergeant during World War I. Although there were hundreds of people reading *Variety* who could attest that Ford had spent World War I at Universal City, he had to cover himself with what he would always feel was the glory of the military mantle.

His eccentricities were also the stuff of common industry knowledge, and he came in for some infra dig kidding when King Vidor's *Show People* prominently featured a director so nervously focused on a scene that he furiously chews a handkerchief. "This was patterned after John Ford," admitted Vidor late in his life.

At home, the mood was usually calm; the house on Odin Street would always be a charming retreat. "When we were children," remembered

Patrick Ford, "the whole street was our family, just about. It was just a little dead-end street, and he had what had been a very small little house, and as he made more and more money, he added on to it. It had carved away hills and tunnels, and it was fascinating for the kids. We loved it."

Most of the visitors to the house derived from the dusty days at Universal. The sharpshooter Pardner Jones would come to dinner at least once a week, sometimes more. Pardner would plunk himself down on a chair in the dining room saying, "Just come a'visiting, just come a'calling."

"He didn't have much to say," recalled Pat Ford. "None of those people were great talkers. And he'd just sit there and my dad would ask him questions: 'What did Pat Garrett look like?' 'He was a dirty, blue-eyed Irish son of a bitch! 'Scuse me, Jack, no offense meant. 'Scuse me, Mary, and 'scuse the son of a bitch.' "

Another frequent visitor was a retired marshal named Wyatt Earp. Jack's primary memories of Earp were of a modest but cold-blooded man. "I'm not a dead shot," Ford remembered Earp saying. "I always walked up pretty close to the other fellow before I fired. The legend has it that I killed a lot of people. As a matter of fact, I never killed anybody. I shot people in the shoulder or the leg, but I never killed them. I left that to my partner . . . who was a dead shot."

(If Earp really said that, he was lying. Aside from the death of one man in Dodge City, Earp almost certainly killed two men during the gunfight at the O.K. Corral, as well as a couple of other men he held responsible for the deaths of his brothers in the bloodbath that followed the showdown in Tombstone. Earp's biographer Allen Barra puts the probable toll at seven.)

The only visitors that set off a steady stream of conversation were Charlie Russell, the great Western artist, and Earp. "I was too young to grasp what Earp was saying," said Pat Ford. "I only remember him saying one thing: 'The only way to be a successful marshal in those days was to carry a double-barrel 12-gauge and don't shoot until you know you can't miss.' "

Keeping mostly to himself and his core group of friends, Ford had no time for the social elite of Hollywood, the Fairbanks-Pickford-Swanson circle. But Ford and his wife did throw Sunday parties, which lasted, according to Mary, "on and on, until the turkey was gone, the ham was gone and the booze was gone." (The illicit refreshment was hidden over the mantel in the den, concealed by a sliding panel.) His parties served as extensions of his hatred of pretense. Once he grabbed a megaphone and yelled at a director who was putting on airs, "Get off that high horse! You're just like the rest of us!"

Ford became rather unlikely friends with Rudolph Valentino, whose heavy-breathing public image was in stark contrast to his quiet, unassuming private personality. Once, Valentino took Mary to a premiere and he was even invited to the house to cook spaghetti.

"Another wop," grunted Ford in his typically corrosive way when he was asked about Valentino near the end of his own life. Then, also typically, he revealed his fondness for the young man. "They made a sauce which I think became famous as Caruso sauce. They also brought their own wine, usually Chianti. We remained fast friends up until the time of his death. Really a fine person."

Also becoming part of his extended family were two new acquaintances. Brian Desmond Hurst was born in 1900 in Castlereagh, Ireland. The young artist was a friend of the director Hugo Ballin, and arrived in Hollywood in 1928 for a visit. While there, he got work doing murals in the libraries and living rooms of various monied members of Los Angeles society. For his own enjoyment, Desmond Hurst had painted a religious image on a screen, which was displayed in a bookstore window. Ford saw it, liked it, and invited Desmond Hurst to his house.

It was the beginning of a friendship that would last till Ford's death, for Hurst was a witty man who could always make Ford laugh. Ford regularly introduced Desmond Hurst to people as his "cousin," which, naturally enough, led many to believe they were related, and was so fond of him that he used him in walk-ons, then got him a job at the studio, where he became an assistant art director. At dinner one night, Ford offered to take Desmond Hurst on as an assistant, but his first paycheck was only $35, when he had been making $75 as an art director. Desmond Hurst swallowed hard and sold his Mercedes.

"I didn't hear you roaring up in that great car of yours," said Ford one night.

"I've had to sell it."

"That's all right, go into the garage and take any car you like." Hurst chose a Chrysler and began chauffeuring Ford to and from the studio in addition to functioning as one of the assistant directors. Hurst was homosexual, and once, when Ford was taunted about his friend, he retorted, "So what? Doesn't everyone have a gay cousin?" In time, Hurst became a more than competent director, with the Alistair Sim version of *A Christmas Carol* as his most noted film, as well as a brave effort called *Ourselves Alone*—a translation of Sinn Fein—based loosely on the life of Michael Collins.

If Brian Desmond Hurst would always be one of Jack's eager acolytes, then Frank Baker would be the thin, harsh voice of conscience breathing good sense in his ear. A typically plain-spoken Australian, Baker had met Francis Ford in the South Seas and accompanied him back to America, where he became part of Frank's moviemaking family for the next four years, turning out B movies and serials as part of a seven-person collective.

"The first meal I had in the United States was at John Ford's," remembered Baker. "In those days, he'd bleed you dry. He'd talk to you and talk to you and suddenly you find half of what you've said appears in the picture that he's making."

Ford offered Baker a small part in *Hearts of Oak*. Baker thought he was giving a superb performance, but Ford took issue with him, asking, "Is that the best you can do? I can go out in that street and pick up a five-year-old child who could show more intelligence than you did. You're the worst actor I've ever seen in my life."

It was a typical opening gambit in Ford's emotional chess game, but rather than sulk, or take it, Baker fired back, telling Ford he was the worst director he'd ever worked for. It was a dangerous thing to say because the only other director Baker had worked for was Francis Ford.

One thing led to another, and Ford ended the argument by saying that as long as Baker worked for him, he'd never receive screen credit. "I'm very pleased to hear that," snarled Baker. "I have some very good friends in different parts of the world and I'd hate to have them see my name on a John Ford production." Over the next forty years, Baker would work on several dozen pictures with Ford. He would be a guest in his house. He would be among the people Ford wanted to see before he died. And he never received screen credit for his work.

"All the Ford family had their troubles," Baker told the historian Anthony Slide, referring to the family's bouts with alcohol. As he pointed out, "They were not [hard drinkers]. They could take a half a glass of beer, and they're in the gutter."

"Although I knew Francis Ford well, I never tried to pry into his affairs. He was an extraordinary man. In some ways, he was very much like John. He and Jack didn't get on very well. . . . Everything that John Ford did, I could see the reflection of Frank. Camera angles and different touches. He'd say, 'How do you like that?' And I'd say, 'I've seen that before,' and he'd go as cold as anything. He had an amazing admiration for his brother . . . but he was completely jealous of him. But John Ford . . . had the touch of greatness. He was perhaps a great man, John Ford. There were many sides to him that people never saw."

Ford's pugnaciousness would never be tempered by success, and very few people could bank the fires like his mother could. Once, visiting him in Hollywood, she watched him get into an argument on the phone that ended when he threw it on the floor. "That's what I get for marrying a temperamental director," observed Mary. "That's not temperament, that's bad manners," said Abby Feeney. "Pick it up!" Ford quietly did. Abby Feeney was a lovable authoritarian, with charm and personality; Ford may have taken after his father physically, but emotionally he was all Abby.

As the silent era drew to a close, Ford's life seemed in good equilibrium, marred only by his binges. For Christmas 1926, Jack and Mary sent out a lovely card wishing people happy holidays "from the little grey house on the hill." Accompanying the sentiment was a pen and ink sketch of the Odin Street house and Ford himself, clad in puttees, hands in pockets, pipe in mouth, looking every inch the commanding director.

On location in Sacramento around the same time, Ford wrote a waggish, loving letter to his wife, addressing it "Dear Claire," then crossing out Claire and inserting "Mary": "Just to say hello, honey and to let you know I love you 'n everythin! . . . I am counting the hours till I see you sweetheart and I'm thinking of you all the time. . . . I love you or as Wingate [Smith, Ford's brother-in-law] would say 'Je t'aime.' " He signed it Bob, Cap, Jimmy, Tommy, Rex, Larry, Joe, Dave, crossed them all out, and finally signed his own name.

Professionally, Ford's life was now bookended by the Wurtzel brothers, Sol and Harry—Sol, the studio manager; Harry, his agent. They were very dissimilar personalities. Working out of his office at 8979 Sunset, Harry had a small but decent group of clients that would eventually include Henry King, Claire Trevor, and Gene Autry. Harry was like his brother in that he was ethical—whenever Sol had one of the studio carpenters do some work on his house, he always reimbursed the studio for their time.

"Harry was a very nice fellow," said Lester Ziffren, Harry's son-in-law. "He'd walk into the Brown Derby and before he could sit down he would have to shake hands with twenty people in twenty different booths. He loved to gamble, and he was a very generous man.

"Sol was a much harder person, much tougher. He'd come up the tough way in the studio, with William Fox. He didn't spend money to spend money." Sol matched Ford in his ability to keep people off balance, while Harry shored up the nurturing aspect of Ford that he worked so hard to conceal.

The relationship between Harry and Jack was closer than the average agent-client bond, and Harry was occasionally called into service as a nurse when Ford went on a binge. "Harry used to go with him to New York on the train," remembered Lester Ziffren, "and from the moment they got on the train, [Ford] was drinking, and he kept drinking all the way across the country until they got to the Sherry Netherland. Harry was guarding him, making sure nothing happened to Ford. He was his client, and Harry was beholden to him. Ford liked him very much."

As what *Variety* would later call a "non-pro," Mary was unimpressed with most movie people and observed their peculiarities with the eye of an amused sociologist. William S. Hart, for instance, was "just a dirty old man." But she grew to adore Tom Mix, because he always sent her flowers on Mother's Day, which Jack never did. She couldn't help wondering, though, about Mix and his wife's habit of keeping loaded guns on every end table in their house.

The big-hearted Mix once ordered two buses filled with champagne to transport a group of Hollywood wives to a San Francisco football game that their husbands had intended as stag entertainment. After the game, they were driven to Gump's, where each wife picked out a present that Mix paid for. Accommodations consisted of a wing at the Palace Hotel. "We had more fun with Tom's money," Mary remembered, "than anyone in the history of the world.

"There really should be a book written about him, and telling the truth. Of course, nobody would believe it, but he was just wonderful and he adored me. . . . I'd get up in the night and go handle him when he'd been nipping too much. He always called it 'loganberry juice.' "

By now, Mary had learned to handle Jack with a combination of patience, humor, veiled exasperation, and an unerring sense of when to look the other way. She had little temper and great forbearance; her response to trouble or frustration was not anger but a sort of sullen depression.

During Prohibition, Mary's method of handling Jack's drinking was to drink with him, and the family knew that when she broke out the Coke and bitters she was about to try to keep up with her husband. In later years, her own drinking moderated; her grandsons never saw her drunk.

The day-to-day operation of the house was Mary's responsibility. The children had governesses, and were sent to private schools. Overall, they were raised in the traditional arm's-length manner of the time that mimicked the Anglo-American aristocracy, who treated children as rarefied eggs that would, eventually, hatch.

As for Jack's family, extended and otherwise, "there were a lot of sore heads when your Grampa married me," Mary told her grandson Dan. "Stepping outside the fold. . . . Ollie [Carey] wasn't nice at all. Everyone was striving to be invited to Harry Carey's ranch on a Sunday. Along about sundown, they'd have a big barbecue. That was where you'd meet the big New Yorkers like Walter Winchell. Jimmy Walker would always be at Carey's. I loved Maine but they never really accepted me. I was an outsider. I was a Protestant. And, I had drawn the pick of the stable."

Mary soon came to an accommodation with her husband's basic priorities. "He loved me and he loved the children, but his mother and father always came first. If there was going to be a shortage anywhere, he shorted us and the house, because they got their thousand dollars a month right on the first, regardless."

Priscilla Bonner had grown friendly with Mary through her proficiency at bridge, and observed a woman doing her best to adapt to her husband's eccentricities. "He was a devout Catholic, she was not. And she was a bridge player. She wanted me to get my sister Marjorie and come over to her house and play bridge. She was lonesome, because he was never home. And when he was, the house was full of priests.

"I was a good bridge player, maybe better than average, but not as good as Margie. So I said that if she wanted to play for as much as 10 cents a point, to leave me out of it. So she and Margie went ahead with somebody else.

"Now, Ford wouldn't give her money, so when she lost at bridge she had trouble paying. She had charge accounts all over town, at any store she wanted, and he never cared how much she spent on the charge accounts, he just wouldn't give her any cash. I've known other men like that too. Mary tried to get me to go to Magnin's and pick out a dress for Margie. She owed Margie a lot of money, and she told me, 'I don't care what it costs, $100, $200, if she'll let me pay her off that way.'

"I wouldn't do it. 'Won't he notice that you bought this dress and you never wear it?' I asked her.

" 'He never notices what I have on,' she said."

When Mary and Jack would squabble, Ford retreated, which drove Mary to distraction. "Jack would go upstairs and do the worst thing a man could do. He just wouldn't speak to me for two weeks. He wouldn't answer my questions. He'd put cotton in his ears and he just wouldn't hear me. What's the use of trying to talk to anyone like that? It's the most aggravating thing you can do."

J ack was that peculiar creature, a periodic alcoholic, able to stay sober for months at a time so long as he had the promise of a debauch down the road. Lefty Hough remembered that, during the production of *Lightnin'*, Ford went on a bender over a weekend and couldn't pull out of it Sunday night. Monday morning, he was still drinking, and a panicked Mary called Hough to come and sober him up so he could get to work.

Hough showed up at the house, but Ford was beyond reasoning. Hough decided to try to find the hidden booze. After some minutes of searching, Hough finally figured out that Ford was hiding it in Mary's riding boots.

Drinking while working would be extremely rare, and Ford would be properly ashamed of himself on those occasions; but drinking at home, or, in later years, on board his beloved boat *Araner*, would be another thing entirely—a designated respite, a safe haven where he could do precisely as he wished, without guilt or recriminations.

"He was not a drunkard," John Wayne would remember. "He was an alcoholic. On occasion, to let off steam, this man just [had to] hit the bottle. . . . But he didn't fight it too much."

The arrival of F. W. Murnau on the Fox lot signaled a quantum change in the style of even ordinary directors. "Fox's directors," wrote William K. Everson, "sincerely in awe of Murnau, literally made their films in his image as a kind of homage to him." Even rough house types like Raoul Walsh went arty in a big way, while Frank Borzage's *Street Angel* doesn't just borrow from *Sunrise*, but from Murnau's adaptation of *Tartuffe* and Lang's *Metropolis*. "Stars apart," wrote Everson, "the first reel of *Street Angel* could pass for authentic UFA at any time!"

For Ford, Murnau's films were a revelation. Jack's pictures had tended toward a collection of medium shots with beautiful compositions as grace notes, but now he saw what was possible—that film was plastic, that light could be sculpted, and that the essence of cinema was a rhythmic succession of striking images. If Universal and Harry Carey had been Ford's primary school, then Murnau constituted Ford's college.

Murnau soon appointed himself a cheerleader for Ford. On February 20, 1927, he wired Ford, on board the SS *Hamburg* headed for Europe, that he had just seen *Mother Machree*. It was a "beautiful picture," he wrote, and he was looking forward to seeing Ford soon. To William Fox, Murnau wrote that another Ford picture, *Four Sons*, would prove to be "one of the greatest box office values that has ever been shown on the screen. . . . I certainly congratulate you on this picture."

Ford was undoubtedly flattered at being considered a peer by such a master of his craft, and responded by supporting Murnau's own work. He told the press that he believed *Sunrise*, which he saw in rough cut, "to be the greatest motion picture that has been produced [and doubted] whether a greater picture will be made in the next ten years."

As part of an overall sprucing up of the studio's image that followed in Murnau's wake, William Fox began a massive upgrading of his facilities by spending $500,000 for a new administration building, a new preview theater, a new wardrobe building, a new still studio, and a new stage. Soon, Fox's films, which, in terms of production polish, were more or less commensurate with Universal's—with adequate but un-innovative lighting and nominal art direction—began to glow with a dark, seductive sheen.

Ford's *Mother Machree*, only half of which survives, features stunning lighting, leagues ahead of most other directors. The deep chiaroscuro prefigures the overtly artistic lighting of *The Long Voyage Home*, as in a beautiful shot where a mother and son, unable to find a place to live because they're Irish, dejectedly descend a staircase in deep focus, moving away from the camera.

The story—an Irish family in 1899 is divided by their emigration to America, and takes years to reunite—would have had enormous appeal to Ford. His use of a muscular, trim Victor McLaglen, whose close-ups disclose a ruddy, weather-beaten face without makeup, give the film a realism and suggestions of tragedy that transcend the surface sentimentality of the material.

*F*our Sons* is one of the rare Ford films that was overtly designed as a prestige "art" movie, the kind of film that is always heavily dependent on critics to find its audience. Ford's feel for this kind of picture was touch-and-go; he would pull it off with *The Informer* and *The Long Voyage Home*, fail miserably with *Mary of Scotland* and *The Fugitive*.

The working title for the film was *Grandmother Bernle Learns Her Letters*, the title of the original short story. In addition to the shooting script by Philip Klein, Ford had Hermann Bing, a Murnau assistant, later a character actor, write a "screen rhythm version exclusive for Mr. John Ford." It's written in the deeply impressionistic, blank verse style of Carl Mayer's script for *Sunrise*. Although the finished film is close to Bing's treatment, he received no screen credit.

Four Sons is an elaborate anticipation of *All Quiet on the Western Front*. A mother and her boys, happy in a small agrarian village in Germany, see their lives destroyed by the virus of militarism until she and her sole surviving child are reunited in America. The Murnau influence is pervasive: Ford uses some of the sets left over from *Sunrise*—the picturesque village, part of the city set—and the actor playing the postman is directed to replicate Emil Jannings in *The Last Laugh*.

But Ford also slows down his brisk storytelling in order to concentrate on Murnau's sine qua non—atmosphere, mood, dramatic texture. After winning the approbation of Murnau, Ford would rarely concentrate on speed again.

Characterization in the film, on the other hand, lacks Murnau's subtlety, as when the evil of the militaristic commander is indicated by his hacking to death a black cat that has had the temerity to cross his path.

The film begins with an elaborate tracking shot that follows the post-man through the town. This luxurious introduction is followed by the sort of arty shots that Ford would have disdained a few years before, or a few years later: a blacksmith plunges a steaming implement into a tub of water, with the camera placed beneath the glass-bottomed tub. The shot is startling, the effect immediate.

No wonder Murnau liked *Four Sons;* it looks like he directed it. According to an item in the *New York Times,* he "gave some advice" during the production. Although the article was referring to matters of technical accuracy—Bavarian architecture, Prussian uniforms and the like—it's not hard to imagine Murnau proffering suggestions, and Ford accepting them.

Although it seems not to have been planned when the film began production in the late summer of 1927 (the script has no indication for a score or sound effects), *Four Sons* emerged in February of 1928 with a soundtrack, courtesy of William Fox's new sound-on-film process called Movietone.

Mostly, Movietone was utilized for background music and the occasional sound effect, as in *Sunrise,* released the year before. Voices were used for joyous songs at harvest time, and a male chorus delicately backed a sequence where the old woman dreams her sons are once again gathered about the dinner table.

But the most innovative use of sound in *Four Sons* comes in a beautiful, misty battlefield scene (probably the swamp set from *Sunrise*), as one of the sons, wounded, cries out for his mother. The disembodied cries of "Mutterchen" are genuinely eerie; even a plaintive clarinet from the orchestra wouldn't have been half so effective as a few words at the appropriate emotional time.

On every technical level, *Four Sons* is a tour de force, but it lacks a certain emotional impact; we never really know the boys who get killed, while the villain, the German colonel played by Earle Foxe, does everything but twirl his mustachios. *Four Sons* is a big, elaborate camera show, full of prestige and full of itself.

Nevertheless, *Variety* called *Four Sons* "profoundly moving" and acclaimed its images as "a revel in beauty and significant detail, with camera shots that are arresting . . . the views of departing soldiers seen marching through the gay village streets from the vantage point of the belfry; the panorama of the farming countryside swathed in morning mists; the church steeple with the tolling bells reflected in the still mill pond and a myriad of such color shots."

Four Sons propelled one Marion Morrison to Ford's attention. Morrison was a USC football player–law student, generally known as Duke, who was earning money by working during the summer as Lefty Hough's assistant propman. Ford enjoyed needling the USC kids, saying things like, "Will you boys with the college education please remove this pile of rubbish?"

It was the second summer Morrison had worked at Fox, and he was beginning to be attracted to moviemaking. "Everybody I was in school with had an uncle or father in law practice," he remembered, "and I was starting to realize that I was going to end up writing briefs for about ten years for fellows who I thought I was smarter than.

"I was getting such enthusiasm out of working with Jack Ford and with the people that were in the business—the prop men, the grips, the cameramen. It was our picture, everybody was working for the picture. There were no departmental heads and union bosses saying, 'Do this.' It was a group, a kind of family."

A scene in *Four Sons* required leaves to blow through the open door of the mother's house. It was Morrison's job to, first, throw the leaves in front of the fan, then sweep up after a take. Suddenly, in the middle of a take, with the cameras rolling and the off-screen trio that played mood music for the actors sawing away, Morrison walked in with his broom and began sweeping.

Astonished and delighted, Ford just sat there enjoying the moment of unvarnished, gauche reality, waiting to see what Morrison's reaction would be. Eventually, the young football player looked up, saw the cameramen cranking, and realized what he had done. "They all looked shocked," he remembered, "and I realized that the real scene [was] going on and they hadn't said Cut."

"But, *why*, Marion?" asked Ford plaintively. A horrified Morrison threw down the broom and began running off the stage. Ford called the young man back, pinned a prop medal on him, and marched him around. "Jack kicked me in the backside and said, 'Now get out.' " But he didn't mean it, and Morrison kept working.

Unfortunately, the accident made everyone giddy; every time Margaret Mann, who was playing the mother of the four sons, looked at Morrison, she'd break up, so the propman was banished from the set for two days so Ford could get the scene shot. "I was never so goddamned embarrassed in my *life*," the old propman told Peter Bogdanovich.

It was the beginning of one of the most productive relationships of Ford's life. He took the big, handsome, good-natured young man under his wing and made him a member of the Ford crew. Morrison, whose own father was a feckless, henpecked pharmacist, responded to Ford's quiet strength and aura of power. The fact that he knew and understood football helped, too.

"I liked Duke's style from the very first time I met him," Ford remembered. "I could see that here was a boy who was working for something—not like most of the other guys, just hanging around to pick up a few fast bucks. Duke was really ambitious and willing to work."

In *Hangman's House*, made a couple of months later, Ford pressed Morrison into service as an extra, and gave him a couple of medium shots as an enormously enthusiastic onlooker at a horse race. Struck by a bad case of hero worship, Morrison began thinking about taking the movie business seriously.

"I really had no intention of being an actor," he would say in later years. "I had no desire for it. I [just] wanted to be like John Ford. I just looked up to this man Ford—he was a big hero to me. He was intelligent and quick-thinking, had great initiative. It was just wonderful to be around him."

In late 1929, Raoul Walsh was canvassing Hollywood looking for an unknown for his epic Western *The Big Trail*. Ford suggested young Morrison. He got the part; under his new name of John Wayne he would get a great many parts.

As the silent era drew to its premature close, Ford made one of his best, most elaborate pictures. *Hangman's House* is a little gem, aptly described by William K. Everson as a "kind of mosaic of *Warning Shadows* and *The Quiet Man* . . . moodily expressionist in its opening scenes, basically old-fashioned melodrama in its plotting."

Ford had dabbled in Irish themes before—*The Shamrock Handicap*, and as far back as 1915, he had acted in *The Doorway of Destruction*, one of Francis's movies, about an Irish regiment saving the British during the Sepoy Rebellion. But *Hangman's House* would be his first full-scale immersion in the land of his ancestors.

The movie was based on a novel by Donn Byrne, a popular Irish novelist of the period, whose foreword to the novel echoed Ford's own feelings about Ireland:

"I am certain that no race has for its home the intense love we Irish have for Ireland," wrote Byrne. "It is more than love. It is a passion. We make no secret of it, and people gibe at us, saying, with a sneer that does not speak well of their manners, 'Why don't you go back to Ireland.' Which is not merited, for every one must know the intricate prison this life is, and how this friendship, that grave, and even the unutterable vulgarity of money matters tie us to an alien land."

Hangman's House tells the story of Citizen Denis Hogan (Victor McLaglen), serving in the Foreign Legion, who receives a letter in the opening scenes that propels him back to Ireland. "I've got to kill a man," he says simply.

"Ireland—such a little place to be so greatly loved."

The beautiful daughter of a cruel hanging judge has been coerced by her father into marrying John D'Arcy (Earle Foxe again) rather than the deeply uninteresting but upstanding man she loves. D'Arcy is an informer, an abuser of animals, an alcoholic, who has previously married Hogan's sister in Paris, and helped put her in an early grave.

Still enraptured by Murnau, Ford mounts long, lateral tracking shots that follow a hooded McLaglen through the studio sets representing Ireland—probably the *Sunrise* set again—dark fog swirling around him. The story isn't much—D'Arcy is so sodden he can't even get his new wife into bed; an immense Irish wolfhound and a loyal butler conspire to preserve her chastity—but the images are ravishing.

The crumbling stone walls, the Celtic crosses, the omnipresence of the Black and Tans, form an effortless, poetic impression of an Ireland of the imagination. Add an exciting horse race, a jailbreak, and a fire that destroys D'Arcy as well as the house and its generational corruption—Hawthorne, anyone?—and you have a memorable picture. "I'm going back to the brown desert," says Citizen Hogan in farewell, "but I'm taking the green place with me in my heart."

Variety raved that "the locale and characters are treated in a fine literary way and the scenic backgrounds . . . are remarkable for their pictorial beauty, so much so that the photographic quality of the whole production is one of its outstanding merits. . . . George Schneideman [sic] has caught some of the most striking touches of composition seen on the screen since those swamp land shots in *Sunrise*, which they often resemble. There are bits of mist-draped landscape that actually inspire real emotion . . . from start to finish, the pictorial side of the production is a revelation of camera possibilities."

Hangman's House is as polished a piece of UFA worship as anything in American cinema, but, even though it contains rough blueprints for both *The Informer* and *The Quiet Man*, it lacks the warmth and humor that Ford's work had displayed as early as 1917. Ford would get that back in talkies, but it would take a few years.

Ford was now a prestige director whose name was beginning to be known beyond the narrow circle of the film industry and hard-core fans. In June 1928, a long feature article appeared under his byline in the august *New York Times*. It was almost certainly ghosted by the studio publicity department—it's far more verbose than Ford's own writing—but it undoubtedly reflects his feelings at the time. It even contains some of his characteristic misdirection—he claims to have been working in Hollywood for twelve years, when he had actually been there for fourteen.

The article rambles from feelings about Hollywood to his ideas about filmmaking: "The quality of universality in pictures is in itself a pitfall, for the director who strives too hard to represent humanity by rubbing down the rough edges of racial and personal traits is likely to make his work drab and colorless. The picture likely to attain great and wide success must have its theme of universal appeal but its people vivid. It is my belief that it should be true in its setting—for instance, that Germany should be represented by the sons, since it is essentially a man's country, but that Ireland, being matriarchal, should be visualized as Mother Machree."

The article concludes with a startling affirmation of Ford's own emotional isolation in Hollywood, his oneness with life's wanderers that looks ahead thirty years to the character of Ethan Edwards: "Knowing it for what it is, a town of success and failure, of aspiration and achievement, of doubt and despondency, I have come to feel that the other [Seven Wonders] have been in their times no more and no less than this town of mine, not high monuments of man's accomplishments, but turbulent plazas of man's unceasing search for the something he can never find."

Six months later Fox released a little Ford programmer called *Riley the Cop*, a pleasant, schizoid time-passer in which J. Farrell MacDonald, as the good-natured title character, travels to Munich to extradite a suspect. It starts out as a mild little comedy-drama, but Ford completely drops the story while the characters run around a back-lot Europe in a fish-out-of-water scenario, with the relaxed, gregarious Irishman butting heads with the authoritarian Germans, resulting in alcoholic hijinks and much cultural confusion.

Riley the Cop has a certain ramshackle charm, but it suffers from the fact that it's almost completely a comedy. Ford's broad Irish humor is indispensable as seasoning but insufficiently varied to sustain an entire film by itself. *Riley the Cop* would be of little interest except for the fact of the accompanying soundtrack. *Mother Machree* and *Four Sons* had both been released with music on the soundtrack, but *Riley the Cop* was the first feature in which Ford had to cope with a music and effects track that was truly intrusive.

Children yell, yodelers yodel, bats hit balls with a loud crack, windows break, people laugh, the crowd at a beer garden joins in a song. No opportunity to match a sound effect with a shot is passed up, although the match is often haphazard—plane engines sound more like boat whistles.

In the latter part of 1928, the sound panic was hitting Hollywood, and Ford had no choice except to go along.

Napoleon's Barber, his first sally into the realm of dialogue film, seems to have functioned as a screen test for the director; he hadn't made a short subject since 1919, but here he was back directing a three-reeler, and not a story he would ordinarily have chosen. Originally a successful vaudeville playlet, *Napoleon's Barber* is about a barber who brags about the horrors he would wreak if he could only get his hands on the Emperor, without knowing that the man in his chair is indeed Napoleon.

It was precisely the sort of one-set drama that the movie companies were buying by the baker's dozen, for this was a period when an art form was being obliterated. The script for *Napoleon's Barber*, dated September 20, 1928, helpfully offers this remarkable suggestion to the director: "The scene in dialogue in chair between the barber and Napoleon should be made in a series of shots from various angles." Ford, who never would have thought of this himself, was undoubtedly most grateful.

Ford rolled the cameras on his first dialogue film on September 29, 1928, and the film was released less than two months later. The results were sufficiently encouraging to the Fox hierarchy to assign Ford to shoot *The Black Watch*, his talking feature debut, in January and February of 1929.

Eight months later, the great bull market exploded in the stock market crash that signaled the beginning of the Depression. As the decade of the 1920s lurched to its end, John Ford had completed a climb near the top of a very slippery profession. He had a solid marriage, two children, a beautiful home, the respect of his peers. As a director whose primary orientation was character and composition, he could not have been thrilled by the arrival of talking pictures, but he would quickly adjust. He had come a very long way from Munjoy Hill, and he was only thirty-five years old.

Ford would make the transition to sound more smoothly than many prestige directors, yet he would always remain loyal to the world of music and silence that he had fallen in love with as a boy. "I . . . am a silent picture man," he would say as an old man. "Pictures, not words, should tell the story."

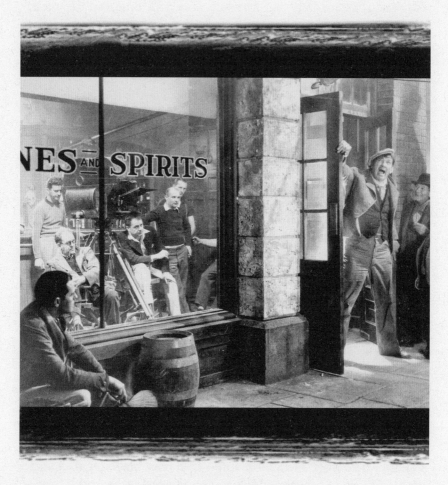

Shooting *The Informer* at RKO studios.

PART THREE

MASTERING AN ART

"I am up to my neck in the creation of a monstrous character called 'Gypo' Nolan—an Informer. I am calling the novel The Informer in his honor. He is a wonderful character and quite original, nobody has touched him. Not popular, though."

FROM A LETTER BY LIAM O'FLAHERTY, JUNE 28, 1924

CHAPTER SEVEN

There were two cataclysms in the last years of the '20s: one on Wall Street, one in Hollywood. The Fords got off fairly lightly in both. "We were lucky in '29," Mary Ford would remember. "A Jewish friend and stockbroker flew out from New York to tip us off. Everyone else went broke but we came out on top." Actually, Ford wrote off about $76,000 in stock losses between 1930 and 1932, but since he earned $268,000 in those three years, he was in considerably better shape than most people in a country where unemployment hovered around 33 percent.

Nineteen twenty-nine was the year Ford paid cash for a new Rolls-Royce. He had called up the showroom and told them he was coming down to pick out a car, but he showed up in khaki pants and a floppy hat. The dealer didn't wait for the disreputable man to identify himself before asking him to leave the premises. An enraged Ford returned home but couldn't bring himself to talk about what had just happened. He called the dealership and told them to throw a mink coat in the back seat and deliver the car to his house.

When it arrived, Ford handed over the cash and told Mary, "Don't ever ask me for anything else." Perhaps because of the humiliation Ford had suffered, he always considered the Rolls to be Mary's car, and carried something of a grudge against it for as long as he owned it. "I don't think they're worth a damn," he would tell one employee. By the late '60s, the car was up on blocks in his garage, and Ford seemed to prefer it that way.

The Depression would decimate the movie business, along with a lot of people that Ford had worked with since he arrived in Hollywood. Frank Baker remembered Ford being accosted outside his office by an old actor from the Universal days whose wife needed an operation. He asked Ford for $200. Ford stared, then backed away, then launched himself at the actor, knocking him down. "How *dare* you come here like this?" he screamed. "Who do you think you are to talk to me this way?"

Baker witnessed this exchange, and also witnessed Ford's business manager Fred Totman coming out of the office door with a check for $1,000. Totman ordered Ford's chauffeur to drive the man home, where an ambulance transported the woman and her husband to San Francisco for the operation.

Baker told the story to Frank Ford, who was amazed. "I've been trying to figure Jack since the day he was born," Frank told Baker. "This is the key. Any moment, if that old actor had kept talking, people would have realized what a softy Jack is. He couldn't have stood that sad story without breaking down. He's built this whole legend of toughness around himself to protect his softness." Later, as the Depression deepened, Frank Baker served as Jack's financial beard, sending checks to more than a dozen families under his own name, so that Ford, who could not bear to be thanked, would never be connected with the stipends.

But the coming of sound couldn't be dodged by any single person's timely intercession. Most of Fox's big directors were masters of the silent form and were understandably reluctant to hurl themselves against the forbidding wall of talkies. The first Fox talkies, and the first talkie mistakes, were made by the studio's journeyman directors, performing the function of stalking horses—not Ford or Borzage, but Irving Cummings, John Blystone, and Crane Wilbur, who responded with some very inventive camera and sound work.

Fox bulked up their staff, adding directors like Henry King, Leo McCarey, Harry D'Arrast, Erich von Stroheim, and William Dieterle. New acting arrivals included the trick roper and monologist Will Rogers, who had made some silent films for Goldwyn and Roach, and a young juvenile named Humphrey Bogart.

Fox maintained niceties that were absent from other lots. Dressing rooms were customized little dwellings of considerable charm. Janet Gaynor had a cottage with a thatched roof redolent of provincial Ireland; Will Rogers had a beautiful adobe bungalow with a cactus garden, tiled roof, and stone fireplace that later would be inherited by composer Alfred Newman. Shirley Temple had a red and white cottage with miniature bathroom fixtures, a baby baby grand piano, and a beautiful mural of . . . Shirley Temple!

All this led Eric Knight, a writer who served a purgatorial stint at Fox and would later write *The Flying Yorkshireman* and *Lassie, Come Home*, to make the comment that "Fox may not make good films, but I'll swear it leads the world in landscape gardening."

Ford had already spent eight years at Fox, and this emotionally conservative man would spend nearly another twenty there. He had worked his way from programmers to A features to epics and back again. He would make something of a grudging transition to talkies, and returned for a number of years to the production of bucolic, essentially Griffithian dramas. Ford the conscious—sometimes self-conscious—artist would not raise his head again until he began working at RKO and abruptly changed his style, returning to the more formal, expressionist manner of Murnau in *The Informer* and *Mary of Scotland*.

Some sense of the paranoia of the early days of sound can be gauged by a note on the script of Ford's *The Black Watch*, an adaptation of Talbot Mundy's *King of the Khyber Rifles*. *The Black Watch* had been slated to be a silent picture in November 1928, when the first continuity outline—by John Stone—had been written. But by January and February of 1929, silent movies were on the endangered species list, so the project was converted to sound. On May 1, 1929, just before the film was released, there was this notation on the cutting continuity: "8580 feet, 4646 words."

The Black Watch did not inspire confidence in his ability to handle the new invention. The premiere was held at the Carthay Circle. The character played by Myrna Loy was named Yasmani, but Victor McLaglen had problems pronouncing the name. "I love you, Jazz Minnie," was the way it came out. "The first time he says this during the premiere," recalled Lefty Hough, "he gets a titter. The second time it gets bigger, and the third time, Christ . . . it spoiled the whole premiere." There was more; Loy's sultry Indian told McLaglen that it was better to be a woman in the arms of a white man than a goddess for thousands of natives.

Word of the derisive laughter got back to Ford, and his natural anxiety over his position in this uncharted new territory nudged him into going off on a drunk. Lefty Hough was delegated to assist Lumsden Hare in reshooting the offending sequence with McLaglen and Loy. There was music in the scene, which required the services of thirty-five musicians, as the music couldn't be mixed with the dialogue but had to be recorded live during the scene.

It wasn't until 4:00 in the morning that they found that the way to get the music at just the right level was to place the musicians outside the soundstage and let the sound bleed through the door. "The picture [had] to be in New York in two days," said Hough, "and I had to stay up all day long and wait till they got the lab open, and rush this film through. I never got any sleep for two days and two nights on account of that damn sequence."

The Black Watch marked the entry of another member into Ford's extended filmmaking family. Mary's brother Wingate, a small, outgoing, very likable man who had been seriously wounded at Château-Thierry, began working for Jack as his assistant director. Along with Eddie O'Fearna, Wingate Smith assisted Ford for the rest of his career.

The Black Watch is a good example of the kind of obstacles directors had to cope with in sound's Brave New World. The film looks exquisite—the great cameraman Joe August demonstrating his unerring touch—and the recording is first-rate, but the proceedings tend to come to a sudden halt for one thing or another.

There are beautiful long shots of some very atmospheric sets, arches, temples, and minarets, usually with foreground objects to give depth to the composition. And Ford gives Myrna Loy a gorgeous introduction—the beautiful woman asleep, her face covered with layers of gauze, the camera lingering on her beauty—a star entrance of the sort he rarely indulged in.

But *The Black Watch* feels stilted, silent film atmosphere infected by (bad) talkie writing, with endless shots of troops marching and pipers piping just to put across the unaccustomed thrill of sound, and with the actors taking looooooonnnngggggg pauses between lines, to let the audience savor the full import of the dialogue.

The film carried the suspicious credit "Staged by Lumsden Hare," one of the many stage actors and directors who flooded Hollywood in the first several years of talking pictures. Ford would tell Peter Bogdanovich that "Winfield Sheehan . . . thought Lumsden Hare was a great British actor—he wasn't but he impressed Sheehan—so he got Hare to direct some love scenes between McLaglen and Myrna Loy. And they were really horrible—long, talky things, had nothing to do with the story—and completely screwed it up." Although the film is not particularly long at ninety-three minutes, its static nature makes it seem longer.

Myrna Loy sensed an interest on Ford's part that he never acted upon. She also noted his "tremendous" sensitivity, which he would have lost a limb rather than acknowledge. After the film was finished, Ford invited Loy to a party at his house. She arrived to a bewildered look from Mary. The party was a stag affair in his den, with Ford surrounded by John Wayne and the rest of the boys. Resolute by nature, Loy stayed and had a wonderful time.

For a film about Annapolis titled *Salute*, Ford wanted to handpick a group of young men that wouldn't look like actors but like young sailors. He told Duke Wayne to recruit a likely group. Wayne hired a gregarious, roughly handsome young football player–engineering student named Ward Bond, who would quickly endear himself to Ford and become a key member of his stock company.

One evening in Annapolis, Ford was in the bathtub when Bond walked into his room and walked over to the dresser, where Ford had left his wallet. "Listen, Jack," Bond yelled, "I'm taking about twenty bucks. I'm going into town drinking tonight. You can go with us if you want to come." Then he was gone. Of all the people in Ford's circle, Ward Bond was the only one who would have dared such a stunt, not out of a matador's courage but, rather, basic obliviousness. Ward Bond believed everybody was like Ward Bond, or wanted to be. Ford found such ingenuous stupidity endearing.

Compared to the flamboyant beauties of late silents like *Hangman's House*, *Salute* is full of lackadaisical camerawork and bad acting. Nevertheless, Ford was still in better professional shape than many other leading silent directors. Major figures like Fred Niblo (*The Three Musketeers*, *Ben-Hur*), James Cruze (*The Covered Wagon*), and Herbert Brenon (*Peter Pan*, *Beau Geste*) would be unable to make the transition to sound for reasons both creative and industrial. In mid-1930, Fox signed Ford for two more years, bringing his salary to $3,250 a week.

Ford was in New York looking at plays for potential screen material when he saw *The Last Mile*, John Wexley's play about Death Row, starring a young actor named Spencer Tracy. "What impressed me the first time was the direction," Ford recalled. "I thought the staging was absolutely brilliant. . . . I knew I had to see it again." The second time he saw it, he noticed Tracy. "More than anything else, I was tantalized by his movement. I don't think many people were ever conscious of Spence's bodily discipline. . . . His catlike agility was something extraordinary. He made every movement sharp and meaningful, and didn't waste a single turn. . . . He had the power of a consummate actor."

The two men went to the Lamb's Club for a nightcap and ended up closing the place. Ford was pleased to find that the Lamb's was virtually an annex of Dublin. William Frawley was there that night, as were Allen Jenkins and Pat O'Brien. Sitting at an adjacent table was John McGraw, the fabled manager of the New York Giants. "So we spent a few hours talking about baseball," remembered Ford.

Ford brought Tracy out to Hollywood to make *Up the River*. The actor had given his word to Herman Shumlin that he'd go back to *The Last Mile* after he made the movie. Script problems kept putting off production, until Tracy's contract expired. "Of course you'll stay out here?" they asked Tracy, only to be alarmed by his answer.

Ford kicked into gear and shot the picture in seventeen days so as to get Tracy back to New York as soon as possible. Ford and Tracy forged a bond, one that wasn't shared by anybody else in the cast. "Spence was as natural as if he didn't know a camera was there, or as if there had *always*

been a camera when he acted before," said Ford. "His speech was decisive. He knew a straight line from a laugh line. If he had a chance for a
laugh, he played it in a way that would get it."

Ford didn't take to many actors the way he took to Tracy. There was,
for instance, Humphrey Bogart, who made the mistake of calling Ford
"Jack" without being invited to. Ford immediately set about humiliating
him. After every take he would call out, "How does that seem to you,
Mr. Bogart?"

Mary Ford helped Louise Tracy find a house, and Ford and Tracy
spent a good deal of time together. In later years, Tracy would blame
Ford for starting his drinking problem. It was meant as a joke—Tracy's
own father was alcoholic—but there might have been a kernel of truth in
it. In 1930, Tracy never drank when he worked, and drank off-hours only
occasionally. By 1935, he had been jailed twice and was widely regarded
as one of the worst drunks in the business.

During production, John Wayne came back on the lot from long weeks
spent filming *The Big Trail.* The starring part in a Western epic was a big
break for a twenty-three-year-old kid, but Ford wasn't happy for him. As
a matter of fact, when Wayne went over to say hello, Ford cut him dead.
Then he did it again. A confused Wayne retreated.

It was part and parcel of Ford's perverse possessiveness. Those people
he cared for had to show an equivalent loyalty, and Wayne, by working
for another A-list director, had somehow violated one of Ford's unspoken
commandments, even if it had been Ford who helped get him the job. It
would be several years before he would be accepted back into the fold.

Ford learned sound fast; all of Hollywood did, for they correctly
surmised that, once the novelty value wore off, no audience would
pay money to see films as clumsily made as *Salute.* Just a year later, with
movies like *Men Without Women* and *Born Reckless,* Ford was finding his
sea legs. *Men Without Women* survives only in a bastardized version that
replaces most of the dialogue with titles. In any case, it seems inferior
to Capra's *Submarine,* which it attempts to replicate. It is an unusually
coarse film for Ford—sailors negotiate prices with Shanghai whores.
Clearly, Ford was treading on the ground Raoul Walsh had made his
own in *What Price Glory?*

In the film, however, are early, faint intimations of better movies to
come: a religious fanatic who goes crazy, like Boris Karloff in *The Lost
Patrol,* and an Englishman with a poignant secret, like Ian Hunter in *The
Long Voyage Home.*

Men Without Women is very much a patchy early talkie, but *Born Reckless* is considerably better, a giddy, energetic minor gem, a genial gangster

movie in the vein of *Underworld* that is well shot on smaller-than-life studio sets. Safecracker Louis Berretti—the unethnic Edmund Lowe—is sent to the Army in lieu of prison. World War I is on, but Berretti comes out of it a hero, then opens a successful restaurant. What nobody knows is that he keeps his hand in with some light crime. When the child of a woman he admires is kidnapped, Berretti sets out to get the kid back.

Born Reckless isn't Ford—the material is closer to Raoul Walsh—but it isn't bad. It's better than most of the 1930 Fox productions; it has atmosphere, picturesque settings, a good-bad hero, and a ramshackle charm. It's one of the few Ford films of this period that's brisk and unexpected enough to hold a modern audience's interest.

Despite the pleasures of *Born Reckless*, as talking pictures settled into a groove the question of what kind of director John Ford was remained very much up in the air. The promise of the early Carey pictures, the fulfillment of *The Iron Horse*, and the faceted excellence of pictures like *Hangman's House* had been accompanied by too many empty assignments, executed with professionalism but little else.

Nearly every first-rank director of Ford's generation, from Griffith to Chaplin to Tourneur to Vidor, had moved quickly, decisively toward self-expression; when they saw an opening, they ran for it. But Ford fought the impulse nearly every time it arose. At this point he was on track toward a career analogous to Henry King or Victor Fleming—a first-rate studio director, but an essentially reactive talent.

Some of it was not his fault, for Ford was a victim of a studio in free fall as well as of his own complaisance. Fox was sinking beneath terrible debts incurred by its founder's unsuccessful attempt to take over Loew's Incorporated in 1929, an attempt submarined by the stock market crash. William Fox was banished from his own studio, which, in the early days of the Depression, was kept alive solely through the box office appeal of Will Rogers. Good stories that cost money went to other studios, to Paramount or MGM; Fox had to make do with second- and third-string material.

Ford had to have sensed the power within him, but he was afraid of the consequences of expressing it. Aesthetically, he had already been exposed to the two alternating strains that would make him an artist—the ease, grace, and homeyness of Griffith, and the conscious aestheticism of Murnau. But for now, in the early '30s, there was a great gift lying fallow—a visual style that was there when he wanted it to be, a few other things in embryo.

The stimuli that would bring Ford's creative personality alive, converting him from a gifted but essentially passive craftsman into an artist, a creator, would consist of several different factors—a woman, and a specific kind of filmmaking: the Western. He must have always known that he had a vision of family, a vision of America, but the Western gave him a central metaphor with which to say it. It would become obvious that no one else could say it quite as well.

And the other stimuli came from two completely different men, each appealing to a different side of Ford's nature. One was Will Rogers. The other was named Merian Cooper.

A year after *Men Without Women*, Ford made another submarine picture, but *The Seas Beneath* is immensely superior to the earlier picture. The story is no better—commander George O'Brien and his crew go after the dreaded German sub U-172, a search complicated by O'Brien's falling in love with the sister of U-172's commander, who happens to be a spy—but the production and Ford's efforts are both on a higher level. *The Seas Beneath* lacks the choppy, tentative quality of early sound, and it's almost completely made on location—Catalina stands in for the Canary Islands.

Ford is in his physical element, capturing the real roll of the sea, authenticity in atmosphere and hardware. The film's underlying theme of a mutual respect between enemies clearly looks ahead to other submarine movies like *The Enemy Below* and *Das Boot*. *The Seas Beneath* is Ford's first really good talking picture.

Even Ford admitted that it had "some good stuff in it," but he never made any large claims for the film because he couldn't stand Marion Lessing, the female lead, who seems to have been cast because she spoke fluent German. "We had a scene . . . in which the German submarine slips up alongside another submarine to refuel, and this girl comes out on to the bridge chewing *gum!* Right in the camera. So we had to go to all the trouble of doing it over again. She just couldn't act."

The Navy had lent Fox a couple of submarines and a minesweeper. Ford slept on board the subs and found he liked Navy life. He responded to the order and discipline, the easy camaraderie of the men, and their competence at their jobs. A good Navy crew was like a good film crew, but with a higher purpose.

And there was another issue; Jack and Mary had been married for ten years, but she remained indifferent to the world in which he was so successful; she had always regarded his movie career and, by extension, him, as "low Irish." Because of her own background, the obvious alternative to the insubstantial world of movies was the military. The Navy began to look better and better to Jack.

• • •

Spencer Tracy visited Ford on the last day of shooting *The Seas Beneath*. Ford, Tracy, and George O'Brien were walking down a pier when Ford asked O'Brien what he was doing next.

"I thought I'd go down to Ensenada and do some fishing," said O'Brien.

"What do you want to do that for?"

"Well, you'd rather I stay in Hollywood and go to the Trocadero and look at other actors?"

"Why don't you come with me?"

"Where are you going?"

"Have you ever been to the Philippines?" Ford was leaving that night. He reached into his pocket and handed O'Brien a ticket. The actor wrote him a check for $200. Tracy, silently observing, must have felt like Sid watching Huck Finn and Tom Sawyer planning their escapades. Ford finally turned to him. "Spence, don't you want to come?"

"If you have a third ticket with you. What are you, a travel bureau?"

Selden West, Tracy's biographer, believes this was an intentional piece of sadism on Ford's part—the director rubbing in Tracy's imprisonment by his obligations, his wife and deaf son. It's also possible that the question was meant perfectly honestly; had the situation been reversed, and Ford's family been similarly on his mind, it would have been entirely characteristic of him to have somebody else take care of the situation, and go on pursuing his own interests. Ford had the solipsism of the essentially selfish artist and couldn't see why Tracy didn't.

Tracy stayed. Ford and O'Brien left. George was carrying a letter of introduction from his father, Dan, the retired chief of police of San Francisco. Dated January 15, 1931, the letter reads, "To Police Officials: This will serve to present my son, George O'Brien, who is making an extensive trip thru the Orient with his close friend, and my personal friend, Mr. John Ford. Any consideration or courtesies extended will be greatly appreciated by all concerned, particularly by myself, for which I stand ready to reciprocate whenever the opportunity may present itself."

That night, they were waving goodbye to Mary, Pat, and Barbara, who were seeing them off. O'Brien noticed that Mary was in tears. "Don't cry, Mary," he yelled. "You'd cry too," she yelled back. "You've got my ticket."

Ford wrote some amiable, lengthy letters home detailing their hijinks on board, and George O'Brien kept a diary of the trip, which ends when the two men got to Manila. The initial part of the trip seems to have been pleasant, with only some bad weather to mar the boyish horseplay: O'Brien noted that they had endured "Worst storm in 3 years, the Captain says. Jack and I slept on our heads!"

Jack's letters home were slightly more forthcoming. "We've had ten days of typhoons, hurricanes, gales, etc. The weather has been terrific—

the ship has been under water all the time. Mountanous waves which broke over the bridge. This is the first time its been steady enough to even write a letter. . . . In spite of that I have had a good time, slept twelve hours a day, ate four meals and five days out I'd read all the books I brought. . . .

"George and I laughed at Mama's suggestion of laying on the deck and getting tanned. If you laid on the deck you'd only get water-logged. . . . The food is very good + and the accommodations swell. I'm glad you didn't come, Mama, ten days of that storm would have caused trouble with that gall-bladder.

"It is quite calm now and the sea is beautiful. I've never seen such magnificent sunsets as we're having. Violent flaming reds which suddenly change to pastel shades of violet blue etc. Yesterday we passed a live volcano fifteen miles away. It was thrilling to see land after nineteen days at sea. The volcano was exactly shaped like a pyramid. O'Brien said 'Gosh! The skipper made a mistake—we're in Egypt!' All last night we could see its reflections—fire against the sky."

The storms had held them up; nineteen days out, the men still had four days to go till they hit the Philippines, and O'Brien said that it was hardly worth the trouble to take off their shoes.

"I'm anxious to see a tree," noted Ford. "O'Brien's behavior has been exemplary. I am proud of him. Never once has he been disorderly or uncouth and at all times is a credit to the industry. . . . Well this trip has done me a lot of good (knock wood!). I've never felt better and certainly never looked better in my life. Even O'Brien looks at me admiringly. (However, it'll do him no good.) I look and act twelve years younger.

"My behavior has been most strict—the beer is very good, and we have regular beer time—with sardines herring etc. Twice a day between lunch and dinner. I am eating like a pig—my appetite's come back with a vengeance."

Ford closed this chatty epistle with a self-caricature of himself staring at a glass of beer.

After twenty-four days at sea, the men finally arrived in Manila on February 10. That day, the Filipino papers made much of O'Brien's presence: "Screen's Dynamic Lover in Manila; George O'Brien, Screen Idol, Slips Quietly into City, Comes with His Director Direct from U.S.; Will Stay Here Awhile."

It was in Manila that something happened between the two men. What is clear is that Ford went on one of his legendary benders. O'Brien later calculated that it might have gone on for ten days. Ford wouldn't leave his bed, occasionally pausing to kick the empties out from under the covers. "Poor Jack . . . just wouldn't stop," O'Brien told his son. "I remember one time, I begged him to quit, we had a dinner to go to, or something, but he just told me to go to hell, you know. It was kind of pathetic."

As O'Brien hadn't taken the trip to hone his nursing skills, he made the fateful decision to leave Jack to his drinking and go on ahead as planned. While O'Brien, on board the SS *Luzon*, visited Dumaguete, Zamboanga, Jolo, Iolio, and Cebu, Ford stayed in Manila. O'Brien told reporters that Ford "lies ill in Manila of dengue fever, but I will rejoin him soon."

After nearly two weeks, O'Brien and the now-sober Ford hooked up again. As O'Brien's son noted, "[He] could have had no idea of the price he would pay for this unassuming show of independence. He did not work for John Ford again for seventeen years, and never had the lead again in a Ford picture."

During the remainder of the trip, there would be no argument between the two men, not even any coolness. It's entirely possible that Ford never even mentioned what he clearly regarded as O'Brien's betrayal. It was Ford's habit to remain congenial and even friendly to people he ostracized professionally. He would remember birthdays, even drop by for visits. The offending party was still a friend, they simply didn't work for him anymore, and it was left to them to figure out why.

And so the two men traveled to Indonesia, specifically the southern archipelago, "where they had a Sultan," said O'Brien. "I had always wanted to meet a Sultan. He had 23 wives. It was embarrassing though because he had them on a Chevrolet flat truck and they sat on boxes. I thought they would [at least] be in sedans."

From there, they caught a boat to Hong Kong on March 9, where they gave an interview expressing their regrets on the tragic death of F. W. Murnau, then traveled to Kobe, Osaka, Kyoto, and Shanghai before turning around and taking a boat to Hawaii, where O'Brien's friendship with Duke Kahanamoku, who had taught him surfboarding, was renewed, to much coverage in the Honolulu papers. The two men arrived in San Francisco on April 11. O'Brien's father was there to meet them, as was a police guard. A newspaper reporter on the scene called them "a pair of rollicking tramps home from the sea."

Over the years, there has been speculation that there was some kind of early-warning spying going on, that Ford and O'Brien were doing reconnaissance of Japanese naval activities during the trip. The notion seems fairly ridiculous, considering Ford's alcoholic intake, and the fact that the entire trip was exhaustively recorded by the press. Certainly, there is nothing in Ford's letters or O'Brien's diary to indicate anything of the sort. George O'Brien thought the idea was hilarious, assuring his son that such speculation was "nonsense."

Thinking back on the experience more than forty years later, O'Brien would say, "I had known him . . . for nearly ten years. Yet after four months in which I was with him every second of every day, I think I knew less about him than ever before. He was the most private man I ever met, and even though I loved him I guess the truth is that I never really understood him."

Ford adored the entire experience, away from "the business," away from the obligations of family, away from filmmaking—living, if only for a time, a Somerset Maugham story.

While Ford was indulging his taste for globe-trotting, his son Pat had been ensconced at the Black-Foxe Military Institute (run by Earle Foxe, the loathsome heavy in *Hangman's House*) in Hollywood. Many show business parents sent their boys there in the hope that the children would be inculcated with the discipline the parents lacked.

Just before Thanksgiving 1931, the ten-year-old Pat wrote a plaintive letter to his parents from the school. "We are having three party [sic]. A minstrel show, a senior xmas party and a junior xmas party. I don't want to go to the Minstrel show, I can't go to the Senior Christmas party, but I can hardly wait until the Junior Xmas party. . . . My weekly grades have just come out they are, Arithmetic 90, English 59, History 90, Geography 91, Spelling 100."

Ford was never a rabid moviegoer, but would attend if convinced the film was of sufficient interest. Around this time, Brian Desmond Hurst dragged him to see Dreyer's *The Passion of Joan of Arc* at an art theater on Vine Street. Ford was seemingly unimpressed, but the next day Desmond Hurst observed Jack entering the theater to have another look.

On a considerably less exalted level, Ford returned to Fox and launched *The Brat*, a variation on Shaw's *Pygmalion*, but with the world's most irritating Eliza. After an arty, expressionist first reel, complete with overhead shots, the film declines into orthodoxy, a photographed play whose slapdash production can be gauged by the simple fact that, in a rear projection sequence of an ambulance racing past various theatrical marquees, the film is projected the wrong way, so all the letters on the marquee are reversed.

The Brat has the worst acting in any extant Ford film: Sally O'Neil is incredibly irritating, with a continual quaver in her voice exactly like Lou Costello's catch phrase "I'm a bad boy," while Virginia Cherrill, Chaplin's blind heroine in *City Lights*, shows up in a supporting part. Cherrill still looks blind, and is completely at sea without the moment-by-moment coaching she got from Chaplin and obviously didn't get from Ford.

Except for the odd flamboyance of the first reel, and Ward Bond and

J. Farrell MacDonald lurking around the edges of the cast, there is no indication that John Ford was anywhere in the vicinity of the set. *The Brat* is Ford's worst surviving film. It can safely be assumed that Sam Goldwyn never saw it; if he had, he would never have hired Jack to direct his prestige picture for the year, starring his greatest box office star.

CHAPTER EIGHT

S am Goldwyn always had trouble finding stories that he and his recalci-
trant star Ronald Colman could agree on. Colman disliked Goldwyn
and usually contrived to deal with him strictly through intermediaries.
Arrowsmith seems to have been one of the easy choices. Sinclair Lewis's
1925 novel had been a popular and critical success, and, although Goldwyn was leery of a story in which the leading lady dies, he was won over
by his star's enthusiasm. With the cast already set, Goldwyn borrowed
Ford from Fox for $50,000, more or less the same amount he was earning
for a picture at his home studio.

Arrowsmith is distinguished more by its photography—by Ray June—
and Richard Day's looming expressionist sets than by its script or acting.
Colman is too old to be playing a young medical student at the beginning
of the picture, and the material—the conflict between idealism and the
real world—is more symbolic than real and better suited to King Vidor
than Ford, who preferred people of the earth and had little temperamental use for metaphoric characters.

The film has odd, random moments of charm—Myrna Loy characterized them as "soft touches"—that have little to do with the overstuffed
narrative. When Arrowsmith asks Leora to marry him, they are in a
restaurant, and she asks him for a nickel for the jukebox, explaining that
"I want soft music." After Arrowsmith has sacrificed her on the altar of
his ambition, he goes into her closet and buries his face in her clothes,
trying to recapture her scent. In the end, Arrowsmith renounces his plush
life and goes off to the woods to indulge in pure research. "Lee and I are
both going with you!" he cries to his friend in valedictory enthusiasm.

If it's not beautifully written or acted, it's certainly a beautifully *spoken*
movie—Helen Hayes and Colman had two of the loveliest, most plaintive voices in the world. Ford adapted himself to Goldwyn's style and

used more close-ups than he tended to when left to his own devices. As was usually the case in this period, Ford let actors give their own performances: Colman is Colman, and Hayes is quite good, but Richard Bennett indulges in a barnstorming theatrical turn as Arrowsmith's mentor. Once again indulging his creative efforts on the margins, Ford found small parts for Ward Bond and John Qualen.

Ford only cuts loose in the last third of the picture, when Arrowsmith and his wife move to the West Indies to stem a plague epidemic. The sets shift from high ceilings and the deco lines of the city to low ceilings, wide-planked floors, latticed doors, and an omnipresent, unhealthy-looking mist. The sequence is a sustained tour de force of voodoo gothic.

Ford and his actors didn't get along. For one scene, Ronald Colman had to appear drunk and throw a vial of serum against the wall. It was a display of raw emotion beyond his preferred personality of polished bemusement. After a number of takes in which Ford attempted to rouse Colman to a display of anger, Brian Desmond Hurst asked, "Do you want anything printed, Mr. Ford?"

"Stick your fingers into that pile of rubbish, take any two out, they all stink." Colman immediately walked off the set amidst a lengthy silence.

Ford and Helen Hayes also had their problems, and she resisted his direction. When Hayes objected to some of Ford's ideas, he charged, saying, "Who's directing this picture, you or me? You go out on that set and do what I tell you to do." Hayes drew herself up to her full five feet and stammered out, "I'm not accustomed to being *speaken* to in that manner!" The set broke up, and the head-butting was followed by what seems to have been one of the occasional crushes Ford developed on an actress. "He got stuck on me a little," remembered Hayes, "and took to calling me all the time." Hayes, who already had her hands full with her heavy-drinking husband, Charlie MacArthur, didn't respond.

The contretemps with Hayes, and Sam Goldwyn's trait of being a very activist producer who liked to pass daily judgment on the rushes, combined to set Ford on edge; his self-confidence was insufficiently strong to deal with anything but adoration or, at the very least, respect.

On September 29, 1931, principal photography was completed except for some second unit shooting and minor retakes. Ford was expected to begin work with the editor, but missed one appointment, then on October 9, showed up in what Arthur Hornblow remembered as a "bruised and battered condition with hangover look, spoke incoherently and rambled, couldn't remember what was said a few minutes before."

Goldwyn figured it might be wise to try again another day, and suggested Ford come in the next morning with some suggestions about cutting out about one thousand feet of the picture. He never showed up, nor did he appear on the 12th to guide Richard Bennett in some retakes. When the studio called, they were told he couldn't get out of bed.

Ford appeared on the 14th, still obviously drunk. He told Arthur Hornblow that he was too nervous to look at the picture and they should go ahead and cut it without him. Ford spent the weekend on Catalina, evidently still drinking, and sent Myrna Loy a telegram: "HAVING A WONDERFUL TIME. WISH YOU WERE HERE. JACK." After missing yet another appointed day for retakes, Ford finally showed up on the 20th, barely audible and incoherent. At this point, Goldwyn threw up his hands, shot another day of retakes, and completed the editing without Ford's input.

Goldwyn got four signed affidavits from witnesses, and forced Fox to refund $4,100 of the money he had paid for Ford's services. Aside from the money, which was minor, Fox was furious about Ford's misbehavior for reasons of corporate psychology. They had sent one of their prize pupils over to the big house on the hill and he had egregiously misbehaved.

On October 22, 1931, John Ford was fired by Winfield Sheehan: "You are hereby notified and informed that effective 10-20-31, your contract is cancelled and terminated . . . because of your wilful failure, neglect and refusal to render the services contracted to be rendered by you . . . you will be held responsible for all damages suffered."

On November 3, *Variety* reported that Ford would be leaving Fox for financial reasons. According to the cover story devised by the studio, they could get three directing teams (production manager Bert Sebell and actor J. M. Kerrigan, Marcel Varnel and Lefty Hough, and editor Harold Schuster and writer Samuel Godfrey) for a total that would equal half of Ford's $3,000 weekly salary.

Winfield Sheehan and Sol Wurtzel knew full well that Ford was one of the top directors in the business, and none of the directorial teams that would be drawing $500 a week between them were likely to repeat his level of skill. But Fox was reeling from a series of box office reverses brought on by Sheehan's preference for thinking big and spending bigger. In 1930, they had spent $1.9 million on Raoul Walsh's 70mm spectacular *The Big Trail*, which had domestic rentals of only $945,000. There were some hits—*The Cockeyed World*, a sequel to *What Price Glory?*, the Gaynor-Farrell musical *Sunny Side Up*—but the studio was bedeviled by out-of-control costs. Fox was regularly spending between $400,000 and $500,000 for a programmer at a time of declining box office revenues.

This was all exacerbated by the talent factor. MGM had Garbo and Crawford and Harlow and the young Clark Gable, among a dozen others. Although Fox had Will Rogers, Janet Gaynor, and the handsome but tenor-voiced Charles Farrell, they had little else. George O'Brien was largely limited to outdoor pictures and Westerns. Then there were Victor McLaglen and Edmund Lowe and Warner Baxter. That's all.

Because of the Depression, audiences were becoming increasingly selective about their moviegoing. Average weekly attendance plummeted from 90 million in 1930 to 75 million in 1931. (It would plunge even further in 1932, down to 60 million, a terrifying one-third drop in three years.) In 1931, Fox lost $5.56 million, in spite of the fact that Winfield Sheehan cut budgets. In 1932, the studio would lose a staggering $19.96 million. Economies had to be made wherever possible, and a high-priced director with a drinking problem that seemed to be flying out of control looked like a reasonable target.

Yet Ford seems to have had a choice of alternative studios. Everybody knew he drank, but they also knew that his pictures were made on time, on budget, and tended to make money; *Arrowsmith* amassed domestic rentals of well over a million dollars, enough to make the expensive prestige picture a break-even proposition, with foreign revenues putting it into profits.

Ford had once again gone to Honolulu, to the Royal Hawaiian, when his agent Harry Wurtzel wrote him that "it would be far more advisable to begin negotiations now than to wait until you return. . . ."

Wurtzel reported that Paramount was interested, as were RKO, MGM, Universal, and First National. "We could close a deal, making it subject to your approval upon your return. I again urge you to give this letter very serious consideration because delaying it may cost you a lot of money. Therefore, cable me what your lowest terms will be, by the week or by the picture, and what company you prefer."

Ford trooped off to Universal to direct one picture. Initially, the project was to be something called *Shanghai Interlude*, but that was altered to a Lew Ayres vehicle called *Mail Goes Through*. By the time it emerged, Lew Ayres was nowhere to be found and the title had been changed to *Air Mail*.

As *Arrowsmith* was just a month from its December release, Ford had another unpleasant reminder of the state to which his brother Frank was falling. "Can I have two hundred immediately," wired Frank on November 24. Now, there were no directorial assignments for Frank at all. Not even Poverty Row was interested in the one-time Serial King. Acting assignments were irregular and, when they did occur, were little more than bits. For the rest of his life, Frank would be dependent on Jack for work or handouts.

• • •

I n her old age, Mary Ford alluded to "unhappy" events from which Ford had helped her recover. One was probably her abortive first marriage; another, no doubt, was the suicide of Mary's brother John at the Odin Street house. Around 11:00 in the morning of January 2, 1932, John Willis Smith went into the garage, closed the door, and turned on the car engine. About 2:30 in the afternoon, after Smith was already dead, something sparked, and an explosion "wrecked the garage." Smith left a note suggesting that his act was the result of a recent estrangement from his wife, Rene.

After Jack drank himself off the Goldwyn lot, he had left with Mary on a trip to the Philippines on October 31 that was meant as a make-good for having left her behind earlier that year. In Hawaii, Ford started drinking again. For five days Jack sat in a dark room at the Royal Hawaiian, drinking, crying, and drooling. Mary finally took him to the hospital.

The children joined them in Honolulu, but Ford and a Fox representative named Larry de Prita—later to marry Ford's niece Cecile—took off by themselves to Bali, Jakarta, and Singapore, then hooked up again with Mary and the kids in Hong Kong, from which point they went on to Shanghai, Kobe, Yokohama, and Honolulu.

Smith had probably been house-sitting while Jack and Mary were away. Mary came back after her brother's suicide, but Ford seems to have continued on his trip—so much for spousal support. While he was away, Barbara became ill, and Ford wrote home that "I *sincerely* hope Barbara is better. Watch her carefully and if she doesn't improve get Mr. Anderson to get the best doctor he can get. More later." On January 28, 1932, at the end of a letter home, Ford wrote of "Rain rain rain. As we approach Bali the sun came out + the view is magnificent. I hope to see you all soon. I miss you + love you so much." None of Jack's or Mary's letters mention her brother's suicide, although the story was fully reported in the newspapers.

U niversal was still the least prestigious of the major studios. Now run by Carl Laemmle Jr., a hypochondriac of flamboyant proportions, even Universal's own stars regarded it as "a shoddy, second-rate place."

Although *Air Mail* was a dry run with material that Howard Hawks would later dress up and claim as his own, it involved a second-string cast and script, the only kind Universal could afford. Still, that was no reason you couldn't have some fun.

"One night we were on location," remembered Gloria Stuart. "I fell asleep with my hair done up to keep the wave in. I was hunched up in my chair and Slim Summerville and John put a flask of whiskey on the arm of my chair and had [the still man] take my picture." The next morning, the company was awash in 8 x 10 glossies of Gloria Stuart looking, in her words, "like a drunk old broad who couldn't hold her head up."

Stuart had come from New York, where she'd been playing Chekhov, and she believed that movies were beneath her and every other sentient person. Her opinion had been confirmed when she had been called into Junior Laemmle's office and informed that they were thinking of developing her as a female Tarzan. She responded volubly before she walked out of the office and slammed the door behind her.

Her first film had been *The Old Dark House* for James Whale, where all the English actors had tea at 11:00 and 4:00. Stuart and Melvyn Douglas were not invited. Douglas and Stuart, left to their own devices, began to talk about the need for an actor's union in the movie business, the nascent birth of the Screen Actors Guild. Only a few months later, Stuart was making *Air Mail* for Ford. Word had already gotten out that Stuart was such a malcontent that she was talking about starting a union, for God's sake. Ford responded by greeting Stuart each morning with a raised, clenched fist and a booming cry of "Comrade!"

"He was dear, but such a reactionary," remembered Stuart. Actually, he was nothing of the sort. Ford was a solid Roosevelt man in 1932 and for as many times as FDR ran, but his true political religion was to be contrary, a one-man insurrection against perceived manners and mores.

As a trained New York stage actress, and a veteran of a James Whale picture, where the director told you when to turn and where to put your hand, Stuart was a trifle nonplussed by Ford's essential trust in the casting process. "John had a handkerchief tied around his right hand. And he would pull on it with his left hand. Once in a while he would chew it. On *Air Mail*, he gave me precisely one piece of direction. Before one particular scene, he said, 'Okay kids, believe it.' I thought it was terribly important."

After shooting *Air Mail* at Universal, Ford trooped over to MGM for another time-killer, a Wallace Beery movie entitled *Flesh*. It wasn't exactly Ford material—Beery was a broad, crude actor who made George Bancroft seem a model of precision. In *Flesh* he played a trusting wrestler led astray by his love for a female ex-con—MGM seemed to be thinking of UFA and Emil Jannings. (*Flesh* is the movie that Barton Fink, the title character of the inspired, deeply strange 1991 movie of the same name by the Coen Brothers, is attempting to write, with a complete lack of success.)

"[Ford] was mad at everybody, especially the producer," remembered Karen Morley, who played the woman who ruins Wallace Beery's life. "I make four for them, no matter what they are," Ford told Morley. "And then I make one for me." *Flesh* was not the one for him. "It's not that he didn't care," said Morley. "He wanted it charming, and Wallace Beery had a rough sort of charm." But Morley, an experienced stage actress, was put off by Ford's manner, the intransigence of the material, and the fact that "none of those silent guys gave you much direction."

Everyone in the film labors under the unconvincing burden of a German accent except Morley, and Ford is able to do little more than avoid the traditional high-gloss Metro lighting and lend *Flesh* some of his *echt* UFA expressionism. Neither Ford nor Barton Fink could do anything at all with a Wallace Beery wrestling movie.

It's probable that Ford took the film as a work-study project, to see what the environment at MGM was like, even though the ice age that had fallen at Fox in the wake of his *Arrowsmith* binge was thawing. He must not have been thrilled with the heavy top-down supervisory methods of the lot, for he would work at MGM very infrequently during the next twenty-five years, when he was at his creative and commercial peak.

In May of 1932, Winfield Sheehan relented and okayed a two-picture deal with Ford that paid him $40,000 a picture. There was one proviso, however—Jack had to waive the story approval that had been in his last contract and shoot the stories Fox wanted him to shoot. The Goldwyn affair had cost him $10,000 a picture and a good deal of his autonomy. Nevertheless, Jack signed the deal.

Ford must have had some concern for the situation in which the industry found itself. Fox was still flailing, MGM was far too bureaucratic, and Universal was in as desperate shape as Fox; on December 20, *Variety* announced that Laemmle's studio had canceled a sequel to *Air Mail* they had been tentatively calling *Skyways* because the budget—$300,000—was too high.

Into this looming professional vacuum stepped a remarkable man named Merian C. Cooper.

When Merian Coldwell Cooper arrived in Hollywood to live in 1931, he had made three pictures—*Grass*, *Chang*, and *The Four Feathers*, but he had lived at least as many lives. Cooper was born in 1893 in Jacksonville and came by his compulsive adventuring honestly; he was a descendant of John Cooper, who had commanded a cavalry outfit in the American Revolution that had been trained by General Casimir Pulaski, the Polish patriot.

After washing out of Annapolis, Cooper had become a newspaperman, then a soldier, participating in border actions against Pancho Villa. Transferring to the Aviation Corps, he trained as a pilot and took part in World War I, during which he was shot down twice.

After the war he stayed in Europe and joined the Kosciuszko Squadron, a ten-man volunteer unit of Americans serving in the Polish air force fighting the Bolsheviks. Shot down again—by a machine gun mounted on a bread cart—he was captured by one General Budienny, who had immense mustachios and was nearly as theatrical a character as Cooper. Cooper was mistaken for someone else and not recognized as an officer, an accident which probably saved his life. He was imprisoned for a year in a forced labor camp. Escaping by bribing the guards in April of 1921, he made his way on foot, under cover of darkness, to Warsaw, where he was decorated for exceptional bravery.

Returning penniless from Poland, Cooper wangled a reporting job on the night shift of the *New York Times*, leaving his days free to spend at the American Geographical Society and to write stories for the *Times* Sunday magazine under a variety of pseudonyms. Cooper's time at the Geographical Society awakened his interest in exploring, which led him to turn down the managing editor's job at the *Minneapolis Daily News*.

Cooper went off to be the second officer on a Singapore vessel that was engaged in taking travel pictures. "I knew nothing at all about motion picture making," Cooper would write years later, "but I set about learning, and, with the conceit of youth, felt confident that I could do a lot better than those aboard, whose job it was to make pictures. . . . I was utterly convinced that the idea of a 'travel picture,' per se, was both stupid and dull, but that in the visual medium of the Motion Picture lay the greatest new teaching idea in the whole field of Human Geography."

When one of the technicians jumped ship in Ceylon, Cooper sent for Ernest B. Schoedsack, a freelance newsreel cameraman he had met in January 1919. Schoedsack was intrepid and fearless. The two men resumed their friendship and broadened it to become a partnership.

With money borrowed from his father ($2,000), his brother ($1,000), and $10,000 in loans, Cooper teamed up with Schoedsack and a journalist-spy named Marguerite Harrison whom Cooper had met in Poland during the war. Their goal was to film the annual summer migration of fifty thousand Bakhtiari tribesmen and their livestock across the Zardeh Kuh mountain range. The result was the stunning 1925 documentary *Grass*, which led Jesse Lasky to commission Cooper and Schoedsack to make *Chang*, a fictionalized documentary set in what is now northern Thailand. That was followed by *The Four Feathers*, also for Paramount.

As a result of his experiences, Cooper was an ardent anti-Bolshevik and, as Kevin Brownlow would observe, "e-x-t-r-e-m-e-l-y right wing." He wrote a book in the 1920s entitled *Things Men Die For*, which contained a passage about blacks that, in later years, he was always careful to obliterate whenever he would come across a copy, in case of a future revolution during which some scholarly Negro, presumably toting a machete, would discover the book and fall upon Cooper and his family.

By 1933, Cooper was regarded with deep respect for his probity and honesty throughout Hollywood, as well as an expert, if unorthodox, filmmaker. He was medium-sized, balding, affable, with immense enthusiasm.

"*There* was a fascinating man," remembered Fay Wray, the leading lady in Cooper's greatest film. "I always looked upon him as a father figure. He was a character, an adventurer. He hated to stay home; he always wanted to be going far, far away. He used to rub his head a lot, trying to keep the ideas in . . . or get them out. He always felt he was full of ideas, bigger ones than anybody else would ever dare to use. He once said to me, 'You think *King Kong* was big? That was nothing. I've got an idea that's bigger by far.' He was a jubilant personality."

In August of 1932, Cooper and his partner began production on *King Kong*, a picture godfathered into existence by RKO's production executive David Selznick. By the time the picture was ready for release in March 1933, it had gone $300,000 over budget. No matter. The picture opened at both Radio City Music Hall and the Roxy and was a huge success, earning a profit of almost $700,000, a very large figure for a movie in the pit of the Depression.

When Selznick left RKO in 1933, his successor as production head of RKO was . . . Merian C. Cooper. Since Cooper felt he had typed himself as a director of outdoor adventures, he immediately set up a widely diversified program of pictures that bespoke a nimble movie mind of rare refinement: *Little Women* (a project begun by Selznick), *Flying Down to Rio*, and *Morning Glory*.

"RKO was like a family, and had a great atmosphere," remembered Jack Hively, an editor and director at the studio. "You wanted to go to work, because it was fun. It was the difference between a big, fairly impersonal operation like Paramount, and a mom-and-pop store. We didn't make great money. I can remember making $100 a week as a first editor, and MGM would have been paying at least $150–$200 for the same job."

Shortly before he ascended to the top job at RKO, Cooper had gone to dinner at the home of Winnie Sheehan. The after-dinner entertainment was what Cooper would remember as "a little cheap picture called *Air Mail*." As the picture ended, Sheehan turned to Cooper and said, "Isn't it a shame this bunch of tripe was directed by Jack Ford?" Sheehan told Cooper that he considered Ford to be "down and out because he has no conception of sound."

Cooper said nothing, but when he was named production head of RKO he immediately instructed his assistant to contact Ford and have him at his office the next morning. "Jack Ford arrived with a chip on his shoulder," remembered Cooper of his future partner, who was nothing if not consistent. Cooper put Ford at ease by flattering him and proposing that they mutually select two stories that Ford could make at RKO. According to Cooper, "within an hour [we] chose . . . *The Lost Patrol* and *The Informer.*"

Just like that, at a difficult crossroads in his career, Ford formed a partnership with one of the most important people in his life. Cooper's *joie de vivre* would nicely balance Ford's more bruised outlook, his enthusiasm countering Ford's low-key professionalism.

In one area, they were in explicit agreement, for Cooper's view of America and its history replicated Ford's: "He believes," wrote Gilbert Seldes of Cooper, "that by concentrating on the life of a few individuals, a single family perhaps, the character and tradition, the habits of life and the sufferings, the accidents and the adventures of a race can be embodied." It was a belief that would provide the foundation for Ford's cavalry trilogy, among other pictures.

The agreement with Ford mandated a very low fee—$15,000 apiece for *The Lost Patrol* and *The Informer*—but Cooper proposed paying Ford 12½ percent of the gross, after the picture had earned double its negative cost. Jack leaped at the deal.

But first he had to go back and make his return to Fox. "The return of John Ford to the Fox company is the occasion for something very special," heralded Louella Parsons, always a booster of Jack's. The name of the film was *Pilgrimage*.

A young man named Robert Parrish was a Ford regular whenever scenes involving children or adolescents were required. One day Parrish went up to Ford and asked him why he always used the Parrish and Watson kids in his films.

"None of your goddamn business," snapped Ford as he walked away.

But Ford took a liking to the eager young man, and continued to use him whenever possible. A year or so after Parrish had violated protocol by asking a direct question, Ford walked up to him. "You asked me a question once—why I always have the Parrish and Watson kids. It's because the Watsons have nine kids, the Parrishes have four, and I can fill a schoolhouse and have only two goddamn movie mothers around."

Ford then asked the boy what he wanted.

"I want to go to lunch," replied Parrish.

"I didn't mean that crap, I mean what do you want to do with your life."

"I wanna be a director like you, sir."

Traditionally, whenever Ford wanted to embarrass someone, or just stall for time, he would fill and light his pipe, a complicated operation that took two or three minutes. Parrish stood there, wondering what momentous burst of wisdom Ford would impart while he was preparing his pipe.

Operation finally complete, he put the pipe in his mouth and said, "Start in the cutting room and work up."

*P*ilgrimage came and went quickly, just another picture to fill a theater for a week, then be retired to the vaults. But seen today, it's an audacious effort with a theme worthy of Henry James.

Hannah Jessop is a mean, Bible-thumping widow in rural Arkansas in 1918. Desperately trying to keep her only son from a woman she doesn't like—we are given to understand that Hannah wouldn't approve of anything in skirts—she gets her boy drafted, in spite of the fact that his girlfriend is pregnant. He is killed in the war, and she spends the next ten years spurning her grandson's overtures.

Nineteen twenty-eight: the embittered woman goes with a group of Gold Star mothers to visit the French cemeteries where their sons are buried. Her experiences during her pilgrimage to her son's grave manage to transform a purebred provincial bitch into something approaching a human being.

Ford manages to avoid the obvious pitfalls of the story, and there are atmospherics that recall the Murnau-influenced *Hangman's House*. The entire opening sequence, in which the relationships of the mother, her son, and his girl is sketched in, is very light on dialogue; the son's simultaneous resentment of and subservience to his mother are communicated by looks, and Ford makes the boy's raw hunger for the girl clear by having him advance directly toward the camera and say, "Tonight? Tonight? After Ma's gone to sleep?" Ford cuts to the girl nodding yes, and we dissolve to leaves trembling outside a window, with the mother reading her Bible inside. When the boy dies in a collapsing trench, Ford makes a direct cut to a storm assaulting his mother's home; she wakes up, screaming his name.

The film was almost completely made in the studio; as only the best directors could do, Ford makes a virtue out of what in lesser hands would be claustrophobic. It is material worthy of Griffith in his best days, made by a visually oriented director who steers the cast into uninsistent, naturalistic acting that lifts the movie above melodrama. Hannah is a fierce old woman, knitting baby clothes for her grandchild but arranging for the clothes to be given to the child by others. She could be the elderly daughter of Ethan Edwards—determined, bitter, unforgiving.

It is the experience of other people and other lands that begins to redeem this Scrooge—being surrounded by people who aren't afraid of her, people possessed by the same grief. She triumphs in a shooting gallery, sobers up a young drunk about to commit suicide, asks forgiveness at her son's grave.

Back home in Arkansas, she gives her grandson her dog and allows him to call her Grandma. Hannah changes, grows—from intolerance to a quieter wisdom, the beginnings of a live-and-let-live beneficence.

In the performance of the unheralded Henrietta Crosman, Ford reveals a skill with actresses that he preferred to keep submerged; William K. Everson called Crosman's "the finest character actress performance in any Ford film, not even excepting Jane Darwell in *The Grapes of Wrath*," and he's not far off the mark. The only serious fault in the film is a slight loss of narrative line, a de-evolution into the episodic that Frank Borzage, who was unmatched in this kind of material, might have been able to avoid.

Lurking in the cast in a small part was Hedda Hopper, still a few years away from starting up the gossip column that would make her famous. Ford and Hopper would always be friendly; once, when he made her mad, she called him an "Irish son of a bitch." He promptly reproved her for being redundant.

On March 3, 1933, the Depression reached its nadir, as investors made panicked runs on banks across the country. Paramount was in receivership, RKO was staggering. On March 5, the newly inaugurated President Franklin Roosevelt declared a four-day bank holiday, instituting a cooling-off period for an economic system teetering on complete meltdown.

In Hollywood, the Association of Motion Picture Producers, housed at the Roosevelt Hotel, proposed that the Academy of Motion Picture Arts and Sciences, the only institution in town whose membership included writers, directors, actors, and producers, approve an industry-wide pay cut: 50 percent for anybody earning more than $50 a week, 25 percent for those earning less. These were draconian cuts, and it was made even more outrageous when the moguls falsely led people to believe that the cuts would apply to the top brass as well as the rank and file.

"We finally realized how the producers were using the Academy and us," remembered King Vidor. After a sudden work stoppage in protest by IATSE, which represented most Hollywood laborers and the projectionists, production resumed in mid-March. A month later, full salaries were restored at most studios, but only Sam Goldwyn retroactively paid his employees the wages that had been held back. Darryl Zanuck, the young production head at Warner Bros., had promised he would do likewise, and resigned in protest when he was overruled by Harry and Jack Warner.

The unilateral pay cut was instrumental in alerting workers of all economic levels that they could not trust the men who held the purse strings of their industry. Even highly paid directors realized that they were not exempt from unacceptable financial behavior on the part of their employers; they needed to have an organization to speak for them and them alone.

On December 23, 1935, twelve men met at King Vidor's house to form the Screen Directors Guild: Frank Borzage, Lloyd Corrigan, William K. Howard, Gregory La Cava, Rowland V. Lee, Lewis Milestone, Eddie Sutherland, Frank Tuttle, Richard Wallace, William Wellman, and John Ford.

The Lost Patrol, the first of Jack's two pictures for Merian Cooper, proved both a commercial and critical success (over $80,000 profit, with more in subsequent reissues) and confirmed for Cooper his judgment of his director, in spite of an unusually confused scripting and shooting process.

When Ford checked onto the RKO lot, he found that the script Cooper had was inadequate, so he called Dudley Nichols and the two men turned out an entirely new adaptation in eight long days and nights. Then, the day before the company was to leave for location outside of Yuma, Arizona, Richard Dix was replaced by Victor McLaglen. Cooper gave Ford a modest budget of $227,703 and a twenty-one-day schedule—very tight for a picture being made entirely on location. The company began shooting on August 31, 1933, not exactly a temperate time in Arizona. The sun was shattering (110 degrees), and the sound equipment generator broke down. For the first day of production, Ford was able to finish only one scene.

On the second day, nothing broke down, but shooting was interrupted by a windstorm. On the third day, work stopped at 9:45 A.M. for another windstorm. To make up for all this lost time, Ford shot some scenes inside a plaster mosque that had been erected, and he worked on Labor Day as well as Sundays. At the end of the first week, the production finally hit its stride. "SHOT OVER SEVEN MINUTES YESTERDAY," production manager Wallace Fox telegraphed Hollywood. "STARTED SIX FORTY FIVE TODAY . . . PROGRESSING NICELY."

The nasty location caused actors and crew alike to collapse, and it greatly eroded tempers; one day Wallace Ford slugged a cook who refused to serve a black laborer. Ford kept moving, shooting eighteen to twenty-two setups every day, cutting scenes out of the script wherever possible. The film wrapped after twenty-three days, just two days over schedule. Cooper instructed Max Steiner to compose a complete score running through every scene. "He wanted me to *paint* in those Arabs with music," recalled the composer.

The setting is Mesopotamia during World War I; a British patrol is set upon by a band of unseen Arabs who pick them off one by one. The first to die is the commander, and the sergeant who is forced to take over has no idea where they are or what their orders were.

"Where are we going to bury him?" asks one man.

"Doesn't make much difference, does it?" is the response.

The men die even when they do the right thing; J. M. Kerrigan's Quincannon loses his temper and charges out into the desert, only to be quickly cut down. Ford liked the moment and repeated it twenty-two years later, with Harry Carey Jr. in *The Searchers*.

The picture is tight, dramatic, and believable. Ford errs only in allowing Boris Karloff, playing a religious fanatic, to plunge deeply into hysteria from his very first scene, which gives him no room to build. There are those who consider Karloff's to be a bravely expressionist performance, but that's just another way of saying it's utterly unnatural. Since everybody else is working in a realistic vein—especially Victor McLaglen, giving a restrained, sympathetic performance as the only man to survive by dint of his brains as well as brawn—it seems a miscalculation.

There is too much Karloff, and there is a little too much Max Steiner, although the composer does pull off a notable *coup de theater* when he introduces a wordless, moaning chorus that eerily underscores the patrol's isolation as the night closes in. Aside from that, *The Lost Patrol* stands firm today, lean, concise, achieving its melodramatic effects with ease and economy.

In September 1933, while Ford was shooting *The Lost Patrol*, Merian Cooper had a heart attack. He didn't return to work until January, but by February he was feeling poorly again. The situation was more complicated than the press releases were letting on. Coping with an insolvent company and having to supervise a slate of between forty and fifty pictures a year was more stress than Cooper was equipped to handle. At least one Cooper intimate believed that the heart attack was a cover story, that the producer had actually had a nervous breakdown and undergone shock treatments.

When he finally came back to the studio in May, Cooper told the board that he was electing to leave his job, which he'd had for only sixteen months, about half of which had been spent on leave. RKO agreed to let him out of his contract and to finance two Cooper adventure films, *She* and *The Last Days of Pompeii*, both of which failed. Cooper's place at the studio was taken by Pandro Berman, who had ably filled in for him during his various leaves. All this affected Ford peripherally; he had a contract, and RKO was happy to have him, but Merian Cooper wasn't around to run interference for him. Nevertheless, the two men had forged a bond and planned to do more pictures together.

It was probably inevitable that Ford would work with Will Rogers. Both men had developed a specialty in bucolic truth telling, and it was quickly evident that they brought out the best in each other. Most of Rogers's films were little more than reassuring showcases of the beloved performer's winning, (but one-note), aw-shucks personality. Ford deepened that, filled in some of the lazier cracks in Rogers's character with intimations of loss and genuine moments of regret. Ford's sense of community gave Rogers's character a reason for his gentle disillusion, his rueful cheer.

The first of their collaborations, *Doctor Bull*, was released in September 1933. Although the story takes place in Connecticut, it is populated by faces that would not have been out of place in Brueghel. *Judge Priest* (October 1934) was a gentle, nostalgic evocation of Kentucky circa 1890, with Rogers playing a widowed jurist with a taste for loose construction and a sympathetic understanding of human frailty. *Steamboat Round the Bend*, shot in May and June 1935, the last picture Rogers made before his death, featured him as a con artist turned riverboat captain.

In all these pictures, the community surrounding Rogers is seen as short-tempered and potentially malevolent; the tempering presence of Rogers is all that saves the towns from disaster. Cumulatively, these three pictures rank with Ford's finest achievements.

Doctor Bull begins by cross-cutting leisurely between the train station, the church, Dr. Bull's home, and the post office. Ford effortlessly creates the sense of an entire social system, a sense of life as it's lived in the town of New Winton; there's an unforced, organic splendor to the shots, similar to *How Green Was My Valley*—beautiful compositions that don't bellow their artistry.

Dr. Bull maneuvers between the senile, the hypochondriacal, the small-minded, and, when necessary, the genuinely ill. (Ford obviously had a high opinion of doctors, for they are invariably portrayed as admirable people, agents of order—*Arrowsmith*, *The Hurricane*, *Stagecoach*, *The Horse*

Soldiers, 7 Women, etc. The only exception is *My Darling Clementine*'s Doc Holliday—half healer, half killer, a man destroyed by his dual nature.)

There is an earthy punch to the dialogue. When Bull comes across a group of people clustered together in a cemetery, he snaps, "Why you all gathered here? Somebody get out?" After tending to a dying woman, he observes that "I've seen a hundred people die. None of them seemed to mind it. They was all too sick to mind it." When he gets an offer of wine after delivering a baby to an exuberant Italian father, he says, just before he tosses it back, "I love to bring Italian babies into the world. Lotta places you go, all you get is a cup of coffee."

This astringency helps the story avoid some of its stickier aspects, and Rogers gives a quietly committed performance. People think Bull and the widow Cardmaker (Vera Allen, who resembles Mary Ford) are lovers, but the time they are together is spent with him stretched out on the couch while she reads to him from *Alice's Adventures in Wonderland*.

When typhoid hits the town, Bull inoculates the children despite the fears of their parents. At the end, sick of the hypocrisies of New Winton, Bull and Mrs. Cardmaker depart the town for a better life.

Ford paces *Judge Priest* (October 1934) in the same laconic, unhurried manner he would direct *My Darling Clementine* a decade later, taking his rhythm from the focused relaxation of his star. In terms of conventional plotting, practically nothing happens, but Ford assembles such a series of charming tableaus that he creates a beautiful evocation of another time and place in a country long gone.

The titles are accompanied by "My Old Kentucky Home." It's 1890, and Judge William Pitman Priest is reading the newspaper on the bench while Stepin Fetchit's Jeff Poindexter slumbers in the witness stand, magnificently unconcerned about the accusation that he stole some chickens. This is partially because Jeff is naturally oblivious, partially because he knows that Billy Priest won't send him up. Jeff's perilous crime somehow gets sidetracked when the discussion turns to the best bait for catfish. Jeff insists that the magic elixir is calves liver. Dissolve to Priest and Poindexter walking down a dusty back road on the way to the river, overgrown versions of Huck and Jim.

As might be gauged from the opening scene, Priest is unconventional, willing to take people as they are. This is not always thought to be such a good idea. "The name of Priest means something in Kentucky!" says his frosty sister-in-law. "I never heard it meant intolerance," he replies. Ford is setting up one of his classic confrontations between propriety and the natural man without whom the perilously maintained order of things collapses.

A state senator is running against Priest, but Berton Churchill, who always specialized in playing oratorical windbags, isn't much of a threat. Mostly, *Judge Priest* is a film of remembrance and longing.

Priest leans back on his porch and puts his feet up (just like Henry Fonda in *My Darling Clementine*), plays godfather to young lovers, does call-and-response with Hattie McDaniel, and lights a candle by his dead wife's portrait, his own sorrowing image reflected in the glass. He goes to the cemetery to fill her in, the first appearance of what would be among Ford's most heartfelt, moving moments. For Ford, death ended a life, not a relationship.

"Been an awful late spring," he tells his wife. "Them honeysuckles sure do smell sweet." Priest is a man without a family—besides his wife, his two children are also dead—but he remains centered by his affection for and duty toward his town, and Ford creates a sense of an upstairs and downstairs, black and white together—taffy-pulls and barber shops with rows of mugs for the customers, a rural idyll that ends with a celebratory parade signifying the vanquishing of all threat. Ford's sense of the gentle rhythm of life was never more acute; nearly twenty years later, when he remade *Judge Priest* as *The Sun Shines Bright*, a much darker picture would emerge.

Judge Priest is a kind of homage to Griffith, the Griffith of *A Romance of Happy Valley* and *True Heart Susie*. It could even be considered a sort of gentle, unofficial sequel to *The Birth of a Nation*, as Ford casts Henry B. Walthall, Griffith's very own Little Colonel, in a stirring performance as an old Confederate soldier, now the town's pastor, recalling the war. Walthall lends resonance to the scene, uniting Ford with Griffith, and Billy Priest with the Little Colonel in one of Lincoln's beloved mystic chords of memory.

As for Stepin Fetchit, there's no question he's a stereotype. So are the white people. Ford often used stereotypes as convenient hooks, then went deep into character and made the stereotypes come alive, confirming Stepin Fetchit's own estimation of the film: "When people saw me and Will Rogers like brothers, that said something to them." As critic Martin Rubin noted, "*Judge Priest* suggests that, by lying around long enough in the dappled Southern sunlight, white and black will overlap . . . without the boundaries of miscegenation ever being crossed."

Steamboat Round the Bend (released in September 1935) is probably the least of the three pictures. The scene is the early 1890s, and Rogers is again playing an old Confederate soldier, now selling patent medicines from his riverboat the *Claremore Queen* (Claremore was Rogers's hometown in Oklahoma, and he worked it into as many pictures as he possibly could). The *Claremore Queen*, like its owner, is genially unkempt and disreputable, which ties in nicely with the plot, involving Rogers's nephew killing a man over a "swamp girl" that the nephew happens to love.

The film is largely about class distinctions, which Americans like to believe they're above. Ford knew better. Here, the tension is between river people and swamp people, with Rogers navigating between them. As always with Ford, the defining unit is not the individual but the family, and Rogers develops one out of an old alcoholic (played by brother Frank), Stepin Fetchit, and the swamp girl, all struggling to raise $500 for a lawyer to help his nephew.

Frank was settling in to playing a long series of drunks for his brother. At one point, he takes the pledge of abstinence, raising his hand for the oath, his sincerity slightly undercut by the bottle he's holding. The climactic steamboat race is stirring and well done, with no recourse to miniatures, as Rogers and his group resort to breaking up the boat itself for fuel: the furniture, the lifeboats, finally the decking all go into the furnace, and there's a very Griffithian race to the gallows to stop the nephew's scheduled execution. (The script for the film specifies that the ship explode at the end, but Ford must have felt that was a little too much Sturm und Drang for such amiable characters.)

Will Rogers didn't memorize dialogue so much as he paraphrased it, which made it hard on the other actors, who never got their correct cues. This delighted Ford, and he just let the camera roll on scenes that were little more than improvisations, especially between Rogers and Stepin Fetchit. "Paht of the time he suhprises me," Fetchit (real name Lincoln Perry) told a reporter at the time. "Paht of the time I suhprises him. But mos' of the time we suhprises each other."

"Nobody could write for Will," remembered Ford in 1972. "He'd read his script and say, 'What does that mean?' And I'd say, 'Well that's rather a tough question. I don't know what it means exactly.' Then we would finally figure out what it meant and I'd say to him 'Say it in your own words.' And he'd go away muttering to himself, getting his lines ready, and when he came back he'd make his speech in typical Rogers fashion, which was better than any writer could write for him. Because no writer could write for Will."

For Ford, Rogers was akin to Harry Carey, an unassuming, unpretentious man who never had to raise his voice to make other people listen. Ford knew that Rogers was beyond direction as such, and tended to defer to the actor.

"He was just a small-town Oklahoma boy," Ford would remember. "That's all he talked about—well, among other things, he talked all the time, but he always brought up the topic of Claremore and Ponca City."

Rogers liked Ford because, as he wrote in his syndicated column of July 1, 1934, "he remembers. Jack used to direct westerns, and made some great ones with Harry Carey, the most human and natural of the western actors. Well, the other day on a big set, a jury and court room trial, Jack had all his old cowpuncher pals, I had known most of 'em for many years, too, and it sure was good to see 'em again."

Rogers may have been a small-town boy, but he had the ear of Franklin Roosevelt (*"Judge Priest . . .* is a thoroughly good job and the Civil War pictures are very true to life." wrote Roosevelt to Rogers in a personal letter of October 8, 1934). More importantly, at least in terms of Hollywood, Rogers had the ear of Fox executives. The studio wanted to release *Doctor Bull* under the title of *Life's Worth Living*, a puerile title that Rogers hated. He fired off a telegram that said, in part, "PUT THE NAME DR. BULL ON OUR NEXT PICTURE. SOME HALFWIT SUGGESTED LIFE'S WORTH LIVING. NOW WE FIND THAT THEY HAVE TRIED TO HANG THAT TITLE ON EVERY FOX PICTURE SINCE OVER THE HILL. SO THEY FINALLY SAID GIVE IT TO ROGERS . . . LIFE'S WORTH LIVING SOUNDS LIKE A GRADUATION ESSAY. AS A MATTER OF FACT, IF YOU DON'T MAKE SOME BETTER PICTURES, LIFE WON'T BE WORTH LIVING." Rogers got his way.

With few exceptions, the three films with Will Rogers helped modify the arty, expressionist side of Ford. The strenuous histrionics of Boris Karloff going mad would be subsumed in an explicit homage to Griffith. It is in these films that Ford achieves the self-realization that defined him for future generations, and enabled Orson Welles to label him as essentially "a poet, a comedian."

From now on, Jack would be able to pick and choose between the two alternate strains of his gift, the one deriving from Griffith, the other from Murnau, first playing off one aesthetic, then the other, ultimately combining them into a classical synthesis that was pure Ford.

Rogers's death in a plane crash on August 15, 1935, shortly before the release of *Steamboat Round the Bend*, was as crushing to Ford as any death outside of his immediate family. Shortly before Rogers took off, Ford had asked him to cruise to Hawaii with him instead. "You keep your duck and go on the water," said Rogers, "I'll take my eagle and fly."

"We had a terrible time with Jack," Mary Ford remembered. "He went all to pieces. He was superstitious, and those last words of Will's kept going through his ears—'You keep your duck and go on the water.'" Rogers's death cut short what would almost certainly have been a long, happy series of reflective rural comedy-dramas, introspective alternatives to the outdoor Westerns Ford would shortly begin making with John Wayne.

Years later, Ford would be asked what the men of the West were really like. "They were like Will Rogers," he said simply.

On September 27, 1934, Ford trooped in to see his doctor, complaining that he was listless, nervous, and tired. The latter was easy to explain: Ford had directed thirteen pictures in four years. Although in basically good physical condition, the examination revealed that Ford's teeth needed some work, he was a little heavy in the abdomen, and his liver was "tremendously enlarged, crowding intestines downwardly and the stomach forward." The doctor's prescription was to abstain from alcohol, especially beer, which accounted for the enlarged liver and abdomen. There is no reason to think that Ford paid any more attention to orders from his doctor than he did to orders from anybody else.

As if he wasn't already feeling poorly enough, Ford made *The World Moves On*, a mushy multigenerational saga that moves from 1825 to 1929 and attempts to replicate the undeserved success of Fox's earlier hits *Cavalcade* and the marginally better *Berkeley Square*. Ford labors beneath the impossible burden of Franchot Tone and Madeleine Carroll gazing soulfully at each other over teacups.

"I'd like to forget that," he would say in old age, echoing the sentiments of audiences then and now. "I fought like hell against doing it . . . but I was under contract and finally I had to do it, and I did the best I could, but I hated the damn thing. It was really a lousy picture—it didn't have anything to say—and there was no chance for any comedy."

Although there may not have been any openings in the script for comedy, Ford was determined to shoehorn some in regardless, which explains the unlikely appearance of Stepin Fetchit in the French army, which sends the entire sober surroundings sky high. The world moves on, but not nearly fast enough.

The Rogers films, and their enormous box office success, helped solidify Ford's position at Fox, as did the arrival of Darryl Zanuck in May 1935. Fox, which had a good distribution system as well as a top-rank theater circuit, had merged with Twentieth Century, which had neither, but did have Zanuck, the best and brightest of the young Hollywood studio heads.

By all rights, Fox should have absorbed Twentieth Century, the company Zanuck founded with Joe Schenck after he left Warner Bros., but Fox was on a financial respirator; although it had assets of $36 million, its earnings for 1935 had been only $1.8 million. Twentieth Century, on the other hand, although it had assets of only $4 million, had earned $1.7 million the same year. A few months after Zanuck arrived, Winfield

Sheehan was sent packing with a check for $360,000, and Zanuck got down to the business of making movies.

Leaden sagas like *The World Moves On* would be rare at 20th Century-Fox, for Zanuck's background as a writer meant that he put a premium on snappy narratives, if possible having something to do with an objective reality with which audiences were familiar.

Zanuck would never be able to compete with MGM and Paramount, and he knew it. He had only one mantra. "Zanuck's whole drive was to do with story," recalled Roddy McDowall. "He very early realized that he didn't have star power. All he had was Will Rogers, Shirley Temple, and Janet Gaynor. And Will Rogers got killed and Zanuck and Gaynor didn't like each other. [Gaynor left Fox as quickly as she could.] But Zanuck knew how to make a film. He was wily, egotistical, and an autocrat. He knew how to run his shop and he ran it very well.

"What Zanuck did, for better or worse, was trust, delegate. 'You do this.' 'You do that.' And he would oversee everything. Sometimes he did damage, and sometimes he was able to exhibit immense insight."

Zanuck once told Philip Dunne that as long as he had a good script he didn't much care who directed it. As far as the remark went, it's probably more or less true. But Zanuck was one of the two or three smartest picture men in the business, and when it came to a great script, he would never settle for anything less than a great director—a Ford, a Kazan.

Alone among studio bosses, Zanuck was loved by writers. "He was wonderful to work with," remembered Winston Miller. "He didn't say, 'I'm the boss, do what I say.' You knew that if there was an argument he was going to win it. But every writer loved to work with Zanuck because he respected writers and you could talk to him as writer to writer. He ignored producers generally in conference, he talked to the writer, which was unusual at the studios. You could argue and he never threw his weight around. . . . You'd go in and he would know your script cold. He would know every minor character, you didn't have to refresh him on anything."

Zanuck had enormous respect for Ford's ability to turn in a commercial picture with a minimum of fuss—with rentals of $1.5 million, *Steamboat Round the Bend* had been the studio's biggest hit of 1935, and *Judge Priest* had done nearly as well—$1.2 million. Zanuck would come to believe that the main thing a producer had to do with Ford was to keep him focused on the material and restrain him from indulging himself, when, Zanuck said, "somebody always sings and you cut to an extreme long shot with slanting shadows."

Zanuck was perfectly comfortable allowing Ford to divide his time with another studio, if that's what it took to keep from losing him entirely. Ford would split his time between Fox and RKO for the next fifteen years, until Howard Hughes began dismantling the latter studio.

Splitting his time led Ford to develop two very specific artistic personalities; Fox was for homespun entertainment (the Will Rogers films, *Wee Willie Winkie*), while RKO was for artistic experimentation (*The Informer*, *The Lost Patrol*, *The Plough and the Stars*). Without the long leash granted him by Zanuck, it is possible that Ford wouldn't have developed a sufficient fluency with his high-art style to enable him, in pictures like *Stagecoach* and *The Grapes of Wrath*, to synthesize both sides of his personality into one whole.

In June 1934, Jack bought a 110-foot ketch called the *Faith*. Built in 1926, the *Faith* had been owned by a Pasadena financier who had been hit hard by the Depression. The ship hadn't been used much, and was in need of maintenance, but the $30,000 that Jack paid still represented a considerable bargain. He promptly rechristened the ship the *Araner*.

She was a thing of beauty, and she quickly became Ford's most valued possession. Her hull was painted white, and her superstructure was all varnished teak, with a central salon anchored by a large poker table. The *Araner* carried a crew of six to take care of the inline diesels that powered the ship. Jack refitted her at considerable expense, overhauling the engines, putting in a new mast, rebuilding the bow and stern, adding a deckhouse, and having the bottom recoppered.

The *Araner* had two fireplaces, two bathrooms, red carpets, a four-poster bed, a dressing room for Mary. Other directors spent their money on gambling or women, but the *Araner* would be Ford's designated luxury. It was a vacation hideaway, an alternate home, a refuge, a cabin in the woods. Here, Ford would while away a good part of the next thirty years of his life, arranging his schedule so that he could spend several weeks or a month at a time on board the yacht, usually docked either at Catalina or Honolulu.

The *Araner* was deeply symptomatic of a particularly Irish-American trait—a proclamation of pride in one's origins, as well as an announcement of a new prosperity. Ford named his luxurious yacht after his mother's homeland—with the possible exception of parts of Albania, the most primitive land in Europe. There was never a boat like the *Araner* in the Aran Islands.

At the same time, Ford enlisted in the Naval Reserve. Chaplain John Brady wrote a recommendation for him stating, "As the director and producer of many famous motion pictures taken on board U.S. Naval vessels and using U.S. Naval material, he had to apply himself and to study as thoroughly as if he were an officer in the Navy preparing for his examinations. . . . He is very much a man's man who makes and keeps loyal friends . . . [and is] keenly alert in evaluating the ability of the thousands of men who have come under his supervision. . . . As the master of a sea-going yacht his experience, training and natural traits and qualifications eminently fit him to be worthy of a position as a Naval officer." There was also a testimonial from Sol Wurtzel, declaring that Ford was "a fine and honorable artist, executive and American gentleman."

Ford got a commission as a lieutenant commander, and couldn't stop himself from some slight puffing of his résumé, wherein he claimed attendance at something called Western Seminary, as well as "a few years spent before the mast." He was consistent in his inconsistency; a few years later, on his annual naval fitness report, he claimed only to be a graduate of Portland High School, and truthfully admitted to a familiarity with French, German, and Spanish, but proficiency in none. A few years after that, he would be up to his old tricks, claiming six months at the University of Maine.

He dove into the life of a gentleman sailor with alacrity, buying every uniform the Navy offered, having them perfectly tailored, and assiduously currying favor with his superior officer. To the Officer's Mess of the Armory in Los Angeles, he bestowed an oil painting of the USS *Constitution;* to his commanding officer, Captain Claude Mayo, he bestowed theater tickets and studio passes, even taking him to Catalina on board the *Araner.* The meaning behind all this was clear: if the movies lacked social status, then the pomp and circumstance of the Navy represented a deeper validation.

Besides, you could have fun on a boat, such as a trip Ford would make with John Wayne, Ward Bond, and a newcomer to the ménage, a young actor named Henry Fonda, on a cruise to Mazatlán. A Christmas tree was set up in the salon, but the main purpose of the trip seems to have been to drink, as is attested by a hilarious gag captain's log in Ford's own hand.

"1:18 p.m. Went ashore—got the owner, Fonda, Wayne, and Bond out of jail. Put up a bond for their behavior.

"9:30 p.m. Got the owner, Fonda, Wayne, and Bond out of jail again. Invited by Mexican officials to leave town."

The next day, invariably designated for hangover recovery by lesser men, was no different:

"Owner went to Mass—brought priest to *Araner*—purpose to sign pledge (to give up drinking); pledge signed—celebrated signing of pledge with champagne, later augmented with brandy.

"Arrived Muertos—great time, 14 hours-35 minutes. This would never have been possible without the advice and help from Mr. Bond, a great navigator who is sneaking drinks. Gave lessons on fishing to Mr. Fonda.

"Mr. Bond started telling Mr. Ford, owner, how to fish from the *Araner*.

"Mr. Ford coins new expression. Told Mr. Bond to go fuck himself.

"Mr. Bond gets fish line tangled in propellor. We drift for 3 hours."

Ford felt entitled to these celebrations. He had just completed what his contemporaries would regard as his most important picture since *The Iron Horse*.

CHAPTER NINE

In April of 1934, Liam O'Flaherty arrived in New York for a cross-country lecture tour that he hoped would put some money in his perennially empty pockets. By July, he was in Hollywood, where he wrote a couple of short stories and got two weeks' work at Paramount. That fall, he sold the film rights to his short novel, *The Informer*, to RKO, for the bargain basement price of just over $2,500.

Ford took Dudley Nichols with him on a cruise to Mexico and back, planning to write the screenplay en route. Nichols was leery of the idea, and properly so; writing is a function of a set routine and environment, and he found it impossible to work while traveling. As a result, he wrote to a friend, "I had to lock myself in a stateroom for eighteen hours a day, for there were other gay, carefree passengers on board!"

Ford approached preproduction carefully. Although there were rumors around town that RKO would cast the reliable but dull leading man Richard Dix in the title role of Gypo Nolan, Ford had other ideas; the part was tailor-made for Victor McLaglen, and he meant to see that McLaglen got it.

Ford had appreciated what Max Steiner's music had done for *The Lost Patrol*, and made sure that he would be available for *The Informer*, going so far as to send Dudley Nichols over to talk to him about the music for the film—the only time, according to Steiner, he ever conferred with a writer.*

As a producer for what was a dangerously uncommercial project, Ford managed to hire Cliff Reid, who, as Joel Sayre remembered, "had more

---

*Steiner was perennially overworked—the same year he did *The Informer*, he did five other films and served as music director for another three, a light load compared to 1934, when he wrote music for a staggering thirty-six films and was the music director for two more.

chutzpah than any other *goy* in Hollywood." Much of the studio's middle management regarded *The Informer* as dramatically pointless and commercial suicide. What was it all about? they would complain, and Reid, a committed Ford loyalist, would take up the cudgel.

"What was *Arrowsmith* about?" Reid would snarl. "Ford was what they were . . . about: F-O-R-D. Never mind the story: just keep concentrating on we got the best damn director in Hollywood working for us. F-O-R-D. Ford."

The Informer was shot quickly, because there wasn't enough money to shoot it any other way. The usually reliable Robert Parrish later spread the story that Ford got McLaglen drunk to capture the befuddlement of his interrogation scene, a story that McLaglen's son Andrew strenuously denies.

"That's so wrong. My father was the furthest thing from the blowhard that story makes him out to be. He was a quiet, soft-spoken man, not an alcoholic. He didn't drink when he was working. I distinctly remember this: I was fifteen, and we were walking across the lawn of our estate. My dad stopped and looked at me and said, 'Laddie, I guarantee you that if I get *The Informer* I will get the Academy Award.' When he got that part, he was the happiest man going."

Late in his life, Ford came clean about the story he had helped to spread. "There is an axiom in the picture business that nobody under the influence of alcohol can play a drunk. And I believe that. . . . You can't play a drunk while you're under the influence. Victor had to run too many gamuts of emotion, bravado, nervousness, fear, sometimes all in one scene, and go back to bravado again and resume the whole thing. He had too much to do to take a drink."

Although Ford usually got on well with stuntmen and other members of the crew, on *The Informer* he encountered someone immune to his rough charm. "Mr. Ford and I didn't like each other," said the stuntman Gil Perkins. "I didn't like the way he picked out a patsy on a picture and gave him a hard time. I thought he was a despot and a professional Catholic. I was a stuntman and got fired every night, so he didn't scare me."

Perkins was playing one of the Black and Tan officers chasing Wallace Ford's Frankie McPhillip through the streets of Dublin. Perkins was to kill McPhillip with a Lewis gun, and had been hired by Eddie O'Fearna on the mistaken assumption that he was an expert with the weapon, which had a tendency to jam. On the first take, Wallace Ford started to climb out the window, Perkins began to fire, and the gun promptly jammed.

"Aw hell, cut it," said Perkins.

Jack reacted swiftly. "Are you the director?"

"No, I'm not," said Perkins.

"What do you mean by cutting the scene?"

Perkins explained the situation, and Ford grumpily let it pass. An hour later, they were shooting the scene where the soldiers run up the stairs looking for McPhillip. At the top of the landing, McPhillip was to shoot, causing several soldiers to fall down the stairs, away from the camera. Ford was handling the blank gun himself, and fired it directly at Perkins; the wad from the blank hit the stuntman in the face.

Ford cut the shot, and yelled at another stunt man for landing on top of Perkins. Although Perkins didn't believe Ford shot him in the face on purpose ("He was fairly careful with stuntmen"), he was nonetheless outraged and did the unforgivable: he challenged Ford in front of his crew. "For such a big shot, you're an inconsiderate son of a bitch!" Ford fired him on the spot. Athough Perkins was one of the top stuntmen in the business, he didn't work for Ford again for twelve years.

Once again, Ford was using Robert Parrish as background talent—one day Parrish would be a member of the IRA, the next a Black and Tan. During the sequence of Donald Meek's interrogation, Ford outlined a pan down a group of soldiers standing with their guns. After the first take, Ford came up with an additional piece of business. "When you get to this guy," he said to Joe August, pointing to Parrish, "stop the camera for a fraction of a second. Bob, when the camera stops, look over at Donald Meek and look mean."

The next day, an assistant director came over to Parrish and said, "Mr. Ford wants to see you in the projection room at noon." Ford was sitting, smoking his pipe. He waved his arms and the rushes from the day before began unreeling, including the shot where Parrish was featured. It looked okay to Parrish.

At the end of the rushes, Ford stood up and announced, "I have directed thirty-one serials at Universal and twenty-four feature pictures, and that is the worst acting I have seen in any of them." A humbled Parrish crept back to the set, where the same assistant told him that Ford wanted to see him at the end of the day. Ford took Parrish to the editorial department, where the chief editor was a man named Jimmy Wilkerson. "Did you see the rushes, Jimmy?" asked Ford.

"Yeah, Jack, they were great."

"Did you see the shot that this guy right here spoiled?"

"I thought it was all right, Jack."

Ford walked over to Wilkerson's desk and began a lecture. "You and I and the extras in the picture are making a picture to entertain the public. If we get paid for it, that's even better. But the job is to entertain people. I don't know that any of the audience wants to be embarrassed the way this guy embarrasses in the rushes."

"Well, Jack, we can always cut around it."

"No. I got a better idea. We finish Saturday. I want you to start him as an apprentice on Monday."

"It's done, Jack," said Wilkerson.

As Ford started to walk away, an overwhelmed Parrish said, "How can I thank you, Mr. Ford?"

"By never putting your goddamn face in front of a camera as long as you live."

Ford had almost certainly devised the entire scenario as a roundabout means of giving Parrish his opportunity to start in the cutting room, putting life in the old Irish saying, "Do good by stealth, and blush to find it known." Shortly after World War II, Robert Parrish would win an Academy Award for editing *Body and Soul*, then go on to a career as a director.

Ford was in his element, working with little money but a great deal of freedom, and with a cast of his own choosing. True, the actors were something of a mishmash; the only authentic Irishman in the cast was J. M. Kerrigan, playing Terry, the wheedling toady who helps Gypo squander his twenty pounds of blood money. Ford adored Kerrigan, an amusing character who had a large repertoire of Irish ballads and kept his pockets stuffed with strange-but-true clippings from provincial Irish newspapers.

Kerrigan earned Ford's gratitude by solving a problem over a scene that rather obviously took place in a whorehouse. Ford was puzzling over how to stage it without having the whole thing cut by the Hays Office, when Kerrigan piped up. "Put hats on the cats," he said. Since nobody had ever heard of whores wearing hats inside, nobody complained.

Ford's old friend George Hively, widely regarded as the best editor at RKO, was cutting the film, assisted by his son Jack. Late one week, George Hively took off for San Francisco to see an old friend. At the same time, Ford decided he wanted to see the interrogation scene. Told that Hively was gone, Ford asked Jack Hively to put the scene together so he could see it.

"I was excited," remembered Hively. "I hadn't cut a picture yet. I had visions of him saying, 'Gee, this is great!' " That night, after shooting for the day had ended, Hively ran the sequence for Ford. When the lights went up, Ford turned to the young man and barked, "Where's your father? Get him down here. You've gotten this so screwed up I can't even look at it."

When George Hively arrived back at the studio, he looked at the sequence and attempted to calm his devastated son. "There's nothing wrong with it," he told him. "He's just angry because I wasn't here. I'll change one close-up and show it to him." That night, George Hively ran the interrogation scene for his director. As the lights went up, Ford nodded and said, "That's what I wanted." Then, turning to the younger Hively, he said, "Well, son, you might make it, but it's going to take a while." The precise difference between the scene as edited by Hively *père et fils* was a few feet of film that the older man had added to a close-up.

Despite the occasional confrontations that Ford devised in order to spice things up, shooting on *The Informer* went smoothly. "The crew knew what he wanted as much as he did," said Robert Parrish. "They knew he didn't want big camera movement and didn't want standard close-ups. He had a thing about the eyes. 'Look in people's eyes, see what they're telling you,' he said. He would talk about the lighting. There was a shot of a street-singer, and Ford came up to Joe August. 'You got any shadows? Paste one on the back wall, there, will you?' "

When Margot Grahame, playing the prostitute Gypo loves, was forty-five minutes late on her first day, Ford greeted her cordially, then said, "I wish you had been here at eight o'clock. We were scheduled to shoot your scene then, but we had to go on to something else. Now we won't have time for your scene. We'll just eliminate it from the script." And he did.

"Some of the stuff he did that you couldn't understand, it wasn't because he was mean," asserted Robert Parrish. "There was a reason. With the Margot Grahame episode, he simply didn't want to shoot the scene. Pan Berman wanted it shot, Ford didn't, and the shooting schedule was too short to wait for an actor to drift in. He was actually kind to her; he told her her hair was wonderful and the makeup was wonderful, but they weren't going to shoot the scene. She was surrounded by people, and the costume designer burst into tears. Then Ford realized he hadn't said anything about the costume and he said, 'Oh, the costume's nice, too.' *That* was a terrible thing to do."

As Patrick Ford was to say of his father, "The only time he ever gave up in any conflict was when he didn't care anyway."

When *The Informer* was previewed, the response was muted; Dudley Nichols heard the head of RKO muttering, "We should never have made it!" Ford and Nichols came out of the theater with every intention of heading for the nearest bar when they were waylaid by the actor Dudley Digges, who stopped them with outstretched arms and tears in his eyes.

The RKO brass may not have believed in the picture, but the critics fell on it with expressions of rapture. *The Nation* referred to its "superb direction." The National Board of Review magazine noted the picture's "grim splendor."

The Informer became something of a sleeper hit. Produced for $243,000—cheap, but not outrageously cheap; *Alice Adams*, an undoubted A picture, cost only $324,000—Ford's picture grossed $891,000 worldwide, producing a net profit of $290,000. It was a tidy sum, especially when RKO had undoubtedly been assuming that *The Informer* would, at best, accrue the same amount of money as *The Lost Patrol*, which had only cost $19,000 more than *The Informer* and produced the smaller net profit of $84,000. Both pictures would be reissued by RKO; as of 1951, Ford had earned $45,128.56 from his percentage of *The Lost Patrol*, and $54,256.68 from his percentage of *The Informer.*

The Informer went on to win McLaglen the Best Actor Oscar, and after directing pictures for nearly twenty years, Ford won his first Academy Award for Direction. Also winning Oscars were Max Steiner and Dudley Nichols.

Ford's reaction to all this was muted; when the Oscars were awarded, Ford and Nichols weren't there—Nichols out of solidarity with his brother writers, who had bolted from the Academy because it was a company union, Ford because he had a lifelong horror of seeming to want the awards he would always proudly display. Like most romantics, he was more attracted to failure than success, and didn't seem to have any idea of how to behave when winning. Nichols refused his award, but Ford accepted, saying, "If I had planned to refuse it, I would not have allowed my name to go in nomination."

The film reestablished Ford with high-brow critics and audiences. As an example of how modest his worldwide profile had been, the 1938 *History of Motion Pictures* by Bardeche and Brasillach hailed Ford as a clever and dependable "newcomer," on the basis of *The Lost Patrol*, *The Informer*, and a few other pictures. More accurately, they also compared *The Informer* favorably to Sternberg's *The Docks of New York* and Hawks's *Scarface*, "or anything in the whole powerful literature redolent of fog and grime and dreariness which the Germans introduced to the Americans."

The Informer was beloved in its day by critics and intellectuals, probably because, in Andrew Sarris's words, "its style was thought to be fused with a worthy theme. The fact that Gypo Nolan was a lower-class character with an empty belly was virtually sufficient in itself to make him a worthy protagonist of the Depression era."

Correspondingly, its reputation has declined over the years, for one generation's shattering masterpiece is another's threadbare warhorse. The film's heavy dramaturgy and rampant Catholicism give it a rhetorical quality that's out of key with the evolution of Ford's career and make it seem a trifle stifling to modern viewers. Certainly, too many scenes are presented for metaphoric reasons, Max Steiner's score is too indicative, and the wanted poster that keeps attaching itself to people's legs threatens to become like an ardent dog.

Yet, *The Informer* still retains a good deal of the compressed, allegorical power of one long, grim night in Dublin. Many of the film's excesses derive directly from Liam O'Flaherty's novel, and some of its most touching moments, as when Katie tells Gypo, "I'll love you when I'm clay," are not in the book at all.

Victor McLaglen's tour de force performance perfectly captures a wounded animal of a man who knows he has done something terrible, even if he can't quite articulate why. There is the wonderful opening out of a silent picture, hypnotically laying on the atmosphere, Ford obviously in love with the beauty of light in the fog, but not forgetting to give a sense of the story's polarities, all without a word being spoken. The film's set-bound, enclosed feel is a perfect corollary to Gypo's increasing entrapment as the consequences of his acts overtake him.

There are no heroes and, with the possible exception of J. M. Kerrigan's Terry, no villains, but there is a wonderful feeling of the ambiguous, treacherous crosscurrents that have always been part of Ireland's struggles for independence. And there's a very rare sense of physical and psychological texture: the drag of a pen moving across paper, Frankie's fingernails scratching the windowsill as he falls to his death, the way Gypo hits a sign hanging over his head, the essential Irish lack of interest in anything that isn't Irish. And there is McLaglen's Gypo in all his brutish, bruised humanity, so stupid, so uneasy in his own skin, failing at being a rebel, failing at being an informer.

Beyond its surprising financial success, *The Informer* gave Jack a critical reputation he would never entirely lose and bestowed on him a leader's role within the industry. It also gave him a friendship with Liam O'Flaherty, a difficult, self-centered, and impatient man.

O'Flaherty dedicated *Famine*, his next novel, to Ford. He wrote him in June 1935, "I thank you for all your kindness, particularly for *The Informer*, but perhaps most of all for yourself. During the past year I have learned to admire you as the great man you are. If I have gone away three thousand miles to say so, that is the Irish way. We are a strange and complicated people. . . . Sorry I'm not going with you on the *Araner*, but I'll time a few pints of stout at Daly's of Kilronan or Lydon's with you, and you drinking down the highways of the western seas under the awning of your great white sail. May God go with you, Jack, and with everyone belonging to you."

John Martin Feeney, of Portland, Maine, circa 1897.

23 Sheridan Street in Portland.
The Feeney family lived on the top floor.

Three of the Feeney boys on a Portland front step.
From the right, Jack, Frank, and Eddie, with cousin John Connelly.
(Museum of Modern Art Film Stills Archives)

Young Jack Ford (left) acting the part of a henchman in his brother's serial,
The Adventures of Peg O' the Ring. (Robert Birchard Collections)

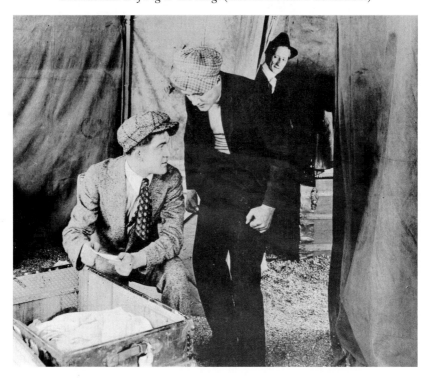

Jack (far right) directing one of his early Westerns with a
typically small crew for the period. (Museum of Modern Art Stills Archives)

Jack (next to camera, hand in mouth) looking worried as he assists Frank
(kneeling) and Grace Cunard during the shooting of the serial *The Broken Coin*.
(Robert Birchard Collection)

Right. The young Mary McBryde Smith in her nurse's
uniform, before she met John Ford in 1920.
(Dan Ford collection)

Left. John Feeney, Ford's father,
holding his grandson Patrick, as
Mary Ford looks on approvingly.
(Dan Ford Collection)

Below. Reveille—mealtime—on location in Nevada for *The Iron Horse.*
To the right, the railroad cars where the cast and crew slept; to the left the
mess hall and first-aid tents. (BFI Films: Stills, Posters and Designs)

Civilization inexorably arriving with the railroad in *The Iron Horse*.
(BFI Films: Stills, Posters and Designs)

Ford and two cameramen making a low-angle shot for *The Iron Horse*.
(BFI Films: Stills, Posters and Designs)

Ford working in the garden at the family home on Peaks Island, Maine, circa 1926. (BFI Films: Stills, Posters and Designs)

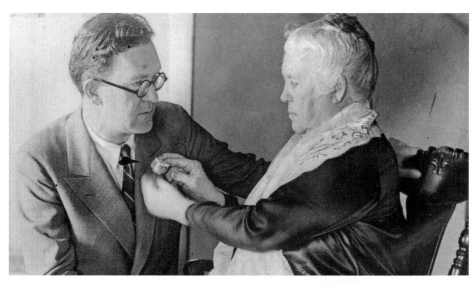

Ford and his mother, Abby Feeney, circa 1928. (Lilly Library)

Jack and Mary Ford, with their children Patrick and Barbara
during the mid-1920s. (Lilly Library)

Ford loved dogs, small or large.
Here with an Irish wolfhound.
(Dan Ford collection)

Jack, Sol Wurtzel (center), and screenwriter John Stone
on location for the *Three Bad Men.*

Jack and his good friend George O'Brien.

Jack and Victor McLaglen, one of the most reliable members of the Ford stock company, during the filming of *The Black Watch*, his first sound feature.

Observing the native mores somewhere in Malaysia. (Dan Ford collection)

John Ford and Will Rogers in a reflective moment on the set. (Lilly Library)

Directing Boris Karloff and Victor McLaglen on location in Yuma in *The Lost Patrol*.

Will Rogers and Stepin Fetchit in *Judge Priest*, one of Ford's most seductive evocations of a cohesive, vanished culture. (BFI Films: Stills, Posters and Designs)

Jack directing Victor McLaglen in *The Informer*.

Mary of Scotland was a failure, but it introduced Ford to the radiant Katharine Hepburn, one of the great loves of his life.

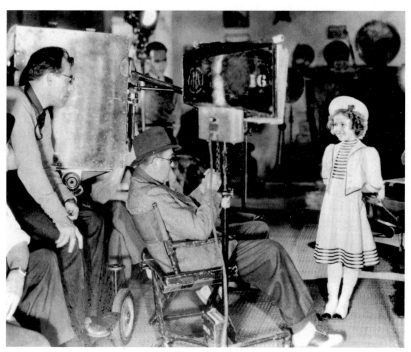

"Ford V-8" directs Shirley Temple in *Wee Willie Winkie*, with Arthur Miller (glasses) behind Ford. (Kevin Brownlow collection)

The *Araner* under full sail. (Lilly Library)

A relaxed pose with typical Fordian body language. (Dan Ford collection)

Good times aboard the *Araner*. Ford with Duke Kahanamoku. (Dan Ford collection)

The cast of *Stagecoach* caught outside the soundstage door.

Although *Stagecoach* was hailed for its action sequences,
what makes the film work is the soft, gentle yearning of the love story
between John Wayne and Claire Trevor.

Ford, with beret and dark glasses on location for *Stagecoach*,
with the firing of a gun serving as a cue for the distant action.
(Museum of Modern Art Film Stills Archives)

The Informer, along with Jack's films with Will Rogers, lifted him to the pinnacle of Hollywood directors. He could direct commercial vehicles with heart and soul, and he could direct art movies that actually made money. By 1935, it seemed that John Ford could direct anything short of the Three Stooges. His income followed suit, rising from $72,903 in 1933 to $121,290 in 1935 and a whopping $192,586 in 1936.

All this success loosened Ford's usually clenched jaw, and he even gave a couple of expansive interviews on that perennial subject, "What's Wrong with the Motion Picture Industry?"

"There's nothing surprising about the difficulty of doing things you yourself believe in in the movies," he told *New Theater* magazine, "when you consider that you're spending someone else's money. And a lot of money. And he wants a lot of profit on it. That's something you're supposed to worry about, too. . . .

"They want you to continue whatever vein you succeeded in with the last picture. You're a comedy director or a spectacle director or a melodrama director. You show 'em you've been each of these in turn, and effectively too. So they grant you range. Another time they want you to knock out something *another* studio's gone and cleaned up with. Like a market. Got to fight it every time."

The problem, he used to believe, was the star system, although he felt that was being broken down. "You don't think *The Informer* went over because of McLaglen, do you? Personally, I doubt it. It was because it was *about* something. I'm no McLaglen fan, you know. And do you know how close *The Informer* came to being a complete flop? It was considered one, you know—until [the critics] took it up. You fellows made that picture."

Ford went on to decry the assembly-line methods being practiced at some studios, most prominently at Warners, where a director might have no more than a day or two to study a script before beginning a production.

He also bluntly told interviewers that any hope they might have of a flowering of social comment pictures was the purest fantasy. "The whole financial set-up is against it. What you'll get is an isolated courageous effort here and there. The thing to do is to encourage each man who's trying, the way you fellows have done. Look at Nichols and me. We did *The Informer.* Does that make it any easier to go ahead with O'Casey's *The Plough and the Stars* which we want to do after *Mary of Scotland?* Not for a second. They *may* let us do it as reward for being good boys."

"Then you do believe," said the credulous interviewer, "as a director, in including your point of view in a picture about things that bother you?"

"What the hell else does a man live for?"

This is vintage Ford, at once iconoclastic—"I'm no McLaglen fan"—

and flattering—"You fellows made that picture." It gives a good idea of how Ford navigated the shoals of studio politics.

A few months later, when Ford was in production on *The Plough and the Stars*, he talked to *Photoplay*. Although the magazine had fallen from the fairly lofty heights imposed by James Quirk, its editor in the '20s, it was still the premier movie publication. The *Photoplay* interview is notable because the writer, one Howard Sharpe, managed to lure Ford into honest admissions of how hard he worked, and how calculated his pictures really were.

Sound, Ford asserted, was of secondary importance. He estimated—undoubtedly overestimated—that 40 percent of the time he worked without a microphone, using a silent camera so he could talk to the actors during a take, as in the silent days.

As he often did, Ford managed to suggest that he had been a swashbuckling soldier of fortune: "Occasionally he mentions (in a noncommittal tone) that he saw this war in China or that revolution in Mexico, and that such and such a thing happened to him in the South Seas."

He admitted to being proud of only one aspect of his talent—his visual sense. "I can take a thoroughly mediocre bit of acting, and build points of shadow around a ray of strong light centered on the principals and finish with something plausible."

For the future, Ford believed that "motion pictures will all be in color, because it's a success and because it's a natural medium. And we'll go out to a Maine fishing port or to an Iowa hill and employ ordinary American citizens we find living and working there, and we'll plan a little story and we'll photograph the scene and the people. That's all pictures should do anyway, and it'll be enough."

Ford retained an easy, companionable feeling for his hometown, and made frequent trips back East, usually unannounced. Aside from visits to his parents and brother Pat, he would occasionally attend the Harold T. Andrews Post of the American Legion, where he was a member. In 1933, he had sauntered into a Portland newsroom and hired a photographer named John Marshall to take photographs around town, which were used as guides for set construction for *Doctor Bull*.

In 1935, Ford was relaxing at Peaks Island with his old childhood friend Tim Donahue. Donahue asked Ford what he thought Roosevelt's second-term chances were. "He'll be elected a second time, and a third and a fourth," Ford replied succinctly.

Donahue was taken aback. "What do you mean a fourth?"

"The whole world will be at war then and if he lives through it, which I doubt, they'll offer him a crown."

The beginnings of myth now began to form around Ford. He was characterized as something above and beyond the ordinary director, gifted with godlike powers of pre-visualizing a film. As any number of Ford editors would later attest, there was an element of exaggeration in these claims.

"The legend about Ford's rushes isn't exactly true," asserted Jack Hively. "It's true that he knew what he wanted, and that he didn't shoot a lot of protection. But there was usually some." Rudi Fehr, editor-in-chief at Warner Bros., where Ford made numerous pictures in the mid-1950s to the early 1960s, said that on some pictures Ford "shot a lot of film, from all sides and angles." Daily shooting reports indicate that Ford shot only one take about 30 or 40 percent of the time. The bulk of the work was completed in two or three takes.

While ego needs undoubtedly played a considerable part in Ford's contribution to his own legend, there may have been an element of self-preservation involved as well. In June of 1938, the Directors Guild issued a fascinating document reporting that the year before there had been 220 producers needed to make 484 pictures; ten years earlier, Hollywood had used a total of 34 producers to make 743 pictures—an 800 percent increase in the volume of producers to make 40 percent fewer pictures. Faced with a metastasizing bureaucracy, Ford's intimidating image was a means of maintaining a controlling hand in the shaping of his work.

Before returning to RKO to make *Mary of Scotland,* Ford made a good picture for Zanuck. *The Prisoner of Shark Island* is the story of Dr. Samuel Mudd, the man who set John Wilkes Booth's broken leg and was imprisoned for treason at Fort Jefferson in the Dry Tortugas, 150 miles from Key West.

The film would mark Ford's initial experience with a cadaverous actor with a sepulchral voice named John Carradine, with whom Ford would have a contentious, amusing relationship over the next thirty years.

"Ford was a peculiar man," remembered Carradine. "You had to know how to handle him. Actors were terrified of him because he liked to terrify them. He was a sadist.

"My agent had been telling me about *The Prisoner of Shark Island* . . .[and] I really wanted the part. Well, I tested for Ford and we didn't get along at all. He was very cantankerous, forced me to play the scene his way, then let me do it my way. I was very unhappy and went back to the dressing room with the actor who had tested with me.

" 'Well,' I said, 'That's one job I won't get.'

"The other actor said, 'You got the part.'

" 'He hated me.'

" 'I'm telling you, you got the part.'

" 'Well, how the hell do you know?'

" 'The director's my brother.'

"And he was. The guy I'd been acting with was Francis Ford!"

Carradine's expert turn as the ultimately sympathetic Sergeant Rankin won him notice and a contract from 20th Century-Fox. Ford took a lascivious delight in baiting actors, but Carradine almost never took the bait. Almost. "Once he called me a stupid, lanky, Galway son of a bitch. I turned around to cold-cock him when Donald Crisp pulled me away. 'He's trying to get you angry,' he told me, 'so he can get the drive into the scene.' He was one of *those*."

Gloria Stuart, who was the leading lady on *Prisoner*, would recall the picture with unease, saying "It was an absolutely perfect script but I'm not sure about the picture. Ford didn't get the script—something was missing."

Nunnally Johnson's script *is* good, but it also displays a startling racism that's considerably tempered in Ford's direction, although, as Richard Corliss noted, "Johnson's is as much a class as a racial bias."

The Prisoner of Shark Island is nearly first-rate, a mini-epic that stretches from Maryland to the Dry Tortugas with nary a slip. The difference between the picture as directed by Ford and the picture as it could have been directed by some other specialist in Americana such as Henry King is the subtlety of the photography and its sense of sympathetic intimacy—these are not actors we're watching, but friends, and the movie is ripe with the gentle, observational jostling of flesh against flesh. Ford uses some intense, almost Wellesian close-ups, and there's a dynamic, beautifully judged jailbreak sequence.

In the long run, *The Prisoner of Shark Island* has proven more popular with historians than with audiences. It did serve as a baptism for the initially uneasy relationship between Ford and Darryl Zanuck. The rushes revealed that Warner Baxter was speaking in an unconvincing Southern accent; Zanuck went down to the set to tell Ford the accent should go. Ford did what he always did when given orders. He told his new boss that if he didn't like what he was doing with the picture, he'd quit.

Zanuck came right back, and twice as hard. "Are you threatening me? Don't you ever threaten me. I throw fellas off this set. They don't quit on me." Screenwriter Nunnally Johnson, who witnessed this confrontation, was horrified. "I thought he was going to punch Ford in the nose, [and] Ford had him outweighed by forty or fifty pounds."

Ford had finally run across a producer who couldn't be intimidated. At the same time, he had run across a producer whose judgment could, for the most part, be trusted. This potentially disastrous confrontation would be the beginning of a professional partnership of equals that re-sulted in a string of great films.

After some years of an uneasy estrangement, Ford cast Harry Carey in the part of the Shark Island commandant. Carey's character is undoubt-edly speaking for Ford when he apologizes to Mudd and tells him he'll work for his pardon. "I love the flag," says Carey, "and I'm jealous of its honor."

In one scene, Carey had to open a letter and read it aloud. Carey was perfect on the first take, so Ford's reaction must have amazed him.

"What did you have to go and learn that thing for," he yelled. "Don't you realize you've never seen this letter before?"

Carey apologized, but Ford remained upset; the letter was a historical document, and he couldn't alter the wording. After chewing on his hand-kerchief for a while, Ford went over to a corner and wrote out another copy of the letter, altering his pleasant, legible hand so that the letter's text was difficult to read. He printed the next take, in which Carey had more of a spontaneous quality.

Gloria Stuart noticed that Ford had not grown any more loquacious in the four years since *Air Mail*. Rehearsing the scene where Mrs. Mudd waits in a courtyard to find out whether or not her husband will be hanged, Stuart underplayed to the point of catatonia. Ford got up from his chair and came over to Stuart. Very softly, he whispered, "Gloria, I think maybe a little more emotion."

"I gave him a little more and I guess it was okay," remembered Stuart.

CHAPTER TEN

As Jack entered his own middle age, inevitably it came time to say farewell to his parents. Abby and John Feeney spent winters in California until the long cross-country railroad trip got too difficult, and they elected to spend their last years in Portland. Abby died in March 1933, and John Feeney followed his wife in June of 1936.

Years of marriage had not warmed up Jack to the responsibilities of marriage and fatherhood. He remained preoccupied and slightly removed. In December 1935, thirteen-year-old Barbara wrote Ford a letter that ended, "P.S. I love you very much. Do you love me? Will you write me on my birthday please."

He was crabby, inscrutable Jack Ford to family and friends alike. Frank Capra told a wonderful story in his autobiography that one would like to be true, involving the March 1933 Long Beach earthquake. When the rumbling began, Capra was getting a haircut at the Hollywood Athletic Club. He ran out into the street and watched the club's tower sway. After it was all over, he went to the steam room, where he found a nude Ford, reading a newspaper.

Capra stuttered out something about the earthquake. Ford kept reading. "What earthquake?" he finally asked. The pose of complete imperviousness was diligently maintained, except for those times when he felt the pressure for a drink, for a dozen drinks, for a hundred, beginning to overwhelm him. Then he would go out on the *Araner* with his friends.

He played around with golf for a time, joining two country clubs, eventually becoming rather good, but there was a clash of temperaments between the game and Ford. He was too compulsive to be able to relax, and far too competitive to lose gracefully. He became well known for shaving strokes, and had a gift for being able to find even the most hopelessly lost balls, usually by dropping an identical ball out of his pocket and saving a penalty stroke.

After John Wayne was expelled from Ford's orbit, the two men didn't see each other for several years. One day in the summer of 1934, Wayne had an argument with his wife, and ended up in Catalina cooling off. He was in a bar called Christian's Hut, when Barbara Ford walked in and told him her father wanted to see him. Ford had spotted Wayne on the dock. "Whoa, wait a minute Barbara, you got the wrong boy—must be Ward." Barbara insisted that her father wanted to see "Duke." Wayne told her to run along; she was too young to be in a bar.

Soon, Mary Ford walked in and told him Barbara had been right, that Ford wanted to see him. Wayne went on board and found Ford with a handful of others. Ford courteously invited him to sit down. Later, he asked him to stay for dinner. Soon the two men picked up the relationship where it had left off. "To this day," Wayne told Dan Ford, "I don't know why he didn't speak to me."

The two men became privately inseparable. At night, before they each went home to their wives, there were saunas at the Hollywood Athletic Club on Wilcox Street. Vacations would be taken together on the *Araner*. Ford would bring along a sack full of books and read for days, with maybe a few hours of cards at night. Conversation was limited, and Wayne would remember that on most of these trips, Ford didn't drink.

But when the gatherings were larger, with additional guests like Ward Bond, Dudley Nichols, or Henry Fonda, the brakes came off, and the agenda was split between serious drinking and serious fishing. There were bonitos and dorados and marlin, Ford's favorite, admired for their strength, endurance, and beauty.

Ward Bond was the designated jester, but a jester unawares. A pleasing actor with a paternal warmth beneath a gruff, working man's exterior, Bond had a child's honest ego; he could never quite understand why others didn't accept him as the great star he clearly was. There are dozens of stories about Ford abusing Bond, making his life miserable, playing practical jokes on him—on a trip to Europe, Ford took photos of the ass of every statue he could find and forwarded them to Bond with a simple message: "Thinking of you."

The overall impression is of alternately hilarious and grueling voyages with a crew of rowdy, overgrown boys. Besides drinking, the *Araner* was the only release that Ford ever found from his internal cauldron. As was obvious from his on-set ritual of chewing and tearing at handkerchiefs, Ford was a man under constant internal stress. "He was very taut and keyed up when working," related Lester Ziffren, the son-in-law of Harry

Wurtzel, Ford's agent. "Drinking was his way of relaxing, closing his mind to everything that had happened."

Before the *Araner*, binges had interrupted his professional obligations—the brief episode of drinking on *The Iron Horse*, the embarrassment of *Arrowsmith*. But with the *Araner* as a safety valve, there would be no alcoholic outbursts while working for the next twenty years. When he felt the pressure building, Ford could process it by counting down the days until he could be back on the ship.

J ohn Ford and Katharine Hepburn had met when he directed a screen test of her emoting in *The Animal Kingdom*. The test survives, in the UCLA film archive, and it reveals no particular chemistry, just Hepburn unsuccessfully attempting to negotiate that thankfully extinct branch of acting called Stage British. She plays a character named Deirdre who asks a man to marry her. What appears to be a slight case of laryngitis doesn't help the dialogue: "A foolish virgin, me." Hepburn works without feeling and can barely be bothered to wait for her cues.

In the wake of *The Informer*, it would only be a matter of time until RKO matched up their most prestigious director with their most prestigious actress. The studio purchased Maxwell Anderson's 1933 play *Mary of Scotland* expressly as a vehicle for Hepburn. The initial idea had been to cast Bette Davis as Elizabeth opposite Hepburn, but Warner Bros. refused to loan Davis out, probably because the actress had recently won the best reviews of her career for *Of Human Bondage*, also on loan-out to RKO. Corporate ego couldn't risk another Davis success at another studio.

Instead, RKO cast Florence Eldridge, the wife of Fredric March, who was playing Bothwell. Eldridge was a stately actress with a vulnerable quality that would have made her a great Birdie in *The Little Foxes*, but she was far removed from the fury that Davis would have brought to her scenes with Hepburn.

There seems to have been a particular kind of tension between director and star almost immediately. Early in the game Ford told Hepburn that "You'll give your best performance or I'll break you across my knee." He was forty-three, regarded as the toughest director in the business. She was twenty-eight, and had been a movie star for four years. Both were casual nonconformists, uninterested in pleasing anyone but themselves. It was strength against strength, the sort of thing that Hepburn loved and Ford usually didn't.

Soon Jack and Kate began meeting at her home in Laurel Canyon or on an occasional weekend aboard the *Araner*. Once the film was finished,

Ford and Hepburn went East, spending a month at the Hepburn family home in Old Saybrook, Connecticut, where they sailed and played golf.

Hepburn was one of the few people of either sex Ford couldn't cow. Once, they were golfing and she refused to concede him a three-foot putt. He missed it, then missed it again. Furious, he heaved his club sixty feet. "If I were you," Hepburn coolly observed, "I'd use an overlapping grip for distance." According to Ford, he refused to speak to her for a week. Even in old age, as he lay dying, they enjoyed sparring: "You are a split personality," he told her, "half pagan, half puritan." "So are you," she retorted. "True," he admitted.

Other than their shared nonconformity, New England backgrounds, and passion for the outdoors, Ford and Hepburn didn't have very much in common. She was a fervent, public liberal and intellectual while Ford always preferred to keep his feelings and beliefs veiled, and was far more conservative, emotionally if not politically. What they had going for them was a deep respect for each other's talent and a considerable degree of emotional passion. Hepburn's essential psychology was that she couldn't respect any man she could dominate, and she couldn't dominate Ford.

Hepburn would later tell Ford's grandson that the relationship was platonic, and Ford agreed ("Oh, God, no, there's no romance there. Kate Hepburn? Oh she's just a dear friend"). Late in life, to friend and documentarian Joan Kramer, Hepburn would be quite open about her lovers—Howard Hughes and Leland Hayward, among others—not to mention her overt selfishness and inappropriateness for marriage. She always said the relationship with Ford was only a friendship. She reiterated this to her niece Katharine Houghton, saying "That's nonsense. You know perfectly well that Spencer was the great love of my life."

Likewise, Mary McLean MacDonald, Ford's niece, who occasionally served as Ford's script supervisor during the '30s, worked on *Mary of Scotland* and characterized the relationship as "an intellectual friendship, not a romance. They were both from New England, were both eccentric in their own ways, and enjoyed verbally sparring with one another. . . . I cannot imagine [the friendship] developed to the point where they considered marriage."

Echoing that was the actor O. Z. Whitehead, a friend of Hepburn's brother Richard, who met Ford at the Hepburn house in 1936 and became a member of Ford's stock company beginning with *The Grapes of Wrath*. Whitehead, whose given names were Oothout Zabriskie, which explains his preference for the nickname "Zebby," was insistent that the bond was nothing more than a deep friendship.

But in her otherwise forthright autobiography, Hepburn turned mysteriously coy when the subject of Ford came up: "Obviously, he was an extremely interesting man. We became friends, and from time to time during his life we met, I would go sailing on his boat *The Araner*. . . . I found him fascinating but impossible. He was definitely the skipper of his own life and you had better not disagree with him too often."

Spencer Tracy's biographer Selden West finds a sexual affair possible if not probable. "She would have lied to [Dan Ford]—she lied all the time, but I think she was probably going by the letter of the law, and meant that they didn't actually have intercourse. That, to me, is believable."

Others find that highly doubtful. "She was too lusty not to consummate it," insisted the director Budd Boetticher, a friend of Ford's in later years. "I can't imagine Jack pulling away like a priest. That wasn't John Ford." In later years, author A. Scott Berg became very friendly with Hepburn, and he remembered that "She talked about Ford frequently, and the only other persons I heard her discuss with that level of emotion were Leland Hayward and Spencer Tracy. I'm sure it was a sexual relationship."

For about three years, from the middle of 1936 to the spring of 1939, Hepburn wrote Ford a series of letters whose tone could best be described as pining. In June 1936, she wrote him a letter of condolence after the death of his father because, she explains, she was afraid to send a wire—clearly, Mary was aware of the relationship. Even more interestingly, Hepburn obviously had known John Feeney.

One indicator that the relationship extended beyond the intellectual was the fact that Hepburn was surreptitious about her letters; sometimes they were sent to the studio, more often to the Hollywood Athletic Club—a mail drop.

The relationship failed to be derailed by the fact that *Mary of Scotland* emerged as an almost complete disaster. Shot by shot, it's beautifully photographed by Joe August, but that's all it is. There is labored exposition that the characters would have already known, and, most damagingly, there is a dreadfully miscast star. Hepburn's patrician brashness is insufficiently submerged in a basically hapless character who never acts, but is relentlessly acted upon.

If one had no idea of the intense relationship that began on *Mary of Scotland*, it could still be intuited, if only because Ford indulged Hepburn with an old-fashioned star entrance, followed by regular injections of immense close-ups that were redolent of the way MGM presented Garbo but were wildly uncharacteristic for Ford, who loathed reflexive displays of star personality. It is the work of a man who has put himself so completely at the service of his star that he doesn't notice the movie is asphyxiating. *Mary of Scotland* sinks beneath the director's reverence.

Mary of Scotland cost $864,000, managed a world gross of $1.2 million, ended up losing $200,000. It was a bitter disappointment to the studio.

After the initial rush of excitement, after the thudding failure of the film, Hepburn continued to write to Ford. In later, chattier letters, she talks about the fireworks she loved as a child, family news, the Fourth of July. She asks Ford to be nice to a friend of hers and lay off the Irish aspect of his personality.

In March 1937, she speaks of a great crisis in trying to reconcile the next thirty years of her life with the thirty she's already lived. She writes of talking to him through the setting sun and keeping a picture of him on her dressing table in Indianapolis, where she was touring with a play. She imagines him positioned just beneath the balcony, where she can focus her performance on him.

By April, she's given up the subtle approach and is trying to budge him off dead-center by telling him she needs him. "Maybe is a feeble way of saying no," she writes. "Clarity is a necessity as everyone gets so mixed up they don't know what is important to them. I used to be a great exponent of clarity, and I shall try to be again." She wants a yes or a no; all Ford was able to give her was a perhaps.

The stalwart defense soon crumbled and Hepburn was back to taking Ford whatever way she could get him: "Oh, Sean, it will be heavenly to see you again if I may, and if I may not, I can drive by Odin Street in an open Ford and think a thousand things. In my mind and heart your place is everlasting."

By August of 1938, she is still contenting herself with maybe. She's a woman at loose ends, having left Hollywood after the bewildering financial failure of the glorious *Bringing Up Baby*. She's occupying herself by golfing, teaching herself to do a one-and-a-half somersault into a pool, and looking for a play. She's obviously lonely for Ford. She's been thinking of going to Ireland and landing in Galway, but has decided to put it off until she can go there for the first time with him—as first mate.

None of Hepburn's letters to Ford are love letters in the conventional that-night-with-you-changed-my-life mode, but they cover every other psychological and emotional component of an affair. There is no mistaking their deeply emotional, tremulous tone. Ford has earned Hepburn's devotion and her fealty.

While Hepburn refers to correspondence from Ford, he didn't keep copies in his files. There is a jocular letter from January 1937, in which Ford makes jokes about Cliff Reid, Dudley Nichols, and Emilie Perkins, a friend of Hepburn's: "We, your friends of the West, are following your career with great pride. I am looking forward with great anticipation to the day I see you again so that I may give you the goddamndest kick in the ass you have ever received and which you so richly deserve."

The people around them obviously knew that Hepburn had some control over Ford. Producer Cliff Reid called on Hepburn to help him sober Jack up after one of his binges. Hepburn got him into her car and drove him to RKO, where she dosed him with whiskey and castor oil. "I thought he was going to die," remembered Hepburn. "And he thought he was going to die. Then he fell asleep and I thought he was dead." But Ford had just passed out. When he woke up, Hepburn carted him to the Hollywood Athletic Club, where they were used to Ford's binges.

According to a letter from a mutual friend of Jack and Kate's, the two were still very much on each other's mind in December 1938. "I got the most devine [sic] letter from Jack," Hepburn said during a night at her house that seems to have devolved into an endless monologue about John Ford. "He sends his love to you and tells me to be very sweet to you. . . .

"How was he when you saw him last? Does he seem well and happy? Is Mary home? Where are the children? . . . Of course I think Mary is a remarkable woman—I think she is insensitive and crude, but still she hasn't had an easy time of it. I think Jack is wonderful but he must be a very difficult man to live with. He probably is better off married to that type of woman than to some facinating [sic] creature with whom he would have been very happy. Had he been happy, he never would have been the artist that he is. . . .

"Did you know Mary? Did you like her? Mary used to be very fond of me until she found out about Jack and me. She thought I double-crossed her. I know she doesn't like me any more because many people have told me all the things she has said about me. But I can't blame her for that. Could you?

"Of course Jack is really wonderful. We were so close. He was so beautifully relaxed with me. I think I'm one woman who could make Jack very happy. I think I could be very good for him. We could have a wonderful life together. I think Jack loved me. Don't misunderstand—he never made a pass at me, but that proves it, doesn't it? I thought a great deal about marriage with him and living with him, but decided against it. I don't think Jack should ever divorce. I think I could have forced the issue, but then I don't know really."

Clearly, Hepburn wanted Ford, but Ford's ultimate feelings are unclear. Aside from his Catholicism—and for men of Ford's generation, Catholicism was never entirely aside—this was a man who loved being centered, loved the comforting rhythm of routine; playing 52 pickup with his emotional life would have been as terrifying as it was exciting.

Mary Ford had not had to endure the serial adulteries practiced by so many directors, but there had been the occasional flare-up—Madeleine Carroll, the star of *The World Moves On*, for one. Mary would claim that the single time she threatened to leave Jack, he promptly went outside, started the car, and began honking in order to speed up her departure. Bluffing, then, was out of the question; the only sensible course was an air of being above it all, with queenly obstinence masking the fact that there was no way Mary would agree to a divorce.

Cecile de Prita, Ford's niece, would say that Mary played hardball. "Hepburn [was] on the make for Jack. It was reciprocated. He wanted out [of his marriage]. . . . Mary threatened to take Barbara, the apple of the old man's eye. Hepburn offered Mary $150,000 if she would give [Ford] the divorce and Barbara, she refused. The old man stayed because of the kids, particularly Barbara."

According to Cecile, Mary told Josie Wayne, John Wayne's first wife, "Jack is very religious, he'll never divorce me, he'll never have any grounds. I'm going to be Mrs. John Ford until I die." Yet, Cecile was living in the Philippines between 1932 and 1945; any information she picked up would have been long after the fact.

Held fast by a lingering sense of duty, and devotion to his daughter, if not to his wife, Ford stayed put. Years later, John Wayne would tell his third wife, Pilar, that Ford "would have married [Hepburn] in a minute, if he had not been Catholic."

In a few years, Hepburn would find the love of her life in Spencer Tracy. The two men were, of course, ridiculously similar. Both were Irish brooders, both were periodic alcoholics—Ford a sloppy drunk, Tracy a mean one. Both were classic introverts, conflicted about the life choices they had made and publicly dismissive about their work. "Learn your lines and don't bump into the furniture," Tracy would snap to young actors who asked him for advice, while Ford gruffly hid his motives and yearnings behind "just a job of work," concealing the deep seriousness of intent that both men believed had to be hidden from the world.

The primary difference between the two was that Tracy had to be drunk to access his dark side, while Ford's dark side was only too familiar to everybody around him. Yet, there is no question that Hepburn understood Ford in that way that a woman understands the man she loves.

"Now, Sean drank more than he should have," she once said, "[and] Spencer drank much more than he should have . . . [but they were] very similar in that they were . . . devastated by the world." Hepburn ascribed Ford's gruff manner to "tremendous self-protection; he's very over-sensitive . . . and when he doesn't live up to [his self-image, it] disturbs him enormously . . . he could be very, very disturbed by people who didn't care for him."

Peter Bogdanovich would come to believe the relationship with Hepburn had an enormous effect on Ford's work as well as his life, with their decision to stop seeing each other serving as a sort of renunciation. "They both would have known the degree of happiness they were giving up," wrote Bogdanovich. "The decision, a kind of glorious and idealistic sacrifice, is echoed in most of Ford's subsequent pictures: the burden of duty, tradition, honor and family is among his central themes. . . .

"The attraction between them, the explosiveness and independence of both their natures, can be seen reflected in several of the key romantic relationships in Ford's subsequent pictures, notably in the extraordinarily rich emotional interplay between Maureen O'Hara and Walter Pidgeon as the forbidden lovers in *How Green Was My Valley*, between Wayne and O'Hara in *The Quiet Man*, *Rio Grande* and *The Wings of Eagles*."

Certainly, it's true that Hepburn helped unlock Ford's ambition, freed it up. Before Hepburn, he was a high-line workaday director, given to expressing himself only infrequently. After Hepburn, he would rarely do anything else. It's not hard to imagine Hepburn exhorting Ford to live up to the responsibilities of his great gift.

Mary Ford's feelings about this period would become clear years later, when friends of the Fords were having marital difficulties and separated for a time. She invited the wife over for dinner and took her aside as soon as she walked through the door. "Jean, you have no idea what I've gone through," she said, "but I'm still Mrs. John Ford. I'm not some ex-wife sitting over in a corner."

Ford would memorialize this agonizing period of indecision when he made his greatest love story. The heroine's name was Ellen in the original story, but in the film it is changed, and the two women Ford loved are permanently united. In *The Quiet Man*, Ford named his heroine Mary Kate.

After *Up the River*, Ford and Spencer Tracy would not work together again for more than twenty-five years, but they nearly united for Ford's intended sequel to the triumph of *The Informer*: Sean O'Casey's *The Plough and the Stars*. MGM had agreed to loan Tracy out to RKO but at the last minute Tracy, up to that point a mid-range featured star, suddenly broke through with the simultaneous smash hits of *San Francisco* and Fritz Lang's *Fury*.

MGM saw no reason to lend their hot young star to another studio, and canceled the loan-out. Forced to scramble, Ford accepted the RKO contract player Preston Foster, a disastrous accommodation that, along with the casting of Barbara Stanwyck, was the beginning of the end for a picture that was born under a dark star. Ford seems to have blamed Tracy for stepping out of the picture. There was a slight coolness on Ford's part for years, a coolness that couldn't have been helped by Tracy's relationship with Katharine Hepburn.

Still, Ford didn't lose heart. On January 27, 1936, he wrote a fascinating letter to Sean O'Casey in which he outlined some of the changes he wanted to make in the play, and also attempted to convince O'Casey of the seriousness of his intentions, not to mention his Irishness.

"We plan to bring Clitheroe back to go out with the coffin of Mollser at the close of the play," he wrote. "To give him an effective speech and to incorporate something in which I am interested could we allow him, as the funeral cortege is moving up the street through the lines of patrolling swaddies, to look back at the Plough and the Stars as it comes down over the blazing Four Courts and utter a prophetic speech to the effect that some day that flag will be hoisted again . . . to the musical undercurrents of 'Keep the Home Fires Burning.' "

Ford then went on to describe two visits to Ireland, the first in 1921, the second in 1934. The first visit was because "we had heard indirectly that our family in Spiddal were in economic and political difficulties." When he arrived in Spiddal he saw the thatched cottage of his cousin Michael Thornton in flames. Thornton's parents were standing by the road watching the Auxiliary lorries depart.

"Michael Thornton," explained Ford, "was a simple country school teacher, a man of small stature, brilliant intelligence and burning patriotism. He became one of the leaders of the West during those sad times and ended up as a guest of the Imperial government in an English prison." After Thornton was released, he went back to Galway, worked for the government for a time, then resumed teaching Gaelic.

When Ford went back to Ireland in 1934, he again visited his cousin. "At the close of a beautiful day I went to meet him at his schoolhouse and found him leaving the building with some forty youngsters making desperate and individual attempts to hang on his coattails. He was older and worn but much happier than I had ever seen him. He had achieved his place in the structure of things. What a difference in the children! Instead of poor, hungry boys and girls, barefooted and red-petticoated that I had known there, he was surrounded by red-cheeked, well-dressed, healthy children in suits of good homespun, proud little emblemed skull caps and all talking the lyrical and musical Irish of the West. . . .

"This change was kindled by the flames of Boland's Mills; since this change came from the people of Coombe, the slums and even Monto, is it wrong of us to assume that Nora or Clitheroe or even Fluther might utter a prophetic sentence that what they fought for would some day come true, that one day the flag of a Free Ireland might fly again?"

Ford closed by asking O'Casey that, if he should "see an Anglo-Irish maniac named Liam O'Flaherty at the Cafe Royale or the Bow Street gaol, please (a) punch him in the nose for me (b) tell him that I have taken the pledge of semi-total-abstinence again."

Ford is simultaneously establishing his bona fides, and constructing a justification for his desired changes. The contrasting scenes of Spiddal in 1921 and 1934 are like *How Green Was My Valley* in reverse, a Darwinian nightmare evolving into a burgeoning middle-class culture.

Whether the story of Michael Thornton is literally true or not, it does express a certain historical accuracy in describing the changes that affected Ireland between 1921 and the mid-'30s. The economic and social position of the Irish did change for the better after independence, and the poor of Dublin went from having the worst death rate in Europe, not far removed from Calcutta, to one comparable to that of any other European city.

"*The Plough and the Stars* is a send-up of Irish nationalism," explained Darcy O'Brien, the author-professor son of George O'Brien. "And here is Mr. John Ford saying, sweetly, guess what, my view is that the battle for national independence you deride in your play actually worked, so . . . you were wrong, we are going to change the end of your play to show this, and please give us permission to do this. . . .

"The play made Irish rebels look like fools; Ford wanted them to look like noble fools, who eventually won, to the betterment of their people." What is most interesting about Ford's letter is how it pits the movie director against the playwright, with the supposed issue artistic integrity, when the real issue at stake is the interpretation of history, in which the movie director was in the long run the more perceptive of the two.

O'Casey responded guardedly on March 29. George Jean Nathan, the only American critic O'Casey trusted, had loved *The Informer* and told O'Casey his play was in good hands. Nevertheless, O'Casey clearly didn't approve of Ford's suggestions. "Of course Ireland isn't yet free in any sense of the word," he wrote, "even politically, for Ulster is yet cut away from her, and kept away by the help of England's power. However, we won't, at present, argue about that point. How to get into the Film what you and I want to get in is the question and it is something of an awkward question to answer."

O'Casey went on to say that to do what Ford wanted would alter the theme of the play, and that Clitheroe, assuming they kept him alive that long, would hardly give a speech at the funeral of his own child.

O'Casey suggested that during one of the battle scenes, somebody could suggest surrendering, but Clitheroe could then make his speech of faith in the future, with perhaps "The Soldier's Song" as background music. "I think I might be able to write out some suitable dialogue for this situation; but don't want to try for fear you'd reject the suggestion, and, for my eyes' sake, I must write as little as possible."

O'Casey's alternate suggestion was to have Lieutenant Langon, wounded in the third act, make a dying profession of faith. O'Casey closed by noting that he hadn't seen Liam O'Flaherty in four or five years, and had no particular interest in doing so.

In a letter the same day to producer Robert Sisk, O'Casey was considerably blunter, calling some of the cuts that had been mandated by the censors "God damn ridiculous. . . . I may say that some of the cuts are the actual words spoken by Patric Pearse, Commander-General of the Irish Volunteers, at a meeting which I helped to organize. I can't see why they should object to this."

Ford and O'Casey were destined to disagree. O'Casey saw all armed struggle as foolish. Ford, on the other hand, had a sense of the inexorable march of individual freedom, whether it was a director feeling his artistic oats, or Irish history.

They were, in almost every respect, two very different kinds of men—Ford had little irony but a strong sense of humor, while O'Casey had only irony. But there was a kind of bond between the two. Whatever the Irish thought of O'Casey, who spent the last half of his life in England, Ford respected him, and at the end of his career he undertook a heartfelt tribute to the writer with the film *Young Cassidy*.

Ford made his changes, without any further input from O'Casey. But if everything had gone right with *The Informer*, everything went wrong with *The Plough and the Stars*. Ford and Dudley Nichols turned O'Casey's tragedy into a sentimental celebration of Irish independence.

Ford and Nichols assumed that everybody knows about the Irish troubles, and that they can therefore serve as the equivalent of the American Civil War—a backdrop for rugged romance. They also expanded the roles of Nora and Jack Clitheroe to make them conventional romantic leads, diminishing the texture lent by the multitude of small parts that give the O'Casey play its distinction.

Although Barbara Stanwyck had wrought miracles for Capra, she and Ford seem to have had little to say to each other. Bonita Granville, who had just brought off a chilling performance with the help of William Wyler in *These Three*, said that Ford's attitude was "very casual, and [he] never, really, with me tried to form a performance. Willie was meticulous about every *line*, every *look*, every *thought*. John Ford was a more general kind of director. It was the feel, the mood . . . he would never try to change a line or tell you anything that you should do specifically."

Only Barry Fitzgerald's Fluther, all jaunty carriage and expert timing, seems at one with the material, and the rest of the Abbey players seem to be in an entirely different movie than the American actors—they're broad, but authentic. They're the movie Ford should have made but didn't.

After RKO previewed the film, they decided that retakes were in order, but Ford was on the *Araner* and didn't want to come back, probably feeling the film was as good as he could make it. "They felt the Hollywood stars did not shine brightly enough with the Irish players," said Eileen Crowe. RKO assigned George Nicholls Jr. to do retakes, which so enraged Ford he instructed RKO to take his name off the picture.

Unfortunately, Ford's contract didn't have a provision allowing him to do that, and RKO executive Sam Briskin reminded Harry Wurtzel that Ford had been asked to put off his vacation until after the preview. The released picture carried Ford's name.

Some of the film's raggedness is undoubtedly RKO's doing. Scenes end abruptly, Stanwyck's eyes fill with tears and she darts off, but we don't know where. There are some clumsily post-dubbed lines to cover continuity problems, and it's easy to pick out the retakes—none of them involve the Abbey troupe, who had gone home by then, and they're shot in a broad, flat lighting that doesn't match Ford's chiaroscuro. Suffice it to say that when Preston Foster is the strongest lead actor in a movie, that movie is in trouble.

Once the retakes were made and spliced in, Sam Briskin tried to mend his fences, writing Ford, "I just returned from New York and everybody there is most enthusiastic about the picture. They are all very doubtful as to its box office, but, nevertheless, feel that it is a picture that we can well afford to be proud of and that, while it may not make us any money, it will certainly give us prestige. I am certainly hoping that the boys in New York are correct and, honestly, I agree with them."

RKO's final cut of *The Plough and the Stars* was a ridiculously brief seventy-eight minutes. The ads were ominous ("A Woman in Love Defies a Nation in Revolt . . . Barbara Stanwyck in a flag-flying show that will thrill your blood, and make your heart beat faster . . .") and the reviews were nearly as bad as the box office. As James Agate wrote in the London *Sunday Times* of February 17, 1937, "O'Casey's play is crammed full of magnificent prose-poetry; there isn't a line of any kind of prose or poetry in the film." "I could have wept when I saw the picture, because I thought it was terrible," said Eileen Crowe.

The Plough and the Stars cost $482,732, and grossed only $316,000. Its failure ended for several years RKO's interest in prestige pictures, including a production of *Juno and the Paycock*, which Ford and Robert Sisk had begun planning.

In spite of the crashing failure of *The Plough and the Stars*, Ford had no intention of swearing off Irish subjects. The same year he came a cropper with *The Plough and the Stars*, he optioned a story by Maurice Walsh that he had read in the *Saturday Evening Post*. It was about a boxer who returns to his native land of Ireland and falls in love with a delightful colleen. It was called "The Quiet Man."

Rather than an awkward lunge for prestige, Ford would probably have been wiser to stay with his original plans to direct a movie called *The Last Outlaw*. As William K. Everson has pointed out, "ostensibly a remake of a 1919 Universal two-reeler written and directed by Ford . . . it actually has no basic connection with it at all. Ford wanted to use some of the characters, and most of all the title, in a much-altered new version." The story—a once-notorious Western outlaw is released from prison after twenty-five years to find the world incredibly different—certainly offers rich possibilities, especially with a cast that includes Harry Carey, Hoot Gibson, and Henry B. Walthall.

But, after *The Informer*, the picture was probably deemed too unimportant for Ford, and RKO tossed it to the hack Christy Cabanne, who didn't exactly obliterate the story's potential, but did handle the material in the flat, by-the-numbers manner of a B movie. One sequence actually works—where the old outlaw (Carey) and the old sheriff (Walthall) go to the movies—*Heart of the Plains*—and are appalled by the apparition of Larry Dixon, singing cowboy.

Ford settled for a story credit on the film, and always had a fondness for it; after World War II, he bought the property back for a remake, but the story was too small to risk doing under the straitened circumstances at Argosy Productions.

Ford must have planned the story for Carey from the beginning—it could scarcely fit anyone else—so it proves his feelings about the actor were not irreparable. Although he certainly didn't go out of his way to hire him personally, he would suggest him for parts to other people, as in a November 1940 letter to Eugene O'Neill, where he suggested Carey for O'Neill's new play *The Iceman Cometh*, probably for the part of Harry Hope. No movie fan, O'Neill claimed that he had never seen Carey, although he had heard of the fine job he did playing the father in a 1939 stage production of *Ah, Wilderness*.

In the mid-1930s, the Fords got on the same bandwagon as thousands of other families and bought a 16mm home movie camera. At first, they used it strictly to document family times, usually on the *Araner*—Barbara as a little girl, with an Irish, Kennedyesque face; Pat, with the ineffably long Feeney face beneath an immense mop of hair; Jack occasionally sliding by, not wanting to be involved, once cheerfully flipping the finger to the camera.

Some of the gatherings seem to be stag, as with shots showing Ford downing beer on the *Araner* with Ward Bond and Liam O'Flaherty. Ford is unshaven, carrying more weight than was usual for his ropy physique, and evidently feeling no pain. Usually, the footage is not markedly different from most people's home movies, except for the people in front of the camera, as in some 1941 footage of John Wayne, Gregg Toland, and Ford in an airplane heading for Mazatlán, their faces beautifully lit by the sun shining through a window. When they arrive, there are some beautifully composed shots of a mariachi band beneath a palm tree that betray Ford's hand. The men go fishing, catch four marlin, and a boyishly delighted John Wayne exults.

The years pass, and Barbara grows to be an almost-beautiful teenager, her radiant spirit leaping through the lens. The *Araner* pitches heavily in choppy seas, or runs smoothly through the seas at dusk, while somebody, probably Mary, who rarely appears in front of the camera and shies away when she does, takes the pictures.

Back home at Fox, the lot was slowly changing under Zanuck's influence. Sol Wurtzel had been relegated to running the B picture unit, the land of Charlie Chan. Wurtzel's operation was known as the Legion of Frightened Men, because of Sol's weird smile that was not a smile, and his habit of firing people more or less for the sake of firing people.

But Zanuck had a gentler touch. He also had big plans for Ford, and handed him the biggest star on the lot: Shirley Temple. *Wee Willie Winkie* seems to have begun as one of those jobs that Ford endured so that Zanuck would be favorably disposed at some point down the road. Ford told of two completely disparate reactions to the assignment, one where he said, "my face fell atop the floor," another where he met the news with what he imagined to be professional imperturbability: "I said 'Great' and we just went out and made the picture." The former response was more likely than the latter. Zanuck attempted to calm his favorite director: "I feel the only way to make this story is to disregard the formula of all the previous pictures Shirley Temple has appeared in to date. We don't want to depend on any of her tricks. She should not be doing things because she is Shirley Temple, but because the situations—sound and believable—call for them."

During the first weeks of the twenty-five days of location work at Chatsworth, Ford made no attempt to ingratiate himself with his star.

Other directors dandled her on their knee; Ford usually just walked right by her, sucking on his handkerchief.

This slightly unnerved the child, who was accustomed to mutual displays of professional charm. She began involving him in conversations. "Ford V-8," she would ask, "did you know you took two minutes and thirty-five seconds to light your pipe that time? The last time you took two minutes and twelve seconds."

The childish coquetry didn't work. Ford would look annoyed and turn away. Other times he would make a halfhearted effort—a thin smile and an unconvincing replica of a laugh. "Usually," remembered Temple, "he seemed to regard me as someone to be endured, not embraced as a colleague." A sure sign of his lack of respect for the child was the amount of detailed direction he would give her, in stark contrast to the minimal instruction he gave the other actors.

The turning point arrived when Temple showed a willingness to master close-order drill, followed by a lack of fright when confronted by a rearing horse that came too close. The child was brave. Good. Ford asked her if she wanted a double for a scene where she was to climb onto a rock island out of the path of some stampeding horses. Temple wanted to do it herself, and, after discussing it with her mother, did. That earned her a smile and a gesture of approval. Temple then gave a very restrained performance in McLaglen's death scene. "Ford came over and put his arm around my shoulder, as he would have a boy," Temple would remember.

She had won over her director like she won over all her co-workers. "Shirley was actually a great kid to work with," remembered Cesar Romero, who was playing the sympathetic heavy Khoda Khan in the picture. "She wasn't a spoiled brat at all. She was also very smart, always knew her lines and yours, too. If you blew a line, she'd tell you what it was! Her mother did a really great job with this child, because she was not the precocious little child star at all."

The off-screen relationship between Temple and Ford was mirrored in the on-screen relationship between Temple and McLaglen—eye-rolling impatience at the thought of being saddled with such a ridiculous apparition, followed by grudging respect, ending in a protective friendship. In 1948, Temple asked Ford to be godfather for her firstborn child. He accepted.

Despite the ignominy with which it is usually regarded, *Wee Willie Winkie* is far from the worst film Ford made in this period. It's forcefully, vividly directed, in spite of some unfortunate exposition ("I'd have sent for you years ago if I'd known you were destitute," says C. Aubrey Smith at one point), the dreariest pair of lovers (Michael Whalen and

June Lang) in the history of Fox, and the plot that was mandatory for a Temple movie—she's *always* looking for a father or grandfather, real or substitute, forever winning over flinty curmudgeons.

But Ford lets us know immediately that the story will be told from her point of view, as he tracks along a train until coming to rest on Temple's wide-eyed face looking out the window. (He was to use her in much the same way eleven years later in *Fort Apache*, where she is up early on her first day on a cavalry outpost. Unfortunately, the nineteen-year-old Temple's repertoire of pouts was identical to her supply at age eight.)

Ford has a great deal of fun with the enormous incongruity between McLaglen and Temple as the two walk hand in hand. There is a beautifully orchestrated buildup to a battle that doesn't happen because two wise warriors (C. Aubrey Smith and Cesar Romero) keep their heads and make peace—the same dynamic that makes the climax of *She Wore a Yellow Ribbon* so unexpected. And there is a restrained, genuinely touching death scene for McLaglen, which gives a human scale to the imperialist comic book derring-do.

"Of all my films," wrote Temple in her memoirs, "I rate *Wee Willie Winkie* the best, for all the wrong reasons. It was best because of its manual of arms, the noisy marching around in military garb with brass buttons, my kilts bouncing. It was best because of daredevil stunts with snipers and stampeding horses." It was, in short, best because Ford injected pageantry, grandeur, and loss into what could have been a perfunctory star vehicle.

Samuel Goldwyn had been planning *The Hurricane* for nearly two years. Initially slated for Howard Hawks, those plans had crashed when Goldwyn replaced Hawks as the director on *Come and Get It*. Ford had also read the book, and actively campaigned for the assignment, wiring Goldwyn from Honolulu, "AM MORE THAN EVER CONVINCED I SHOULD WORK WITH YOU ON IT STOP WISH YOU COULD CONVINCE DARRYL. . . . REGARDLESS WHO MAKES PICTURE POSITIVE IT WILL BE SUPERB AND REBOUND TO YOUR GLORY." In spite of Ford's drunken outburst at the tail end of *Arrowsmith*, Goldwyn hired him for $100,000 and 10 percent of the profits for ten years.

The casting process was smooth, a combination of stalwart character actors (Thomas Mitchell, Raymond Massey, Mary Astor) and attractive newcomers (Jon Hall, Dorothy Lamour). Lamour, on loan from Paramount, went in to meet Ford, who asked her how long it would take her to get a tan. She estimated about ten days. He asked if she liked his tan. As it happened Ford didn't have a tan—he had that delicate Irish skin that burns rather than tans. Nevertheless, Lamour was an actress trying to get a part, so she said he had a very nice tan indeed. Where did he get it?

"In Honolulu," he replied. "They have beautiful sunlamps in the bars there."

Ford and Goldwyn had not had a smooth working relationship on *Arrowsmith*, and *The Hurricane* was to be more of the same. The problem wasn't the script or cast; the problem was what Ford took to be a changing of the rules after the game started. "Ford wanted to make the picture in the South Seas," remembered Sam Goldwyn Jr. "My father thought he was going to make it in the South Seas, but then decided to do second unit there and shoot the majority of the picture in Hollywood. He was terrified of the control issue."

"Sam was scared," groused Ford. "He never trusted a director on location." (This was eminently true; over the years, Goldwyn rescinded permission for William Wyler to shoot *Dead End* in New York, and Rouben Mamoulian—before he was replaced by Otto Preminger—to shoot *Porgy and Bess* in Carolina, leading both pictures to have the entombed feel of the sound stage.)

Ford was infuriated by what he took to be a double-cross. Goldwyn should have known that, in Ford's words, "I always get the picture made on time." With *The Informer* behind him, Ford had considerably more prestige than he had at the time of *Arrowsmith*, and, for the most part, he ignored Goldwyn, except when the producer gave him no alternative.

Goldwyn liked to come on the set and kibitz, which was anathema to Ford. Once the producer came on the set and complained to Lamour that her hair looked like a cheap wig, which infuriated the actress because she spent several hours every night washing and braiding it. Ford strode over and gruffly told Goldwyn that Lamour's hair was just fine and was not going to be cut, permed, coiffed, or altered in any way. Goldwyn slunk away but refused to take the hint.

Later, concerned that Ford wasn't shooting enough close-ups of Jon Hall and Lamour, Goldwyn walked onto the set accompanied by Ira Gershwin. Ford was on a crane; when he noticed Goldwyn, he halted work and had himself lowered to the ground. "There aren't any close-ups," said Goldwyn. Ford stared at him for a beat, then poked him in the stomach. "Look, Goldwyn. When I want a long shot I aim the camera here." Poking him a little higher in the stomach, he said, "When I want a medium shot, I aim here. And when I want a close-up," he concluded, jabbing Goldwyn in the chest, "I'll put the camera here." Then he shoved Goldwyn toward the door.

"Well," said Goldwyn to Gershwin, "at least I put the idea in his head."

In fact, Ford shot *The Hurricane* in a more or less conventional manner, with the usual number of close-ups.

Ford shot the "book" scenes first, then moved on to the special effects extravaganza of the hurricane. "Terse, pithy, to the point," was the way Mary Astor characterized her director. "Very Irish, a dark personality, a sensitivity which he did everything to conceal." Ford proved himself to Astor one day when he told her, apropos of a scene with Raymond Massey, "Make it *scan*, Mary."

Another day, he spent a lot of time working with a small Polynesian child for a scene where he was being severely questioned by Raymond Massey, playing the martinet governor of the island.

"Where were you, boy?" Massey was to inquire. Ford stood close to the child and repeated over and over the child's response, "Fish-ing, fish-ing," separating the two syllables with a musical lift in the second half of the word. The boy parroted back the intonation, while Ford, instructing the camera crew with hand signals that the child couldn't see, sculpted exactly the right bold-faced, duplicitous reaction he wanted.

Although credit for the hurricane sequence has usually gone to James Basevi, Ford rarely relied on second units and adored shooting action footage of any kind. Mary Astor mentioned only Ford directing the still-impressive sequence and Samuel Goldwyn Jr. said, "I remember seeing Ford on the set. It was designed shot by shot, and he had a good relationship with Basevi."

Because of his frustration with Goldwyn, Ford shot the picture in a state of controlled irritation; when Goldwyn assembled a rough cut, Ford refused to show up at the screening. Nevertheless, he agreed to help out Goldwyn by shooting some second unit footage for *The Adventures of Marco Polo*, a lavish stiff being shot concurrently on the lot. Ford's footage involved a blizzard and Marco Polo crossing the Himalayas. "I went for six days and did this stuff with Gary Cooper which I think gigged up the picture a bit. I wasn't paid for it." In later years, Ford put *The Hurricane* behind him. He and Goldwyn agreed on a wary mutual respect for one another, while avoiding working together again.

The Hurricane is a South Sea idyll in the tradition of *Moana* or *White Shadows in the South Seas*—the depredations the white man visits on the innocent children of the sun in French Polynesia, with a climax that is brutishly terrifying, then suspenseful, finally happy.

Ford manages to create deeper characterizations than the norm for this kind of picture. Raymond Massey is the putative heavy, but he genuinely loves his wife, played by Mary Astor, who in turn is sympathetic to the natives. As a result, Massey relents at picture's end and allows the lovers to escape.

With actors like Thomas Mitchell as a good-hearted tosspot doctor, and John Carradine, it's recognizably a Ford film, as is the theme of the natural man (here, the Polynesian natives) struggling against the strictures of authoritarian civilization.

For Ford, it was something of a return to the silent days, and among the most sensual of his films of this period. The setup is verbal, but after that there are long stretches of the film that are entirely visual—a lovely sequence of a marriage feast followed by the wedding night, or a lengthy, expressionist montage involving Jon Hall's attempts to escape from prison. Pictures, mood, and rhythm were always Ford's supreme gifts.

Politically, Ford was firmly ensconced in the Roosevelt camp, as was most of the Hollywood community. In a letter to his nephew Bob, who was fighting in the Spanish Civil War, Ford categorized himself as "a definite socialistic democrat—always left. Communism to my mind is not the remedy this sick world is seeking. I have watched the Russian experiment with great interest. Like the French commune I am afraid it might lead to another Buonoparte—Mussolini was in early manhood an anarchist—Hitler almost."

Ford was writing from someplace called Bill Brown's Physical Training Farm, in Garrison-on-Hudson, New York, where he had gone to dry out after the stresses of *The Hurricane,* or as he put it, "getting my liver shaken up by hiking and riding."

With enforced leisure, away from both work and drink, he took the time for some unsparing self-analysis. "I am glad you got the good part of the O'Feeney blood. Some of it is *very* god-damned awful. We are liars, weaklings and selfish drunkards, but there has always been a stout rebel quality in the family and a peculiar passion for justice. I am glad you inherited the good strain."

Ford bewailed his isolation: "Owing to the very hide-bound and conservative papers we get little or no information as to what is happening in Spain. Your letter is very illuminating. I got some idea of it from Hemingway—have you met him?"

He told the young man that as soon as his sabbatical at Bill Brown's was over, he was heading for Portland to see his family, then it was back to Hollywood. He closed with the fatherly admonition that Bob should keep a diary and his head down—"look for the humerous [sic] & dramatic side."

Ford's attitude toward his alcoholism remained deeply ambivalent; in his films, whenever one of his heroes drinks to excess, it's a sign of weakness or spiritual fatigue, but with the supporting players, it's more of a raffish character trait, not a flaw. Ford bought into both views, believing his drinking was a necessary part of his character, as well as "very god-damned awful" and "selfish."

The war in Spain served as a radicalizing agent for much of Hollywood, and it brought Lester Ziffren into Ford's orbit. Ziffren had been a United Press reporter in Spain when the war broke out. The UP office in Madrid must have been an interesting place; as Ziffren recalled, "Our office had a Monarchist, a Socialist, a Trotskyite. These people would come in from their day's duties and I'd compare notes with them."

Ziffren fell in love with Harry Wurtzel's daughter Edythe, who was passing through Spain in the early spring of 1936. When she left for Hollywood, Ziffren followed.

Having witnessed the carnage in Madrid and elsewhere, Ziffren was asked to speak about his experiences at a gathering of screenwriters. "I didn't know who these people were," said Ziffren. "I didn't even ask about their politics. The meeting was at the home of a woman writer. There was coffee, soft drinks, a few cocktails, about thirty people in this very nice house.

"After I spoke there was a question period. 'Tell us about the assistance given to the Loyalists by Russia.' I said that, strangely enough, Russia had put a price on their assistance and demanded to be paid in gold, in contrast to Mexico, who shipped the arms without any financial conditions. That didn't sit well with them; I cooled their enthusiasm a little."

After Ziffren and Edythe married, he was put to work writing Charlie Chan movies for Sol Wurtzel. Later, he went to work for Harry as an associate agent. Over the years, he observed Ford in both social and business situations. "Ford was a baffling man," he asserted. "Conservative, but liberal on the Spanish Loyalists. A difficult man to characterize or analyze. I do believe he bought an ambulance for the Loyalist Medical Corps. I'm pretty certain of that."

Contradiction upon contradiction. In November 1938, Leni Riefenstahl arrived in Hollywood bearing a print of *Olympia*. Ford's interest must have been piqued by the press coverage, which was favorable in New York and Chicago, virulent in Hollywood. Ford invited Riefenstahl and her two traveling companions, the journalist Ernst Jager and a Mr. Klinkenberg, from the German Sport Association, to meet with him at his house, where he showed them some of his films. Riefenstahl's impression of Ford was "a man of big Socialist idealism, not at all a capitalistic man. His wish was to produce . . . automobiles for those people who didn't have much money."

By this time, it was clear to everybody but Neville Chamberlain and the Republicans in the American Congress that war with Hitler was inevitable, so it is possible that Ford was availing himself of an opportunity to do a little light inspection of the Third Reich's greatest filmmaker. But by showing Riefenstahl his own work, he was also clearly hoping for peer approval, which he seems to have received—when she got back to Germany, Riefenstahl sent him an autographed portrait inscribed "Unter John Ford mit herzlichen grus aus Deutschland. Leni Riefenstahl." (For John Ford with hearty greetings from Germany. Leni Riefenstahl.) He kept the portrait for the rest of his life.

To an impartial ex-journalist, Ford presented himself as conservative; to a nephew, and to the house filmmaker of National Socialism, he presented himself as a Socialist. Ford's enthusiasm for the left-wing, anti-Franco forces was a simple transposition of a political situation near to his heart: Franco equaled England, while the Spanish Loyalists equaled the IRA. Bobbing and weaving, always covering up, the main object for Ford was to prevent anyone from glimpsing his closely guarded core.

In late 1934, sandwiched in between *Judge Priest* and *The Informer*, Ford had directed *The Whole Town's Talking*, a light comedy about a meek accountant who is suddenly found to be the double of a homicidal gangster—both parts being played by Edward G. Robinson.

The material is coy, and it's clear the film was done for the sake of staying busy. W. R. Burnett, one of the writers, noted that Ford "didn't say anything" during story conferences, a dead giveaway. "I don't even know why he took the picture."

Likewise, after the professionally stylish *The Hurricane*, Ford marked time for a year with two regressive scripts—*Four Men and a Prayer* and *Submarine Patrol*. Ford was extremely critical of directors who didn't stay at bat. He admired Lewis Milestone, for instance, but would say that "Milly's problem is that he fusses too much over script." He took pride in being a working director, emphasis on working.

Submarine Patrol is particularly dire, with a trite script—spoiled World War I era playboy made into a man by the Navy as represented by a 110-foot sub-chaser—that Darryl Zanuck knew wasn't any good: "Try the script out on several different directors," Zanuck noted on December 22, 1936. "Somehow it doesn't come off—as a programmer very good, but not as a big special. WORK ON IT!"

It didn't help, and Ford responded in kind. Except for the presence of John Carradine, Ward Bond, and J. Farrell MacDonald playing a character named Quincannon, Ford compliantly directs the ordinary material. It was a bewildering lack of discrimination, as if George Stevens, having proven his mettle with *Alice Adams*, had gone back to directing Wheeler and Woolsey.

Perhaps it was a kind of hibernation, after which Ford would emerge invigorated and reborn. Certainly, a brief run of mediocre time-passers didn't make any difference to his prestige or his income. About the same time he was making *Submarine Patrol,* Harry Cohn offered him *Golden Boy,* and well into the '50s, Ford would regularly be asked to direct prestigious pictures such as the *War and Peace* eventually made by King Vidor. In 1938, Ford earned $196,791, the fifth-highest salary paid to a Hollywood director (after Capra, W. S. Van Dyke, Roy del Ruth, and Wesley Ruggles) and considerably more than such talents as Clarence Brown, Victor Fleming, King Vidor, and William Wellman.

Once past this temporary malaise, Ford embarked on probably the most prodigious feat ever accomplished by a motion picture director. In the space of the next two and a half years, he would direct seven films. Three would be acknowledged masterpieces, two merely excellent, one a highly professional entertainment. Only one would be an aesthetic failure. He would win two consecutive Academy Awards for Best Director. Finally, well into middle age, the promise of John Feeney's son would be fulfilled, and John Ford would stand at the pinnacle of his profession.

CHAPTER ELEVEN

Merian Cooper, Jock Whitney, and his cousin C. V. "Sonny" Whitney had formed Pioneer Pictures in 1933. Among the first things Cooper did was sign a two-picture deal with Ford for $85,000 a picture, which, as Cooper recalled, "aroused the ire of every studio head in Hollywood, particularly Dave Selznick." Cooper was informed that he was setting a ruinously inflationary price for directors. Didn't he know there was a Depression on?

After producing a couple of more or less unsuccessful pictures in Technicolor (*Becky Sharp* and *The Dancing Pirate*), Pioneer merged with Selznick International. David Selznick thought Ford was a good director, as directors went, but the merger was to be the beginning of a very amusing series of maneuvers—Selznick assiduously trying to get Ford to make a picture for him, Ford deftly dodging. He had made a deal with Merian Cooper, not David Selznick, who was already known for compulsively directing directors—Ford's idea of hell.

Ford's contract with Pioneer called for his first picture for the company to start on or before November 1937, with the second to follow within a year. But, as of January 1936, Ford was under exclusive contract to Fox for three pictures, a deal that would take him until August of 1937 to fulfill. Furthermore, he had already had all the loan-outs permissible under his agreement. The sound of grinding teeth could be heard coming from the direction of Culver City.

By late September of 1936, Ford was in serious negotiations with producer Walter Wanger for yet another commitment, while still managing to stiff-arm Selznick. At the end of the year, it was announced that Ford would be directing *The Hurricane* for Goldwyn, which Fox let him make because Ford agreed to extend his contract, in addition to Goldwyn agreeing to lend them a star and sell them a "very important" property.

After *The Hurricane*, Ford still had two pictures to make for Fox before he could even discuss working for Pioneer-Selznick, which, at this point, was planning an adaptation of *The Sea Wolf* for him, tentatively to star Paul Muni. Part of the deal—and part of the problem—was that Ford was insisting that Merian Cooper act as the producer for any picture, i.e. serve as a buffer between him and Selznick.

By February 1937, Selznick's never-generous supply of patience was disappearing fast. He ordered Merian Cooper to get a definite date when Ford would be able to go to work for him. *The Sea Wolf* disappeared as a potential project when Selznick sold it to Warners for $15,000. Selznick had Ford penciled in on another, slightly larger-scaled picture: "Ford may be on *Gone with the Wind* as late as the end of May," he dictated on February 23, 1937, "and it would be at least three months beyond this before we could have Benedict Arnold script ready."

Ford had other plans. On April 10, 1937, Ernest Haycox had published a short story called "Stage to Lordsburg" in *Collier's* magazine, and Ford quickly bought the movie rights for $7,500. He could afford it; in May, he signed an eight-picture deal with Fox that was later amended to ten pictures; Jack was to earn $45,000 per picture for the first two, $75,000 for the next four, and $85,000 for the last four. It was a nonexclusive agreement; after completing four pictures for Fox, he was free to make two films for Pioneer and one for Wanger.

Ford invited John Wayne for a weekend on the *Araner*. Wayne expected to find the usual gang of reprobates, but he found himself alone on the ship with Ford. The director handed Wayne the original Haycox story and a screenplay adaptation written by Dudley Nichols. What, he wanted to know, did Wayne think of the story?

Wayne could tell that he was a natural for the part of the Ringo Kid. He could also tell that Ford was not about to give him the part. Or was he? Ford and Wayne played cards and drank gin. Finally, Ford got to the point. "You are acquainted with some of the new young actors. I was wondering if you knew of one that could play the Ringo Kid."

Tired and irritated, Wayne (facetiously?) mentioned Lloyd Nolan.

"Nolan?" said Ford. "Jesus Christ, I just wish to hell I could find some young actor in this town who can ride a horse and act. Goddammit, Duke, you must know somebody. But then you've been out at Republic. You're not likely to see a hell of a lot of talent out there." Ford got up and said good night. For the rest of the weekend, Ford baited Wayne with cracks about abysmal Westerns at Republic and his casting difficulties with the Ringo Kid. Finally, as the ship was pulling into San Pedro harbor, Ford said, "Duke, I want to tell you something. I have made up my mind. I want you to play the Ringo Kid."

Of course, Ford had intended to cast Wayne the entire time, probably from his first reading of the story. The game-playing that Ford was to indulge in all his life was part cruelty, but it also was intended to create a complete awareness of Ford's power and significance.

And there was still another aspect of it: the way such behavior could focus an actor's attention away from himself and his career, and onto the part and the picture, where it belonged. "He knew what he was doing," Wayne would tell his biographer Maurice Zolotow. "First of all, he was makin' me feel emotions. He knew he wouldn't get a good job of work out of me unless he shook me up so damn hard I'd forget to worry about whether I was fit to be in the same picture with Thomas Mitchell. . . . Mr. Ford only wanted to do one thing and that was to make good pictures, and to do this he would do anything, anything."

Cooper told Ford he could commit to both Wayne and Claire Trevor, a minor actress at Fox who had created a stir in William Wyler's *Dead End*. "I'd see him on the lot very often," Trevor told John Gallagher, "and he'd say, 'I got a picture for you.' Never tell me what or anything, but he did keep me in mind for many years before we got together on this picture."

Cooper's deal with Selznick gave him the right to pick his own pictures, over which he would have full authority once Selznick had agreed to the project. Selznick, however, did have veto power over the project in its initial stages.

In late June 1937, Ford and Cooper went to Selznick's house for dinner to pitch the project. Selznick loathed it. First, he explained to Cooper, there were no big stars. Secondly, it was "just another western," a genre in which he had next-to-no interest. Why not do something else, he asked Cooper, perhaps a classic?

Ford and Cooper mounted a spirited counteroffensive. ("Jack Ford can state a case as well as anybody who ever lived, when he wants to take the time to do it," asserted Cooper in 1971.) They explained that the story was nothing but a vehicle into which they planned to inject a group of characters stolen from Bret Harte. The characters were classics, so the film could not help but be a classic. Cooper pointed out that the picture would have the most appealing love story in the world, the growing love between a good bad man and a good bad girl—"a sure-fire star-making formula." After an hour of intense lobbying, Selznick capitulated and gave the picture the go-ahead.

The next morning, Selznick told Cooper that, after deep thought, he had come to the conclusion that "your and Ford's Western" wouldn't get its costs back without big stars. He believed, he said, that he could get them Gary Cooper and Marlene Dietrich instead of John Wayne and Claire Trevor. Selznick's thinking was revealed in a memo he sent to Jock Whitney, his principal financial backer in Selznick International: "FEEL VERY STRONGLY, AS I EXPRESSED TO COOP, THAT WE MUST SELECT THE STORY AND SELL IT TO JOHN FORD, INSTEAD OF HAVING FORD SELECT SOME UNCOMMERCIAL PET OF HIS THAT WE WOULD BE MAKING ONLY BECAUSE OF FORD'S ENTHUSIASM. . . . IF THIS MEANS WE ARE TO LOSE FORD, I WILL SUPPLY COOP WITH AS FINE A DIRECTOR AS POSSIBLE. . . . I AM WILLING TO CONCEDE [FORD] IS ONE OF THE GREATEST DIRECTORS IN THE WORLD, BUT WHOSE RECORD COMMERCIALLY IS FAR FROM GOOD. . . . BALANCED AGAINST ONE REALLY GREAT PICTURE, 'THE INFORMER,' WHICH CERTAINLY COULD NOT BE TERMED A COMMERCIAL SMASH, AND A COUPLE OF GOOD PICTURES THAT DID FAIRLY WELL, SUCH AS 'THE LOST PATROL' AND 'THE WHOLE TOWN'S TALKING,' ARE SUCH OUTSTANDING FAILURES AS 'MARY OF SCOTLAND' AND 'THE PLOUGH AND THE STARS.' "

Selznick was not completely off track; within the context of the period, "Western" meant little more than a B movie, and "classic Western" was an oxymoron. The use of the phrase by Ford and Cooper clearly showed that they intended to do nothing more or less than reinvent a genre, which, for all of his gifts, was not Selznick's business.

"I was dumbfounded," remembered Merian Cooper. Aside from the fact that he believed Gary Cooper and Marlene Dietrich to be too old, Cooper had made a commitment to Wayne and Trevor. As he once said, "I didn't learn anything really at the Naval Academy, except, 'not to lie, cheat or steal—and never to break your word, no matter what the cost.' "

Cooper argued with Selznick for hours. He was amazed that Selznick would go back on his previous agreement, while Selznick was amazed that Cooper didn't want Gary Cooper and Marlene Dietrich in his movie. Neither man budged.

Cooper felt he had no alternative but to resign from Pioneer Pictures, walking away from $64,000 in salary, which he had postponed taking until the start of production. He tossed that money, and a long-term contract that paid him $2,500 a week, plus a percentage of both companies (Pioneer and Selznick International) overboard on a point of honor. And then Ford and Cooper simply moved "Stage to Lordsburg" over to Wanger and began preproduction, which had probably been their hope, if not their intent, the entire time.

Selznick washed his hands of the deal, and of Ford: "He is an excellent man, but there is no point in treating him as a god, and if he doesn't want to be here I'd just as soon have some other good director." Selznick never seems to have grasped Ford's horror of his intrusive working methods. As late as 1941, Selznick was still noodling around with projects that might lure Ford to the studio; perhaps *The Ox-Bow Incident*, or *Anna Christie*, with the spectacular cast of Ingrid Bergman, John Wayne, Thomas Mitchell, and Laurette Taylor, with a Dudley Nichols script and Gregg Toland on the camera.

As for Walter Wanger, he had nearly as much class as Selznick, but not as much ego. He had gone to Dartmouth, and never let anybody forget it. He had produced prestige films at Paramount, Columbia, and MGM before going independent at United Artists, where he quickly ran into trouble. From 1936 to 1938, UA had dropped $6 million into nine Wanger productions and received not a dime of profit. For Wanger, "Stage to Lordsburg" must have looked attractive—a prestigious director with a not terribly expensive property.

The Ford and Nichols adaptation of "Stage to Lordsburg," soon retitled *Stagecoach*, differs significantly from Ernest Haycox's original. All the character names are changed; the whore Henriette becomes Dallas, and the good bad man Malpais Bill becomes the Ringo Kid. The plot skeleton is the same, but characters are added, as is the entire subplot of the Ringo Kid seeking revenge against Luke Plummer. In the Haycox original, there's no driving motivation; no one wants to chase anybody out of Tonto in the very beginning, and the stage hasn't been running for forty-five days, so everybody is aware that they're traveling at their own risk. Ford adds urgency, and deepens the characters of Hatfield and Peacock. In the story, Lucy Mallory is only engaged to her soldier, not married, thus not pregnant. In other words, Ford and Nichols added a new narrative strand coexisting with the one about the menace of the Indians.

Although some later critics pooh-poohed Ford's claim that the story derived from de Maupassant's "Boule de Suif," as Edward Buscombe has pointed out, the two stories both feature an acute class consciousness between ordinary people and the vanities and pretensions of those who imagine themselves to be the pillars of society.

Wanger usually favored a hands-off attitude toward his directors, and he also had a respect for Ford that was similar to Cooper's. "I read the story," Wanger wrote to United Artists publicity head Lynn Farnol, "but after Ford had purchased it and brought it to me. Again, it was Ford who worked with Dudley Nichols in creating a fine script; and John Wayne as the Ringo Kid was also Ford's idea. While I am proud to be the producer of *Stagecoach*, will you please do everything in your power to see that the picture is known as John Ford's achievement."

That, at least, was Wanger talking after it was clear that the film was a success. Before production, he echoed Selznick in his belief that Wayne's stock had been fatally devalued by nearly a decade of cheap Westerns. Wanger wanted somebody else—Joel McCrea, anybody. Ford even went so far as to test a few actors out of courtesy to Wanger. Bruce Cabot was put on top of the stagecoach in front of a process screen for a sample scene. "I went up to John Ford," Cabot remembered, "and I said, 'Well, Pappy, how did I do?' And he said, 'You did great, Bruce, but Duke's got the part.' "

The Breen Office rejected the treatment completely—it sympathetically portrayed a prostitute and an alcoholic, and sanctioned violent revenge. Ford and Nichols gave a little—the script never specifically refers to Dallas's occupation, and they planted information about Luke Plummer's murderous past, making his death a question of retribution—and the Breen Office gave a little in the matter of Doc Boone's alcoholism.

While all this was going on, Ford and Cooper were forming their own company. Ford had been tempted for some time by the possibilities of independent production. In June 1937, the trade papers announced the formation of Renowned Artists, a group that would include both Ford and Tay Garnett, whose film *Trade Winds* was announced as the initial release from the company. Renowned Artists fell through, but Ford and Cooper didn't give up. They chose for their logo a silhouette of a three-masted ship in full sail. They called their company Argosy.

In the summer of 1921, a tall, slender man named Harry Goulding arrived in Monument Valley, Utah. Except for John Wetherill, who lived in Kayenta, Arizona, twenty-five miles south, where he provided lodgings for visitors, Goulding and his wife were the only white people for hundreds of miles.

The area around the Valley was known as the Paiute Strip, but in 1922 the Paiutes headed north, and the land became public domain, open for homesteading. Goulding and his wife, Mike—her given name was Leona, but Harry had trouble getting that out, so he rechristened her—moved in.

For the next four years, the couple lived and worked in tents. Harry would go to Kayenta perhaps once a month for mail and supplies, while Mike tended flocks of sheep and learned the language of the Navajos who began showing up at the Gouldings' tent to trade. The Navajos, who had numbered only about seven thousand in the mid–nineteenth century when they were subdued by Kit Carson, now had a population of close to 100,000, many of them living in the Four Corners area. They came to trust the Gouldings as friends.

Slowly, Goulding accumulated enough capital to buy his land in 1936. But the Depression devastated the always fragile economy of the Valley;

both Goulding and the Indians struggled to survive. The Indians couldn't sell their wool, so they took to selling goatskins to get coffee. There was no food, no water, no rain.

Occasionally, however, there was a movie crew. Zane Grey passed through the Valley in 1913, and in April of 1922 he took Jesse Lasky, who was producing a series of films for Paramount based on Grey stories, and producer Lucien Hubbard on a trip into Navajo country—the Painted Desert, Paiute Canyon, Rainbow Bridge, and a few other places. The story for *The Vanishing American* was conceived on this trip, and the shots of Monument Valley featured in that film were probably Grey's idea.

In 1938, Harry was told that a Hollywood company was planning on making a Western around the Flagstaff area. "A rider came in and told us," remembered Mike Goulding. "Harry went to Flagstaff, [and] sure enough . . ."

It is at this point that history gets a little cloudy.

In one of several variant versions, Ford told his grandson Dan that it was George O'Brien who saw Monument Valley first and came back raving about it. "Harry Goulding had given him a lot of pictures and I was entranced," asserted Ford.

Mike Goulding's story has her husband packing up a bunch of stills of the Valley and driving to Los Angeles, where he presented them to the staff at Walter Wanger Productions. As it happens, this story was corroborated by photographer Josef Muench, who remembered that Harry's original plan was to use simple snapshots, until Muench offered to print up a batch of 8 x 10s of his professional photographs and mount them in a spiral notebook. "Harry said, 'That should do the trick,' " remembered Muench.

Moreover, Mike Goulding's memories were very specific. She had an older brother in Los Angeles with whom they could stay, and she distinctly recalled sitting in the car while Harry went in and told the secretary at the United Artists studios that he wanted to see Walter Wanger. He didn't see Wanger, but was introduced to Ford, who examined the portfolio and told Harry, "I'd always wanted to do a picture up there."

From documents in the Wanger papers, it seems that the company made their initial contact with the Gouldings through Wetherill, who didn't have enough room to house everybody at his particular trading camp; Harry Goulding took the overflow. The existence of Wetherill doesn't negate Harry's story so much as amplify it. Once the company got to the Valley, it made more sense to headquarter at the Gouldings', who were right there, and skip the twenty-five-mile commute from Kayenta.

When he first examined Monument Valley's 96,000 acres, Ford found the ultimate frame for his pictures: sandstone buttes like fists punching through the earth's crust, as well as delicate architectural spires rising toward the sky—a place of majesty and repose. Monument Valley gave the impression that it is as it has always been—permanent, implacable, sacred.

At night, clouds descend and settle over the buttes and pillars like gods visiting their creation. Even the watchful, uncommunicative Navajo people must have appealed to Ford. This was not Newhall, as much rural as Western, this was *out there*, a full 180 miles from the nearest railroad, with an endless series of compositional possibilities. Here, finally, were mountains to match the men Ford could put on the screen.

In the years to come, Ford would ritualistically return to Monument Valley, even when he wasn't working on a film. Harry Goulding reserved a little stone building for him that was visible from the front door of the trading post, a small piece of land at the base of a butte looking over the valley. The noble geological features—Rooster Rock, Meridian Butte, Totem Pole, the Mittens, the King on His Throne, the Big Indian, Bear and the Rabbit—became a landscape given meaning through Ford's camera.

Until Harry Goulding sold the lodge in 1963, Ford used Monument Valley more than any other location. Aside from its innate beauty, he loved the isolation—no interfering executives, no family pressures, no telephones, no competition for the position of authority figure.

Harry Goulding became the location liaison because of his fluency in Navajo. Ford would explain the scene, then follow Harry out to a couple of likely spots. Ford came to consider the Gouldings as more than a necessary part of his filmmaking mechanism; they were friends. Once, years after *Stagecoach*, he stopped by the Gouldings' with Mary and Brian Desmond Hurst in tow. It was February, it was his birthday, and the unprepared Mike quickly baked a batch of Ford's favorite biscuits, stuck some candles in them, and everybody sang "Happy Birthday." "That went over big," she recalled.

Audiences have traditionally assumed that great movie stars are just playing themselves, a gross oversimplification that ignores the vast amounts of contemplation and adjustment that changes Archie Leach into Cary Grant, or Marion Morrison into John Wayne. As the briefest glance at any of Wayne's early B Westerns shows, the easy, likable personality was there from the beginning, but so was a lumbering gaucheness. The accoutrements that spelled John Wayne were added incrementally, and not just by John Ford.

Ford has perhaps been given a bit too much credit for creating the man who usually called him either "Pappy" or "Coach." While the

Wayne of 1932–33 has little to offer save his personality, the Wayne of 1938 is greatly improved, acting with authority and concision, even if he is marooned by Republic's hopeless scripts. What Ford did was provide a setting in which this rough jewel could shine.

Take, for instance, the walk. "Duke got his walk from my wife's father, [the character actor] Paul Fix," asserted Harry Carey Jr. "Paul coached Duke. Duke had said, 'I don't like my walk; I look awkward when I walk.' He was very aware of these things. Paul said, 'Point your toes when you walk, point them in the ground.' Well, you point your toes like that you're going to stab them into the ground." The rolling hips and shoulders that made Wayne's movements so distinctive were his way of adapting to Fix's suggestions about his feet. "He worked so hard to be a very graceful huge man. It didn't just happen."

As a man, Wayne could be demanding and impatient, but he had an innate gregariousness, an interest in other people, that was unexpected and charming. "What was different than the roles that he played," said his oldest son, Michael Wayne, "was that he would listen to people. He wanted to hear what they thought. He was a listener as well as a talker."

Although Ford liked to give the impression that Wayne was a sub-verbal oaf, the actor was not what he played. "He was an expert in Western Indian tribes," remembered Toni La Cava, his daughter. "He was a history buff, he knew all about the Civil War. He knew what battle was where, and how many men were taken at this place. He knew an awful lot about Oriental art, about Native American art. He knew an awful lot about a lot of things."

Wayne was well known as a demon chess player. Although he wasn't tournament caliber, he made up for technical flaws by psyching out his opponent. "Is *that* the move you're gonna make?" he'd inquire with an air of deep regret. "Are you sure you wanna make *that* move? OK." Nudged along by Wayne's own habit of pretending his every move was worthy of a Grand Master, the opponent was soon convinced he had blown the game. He'd do the same thing at bridge.

Forged by years of working for little money and less acclaim, Wayne would become a compleat professional. Like Ford twenty years before, he had propped, he had stunted, he had worked for the worst directors and was about to work for the best. He would always cast an eagle eye on all the crafts that made up a motion picture crew. He expected the same level of skill he demanded from himself and he never put on airs. As the cameraman Bert Glennon would remember, "I've seen him put his shoulder to a location truck that was stuck, or hold a pair of shears and a comb for a hairdresser when she had to make a hurried change on one of the characters."

"He was a professional," said Dobe Carey. "I never saw him miss a word, I never saw him late, I never saw him with a hangover. Oh, one time I saw him with a hangover, but he was really a good man to work with."

The relationship between Ford and Wayne was already deep—part father-son, part demon-mentor. "Duke paid quite a lot of attention to him," said Ben Johnson, "and [Ford] demanded that, really."

"He often asked for and took Mr. Ford's advice on things," said Michael Wayne, "both with respect to his personal life and also his career. And whenever Ford wanted him, all he had to do was [crook his finger] and my father came running. . . . They weren't politically aligned at all; Ford was a big . . . Democrat and of course my father campaigned for Richard Nixon, so they had their differences."

When Wayne's back was turned, Ford's attitude shifted to affectionate fatherly concern, as when, in 1946, Howard Hawks hired the actor to star in *Red River*. Ford dashed off a note wishing Hawks "all the luck in the world on the picture . . . and take care of my boy Duke and get a great picture."

Ford grew to appreciate the way Wayne could effortlessly command a scene simply by entering it, the way he could communicate complex emotions without using many words, the undemonstrative way he expressed attraction to a woman. The screen character the two men carved was, in most respects, similar to the part Ford played on a film set—strength and isolation in equal measures.

Ford had discovered him; now he made it his job to shape Wayne into a film hero, a character big enough to serve as a battlefield for civilization's conflicting desires.

Preproduction for *Stagecoach* was as carefully monitored as everything else. Ford wanted little touches of reality amidst the drama. A test was made of Claire Trevor modeling her plaid dress and costume designer Walter Plunkett was horrified to see that her petticoat was clearly visible on one side. Plunkett said he'd fix it immediately, and Ford turned on him, saying that he had loved the idea, that the dangling petticoat was a touch of genius, and that he regretted to see he had misplaced his admiration for Plunkett's skills.

Ford shot a test of Wayne and Claire Trevor to see how they looked together, and he was unhappy with what he saw. He took Wayne by the chin and shook his head. "What are you doing with your mouth?" he demanded. "Why are you moving your mouth so much? Don't you know that you don't act with your mouth in pictures? You act with your eyes!"

Ford shot *Stagecoach* from October 31 to December 23, 1938, a total of forty-seven shooting days, four days over schedule, for slightly less than $550,000. Ford got $50,000, Dudley Nichols got $20,000, and the cast, in toto, received $80,000, with Claire Trevor's $15,000 being the largest salary. John Wayne got a grand total of $3,700, just about what he was getting at Republic and less than supporting player Tim Holt, who got $5,000.

As the film got under way on location, Ford stayed open to happy accidents. Early on, near Caliente, Arizona, Wingate Smith was awakened by a production man who told him it was snowing. Smith fully expected to have Ford cancel shooting, or mobilize everyone to brush away the snow.

But instead of being angry over continuity problems, Ford was delighted. "Great! That's just what we needed." Ford and crew got some shots of the stagecoach rumbling through landscapes heavily dusted with snow, while, back at production headquarters, Merian Cooper was asking on the shortwave radio just how Ford intended to use those scenes. Ford refused to answer. Back at the studio, he had stagecoach driver Andy Devine deliver a line about taking the high road, because Apaches don't like snow. A small thing, but a way to work in some striking images without jabbing the audience in the ribs.

During production, all the actors had to be on the set all the time, whether they were scheduled to work that day or not. The enforced intimacy created a family atmosphere; people got to know each other while sitting and talking. Also contributing was Ford's habit of filling up the extra ranks with old friends from the silent days. The small parts and extras in *Stagecoach* included such once-familiar names as Bryant Washburn, Helen Gibson, Buddy Roosevelt, Bill Cody, and Franklyn Farnum, not to mention old Ford cohorts such as Vester Pegg, Duke Lee, and Frank Baker.

Most of the creative work was done during rehearsal and blocking. Ford took longer rehearsing than most directors, but it enabled him to get a printed scene quickly. Most of his work on the script was in cutting it back slightly, compressing six lines into three.

Ford rode Wayne mercilessly. He was "a big oaf," a "dumb bastard." "Can't you walk, for Chrissakes, instead of skipping like a goddamn fairy?" "[He was] very tough on Wayne, very tough," remembered Claire Trevor. "I felt sorry for Duke because he wanted to succeed so badly, and this was his big chance. . . . Duke took it. He took it like a soldier. Because he knew he was helping him."

Ford allowed the actor to look at the rushes, then asked him what he thought. "Wonderful," said Wayne. Ford asked about some of the other actors, who Wayne thought were also wonderful.

Wasn't there anything Wayne found wanting? Casting about for something insignificant and safe, Wayne mentioned the reins that Andy Devine was holding. They seemed too loose, they needed more tension. Ford immediately yelled, "Come on down everybody. Our star thinks he's fine but he can't stand Devine's performance!" This was a gambit that Ford would use to ensnare the unwary for the rest of his career. It provided the spur for Ford to work Wayne over every day of the production until even Tim Holt told Ford to "Stop picking on Duke." It didn't help. Ford kept picking on Duke for the next thirty-four years.

At the same time Ford was making Wayne's life miserable, he was taking care of him. Anytime there was a chance for a reaction to a moment in the film, or another character, Ford would insert a shot of Wayne, making his response the focal point of the scene. And Wayne would loyally point out that Ford only harassed him about minor things—his walk, the way he washed his face in a throwaway moment. "But when I had a scene to do," said Wayne, "he treated me like a baby. Which was really his style. But he'd do anything to get a performance."

Ford explained to Wayne that context was everything, that he didn't have to express all that much, that the audience would read into him whatever emotion the scene indicated. A soundman remembered that for a scene Wayne had particular difficulty with, an exasperated Ford finally said, "Just raise your eyebrows and wrinkle your forehead," a mannerism that worked so well Wayne used it the rest of his life.

Of all the actors, Thomas Mitchell seemed the best able to handle Ford. When the director began riding him one day, Mitchell silenced him with one sentence: "Just remember: I saw *Mary of Scotland.*"

Wanger assigned an inexperienced twenty-four-year-old contract actress named Louise Platt to the picture. Platt was playing a pregnant cavalry wife trying to get to her husband before the baby is born. She immediately got off on the wrong foot with Ford when she took offense at the rough-and-tumble atmosphere.

"My mother had been something of a Southern belle and my father was in the military," remembered Platt. "So when I learned my character was from Virginia and was taking the stagecoach to meet her husband who was in the cavalry, I had a great deal to draw from. It was my experience that Southern women were very strong, but never hard. I wove that into my characterization and worked on a very light Southern accent."

Nevertheless, Ford didn't like what he saw as Platt completed her first scene. He took her aside and said that her character had to be hard, "hard as a rock. She wants only one thing. To get through. To get to her husband." That, said Platt, was the only direction he gave her throughout the filming.

"He understood the medium. Remember the scene just after my baby was born? Ford spent a long time getting the light to glint in Claire's eyes for her close-up. She only said three words. 'It's a girl.' From those three words and that close-up, you knew everything about Claire's character. Whatever life had done to her she would be a wonderful mother. It was brilliant acting and brilliant direction."

For the landmark chase scene across the flats, Ford took the crew and John Wayne—the other actors were all shot back at the studio in front of a process screen—to Muroc Dry Lake near Victorville. Ford followed Wayne's recommendation and hired Yakima Canutt, who had been working with the actor on Poverty Row for years, as primary stuntman and wrangler. When Canutt walked into Ford's office, he was greeted with "Well, Enos, how are you?" Canutt was immediately on his toes, for very few people knew his real name—Yakima was a nickname from his days as a champion rodeo rider.

Although Ford had been planning to jettison a sequence in which the stagecoach has logs strapped to it for a river crossing, Canutt assured him it was do-able with a classic piece of movie magic: the logs were hollow props, and the coach was actually towed across the river by an underwater cable hooked to a truck. Ford was so pleased by the result that he gave Canutt carte blanche to design the stunts.

Canutt had a tractor dig up about fifteen acres of the lake bed to soften the soil for the stunt falls. Canutt came up with the classic and still remarkable sequence in which he, as an Indian, transfers from a horse to the team pulling the stagecoach. Wayne fires from the top of the coach and Canutt falls, dragging his feet on the ground, holding on to the harness between the two lead horses. Wayne shoots again, and Canutt lets go, allowing the stagecoach to pass over him.

The space between the horse's hooves was only three feet, and Canutt was a big man, nearly as large as John Wayne. It was mandatory that the horses be running absolutely straight, and even then, there was very little margin for error. "You have to run the horses fast," Canutt said, "so they'll run straight. If they run slow, they move around a lot. When you turn loose to go under the coach, you've got to bring your arms over your chest and stomach. You've got to hold your elbows close to your body, or that front axle will knock them off." Canutt had chosen a section of the lake bed that had not been softened up, so the stagecoach wheels would not sink into the ground any more than was absolutely necessary.

Ford was using three cameras on the camera car. Because he didn't like to rehearse stunts, feeling it made them look too polished, he asked Canutt about speed. "How fast will that team be traveling?" he asked Canutt. "I don't want any mishaps." Canutt figured thirty-five to thirty-seven miles an hour.

At the conclusion of the stunt, Canutt, a good showman, added a little tag: as the coach passed over him, he rolled over, tried to get up, then collapsed again, just to show the audience that it hadn't been a dummy.

Canutt walked over to the camera car to find Ford leaning against it, looking at the ground. One of the cameramen said he'd probably missed the tag, a second wasn't sure, and a third thought he'd gotten it. Canutt volunteered to do it again. "You know I love to make money."

Ford looked up. "I'll never shoot that again," he said flatly. "They better have it."

Ford broke one of direction's primary rules by switching the position of the camera during the chase scene from right of the stagecoach to the left, thereby making it appear that the stagecoach had changed direction. It's the sort of thing audiences rarely notice, but critics always do, and Ford, defensive as always about any perceived shortcoming, had a commonsense explanation: "It was getting late and if I had stayed on the correct side, the horses would have been back-lit, and I couldn't show their speed in back light. So I went around to the other side where the light was shining on the horses. It didn't matter a damn in this case. I usually break the conventional rules—sometimes deliberately."

In spite of the dangerous stunts, everything worked the first time. As the production wrapped up, Ford called Canutt into his office and told him, "You can go home and put this in your notebook. Any time I'm making an action picture and you're not working, you are with me."

At the wrap party, Bert Glennon, Ford, and Canutt were talking when editor Otho Lovering announced that he'd looked at all the footage and thought Ford had one of the best Western pictures ever made. "Yes, thanks to Yakima Canutt," blurted Glennon. Canutt saw Ford glaring at Glennon and later told him that he'd cut both their throats. Ford never called Canutt to work for him again; the only times Canutt worked on a Ford picture—a stunt on *Young Mr. Lincoln,* and directing a third unit on *Mogambo*—he was hired by the studio.

Claire Trevor remembered seeing *Stagecoach* in rough cut form before it was released. Ford was in the screening room, and after the film was over, he turned to her and said, "It's going to be great. And *you* are so good in it, they're not even going to realize how good you are." Trevor left the screening room on an unaccustomed high.

Unlike many of his pictures, Ford stayed with this one through the editing process. Sound editor Walter Reynolds had dubbed in a lot of war whoops during the chase scene, but Ford told Reynolds to take them out. *Stagecoach* previewed in Westwood on February 2, 1939, barely a month after it finished shooting, and was released a month after that, with a promotional campaign that emphasized the director ("The director of *The Hurricane* now gives you lusty excitement and roaring adventure") and suspense ("Due to the tremendous suspense developed in *Stagecoach*, we recommend that you get to the theatre for the start of the picture").

The response was instantaneous. "I cannot tell you what a thrill that was," remembered Claire Trevor. "I expected it to be a good picture, but I didn't expect to be swept up and carried along with such joy! I was overwhelmed by this picture. I thought it was the best thing I'd ever seen. I forgot I was in it. When I was leaving the theater, [the columnist] Jimmy Starr said, 'That's a damn good *western*.' I almost hit him right in the face. To me, it was a symphony, a marvelous piece of work that used the motion picture camera in the best way that I'd ever seen it done. It used the medium so perfectly that it couldn't ever have been that good in any other medium."

From the trade papers to the newspapers in America and Europe, the film was hailed as an instant classic, especially the eight-minute, forty-eight-second chase. Certainly, it made John Wayne a major star, and from the stunning entrance given the young actor, the camera rapidly dollying into a tight close-up as Wayne flourishes his rifle, that was obviously Ford's intention.

There are those who dislike *The Informer*, *Stagecoach*, and *The Long Voyage Home* because they dislike the writing of Dudley Nichols. Certainly, Nichols's and Ford's collaborations are more consciously artistic than the director's work with other writers. It seems obvious that Ford regarded Nichols as someone who could enable him to develop his talents in specific directions that were very desirable to Ford, less desirable to posterity.

This position has been eloquently summarized by Richard Corliss, who wrote that, "Nichols' world is a rigorously schematized place where Good and Evil are rarely allowed to interact within one person, and where Big Brother Dudley is forever whispering slogans of moral uplift into the ears of the mass audience he sought to liberalize but ended up insulting."

Nichols *was* fond of using people as symbols, the 1930s agit-prop equivalent of High Concept, and the film's rhythm *is* rigid—scenes of action followed by scenes of character, and so forth. Everything comes together very neatly—too neatly, for an artist of ambiguity like Ford. *The Informer* ripened elements of Ford's style that, in retrospect, are far from his most enduring contributions.

But these films arrived when the artistic credentials of American films were far from firmly established, and self-conscious style and messages delighted the film art evangelists. Conversely, it was their lack of self-consciousness that caused the unpretentiousness of many of Ford's later films, especially the Westerns, to be consistently undervalued at the time they were made.

Nichols and Ford juggle a lot of characters and a fair amount of plot, but everything is written and played with delicacy and truth. Ford has less time for the photographic beauty that would come to dominate his work; the camerawork is more functional than pyrotechnic, except for the rapid track-in to John Wayne, Ford's proudly emphatic announcement of a star being born.

There are echoes of Ford's past here—the stagecoach goes through the Newhall cut that he used in *Straight Shooting*, and the gun at the head of Louise Platt just before the cavalry rides to the rescue copies a shot from Griffith's *The Battle of Elderbush Gulch*. It's also a covert New Deal movie, with constant appeals to collective wisdom—and with a banker as the heavy.

Perhaps the crux of the matter is the one specified by Randy Roberts and James Olsen, in their biography of John Wayne. "*Stagecoach* is at its core a B Western—the best B Western in movie history, but a B Western all the same." That is to say, there's a whore with a heart of gold, a good bad man, the drunken doctor quoting Shakespeare, a crooked banker, a courtly Southern gentleman.

But B Westerns didn't look like *Stagecoach*, B Westerns didn't have casts like *Stagecoach*, and B Westerns didn't have the distinctly egalitarian message of *Stagecoach*—that it is society's outcasts who do the hard work of American civilization. And B Westerns didn't have *Stagecoach*'s audacious premise. As Garry Wills points out, the film really belongs to the *Ship of Fools* genre, in which a group of isolated strangers are forced into confrontation and are therefore altered, or at least exposed. That's why the casting of a major star like Gary Cooper would have altered the chemistry toward a star vehicle and away from the ensemble piece Ford was determined to make.

Stagecoach remains the paradigmatic Western. As André Bazin wrote of the film, "Art has found its perfect balance, its ideal form of expression." Bazin found the film the ideal fusion of form and content, that, like a wheel, "remains in equilibrium on its axis in any position."

Ford would make deeper films than *Stagecoach*, and he would make more virtuosic films than *Stagecoach*, but he would never again make one so nearly perfect, more filled with an easeful grace, with perfectly inflected camera and characters. It's a film as pure and refreshing as deep breaths of mountain air. It's his *City Lights*, his *Rules of the Game*, but unlike those pictures, which don't fall into any neat genre classification, the characters and settings of *Stagecoach* could be all too easily replicated by other, less expert hands.

With *Stagecoach*, Ford found the subject that meshed perfectly with his calm style. Ford had been experimenting with two- and three-plane composition for some time, often holding sharp focus throughout, and his collaboration with Gregg Toland on *The Long Voyage Home* and *The Grapes of Wrath* would extend the style still further. But *Stagecoach* was a more integrated example—one of the reasons Orson Welles looked so intensively at the film before embarking on *Citizen Kane*.

It was a style particularly suited both to Ford's aesthetic and emotional sensibilities—meditative compositions in depth, usually medium shots, with the characters reacting to each other within the shot. It gave the actors more to work with, and gave the studio less. From this point, Ford's camera would be predominantly still, so that when he did move it—the sudden, quick pan to the Indians on the cliff, the furious tracking shots during the attack—the simple fact of the movement would add excitement to the scene.

Even the music score, a compendium of traditional folk tunes, would prove emblematic. It didn't matter whether the movie took place in Wales, Ireland, or Oklahoma, henceforward the music would be organized around folk tunes. Ford would tell his friends that he'd rather listen to good music than bad dialogue, but the gambit was about more than personal preference; the music evoked a sense of the past, of tradition.

The picture was an immediate success with critics. *Variety* called it "[a] sweeping and powerful drama of the American frontier." The *New York Daily News* said that "every part is admirably acted. . . . John Wayne is so good in the role of the outlaw that one wonders why he had to wait all this time since *The Big Trail* for such another opportunity." Even the *Daily Worker* was impressed, saying that "You'll comb the Hollywood hills many a day to find a more brilliant team than Walter Wanger and John Ford. . . . Ford has done wonders with the material in the script."

Yet *Stagecoach* ended up as a hit, not a smash. It grossed $1.1 million, for a net profit of nearly $300,000. Since Ford had taken 20 percent of the profits in order to keep the budget modest, by 1949 he had collected more than $100,000 on top of his $50,000 salary. Still, given the reviews, the industry seemed to feel that the film had fallen short commercially. *Variety* noted that "*Stagecoach* at the boxoffice has not sustained the enthusiastic reviews it received from the press. Lack of strong names in the cast and a trite title are the reasons given for the *Stagecoach* fade."

Stagecoach added yet another component to Ford's expanding extended family—the Navajos of Monument Valley. Now, he would always have

Indians that he knew and trusted to play parts in his Westerns. The qualifications were simple—the Indian had to ride well, and, most importantly, he had to have what Ford called "a great face."

Two of the regulars were the Stanley boys, John and Jack. Of these,
Ford's favorite was John; he could speak English well and had a good
working relationship with white men. It was Jack who gave Ford the
name *Natani Nez*—"Tall Leader." With the Stanley boys at the core,
Ford had about fifty Navajos that played all the Indians in his pictures,
whether they were supposed to be Navajos, Comanches, or Mescaleros.

For Ford, the Navajo in Monument Valley were friends. After the
location work for *She Wore a Yellow Ribbon* was completed in late 1948,
the Valley was paralyzed by a snowfall that the Indians called "two men
deep."

Ford made some calls and military planes dropped food to the
stranded Indians in what came to be called Operation Haylift. "Thanks
to Mr. Ford and the payroll he brought into the Valley, there was food in
the hogans," said Dolly Stanley Roberson, Jack Stanley's niece.

Stagecoach changed everything for its star. Wayne chose to develop a
specific image, a screen personality that overlapped his off-screen
personality but not as much as, say, George O'Brien's or Harry Carey's
overlapped theirs. "He would analyze every script from the point of view
of 'Is this what my audience wants to see me in?' " said his son Michael.
"He would never trick the audience and deviate from playing a man with
a code. Surprise, yes; trick, no."

As for John Ford, no more would he direct make-do projects—*The
Whole Town's Talking, Submarine Patrol*—which he could only make as "a
job of work." He chose now to unleash a fully developed directorial personality: picturesque, ample, meditative, self-assured films of history and
longing composed with what John Wayne would call Ford's "simplicity of
delivery." His characters would go about their business with a mournful
weight, befitting the grandeur of the stage on which they were playing.

For Ford, America and democracy grew out of the encounter between
wilderness and civilization, and Monument Valley would be the meeting
ground for the palpable and the possible. The complexity of the pictures
he was about to make meant that John Ford's themes were, at long last,
the full equal of his images.

CHAPTER TWELVE

Always setting a relentless pace from film to film, Ford was now setting a relentless pace from studio to studio. Fox, RKO, and Wanger were all competing for his services, but, because of their ten-picture contract, Zanuck and Fox had favored-nation status.

When Ford wasn't directing, he was scouting projects, as in a memo that raved about Jean Renoir's *Grand Illusion*, which he called "one of the best things I have ever seen." He wanted to direct an American remake that would have changed the nationalities of the prisoners from French to English. Victor McLaglen, he suggested, could play the Jean Gabin part, J. Edward Bromberg the Jewish part, and "possibly Romero or Niven playing the aristocrat."

Zanuck saw the picture the very next day. He thought it was "one of the most magnificent pictures of its type that I have ever seen," but he also wisely thought a remake of another director's great film was a fool's errand. "I think it would be a criminal injustice to attempt to remake the picture in English," he wrote Ford. "The most wonderful thing about the picture is the fine background, the authentic atmosphere, and the foreign characters, who actually speak in the language of their nationality. Once you take this away, I believe you have lost 50% of the value of the picture. . . . I . . . feel that we could never get anywhere near this picture."

Four days later, Ford wrote a letter to an executive at Fox, taking exception to comments made by the publicity department that the press shouldn't judge Nancy Kelly by her performance in (Ford's) *Submarine Patrol*, but wait until they could see her in (Henry King's) *Jesse James*. The comments found their way into print, and Ford, always touchy about criticism, reacted as might have been expected:

"Naturally, this coming out in print is an adverse criticism from my own studio of my direction. So I am taking this means of conveying to you, Bill, that I presume I am no longer wanted at 20th Century Fox to direct pictures, especially pictures with women. I am terribly sorry that the studio should have to take this means of protecting their stars, but perhaps they know best. Naturally this affair coming out in print has caused me much humiliation. . . . In the future if you have a picture without women please think of me."

After the appropriate soothing of his ruffled feathers, he went back to preparing "two swell pictures" for Darryl Zanuck.

Young Mr. Lincoln had been in the works as far back as 1935, when Howard Estabrook prepared a treatment. Zanuck decided to let the project lie fallow for a while; when it was picked up in 1938, Lamar Trotti was the writer, and he streamlined the film's first half into a serene progression that emphasized character and amplified the courtroom drama by including details from a trial Trotti had covered as a journalist.

What never changed was the casting, for as far back as the Estabrook treatment, Henry Fonda, just arrived on the Fox lot, had been penciled in for the part of Abraham Lincoln. As of January 1939, with *Stagecoach* just completed, Ford was trying to dodge Lincoln: "Ford does not want to do Lincoln film and is looking for another director," reported William Goetz to Sol Wurtzel. "DFZ has not decided what Ford is to do next but will know in a week." A week later, Ford had changed his mind—or had had it changed for him—and began preparing the picture.

Ford and Zanuck settled on a light makeup for Fonda, mostly around the nose, that suggested Lincoln more than it replicated him. Although Ford never explicitly required his actors to do research when playing historical characters, it was clearly expected. Milburn Stone was playing Stephen Douglas, and one day Ford suddenly appeared and asked him, "Who held Lincoln's hat when he was inaugurated?"

"Stephen A. Douglas," answered Stone. Ford nodded and walked away, but was soon back. "Who was the first man President Lincoln sent for when Fort Sumter was fired on?"

"Stephen A. Douglas," answered Stone.

It is New Salem, Illinois, in 1832, and Abraham Lincoln, aged twenty-three, is running for Congress. Ford emphasizes the homey details that believably create an image of a great man in chrysalis form—Lincoln trades a roll of flannel fabric for a barrel of books; when he gives a campaign speech, he's unsure about what to do with his hands.

Abe goes to visit Ann Rutledge's grave, bringing along some flowers and some questions about his future. He makes up his mind by dropping a stick; if it falls toward him, he'll stay where he is; if it falls toward Ann, he'll leave town and practice law. The stick falls toward the woman he loved.

Lincoln's future derives from his past—from his memory of Rutledge. In Ford's work, the dead are palpable influences, if only because their hopes and dreams must be carried forward by the living. Many writers have opted for a simplistic view of Ford, noting how his work progressed from optimism toward disillusion as the director aged. But Ford always qualified the optimism in even his early work with a sense of loss. In any case, Ford's celebrations of community and the future are always set in the past, never the present. The greater the optimism, the further in the past the story. Filmmaking, not alcohol, was Ford's primary narcotic, and nostalgia his primary emotion.

Five years after leaving New Salem, Lincoln is practicing law, his long legs up on the table, a genial man with good humor and an inherent prairie integrity. Ford's Lincoln is never in a hurry but always contrives to win, whether it's a rail-splitting contest, a tug-of-war, or a murder case. The murder case gives the film its only narrative hook, and, as always, Ford tends to overplay the rhetoric and reactions of courtroom drama.

Nevertheless, there is something that feels right about this Lincoln; he imposes his will without seeming to, has a gift for the jugular as well as for leisure. The influence of Carl Sandburg's biography is felt in Lincoln's habit of gazing out over the landscape and sensing the tug of a vague, mystical call, but he's no backwoods saint—he takes money for defending his client even though the family is poor. This is a Lincoln who lives in the real world—even lawyers have to eat.

Ford and Henry Fonda had been off-screen friends for several years, but now extended that friendship into their work. They would make three classic pictures back to back. At this point, Fonda's career had encompassed more than a dozen pictures, but none of the people he had worked with were anything remotely like Ford. "He cast actors if they were good [card] players," said Fonda with some amazement.

Ford would use Fonda in a very different way than he would John Wayne. Wayne's characters were earthy and warm, brawlers by temperament, capable of love and rage. Fonda's characters burned with a cold fire—they displayed strength, but a removed, abstracted, rather asexual strength, tempered by the actor's instinctive austerity.

For their next collaboration, Ford and Fonda moved into *Drums Along the Mohawk*, an adaptation of the best-selling historical novel by Walter Edmunds. The film had gone through various typewriters on the way to a final shooting script, including those of Bess Meredyth, Sonya Levien, and even William Faulkner. All the early scripts are a bit leisurely, and Faulkner's treatment is the furthest removed from the final product.

By early December 1938, Zanuck realized where he had gone wrong with the script. "Made an error in endeavoring to become an epic . . . we must see it over the shoulder of our two characters . . . we must not lose sight of that for one second." In adapting the novel, Zanuck decided to emulate the method of *The Good Earth*, where "they discarded chapter after chapter and concentrated on the personal story."

The fine-tuning of the script went on for four more months; Zanuck's notes on a later draft show a lessening of patience: "Mr. Z could not be emphatic enough in bringing home that we are in the business to GIVE A SHOW—that our first job is to MAKE ENTERTAINMENT. . . . Mr. Z does not like montages and they should be dropped . . . it will be far more exciting [if] the run at the climax [is] made by one person rather than two." The story was largely structured by Zanuck, with Ford coming on to polish the final draft and make various dramatic and character adjustments.

That contribution was generally all-important. For instance, *The Informer* is a relatively brief (ninety-one minutes) film whose script runs a lengthy 138 pages, due mostly to Dudley Nichols's purple scene-setting.* Ford contrived moments of emphasis and inflection—Gypo spreading his arms in a pose of crucifixion as Frankie's mother forgives him.

In *Stagecoach*, his touches were even sharper, and more in character. After the drunken Doc Boone coerces Luke Plummer into giving him his shotgun before going out for the gunfight with the Ringo Kid, Nichols's line was "Gimme a drink." Ford changed it to the sharper, funnier, "Don't ever let me do that again." He also added Doc's line in the final scene: "They'll be saved the blessings of civilization."

Ringo's dive into the ground-level camera as he fires his rifle is a Ford addition, as is Luke Plummer walking into the saloon after the fight, then dropping dead. Ford is not just composing shots, he's shaping the characters, sharpening them with his native picture-sense.

And sometimes he's smart enough to cut material that's clearly extraneous, as in *Young Mr. Lincoln*, whose script ends with superfluous dialogue from onlookers gazing at Lincoln on the top of the hill amidst the lowering clouds, followed by a dreadful scene of Lincoln conversing with a disembodied voice of destiny who lays out his future for him.

Ford went to Hawaii for a short vacation after finishing *Young Mr. Lincoln*, and returned in mid-June 1939 to begin *Drums Along the Mohawk*. When the company arrived on location in Utah's Wasatch

---

*"We see him come out of the fog like some strange fish out of a mysterious ocean of mist. . . ."

Mountains, the weather refused to cooperate; Frank Baker remembered six consecutive days of rain beginning the day he arrived, with Ford refusing to speak to him for weeks as punishment. Ford named Henry Fonda "Director in Charge of Entertainment," and Fonda organized a series of songs in three-part harmony around the campfire at night. Every evening at 9:30, a bugler would walk into the woods and blow a quiet taps.

A new addition to the crew was propman Joe Behm, who had to undergo the usual hazing. Behm met with Ford to show him some of his designs for props, and Ford barked, "What do you want me to do? Prop the show for you?" Behm made some conciliatory noises, and Ford responded by telling him that his work showed imagination and that he, Ford, would okay everything the propman wanted to do, sight unseen.

Once they got to the location, Ford's first request of Behm was that he get a baby grand piano for the recreation tent. Behm was stunned; if Ford had told him this in Hollywood, they could have just loaded a piano onto the trucks bringing the rest of the equipment, but where was he supposed to get a baby grand in southern Utah?

It was, of course, a test, which Behm passed splendidly. He made a trip down a long, winding road to Cedar City and went door to door until he found a resident willing to rent their piano to the film company.

Ford's next request was for a Model T for a gag shot that, he hoped, would elevate Darryl Zanuck out of his chair in the screening room. Behm found the car, Ford got his shot, and Zanuck was suitably amused. Unfortunately, the film's production manager was not. One day at lunch, he yelled at Behm for unauthorized expenditures for pianos and cars, then ordered the piano sent back to Cedar City.

When Ford found out that the piano had been sent back, he asked why, then immediately sent for the production manager. "This is your company, you're the boss, no one countermands your orders," Ford began. "You've questioned my integrity, you sent the piano back, you criticized Mr. Behm for following my orders . . ."

"But Skipper," said the hapless production manager.

"Don't Skipper me. I'm Mr. Ford to you. I want to clarify this situation; I'm running the company. When I give an order it's followed. . . . Bring back that piano—now!"

The production manager told Behm to get the piano, but was promptly interrupted by Ford. "I don't think you heard me straight. *You* bring the piano. Mr. Behm is through for the day. And another thing: you're barred from my set." Loyalty had been rewarded, arrogance punished, and a clear line of authority established—the actors didn't make the picture, nor did the producer, and especially not the production office. Ford made the picture.

Drums Along the Mohawk would be Ford's first experience with Technicolor. The film benefited from the addition, but he would always remain somewhat distrustful of color. "It's much easier than black and white for a cameraman," he would say. "It's a cinch to work in, if you've got any eye at all for color or composition. But black and white is pretty tough—you've got to know your job and be very careful to lay your shadows properly and get the perspective right. . . . There are certain pictures, like *The Quiet Man*, that call for color—not a blatant kind—but a soft, misty color. For a good dramatic story, though, I much prefer to work in black and white; you'll probably say I'm old-fashioned, but black and white is real photography."

Drums Along the Mohawk is Ford's sole excursion into the sadly under-dramatized subject of the Revolutionary War, and if Claudette Colbert's innate stylishness feels too artificial for a Ford film, it's hard to criticize it otherwise. The film does exactly what it sets out to do, does it with humor, emotion, and theatrical dash. John Carradine's villain is nothing if not picturesque in a black cloak and eyepatch, and there is the glorious Edna May Oliver, snapping off her lines ("I've got a long face and I poke it where I please"), a blustering, salt-of-the-earth hardcase with a heart of gold—in essence, the Victor McLaglen part. Ford steals a lovely shot from King Vidor's *The Big Parade*, as Claudette Colbert falls to her knees in supplication as her man goes off to war, just as Renee Adoree did with John Gilbert.

The extensive location work gives the film an airy, relaxed feel, meshing well with the vigorous action footage and making *Drums Along the Mohawk* a fine example of Ford the professional filmmaker.

In early 1938, John Steinbeck and photographer Horace Bristol toured the migrant camps of California, gathering material for a *Life* magazine feature. But Steinbeck wasn't satisfied by the magazine story, and quickly wrote *The Grapes of Wrath*, fueled by his prolific notes and considerable outrage. The novel was published in 1939 and quickly became a sensation. Zanuck purchased the movie rights and assigned the script to Nunnally Johnson.

Johnson was intimidated by the quality of Steinbeck's book, and told his girlfriend Dorris Bowdon that he felt it had a "biblical" quality. Unusual for any period of Hollywood, the first draft was more or less the only draft. Zanuck's script conference notes for Johnson's draft of July 13, 1939, are marginal but well taken: "Suggest that we see Tom walk into the first scene. . . . We are going to drop the element of Uncle John's sin . . . clarify farewell scene—don't give the impression that Tom is running away—he is making a sacrifice." (The dialogue is the same in the film as in Johnson's script; the emphasis was in the acting and direction.)

Zanuck told Johnson that he felt he had not been harsh enough in depicting the difficult, dispiriting conditions of the Okies. Zanuck outlined a new sequence that he felt would communicate what he wanted:

"Their money practically gone—gas low—and the terrible realization that what they were told [about there being no jobs] is true. . . .

"We come in on them driving into town and asking somebody where they should go about finding work—maybe showing the fellow the handbill. The man just looks at them and laughs. Somebody else comes along and they ask him. We see the fellow look at the car and down on the license plate. 'Oh—Oklahoma. There's a camp on the edge of town—maybe somebody there will tell you.'

"Their hopefulness and terrible disillusionment. They drive into the Hooverville camp and their hearts drop at the terrible sights. The futility of what has occurred. They just look at each other as the stark truth dawns on them. 'Don't seem very encouragin', does it?' . . . Ma snaps them out of it—they'd better pitch the tent, etc."

It was this latter scene that Ford would stage with a slowly advancing camera shooting through the windshield of the Joads' battered truck, the people of the camp warily, wearily shifting out of the way as they eye the new arrivals, whose presence will mean even less food for the rest of them.

When Zanuck and Johnson were in agreement, the producer issued strict instructions to the writer: "I want complete secrecy in reference to *The Grapes of Wrath*. . . . I want you to make only three copies—one for yourself and two for me. A number of more or less unfriendly newspapermen are waiting to grab our first script to actually find out what we have done with this great book." Johnson sent Steinbeck a copy of the script along with an apology, explaining that he felt it necessary to invent a scene that wasn't in the novel—the one in the roadside restaurant, where Pa Joad and the children try to buy a nickel's worth of bread. Johnson was proud of the scene, but wasn't sure about Steinbeck's reaction.

As it happened, Steinbeck loved the scene and the script; when he later sold Fox the rights to his propaganda novel *The Moon Is Down*, he asked if Johnson could do the adaptation. After Johnson was assigned the job, Steinbeck sent him a telegram: "Tamper with it."

Nunnally Johnson's script was a gem of compression; he made changes, but they largely centered on reordering scenes and transposing dialogue from one character to another.

Although later memoirs would claim that the part of Tom Joad was earmarked for Tyrone Power, early casting notes from mid-1939, when the script was completed, mention only Henry Fonda for the part. Other parts were up for grabs: Walter Brennan or James Barton for Pa, Beulah Bondi for Ma, John Carradine for Casey, Jimmy Stewart for Al. Ford's main contribution to the casting process seems to have been Jane Darwell. Steinbeck had written Ma as a tough old bird, and the proposed casting of Beulah Bondi would have been true to the novel, but Ford wanted something more expansive, more of an earth-mother, and he got it.

There is a notation on the shooting script preserved in the Fox studio files at the University of Southern California: "Clarence Brown?" Clearly, Ford was not necessarily Zanuck's first choice, at least not if the prestigious MGM director could be loaned out to Fox, as he had been for *The Rains Came.*

Zanuck made his decision in mid-July 1939, while Jack was still on location with *Drums Along the Mohawk.* "If I were assured of a month off, I would leap at the chance of doing 'Wrath,' " replied Ford, but he was worried about his current picture, and couldn't quite bring himself to commit to another right away. "Your letters and wires about tempo frighten me," Ford wrote Zanuck. "Both the script and the story [of *Drums Along the Mohawk*] call for a placid, pastoral, simple movement which suddenly breaks into quick, heavy, dramatic overtones. All this requires care." Ford closed by suggesting that they wait until he returned from location, look at the footage and see what adjustments and added scenes might be necessary before he seriously contemplated *The Grapes of Wrath.*

The more Ford thought about it, the better he liked it. "I'd read the book—it was a good story—and Darryl Zanuck had a good script on it. The whole thing appealed to me—being about simple people—and the story was similar to the famine in Ireland, when they threw the people off the land and left them wandering on the roads to starve."

Once he'd agreed to direct, Ford was not left alone to devise an approach to the film, mostly because there wasn't much time. Ford finished *Drums Along the Mohawk* on September 5, 1939, and had only four weeks before the beginning of production on *The Grapes of Wrath.* Fox provided him, Gregg Toland, and art directors Richard Day and Mark Lee Kirk a vast array of research photographs and documents separated into files labeled, variously, "Soil Erosion," "Dust Storms in Action," "Condition of Land," "Cars on Highway," "Transients in General," "Dance," "Migrants at State Line," "Govt. Camp," "Squatters Camp," "Eating Places." Most of the photos, including the brutal, heartbreaking work of Dorothea Lange, derived from the Farm Security Administration.

Amongst the material were written vignettes, snippets of reportage that could have come directly from Steinbeck's great novel: "All a transient hears is 'No work. No relief. Keep Moving.' " Or this, from a Dust Bowl refugee: "We was starved out and we live on perhaps. We could maybe find a little work if we could afford to roll."

Ford's approach to the story was to follow his natural bent and subtly de-politicize it through a different emphasis. "I was only interested in the Joad family as characters. I was sympathetic to people like the Joads, and contributed a lot of money to them, but I was not interested in *Grapes* as a social study."

Production began October 4, 1939. Working efficiently, Ford and the great cameraman Gregg Toland fell into a perfect rhythm; mornings were taken up with long and medium shots, to get the delicate slanting light. Midday was reserved for close-ups, and then late in the afternoon it was back to long and medium shots. There was no makeup on the actors, no diffusion on the camera. Toland was shooting the picture sharp, hard, and cold.

Ford's main source of irritation on *The Grapes of Wrath* seems to have been John Carradine. "[Ford] didn't like John very much," remembered Dorris Bowdon, who was playing Rosasharn, "because John was one person that was totally oblivious to Ford's needling. He would treat it with patronizing contempt. He was very skillful at overreaching Ford. John Carradine had such ego, he was a marvel. He thought of himself as Barrymore, and he was impervious to anything Ford did to him. Ford used to make him behave in silly, pretentious ways, but if Carradine didn't like it, he would do something else during the scene, or overdo it in rehearsal, so it was ridiculous, and even Ford would laugh."

Carradine's take on all this was a principled resistance to Ford's vision of Casey as a grotesque. "No matter what part Ford hired me for, he'd always want me to slobber, drool, or squint. I used to fight him, not verbally, because you didn't do that with Ford, but just go ahead and do it my way."

Carradine had devised a piece of business for Casey, but he knew he couldn't suggest it to Ford. He therefore started a conversation with Henry Fonda. "It was the scene where Casey's talking about another preacher, and to illustrate a point, I wanted him to jump over a fence.

"Ford comes over, just like I knew he would. 'What was that?'

" 'Oh, nothing, just an actor's pipe dream.'

" 'What was it?'

"So I told him while he was chewing on his handkerchief. And he said, 'Oh, all right, go on, do it.' But I had to make *him* ask *me*. . . . He was an Irishman through and through."

"I don't think Ford ever understood my father," theorized David Carradine. "Ford was such an ambivalent guy. Fiercely loyal, and also cutthroat. Mean, especially to people he loved. My father played Casey's death scene, and says, 'You guys don't know what you're doing,' which is Steinbeck's way of saying, 'Father, forgive them . . .' After it was over, Ford told my Dad, 'John, that was a really great scene.' And Dad said, 'If I'd done what you'd told me to do I couldn't have played that scene at all.' They were always back and forth at each other. They were both very hidebound people, very stubborn, very Irish. Full of mysticism, poetry, temper, and a sense of impending doom. My father loved him, in a shanty-Irish sort of way."

Ford was always directing Carradine to "Get down on your haunches. Now spread your arms like a spider." Bowdon thought Ford was enjoying making Carradine look grotesque, but the effect isn't silly, it's startling, fascinating; Casey is a man in his own space, in his own world, living by his own rules, unconcerned about what others think. His sprawling, relaxed physicality is the yin to Tom Joad's tightly coiled yang.

Ford moved calmly but deliberately through the film, rehearsing shots three and four times before he rolled the camera. He was at the absolute top of his game, creating indelible moments, as when Jane Darwell's Ma looks over her meager belongings as they leave their house, then holds up a pair of earrings to see how they look reflected in a dirty window. It's a perfect example of Ford's refusal to go outside the immediate dramatic context for a symbol or metaphor, a rigor that gives his films a poetic meshing of meaning and moment unusual even for a lyric artist.

Eddie Quillan, playing Rosasharn's hapless husband, remembered an unaccustomed specificity to Ford's directions, an attention that was total. At one point, Ford directed him to "Get your voice a little on the Southern." Then, after another rehearsal, "Make it stronger." For a reaction shot of a group of men, Ford told them, "I want everyone's eyes forward." But Quillan had shifted his eyes downward because it struck him that the line he was reacting to would embarrass his character.

"Cut," said Ford. "I said everybody's eyes straight ahead."

Detail was everything. During the scene where the Joads pull into the camp and settle down to eat while hungry children watch, Ford caught Frank Darien, who was playing Unc, emoting. "You working with Theresa Helburn [the head of the very upscale Theater Guild] last night?" he snarled. "Had Theresa Helburn over at your house last night, huh? Working on the scene, huh?"

"He shamed this poor sonofabitch," said Henry Fonda, "so that when he did it again there was no emotion, he was drained, which was what Ford wanted, of course."

If Carradine's obliviousness was a burr under Ford's saddle, then Dorris Bowdon was his object of displeasure. Although she had worked for Ford on both *Young Mr. Lincoln* and *Drums Along the Mohawk*, when Ford told her she reminded him of his daughter, now he began to turn on her, possibly because Bowdon committed the offense of telling Ford that Zanuck was giving her the plumb part of Rosasharn. So much for the director's prerogative.

There had been some discussion about Nunnally Johnson producing the film himself, but the writer was unhappy about his growing relationship with Bowdon, unhappy about the prospect of butting heads again with Ford. Johnson bailed out, telling Zanuck that he was going to New York to work on a play with Charles MacArthur. "Nunnally was a two-time loser at marriage, and he walked out on the film and he walked out on me," was the way Bowdon remembered it. "I was very pained and upset, and John was an extremely perceptive man. He knew that Nunnally was not producing anymore, and I guess he felt safe in humiliating me."

Bowdon could do no right. If she was on the set, Ford would remonstrate with her: "Your hair is sloppy. Why don't you get it checked before you come on and hold us up." If she was off the set getting her hair checked, Ford would say, "Well, let's everybody wait it out. Miss Bowdon is holding us up at $15,000 a day." Bowdon wasn't his only target; also coming in for abuse was O. Z. Whitehead. Bowdon and Whitehead were always being criticized for picayune things, but Bowdon noticed that "the devil in him" made Ford select times when there were a lot of people on the set. "Maybe he wanted an audience, or maybe he resented having to work with large crowds, but it always happened when a lot of people were around."

Henry Fonda's concentration on his part was so complete that he could ad-lib in character. During the dance scene in the government camp sequence, Ford told Fonda to tease Rosasharn a bit before he read his lines to Ma. "Now remember," Ford told Bowdon, "you're a pregnant girl who's a little self-conscious about it, so you work out some business with the shawl and stay close to Ma, because a girl in your condition is not going to walk freely among the fellows."

"Jane Darwell and I had become friends," remembered Bowdon. "She was so warm and helpful to a young actress. She would tell me things, and warn me about things with John. She knew his temperament. I loved her very much. She turned to me before the scene and said, 'I dread this scene. I'm such a fat old lady and I have to dance and say lines at the same time and I know I'm going to screw it up.' "

Darwell and Bowdon were sitting on a bench by the dance floor; Fonda walked up behind them and touched Rosasharn on the shoulder, then stuck his head through on the opposite side. "It was building the scene to show a good family relationship," remembered Bowdon, "and a family that didn't know how to express affection with tactile gestures. . . . It heightened the scene enormously."

Fonda and Darwell did their lines, then moved out onto the dance floor, where Darwell did everything perfectly. When Ford yelled "Cut," Darwell smiled and rolled her eyes in pleasure and a delighted Bowdon applauded her friend. Ford promptly exploded, yelling out "Who did that?" Then, using the set's public address system, he excoriated Bowdon in front of the entire cast and crew. "You amateur! You dumb, stupid, green amateur. Don't you know how to behave as a professional? Don't you know you never clap on a set?"

"He went on and on, saying the most painful, degrading things," said Bowdon. She *was* little more than an amateur, and one, moreover, who was already in an emotional state because of the situation with Nunnally Johnson. Ford angrily called a wrap for the day, and Bowdon went to her dressing room, closed the door, and dissolved into tears of humiliation and rage.

It was a Friday, and Bowdon stewed over the weekend, "crying my heart out," as she put it, over her director's displeasure, over her lover's inability to commit, over her own inadequacy. On Monday, Bowdon's face clearly showed how difficult her weekend had been. Ford came up to her and took her by the shoulders.

"You've been crying," he said.

"Thanks to you."

"I'm going to make you smile."

"I don't think anything you could say would make me smile. Nothing you could say would amuse me."

Ford gazed at her for a moment, then said one word: "Fornication!" Bowdon broke up and the two walked back to the set and were friendly from then on, although, remembered Bowdon, "I was glad I never had to work with him again."

Saying he was sorry without saying he was sorry was a particularly Fordian trait. Yet, for Bowdon's one big scene, Ford could easily slip into the part of father confessor. Rosasharn's baby had just been born, and her husband had left. The day before the scene was to be shot, Bowdon developed a sore on her face. She asked Ford not to shoot her close up until the sore disappeared. He told her to take her place on the set, he'd light it and see what it looked like.

Bowdon and Jane Darwell took their places, Ford came over to the young actress, sat down just out of camera range, reached out and took her hand. "Poor Rosasharn," he murmured. "She has so much to deal with. He's just left you. He walked out. It was too much for him. He couldn't face not being able to feed you, and having a baby. You're alone now, and although you've got Ma and Tom and Pa, Grandma's gone, but you know that you may not be able to feed your baby . . ."

As Ford talked, Bowdon receded into her character. "You're lost, you're lost. You don't know this land. Ma may not be able to hold on." And then he said, "This is for the long shot. Now you read those lines to me." Bowdon's face reflected the moment; her tears were real. She spoke her lines, Darwell spoke hers, Ford said "Cut." It was the only take he made. Faced with an inexperienced, shaky actress, he had reverted to the directorial technique of the silent days, talking the actor into the emotional moment.

"John had everything he wanted," said Bowdon. "The pain in my face, the sore on my face, the misery of my position. And he was perceptive enough to make use of my wanting to look better than I did. He was a superb director. I worked for everybody at Fox, either when I was in the stock company or when I was featured, and I never saw another director work in a way that was as skilled."

Did Bowdon believe that Ford's sadistic side was displayed because of professional necessity or because of something inside him?

"It was because he was an SOB. He was a demonical man. Part of his mercurial personality was to do something he knew was mean or mischievous and then try to justify it. Jed Harris liked to break a person down, or make them uncertain, to control them, and I think Ford had some of that. I believe the real reason he picked on me was that he disliked the man I was going with. Nunnally and he had feuded on *The Prisoner of Shark Island*. Nunnally disliked him, and I think that was one of the reasons he turned on me after *Young Mr. Lincoln*." Dorris Bowdon and Nunnally Johnson married soon after *The Grapes of Wrath* and stayed married until Johnson's death in 1977.

Ford was at his best, prodding those who needed prodding, leaving Fonda alone because the actor—proud, stubborn, slightly chilly—felt Tom Joad without prompting from a director. Fonda's Tom Joad combines the Midwestern sincerity of his Lincoln with an ex-con's stone-cold paranoia. He's no victim, is, in fact, perfectly capable of making trouble. Fonda's lean equalizer is the reason the film never subsides into a morass of little-people sentimentality, the reason it still speaks with a surprising immediacy.

Dorris Bowdon remembered Ford's care with the point-of-view shot of the Joads' truck pulling into Hooverville, with the extras glaring at the truck/camera as it forces them to the side of the road. "Every one of those extras had been carefully directed," remembered Bowdon. " 'You have arrived here from a land that has blown away from you. You've got to show you're hungry, you're confused, you're ignorant . . .' "

The script was altered only in minor ways, but it's hard not to regret the omission of a speech Nunnally Johnson dropped into the scene between Tom and other migrants laying pipe. Tom asks, "What is these reds?" and one of the other migrants responds:

"Well, I tell you. They was a fella up the country named King—got about 30,000 acres an' a cannery an' a winery—an' he's all the time talkin' about reds. Drivin' the country to ruin, he says. Got to get rid of 'em, he says. Well, they was a young fella jus' come out an' he was listenin' one day. He kinda scratched his head an' he says, 'Mr. King, what is these reds you all a time talkin' about?' Well, sir, Mr. King says, 'Young man, a red is any fella that wants thirty cents an hour when I'm payin' twenty-five.' "

For the all-important final scene between Tom and Ma Joad, Ford let the tension build. "Ford didn't even watch the rehearsal," remembered Henry Fonda. "Both Jane Darwell . . . and I knew the scene was coming up on this particular day; it was on the schedule. We knew that this was the key scene in the picture for both of us. It was an emotional scene and we were looking forward to doing it. We each knew our lines and we thought they were incredibly fine, we were eager to get on with it. . . .

"I had to light a match, and then the cameraman, Gregg Toland, rigged a light in the palm of my hand with wires going up my arm. The light, which was supposed to be the glow from the match, had to light Ma's face just right. It took an hour and a half to set up that piece of business.

"Then I tapped her and she opened her eyes and she went outside with me. We walked around the tent and up to the bench that was at the foot of the dance floor. Ford wouldn't let us get into the dialogue. By the time he was ready Jane Darwell and I were like racehorses that wanted to go. . . .

"Then with Ford's intuitive instinct, he knew when we were built up. We'd never done it out loud, but Ford called for action, the cameras rolled, and he had it in a single take. After we finished the scene, Pappy didn't say a word. He just stood up and walked away. He got what he wanted. We all did."

Fonda's haunted face, and Ford's ability to hit a peak moment without seeming to strain for it conspired to create one of the screen's indelible scenes. "I'll be all around in the dark," says Tom Joad. "I'll be everywhere. Wherever you can look—wherever there's a fight, so hungry people can eat, I'll be there. Whenever there's a cop beating up a guy—I'll be there. I'll be there in the way guys yell when they're mad. I'll be there in the way kids laugh when they're hungry, and they know supper's ready, and when people are eatin' the stuff they raised, and livin' in the houses they built—I'll be there too."

After forty-three days of principal photography, Ford wrapped *The Grapes of Wrath* in mid-December. Although Ford would claim that he ended the film with Henry Fonda going over the hill, and that Zanuck added the last scene with Jane Darwell and Russell Simpson, Johnson's script dated July 13, 1939—the week that Ford was still circling around the idea of directing the movie—includes the last scene in the truck. It might have been directed by Zanuck, but it certainly wasn't an after-thought.

Although Ford pretended to disdain such things as politicking, he was too skillful a filmmaking general not to realize that it was part of the job of anybody who had any claim to a lengthy career. On *The Grapes of Wrath*, Darryl Zanuck knew very well that there wasn't much he could add to the extraordinarily concise and vivid footage Ford was turning in, so he turned his attention to the sound. He decided to invent the sound of the Joads' truck. "He was determined to make it the best truck sound anybody had ever heard," remembered Robert Parrish.

Zanuck ordered a replica of the Joad truck, loaded it up with the sufficient amount of weight, and sent it and a six-man sound crew out to Oklahoma to record the grinding and shifting of gears in all its authentic glory.

While the sound crew was still out on the road, Ford came in and told Parrish that he had scheduled a screening of a rough cut to show some exhibitors. "I want you guys to start putting in some temporary sound effects," Ford said. Parrish and Phil Smith went to work putting in sound out of the stock library. For the truck, Parrish and Smith went out to the parking lot and recorded various engine sounds, and, for the sequence where the Joads' truck breaks down, tools being dropped.

The screening was a smashing success. Then as now, nobody noticed that Tom's brother essentially disappears, as does Rosasharn's baby. People applauded; Zanuck spoke, then Ford spoke. "I want to thank you, Darryl. The sound you got for the Joad truck makes it the star of the picture. It really is terrific." Zanuck beamed. "When the sound crew finally came in from Oklahoma," said Parrish, "it was great, but we didn't use a bit of it."

For the publicity campaign, Zanuck got the idea of hiring Thomas Hart Benton to do a series of illustrations for the ads, setting the film apart from its competition, as well as creating a sense of mystery about what the film actually looked like.

When it opened on January 24, 1940, a bare five weeks after finishing production, *The Grapes of Wrath* was immediately acclaimed as a master-piece. The *Times* called it "One of the cinema's masterworks," the *Herald Tribune* said it was "A genuinely great motion picture." John Mosher in *The New Yorker*, whose disdain for the movies approached the universal, said that "It is a great film of the dust plains, the highways, the camps, of the sky above, and of a nameless, evicted people."

Even Eleanor Roosevelt, in her *My Day* column, wrote about seeing the film in Golden Beach, Florida. "I think it is well done," she fretted, "but I wonder if it will convey to many people the reality of what they are seeing. . . . I did not feel the tragedy gripped the audience. They did not seem really to know what this story actually meant."

As the reviews came in, Zanuck altered the ads to a series of Benton heads of the characters with the line "Us Joads Thank New York!" One of the few dissenting opinions came from Martin Quigley, editor of the *Motion Picture Daily*, an ardent Catholic and one of the co-authors of the censorship code. "If the conditions which the picture tends to present as typical are proportionately true," thundered Quigley, "then the Revolution has been too long delayed. If, on the other hand, the picture depicts an extraordinary, isolated, and non-usual condition . . . then no small libel against the good name of the republic has been committed."

Although *The Grapes of Wrath* made some money, it was not an enormous popular success, grossing $1.59 million—around double its cost. It was a little too rigorous, a little too uncompromising. Certainly, it confirmed to Hollywood conservatives that Ford had dangerous populist sympathies. George O'Brien believed that his friend Jack had allowed himself to become a purveyor of Communist propaganda. Met with a protest that the film was a work of art, O'Brien replied that was just the trouble.

Nunnally Johnson's script subtly shifted the focus from Ma to Tom Joad, to accommodate the fact that Ma was being played by a character actress while Tom was being played by a star. Ford emphasizes the dignity of the people that work the land, and their sense of loss when that work is taken away. The film lacks the sociological sting of the novel, but it compensates by creating a feeling of universality, making the Joads archetypes of dispossession. Accomplishing this was easy for Jack—an empathetic feel for rootless souls would enrich his Westerns, of course, but it would also inform *The Quiet Man* and *They Were Expendable*.

Ford's touch for metaphor was never as sure or delicate; the people who come to throw the Okies off their lands remain encased in their cars or their caterpillar tractors, agents of the machine; Muley and his family stand on the ground they have struggled to farm, defenseless, without armor.

As Zanuck had promised, John Steinbeck was given a pre-release screening of the film. He wrote his agent soon afterward, "Zanuck has more than kept his word. He has a hard, straight picture in which the actors are submerged so completely that it looks and feels like a documentary film and certainly it has a hard, truthful ring. No punches are pulled."

Steinbeck, remembered his widow, "adored the film." The Steinbecks and the Nunnally Johnsons remained very close, and Steinbeck and Fonda stayed friends to the end of their lives. Fonda read poetry at Steinbeck's funeral, and, when the actor died in 1982, Tom Joad's final speech was read at his funeral.

At the end of the book, Casey is dead, Tom has been beaten, and Rosasharn's stillborn baby is floating down a river. At the end of the movie, Tom leaves his family to organize a union. Tom Joad moves from objective reality to a more mythic realm, but Ford makes his gradual abstraction seem as real as the dirt that the desperate, blasted Muley sifts through his fingers. Tom is one of Ford's men on the border, doomed, like Ethan Edwards in *The Searchers*, to live his life poised between wilderness and society. When Tom goes over the hill, he becomes a fierce ghost in the American darkness.

Today, sixty years after it was made, *The Grapes of Wrath* retains nearly all of its concentrated humanist power. Few films, whether made in or out of Hollywood, have the film's cold, seditious anger. "Every image is so moving," Lindsay Anderson said. "It's like looking into the Garden of Eden, looking at our own lost innocence."

CHAPTER THIRTEEN

S ince Ford had given Walter Wanger a hit, both financially and creatively, the producer was anxious to keep Ford working for him. In
February 1940, Wanger signed a contract with Argosy. The deal was for
two pictures, one to be directed by Ford, one to be "coproduced and
personally supervised by Merian C. Cooper on behalf of Argosy." The
former was to be *The Long Voyage Home*, an adaptation of several one-act
plays by Eugene O'Neill, the latter *Eagle Squadron*, about twenty-four
American pilots who joined the RAF in early 1940.

The RAF picture appealed to Cooper because of his own flying experience and the innate heroism of the subject; it appealed to Wanger
because it would enable him to use some blocked funds in England. Cooper's idea was to film the picture documentary style, without a shooting script. Both projects were naturals for their respective makers, and
Wanger was cutting Argosy in for 25 percent of the net profits.

By the time Argosy signed the contract wth Wanger, Ford already had
Dudley Nichols working on converting four O'Neill plays (*The Moon
of the Caribbees, Bound East for Cardiff, The Long Voyage Home*, and *In the
Zone*) into one script. Nichols signed his contract January 12, and Argosy
agreed to pay him $12,500 up front. Time was clearly of the essence,
because the contract stated that Nichols believed he could do the job in
five weeks. If, however, it took longer than that, they grudgingly agreed
to pay him an additional $2,500 for each week, until he reached a ceiling
of $25,000.

Nichols did a very expert job. The film's opening derived from *Moon of
the Caribbees*; the death of Yank from *Bound East for Cardiff*; the episode of
Smitty and his secret from *In the Zone*; while the film's concluding section
mostly derived from *The Long Voyage Home*.

Although Ford and Victor McLaglen had made seven pictures together, there now came a slight rupture in their relationship. Ford asked McLaglen to play Driscoll, the part eventually played by Thomas Mitchell. McLaglen was then making the biggest money of his career, $50,000 a picture, and Ford offered him only $25,000. McLaglen refused, and Ford took it amiss. Ford would stay miffed until he cast McLaglen in *Fort Apache*.

Ford added John Wayne to the cast, playing the sweet young Swedish sailor named Ole who's mothered by the older, tougher sailors. "I was still under contract to Republic at the time," remembered Wayne in 1972. "*Long Voyage Home* was right after *Stagecoach*, but I was still doing six-day Westerns. I'd finished one at twelve o'clock at night and the next morning I had to start a picture where I was a Swedish sailor, presumably with an accent, with no chance for coaching. I had to play a straight part as a Swede and my accent couldn't clash with John Qualen's, who was playing a comic Swede. I wanna tell you, that was quite a switch from the night before, knocking people around and jumping on a horse." Ford didn't make it any easier for him by retaining most of Ole's dialogue from O'Neill's play.

Wayne was worried about his big scene in a bar, when he has to tell the story of his life to a whore. Finally, he asked Ford for help. "Well, Jesus, all right, if you want to be a goddam actor. But you don't need it." Ford arranged for Wayne to spend a couple of weeks being tutored by the actress Osa Massen, so he could pick up the rhythms of Swedish speech.

One day Ford was idly mumbling that he wished he could find a young Una O'Connor, whereupon a mutual acquaintance suggested he take a look at an actress named Mildred Natwick. Like O'Connor, Natwick had sharp, unbeautiful features, but there was a gentleness and natural warmth to her personality that was unlike the older, more grotesque actress.

Ford hired Natwick for *The Long Voyage Home*. It was her first film, she was scared of the new medium, and she had probably heard enough about Ford to be at least a little leery of him as well. But Ford sensed that this was a true, gifted actress, and always treated her with the greatest respect.

"He told me everything to do," remembered Natwick. "It was like marvelous coaching. And I remember he said, when I had to [make an entrance] he said, 'Why don't you have your sweater down and sort of be pulling it up over your shoulder.' And then he would put in lines; the line in the play, I think, was 'A drop of gin, Joe,' and then he said, 'And with a beer chaser'. . . . He just made me so comfortable and so easy, that it was a wonderful way to do one's first movie." For Natwick, Ford would always be "funny and delightful. He could bark at people, I always thought it was to bring out an effect, to make an effect."

A visitor to the set noticed how quiet and alert the production was, with none of the rough kidding and lightness endemic to movie sets between shots. When the crew began shifting lights, Ford and cameraman Gregg Toland would huddle, Toland looking through his viewfinder, then passing it to Ford, who nodded in agreement.

When the lights were set, the actors would rehearse while Ford watched, rubbing his face as if it itched. Toland moved in and out of the group, taking readings with his light meter. Ford would finally say, "Let's try it." After a run-through that didn't satisfy him, Ford began minute adjustments, telling Barry Fitzgerald to nod his head a specific way, even demonstrating it for him. And when Fitzgerald finally did it the way he wanted, there was no praise, just the instruction to go for a take. The take was followed by a pause, and then a quiet "Print it."

The latitude Ford gave Toland to work in his favorite deep-focus style disproves the myth of Ford as a rigid technical authoritarian. (He was much harder on actors than he was on his crew.) While the compositional style would be the same, there is considerable difference in texture on Ford's films, even in the same period, from the shadowed, soft look that Joe August gave Ford (*The Informer*), to the diffused and glowing Bert Glennon pictures (*Hurricane, Young Mr. Lincoln*), to Toland's high-contrast, razor-focus work in *The Long Voyage Home* and *The Grapes of Wrath*.

The observant Wayne once again appreciated the way Ford could orchestrate a disparate group of craftsmen until they were all resonating to one single note. "As an administrator, he could have been anything he wanted to be. Not necessarily in business, but in the military field, handling personalities and people. Nobody could handle actors and crew like Jack. He was the finest editor I've ever seen. He'd make [Dudley] Nichols write a scene five or six times until Nichols was just about drenched. And then he'd find three lines out of three scenes that Dudley had written and use them for [one] particular speech. He knew how to draw lines out that give character and progress your story at the same time."

On the set, Wayne explained, there was always the soft accordion music of Danny Borzage serenading the cast and crew, gently underlining the emotion of the scene being worked on. "Ford, while they're lighting a set, talks to the actors very quietly, puts them through a scene. Now he calls the cameraman over. He watches them go through the scene. He talks to them. 'Do you think you can go down over there instead of here?' 'Yeah, sure.'

"Now, when you start to do the scene you're at complete ease. You've walked through it, and as you're setting your lines you're in the right position. Some directors line the whole scene up the night before and say, 'You stand here and you stand there and when you say that line come over here.' Well, when you say, 'Come over here on that line,' instinctively it affects your performance. The other way, you're eased into it so beautifully; you're where he wants you for composition, but you're also where you want to be for the lines. Ford wants the action to come out of the actor in a manner that's comfortable to him. After that's done, then he gives you the little touches that he wants. But he gets you at ease first."

Watching the film take shape, Dudley Nichols was moved to write an appreciation: "Dear Sean, The rushes are so wonderful I can't resist telling you again in a note. I'd rather look at any day's rushes than see the best film of the year. I didn't think any picture could ever be as good as 'Grapes' but I have a crazy feeling that this is going to be better, at least for a mugg who isn't 'normal.' (And who the hell wants to be normal, you anarchistic Tad?) . . ."

The world of Ford's *The Long Voyage Home* fully reflects O'Neill's aura of ordained doom. John Wayne's Ole is the pampered child of the other crewmen, protected from drunkenness, rescued when shanghaied. It may be too late for the others, but, by God, Ole will survive and thrive—they will see to it. It is this dynamic that gives the film its through-line, gives the characters the feel of self-sacrificing family. Otherwise, as Janey Place observed, the overriding impression is of a sensationally sensual mood rather than a specific story.

Ford adored Gregg Toland; like Ford, he had an innate eye for composition; like Ford, he worked decisively. And they shared another bond—drinking. Toland was an alcoholic, although he would later dry out.

Because the two men thought alike about so many things, Ford gave Toland his head. *The Long Voyage Home* would be among the most relentlessly photographed movies in Ford's career; every shot is a knockout. David Thomson believes that it is a movie in which "the . . . photography is out of control," that is to say that the tail of the image is wagging the dog of the story. But at least *The Long Voyage Home* has a story; the next time Ford let his cameraman and pictorial imagination off the leash, the result was *The Fugitive*, a movie that asphyxiates in allegorical excess.

It's clear that there could have been no *Citizen Kane* without Toland's experiments on *The Long Voyage Home*. Aside from the virtually identical photographic style, Toland, undoubtedly thinking of Ford, was constantly telling Welles to play a scene in one shot whenever possible and avoid unnecessary editing.

From the opening, with "Harbor Lights" on the soundtrack, and native women writhing sensuously on a tropical night as the *Glencairn* lies off an island in the West Indies, *The Long Voyage Home* sets a tone of lyrical yearning. The men are largely either reformed or haunted alcoholics, united only in their resolve to make sure that young Ole isn't trapped like they are. The rest of them are caught between their mutually exclusive desires for home and their yearning for the sea.

Ford and O'Neill are something of a dream mating, sharing an essentially tragic view of life born out of an Irish Catholicism that is equal parts guilt, anger, repression, and submission. Ford captures the mutual dependence of men at sea, the bonds of trust and reciprocal discretion, the unspoken devotion, as well as the vulnerability that lies just beneath the skin—as Ward Bond's Yank lies dying, he doesn't want to be alone.

The Long Voyage Home is filled with the depressive knowledge of inevitable war. "Everywhere people stumbling in the dark," cries out Thomas Mitchell's Driscoll. "Is there to be no light in the world?" The film is entirely made on the stage but it never feels stagey—the ship is constantly creaking and rolling, and the images are filled with damp iron.

In the end, Ole is saved from being shanghaied and is sent home, but Driscoll is captured by the dark ship *Amindra*, which is sunk by the Germans with all hands lost. The remaining men ship out again on the *Glencairn*, as the clouds blot out the early morning sun and "Harbor Lights" comes up again on the soundtrack. *The Long Voyage Home* is a film of fate and dark diagonals, a visual masterpiece and, except for the Smitty sequence, which goes on too long, a dramatic one as well.

Wanger knew he had an art-house film. He attempted to capitalize on Ford's growing aura by spending $50,000 commissioning nine major American artists to come to Hollywood and paint scenes from the film for an exhibit that would travel across the country as part of the promotion.

Thomas Hart Benton, Grant Wood, Raphael Soyer, George Biddle, James Chapin, Ernest Fiene, Robert Phillipp, Luis Quintanilla, and Georges Schreiber turned in some beautiful work, especially Benton, Wood, and Chapin.

United Artists attempted to tie the picture's fate to the rising public profile of its director. "John Ford gives you box-office drama with the kick of dynamite!" proclaimed the pressbook enthusiastically, if ungrammatically. "The genius of John Ford becomes the business partner of your showmanship in realizing sweeping profits."

The Long Voyage Home was far more a critic's picture than an audience picture. Bosley Crowther in the *Times* wrote that it was "a stark and tough-fibered motion picture which tells with lean economy the never-ending story of man's wanderings over the waters of the world in search of peace for his soul. . . . It is harsh and relentless and only briefly compassionate in its revelations of man's pathetic shortcomings. But it is one of the most honest pictures ever placed upon the screen." The other critics followed Crowther's lead and basically threw their hats in the air.

Eugene O'Neill was properly appreciative of Ford's achievement. "My congratulations on a grand deeply moving and beautiful piece of work," O'Neill wired Ford after a preview screening. "It is a great picture and I hope you are as proud of it as I am. Carlotta is equally enthusiastic. Our one disappointment tonight was that we missed seeing you again. All cheers to you and much gratitude. Gene." A few weeks later, Carlotta Monterey O'Neill amplified her husband's comments: "We were deeply moved and proud that you had directed it."

Both *The Long Voyage Home* and *The Grapes of Wrath* received Oscar nominations, but Ford got a Best Director nod only for the latter picture. On the night of the awards, presenter Frank Capra called all the other nominees to the podium: Alfred Hitchcock, Sam Wood, George Cukor, and William Wyler. The winner was Ford, the man who wasn't there. He was fishing off the coast of Mexico with Henry Fonda, where, he said, he planned to stay "for as long as the fish are biting."

Shortly after *The Long Voyage Home*, O'Neill grew enthusiastic about a suggestion from Robert Sisk: a stage revival of *The Hairy Ape*, starring Victor McLaglen, to be directed by Ford.

The Theater Guild's Lawrence Langner countered with Charles Bickford for the part of Yank but expressed some doubts about Ford's drinking. "From all I've heard of him," replied O'Neill on August 24, 1941, "and from meeting him myself—I'd say he never lets his binges get between him and any job he regards with enthusiasm. The question is, will he regard a stage Hairy Ape with enthusiasm? I know he would a film of the play."

There is some question as to whether an offer was actually made to Ford, or if O'Neill and Langner thought better of the idea. In any case, Ford would have had to turn the offer down, because he was in the midst of shooting *How Green Was My Valley* for Zanuck, after which he went directly into the Navy.

*T*he Long Voyage Home was a financial flop. It cost $689,495, grossed $580,129, for a net loss of $224,336. Along with several other failures that should have been successes (Hitchcock's *Foreign Correspondent*, which lost $369,000), the Ford film permanently soured Walter Wanger on United Artists, who had insufficient clout with the large theater circuits.

In the fall of 1940, Cooper told Wanger that Argosy wanted to go ahead with *Eagle Squadron*. Wanger promptly panicked. His company was in difficulties, he explained to Cooper, and he couldn't see his way clear to make the picture. Wanger paid Argosy their $35,000 option fee, and went off to try to drum up financing and a releasing deal elsewhere.

Informally, Cooper told Wanger that he would undertake a picture for Wanger anytime, so as to earn the $35,000 that Wanger had paid.

Wanger signed a lucrative deal with Universal and set up *Eagle Squadron* there, but the two men didn't want to make the same picture. Cooper still wanted to make it documentary style and cheap; Wanger wanted a conventional fictionalized Hollywood aerial epic. The picture was eventually made following Wanger's vision and made a profit of $697,607. Although contractually Argosy was in for 25 percent, it seems that Cooper let it go, as the picture that resulted was far from his ideas. It was admirable, it was idealistic, but that money would have come in handy in a couple of years, when Argosy hit very rough water.

I n October, Ford wrote out a new will, leaving everything to Mary. He signed himself "John Ford (Sean Aloysius O'Feeney)." Ford's investments were minor. He had bought five hundred shares of Western Costume in 1926, and there were other stock purchases over the years, mostly AT&T and other blue chips, but far fewer than might be expected from someone with his income. The 1929 crash seems to have disabused him of putting a lot of stock in stocks.

Ford got a wake-up call about just how important it was to hold on to your money when Tom Mix showed up on his set one day. Mix hadn't made a movie since 1935. He had four ex-wives, and was just scraping by; there was no demand for a sixty-year-old Western star in the Hollywood of 1940.

"What do you think I could do in this business?" Mix asked Lefty Hough. "I need a job." Hough hemmed and hawed and took Mix down to the set where Ford was working, where he asked him the same question. "Jesus, Tom, we don't make pictures like we made with you years ago. They're talking pictures and not the action stuff we used to do." In fact, Mix had made a lot of talkies, but it is a mark of how he had fallen that Ford didn't seem to know he had.

Mix went to see Sol Wurtzel and got the same response. When he came out, Lefty Hough was waiting for the shaken actor. "Jesus," he said, "I made millions for this outfit . . ." It was an eerie, uncomfortable scene that would be played out innumerable times in this period, as survivors of the silent period hovered on the fringes, asking old friends for jobs.

Shortly afterward, in October 1940, Mix was killed when his Cord went off the road in Arizona and an aluminum suitcase on the back deck shot forward and broke his neck. The man who had once made $7,500 a week, with virtually no income tax, left an estate worth about $115,000. His attorney estimated that after the debts were paid off, only about half of that would remain.

Mix's estate tried to get a flag from the Veterans Administration to cover the coffin, which proved to be an unfortunate idea. Since First Sergeant Mix had deserted from the U.S. Artillery in October 1902, the Army, although it seems not to have pursued Mix either at the time or after he became a star, became retroactively snippy about the request for a flag. Ford intervened and wrote the VA. Tom Mix got his flag.

The only outright failure Ford would direct in this period was a terrible adaptation of *Tobacco Road*. Bound on the one hand by the enormous success of the play and novel, and on the other by censorship requirements, Ford was defeated by the material. The characters are relentless caricatures, and the tone shifts from scene to scene; elegiac loss segues to slapstick—at one point Jeeter Lester steals food from his own son. It's unworkable and Ford is reduced to repeating previously successful moments. Charley Grapewin's speech about the tragedy of losing his land plays as a feeble echo of John Qualen's similar speech in *The Grapes of Wrath*.

The material is basically raucous comedy—Jeeter estimates his offspring as numbering "seventeen or eighteen"—but Ford and cinematographer Arthur Miller can't find the right tone, and end up shooting it as if it were a drama, with a particularly beautiful infinity of grays. Ultimately, however, the meditative style—there are enough low-angled shots and falling leaves for Ma Joad to begin packing for California all over again—works against the material.

Nunnally Johnson thought the problem was a basic misalliance between Ford and the characters: "John of course hadn't seen the play and he didn't know the first thing about a Southern shack hollow. But I was hardly prepared for what he started giving me, which . . . was a lot of wild Irishmen, and there would be shouts—why, these people wouldn't have shouted once in two years."

Johnson was fairly circumspect about all this when talking to Ford's grandson, but when speaking to his own daughter, he was considerably blunter. "He was much too powerful for me, and it was just as if I were talking to him in Greek. To him, a low, illiterate cracker and a low, illiterate Irishman were identical. They reacted the same way. Since he didn't know anything about crackers, except me, and he did know about the Irish, he simply changed them all into Irishmen. The whole thing was a calamity."

Although 1939 has, by common consent, been canonized as the ultimate year of what everybody persists in referring to as Hollywood's Golden Age, you could make a strong case for 1941 as well. Besides *Citi-*

zen Kane, there was *The Maltese Falcon, The Lady Eve* and *Sullivan's Travels, The Little Foxes, The Strawberry Blonde* and *High Sierra, Meet John Doe, Penny Serenade, Sergeant York* and *Ball of Fire, Man Hunt, Suspicion, The Devil and Daniel Webster, The Sea Wolf,* and *Dumbo.* And *How Green Was My Valley.*

Of all these pictures, it was *How Green Was My Valley* that dominated the awards ceremonies, winning Oscars for Best Picture, Best Director, Best Supporting Actor, Best Black and White Cinematography, and Best Black and White Art Direction. Thirty years later, Andrew Sarris maintained that while *How Green Was My Valley* would not have gotten his vote over *Citizen Kane*, it was still, *Sunrise* excepted, the best film ever to win the Best Picture Oscar.

The history of *How Green Was My Valley* is of a series of potential creative disasters narrowly averted. Zanuck's original plan had been to shoot as much of the picture as possible on location in Wales, but the outbreak of the war in Europe killed that idea. Instead, Zanuck had the great art director Richard Day build a Welsh village on the Fox ranch in Malibu, an extraordinary set that was as much the star of the picture as any of the actors. Zanuck also wisely abandoned his plan to shoot the picture in Technicolor, probably for financial reasons. Visually, the dry brown slopes of the Santa Monica mountains would have belied the title and rendered the illusion of a lost paradise a little less convincing.

Zanuck fussed with various drafts of the script beginning early in 1940, and was obviously uneasy about it because he sent drafts to various producers around the lot. The responses were unanimous. Robert Bassler wrote that "Some idyllic society is lost; let's see more of life in the valley before the labor conflict." Henry Lehrman, Charlie Chaplin's old nemesis from the Keystone days, wrote that it was "inopportune to make this film now. Shouldn't throw stones at England. Postpone until after hostilities are over."

At a conference on May 22 regarding the initial script by Ernest Pascal, Zanuck said that he was "very disappointed" that Pascal's version turned into a story of labor rather than of a family. "We should see this through the eyes of Huw, offstage commentator. We could open with a beautiful long shot, the voice of the boy telling of walks with his father, the scene dissolves into walks, etc."

Two months later, Philip Dunne, writing of a still-later draft, told his boss that he felt the script was still heading in the wrong direction, "giving a sense of dreariness, which need not be there. The real trouble is that the script fails to catch the atmosphere of the book. I don't know exactly why. I can't put my finger on what is exactly wrong because it consists of thousands of little omissions. I think a fresh start should be made."

A fresh start was made, by Philip Dunne. For the rest of the year, Dunne and Zanuck went back and forth on the script. Zanuck's notes on an August 23 draft: "No attempt yet to cast. Write and judge on merit. Voice device overdone. Labor and trouble to a minimum. This should be history of a family, not a labor dispute. Needs cutting and condensing, tempo. Too much Welsh dialect; just the flavor is what we need."

On November 11, 1940, Dunne turned in a revised temporary script that ran a whopping 246 pages. Zanuck's comments on this version were modest, noting that heavy cuts needed to be made. "My only complaint about Gryffyd is that he is still pretty much a stick." And there is this notation: "Set Wyler right about retakes."

Zanuck had borrowed William Wyler from Sam Goldwyn to direct, and it was Wyler who was guiding the writing of Dunne's script. As Dunne said, "[Wyler] did everything except actually shoot it." Zanuck wasn't always happy with Wyler's taste for elaboration in the script and strove hard to concentrate on the people. As he sternly addressed the two men about a scene in which Huw gets his first suit with long pants, "The tailor business is amusing but good heavens, we are in the middle of a story and we cannot stop for vaudeville acts. . . . Let's take the bull by the horns and get it over with one short silent scene with the Voice over it. . . . .What good is there in showing this? It is only background to our real people."

It seems that Zanuck did the final polish on the script himself, in a draft dated December 3 that closely follows the finished film. At that point, casting was moving forward. Zanuck had already arranged the loan of Walter Pidgeon from MGM, and was giving some thought to Greer Garson for the part of Angharad. Zanuck's other casting ideas were random: Martha Scott or Geraldine Fitzgerald for Bronwen. Sara Allgood was always first choice for Beth, as was Donald Crisp for Morgan.

But the most important part was the child through whose eyes the story is told, and that was settled through a pure fluke. "I had made films in England," remembered Roddy McDowall, "and I made a test in New York. It was sent out here at the end of 1940. Wyler was in the projection room running four different tests of children and the last one was mine. The casting director stood up and put his hand in front of the projector light and said, 'You don't want to see this kid. He's bandy-legged, he's not attractive, and he has a turned eye.' In those days, a child actor had to look like Freddie Bartholomew. But Willie said, 'As long as we're here, let's see it.'

"Well, Willie wanted me shipped out to California, and I did another test, with Alexander Knox in the part of Mr. Gryffyd. It was a scene where they're working on some wood project; it didn't make it into the actual film." Wyler and Zanuck were in complete agreement—the boy had an unforced sweetness, an attentiveness, that made him perfect for the part of Huw. McDowall was placed under contract.

Shortly afterward, Wyler left the picture. New York didn't like the script, didn't think making a movie about labor unrest was wise, didn't like the lack of star names in the cast, and they especially didn't like Wyler's reputation for extravagance in production time. They refused to spend the budgeted figure. Zanuck fumed, informed them that *How Green Was My Valley* was the best script he had ever had, and he would make the movie one way or the other, even if he had to make it at another studio. Zanuck, as always, trusted the story.

That got New York's attention. There was only one director who could shoot *Valley* for the money Zanuck could spend and not cut corners. Zanuck offered Ford $100,000 on a separate contract for this one film only, $15,000 more than Ford was currently making per picture. And so it was that in January 1941, Philip Dunne was called to a meeting with his friend John Ford. The two men had met in 1930 and been close friends ever since, united by their common interest in Irish history.

Ford tweaked some of the script; he suggested paraphrasing one of FDR's recent lines regarding unions, and he heartily approved of the line suggested by Philip Dunne for Gryffyd: "My business is anything that comes between man and the spirit of God." Furthermore, Ford wanted to write in a part for Barry Fitzgerald. "He has no lines, but Mr. Ford will give him business throughout." Otherwise, Ford left it alone, for, as he would later write, "It was as nearly a perfect script as could be possible."

A young actress named Anna Lee had interviewed unsuccessfully for the part of Bronwen, but was called back after Ford took the picture over. All her friends told her that she was never going to get the part because Ford hated the English and only liked the Irish.

Lee promptly devised an entirely mythical grandfather named Michael O'Connor. Ford seemed to believe her and said he didn't want to test her, but wanted to see her with Roddy McDowall, who was brought into the room. Lee sat in a chair with Roddy at her feet, and the two improvised a scene. "The next thing I knew, I had the part," remembered Lee. "Years later, I told him my Irish grandfather was all a spoof, but I don't know whether he believed me or not."

Lee would become among the most prominent female members of the Ford stock company. Ford's pet name for her was Boniface, her middle name (Joanna Boniface Winnifrith). She became familiar with his multiple eccentricities, and loved him all the more for them.

Ford's feelings for Lee were cemented when she had a miscarriage while shooting the film, brought on by collapsing during the scene where she learns her husband has died. She hadn't told Ford that she was pregnant, but he nevertheless blamed himself. The result was that on every picture Lee worked on with him, Ford would assemble the cast and crew, then ask her if she was pregnant.

"No sir," she would reply.

"I just wanted to make sure."

Also cast was Maureen O'Hara, in the first of five films with Ford that would make her a member of his extended family, which didn't exempt her from a turbulent relationship she would characterize as "love/hate."

A few days before Ford began principal photography, he lined up the cast in their costumes and had Arthur Miller shoot a test, panning down the line. Miller was confused, but knew better than to ask Ford about his reasons. Then he realized that he was doing it to see if there was a believable family resemblance.

Although the two men only made a pair of movies together, Miller would remember Ford as "the director I liked working with better than anybody in the industry. You'd only talk, I think you might say, fifty words to him a day; you had a communication with him so great you could sense what he wanted. . . . He never once looked in the camera when we worked together. . . . He was a man whose veins ran with the business. . . .

"He had one odd thing: he'd talk to someone way across the studio about a character to be played by someone sitting next to him, instead of talking to the man next to him about it, and the man next to him would of course listen to every word."

Zanuck kept an attentive eye on the rushes, sending memos to Ford about how he was shooting the various scenes. He liked the way Ford directed the scene of Roddy McDowall's initial attempt at walking, played entirely in long shot, but wanted two close-ups as well, one of McDowall, one of Walter Pidgeon. "I feel certain it will intensify and build up the emotional value of the scene," wrote Zanuck. "It will also make people cry. . . . Perhaps you considered this and disregarded it for some reason." Zanuck went on for another paragraph about the various and sundry reasons the close-ups were a good idea, ending with a tentative "If you agree with me . . ."

Ford circled the sentence beginning "Perhaps you considered this . . ." and scribbled a reply in the margins: "dear darryl—the sun goes down out here at six-thirty—Jack." The close-ups were shot back at the studio and cut in. Zanuck was thrilled by the rushes, and told Ford that if he were to "keep it up like it is going it will be the greatest directorial job that you have ever turned in."

Ford, remembered McDowall, "was psychologically very, very sophisticated in how to treat his actors. All of them were treated differently. Sometimes abuse was involved, sometimes tremendous wheedling. I'd made a lot of films by then, and I wasn't a neophyte, and I don't remember him directing me at all, which is really the greatest compliment you can pay a director. He was a tremendous magician with people."

McDowall was perfect for the part and perfect in the part. Philip Dunne was only on the set a few times, once when he was called down to rewrite a line in the school sequence. Dunne watched the rehearsal, and Ford said, "See that? See how the kid sort of felt for the stool with his ass while keeping his eyes on the teacher? I didn't tell him to do that. He just naturally does everything right the first time."

Ford wasn't entirely sure about Walter Pidgeon; the director prided himself on being able to spot an actor from a mile away, and he believed he had to keep a vigilant eye on the MGM star, who he felt wanted to be the center of attention. But Ford's only real problem was with Sara Allgood, with whom he had a prickly relationship. One day she complained that a scene "wouldn't play." Ford called Dunne to the set and explained the situation, whereupon Dunne, spinning off the most famous Ford anecdote of all, ripped the scene out of the script and said, "Now it plays!"

"See?" Ford said. "The sonofabitching writer won't do anything to help us, so we'll have to shoot it the way he wrote it."

Ford reined in most of his native sarcasm, because he couldn't afford to do or say anything that might cause Roddy McDowall to freeze up. The story was told through his eyes, and he needed the boy emotionally open.

Anna Lee noted that he would never tell an actor he respected or had confidence in what, directly, he wanted from them in a given scene. For a scene after her husband's death, Lee had an emotional little speech about her loneliness. "He came up to me and talked about something completely different. Then he would always take this grubby handkerchief that he carried, which he chewed the corners of, and he would tie it around you somewhere. . . . I think he tucked it in my apron or somewhere, and you knew that was his mark of approval, a sort of good luck token."

One day Howard Jones, the USC football coach and a friend of Ford's, visited the set. Ford, Jones, and Arthur Miller took box lunches up to the top of a hill and ate, and Jones asked his friend if the picture was going well.

"Everything seems fine," Ford muttered, but then he went on to enumerate the misfortunes and tragedies that made up the narrative. Irreparable breaches between generations, a father killed, a son killed, a daughter marrying a man she doesn't love. "I have to find some way to bring the family together as far as the audience is concerned for them to really enjoy the picture." It was one of the few times Ford verbalized the anxieties that led him to wear out thousands of handkerchiefs over the years.

A few days later, the sky was filled with gorgeous clouds, and Ford asked Miller if it would be possible to get some footage of the clouds, then enlarge them via rear projection. Ford played the last several shots of the film in front of the clouds, giving a sense of sylvan grace and healing to what was actually a tragedy.

He was always thinking, sometimes out loud. As Maureen O'Hara comes out of the church after her wedding, Ford's camera pans slightly to find Walter Pidgeon on a hill, framed by an oak tree. Looking at the shot for a few seconds, Ford mumbled, "If I make a close-up, somebody will want to use it." He stayed with the long shot. Philip Dunne would remember that he had specified a close-up of Huw when his older brothers leave the house for the last time. "Ford never cut in. He played it in a long shot. I don't know if that was deliberate. I never asked him. But what he *didn't* do was brilliant."

For the most part, *How Green Was My Valley* was a blessed picture, all the gears smoothly meshing, oiled by a healthy application of Ford's Irish luck. "There were extraordinary accidents that happened," remembered Roddy McDowall. "Like planning a whole crowd coming down that hill of the Welsh mining town, and they'd start the smokestacks going. All of a sudden when the cameras would be rolling, the wind would shift, and the smoke would do the most amazing things, and the sun would shine through it. The most incredible accidents happened to make that film just a little bit better than if they hadn't occurred."

There was one flurry of outright hostilities between Ford and his brother, Eddie O'Fearna, during the filming of a brief scene in a toffee shop. The actress behind the counter was very small and needed to stand on a box. There was no box on the set, causing a delay. Ford laid in to Eddie, and the normally amiable man fired back. "That's not my responsibility and you know it!" One word led to another, and without warning Eddie threw a punch that knocked Ford flat. "Ford got up, never said another word," remembered Arthur Miller wonderingly. "The two went on working as if nothing had happened. I guess at heart they were just a couple of 'Shanty Irish' brothers who had done this sort of thing before."

At the end of August 1941, eight weeks after the cameras began rolling, the last shot was completed. "It was the most succinct production experience I have ever encountered," remembered Roddy McDowall. Ford had taken two months to shoot a picture that any other director would have shot in three, and for which Wyler would probably have needed four.

"I remember the day we finished it," said McDowall. "I went right to work on another film. It was a terrible day . . . [because] Ford had created such an extraordinary sense of being together. It was a total belonging."

In December, the film was released to rapturous critical praise. It was the sort of production that could only have been accomplished under the studio system, where the departments dovetailed, when people were used to working with one another with knowledge and some affection, when every movie didn't have to be built from the ground up. When Ford was congratulated by various people at the studio, he said, "Nonsense. It took me 26 years to know how to do that job in eight weeks. Congratulate the actors! I'm only a slave-driver, a kind of Legree."

Richard Day's production design gives *How Green Was My Valley* an epic sweep, and Ford's eye gives it a sense of reality. Ford gets such a sense of both emotional and physical detail in it, does so many things right: the men tossing their pay into the mother's apron as she waits by the door of the house; the women of the town reaching out to touch the splendor of Bronwyn's wedding dress; the chirruping fear of Huw when he believes he won't walk again; the sluggish, stunned movements of the men after they've gone on strike, tradition breaking apart on the shoals of the twentieth century.

How Green Was My Valley is a story of dispersal and dissolution, but it's a tribute to Ford's powers of suggestion that he could convincingly create an aura of warm nostalgia around a movie about bad marriages, poverty, fatal mining accidents, and violent, family-rending labor disputes, without ever actually betraying the tone of the material.

Ford could glide from the more or less scathing left-wing point of view of *Grapes of Wrath* to the uneasy centrism of *How Green*, where unions are justified but bring a heavy cost, because his vision was always more communal than collective, and almost never ideological. In that sense, his lionization by the left in the mid-1930s was a misunderstanding that worked to Ford's critical advantage.

Criticisms about the film being an inaccurate depiction of a mining town are irrelevant; it is life seen through the eyes of a child. Although it is narrated by a man, the characters are drawn with the broad strokes of an awestruck boy, bathed in the golden glow of an adult's remembrance of his childhood. And it is one of the most cogent statements of one of Ford's deepest themes: the way that time's flow destroys the old ways, which must die in order for the future to take hold. Ianto stands up at the dinner table and says that if manners prevent him from speaking against injustice, then he will be without manners, and we understand both his anger and the pain of his father's loss of control of his sons, his house, and his life.

Working with material that was inescapably dour, Ford turned it into a masterpiece about the tenacity and universality of family feelings. "The shining spirit of those people is irresistible," said Roddy McDowall. "And Ford's film language!" At the film's beginning, we see the bleak, blasted place the valley has become, so that, when Roddy McDowall's Huw walks again, in a bower of trees framing a meadow filled with hundreds of daffodils, we weep as much for what will be lost as we do for a child's resurrection. Ford was aided enormously by Arthur Miller, whose work, as fellow cameraman Robert Surtees noted, "had the quality of fine black and white etchings."

Although Philip Dunne felt that Ford had directed the love scenes between Pidgeon and O'Hara magnificently, to his dying day he felt that Ford let some of the bit players go over the top: "When the postman brings the invitation from Queen Victoria, he has him hold out the envelope and throw a big salute . . . things like that, these broad strokes. There's no reason in the scene where they're washing up after the mine, for the wife to pass her husband who's smoking a pipe and dump a pail of water on him. That is not motivated, and I never liked unmotivated actions."

Dunne pined for the film that might have been had William Wyler directed it. Wyler was a very different kind of director—analytical, narrowly focused on a film's central dramatic conflict. By having Ford take over the picture, Zanuck not only assured himself of having it made on time and on budget, he made sure that the film would have an emotional as well as a dramatic component. "Ford changed the canvas of the film," said Roddy McDowall. "He made it much broader."

Philip Dunne could never quite admit that Ford did a more empathetic job than Wyler would have. "Willy was *not* . . . a corny director, and that was both Jack's strength, when he controlled it, as in our movie, and his weakness, when he didn't, as in *Grapes of Wrath*, specifically Jane Darwell's dreadful performance, which won her an Academy Award. Nunnally Johnson, in private, waxed almost poetic in his anathema on the subject. The Academy membership loves corn, or they'd never have bestowed their laurel on *Going My Way*." Had Wyler directed the picture, "we would have had a more honest movie, a more dramatic one, a more thoughtful one—and probably one less successful at the box office. Audiences too love corn."

For years Ford would give a party for the group he called the Ladies of the Green Valley. O'Hara, Lee, and the rest of the women members of the cast would attend, as would Philip Dunne and Roddy McDowall. So would Jane Darwell; although she hadn't been in the picture, Ford would probably have preferred her to Sara Allgood, so she was in on a pass.

By the fall of 1941, Hollywood was changing. Writers like John Huston and Preston Sturges were becoming directors, and a rank outsider like Orson Welles had been given the keys to RKO's kingdom. Ford didn't care for either Huston or Sturges, but he was fond of Welles, possibly because Gregg Toland vouched for him and told Ford how often Welles had looked at *Stagecoach* in preparation for *Citizen Kane*.

Ford turned up on the set of *Citizen Kane* early in the shooting and promptly exclaimed, "Well, how's old snake-in-the-grass Eddie?" warning Welles that Eddie Donahue, his assistant director, was a spy for the front office. After Welles had made a couple of his own movies, he received a citation of sorts that had been put together on the back of a piece of cardboard in Baja by the Ford clique in high alcoholic spirits. "Many ornate and official looking stamps were pasted all over this document," Welles told Peter Bogdanovich, "including several Mexican beer labels. . . . The text was brief. There was just this simple statement: 'Orson Welles has been elected.' "

Welles adored Ford's work and seems to have adored Ford as well. "Sentiment is Jack's vice. When he escapes it, you get a perfect kind of innocence. . . . And what a sense he always has for *texture*—for the physical existence of things."

How Green Was My Valley has maintained the reputation it began building that year, when it won over one of its more unlikely fans. "We went to a movie, *How Green Was My Valley*," wrote General Joseph Stilwell in his diary. "It is one of the best films I ever saw." It remains among Ford's most powerful achievements, as was attested by the black critic and commentator Stanley Crouch, who wrote an essay nearly sixty years after the film was made about how the film moved him the first time he saw it as a child, and has continued to move him through repeated viewings as a man:

"There was something in the tale that spoke to the world surrounding me even though the people, superficially, were so different. The cinematic depth gave me one of my earliest experiences of the meaning of the universal achieved through aesthetic form. . . . I can see my younger brother . . . that street and those people, some of whom are now gone (my brother from the complications of a gunshot wound . . . my mother cremated in Houston, Texas, after her 1992 death on Bloomsday), rise into asphalt, concrete, fences, lawns, bricks, homes, and life once more, crossing the dark breech of eternity. I am back there just as the boy was in *How Green Was My Valley*, and nothing is dead, nothing gone, all is made perpetual through the regeneration of memory."

The run of films that had begun with *Stagecoach* and concluded with *How Green Was My Valley* completed Ford's transition from excellence to greatness. He would win back-to-back Academy Awards for direction, an achievement that has not been equaled since, and he stood at the apex of the American film industry, in complete sync with his industry and American culture. Movies like *The Informer, Stagecoach, The Grapes of Wrath*, and *How Green Was My Valley* meshed with the rising of a social conscience in the country at large, as well as with a growing awareness of film as art.

World War II and its aftermath would end all that; by the late '40s, there would be no general cultural consensus, no sense of social and aesthetic unity that could simultaneously encompass political radicals and mainstream values. America's divisions became more pronounced, and John Ford's belief in America's lambent promise would begin to darken.

While Ford had been turning out great movies with nonchalant ease, he had one eye on the storm that was coming from Europe. From a document in the Ford papers that has been dated as December 1939, it is clear that he had been doing some light reconnaissance for the Navy during long cruises on the *Araner*, as in this report about a recent trip to Baja:

"*Cape San Lucas*. The usual Japanese photographer. Same one that has been there for the last six years. . . .

"*Guamas*. When entering Guamas harbor I thought for a moment I was in Moji Straits. The Japanese shrimp fleet was lying at anchor. Fourteen steam trawlers two to two hundred and fifty tons . . . two mother ships five to six hundred tons. . . . The most striking point concerning this fleet is its personnel. This has me completely baffled. The crew come ashore for liberty in well-tailored flannels, worsteds and tweed suits. . . . The men are above average height . . . young . . . good-looking and very alert. All carry themselves with military carriage. . . . For want of a better word I would call them the Samurai or military caste. . . . I am positive they are Naval men. . . . They constitute a real menace. Although I am not a trained Intelligence Officer, still my profession is to observe and make distinctions. . . . I will stake my professional reputation that these young men are not professional fishermen."

As a committed Roosevelt man, Ford was far from an isolationist, but when Philip Dunne, representing the William Allen White Committee, an interventionist group raising money for England, asked him for $500, he demurred.

"What if Hitler invades Ireland?" Dunne asked.

"They'd repel them," said Ford.

"How?"

"By throwing their rosary beads at them."

Ford ended up giving Dunne the $500. "He was a sound man," remembered the writer. And an irascible one. Jean Renoir arrived at Fox in the spring of 1941 after fleeing France and Hitler. Since Renoir's English would never be more than pidgin, he was always at a disadvantage working in America. When they were introduced, Ford paid him the tribute of speaking in French: "Dear Jean, don't ever forget what I'm going to tell you. Actors are crap."

On September 9, 1941, William "Wild Bill" Donovan, head of the newly created Office of Strategic Services in Washington, wrote Frank Knox, the Secretary of the Navy, that he wanted John Ford put on active status and assigned to his office as soon as was convenient.

By mid-September, Zanuck was editing *How Green Was My Valley* together for its December premiere. Ford was in Washington, D.C., when Harry Wurtzel wrote him with the happy news that the phone had been ringing off the hook with job offers. "Colonel Joy has approached me a couple of times about making a new deal—he said it was at the request of Zanuck and Bill Goetz. . . . Joe Breen called me again yesterday and wanted to know when you were going to return. . . . He is very anxious to make a deal with you direct—or with Argosy—for two pictures a year. Jesse Lasky, talking for Warner Brothers, has spoken to me regarding your doing MARK TWAIN for him. In fact, all of the studios have called and to all I have given the same answer—we will discuss everything upon your return here."

But Ford was about to walk away from the work he loved and needed. Movies would have to wait. At the end of September, he wrote to his wife: "Dear Ma—Things are moving apace. Kids gradually getting here—hum of preparation and excitement. . . . Mary, it would take volumes to say what I think of your unselfish courageous attitude in this present emergency. Words literally fail me. I am very proud of you. 'Nuff said except I love [and] admire you more than ever. Be proud—but under no circumstances deprive yourself or Barbara of anything. Will write often. Bushels of love, Jack."

A few weeks later, Ward Bond sent "Seaman First Class John Ford" a joking telegram: "Have managed to sell *Araner.* Proceeds do not cover round trip to Avalon. Please wire difference $4.29 Mexican."

On Sunday, December 7, Ford, his wife, and daughter were having dinner at the home of Admiral Pickens in Alexandria, Virginia. The maid came in with the telephone but the admiral said that he didn't want to be disturbed when he was eating. This is different, the maid said. This is the War Department. The admiral picked up the phone and listened. "Yes, yes, yes," he said, and then he hung up.

"Gentlemen," he announced, "Pearl Harbor has just been attacked by the Japanese. We are now at war."

"Everybody at that table, their lives changed that minute," remembered Mary Ford. People got up and left the dining room, which dismayed the admiral's wife. "It's no use getting excited," she said. "This is the seventh war that's been announced in this dining room." Two weeks after Pearl Harbor, Ford was on his way to the Canal Zone via Miami.

In February 1942, *How Green Was My Valley* went into wide release, but by that time Ford was, for the first time, preoccupied by things besides the next movie. It was time to go to war. For the next three and a half years, his headquarters wouldn't be Odin Street in Hollywood, but the Office of Strategic Services, at 25th and E Streets in Washington, D.C.

Pearl Harbor brought America into World War II, but John Ford was already there.

The Ford Family
LILLY LIBRARY

PART FOUR

AT WAR

"Ford never liked being an administrator. He would go out and do things."

ROBERT PARRISH

CHAPTER FOURTEEN

In 1939, Ford began organizing what became the Eleventh Naval District Motion Picture and Still Photographic Group. The unit would eventually consist of about two hundred men—thirty-five officers, one hundred seventy-five enlisted men, all recruited from the studios, who began receiving training and military indoctrination two and three times weekly.

They were, remembered Mary Ford, "over-age and rich, people who could never have been drafted, but when Jack said, 'Let's go,' they obeyed him." The idea was to form a photographic unit for the Navy made up of some of Hollywood's best and brightest. The unit would take charge of documentary, propaganda, and reconnaissance photography—one-stop shopping for moviemaking, writers, directors, cameramen, makeup artists, editors, and crews. The objective was "to record the history of the Navy in World War Two."

On January 24, 1941, Ford wired Merian Cooper his estimates for what it would cost to run the Field Photographic Unit: "FOR FIRST YEAR A TOTAL OF FIVE MILLION DOLLARS CONSISTING OF RESEARCH ONE MILLION FIVE HUNDRED AND TWENTY SEVEN THOUSAND. CAMERAS INCLUDING DEVELOPMENT OF NEW TYPES ONE MILLION TWO HUNDRED AND FIFTY THOUSAND. NEGATIVE RAW STOCK AND DEVELOPING TWO HUNDRED AND FIFTY THOUSAND. . . . TOTAL FOR SECOND YEAR THREE MILLION SINCE MOST EQUIPMENT AND TRAINING IS IN FIRST YEAR. THIRD YEAR TOTAL REDUCED TO TWO MILLION SIX HUNDRED FIFTY THOUSAND FOR SAME REASON."

Serious recruiting began. Among the first recruits was Gregg Toland. Ford and Cooper mutually proposed members of the unit and decided on duties and rank, as in this wire from Ford the same day as the budget wire: "SUGGEST ADD HALF STRIPE FOR AUGUST TOLAND SIEGLER ROSSON

AND ONE OTHER. TALKED TO DOROTHY ALL WELL AT HOME. THANKS COOP AND GOD BLESS YOU."

Ford asked the great cameraman James Wong Howe to join. Howe wanted to go, but he was Chinese; although he had lived in America for thirty-nine years, the Exclusion Act forbade him from becoming a citizen. Because he wasn't a citizen, the War Department couldn't give him a commission; the only way he could get to Ford's unit would be to enlist in Chiang Kai-shek's Nationalist Chinese army, and then be "loaned" to the Americans. But Howe didn't trust Chiang Kai-shek or his army, so he had to turn Ford down.

Ford also went after a camera operator named William Clothier. Ford offered him a commission, but when Clothier came home to talk it over with his wife, Carmen, she immediately bridled. "What are you going to do if you're out in the middle of the ocean and the boat sinks?" she asked. "You can't swim to shore." Clothier backed out of the Navy but got a commission in the Air Force. When Ford saw him again in Washington, he got up from his chair and kissed Clothier on the cheek. "I'm sorry you're not with us, but I'm glad to see you're in uniform," he told Clothier. After the war, Clothier would become one of Ford's most trusted collaborators.

A young actor named George Hjorth intended to enlist in the Air Force, but when he was making the rounds of the studios to say goodbye, someone suggested he join up with Ford's outfit instead. "That way you can serve your country and live at home," he was told. It sounded good, so Hjorth signed up and was promptly ordered to report to Washington. He never got back to Hollywood for the rest of the war.

Conspicuously absent from the unit was George O'Brien. According to O'Brien's wife, Marguerite, O'Brien, at the age of forty-two, rushed from his Malibu ranch to enlist in the Navy as soon as he heard of the formation of Ford's unit. Marguerite took this personally, as a willful abandonment of the family, and she seems to have been glad when, as O'Brien believed, Ford refused to tap him for the unit.

In fact, Ford hadn't ignored O'Brien, and tried to get him assigned to the unit long before Pearl Harbor, despite the "abandonment" episode in Manila years before. "He would be of great value to me with his knowledge of photography and of naval affairs in general in command of a Mobile Photographic Section," wrote Ford in a vain attempt to get O'Brien transferred to his unit. "If it could be arranged so he could transfer to our Unit you would be doing us a great favor."

As a father of two, O'Brien could have easily stayed in Hollywood, but he was at something of a life impasse—his RKO contract had ended, and his marriage was none too healthy. O'Brien was first sent to San Diego to get recruits in good physical condition, then became a beachmaster and participated in more than fifteen invasions, eventually rising to the rank of captain.

For a year, the men in Ford's unit underwent training in whatever aspect of film work they didn't already know. Training sessions were held on soundstages at Fox or some other studio, sometimes in the Naval Reserve Armory in Los Angeles. At the end of the year of training, each of the nine divisions was a complete camera unit, able to undertake all aspects of documenting a war with motion picture or still cameras, from 35mm Mitchells and Bell & Howells to 16mm Eyemos, Akeleys, and DeVrys. They could develop and print their work in the field or on board ship. They were even indoctrinated in Navy routine, although Ford's grasp of that would always be casual, to say the least.

By mid-March of 1941, enrollment was 50 percent complete. It was inevitable that Ford would invite his ambitious young friend Robert Parrish to join. "He said, 'I've got Gregg Toland and Joe August in the unit and they'll teach you how to use a camera,' " remembered Parrish. "He set it up as a Naval Reserve Unit, but it never occurred to us at the time that there would be a war."

Ford, however, thought otherwise. On September 11, 1941, he had been inducted into the Navy as a lieutenant commander "for the duration of the emergency." By this time, units of the Field Photo had already done time at places from San Diego to Pensacola, Panama to Pearl Harbor. One crew had even gone to England, already in the war, to observe how their British equivalents handled their tasks.

John Wayne wanted to join, but according to his son, "he was too old with too many dependents, plus he had an ear infection from a film he made called *Reap the Wild Wind,* an infection that never left. Everytime he'd get in the water it would come back. So he was actually 4-F."

Bad ear or not, Wayne kept tiptoeing to the edge of enlistment but could never quite bring himself to do it. In early October of 1941, Ford wrote Mary of his disgust with Wayne and Ward Bond's continuing hijinks at a time when the world was sliding into chaos. Three months after Pearl Harbor, he wrote Mary again, this time more contemptuously, saying he was "delighted" to hear about Wayne and Bond perched on a mountaintop as lookouts for a potential Japanese invasion of California. "Such heroism shall not go unrewarded," he wrote sarcastically. "It will live in the annals of time." (Bond was an epileptic, hence an authentic 4-F.)

The pattern was set. Every once in a while, Wayne would write of his interest in serving, as soon as he wrapped up another picture. Or two. In May 1942, Wayne wrote a "Dear Pappy" letter asking about any direct suggestions Ford might have about how Wayne could get in, finally asking if the Field Photo would take him. If Ford replied to Wayne's letter, it's lost. In the spring of 1943, Wayne again wrote about openings in the unit, and an official replied that, while the Navy and Marine allotments were full, Wayne could, if he wished, enlist under the Army's allotment. Republic sent him to Utah to make a movie, but not before Wayne wrote Ford that he would be ready to serve by October.

October came and went, and Wayne kept making movies, letting Republic file draft deferments for him, telling Ford he needed one more cinematic "fling before going off to battle." Wayne kept having flings until the war was over, never appealing the deferments filed by Republic, who were frantic to keep the money rolling in from Wayne's consistently successful movies. His inability to bring himself to enlist must have been a disappointment for Ford, not to mention serving as handy leverage that he could use to cow the actor when he threatened to get too full of himself.

If Wayne failed himself, he tried not to fail Ford. He went on a USO tour of Australia, New Britain, and New Guinea, and put in time at the Hollywood Canteen. At Christmas, he and Bond filled the house on Odin Street with flowers, perfume, and presents.

The Navy was leery of a bunch of Hollywood amateurs, however well-meaning, but finally Colonel Donovan accepted Ford's unit as the photographic component of the Office of Strategic Services. Ford's only superior was Donovan; Donovan's only superior was Roosevelt.

Although Donovan's nickname was Wild Bill, the wildness was strictly intellectual. He was a Wall Street lawyer, a Republican, who filled the OSS with a mix of bluebloods and brilliant amateurs. Donovan didn't care about the politics of his people, and in fact had some Communists working for the OSS.

Personally, Donovan was a dumpy-looking but charismatic man with a quiet voice. "He was rather small and rumpled [with] piercing blue eyes," remembered Julia McWilliams, who worked in the OSS and would achieve her own measure of fame under her married name of Julia Child. "It was said that he could read a document just by turning the pages, he was so fast at it, and he was . . . somehow fascinating [to people]. He gave you his complete attention and you were just fascinated by him."

Donovan valued creativity, intelligence, and a love of adventure, and in return gave his people a great deal of autonomy. Besides Ford, Donovan's recruits included the baseball catcher Moe Berg, Harvard president James B. Conant, and diplomats David Bruce and Allen Dulles. Donovan's friendship with Roosevelt made him anathema to J. Edgar

Hoover, among others. Douglas MacArthur would never allow the OSS into his theater. West Pointers called the OSS "Donovan's dragoons," Charles Lindbergh said the organization was "full of politics, ballyhoo, and controversy," and Joseph Goebbels characterized it as a "staff of Jewish scribblers." William Colby, later head of the CIA, called the OSS, "an exercise in improvisation."

Once again, John Ford was in the right place at the right time.

The first year he worked for Donovan, Ford's home in Washington was a 14 x 38 foot broom closet (actually Room 501) in the Carlton Hotel. Later, in 1943, he found an apartment on Connecticut Avenue. The official address didn't fool Mary. Although she was used to being separated from Jack while he was on location or on one of his jaunts with the boys, his going off to war caused her understandable anxiety. She lost a good deal of weight ("at first I didn't know her, she is so very thin," wrote Louella Parsons in June 1942) and began indulging in long-distance phone calls.

"Honey, it was swell hearing from you last night, but Ma, you can't call up long distance just when you're blue and lonesome," wrote Ford. "It's too damned expensive. We've really got to adjust—not financially necessarily—but mentally. To hell with the Bonds and the Waynes. They don't count. The blow will hit them hard next year. . . . I'm terribly disappointed about May leaving you alone in the house when Barbara went out, because I know how scared you are to stay alone."

Ford then turned around and immediately penned a note to Barbara: "Keep Ma happy. She called last night, saying she was alone in the house, you having gone out etc. Kinda feeling sorry for herself. . . . I love you + I miss you much. daddy." Then, in a P.S., "Don't let Ma read my letters to you or vice versa. You are old enough now to have your own privacy."

In a sense, Ford's service in the military would replicate his work in Hollywood: downtime in Washington followed by spurts of excitement doing what he was put on earth to do—shoot film, command men, insult anybody asking for a compliment. Helen Hayes came to Washington late in 1941 with a Maxwell Anderson play called *Candle in the Wind*. Ford went to see the play and afterward the two went over to the Lincoln Memorial, Hayes's favorite Washington landmark.

After waiting for the requisite praise which never came, Hayes finally asked Ford what he thought. Ford looked at her affectionately and said, "Baby, do you stink!"

"That was Jack," remembered Hayes.

The war brought Ford into contact with a young recruit to the Field Photo named Mark Armistead. For a time, the two lived together on an abandoned yacht called the *Saramia* anchored in the Potomac River while Ford waited for the space at the Carlton to come open. Armistead had initially rented out the cabins to other officers, and kept the master bedroom for himself. But when Ford heard about the yacht, he insisted on inspecting it, then commandeered Armistead's room for himself.

Armistead had to adapt to Ford's nocturnal tendencies. "He didn't sleep at night," remembered Armistead. "Only naps during the day." All through the night, Ford would talk, breaking up the conversations by alternating between Hershey bars and his pipe, filled with Virginia mixture tobacco.

On February 24, 1942, Ford wrote Mary from Honolulu in some wonderment. " 'My gawd' you'd never recognize it. The old Honolulu we loved so much has changed—I think for the better. The trip over was uneventful but very exciting. Our gang had to stand watches and they made me very proud and happy. Strange seeing old Hawaii loom up in the morning mist—the absence of leis and music—no crowds. . . .

"Naturally one can't write a great deal of what is happening here, but somehow I like this place now better than ever. All our old friends were elated to see me and were astonished to see me as 'Kelemoku' (sailor boy). Our work is terrifically vital & we have been accorded a most welcome reception by everybody.

"The only things I miss are you & Barbara—seems strange not to see you on the beach with sun-tan oil—or Babs running around in shorts in a terrible hurry to grab a sandwich or go to a movie. I guess I must love you all very much. Nevertheless I am very close to you all—much closer than I've ever been."

Two days later, the Oscars were awarded. Ford remembered that when he heard that *How Green Was My Valley* had won Best Picture and he had again won Best Director, he was somewhere in the Pacific on board the USS *Salt Lake*, where Captain Elias Zacharias ordered ice cream be served for dinner, and Admiral Bull Halsey flagged congratulations. It's more likely that he was still in Honolulu, for he told Mary in the letter of February 24 to continue addressing him at the Moana Hotel, that he was "going to make it general head-quarters for a bit."

Ford ran his unit pretty much the way he ran a film set, but on a larger scale. "His enjoyment was crossing people up," said Mark Armistead. "*If* he liked you. If he didn't like you, he just ignored you, but if he did like you, he gave you some pretty bad times."

"I thought I was joining the Navy," said Robert Moreno, who had been an assistant cameraman at MGM, "but it turned out not to be the

Navy at all. Ford could do whatever he wanted, as long as he kept Wild Bill Donovan happy."

The fact of the matter was that Ford had been given official carte blanche by Donovan: "You are hereby authorized to exercise full responsibility relative to the carrying out of the projects assigned you," wrote Donovan in a directive of May 12, 1942. "This authority includes authorization to serve as certifying office for purchase vouchers, payrolls and other vouchers and official documents and to enter into necessary contracts for supplies, space and service relative to the above duties.

"You are further authorized to direct and control official travel to such points as may be necessary to carry out your said duties."

So, aside from Ford's native ability to get what he wanted, was added the official imprimatur of Wild Bill Donovan. This was to be a continuing source of frustration for other filmmakers with less power, or with a less devious nature. William Wyler, attempting to get rolling with *The Memphis Belle*, his movie about a B-17 Flying Fortress, found it impossible to get equipment. For weeks he stood on a runway, with no cameras and no film, watching bombers take off.

"My equipment had a very low priority," Wyler remembered years later. "It was coming across on a surface vessel. Suddenly John Ford showed up. . . . He was in the *Navy* and his equipment was *flown* over by the Army Air Force. I don't know how he did it." Wyler vented to his wife, who said that "Willy didn't know the Army ways. He couldn't requisition even a typewriter, much less cameras. When Ford came over with *two* camera crews, it just drove Willy crazy."

I n the spring of 1942, the Japanese admiral Yamamoto convinced his colleagues to go for broke—a single, decisive battle that would decide the course of the naval war in the Pacific. As the focal point for the offensive, Yamamoto chose the obscure island of Midway, one thousand miles northwest of Honolulu.

Yamamoto's reasoning was that Midway, on the perimeter of the Hawaiian waters, would give his country a base in the Pacific that could not fail to worry the Americans, as well as provide the Japanese with the possibility of harrying the West Coast of America. He began assembling an armada of more than a hundred warships, including eight aircraft carriers and eleven battleships, in addition to transport and supply vehicles—the most powerful force in Japanese military history.

As with Pearl Harbor, the Japanese were relying on the element of surprise, but they were unaware that the Americans had broken their code. The Americans could tell a Japanese strike was approaching, but they weren't sure where—the Aleutians, the central Pacific, and Midway were all possible candidates. All the Americans knew was that the target was designated "AF." Operating on gut instinct that the target was Midway, an analyst instructed Midway to send a radio message saying the island was short of fresh water. The next day, the Americans picked up a Japanese radio signal saying that "AF" was running short of fresh water. Now, Admiral Chester Nimitz knew where the attack was headed and had time to prepare.

And so Ford and Jack Mackenzie Jr., the twenty-year-old son of a Hollywood cameraman, were sent to Midway from Hawaii two weeks before the Japanese raided, making the journey via mosquito boat. Ford had wanted to go to war, and now, by God, he was about to.

At one point it looked as if Mackenzie was going to be reassigned to Wake Island, but Ford intervened to keep Mackenzie on Midway. Mackenzie was unhappy; the action was on Wake, and all Midway could offer was day after day of perfect weather, with stunning sunrises and sunsets—perfect for color photography, not so perfect for a young buck anxious for action.

On the evening of June 3, as Yamamoto's ships neared the island, Captain Simard, Commandant of the Naval Air Station on Midway, asked Ford to act as a forward observer and stay in the powerhouse equipped with his 16mm camera and two phones so that he could report the battle's progress to the officers on the ground.

The battle began early the next morning. Mackenzie was jolted from his sleep at dawn by all hell breaking loose around him. Wave after wave of Japanese planes launched themselves from the carriers to pound the island while American planes dove, darted, and bombed the ships.

Mackenzie had been bunking with Ford in the powerhouse, where he had an unobstructed view of the entire island all the way to the ocean. He was using a Bell and Howell Filmo 70 loaded with Kodachrome. After the initial wave, Mackenzie went to the airfield control tower, while Ford kept grinding with his own Filmo at the powerhouse as several Japanese fighters stitched the building with machine-gun fire. Ford was shooting the bombardment from one of the primary targets.

Mackenzie began moving around, catching as much as he could on the run, looking through windows, peeking around corners. Ford was hit in the head by a piece of flying concrete and knocked out. He recovered, picked up his camera and kept shooting, then was struck by shrapnel that ripped a three-inch hole in his upper arm. The arm quickly began turning color as it bruised from elbow to wrist.

Soon, the island's aircraft hangars caught fire from the bombardment, and the hospital was burning. An oil tank exploded, sending heavy waves of black smoke toward the sky. "It was a merry little hell all around," remembered Mackenzie.

Ford made his way to the infirmary, where doctors treated his arm and dosed him with some tetanus vaccine. The medical report noted that he was "not incapacitated for duty. To return for treatments."

For a time, it looked as though the Japanese would triumph, but then, swooping down from fourteen thousand feet, American dive-bombers caught the aircraft carriers at their most vulnerable moment—the decks were crowded with airplanes refueling, and gas lines were strung across the decks. It was the fatal five minutes of the battle, and of the war in the Pacific. Three Japanese carriers were sunk; a fourth went down the next morning. At that point, Yamamoto turned his fleet around. He had suffered a crushing defeat, the first in Japanese naval history.

The Americans lost one carrier (the *Yorktown*), a destroyer, and more than a hundred planes, but it was a massive logistical and moral victory. The Japanese had forced a battle, had swung into it with superior strength, and they had lost. Instead of threatening Hawaii and the West Coast of America, the Japanese found themselves on the defensive.

"From that historic moment," wrote Stephen Ambrose, "the U.S. counteroffensive began to gather force and to move relentlessly towards the home islands of Japan. . . . Everything before Midway was an immense Japanese success, and everything afterward, a failure."

Ford cabled Mary: "OK LOVE. JOHN FORD."

"HOLLYWOOD NOTABLE HURT" screamed the headline in the *Los Angeles Examiner* on June 10, 1942, over a three-column picture of Ford and a story by Louella Parsons. The front page of the *Hollywood Reporter* carried the story of how Ford filmed the Battle of Midway. On June 30, Mary wrote her husband, "I love you more than ever and am even more proud of you today than on July 3, 1920. . . . You've been so wonderful to me and after all, the only words are thank you . . . for 22 marvelous years."

Word of Ford's exploits in shooting the battle that raged around him quickly spread. A bulletin marked "SECRET" was sent to William Donovan on June 15. "The pictures [Ford] took on Midway are remarkable. I think and believe Jack will be given the Navy Cross as a result of his conduct in the Midway action. He was stationed at an observation post with one enlisted man. The observation post was on top of the power house which is a hot place to be during an air raid where the first objective is the power house. He kept in communication with Command Headquarters throughout the engagement although he was knocked down three or four times during the action from bomb explosions and was wounded early in the battle. Not only that, but he and his man managed at the same time to photograph the action."

Ford, bandaged arm swollen to twice its normal size, returned to Los Angeles on July 18, just long enough to have the arm looked at by a doctor, then flew to Washington with the film he and Mackenzie had shot. There was, he believed, a good documentary in it.

Ford became friendly with Admiral Chester Nimitz, who spent the war caught between the ever-present rage of Admiral Ernest King, Chief of Naval Operations, and Douglas MacArthur, whose preference was always to win the war against Japan single-handedly. Despite his growing network of relationships, and the fact that he was a passionate believer in the military and the cause for which he was fighting, Ford could no more drop his suspicion of supervision in Washington than he could in Hollywood. A film shot by Ford would have to be edited and scored Ford's way.

"He wouldn't let the Navy people see any of the *Battle of Midway* until he'd found a way to show it to the President," remembered Robert Parrish. "He was in the Navy and under orders but hid what he was doing. He told me, 'I don't want any admirals coming around this project acting like associate producers.' He trusted the Navy but he didn't trust them to let them know what he was doing any more than he would let Zanuck or Cohn know what he was doing."

Parrish remembered that the raw footage of *The Battle of Midway* was somewhere between twenty to thirty thousand feet, enough for a feature. "It should run about eighteen minutes," Ford told him. By the time Parrish was through with his rough cut, which took about three months, he and Ford had fine-tuned the film to run seventeen minutes.

Ford shamed Dudley Nichols into working on the narration by muttering, "We're the ones who are out there getting shot at." For dialogue, he called on James Kevin McGuinness, a successful producer at MGM.

Ford took the contributions of both men and edited them down to what Parrish remembered as two typed pages. "He'd say, 'Run the film; when I point at you, say this. . . .' And he'd point at [Henry] Fonda, or point to Phil Scott, the sound effects cutter. 'When the planes lift off, yell, "There go the Marines." ' "

"He'd have us do things without orders," said Parrish. "He'd just say, 'Go do it.' I was chasing back and forth across the country cutting *The Battle of Midway*." One day Ford pulled a small roll of film out of his pocket and told Parrish where to splice it into the film. It turned out to be a close-up of Franklin Roosevelt Jr., clearly implying that Roosevelt had been on the scene. "I don't know to this day if FDR Jr. was at Midway," remembered Parrish.

Most of the film consisted of the footage Ford and Mackenzie shot, but Parrish added some shots of the sea action that had been photographed by Lieutenant Kenneth Pier. When the film was edited and sound added, Parrish and A. J. Bolton, the naval attaché in Los Angeles, bicycled their one print from studio to studio to gauge reaction. "It is not possible to tell you of the wonderful reception the picture got everywhere we went," Bolton wrote Ford. "Even Harry Cohn only had one or two criticisms to make of it. He was quite upset that you didn't have any miniatures of . . . plane crashes. Bob and I thought we might cut in a few but decided not to until consultation with you."

Ford wisely opted to keep the film completely authentic; no studio re-creations, no miniatures. *The Battle of Midway* doesn't attempt reportage as such, and offers no broad perspective of the battle. (In a sense, the film misrepresents the battle, for the air attack on Midway itself, the centerpiece of the film, was a comparatively insignificant part of the overall battle.) As William Murphy noted, "the film substitutes moral and emotional feelings for information," which sets the film apart from Frank Capra's *Why We Fight* series, or other wartime documentaries such as *Desert Victory* and *The Stilwell Road*.

Judged as a documentary, it's unusually impressionistic; judged as a John Ford film, it's one of his best, offering the rough essence of Ford's spirit and the way he perceived the valor of battle. It also has the necessary authenticity; as the explosions go off, the frame line of the 16mm film jumps within the camera mechanism. It has a very spare, aphoristic narration compared to other, invariably hectoring wartime films; Ford trusts the image, trusts sound, trusts the mood conveyed by "Red River Valley" played at sunset, trusts the feelings associated with the voices of Henry Fonda, Jane Darwell, and Donald Crisp.

Usually, Ford takes his time setting a mood, but the short running time forced him and Parrish to adopt a clipped pace that still had room for typical Fordian moments—distant thunder over a sunset, comic relief in the form of some birds, low-angle close-ups that emphasize the nobility of a face, a flag raising, the burial of the dead. Ford didn't have time to characterize the soldiers, but he managed to personalize them by showing us their families back home.

In November 1942, Ford arrived in Algiers to find Darryl F. Zanuck waiting for him. Zanuck was a colonel in the Signal Corps and was working on a documentary about the North Africa campaign. Ford feigned dismay. "Can't I ever get away from you? I'll bet a dollar to a doughnut that if I ever go to Heaven, you'll be waiting at the door for me under a sign reading, 'Produced by Darryl F. Zanuck.' "

Between November 16 and December 6, Ford and Jack Pennick were attached to Company D of the 13th Armored Regiment in North Africa, moving through Algeria in tanks, on their way to Bône, Souk el Arba, and Medjez el Bab, where they encountered German resistance. Company D pushed forward until Tĕbourba, which they reached on November 29, where their advance was stopped by tank fighting, artillery fire, and dive-bombing. A week later, Ford and Pennick were ordered to the rear.

Those were the facts as related in a memo from Ford's commanding office. But by the time Ford was through mythologizing the episode, he had been under fire twenty-four hours a day for six weeks, had subsisted on tea and English biscuits, and had somehow managed to lose thirty-two pounds off his already lean frame.

On Christmas Day that year, Mary wrote Jack about the holidays on Odin Street. "We had a beautiful tree and big fires in the fireplace and Christmas carols in the music box. Ward and Duke were over generous . . . gorgeous bags for Barbara, and Ward filled the house with flowers and perfume bottles, and in return we spent the night before Christmas helping Josie and Doris [Wayne's and Bond's estranged wives] keep their chins up. . . .

"I've done my 100% best this Christmas. Maybe I've succeeded, who knows. The house looks so pretty in its Christmas finery. Fires in all the fireplaces, the wind outside blowing like heck makes it seem even more homey. Your brother Frank is drunk and telephoning every few minutes, but no one is letting him come up. We all feel we will see you soon. We love you so awfully much and miss you so."

Being away from the familiar routine of home and work loosened up the normally taciturn Ford. His nephew Francis Jr. had been at Pearl Harbor during the Japanese attack, and was seeing a very active war. After Jack got back from Midway, he had Frank Jr.'s commander send him over to his hotel in Honolulu. The young man knocked on the door, stepped in, gave his uncle a snappy salute, and was astonished to have him walk over and throw his arms around him. "Gee, I'm glad to see you," Ford said. All he wanted was to have a heart-to-heart, so he could tell his brother that Frank Jr.—known to the family as Billy—was okay.

Likewise, his letters to Mary had always been chatty and companionable, but Ford's wartime correspondence carries more warmth: "Dear Ma, Enjoyed talking to you on the phone just now—your letter written Tuesday pleased me—gave me pictures of our beautiful home—the home and family we are fighting to preserve—Will keep in touch . . . hope to see you in a few days or a few weeks . . . all my love miss you so much. Daddy."

Or this: "Well, Ma, I sure fall in love with you more than ever . . . you've got plenty of guts, Ma, the right kind. . . . I pray to God it will soon be over so we can live our life together with our children and grandchildren and our Araner—Catalina would look good now. God bless and love you Mary darling—I'm tough to live with—heaven knows & Hollywood didn't help—Irish and genius don't mix well but you know you're the only woman I've ever loved."

Occasionally, he even permitted himself a rough form of romantic enticement: "Ma—I think I'll even sleep in the same bed with you if we get together one of these days—"

Ford had never been so naked about his need for the order and stability of family, and would never be again. Likewise, it is the only time he would let his crusty guard down and call himself what he was—a genius. Another letter proclaimed one of his infrequent bursts of pride in Pat, when the boy sent him a letter that "made my heart swell with joy and stuff. It's so sweetly pathetic—so Irish! . . . I love you & miss you more than a mere pen can tell."

Ford also took the trouble to keep in touch with colleagues. "Just had the extreme pleasure of seeing the Ox-bow Incident," he wrote William Wellman, "and I was certainly thrilled. It is the best picture I have seen for longer than I like to remember. Billie, it was really swell and it did my heart good after reading all the publicity about these new genius boys like Pisston Sturges and the like, to think that an oldtimer should come along and put out the best direction of these recent years. . . . The only thing in the picture that didn't strike me as being real, Billie, was my brother Frank refusing the drink and making such a fuss about getting hung. After all, most of his ancestors have been hung, and I just can't see Frank refusing a drink."

Dudley Nichols had evidently sent his script for *This Land Is Mine* to Ford and asked for his opinion, which Ford gave, but not before reminiscing. "I ran *The Informer* last week, and boy, did I get a bang out of it. You know, Dudley, I never did see it except for that night at the preview when I was horribly sensitive to the hostility of the Hollywood reactionaries, who clustered around us wailing that any one should tear down their Gods. . . . To look back and to think how quickly the script was written and the picture was photographed. I have been thinking a lot about pictures lately. My work here, of course, is of a confidential, technical nature, but especially in North Africa in that freezing zero weather when every portion of your body would freeze and only the mind remained active then as a self-hypnotic gesture [I] would work on the scripts. How I want to talk them over with you!

"Dudley, please believe me when I criticized your production as though I were criticizing my own work. For you to make the greatest picture of all times would be of keen delight to me, because after all as Fluther said, 'You're the blood of my heart.' Christ! How I would love to have you succeed in your production, but Dudley, stay away from war stories. They are a drug on the market and can follow only one pattern."

Back home in Hollywood, Mary was vice president of the Hollywood Canteen, where she ran the kitchen. The Canteen was open every night from 7:00 to midnight and on Sunday from 2:00 to 8:00, hosting about six thousand servicemen per night; she didn't have an awful lot of spare time on her hands.

"It started out as nothing," Mary told Anthony Slide. "It was a deserted roller skating rink, and we fixed it up a little bit. Mrs. [Jules] Stein and two or three other women were struggling to get it in order . . . and I came in and said, 'I've had my vacation. What can I do?' And they just threw themselves on the floor and said, 'Will you take over the kitchen?' "

Mary called in one of her best friends, Mrs. Joe E. Brown, and the two women were soon running the operation with quasi-military precision. Reginald Gardiner was the chief dishwasher, and Spencer Tracy would even drop by to help out.

Outside, on the main floor, Kay Kyser was in charge of the music and he enlisted the best bands in America to handle the entertaining—Freddy Martin, the Dorsey Brothers, and Rudy Vallee, with Harry James holding down a regular Monday slot. Leopold Stokowski would give concerts, as would Frank Sinatra, and Lady Mendl would serve coffee. Marlene Dietrich came regularly, and learned how to jitterbug. Most days, Mary went in around 4:00 in the afternoon and trooped back to Odin Street around midnight.

"Mary is always there," wrote A. J. Bolton to Jack. "In fact, she is Miss Hollywood Canteen. It is a good thing for her as I think she was pretty miserable just sitting on the hilltop worrying about you and waiting for you to come home." From her vantage point at the Canteen, Mary was able to keep up on doings in town, and wrote her husband spiky letters about chicanery on the home front—Duke Wayne's infatuation with the woman who would be his next wife, and Ward Bond's divorcing his wife because she was "sloppy."

"Hold your hat when you read this," she wrote Jack on January 24, 1944. "Fred told me I'd done a swell job [at the Canteen] the past year and he knew you'd be proud of me . . . the acacia trees are in bloom and I think the hill is beautiful. . . . I love you terribly. All my love and Aloha."

A month later, Pat Ford's first son, Timothy, was born, making Jack a grandfather. He responded with a letter proclaiming his strong emotions at the extension of the line.

While Ford was preparing *The Battle of Midway*, a sudden bureaucratic crisis presented itself. *December 7th*, a docudrama Gregg Toland had made about Pearl Harbor, had turned out to be a rather lengthy eighty-five minutes long. The project had begun with a letter from Secretary of the Navy Frank Knox to William Donovan requesting "a complete motion picture factual presentation of the attack upon Pearl Harbor. . . . As you well know, the President has stressed the highly historical import of this date and I believe it should be handled by the best talent available." Ford, Gregg Toland, Ralph Hoge, Jack Pennick, James Mitchell, Robert Parrish, and James Saper were assigned the task of making the movie and promised "all necessary cooperation."

Toland, Sam Engel—later the producer of *My Darling Clementine*—and operator Eddie Pyle arrived in Hawaii in February 1942, and were joined a few weeks later by Ford. (It was while he was in Honolulu that Ford picked up rumors of the impending Japanese advance on Midway.) Ford seems to have set things up, then left Toland to make the movie. The uncut version has survived, and it's an extremely odd, humpbacked piece of work, a dramatized documentary with Walter Huston as Uncle Sam, Harry Davenport as a folksy Mr. C (for Conscience), and Dana Andrews as an Unknown Soldier.

It opens on December 6, 1941, as Uncle Sam and America's conscience engage in a colloquy that mixes a quick history lesson about Hawaii with accusations. Japanese-Americans in Hawaii (37 percent of the population, we are informed) are portrayed as potential traitors; gardeners listen to officers kibitzing about their ships, amassing information about Hickam Field, the target of the Japanese attack that came within twenty-four hours.

It's all quite inflammatory, and, by the time it was ready for release in late 1942, rather beside the point. Ford had considerable input into the film, because after the elaborate—and quite effective—sequence of the attack on Pearl Harbor, Irving Pichel becomes the narrator—he was the voice of the adult Huw in *How Green Was My Valley*—and the film moves into some definitively Fordian moments: a sequence of the dead identifying themselves, followed by shots of their parents—an idea Ford would help himself to for *The Battle of Midway*—and the reverent consecration of graves.

After this, the film moves quickly to scenes of reclamation, the righting and salvaging of ships. The film finally declares Hawaii the greatest military fortress in the world—a classic case of locking the barn door after the horses were gone.

As the film circulated amongst the brass, people—important people—began clearing their throats. One lieutenant colonel said that "the proportion of the picture's time and the attention given to the local Japanese problem is unwarranted when compared to the overall significance of the December 7th attack." Julian Johnson, of 20th Century-Fox, said that "the graveyard stuff might be good in some other picture, but here, after all the hell we have just seen, it is bad anti-climax." And Admiral Stark, commander of Naval Forces in Europe, went even further:

"This picture leaves the distinct impression that the Navy was not on the job, and this is not true. . . . I am not concerned with minor inaccuracies but great harm will be done and sleeping dogs awakened if the picture is released as it now stands."

The film was judged to be disruptive and designated unreleasable. Roosevelt issued a directive saying that all future Field Photo material be subjected to censorship, lest it injure morale. Since Ford had never had official permission to shoot the battle of Midway, and Roosevelt had just come down hard on the unit's work, he felt he had to play cloak-and-dagger games with the Midway footage and the editing process. (It was at this point that the magical close-up of FDR Jr. came into play. That, Ford knew, would make any presidential hard feelings vanish in a hurry.)

Robert Parrish told John Baxter that after *The Battle of Midway* was edited, Ford sent him to California with specific instructions to show it to Toland and Sam Engel. When the film was over, they both got up and stalked out without a word. When Parrish cornered Toland, the cameraman simply told him, "I don't wish to discuss it."

"What I didn't know," said Parrish, "was that many of the ideas in *The Battle of Midway* were part of *December 7th*. My guess is that Toland, Ford, and Engel had worked out the story for *December 7th* . . . then when Ford was presented with the opportunity to make *Battle of Midway* he used some of the same ideas that he had developed with them."

Ford may well have cribbed some ideas from Toland's film, especially if they had been his contribution in the first place. Beyond that, Toland had made a movie of feature length about America's worst military disaster, whereas Ford had shot a snappy short about our quick recovery.

Ford's friend James Kevin McGuinness offered his thoughts about Toland's effort. "The best general observation I can make in relation to Gregg's picture," wrote McGuinness, "is that, in the nature of present events, the U.S. Navy can deal only in facts. . . . It must not editorialize, or fictionize. . . .

"I'd crowd in every interesting foot of the salvage operations I could and finish off with a burst of glory when the battle wagons put to sea again. . . . As you said, the question of the Japs in Hawaii doesn't belong in this picture. You can't report it accurately, and there is no final determination of their loyalty or disloyalty which enables you to say they were, or were not Fifth Columnists. Probably they were both, but saying so is confusing. . . .

"I would, of course, hold on to every foot of the emotional film—the church services, the burials, etc. That's swell and very moving."

Ford and Robert Parrish cut *December 7th* down to a manageable thirty-four minutes, concentrating on the scenes of salvage and repair, reducing Toland's attempt at a documentary epic to a footnote. Walter Huston disappeared, as did Harry Davenport and any analysis of what had gone wrong.

Ford's shortened version of *December 7th* won the Oscar for Best Documentary and seems not to have come between him and Toland, at least not for long. By September of 1944, Ford was forwarding a decoration Toland had earned called the Cruzeiro do Sul. "Wear them with honor, my boy," wrote Ford, "but don't forget you wear them last. Despite the importance of the decoration, it is still foreign and must come after your American Theater ribbon." He went on to ask Toland if he could make arrangements with Sam Goldwyn to co-direct an MGM project called *They Were Expendable* with him. "I think it would be to his best interests for you to undertake an assignment of this sort, as it would be a great experience for you when he starts you directing."

Goldwyn obviously wasn't crazy about the idea, which led Ford to suggest a little further politicking: "Mr. Goldwyn must understand that one of the prime factors for your obtaining inactive status was the possibility that you might be assigned to this Navy picture. At least, I would try that gambit on him and hint that you might possibly be recalled if he didn't acquiesce."

Ford seems to have realized that Toland's full-length version was not negligible; on December 6, 1946, he wrote a letter to the Bureau of Archives asking them to preserve a print of the long version, "eight reels, I believe," thereby ensuring its survival.

The Battle of Midway was released months before the shortened version of *December 7th*, and earned superior notices. The *New York Times* said, "For 18 tingling and harshly realistic minutes the spectator is plunged into the front line amid the thunder of exploding bombs, the angry whine of fighter planes locked in combat and the relentless bark of anti-aircraft guns aboard surface vessels."

"The impact is quick as a wound and deep as loneliness," wrote James Agee in *The Nation*. "The result is a first-class failure to film the most difficult of all actions—a battle. But it is a brave attempt to make a record—quick, jerky, vivid, fragmentary, luminous—of a moment of desperate peril to the nation."

It remains a remarkable picture—along with John Huston's marginally superior *The Battle of San Pietro*, it's one of the World War II films that carries the real reverberations of battle and death.

In retrospect, it can be seen that *The Battle of Midway*, along with the Huston film, served two concurrent purposes: they created a symbiosis between fiction and nonfiction films that enabled Hollywood filmmakers to be more realistic in their depiction of battle and war; and they served as a powerful propaganda antidote to the conservative Congress that had been elected in November 1942, which viewed most war documentaries as far too liberal—that is to say, pro-Roosevelt. *The Battle of Midway* showed the costs and the trials, the dead and the dying, as well as why it all had to be endured.

Even now, far removed from Midway and the war, *The Battle of Midway* resonates. It remains one of Ford's great achievements.

CHAPTER FIFTEEN

From January to August 1943, Ford was in Washington running his unit, adeptly fighting what he called "the paper war." He and William Donovan had clearly grown close: on April 27, Donovan wrote to Rear Admiral Harold Train, the Director of Naval Intelligence, that Ford "inspires real devotion among his men. . . . He has evidenced his leadership and his courage in his photographic work with the fleet in the Pacific, as well as with the invading forces in Tunisia . . . both as a man and as an officer, I consider Commander Ford superior and outstanding."

In early December, Ford accompanied Donovan to Chungking, Chiang Kai-shek's wartime capital. Donovan wanted a serious OSS presence in China, but Chiang Kai-shek wasn't interested. Ford, through his friendship with General Claire Chennault—Merian Cooper was Chennault's chief of staff—set up a program in which OSS operatives were smuggled into the country under the pretense of being Chennault's airmen. Donovan returned to Washington, but Ford stayed on for two more months, photographing the terrain between Chungking and Kunming and flying aerial reconnaissance as far west as the base of the Himalayas. On January 14, he and Jack Pennick flew back to New Delhi, then began the long, incremental trip home.

William White's *They Were Expendable*, the nonfiction account of the PT boat effort during America's losing campaign in the Philippines, began to be talked of as a Ford project almost as soon as it was published in 1942. In March 1943, Ford received the first direct feeler from MGM's Eddie Mannix about getting a furlough to do the picture. On March 9, Frank "Spig" Wead, already working on the script, wrote that "We all feel that Jack is the *one* man to direct this picture . . . we're trying to make it the best Navy picture ever made."

Donovan dug in his heels about releasing Ford, and, in any case, MGM didn't care for Wead's first draft. They handed off the project to Sidney Franklin instead of Ford's preferred producer, James Kevin McGuinness. "Frankly, it reminded me of Winnie Sheehan in the old days," wrote Ford to McGuinness. "Typical old producer, old MGM. 'We'll fix the script up'—'round it out—more character' etc."

That seemed to be that, but during the next year, Donovan relented and agreed to let Ford go, and MGM relented and agreed to give Ford and Wead their heads.

It was about the same time that Ford began mulling over an idea to build a private residence *cum* clubhouse after the war for the men that had served under him. He told Harry Wurtzel to check around for likely sites; Wurtzel suggested the old Conway Tearle mansion in the heart of Hollywood. "I know the old Tearle place," Ford wrote. "Frankly I don't think it would do. The cost is too high and I think we would do better either out in the valley or around Beverly." (The Tearle mansion later became the headquarters of the American Society of Cinematographers.)

The time away from his steady, sizable paycheck began causing financial problems. Ford had been earning more than $3,000 a week in 1941, but he was making about $4,000 a year in the Navy, plus whatever his investments kicked in—about $36,000 in 1941. Besides his own family obligations, Ford contributed a monthly stipend of $100 to his brother Pat, and a similar amount to his sister Mary Agnes, although that was cut to $50 because her children were all working. The Navy took over the *Araner*, using her as an antisubmarine vessel for patrols off the coast of California. That helped, but there were still cash-flow problems.

In August 1943, Fred Totman, Ford's business manager, wrote him that he had had to overdraw on the bank while waiting for a dividend from AT&T. After the check finally arrived, Totman paid Harry Wurtzel's commission, made an income tax payment of nearly $10,000, and paid a bill for life insurance that left only around $12,000 to carry all the rest of Ford's responsibilities for the year.

Ford reacted with frustration and anger. "All I can say is, after making the amount of money I have for the last twenty years, it seems incredible that with a war on, my family can't live comfortably while I am away." Ford's only idea about economizing involved asking Harry Wurtzel to either forgo his commissions until the end of the war, or lower his rate to 5 percent.

As Totman pointed out, the primary problem was the tax bill for 1941, when Ford had earned $168,000. As Totman didn't point out, even with the *Araner* off his back, Ford was liable for all the usual expenses for someone in his income range. Totman assured Ford that Mary was wanting for nothing, but had cut down on many things and was doing wonderful work at the Hollywood Canteen, but that "everything is awfully high, the common laborer is now getting $1.00 per hour and hard to get."

Although Ford had his hands full, he clearly enjoyed hearing about doings back home. In August 1943, he wrote a letter to his frequent script supervisor Meta Sterne that noted "Katie Hep is at Fernwick, I hear (pronounced Fennick) I am looking forward to seeing her playing a Chinese peasant. 'Reaaaly, Hung Low, peach blossoms are not blooming again!' ..." Later, he wrote a letter to Bing Crosby congratulating him on *Going My Way*. "As for the picture well I understand that after seeing it Jim McGuinness went to early Mass."

Ford would drift from place to place, leaving much of the day-to-day operation and planning to trusted lieutenants such as Ray Kellogg and Mark Armistead. Like Bill Donovan, Ford believed in delegating.

Armistead came up with the idea of having Robert Moreno photograph the entire coastline of Western Europe, starting in Denmark and moving all the way down the coast of France. Moreno and his unit flew in a pair of B-17s about a thousand feet in the air, taking large-negative stills, looking for munition placements. In essence, he was methodically scouting likely locations for the invasion of Europe.

The unit presented these photographs to Eisenhower. The photos were enlarged to 16 x 20 and mounted in a beautiful album. One of the men stood there, flipping through the album, showing Eisenhower what they had done, while Ford stood proudly by. "Here's Le Havre. . . . Here's Cherbourg . . . here's Brest. . . ." Le Havre and Cherbourg were very nice aerial photographs, but Brest was represented by a beautiful, nude woman. Eisenhower's half-smile didn't waver, but Ford turned beet-red. The little joke his men had cooked up behind his back had fallen flat, and they realized they were in serious trouble.

"Ford was going to court-martial all of us," remembered George Hjorth, "but two weeks later we got a letter from Eisenhower thanking us for the presentation. 'I especially enjoyed the port of Brest,' he wrote. And the threat of court-martial went away. You see, most of the guys in Field Photo were nuts; we had tremendous imagination, and sometimes it got us into trouble. I was almost court-martialed three separate times."

Not all of Ford's postings were as grim as China; there was some time spent in Rio, and Ford wrote home that "This is quite a joint . . . really breath-taking in its grandeur + beauty—is quite like Honolulu—palms, water, sky etc. . . . These so-called Brazilian beauties are from hunger. . . . Am feeling fine—bowels OK. Food here is good + plentiful—will start inland tomorrow for a few days—mining rubber gold etc."

Ford's letters convey an impression of burdens manfully undertaken, with an undertone of a man having the time of his life; as he wrote in a letter to the captain of the USS *Brazos,* "Please give my regards to Admiral Nimmetz [sic]. He is doing a truly great job. By the way, who does he bawl out now that I'm no longer there? Don't you think he needs me to yell at when things are going good?"

There were some activities he somehow neglected to report to Mary. Robert Moreno remembered one episode in England where Ford, *sans* cap and tie, volunteered to accompany some enlisted men on a pub crawl. His method of volunteering was to say, "I'm coming along. I want to see the local color."

At the first pub they went to, Ford started making acid remarks about the British, just loudly enough to be overhead. As the pub was full of said British, the atmosphere grew a trifle thick. The other Americans thought moving on might be the discreet thing to do. This behavior, however, was repeated at three more pubs. The group hadn't been able to do any serious drinking, let alone have any fun, except for Ford, who seemed to be enjoying himself hugely. Moreno finally asked him, "Do we have enough local color now?"

"Yeah, I'm sick of these limeys."

George Hjorth went out drinking with Ford and Brick Marquard, and found him "crusty, but not mean. Severe. Underneath the crust, he was a hell of a nice guy, and quite shy. We were drinking and I asked him about his reputation; he'd won all these Oscars, and everybody thought he was a hell of a director. And he told me that he didn't think he was such a great director, but that he just had a talent for surrounding himself with the best people. And then he got sloshed and Brick and I had to put him to bed."

From mid-1943 to the end of the year, Ford visited Portland, Boston, Rio, Brazil, Trinidad, back to D.C., then was off to India, where, in December, he wrote a letter raving about the beauty of the Taj Mahal. In January 1944, he was in New Delhi, Karachi, Aden, Khartoum, Accra, Natal, and Brazil again before returning to Washington on the 23rd. In March, he spent two weeks in Los Angeles, his first real time off since a couple of days after the Battle of Midway.

Soon afterward, he had to write a letter of condolence to George Meehan, a cameraman at Columbia, whose son Arthur was in the Field Photo and had been killed in action. "We are stunned with grief back here, but of course our sorrow is nothing compared to yours. . . . I am trying to get several days leave so I might come to the Coast and see you and your wife, if you wish. Perhaps I could tell you better in words what I'm trying to say on paper, but I know nothing I can ever say or write will ease the cold fact that our Country, our Navy, and our hometown Hollywood has lost the bravest, cleanest, most lovable boy that ever made the Supreme Sacrifice for the things he loved and for which he fought."

With his enlarged sense of responsibility for those under his command, either on the set or in the war, such letters must have been agony to write, and the losses greater agony to experience. "The Japs are a lot smarter than we give them credit for," Ford commented in a letter to Frank Wead. "They are careful, cautious, and not impetuous—and when they hit, they hit hard."

Ford must have been taken aback when Ollie Carey wrote him to see if he could do anything about her only child's assignment in the Navy. "Have been working like hell on Dobe's case," he wrote her, "but it looks as though he will shove off before we get definite word. . . . Goldie, don't let Harry worry about the kid. It's a serious matter trying to play around with Fate. We have checked his situation and he is with a CASU outfit [casualty outfit; Carey was a medical corpsman] and will no doubt be stationed on one of the Islands in the Southwest Pacific, a long way from the actual sea frontier, which, at present, is very liquid and moving farther and farther east. In other words, he won't be in any landing parties. . . . He will be at a base hospital and I honestly think the kid will be a better man for the experience. . . .

"Goldie, you know that I am Irish and fey and I know everything will be alright. Keep the old man cheered up. I expect to be out there in a couple of weeks and I will get in touch with you immediately. . . . All my love and affection—and God Bless you all."

This was dicey. On the one hand, removing Dobe from anywhere near the front lines meant another man, one without equivalent connections, would have to endure the risks; on the other hand, Ford owed Harry Carey everything and knew it. There wasn't much choice.

After a stretch in the Caroline Islands, Dobe Carey was suddenly ordered back to the States. "Who in the hell do you know in Washington?" asked a friend in the personnel office. Carey was devastated; he'd grown fond of his fellow soldiers and didn't want to be thought of as a slacker. But there was no appeal; he flew to Guam, then Pearl Harbor, then took a boat to Vallejo, California. After twenty days' leave, he reported to Washington, to the Field Photo unit, where he was assigned to develop classified government film for the last eleven months of his military career.

"Ray [Kellogg] says you're doing a good job here," Ford told him after he called him to his office. "I told your Ma and Pa. They're both fine. OK, that's all kid. Get back to work."

• • •

On April 18, 1944, Ford was off again—Newfoundland, Scotland, London, mostly preparing to cover the coming invasion. Ford asked his men who among them had small-boat experience, and Robert Moreno raised his hand. "I told him I had, and that was about it. He didn't tell us how to cover it or anything."

Mark Armistead had become friendly with John Bulkeley, the hero of *They Were Expendable*, and brought him by to meet Ford at Claridge's. Ford was lying in bed naked, but he insisted on getting up and saluting Bulkeley, a winner of the Medal of Honor. Bulkeley was assigned command of a squad of PT boats working the English Channel during D-Day.

Ford's unit was in charge of documenting Operation Overlord, 176,000 Allied soldiers invading the beaches of France. Since photographing any battle is always an exercise in improvisation, Ford's job was to make sure that everyone who should have a camera had one. He assigned Brick Marquard and Junius Stout to be lead cameramen in the first wave, and supervised fitting some of the landing craft with automatic cameras that would start filming as soon as the ramps lowered.

Since George Hjorth had already made some nine drops behind enemy lines, he was assigned to go in before the invasion, find a spot on the beach, and photograph the incoming troops. "All Ford told me was, 'Photograph what you see. If you can see it, shoot it.' "

The invasion was originally planned for June 5, so Hjorth went in on the 3rd, when some Free French picked him up and hid him in a farmhouse. On the morning of the 6th, about two in the morning, he was taken down to the beach. Hjorth had an Eyemo and about twenty rolls of black and white film. He was about fifty yards from the water, behind a tuft of bushes.

"I could hear motors. It was the minesweepers cleaning out the area. They had a big, wide strip they cleaned out, then two Y shapes on either side of the main strip, one for coming in, one for going out. When it started getting light, I looked out, and it seemed there were islands out there in the channel. But I remembered that the only islands in the channel were Jersey and Guernsey, and those couldn't be seen from the shore of France. And then I realized those weren't islands, those were ships, dozens of them, hundreds of them. That's when I realized it was the invasion.

"It was pretty light when the invasion started, maybe seven o'clock. And I started cranking away. All I was thinking was 'Am I in focus? Is the camera too high or too low?' The fact that I was photographing guys getting killed didn't hit me until I got onto a destroyer later that day, around noon. Then it hit me hard. That was the day I started smoking."

Ford was on board the battleship *Augusta*, which was serving as invasion headquarters. But as the barges disgorged their men to the slaughter that awaited the first wave, as the battle wore on, Ford grew restless. He radioed Armistead, on board Bulkeley's PT boat, to come and get him. The last thing Bulkeley wanted was a Hollywood director as his responsibility in the middle of the most important battle of the twentieth century, but Armistead vouched for him.

Bulkeley was surprised at how quickly Ford absorbed the requisite information. Armistead thought Ford seemed unusually happy, even when the PT boat fought a machine-gun duel with German E-boats off Cherbourg. Ford genially accused Bulkeley of planning to take the first picture of the dead body of a famous director. The two men became friends, and Ford realized that Bulkeley would indeed be a great subject for a movie.

Although Ford would later imply that he was dodging bullets on Omaha Beach ("My memories of D-Day come in disconnected takes like unassembled shots to be spliced together afterward . . ." he said at one point), he seems not to have actually landed for several days. Certainly, his grandson Dan, who would be decorated for his own service in Vietnam, never heard any stories about Ford's exploits on D-Day, which he is certain he would have had Ford been in the first or second waves.

Two days after D-Day, Ford wrote Mary in veiled terms: "Been up country for a coupla days—lovely weather—enjoyed the English summer. Feel wonderfully well + rested—lots of milk + eggs etc.—put on weight. . . . Well my darling I miss you terribly + our home + our family, but I guess that's what we're fighting for. Carry on my sweet. I hope to be with you all again before many weeks. This thing is going great. Jerry is bound to crack up any day. I love you."

Ford began moving inland with the American troops. The other directors serving in the same theater were astounded at Ford's bravado. George Stevens remembered sheltering himself under a hedge in Normandy when he looked up and saw Ford standing full-height, calmly observing some fighting.

Although the duties and responsibilities of command and combat might have been expected to keep Ford away from the bottle, his pattern remained the same: long months of sobriety followed by an alcoholic debauch. After D-Day, he went off on a major drunk. William Clothier had his quarters commandeered by a drunken Ford, who shortly began pissing and vomiting all over Clothier's sleeping bag.

Clothier, a pugnacious man completely without the gift of fear, went storming out to accost Ford's men. "I don't give a shit if he's your commander, get him the hell out of here," he screamed. "He's throwing up all over my room." Moreno's crew dragged Ford away from Clothier, but Ford accused his men of stealing his whiskey.

"The next thing you know, he's on a plane back to London," recalled Moreno. "Mark Armistead comes to my crew and asks, 'Where did you leave Ford?'

" 'He left us.' "

Armistead began worrying. He continued worrying after Ford, still drunk, called from London and told Armistead to come and get him, even though Ford rang off before he could tell Armistead where he was.

"How am I going to find him?" wondered Armistead aloud.

"Look in the pubs," suggested Moreno. Armistead finally found Ford out of uniform, without identification, barely conscious. Armistead sobered him up and shipped him off to America from Weymouth on June 19. "I liked Ford when he was sober," remembered Robert Moreno. "But when he was drinking he got pretty rough."

Had William Donovan wanted, he could have tossed Ford out of the service for dereliction of duty, although Donovan clearly didn't want to, perhaps because he liked Ford's attitude. He seemed afraid of nothing.

General Albert Wedemeyer, who would become a pillar of America's right wing in the 1960s, observed Ford at war. "He photographed two or three air raids in Burma and China. He was in New Delhi. . . . The thing I admired about him was there was not a lot of fanfare. . . . He didn't show off. He played down the things he did, he never bragged about them. When the chips were down and bullets were flying, the guy was around and he wasn't showing off."

Ford's demeanor in uniform was consistent only in its inconsistency, Robert Parrish remembered that some days Ford would ream a man because his shoes weren't shined. The next day Ford would be sitting with his bare feet propped up on his desk.

"This was John Ford's [unit]," asserted Mark Armistead, "and we did things the way he wanted them done and that was it. . . . To him, the most important thing was to get the job done and if it was necessary to go through red tape or protocol, the results to him were far more important than observance of . . . regulations."

Ford was back in France on July 29, 1944, went to London for a week on August 4, then went home through New York, arriving in Los Angeles on August 14 for two weeks. On September 1, he was back in Washington.

By September 1944, the tide had clearly turned in Europe, and an Allied victory was widely assumed to be just a question of time. Ford began thinking about the resumption of his career. On September 12, he wrote to the art director James Basevi: "I might see you in a few weeks. If you should see Bill Goetz and Nunnalley [sic] ask them if they will have room, when the war is over, for an old broken down second unit director. Salary no object."

That same day, he wrote a memo to the Chief of Navy Personnel requesting permission to wear the Naval Reserve Ribbon in a few weeks, when he would complete ten years in the Reserve. It was the first sign of a pride in decorations that would increasingly manifest itself in the future.

Plans for *They Were Expendable* were once again hanging fire. On September 12, James Forrestal, the Secretary of the Navy, wrote the acting director of the OSS that MGM had requested the services of Commander John Ford. "This picture would be helpful to the Navy, and, because Commander Ford is ably qualified by reason of his motion picture experience and his Naval service, I hope that he will be made available."

A month later, Ford was at Fox, lobbying for a waiver to do the film on loan-out at MGM. "Ford stated that he had just recently returned to the US to recuperate from shock and wounds sustained in combat," wrote a studio functionary to Darryl Zanuck. "If MGM does use his services, he will not receive any compensation, but the money would instead be turned over to a club which Ford is interested in sponsoring as a memorial for war cameramen."

Zanuck knew his man. "I do not choose to believe all the facts as related by Ford," he replied, "including the wounds." Nevertheless, Fox gave him the waiver.

Contrary to Ford's later remarks, which indicated he left the service grudgingly and would rather have been on the front lines than back in Hollywood, he went enthusiastically, both because of the subject matter of the film and his plans for his $300,000 fee.

Eight days after Forrestal's letter, Ford wrote a memo to the Chief of Navy Personnel requesting temporary inactive duty while he made the film. "The Secretary of the Navy and Rear Admiral Merrill are anxious to have this film produced as a matter of naval policy," Ford wrote. "The Metro-Goldwyn-Mayer Company refuses to do the picture unless I personally direct the film.

"Personally, I concur heartily in their request as the picture would have a big Navy motif which at the present would be very timely. If this request is granted, it is understood that I shall return to my active duty with the Office of Strategic Services immediately the picture is finished. It is also understood by the aforementioned gentlemen that all remunerations I receive from the film will be turned over to a charitable fund for service men and that I shall not retain any part of the resultant financial returns."

To others, Ford played the part of an embarrassed Hollywood pro overruled by his superiors. "My militaristic ego has been somewhat deflated," he wrote General Wedemeyer in October 1944. "I have been ordered to Hollywood to do a commercial picture called 'They Were Expendable,' and I am leaving tonight. While I will at least get a chance to spend Christmas with the folks and play with my grandson's electric train, still I'm a bit abashed that a great warrior like me should be in mockie-land while the good people are fighting. However, the picture won't last forever, while the war seems a bit indefinite as yet. I am getting a big chunk of dough for the picture, which I am turning over into a trust fund for Pennick and the boys. That at least clears my conscience a bit. It will give Pennick a place to store his loot."

There was one last tragic death to add to the dozen that had been amassed by the Field Photo Unit. On January 22, 1945, Junius Stout, the son of cameraman Archie Stout, was shot down over the island of Guernsey. He was in a DC-3, doing reconaissance photography, when the pilot got lost and wandered over the German-occupied island.

For many Hollywood filmmakers, the war was a thorny psychological problem. Frank Capra never really recovered from his experiences, and it deeply affected George Stevens, nudged him into being a far more serious, heavier filmmaker than he had been before. For a man like John Huston, the problem was more intellectual than psychological—to hate it and glory in it simultaneously.

The war changed Ford as well. For him, it was a crucible in which he tested himself and earned better than a passing grade. It enveloped him with a sense of large purpose that was absent from a career in Hollywood. And it let him earn a share of valor for himself. Well into secure middle age, John Ford had put himself in harm's way, fought in a great war, and survived.

It also stiffened his resolve about the kind of director he wanted to be. The John Ford of the 1920s and 1930s had been happy directing three or four pictures for the studio for every one he directed for himself. No more. From now on, the proportions would be reversed.

While his professional identity would always be that of a filmmaker, Ford's emotional allegiance seems to have shifted to that of the profession of arms, a conversion that was only amplified when, on June 29, 1945, James Forrestal promoted him to the rank of commander. As Mark Armistead would note of Ford's 1951 promotion to the rank of rear admiral, "He was probably more proud of the Admiral's stripe than he was of all his Oscars combined."

Most men wrap up their war experiences and place them on a mental shelf, to be taken down at appropriate moments. But Ford wanted more than that, wanted a tangible representation of the work his men had done—and, perhaps, maintain his aura of command, give him yet another area where he would be greeted by salutes.

As Ford began shooting *They Were Expendable* in February 1945 in Key Biscayne, Florida, he became a grandfather for the second time, as Pat's wife, the former Jane Mulvaney, gave birth to Daniel Sargent Ford. That same month, he received a cable from Frank: "READY AND RARING TO WORK LOTS OF TALENT FOR YOU HOPE YOU CAN USE ME."

As the cast and crew of *They Were Expendable* discovered, four years in the Navy had not mellowed John Ford. He still delighted in reducing John Wayne to quivering pulp, he still would make things up as he went along, still inveigled people into making suggestions, after which he would pretend to be livid at their impertinence. He remained a truculent enigma.

One day, Ford began berating Wayne about the way he saluted, and kept the abuse coming. Finally, Robert Montgomery walked over, placed his hands on both sides of the director's chair and said, "Don't ever talk to Duke like that. You ought to be ashamed." The set fell silent. A break was ordered, and Ford ended up in tears.

He was no more respectful to Donna Reed. When the wardrobe people made the mistake of bringing her around for his approval, Ford snarled that no one cared about costumes in the picture they were making. But Reed was intelligent and tough, and used Ford's attitude as something to work against, to give her a sense of fortitude. Within a few weeks, she had won his respect. Before a touching dinner scene with John Wayne, where all the emotions of love in war remain unspoken, Ford pulled a string of pearls out of his pocket and gave them to her to wear—one of his talismans, as well as a touch of formality in the midst of chaos.

Robert Montgomery was one of the chilliest actors in Hollywood; his patrician airs would, under normal circumstances, have made him a prime candidate for a lengthy series of scathing put-downs, but Ford seems to have respected him, probably because Montgomery was a hard-core Navy man. During the war he had been a naval attache in London, worked on PT boats, and finally served aboard a destroyer during the D-Day invasion. He had earned the right to play a hero.

But as production got under way, Montgomery was seized with an overwhelming panic attack. "I realized I'd forgotten everything, forgotten acting, forgotten what the whole thing was about. I felt I couldn't do it anymore. I was desperate."

Pacing back and forth in his room at the Blackstone Hotel in Miami at four in the morning, Montgomery was interrupted by a knock on the door. It was Ford. "You in any trouble?" he asked.

Montgomery unloaded, telling Ford to get another actor and fast. Ford suggested that Montgomery just concentrate on running the boats that he knew so well, that he focus on mechanical tasks while Ford shot footage of maneuvers. When the familiarity of the surroundings and the rhythm of production asserted itself, Montgomery would relax, be it a couple of days or a couple of weeks or a couple of months. Then Ford would get around to shooting Montgomery's scenes.

On the third day of shooting the long shots of battle, Montgomery felt the viral panic begin to fade. He walked over to Ford and told him he was ready to begin acting. It was another example of the sensitive, intuitive side of Ford he worked hard to conceal. It is also possible that he was feeling more than a touch of uncertainty himself, which helped him relate to Montgomery.

The mood was somber, for Ford was making a somber film. That winter of 1944–45, the Allies were pushing on toward Berlin, but there was still savage fighting in the Pacific. The rough estimate for an invasion of Japan was November, about the time the film would be playing in theaters. Ford filled his film with a sense of grim purpose, of the moral weight of war, and he managed to completely avoid any race-baiting—no Japanese soldier ever appears on screen.

On May 14, back at MGM after completing the Key Biscayne locations, Ford was making process shots when he slipped between two camera parallels and fell, breaking his shinbone. Montgomery and Wayne accompanied him to the hospital. Going up in the elevator, a woman kept staring at him. Finally, he looked back at her and growled one word by way of explanation: "Alcoholic!"

There was one major sequence left to shoot. While Ford was laid up at the hospital, Robert Montgomery took over the direction for a week. Ford wrote Gene Markey from the hospital that he expected to be out of the hospital on a Sunday and back on the set on the following Wednesday.

While Ford was in Hollywood, while the war went on, the work of the Field Photo Unit went on as well. Ray Kellogg, who had been in the Fox special effects department when he joined up, was chief of the unit in Ford's absence, and was supervising the collecting and analysis of German newsreel film as evidence for the coming war crimes trials.

It was an immense job; Ford and Kellogg assigned Budd and Stuart Schulberg, Bob Parrish, Robert Webb, and others to the project. Ford wanted to take a more active role in this effort, as well as attend the Nuremberg trials, but his work on *They Were Expendable* and his efforts in setting up what became the Field Photo Farm kept him in Los Angeles.

The war in the Pacific was quickly brought to a close by the bombings of Hiroshima and Nagasaki on August 6 and 9, respectively. On September 2, 1945, Douglas MacArthur accepted the surrender of the Japanese. World War II was over. On September 27, Ford was called into Bill Donovan's office and presented with the Legion of Merit. The next day, the Field Photographic was officially disbanded; the day after that, its commanding officer was released from active duty. John Ford's war was over.

Ford knew full well that he had succeeded beyond the measure of most men during his war service; he just wanted to make sure that everyone else knew it too. Ford would always maintain a full selection of naval uniforms, beautifully tailored and immaculately maintained, which he wore at the drop of a VFW convention—an amusing alternative to his work apparel, which would become increasingly ragged through the years.

He began maneuvering to get medals, decorations, and awards. He got Bill Donovan to recommend him for a Silver Star for his service at Midway, but he didn't get it. He wrote a painfully sanctimonious letter to a friend in the Navy about the Commendation Ribbon, which he said he wanted "to be buried in . . . perhaps in a leisure moment [if] it was brought to Jim Forrestal's attention it could be done. . . . John it's very brash of me to take up your time and I apologize most humbly. I can only say that I would like something for Mary & the kids to be proud of."

A few years later, he wrote to Alan Kirk, formerly an admiral in the Navy, now the American ambassador to Belgium, asking to be advanced from Chevalier of the Order of the Crown to the rank of Officer. Ford offered several reasons for the promotion, among them "I have won the Prix du Roi, Belgium's premier award to film makers more than any other director in the motion picture business. . . . I am recognized by the Belgians as the leading director of the world. Believe me, I say this with all due modesty."

As if all this wasn't enough, he also dropped the fact that he had had dinner with "your friend and admirer, His Eminence, Cardinal Spellman."

Such letters make clear Ford's naked desire for the validation represented by medals and rank. Like many old soldiers, he would on occasion exaggerate the scope of his war wound; a brief synopsis of his war record claimed that he was "severely wounded" during the Midway battle and was "invalided home [with] injuries due to enemy action late 1944."

Mostly, the entreaties and posturing were to no avail. He was awarded the Naval Reserve Ribbon, but his request for a Commendation Ribbon was rejected by everybody, including Chester Nimitz. There was also an effort to get him the Distinguished Service Medal for preparing the photographic coverage of D-Day, but that too seems to have produced no results. Ford ended up with the Purple Heart, the Legion of Merit, the American Defense Service Medal, the Asiatic-Pacific Area Campaign Medal with a bronze star, the American Area Campaign Medal, the European–African–Middle Eastern Area Campaign Medal, the World War II Victory Medal, and the Naval Reserve Medal signifying ten years of service.

However, the Navy was willing to lavish him with praise: "Personnel of his organization performed with outstanding distinction and valor in clandestine operations and in combat in the world's battle fronts," wrote his commanding officer in Ford's final Officer's Fitness Report on September 28, 1945. "This record of high accomplishment results from Captain Ford's outstanding ability, his devotion to duty, his loyalty to and love for his subordinates. The discipline of his organization was outstanding; their accomplishments superb. This could result only from great leadership."

They Were Expendable opens in Manila in 1941. Pearl Harbor is attacked, and torpedo boat squadron #3 has to earn the respect of the brass, because nobody believes in PT boats. The Pacific is vulnerable from the loss of ships at Pearl, so PT boats are pressed into service; the commanding officer of John Brickley (the name the film gives Bulkeley) tells him that the Japanese did to the American Navy what the British did to the Spanish Armada.

"You and I are professionals," he tells Brickley. "If the manager says sacrifice, we lay down a bunt, and let somebody else hit the home runs."

Ford tells a quiet, impressionistic saga of the PT boats and their scrappy struggle in the Pacific, of Subic Bay and Corregidor and Bataan, a time when America was being continually battered. Ford believed in heroes, and he creates a couple of believable ones in Brickley and Rusty Ryan (Wayne), his restless, irritable second-in-command. He does less well with his idolatrous portrayal of MacArthur, who is shown evacuating the Philippines backed by "the Battle Hymn of the Republic" and accorded a reverence that would seem extreme for Lincoln. (Ford undercuts his own worshipful mood somewhat when he has a starstruck sailor ask MacArthur to autograph his hat.)

The film is at all times superbly shot by Joe August, with a far gloomier lighting than the ubiquitous MGM high key. It reflects a grave formal beauty, and the images of battle capture the phosphorescence of the water in the Far Pacific. In the largely unspoken romance between John Wayne's Rusty and Donna Reed's nurse Sandy Davis, Ford captures a quality of muted longing that beautifully suggests the impossibility of sustaining any kind of satisfying relationship during war.

Men die, John Wayne intones Robert Louis Stevenson's "Home Is the Sailor," Bataan surrenders, and the Japanese move on to Corregidor. Brickley and Ryan are airlifted out, leaving their men behind. "The job," Brickley tells Ryan, "is to get ready to come back." Thus ends one of Ford's most stirring tributes to a lost campaign.

They Were Expendable is, perhaps, too much in one mournful key, but Ford is documenting a losing campaign and one, moreover, that was in the very recent past, which forbade him from taking the liberties he might have imposed had there been more time between the events and the film commemorating them.

MGM didn't release *They Were Expendable* until December 1945. The melancholy picture was apparently out of key with the celebratory public mood, but the film captured the weary resignation that was the rich soil out of which film noir would shortly flourish. The picture certainly couldn't be considered a financial failure; it grossed $4.1 million worldwide against costs of $2.9 million.

With his money from *They Were Expendable*, and with a contribution of $10,000 from John Wayne, Ford bought eight acres of land at 18201 Calvert Street in Reseda in the San Fernando Valley. The land cost $65,223.50; improvements and additions added up to a total of $114,261.56.

Ford paid for an elaborate clubhouse complete with bar, swimming pool, tennis and badminton courts, and baseball diamond, all surrounded by eucalyptus trees. The master bedroom was permanently reserved for Bill Donovan, and the den was decorated in early American antiques. In the den were thirteen glass cases, holding the medals awarded to each member of the unit killed in the war.

Inside the clubhouse, there were five bedrooms, and a large pine-paneled room with a huge fireplace at one end. Over the fireplace was the large portrait of Ford painted during *The Long Voyage Home*, showing him with hands on hips and pipe in mouth. "It was as if the whole man filled the room through that portrait," remembered the wife of one of Ford's men. Nobody was likely to forget who was responsible for the farm's quiet comforts.

When it was all built, there was about $75,000 in cash left to keep the place running. Since the place cost a little more than $10,000 a year to operate, the Farm did not have all that much financial breathing room.

Ford christened it the Field Photo Farm, and farm it was, in spirit if not actuality. Although today the area has been subsumed by the endless urban sprawl of Los Angeles, in those days it was quite rural; Jane Darwell, who lived nearby, had chickens pecking around her rustic front yard.

The idealistic intent was to maintain the ties between the men that had formed Ford's hearty band of brothers, and broaden it out amongst their wives and children—and, if possible, have at least two beer blasts a month.

Ford took an extremely active position in relation to the Farm; in 1948, he paid $12,000 for improvements out of his own pocket, and he delighted in planning the Memorial Day services himself. Here, as Dan Ford wrote, the service would be called to order at 11:00 A.M. sharp. "The men would stand in formation, and the flag would be flown at half-staff; an invocation would then be read as a choir softly sang 'America,' following which there would be a reading of some sort of patriotic literature, a traditional folk hymn, and a speech by a visiting military dignitary. In closing, the names of the thirteen fallen members of the Field Photographic would be read, with a muffled drum roll and the utterance in unison of 'Died for his country' after each name. The services closed with a bugle sounding taps, and the lonely sounds would echo hauntingly among the Farm's eucalyptus trees."

For the Christmas parties, held on the Sunday before December 25, Santa would always arrive on a stagecoach, with Ford personally choosing the actor for the part. Andy Devine did the job for a while, as did Alan Hale Sr., Charles Kemper, and Mike Mazurki. Ford would inspect the preparations, then drop his handkerchief, signaling the cowboys to escort the stagecoach carrying Santa, with Danny Borzage and James Stewart on top, each playing "Jingle Bells" on the accordion. The stagecoach would stop in front of the clubhouse, Santa would get out with a large bag of presents, and everyone would follow him into the house. After cake and ice cream, Santa would depart, get into street clothes, and come back for the continuing party. The kids never knew.

The Field Photo Farm soon started up a newsletter entitled *The Starboard Club*, full of chatty news and notes about doings on the Farm. Most of the social activities were on weekends and holidays—Sunday dinners followed by a movie or a square dance, a Friday camera night, a Hobby Show, or the occasional Stag Night, ominously promising "Refreshments—Entertainment??????"

"In a sense he re-created the world in his pictures out there," said the actor Ken Curtis, later Ford's son-in-law. But Ford's dream of a cross between Camelot and a boys club was always problematic; almost from its inception, the bulletin would run the names of people who weren't attending—Ray Kellogg, Jack Pennick, Mike Luciano, perhaps fifteen others—and wag a finger at the miscreants: "Procrastination is the thief of time and if it has been delaying your trip to the Farm, it's robbing you of the time of your life! I can't for the life of me see why anyone puts off a little jaunt that can mean so much. Call and tell us you're coming now."

When people weren't being scolded for not showing up, they were being scolded for showing up and causing wear and tear: "There is much gross negligence by non-thinking members, who enter the house and clubrooms in wet bathing suits—who leave bottles and glasses strewn on the grounds and in the pool—who carelessly leave cigarettes to burn the window-sills, the seat-pads in the Ballroom, and even some of the furniture."

The problems inherent in the Farm were perfectly captured by an exchange Ford had with Bob Parrish. Ford had invited Parrish over to Odin Street for dinner, and asked for suggestions about improvements to the Farm and the chapel, where, he told Parrish, everyone would be welcome, regardless of race, creed, or color.

A reckless Parrish blurted out exactly what he thought. "I think you should bulldoze the farmhouse, the chapel, the hitching post, the stained glass windows, the swimming pool, the stables—the whole thing. Then I think you should subdivide the eight acres into fifty-foot lots and build low-cost duplex houses for returning veterans."

The silence, as they say, was deafening. Parrish believed that Ford used four kitchen matches while lighting his pipe and, undoubtedly, struggling to control himself. Finally, he said, "Like I said before, everyone will be welcome, regardless of race, creed, or color."

Parrish's attitude was symptomatic of many of the returned veterans. "It was something he loved; he was passionate about it, and he wanted it as a hangout for the sailors. Wives could come from time to time when invited. But I was passionate about a place to live that wasn't my mother's spare room." Ford would punish Parrish for his insolence soon enough.

Ford's home movies show an amalgam of several successive July Fourths at the Farm, fragments of lazy holiday afternoons: regimental pipers, a black chorale, a cat lapping at the puddles from a nearby swimming pool. The grounds are manicured, with white picket fences and arbored walkways with wheelchair ramps. There are square dances and the Sons of the Pioneers, and, in a brief shot or two, Ford can be seen picking them up and laying them down in a fairly lightfooted fashion.

The emotional centerpiece of the Farm was the chapel, a small wood frame structure with miniature porticoes. The chapel was nondenominational; the altar had a cross, a crucifix, and a Star of David. On the wall of the chapel, Ford inscribed these lines from A. E. Housman:

Here dead lie we—
Because we did not choose
To live and shame the land
From which we sprung . . .

The Farm was open to a great many veterans who weren't part of Ford's unit. Among them was Pat Grissom, who was in the Third Infantry and moving toward Munich when he was paralyzed by a German bullet.

Grissom was undergoing rehabilitation with Herb Wolf, one of the Field Photo men, who had been injured in a jeep accident. Ford asked Wolf if there were any other men in the hospital who might enjoy Sunday barbecues.

"About three wards of them," replied Wolf. Ford told him to bring them around.

"Ford would come around nearly every Sunday," remembered Grissom. "He called us 'Herbie's Boys,' and always made us feel welcome. They started a square dance club, and we would go out to watch. We were sitting outside the clubhouse, by the large windows where you could see what was happening on the inside.

"Ford came by and asked if any of us smoked cigars. I was the only one that did, so he gave me this cigar, a Corona Belvedere. The first Cuban cigar I ever smoked. It cost 20 cents. From then on, that's all I smoked."

Ford lent a hand in drumming up support when the Veterans Administration closed Birmingham Hospital in Van Nuys, where Grissom and many of the paralyzed veterans got their therapy. Grissom became particularly close to Wingate Smith, which meant that Mary liked him as well.

"Ford and I got to be very friendly, but not intimate. I've always said that John Ford saved my life. Not literally, but by inviting us out to the Farm, paying attention to us. I met people like John Wayne and Gregory Peck and Maureen O'Hara and Ollie Carey and Cliff Lyons. Being there did more for our rehabilitation and getting us ready to go back to life than anything else. It gave us a drive, an impetus, it made a significant impact on our lives. Because of John Ford, we realized that we weren't just old soldiers waiting to die."

Ford had earned virtually no money in four years, and *They Were Expendable* had done nothing to alter that. He had a career to resume. Under the ten-picture deal he'd signed in 1937, Ford still owed Fox one picture for which he was to be paid $85,000, but Zanuck generously tore up the contract and gave Ford $150,000 for the last picture under the old deal.

Zanuck then dangled all sorts of projects in front of him: an adaptation of Wendell Willkie's *One World*, with an accompanying note that said, "If ever the world needed a picture with the theories of Wendell L. Willkie, it certainly needs it now." Ford remained unconvinced. Then there was the lavish costume epic *Captain from Castile*. He wasn't interested.

On November 1, 1945, Ford reported to Zanuck that he had read a story entitled "The Stranger on the Highway," and looked at an old Allan Dwan movie called *Frontier Marshal*. Ford thought "Stranger on the Highway" might make an artistic success, but not a commercial one. *Frontier Marshal*, on the other hand, was much more to his liking. "I agree with you and I think it could be made into a great Western in Color. With Fonda as Wyatt Earp and Ty [Power] as Doc Holliday and the rest of the cast you suggest, I think it would be a wow.

"Perhaps it needs a little more historical flavor and perhaps you should have more exterior scenery. The background, for instance, like Monument Valley or the Painted Desert. Basically there is a swell picture in it. Of course, more than forty percent of it is true. I am really enthused. . . ."

"Suppose we have a chat."

It was time to go back to work.

The cast of *My Darling Clementine* gather for a group portrait, with Ford on top of the stagecoach.

PART FIVE

THE PERILS OF INDEPENDENCE

We're students of the great John Ford,
Disciples of the sage-brush bard;
We ride all day and shoot all night,
Then lap-dissolve to another fight.
Though other actors may get bored,
It's different when you work for Ford.
Like Bogey winds up with Bacall,
And Gable grabs Claudette,
We finish in a bar room brawl
Walter Brennan's what we get.
And until the picture is scored,
We're the ghosts of Art Acord.
Our lingo never gets obscene,
But don't blame John, blame Joseph Breen.
We love him like we love the Lord.
We're students of the great John Ford.

LYRICS TO UNKNOWN MELODY FOUND IN FORD PAPERS,
DATED FEBRUARY 1948, AUTHOR UNKNOWN

CHAPTER SIXTEEN

John Ford was fifty-one years old when World War II ended. He was six feet tall, weighed 175 pounds, was missing ten teeth, had eyesight rated a medium-lousy 6/20, had two children and two grandchildren.

Despite the leg fracture incurred on *They Were Expendable*, Ford retained an easy grace about his movements. He wore blue dress shirts that had been expensive when originally purchased, years before. The sleeves were usually slightly soiled, as were his preferred cream-colored flannel pants. Sometimes he would wear a belt, other times he would adopt a motif from Fred Astaire and wrap a necktie around his waist, with the knot at the side. He liked brown and white saddle shoes, but tended to leave the laces untied, and mismatched socks were par for the course. He liked a windbreaker or a military-style combat jacket, and a dirty slouch hat that had also once been of superior quality. Sometimes, the slouch hat would be replaced by a St. Louis Cardinals baseball cap, or a tweed cap. Where once he had used Bay Rum as an aftershave/cologne, now his predominant scent was tobacco.

At work, Ford's manner and style were codified and would remain so for the rest of his career. The casting process was simple: when word got out that Ford was about to make a movie, the members of his stock company went to his office for a visit. The supplicant would sit there until Ford told them if they were going to be working or not. If so, he would tell them about the story and their part in it.

On the set, rehearsals were fine, but after that he wanted to shoot, and he preferred to print the first take. "The first take, even with fluffs, is always the best," he would say. The atmosphere was tense. "There was always an essence of fear in every Ford camp," said Frank Baker. "You're waiting for him to jump on you. . . . He was doing it for a purpose all the while. He's getting [better] discipline out of that company than any company that ever went before a camera. He just had to open his mouth, and 'Yes sir, yes sir.' "

On the set, he was decisive. "He would come in," remembered Andrew McLaglen, Victor's son, "and he would set the camera and rehearse. There wasn't a lot of camera movement, maybe a little in-and-out dollying. He was a good rehearser; he'd block it, but he wouldn't over-rehearse. As long as the actors knew their lines and the cameraman had lit it for what he blocked, he was ready.

"He knew what he wanted. He had the courage of his conviction in a scene. He'd say, 'Cut. Print it. If we want a better take, we need better actors.' The actor would say, 'Huh? It was the first take!' Ford would hand him his DGA card and say, 'Here, you take the chair.' He came in prepared. If you had an eight o'clock call, you didn't wait till noon to get your first shot."

"He shot all his own action," said William Wellman Jr., who would act in a number of pictures for him. "You could see him get excited when there was a stunt going on. And he always had Danny Borzage playing the accordion in the morning and between shots. 'Bringing in the Sheaves.' He loved that music. And he would always break for tea around 4:00 although only a few people would be invited, usually the major players."

Although Ford liked to give the impression that he never looked at the rushes, he did, but very quietly, and only with the editor or his assistant. "If anyone else walked into the projection room," Robert Parrish remembered, "he would stop the screening and ask the intruder to leave."

Like any truly smart man, he asked a lot of questions and was a good listener. Dobe Carey, along with many others, believed that Ford was a very lonely man, always wanting to be one of the boys but unable to give up the persona of mystery and authority he had painstakingly created for himself.

As rough as he could be with actors, women usually got a pass. "He had a strange, old-world quality with women," Frank Baker told Anthony Slide. "He was always very nice to women, always very courteous to them. . . . God! If you used bad language in front of women, he'd throw you right off the set. . . . I guess that was the Irish blood in him. And John Ford, the same as his brother, had great physical courage, and had a lot of moral courage too."

He was very self-conscious about his looks, and would often use a loose kind of body language or bizarre expressions to communicate with an actor. That, plus his nervous habit of chewing on a handkerchief, caused him to forbid still photographers to shoot his picture without his knowledge.

He despised what he called director's touches, self-conscious or elaborate shots. "I try to make people forget they're in a theater," he said. "I don't want them to be conscious of a camera or a screen. I want them to feel that what they're seeing is real." He despised cheap irony: "A lot of scenes are corny, Duke," he told John Wayne. "*Play* 'em. Play 'em to the hilt. If it's *East Lynne*, play it! Don't avoid 'em, don't be self-conscious about 'em. *Play* 'em!"

Conversations about even the craft, let alone the art, of directing were *verboten*. Ford only seems to have lowered his guard with two or three people. After seeing Fred Zinnemann's first film, he snarled, "You could be a pretty good director if you would stop moving the goddamn camera all the time. There has got to be *a reason* for moving it. Use the camera like an information booth."

Ford also opened up with Elia Kazan, and, years later, with the young Bertrand Tavernier. When Kazan cornered him at a party, Ford said he got his staging ideas from the set. Not the script, not the actors, not the theme. The set. "The settings he chose were already poetry," said Kazan. "He lifted his action to fit them."

When Kazan made *Viva Zapata!*, he enlisted as many of Ford's crew as possible, and quizzed them relentlessly about his methods. "Get out early, before anyone else," he was told. "Use the day as it comes up. The accident of each day's weather is a dramatic effect. Don't duck it, use it.... Get out on the set before anyone else, walk around it. Look this way, look that. The set is your main source."

"Not too many camera moves," Ford told Tavernier. "All the young kids who are starting out want to do crazy things with the camera. It's useless. The simplest continuity is the most efficient: a shot, then a reverse shot. You must spend more time with the actors and the dialogue than with the camera. Anybody can think up a difficult camera move, but very few people manage to retain the same feeling between a long shot and a close-up, to keep up the quality of the emotion."

He held himself to a high standard, with the emphasis on a focused comprehension of the material and of his approach. He told Jean Mitry, "You can change a cue, modify an incident, but the movement of the camera, like its position, is determined in advance. A director who changes his mind is a director who loses time. You should make your decisions before, not during shooting.... What would you think of an architect who arrived at his building wondering where to put the staircase? You don't 'compose' a film on the set; you put a predesigned composition on film. It is wrong to liken a director to an author. He is more like an architect, if he is creative. An architect conceives his plans from given premises—the purpose of the buildings, its size, the terrain. If he is clever, he can do something creative within these limitations."

His treatment of writers, indeed, of most of his co-workers, was pointed and rather in the manner of a lofty professor drilling sense into the mushy heads of freshman. "If you didn't cut the mustard," remembered Mark Armistead, "he'd have nothing to do with you. If you did cut the mustard, you became an unhappy man. He'd sit on your back, making you do a bit better. He was a perfectionist."

Frank Nugent's story about Ford's method of breaking him in on *Fort Apache* is well known but bears repetition. After Nugent had read every book extant on the American Southwest, Ford "sent me hotfooting to Tombstone and Apache Pass and Cochise's Stronghold and to the pathetic little markers showing where men had been spreadeagled and submitted to the small Apache torture fires. After seven weeks of this I returned to Hollywood full of erudition, steeped in Indian lore and cavalry commands."

"You're satisfied with yourself?" Ford asked. Nugent answered in the affirmative. "Fine, now forget everything you've read and we'll start writing a story about the cavalry."

Likewise, when Nugent and Laurence Stallings collaborated on the script of *3 Godfathers*, Ford listened to them read the first ten pages, of which Stallings and Nugent were inordinately proud. Then he let loose the dogs of war.

"Has it ever occurred to either of you that the first motion pictures were Leland Stanford's studies of a running horse? Well, for your information, a running horse remains the finest subject for a motion picture camera. Now forget this dialogue stuff and give me some horses and real estate."

"Ford never quite forgave us for the wordy beginning," Nugent remembered, with the air of a man gingerly fingering a scar earned in battle.

Ford's writers worked a few hours in the morning, a few in the afternoon, with the director guiding, making the writer talk out each sequence in detail before it was actually committed to paper. Usually, the scripts were written fairly quickly: the final script for *The Quiet Man* was written in ten weeks, *3 Godfathers* was written in a month, *Yellow Ribbon* in seven weeks. *Fort Apache* took about fifteen, but half of that time was spent on research and discussion.

Winston Miller, who wrote *My Darling Clementine* with Ford, remembered that "We sat around in his office every day for about four or five weeks, just kicking it around. All we knew was that it was about Wyatt Earp and it would end with the gunfight at the O.K. Corral, and from there on we were on our own.... We just made it all up."

Among the upper echelon of writers who had worked with Ford, there was a loose theory best enunciated by Nunnally Johnson. "I think John

Ford almost dies because he can't write. It just runs him nuts, that he has thoughts and ideas and has never trained himself to put them down on paper. . . . The town is full of legends of John Ford mistreating his script. You know, tearing out twenty pages and saying, 'Now we're three days ahead of schedule.' Or saying to somebody, 'God damn it, this fellow has been reading the script.' All of these things to belittle the script, and of course, it's a perfectly clear indication that he hates the fact that he didn't write the script."

If not completely true, Johnson's assessment is close enough. Ford could outline a story in sequence progression, he could add dialogue touches, but he thought in images, not words.

"He saw things through his own prism and nobody else had that same prism," remembered Winston Miller. "He would sit there chewing his dirty handkerchief. . . . One day he said, 'I always wanted to do a scene of a whore's funeral in a small Western town. The casket is on a wagon and it starts down the street and only the madam and the other girls are following it. It goes down the street, and . . . the banker looks out and his conscience gets the better of him, and finally he goes and falls in line. And the blacksmith, when it goes by, his conscience gets the better of him. Pretty soon all the men in the town are following the casket.'

"I said, 'That's fantastic, that's wonderful, I love it.' And later on while I was writing the script, I didn't see him much then because he went his way and I went mine. I ran into him on the lot one day and he said, 'How's it going?' I said, 'Fine.' He said, 'How's the whore's funeral working out?' Then I made a mistake, I said, 'It didn't work out, because she's not a whore with a heart of gold. She's really a mean, vicious, lying girl. She isn't the kind of girl you had in mind.' He made me go and explain in great detail why I wasn't using it. When I finished, he said, 'I don't know what you're writing, but on the screen it's going to look a hell of a lot like a whore's funeral.' Actually, he didn't use it, because it didn't work, but I wasn't going to be the guy to tell him it wouldn't work."

Directors needed writers, but they didn't—couldn't—allow themselves to admit it. "They were always knocking the screenwriter," remembered Stephen Longstreet. That was bad enough, but in those days there was a fair amount of credit-stealing as well. "I wrote *Duel in the Sun* with Niven Busch, but on the screen it says that David O. Selznick wrote it. Most screenwriters were hacks, but they were great mechanics and always underappreciated."

Longstreet's estimation of Ford's writers was more forgiving than, say, Nunnally Johnson, who thought they were little more than amanuenses. "Frank Nugent—maybe. Laurence Stallings was not a competent screenwriter, and Dudley Nichols was an intellectual who felt he was inventing screenwriting." Nevertheless, Nugent, Stallings, and a strange, warrior personality by the name of James Warner Bellah were the writers that Ford would turn to repeatedly in the next fifteen years, perhaps because they understood his idiosyncrasies and their writing left plenty of air for Ford to insert the visual equivalent of pages of dialogue.

Ford's sense of structure was unorthodox. As Joseph McBride and Michael Wilmington noted, the opening reel of a Ford film is often a methodical, silent affair in which the audience is marinated in the textures of a place and the roles of the people in that place. Conflict is planted, but not actually verbalized.

Winston Miller pointed out that *My Darling Clementine* violates all the conventional rules of screen narrative. Earp comes to Tombstone, refuses the job of sheriff, his brother is killed, he decides to be the sheriff. With the story set, Ford basically drops it for several reels and plays with characters. "[Henry Fonda] sits on the porch with his feet up," complained Miller, "and you have John Ford vignettes. You have interesting scenes, but there's no urgency, [just] a lot of shambling around."

Ford's likes and dislikes in movies were clear. "I like a story that has a . . . good beginning and a good finish. I feel quite confident of making the in-between interesting. I like a story that happens in 24 to 48 hours. I despise pictures where the heroine has 46 changes of costume, 15 different hairdos and where the hero comes to the houseparty with one small bag and has 20 changes. I prefer stories laid in the United States. I like the chase motif."

With Ford, the antennae were always up, the machine was always running. Dudley Nichols remembered being on a streetcar with Ford one night when he noticed the director fascinated by a double reflection on the glass in front of them—the passing street outside as well as the people in the seats behind Ford and Nichols. The two men discussed the image, and Nichols realized Ford had made a mental note about using that lighting scheme the first chance he got.

As with any top director, the most important issue was control. He could control himself only when he was controlling others. If he had to quit drinking to work, by God they would too, and share the sacrifice. Ford did so well in the military because his methods of filmmaking had served him as a self-imposed basic training. Every day was a battle, and the results nearly life and death, hence the terrible stresses that buffeted him, and the strange, nervous habits he developed to cope with them. Only people terrified of losing control insist on absolute control.

What made his abuse worth enduring? Aside from the feeling, rare in Hollywood, of perhaps creating something truly worthwhile, there was the humor, the ferocious loyalty, the enveloping feel of family, and

Ford's endearing trait of revealing weaknesses that he always pretended he didn't have.

"Inside, he was one of the most considerate, generous [people]" remembered Ruth Clifford, who started acting for Ford in the Harry Carey days and was still at it forty years later. "His memory was like an elephant's. The cowboys that worked . . . in the Universal days grew up and became old . . . extras or bit players. In every John Ford film up until he died, he would have those old faces sitting on a porch, riding a horse with their back to the camera into the sunset . . . not heard, but there, because it gave them an income, residuals, unemployment benefits.

"I couldn't possibly remember the number of films I've made, but . . . Mr. Ford always gave me a spot and a challenge in so many, many pictures. I once said to him, 'I'm grateful.' And he said, 'You deserve it. If you weren't any good, I wouldn't have you.' In the long run, he would befriend anyone. . . . He was without a doubt one of the most wonderful persons I have ever known in my life."

Frank Baker recalled an example of Ford's eerily retentive mind. On *Four Sons*, they had an argument about a button on a military uniform. Ford believed the eagle on the button should be facing left, while Baker believed it should be facing right. In any case, Baker pointed out, the camera couldn't see which way the eagle was looking. Fully twenty years later, when Ford was sitting in his armchair, books stacked on either side as usual, he pulled out a book, opened it, and handed it to Baker. "You see, it turns to the left!" Baker didn't know what he was talking about. "What turns to the left?" "The eagle's head," said Ford triumphantly.

Yet even the old-timers among the stock company had to be careful. When Ruth Clifford was hired for *Wagon Master*, her agent read the script and thought another client of hers would be perfect for the part of the ham actor, which had been written expressly for Alan Mowbray. The agent began calling Meta Sterne, Ford's secretary, and pushing her client.

When Clifford showed up at the studio for costume fittings, Ford came to the door and said what she would later remember as "the only unkind thing he'd said [to me] in his life: 'Since when are you casting my pictures?' " Ford must have had a few other remarks to make, because Clifford was reduced to tears. Meta Sterne came in and told her she was just taking her turn and to forget about it. "He bites everyone just once," said Sterne. Shortly afterward, Ford came over and put his arms around Clifford and said, "I just wanted to see you cry."

To his grandsons he was Grampy or Gramps, and Mary was Nana. He had lived in the house on Odin Street for more than twenty years, and, as he told one reporter, "After being in pictures that long, I consider myself lucky to have a house at all." The household staff was small, usually just two people, one of whom was James Jackson, Ford's chauffeur and a decorated black veteran of World War I.

Ford's den, where he held his story conferences, was set off from the dining room by a sliding panel, and furnished in the masculine manner of a sea captain. Bayonets, spears, and old ship's wheels were on the walls, and the tables were littered with trophies and souvenirs of his travels. There was a deerskin given him by the Navajos, and a luxurious rodeo saddle. On the wall over the mantel was a framed Indian headdress, and nearby was a drawing of flowers in a pot with the inscription, "To Mr. Ford. Love, Shirley Temple."

Ford's patriarchal concept of family was deeply romantic, one of the reasons he was unable to replicate the idealized feelings of his movies in real life. "Papa was not a nurturer," said Joanne Dru, a good friend of Barbara's. "The family never really communicated . . . maybe because he couldn't relax. He really didn't relate to women. I've often thought that Papa had tremendous insecurities—never regarding his talent, but as a man. He surrounded himself with these big, strong bruisers."

He had no hobbies, and no diversions other than the *Araner* and reading, which was often fuel for his films. For companionship, Ford and Mary kept Irish wolfhounds for a number of years. The aristocratic wolfhounds were succeeded by a pair of dachshunds from Barbara's dachshund, Sunday. Jack even allowed the dachshunds on his bed, where he enjoyed playing games with them. (Ford loved dogs, but his brother Frank had a remarkable rapport with anything on four legs, including horses.)

Although he had a number of his films at the house in 16mm prints— *The Informer, The Long Voyage Home, The Lost Patrol,* and *Stagecoach,* among others—nobody ever mentioned him watching them.

At the house, there were strict rules. Pat and Barbara were always sure to tell their friends, "Now, listen, when you walk in the front door, don't mention anything about movies." (Later in his life, Ford would be the one who broke his own rule.) He was a great fan of Laurel and Hardy, and would sometimes say that his favorite movie of all time was Leo McCarey's *The Battle of the Century,* a two-reeler featuring the greatest pie fight of the silent era. He also adored the Marx Brothers.

The mood around the house could be pleasant and convivial, and he could be enormously charming in dodging Subject A. Once, Mel Ferrer asked Winston Miller to arrange an interview with Ford so the ambitious young actor could have an in-depth discussion on the art of film.

"Ford guided the conversation, and he never got around to moviemaking," remembered Miller. "He talked about everything under the sun—college days, he sang the Maine Stein song. And it was very frustrating to [Mel] because [he'd] come to sit at the foot of the master to learn about what was the secret of his success. And he would not get on that subject at all, he was adamant."

Serenely presiding over Jack's moods and Jack's rules was Mary, "a great lady," according to Patrick Wayne, John Wayne's son. "She had the patience and forbearance to put up with this crazy guy. And she was there all the time. What makes a good marriage? Common interests, common goals. [But] Ford was married to work, either shooting a film or preparing a film, in the office working and writing. He would edit scenes like crazy, edit on paper. Did it work for her?" Pat Wayne left the question hanging. Clearly, he didn't see how it could have; clearly, on some level, it must have.

"Mary was striking, a gracious hostess, a charming woman," remembered Jean Nugent, the wife of Frank Nugent. "And she had the best collection of jade jewelry I've ever seen in my life."

"Mary was wonderful," remembered Kathleen O'Malley, who went to school with Barbara. "Once, my sister was supposed to bring a picnic lunch for a class outing and forgot all about it. So she said to me, 'Let's go home and get something,' but by the time we got back we had missed the picnic. Mary was standing there and said, 'Why don't you girls come to our house on Saturday and we'll have a little picnic lunch with Barbara?' And we did and had the most marvelous time.

"She and Mr. Ford had a give-and-take. Once, Anna Lee was upset because her son was being inducted into the service. Pappy said, 'Don't worry. Mary, tell her what you used to tell me when I went into the service.' And Mary said, 'I just always told him to pack enough underwear.' They were like George Burns and Gracie Allen."

Jack and Mary had evolved into serious bridge players and affectionate partners, the stresses and strains of the Hepburn period filed away, if not forgotten. "They genuinely liked each other," remembered their grandson Dan. "They would do card tricks, one in particular where he would be out of the room and she would pull a card and show it to everybody in the room, then shuffle the deck, and he would come back into the room and pull the card. They had everybody convinced they had a telepathic way of communicating because nobody could figure out how they did it. They were very friendly and funny together. And he loved to play 20 Questions; any subject, no matter how obscure. I remember one time it was Hermann Goering's hypodermic needle. Other times it would be something relating to Sherlock Holmes."

When he wasn't preparing a film or on location he was on the *Araner*. During the war, the Navy had painted the ship gray but Ford restored her to yacht trim, although he was proud she had been in service and could officially be called the USS *Araner.* "He was a Navy man from the word go," was how one employee would put it, and that would never change.

Two or three Sundays a month he'd attend Church of the Blessed Sacrament, then visit his sisters Jo and Maime, who, along with Cecile de Prita, lived in an upscale tract house in the Valley. After the Fords moved to Bel Air, he attended St. Martin of Tours in Brentwood. He liked family, but was more favorably disposed toward family that he didn't have to support.

When it came to sports, he loved baseball—when the Dodgers moved to Los Angeles in 1958, he became a regular season ticket holder. When it came to food, he liked lobster, or meat and potatoes, and his preferred nonalcoholic beverage was ginger ale. He ate a very light breakfast, no lunch, and a big dinner. Like most alcoholics, when he wasn't drinking he had a tremendous sweet tooth, and loved chocolate and vanilla ice cream, with frequent Hershey Bar snacks.

When not working, he was nocturnal, and would plow through several books every night, often history. For fiction, he preferred P. G. Wodehouse or Irish writers. Music tended to be for when he was drunk, and then it was lachrymose Irish ballads. He spoke mediocre French, and Spanish with a Maine accent. Mary's main form of relaxation was horseracing, which she bet on often and badly.

For all of his studied harshness, he was capable of a kind of rough tact. Although his good friend Brian Desmond Hurst was homosexual, the subject never came up. Once, Hurst was staying with Ford when he told him he was having dinner at George Cukor's house. "What do you want to go there for?" grumbled Ford. "There's a perfectly good steak waiting for you in the kitchen."

When Hurst returned, Ford gave him the third degree, a parent grilling a frisky teenager. "What was the dinner like? Who was there?" Hurst told him that Spencer Tracy was there, which Ford didn't understand at all. Ruth Gordon's and Garson Kanin's attendance was noted with "Oh, they'll go anywhere for a free dinner." Clifton Webb was there and Ford nodded. "Oh, you might expect *that.* What's the house like?"

Hurst described the enormous pool, the drawing room with the hand-painted chinoiserie wallpaper, the Manet over the fireplace, the paneled study. He finished by saying, "I can't give you any information about the bedroom, Jack, because I didn't go upstairs."

"Brian, I'm proud of you," Ford said, the first time Ford had ever referred to what Hurst called "that side of my life."

Ford also enjoyed the Emerald Bay Yacht Club, which had grown out of a group who liked to spend the occasional afternoon in the steam room of the Hollywood Athletic Club. The club motto was "Jews But No Dues"; besides the stock company, the members included Frank Morgan, Frank Borzage, Gene Markey, Philip Dunne, Preston Foster, William Gargan, Johnny Weissmuller, Richard Day, Victor Fleming, Dick Powell, James Cagney, George Brent, Donald Crisp, Tay Garnett, Ronald Colman, Howard Hawks, Frank Capra, and William Wellman.

It was, needless to say, a heavy-drinking crew, and they meant to keep it that way. In something of a running joke, the club consistently refused to admit Dudley Nichols because he had never been treated for alcoholism. Not a man to take it lying down, in 1946 Nichols wrote a desperate letter naming six co-sponsors for his application in the club: Leo McCarey, W. C. Fields, Gene Fowler, Gregory La Cava, Marshall Neilan, and Wilfred Lawson—a Who's Who of Hollywood alcoholics.

Ford enjoyed dropping in on people unannounced. Harry Carey Jr. remembered one typical afternoon. His son Tom was on the floor playing with Civil War toy soldiers when Ford showed up and immediately focused on the soldiers.

"Uncle Jack," asked Tom, "why did John Wilkes Booth shoot Lincoln?"

"You mean you never heard that story? Well, what was the name of the play Lincoln was watching?"

"*Our American Cousin,*" replied the young history buff.

"Well, John Wilkes Booth was a very good actor. And your grandmother Ollie was in that play and she was very bad. She was so bad that John Wilkes Booth took out his gun and tried to shoot her, but he missed and killed the President instead."

Although Ollie Carey was not amused by the reference to her age or her professional ability, it was a good example of Ford's humor—pointed, funny, and at somebody else's expense.

A good sense of Ford's life away from the studio can be gauged by the Ford home movies. They document a leisure life lived largely on Catalina, the *Araner,* or both. Seaplanes take off from San Pedro; Ward Bond, stomach sucked in, strides manfully on the deck of the *Araner;* John Wayne, an unglamorous slab of sunscreen on his nose, and his second wife, Chata, struggle to bring in a sizable swordfish. Pat's sons show the camera their favorite toys; a close-up of a shapely, anonymous female bottom as its owner bends over the side; Dan Dailey water-skiing; the *Araner* in rough seas; Maureen O'Hara and her children on the *Araner's* motorboat, with a nearly deserted Catalina in the background, the 16mm Kodachrome showing the smogless skies as a lustrous royal blue; Barbara, very spritely, very cute, dances past the lens; a beautiful shot of a moonlit night on Avalon Bay.

Occasionally, Ford or Mary would take the camera to the Field Photo Farm, and get some shots of a stagecoach full of children or Danny Borzage on the accordion, or Ford himself, with his loose, rolling sailor's stride, ambling through, nodding at the camera. There's one delightful shot of Ford and Pat, moving toward the camera on the deck of the *Araner*, with identical walks.

Ford was no less of an enigma to his family than he was to his actors. "He wasn't much of a talker," Patrick Ford told James D'Arc. "A very strange man. He was . . . a man with the ability to concentrate almost wholly on his profession, excluding a lot else. . . . He used to sit [and] sketch with charcoal: faces, faces and scenes. . . . Indian faces, western faces . . . sometimes people like the Welsh people in *How Green Was My Valley* . . . or scenes of trains crossing the mountains in the background. He was doing it and thinking. . . . He was a very brilliant man. He was single-minded, he only cared about pictures. He saw without having to sit and talk, he saw an awful lot that I didn't see.

"My conversations with him as his only son—that I know of—was 'Yes sir,' until one day I said 'No sir,' and then I was no longer around. . . . Our family life was pretty much like that of a shipmaster and his crew, or a wagonmaster and his people. He gave the orders and we carried them out. . . . His whole [life] was movies, you know."

Ford confirmed his son's opinion of his utter lack of interest in a domestic life. "I eat, sleep and drink whatever picture I'm working on," he said. "Read nothing else, think of nothing else; which is probably the reason the continuity and mood of my products stays at an exact level." But the only trait he would ever allow himself pride over was the quality of his images; "I still think I'm the best cameraman in the business," he would say.

He was present but not present, constantly preoccupied with his own thoughts. In the hundreds of family snapshots preserved in the Ford papers at the Lilly Library, Ford is rarely smiling—the most he seems able to summon at will is a quizzical lightness around the mouth.

"He kept to the studio, and he kept to his boat," said the director Andre de Toth. "He was not a social person."

As for his brothers, in all the years Lefty Hough knew him, he never saw either Frank or Eddie at the house. On balance, this might have been a good idea because Eddie, normally a mild-mannered man, got crazy when alcohol was involved. "Eddie was a mean bastard when he got drunk," said Wingate Smith. "The only way to handle him was to hit him with a club."

Andre de Toth had met Ford just before the war through their mutual friend, Jack Daniel's. ("He wouldn't insult it with the rocks. He was a sailor and rocks were to be avoided.") One day in 1946, de Toth was having a drink at the Garden of Allah when Ford came in. After one drink—"unusual for him" dryly noted de Toth—Ford said, "Come on." Ford and de Toth then piled into his car and he careened over to a studio on Melrose and Bronson. "He didn't drive the car, the car drove him," observed de Toth. Without slowing down, Ford drove past the security gate and came to an abrupt halt in front of a pleasant little Spanish bungalow.

Ford got out, leaving the engine running, with de Toth trotting after him. Walking through two outer offices without pausing to introduce himself, he marched into the private offices of Charles Einfeld and David Loew, founders of the nascent Enterprise studio. "Charlie, David," said Ford, "he's going to direct *Ramrod*, I can't get rid of my commitment. Talk to him, give him a script, I lost mine. He'll be all right." He promptly turned around and went back to his car.

"That was Ford," remembered de Toth. "He knew I had earned my living riding herd and he knew I was in love with Westerns. That's the way I got into Westerns. God, I loved it." Typically, after Ford did de Toth the favor, he ignored him. "He acted like he didn't know me, the son of a bitch," de Toth said with a sigh more than a half century later. "He had to do everything by way of the back door, because he had slammed the front door in your face. I think he was a very lonely man; he was sure of the art he wanted to make, but not much else.

"You know, a phrase that is very misused is 'I know him.' People say hello to someone and they think they know them. Jack Ford was a very complex man; if you ask me did I know Jack Ford, I say, 'Hell, no.' And I honestly believe if you had asked Jack Ford if he knew Jack Ford he would have said, 'Hell, no.'"

Because of his unresolved—and unresolvable—internal conflicts, Ford was a man in perpetual flight from his fragile inner life to his rock-solid professional life. Pain was to be concealed; malice was to be displayed. And he arranged things so carefully that he could easily present a deceptive facade, the quality of glide.

As his grandson Dan observed, "To catch a plane he always leaves the house at the last possible moment, he is always the last one to walk on the plane, he never misses the plane and they never have to hold it for him either. He's just one of those people that goes through his life as though it was prepared for him in advance . . . as though there was a path and all he had to do was walk down the path." Everybody who knew him knew they didn't really know him.

His friendships, such as they were, were extensions of the relationship he had with his actors and crew—the fierce father figure and his trembling acolytes. He had virtually no intimate relationships among his peer group. There were cronies and acquaintances, but few friends. "All these people were beholden to him and they were afraid of him," said Andrew McLaglen. "These were guys like Jack Pennick. Who else could they work for? Jack felt he had power over them and he felt their fear. Why he needed that, I don't know."

As for his real family, as opposed to his extended family, Ford continued to make yearly trips back to Portland, where he would check into the Eastland Hotel and make a pilgrimage to Sheridan Street to see his brother Pat, after which he'd fan out. He stayed in touch with Lucien Libby, his old high school teacher. Ford usually traveled alone—his niece remembered Mary coming with Ford only a few times, once at Christmas. "Mary was very beautiful and nice," remembered Mary McPhillips. "Uncle Jack never talked about movies. *Never.* He treated me like any uncle would. 'How's school?' How's everything?' "

Ford seems to have been disinclined to import any more Feeneys to California. Only once did he invite Mary McPhillips out, and then it was a quid pro quo. "It was the end of Pat's junior year at the University of Maine," remembered McPhillips. "Uncle Jack called and asked me to drive back to California with Pat and 'slow him down.' When we got there, he invited me on the set of *How Green Was My Valley.*" "You're the only member of my family allowed on my set," he told her. He invited John Wayne over to the house to meet his niece, who was suitably impressed. Mary noticed that the Odin Street house was unpretentious, with a big living room and lots of books. Ford's only real concession to his status and income remained a chauffeur—Mary didn't drive—and the *Araner.* "I think he was in love with that boat more than he was his family," said Ben Johnson.

The *Araner* was where he unwound, where he relaxed, where he drank . . . but not exclusively. Ford met a lot of interesting people because of his ship. He once recalled sailing into Pearl Harbor before the war and docking next to the yacht of George Patton. "We exchanged books," Ford said with some wonderment, "so when he became Blood and Guts, to me it was a complete metamorphosis, because actually he was a . . . gentleman. And he didn't have much to say around the house, around the ship. His wife wore the riding breeches and the ivory-handled guns."

Although Ford's admiration for Frank Capra was well known, they were very different kinds of men and saw each other most frequently at

St. Martin of Tours church, and only occasionally socialized. The people that were frequent visitors to the Capra house were William Wellman, Bing Crosby, Dave Chasen, and the writer Myles Connolly. Capra's son Tom remembered one long night when Duke Wayne and Ward Bond got into a fight in the middle of the Capra living room and totally destroyed the carpeting. Mrs. Capra put her foot down and made Wayne and Bond install a new one.

There was something more between Ford and William Wellman, the legendary Wild Bill, but it was surreptitious. "I'd call it an unspoken friendship," remembered William Wellman Jr. "They had certain similarities about them, their backgrounds, where they came from. Ford would come on Dad's sets, and for Dad to let another director on his set . . . that was Big Time; that tells you something about his feelings for Ford."

Yet, even there, Ford had difficulty with the equivalent give-and-take necessary for a true friendship. "Occasionally, Ford would have parties, and Dad would go," remembered Wellman Jr. "But Ford never came to his. In thinking about it, I guess you could call it a mutual respect and admiration. But it was hard to be a friend of Ford's."

Within the industry, Ford's alcoholism was common knowledge, but, as the journalist Joe Hyams recalled, "nobody gave a damn. He was ready in the morning with his setups." It should also be noted that attitudes toward alcoholism, the primary occupational hazard of the industry, were considerably less censorious than they are now. "In those days, everybody drank," said Hyams. "Drinking was a form of convivial time spent. As long as you didn't miss a call, nobody thought it was a bad thing."

Ford could be rather funny when sticking to beer or wine; a little buzz made him genial and slaphappy, but hard liquor unleashed something else entirely, a ridiculously serious, maudlin drunk on his way to oblivion. "I remember getting long lectures about the importance of my religion," said Dan Ford, "with him drooling all over himself."

Once he started on hard liquor, Ford could not stop until he collapsed, "until he would be a slobbering, helpless drunk," in the words of Charles FitzSimons. "It was tragic. You would look at him and you couldn't believe it was the same man. You'd see the fastidious Ford—despite his eccentric clothing—and then you'd see this slobbering drunk with his head hanging and the drool going down his chin. It was heartbreaking."

Ford was aware of what he was like at these times, because he would only allow his family or inner circle to see him in this condition. Many co-workers and acquaintances never saw him drink at all.

The fact that alcohol completely dissolved the otherwise rigidly maintained facade of Ford could be terribly disconcerting to people who weren't used to him. "The first time I met him," remembered Marilyn Fix Carey, the daughter of character actor Paul Fix, the wife of Harry Carey Jr., "I was terrified. It was 1944, at Harry Carey's ranch. Ford was terribly drunk; slobber was coming out of his mouth. He had peed his pants."

When Ford was on a binge, nobody was safe. Propman Ace Holmes once recounted a story he undoubtedly heard from Wingate Smith. Ford and Smith, both drunk, were on the *Araner* when Mary and Barbara pulled up in a ketch. Climbing on board, Barbara kissed her father and the two women went back to their cabins. Ford turned to his brother-in-law and said, "Who are those two cunts?"

Likewise, Joanne Dru recalled a time when Ford had locked himself in his bedroom, the better to focus on his drinking. Dru and Barbara were outside talking when they heard a drizzling noise and looked up. It was Ford, relieving himself out of the window. "Good afternoon, girls," he said companionably.

The family wasn't much help, not that anyone could have been. With the living-in-denial obliviousness that foretold her own alcoholism, Barbara Ford told her nephew that, "He would come to my mother and say . . . 'I've cut the picture, the music is OK'd, Zanuck's OK'd it, it's shipped for negative. . . . Here's $1000 for you to do what you want,' and then he got drunk. And he drank for three weeks. So he was not a problem drinker."

What was he looking for when he drank?

"Escape. Oblivion."

Aside from the genetic and cultural factors that entered into his alcoholism, Ford was undoubtedly also drinking to relieve the pressure induced by his increasingly neurotic psychological makeup. As James Warner Bellah would note, "As a young boy, he was a Catholic in a Protestant state . . . his father was a saloon keeper in a teetotal state. He wasn't just a Catholic, but an immigrant Catholic. He had enormous tensions."

Dealing with this uneasy combination of elements, this confused, inner sweetness and outward purgatorial sadism, must have been nearly impossible, but Mary Ford tried. "He truly adored her," said Robert Parrish. Although Mary was a quiet woman who didn't appear aggressive, she had the necessary steel to handle Ford, and he would generally listen. "Mary could get at him," recalled Andrew McLaglen. "She wasn't afraid of him at all. Barbara absolutely worshipped him, and Pat loved him a lot, but he suffered from being in his father's shadow. He wouldn't be the first child to have been overshadowed by a parent."

"Mary was a good wife to him," remembered Mary Lou Whitney, the wife of C. V. Whitney, Ford's friend and financier of *The Searchers*. "She would sit there, very stoic, until she'd had enough, and then she'd say, 'John, you're absolutely wrong.'

"John would say, 'Are you sure?'

" 'I'm sure. Apologize.'

" 'Well, Mary says I'm wrong,' he'd say, and then he'd apologize."

CHAPTER SEVENTEEN

For a generation of serious, artistically inclined directors who had gone off to war, quietly going back to work for the Zanucks and Warners of the world was an impossibility. Within a year or two of war's end, David Loew and Charles Einfeld would form Enterprise Productions; John Huston would be partnered with Sam Spiegel in Horizon Pictures; Frank Capra, George Stevens, and William Wyler would be allied in Liberty Productions; Hitchcock would form Transatlantic Productions with Sidney Bernstein; and Ford and Merian Cooper would reactivate Argosy Productions.

Of all these companies, Argosy was well calculated to succeed, if only because Ford's record of observing the verities of budgets was unmatched, and Cooper had both a creative and financially astute side. Argosy had already made two artistically successful pictures—*Stagecoach*, an Argosy effort in everything but name, and *The Long Voyage Home*—so Ford and Cooper had a matrix for what they hoped to accomplish.

The initial Argosy picture was to be Ford's old favorite from the Universal days, *The Last Outlaw*. United Artists bought the story rights for $25,000 and was going to distribute, while John Wayne and Harry Carey agreed to star. The cost of the picture was to be $800,000, and Argosy was to receive 70 percent of the profits.

Unfortunately, the deal fell through, probably because Cooper felt a multi-picture deal would be more advantageous than a succession of single-picture contracts. While Cooper got Argosy up and running, Ford went about working off the last picture he owed Darryl Zanuck.

The man who has been the subject of more films than all American presidents combined was born in Illinois in 1848 and followed his family West in 1864. Arrested in Indian territory for horse stealing, Wyatt

Earp jumped bail and fled to Kansas. In 1874, he turned up in Wichita, where he went to work as a policeman; in 1876, he moved to Dodge City, where he met John "Doc" Holliday, a tubercular gambler with a terrible temper. Earp's older brother Virgil got an appointment as a marshal in Tombstone, Arizona, so, in 1880, his brothers joined him there, followed by Doc Holliday. Although he was working as a deputy sheriff, Wyatt Earp was really hoping to strike it rich as an entrepreneur and gambler.

The most famous thirty seconds of the Old West took place in October 1881. The gunfight at the O.K. Corral ended with everybody but Wyatt Earp either dead or wounded. A few weeks later, Virgil Earp was shot again, while Morgan Earp was killed. Virtually every version of the story would reverse the events, and have the O.K. Corral as the end of the conflict rather than the beginning, with the death of Earp's brother as primary motivation.

Various interpretations of the events in Tombstone would make it a blood feud, or an athletic contest, but the ascertainable facts strongly indicate it was a blown arrest. Tombstone had an ordinance outlawing guns within the city limits and the Clanton faction had been walking around town for two days, armed and threatening to kill the Earps. The Earps were attempting to arrest the Clantons, with Doc Holliday watching their backs.

The facts of Wyatt Earp and the O.K. Corral would probably have been relegated to the morgues of Southwestern historical societies were it not for Stuart Lake's 1931 book *Wyatt Earp: Frontier Marshal*, which characterized Earp as a Hercules of the West, cleaning out Augean stables in town after town. (Although Earp died in 1929, and was in fact a lawman for only eight of his eighty years, he seems to have cooperated with Lake in the early stages of his own enshrinement.)

Lake's book served as the basis for a 1939 film called *Frontier Marshal*, with Randolph Scott as Earp and Cesar Romero as Doc Halliday (the film's spelling). As efficiently but anonymously directed by Allan Dwan, it's a movie of limited interest, departing from history in a manner that makes the impulses behind *My Darling Clementine* seem rigorously documentarian by contrast.

The Dwan film feels crowded; the plot jettisons Earp's brothers, but the brief seventy-one-minute running time makes it seem jammed with plot—the filmmakers didn't trust the characters, unlike Ford, who rarely trusted anything else. Yet several sequences of the Ford film derive directly from the Dwan, in particular the entire opening, with a drunken Indian terrorizing the town—Ford even hired the same actor, Charlie Stevens, an old compatriot of Douglas Fairbanks's—and using a visiting vaudevillian as a frayed bone of contention between the two warring camps of Tombstone. In *Frontier Marshal*, Eddie Foy Jr. plays Eddie Foy Sr., while Ford and his writer would dream up a rather more delicious character they called Granville Thorndyke, an "eminent tragedian" played by Alan Mowbray as a ham actor with a soul.

Ford's Earp is one of the last times he would draw a man of the West without a character conflict; Earp has no particular nostalgia for the past, and, except for the scene at his brother's grave—an add-on not directed by Ford—never expresses any interest in the future. The Wyatt Earp created by Ford and Henry Fonda is a self-possessed, pragmatic man, interested in a clean shave and a quiet town. If nobody else will give him those things, he'll have to get them himself.

The conflicts are embodied in the nearly urbane Doc Holliday, who inspires Earp with his education and covert graciousness even as he spirals down to self-destruction, while the Clantons are simply brutish and nearly subhuman.

Ford cast history aside, and used only the premise, for he knew that audiences—not to mention irascible film directors—want meaning more than facts. (As demonstrated by a dozen or so thankfully forgotten self-important Westerns of the 1960s and 1970s—*Doc, Soldier Blue, Little Big Man*, etc.—the last thing anybody needs from a movie is a cynical history lesson.)

To help him construct this vision, Ford chose Winston Miller, the brother of silent star Patsy Ruth Miller. Miller had only the most minor writing credits—a couple of serials and *Home in Indiana*—but he also had a trump card: he had played the young George O'Brien in *The Iron Horse*.

This was the beginning of a new phase in Ford's career, where his screenwriters would predominantly be people named Nugent or Bellah, not Nunnally Johnson or Dudley Nichols. This meant something different to both Ford and his actors.

"When there'd be a scene maybe a little bit on the rough side," remembered James Stewart, "right in the middle of it he'd say, 'Cut. Everybody's talking too much. You must have different scripts than I do. I don't have all this stuff.' Which of course is an absolute lie, because *he'd written it, he had done the writing of it.* . . . Lots of times he'd cut eight or ten lines out of a four or five-minute scene" (emphasis added).

The central idea for Ford, as he came back from the war, was to make the movies he wanted to make, untrammeled by the interference of a studio or the competing or even complementary visions of a strong-minded writer with his own take on a story.

Miller's first draft for *My Darling Clementine* is reasonably close to the film, although there are some differences: the script has Doc Holliday killed before the gunfight; the Clantons never openly challenge Earp;

Earp still leaves at the end, but the final words to Clementine aren't there; the character eventually played by Linda Darnell is killed, but another girl is wounded by the Clantons, and Holliday successfully operates on her.

Zanuck added his usual pointed touches, sharpening and defining the material, as in this dialogue addition:

"Clanton: Well, good luck Mr? Mr?

"Wyatt: Earp. Wyatt Earp.

"Wyatt walks out. They stare."

Other than Henry Fonda, who was always set for the part of Wyatt Earp, casting was more of a struggle than Ford was used to. He asked Zanuck for Anne Baxter for Clementine, but had to settle for the bland Cathy Downs. Likewise, he was never happy with the heavy-lidded Linda Darnell as Holliday's Mexican lover.

Yet, some of Ford's own ideas tended toward the bizarre. For one reason or another, Tyrone Power as Doc Holliday disappeared from the list of possibilities early on. Among Ford's enthusiasms for the part was Douglas Fairbanks Jr. ("He might be really terribly good in it. He would look about the same age as Henry and as it's a flamboyant role it is quite possible he could kick hell out of it. Think it over well.")

Ford then developed a fixation on Vincent Price. He was, he told Zanuck, concerned about Victor Mature—Zanuck's preference. After Mature met with Ford, the director's concerns were smoothed over. "I am not at all worried about Mature," he wrote Zanuck on February 28. "I really wrote the note to see that a little discipline was performed on Junior."

There was only one instance of Ford's legendary touchiness during the writing. It concerned a scene where Earp stops Holliday from leaving Tombstone because he believes him to be implicated in his brother's death. "Ford was discussing with Zanuck how he wanted to do it with Holliday on the stagecoach with a driver," said Winston Miller. "I said, 'Shouldn't it be just Doc Holliday riding his own horse because it would be better with two men instead of having the stagecoach driver there too.' I made the mistake of saying, 'It seems cluttered.' Well, that was the key word that gave Ford his opening. He gave me a ten-minute dissertation that he had been known to direct scenes with as many as five people in them without it being cluttered. . . . He was volatile; he could be the nicest guy in the world and he could be the meanest. You never knew which was going to happen." As Miller remembered, "Sooner or later he wanted to dominate you."

Miller observed that the way Zanuck controlled Ford was through flattery. "Zanuck had an idea that he suggested and Ford thought it was terrible. Zanuck said, in effect, 'Jack, if any other director was going to do the picture, I wouldn't even suggest it to him, but you can pull it off.' . . . Ford ate it up. Zanuck played him like a flute."

Ford and Miller wrote in the church scene so Fonda could do the same endearing high-stepping dance he had done in *Young Mr. Lincoln.* "Ford simply thought it made a good shot," remembered Miller. "He shot the long scene with the two of them walking because he liked to watch Fonda walk."

One day during the writing phase, Ford suddenly asked Miller, "If this picture doesn't turn out well, it won't hurt you in the business, will it?" Miller's credits were so minor he was barely in the business, but he didn't pick up on the fact that Ford was fishing for a compliment. "No, I've got other credits I can fall back on," Miller said. "Ford kind of dummied up for a while. . . . He kind of froze; he wanted me to say, 'Oh, no!' "

As the picture moved toward production, Ford, obviously glad to have the old gang gathered around him once more, began displaying his humorous side. He wrote a letter to Frank Capra, who was shooting *It's a Wonderful Life,* in which Ward Bond had a good supporting role: "I am writing you regarding using Ward Bond in your picture. As you know, he has already signed a contract to work in my forthcoming production. . . . I have talked it over with the various members of the cast and they are enthusiastic and wholehearted[ly] in accord with the idea of Bond working for you. In fact, a delegation . . . just left my office. They are willing to advance you as much as $890.00 if you can get him out of our picture to work solely in yours. Hank Fonda, an actor who is also working in the picture, offers to throw in a Radio Victrola, hardly used. A Mr. Victor Mature also offers in compensation and beyond various presents, the phone number of a very interesting young lady (colored)."

Ford and Capra rearranged their schedules so that Bond could do the two films back to back. There is no record of whether or not Capra took delivery of the Victrola.

The Tombstone set constructed in Monument Valley cost $250,000. Ford's desire to help the Navajos played a considerable part in determining the location. It was the first film he'd made there since *Stagecoach,* and this time he was greeted on the steps of Goulding's as a friend. Once again Ford sat at the head table in the dining hall, his bone-handled jacknife beside him, presiding over the company. Wingate Smith helped out in the kitchen; Ward Bond assisted Harry Goulding at the trading post, as did Linda Darnell.

Ford brought a priest eighty-six miles over a dirt road to say Mass on Sunday. Attendance was mandatory for Catholics, Protestants, and Jews alike, as was a contribution when the hat was passed. As always, the nights were magical—silent except for Danny Borzage's gentle accordion airs, dark except for flashes of lightning far away in the Valley.

For a scene where the Clanton gang rides into town, Ford got a wind machine to create a dust storm, and instructed the actors to fire off their guns and shotguns close to the horse's ears so they'd ride wild. He wouldn't allow stuntmen to do the scene, but insisted that Walter Brennan, John Ireland, and Grant Withers do their own riding.

They managed to pull the scene off, but then Ford asked for a retake. Grant Withers was hanging behind, and Ford nudged him. "Come on, Grant, dammit, hurry up. Which is your horse?"

"The one with the shit in the saddle," said Withers.

It was requests like that, not to mention Ford's overall demeanor, that alienated Walter Brennan. "Can't you even mount a horse?" yelled Ford when Brennan was having trouble. "No, but I got three Oscars for acting," retorted Brennan.

Despite their mutual dislike, Brennan was giving a memorably cold, homicidal performance as Pa Clanton, possibly because he was transferring his loathing of Ford into his character's loathing of Earp. Brennan went through the film in a professional manner, and refused to ever work with Ford again. (Ford's home movie footage of the production shows a few random but beautiful shots of the Valley at dusk, Jack Pennick and Tim Holt relaxing, Victor Mature and Ward Bond gagging it up, and a notably solemn Walter Brennan not gagging it up.)

Winston Miller didn't go on location, but producer Samuel Engel did, making some minor dialogue changes. Later, he successfully petitioned for a writer's credit, sending Ford and Miller into a snit. "I asked him once why he was trying to muscle in on my credit," said Miller. "He said, 'On a John Ford picture a producer credit doesn't mean a thing. Everybody knows he's the producer.' "

Later, Ford would accuse Miller of lying down during the credit arbitration. As always, he personalized it: "Didn't you think a Ford credit was worth fighting for?" he asked Miller. "Why didn't you call me?" "I didn't want to bother you," said Miller. "It wasn't your problem."

The expected patsy on the picture was Victor Mature, a big, easygoing actor more renowned for his physique and knack for publicity than his acting talent. But Ford was surprisingly easy on Mature, perhaps because the actor had served in the Coast Guard during the war and done active convoy duty in the North Atlantic for fourteen months.

When Mature began running a high fever, Ford took him back to his studio dressing room, where the actor, who had just returned to Hollywood, was currently living. When Ford saw the cramped quarters, he insisted that Mature live in his house for the remainder of production.

Winston Miller's script stayed close to history in at least one regard, and that was by making Earp fairly laconic. Ford, however, made him even more so by trimming passages in which the character explains himself or makes a joke. He cut a lot of Doc's dialogue as well, cut a long speech of Russell Simpson's at the church service, and toned down various flamboyant elements in the script: Doc's first appearance—in an opera cape!—and a catfight between Chihuahua and Clementine.

Ford's sense of the texture of a scene, of the qualities an actor could project if you just stood back and watched, was never sharper. Fonda leaning back in his chair on the sidewalk, balancing himself on a beam; the lengthy tracking shot of Earp and Clementine walking toward the half-built church, Fonda moving with the deliberate stride of a graceful stork.

As Terence Rafferty has observed, Ford paces the entire picture to the purposeful, elegant rhythm of Fonda. *My Darling Clementine* is a Westerner's Western, laconic, unfussy, large-spirited, perennially modern in its quiet, contemplative mood and dark undercurrents. Nearly every exterior shot is framed to include vast expanses of sky, and, in a particular masterstroke, the gunfight at the O.K. Corral is played without blaring music, but with natural sounds—wind, boots scuffling for purchase in the sand. The silence is eerie and haunting.

When the location shoot was over, Fox and Ford handed over their beautiful Tombstone set to the Navajo tribal council to be disposed of as they saw fit. It sat there for five years, until 1951, when it was sold for salvage and carted away.

With $2 million at stake, Darryl Zanuck had some problems with the film. "You have in the film a great number of outstanding individual episodes and sequences," he wrote Ford on June 25, 1946. "You have a certain Western magnificence and a number of character touches that rival your best work, but to me the picture as a whole in its present state is a disappointment. It does not come up to our expectations."

Zanuck went on to state that the picture faced a radical recutting, that his primary concern was the story construction. "If the picture does not live up to my own personal anticipation, it will not live up to the anticipation of a paid audience." Zanuck said that Ford had given him enough raw footage to enable Zanuck to make 95 percent of the changes he felt were necessary, but—and this was a very big but—he wanted to make the changes himself, without Ford's input. "You trusted me implicitly on *Grapes of Wrath* and *How Green Was My Valley*. You did not see either picture until they were playing in the theaters and innumerable times you went out of your way to tell me how much you appreciated the Editorial work."

Zanuck always prided himself on his skill as a film editor and the changes he made on *Clementine* tend to bear him out. He used the scissors carefully, sometimes cutting little more than a few words at the end of a sentence. Either because Ford refused or was unavailable, Zanuck added one scene, of Henry Fonda at his brother's grave, that was actually directed by old studio hand Lloyd Bacon in an effective imitation of Ford's style. Zanuck also insisted that Fonda and Cathy Downs kiss in the last scene, a clinch Ford had strenuously resisted.

It might be the reshoots that give the film some continuity problems unusual for Ford—Earp mysteriously going from unlathered to completely lathered in the barbershop, Chihuahua's black stockings vanishing just before Wyatt dunks her in the horse trough. All of Zanuck's changes are clearly focused on giving the picture a firmer narrative foundation, making it easier for the audience to grasp the movement of the story.

None of this mattered to Ford; as Lindsay Anderson said, "he didn't like what Zanuck did to *Clementine*. Remember, all through the war, he'd been his own boss." Zanuck would offer Ford the staggering sum of $600,000 a year to stay at Fox, but he had violated his star director's growing need for autonomy. Ford was determined to cast his lot with Argosy Productions.

Ford would drift back to Fox a few times, but the days when he and Zanuck worked in close harmony were over. The best pictures that Ford would do in the last third of his career were personal projects—*The Quiet Man*, or *The Searchers*. Studio assignments—*Mogambo, The Long Gray Line*—would all seem slightly lacking. Ford would not exactly toss them off, but the lack of spark would be noticeable.

"I have this theory," said Roddy McDowall, "that certain combinations—Ford and Zanuck, Capra and Cohn, Wyler and Goldwyn—abrased each other in a very creative manner, like Michelangelo and Pope Julius. They were constantly criticizing each other, and there was conflict, but the end results were astonishing."

My Darling Clementine opened to good reviews and average business, grossing a little over $2.8 million. Basically, it did little better than break even. Bosley Crowther in the *New York Times* liked it, while Richard Griffith, in *New Movies*, correctly said that, "on the surface, and to millions of its audiences, it will appear as no more than a jimdandy Western. . . . It's also a sustained and complex work of the imagination."

It is that. From the El Greco skies of the opening scene, to the eminently jaunty, eminently soused tragedian Granville Thorndyke, to the resolutely underplayed ending, Ford keeps the focus on the people. Ford's direction is like the look on Fonda's face as Mature finishes a Shakespeare soliloquy—attentive, observant, focused, but also a little awestruck and quite beautiful—beyond acting, beyond analysis. The meditative pace makes the spasms of savagery and violence, unusual for Ford's work, feel genuinely brutal.

On the other hand, he's clearly helpless to do anything with the placid Linda Darnell and doesn't really try very hard. Most of his coaching seems to have gone into Victor Mature, who responds with his best performance, although he's about as tubercular as a Kodiak bear. His Doc Holliday is on fire with a bad temper, furious with self-loathing over his illness and alcoholism.

Although Ford would boast to Peter Bogdanovich that he stuck closely to history in the film, *My Darling Clementine* is fanciful even by the limited standards of Hollywood. In real life, Old Man Clanton died several weeks before the O.K. Corral, there was no Clementine, and Doc Holliday didn't die in the gunfight. What Ford did get right, according to Allen Barra, Earp's biographer, was the temperament of the times and the men. "He got the good guys right and he got the bad guys right," said Barra.

"Ford always said documentaries were boring," remembered Harry Carey Jr. "He liked color and romance and movement." What Ford did with *Clementine* was give human dimension to a myth. *Stagecoach*, Lindsay Anderson observed, is very good prose, but *Clementine* is poetry. Bit by bit, film by film, Ford was beginning to create a living tapestry of the great American legend of the West.

CHAPTER EIGHTEEN

While Ford was tussling with the Earps, the Clantons, and Darryl Zanuck, Merian Cooper was setting up Argosy. On May 30, 1946, he wrote United Artists president George Bagnall about the possibility of buying *The Long Voyage Home* and *Stagecoach*, but not before some complaints about U.A.'s handling of the former picture.

"It was sure to lose money if thrown into regular distribution channels, and, in my opinion, it was sure to make a little money if exploited as the winner of the New York critics' award for 1941 and handled as a specialty. Whether there is any money left in it now, I doubt very much; however, Jack and I would like to buy it for a few dollars just to own what we think is one of our finest pictures."

Since *Stagecoach* had already been reissued once, Cooper believed that it was "about played out," while *The Long Voyage Home*, at this point, was carried on the U.A. books as being $143,000 in the red.

The plan to purchase the pictures never went through, but Cooper and Ford were clearly intent on Argosy being more than just a production organization; they wanted to own their own pictures, as Chaplin, Goldwyn, and a few other producers did. The idea was both psychologically and financially sound; the pride deriving from ownership was good, but the steady monies to be derived from working a film library were already evident—television could be sighted in the middle distance. Even in 1946, the future was clear; the $143,000 deficit on *The Long Voyage Home* would be cut to $82,570 in just two years, but that $61,000 of revenue went into the pockets of U.A., not Argosy Productions. Cooper and Ford meant to change all that.

Several times a year, Ford would travel to Harry Carey's ranch in Saugus, thirty-five miles north of Los Angeles, or there would be reciprocal visits to Odin Street or the *Araner.* The meetings could be slightly uneasy until the two men began drinking. Harry Carey Jr. didn't like Ford's visits because he scared the young man, always crooning "Mel-woooood, l'il Melwooooood" whenever he saw him, in memory of the night he was born and Ford and Carey had gotten drunk on Melwood whiskey. "There was a cockiness about him that reminded me of the kids I'd wind up getting into fights with at school," Carey Jr. would remember.

In retaliation for Ford not hiring him, Carey wouldn't go to see Ford's movies, which in turn irritated Ford. They were like an old married couple who couldn't really get along with each other, but couldn't really get along without each other either. One time they got wildly, falling-down drunk. Ollie Carey got her husband to bed, but Mary had long since retired, which left Ford and Ollie.

Ford was sitting in the kitchen, overwhelmed by maudlin waves of emotion as he often was when drunk, crying, drooling, talking about how Dobe and Barbara should get married and carry on the noble tradition of the Ford and Carey families. It was not to be. Dobe married Marilyn Fix, while Barbara went on to her own marital misadventures.

In the early part of 1947, Harry Carey was diagnosed with lung cancer. He failed quickly. About two days before he died, Carey was sinking into a coma, mumbling about Jack. Ollie Carey called Ford and told him that if he wanted to say goodbye to his old friend, now was the time. As Harry died, Ford was on his knees alongside the bed. Ollie Carey was on the porch of her house when Ford came out and began sobbing like a heartbroken child, holding on tight to Ollie. On and on it went, for fifteen or twenty minutes. "The more he cried, the stronger I got," said Ollie Carey. "It was very good for me. He shook and cried."

At the wake, Ford sidled up to Ollie and told her he was going to remake *3 Godfathers* with John Wayne, Pedro Armendariz, and young Dobe as the third lead. Ford intended to pass the torch to another generation; he didn't know that Ollie didn't want her son to become an actor. Nevertheless, she went along with her old friend's plans.

Dobe Carey asked Bob Parrish to come to the funeral, which was being held at the chapel at the Field Photo Farm. Parrish came with writer Daniel Fuchs, and found Harry Carey's horse tied up at the hitching post outside the chapel. The horse had been standing there all night, accompanied by an honor guard.

After the service, Parrish was chatting with old friends from the unit when Ford came up and acted like he didn't know who Parrish was. After lighting his pipe, he turned to a warrant officer and said, "As soon as the morbidly curious civilians leave, we'll break out the beer and start the wake." Ford and Parrish didn't speak for the next twenty years.

• • •

After the initial flirtation with United Artists, Cooper opened discussions with lowly Monogram Pictures. The proposed agreement entailed using 50 percent bank money, 35 percent Monogram's money, and 15 percent Argosy's. That Cooper was having talks with Monogram, a company neither he nor Ford would have deigned to do business with as employees, shows how committed they were to independence, whatever the costs, as well as how unsympathetic a reaction they must have gotten from the major studios.

In mid-September 1946, Argosy bought the rights to Graham Greene's 1940 novel *The Power and the Glory* from Alexander Korda for $50,000. Two weeks later, they signed a distribution deal with RKO. The contract mandated four pictures: *The Fugitive*—the adaptation of the Greene novel—*The Family* (the U.S. Marines and exiled White Russians in China circa 1937, "a tragedy full of belly laughs," according to Ford, with John Wayne and Ethel Barrymore tagged for the leads), *Uncle Mike Meets Murder,* and *The Quiet Man.*

The first picture up would be *The Fugitive*, and Argosy would get 66⅔ percent of the profits. At the same time, Argosy was investigating a deal with Walter Wanger whereby Argosy would produce four pictures, three of them in foreign countries, all in Technicolor, with budgets topping out at $650,000. Special provisions would be applied if Ford decided to direct one of the pictures. Wanger would supply financing and the profits were to be split 50-50. Release would be through Eagle-Lion. The contract was never signed, possibly because Ford feared becoming overextended, possibly also because the likelihood of producing Technicolor pictures on location for $650,000 became more remote by the month.

At the same time, Ford and Cooper set about amassing a reasonable supply of properties suitable for adaptation into movies. As far back as 1941, Argosy had optioned C. S. Forester's *The African Queen*. Katherine Cliffton, Argosy's story editor, told Cooper he should consider a new novel called *Mister Roberts*, and Cooper thought about doing a remake of *Grass* as well as a biopic about his fellow explorers Martin and Osa Johnson. *The Glass Menagerie*, in the form of a 151-page screenplay by Tennessee Williams, would be submitted in 1949. Cooper also was thinking about Argosy being something other than a convenient shop for John Ford, for he was interested in filming a murder mystery and seems to have contemplated Dorothy Hughes's *In a Lonely Place*, which Nicholas Ray would make in 1950.

But they decided that their initial production would be an adaptation of Graham Greene's novel of a tortured whiskey priest. Ford and Cooper had actually been mulling over the idea since 1941, when they had made some feints in the direction of preparing a production that would star Thomas Mitchell, with photography by Gregg Toland and financing from Jock Whitney.

The screenplay assignment went to old friend Dudley Nichols, who was at RKO preparing his productions of *Mourning Becomes Electra* and *Sister Kenny*, both doomed to critical and financial catastrophe. Although Nichols had more than enough on his plate, he told Cooper that he was willing to do the adaptation of the Greene novel because of "my unbounded admiration for our top director, Jack."

Argosy was paying Nichols $50,000 to "write, compose and prepare" *The Fugitive*, with an optional second script to follow, but half his salary was deferred; Ford and Cooper were also deferring portions of their salaries. In return for his goodwill, Argosy gave Nichols 10 percent of the net profits on the film.

Working with Nichols seems to have been much more of a marriage between equals than working with Frank Nugent or Laurence Stallings; the writer's correspondence with Ford has an easy, relaxed swing, and, while Nichols clearly respected Ford, he didn't particularly defer to him.

Nichols completed his script in October 1946. "In all honesty," he wrote Ford, "your name should be on it. It is as much yours as mine." Ford seems to have had qualms about the project's commercial, if not aesthetic, potential. He wrote Darryl Zanuck that same month that "It is really not a sound commercial gamble but my heart and my faith compel me to do it."

"The following photoplay is timeless," reads the foreword to Nichols's script. "It is laid, for the purpose of clarity, or to be honest, for economical reasons, in a Latin American country. . . . The story happens to be true. It is a very old story with its roots way back in Biblical Days. It is timeless . . . topical. Even now it is a Passion Play in Yugoslavia, Poland, Russia, Germany, China and God help us, in some parts of the United States."

Because of the paucity of dialogue, the script is very visual, more like the script for a silent movie than a talkie. It also includes plentiful hints that Ford and Nichols were completely under the sway of the flamboyantly picturesque Mexican films directed by Emilio Fernández (*The Pearl*, *María Candelaria*), who was hired to serve as associate producer. Fernández clearly had a great deal to do with the visual look of the picture, in terms of both inspiration and second unit shooting. Regarding the long shots underneath the credits, Nichols's script notes: "NOTE TO FERNANDEZ [cinematographer Gabriel] FIGUEROA FROM NICHOLS: Ford and I suggest that you two men take a week or ten days with a double and get these shots at the end of the picture."

The sets were lightly characterized ("These sets are white-washed sets with low ceilings"), but the look of the film was firmly set in the film-makers' minds. "This is a tableau," notes Nichols, or "All this should be photographed in a striking fashion. Suggest a camera pit dug in the floor. Camera level is just a few inches above the floor," or "CLOSE SHOT—Maria holding her baby and wondering what he is going to do (Strictly Figueroa!)," or "NOW WE GO UP A MEAN LITTLE STREET where we see the lighted window of a cantina. (Get going, Gaby. Do your stuff.) . . . We have a scene here where lights grow and grow in the darkness ala *Maria Candelaria*. (NOTE FROM FORD AND NICHOLS: This is a direct swipe.)"

It is very much a High Art script, and there was no interest in compromising the film's look and meaning. "NOTE TO EMILIO, GABY AND AL YBARRA FROM FORD AND NICHOLS: The foregoing scenes should not be hurried. Even if we have to travel for days, we must find the location. Let us photograph early morning and late evening. We must be patient and wait for the proper light to make these scenes memorable. The lighting should be stark and simple. Pure motion pictures here." What Ford and Nichols were clearly after was a Catholic story of redemption á la *The Informer*, but with a bigger budget.

Unfortunately, the compromises were all in the story. Graham Greene's story of a whiskey priest stumbling toward Golgotha was radically altered to the story of a priest whose only sin was an inability to believe in the coming of evil.

"The first year," Nichols has the priest say of the dictatorship, "well, the whole thing seemed fantastic. I couldn't believe there was any real reason to leave the country. Things like that have happened before. I thought I'd stay another month—and see if things got better. Then another month, and another month. . . . Then I began to lose grace. I began to have pride. I began to think I was a brave man. . . . I thought I was a fine fellow to stay when the others took to their heels. . . . When the real test came I couldn't measure up. I didn't have the courage. . . . I let men die for me. . . . Then I committed the unforgivable sin. Despair."

By changing acts of commission—drinking and whoring—to a single sin of omission—silence—Ford and Nichols made it impossible for the priest to command the fascination of the audience in the way that Gypo Nolan had. (Some of this was because of the censorship restrictions of the Production Code, but Ford's treatment of alcoholism would never be realistically sodden. Ford was dodging the reality and consequences of alcoholism in his art just as he was in life.)

By slathering transfiguring photography ("It is Mary Magdalene on the road to Calvary," Nichols rhapsodizes over a final close-up of Dolores Del Rio) over an already aestheticized story, Ford and Nichols further diminished their main character. By the time Nichols gives the priest his single eloquent line ("I want to live my death," he says, refusing a final drink of brandy), it's the last scene in the picture, and it's too little too late.

Ford knew he needed a box office name to anchor the script and provide some semblance of commercial appeal, but RKO's list of contract leads stopped after Robert Mitchum and George Raft. Following a flirtation with José Ferrer, Ford settled on Henry Fonda. But Zanuck had him penciled in for an innocuous picture called *Chicken Every Sunday*. Ford called in years of friendship and asked for Fonda on loan-out; if that wasn't enough, he offered to direct a picture for Zanuck in return. Suddenly, the scheduling problems were resolved.

The budget was set at $1.13 million, with Argosy putting up a total of $782,000, including $100,000 in cash. RKO dropped in a quarter million, and Fonda deferred half of his usual $100,000 salary.

Fonda was a very good actor, but his forte was quiet resolve; tortured self-doubt was not in his acting vocabulary, and it would have taken more than hair dye to make him look Latin. He was egregiously miscast. Ford wanted Gregg Toland to photograph the picture, and Toland and Ford went so far as to plan a location hunt in September of 1946, but once again Toland couldn't escape from his commitments to Sam Goldwyn. Ford ended up with Gabriel Figueroa, who had shot the Mexican pictures Ford had admired.

Production began on December 2, 1946. The American crew consisted of a half-dozen actors, a production manager, an editor, an art director, a couple of assistants. Everybody else came from the newly opened Churubusco studios, on the edge of Mexico City.

They shot at an old Spanish fort at Perote, the plain at Cholula, a cathedral at Tepoztlán, and the shoulder of the mountain called Sleeping Woman. On location, the unit lived off the land. A jeep foraged ahead, buying chickens from one village, vegetables and bread in another. The food was collected by truck and brought back to the location after being cooked over charcoal.

Ford found that the Mexican technicians were good, with an indifference to union jurisdiction that warmed his heart. Propmen picked up hammers, electricians helped push a camera dolly. Ford told Figueroa, "You've got the fastest camera crew I've ever worked with."

But some of the finer motion picture crafts were not a Mexican strong point: a church was built with real, foot-thick adobe; a cobblestoned street was laid with real cobblestones cemented with mortar. It was nice for authenticity, but it meant that every set had to be taken apart, not with screwdrivers, but with sledgehammers, and none of them could be reused.

Fonda knew Ford's peculiarities well, but J. Carrol Naish had never worked with the director before and showed up with a carefully worked out accent and characterization. Ford lit into him with a vengeance, using, according to Henry Fonda, "the most embarrassing language! I can't remember all the dirty words. Just shameful, rude, everything. Well, it just destroys an actor to be talked to like that. And whenever Naish would want to talk about a scene, Ford would say 'I'm not gonna do it.' He'd just tear the page out of the script and throw it away! . . . He was an incredible man, but he wouldn't talk about your problems as an actor."

Ford had to rely to an unusual extent on Emilio Fernández, a theatrical figure who worked with great fanfare at the top of his lungs. A sentence or two from Ford somehow resulted in a peroration from Fernández that took a full minute. After a few days, Ford noticed that the Mexican crew were referring to Fernández as "Jefe"—chief.

One day, after Fernández had given a long string of ostentatious orders and bawled "Silencio!" he waited for Ford to mutter "Roll 'em." But Ford had walked away and was examining a speck on the studio wall. Fernández waited, and the crew saw Fernández waiting. When Ford had waited long enough, he calmly walked back to the camera and said, "Roll 'em." At that point, Ford became "Jefe."

Cooper and Ford realized that if both of them were to attend to production matters, there would be nobody left to mind the Argosy store. Cooper went looking for an executive and found one in Donald Dewar, a young lawyer who was a protégé of Dan O'Shea, David Selznick's vice president. Dewar had found working with Selznick so difficult that once he had passed out from hypertension, so a change seemed to be a good idea. From Argosy's point of view, Dewar was close to Security Pacific and Bankers Trust, the banks where the bulk of Argosy's financing was coming from. Dewar came on board as vice president of Argosy Pictures on January 1, 1947. He was not immediately intimidated by Ford, although people told him he would be.

"The point was made to me that I would find him a very difficult guy to work with," remembered Dewar. "Which wasn't the case. There were people who took a brutal beating, but I never had a single difficulty. He never even raised his voice, did nothing of a negative nature as far as I was concerned."

While Ford and Cooper finished shooting and began post-production, Dewar reconnoitered the Argosy territory. "The relationship between Cooper and Ford was hard to describe. They were good friends, but I wouldn't put them in the category of pals. Ford was the dominant person, but he dominated smoothly, unlike Selznick. People still called Cooper Colonel, but nobody ever called Ford Captain, or whatever rank he had earned in the Navy. Did Coop like being called Colonel? He didn't dislike it.

"Coop spent a hell of a lot of time on the stock market. I can remember going into his office, before I knew anything about the stock market, and he would be on the phone with his broker. He also subscribed to a chart service, charts that were four feet long. He loved to put his feet up on his desk, spread this chart out in front of him, and talk on the phone to his broker."

Around this time, Ford received a fan letter from a young English film critic named Lindsay Anderson, who had fallen hard for *My Darling Clementine*, due to Henry Fonda's subtlety and simplicity, as well as what he would call the "moral poetry" of the film. Ford wrote back, saying, "It gives one's soul a fillip to hear such intelligent praise. Thank you . . . I am as yet unable to write longhand, due to a bathing accident at Omaha Beach," and mentioned that he had just completed a picture in Mexico called *The Fugitive*, "a very simple picture about a very simple man." He asked Anderson to let him know what he thought of it.

B y 1947, the beginnings of the Red Scare were clearly visible in Hollywood. Hedda Hopper, the Madame Defarge of the Hollywood Right, asked Ford if it was true that labor unions had forced him to hire known Communists on location in Mexico. "A Communist wouldn't touch [*The Fugitive*] with a ten-foot pole," Ford snorted. "We fully expect to be panned by every left-wing reviewer in the country. The picture is anti any political party that forbids the complete freedom of worship."

Ford then paraphrased a line from *The Grapes of Wrath* for Hopper's benefit. "You may hear much about Communists in Mexico, but if they are causing any serious trouble, I never noticed it. Of course, there is plenty of rumor. If a man merely asks for a raise in pay, he's likely to be tagged a Red."

Because of the alterations that Nichols and Ford made in Greene's priest, the publicity was able to take advantage of the House Committee on Un-American Activities hearings that were getting under way in late October of 1947. Louella Parsons burbled that the picture "takes an unforgettable punch at the kind of Red Fascism which is spreading over Europe today. . . . It is the story of man's intrinsic right to worship his God in the face of political pressure." Well, maybe. The picture actually seemed more to be about Gabriel Figueroa's intrinsic right to have his photography overwhelm every other aspect of the movie.

Just before the film was released, Ford did a radio broadcast in which he defiantly proclaimed, "My partner Merian Cooper and I expected to lose our shirts on *The Fugitive*. We wanted to make the picture anyway and we did. Now that I've seen the finished product I'll just add this to my economic report—fifty years after Merian Cooper and Jack Ford are in their graves people will still be looking at *The Fugitive*."

The film opened Christmas Day 1947, with an unimpressive ad in the *New York Times*. As far as a promotional tag line, the best RKO could do was, " 'This is my finest motion picture!' says John Ford." Many critics liked the picture; the *New York Times*'s influential Bosley Crowther wrote that *The Fugitive* featured "the best direction of the year; brilliant, inventive, symphonic. . . . Mr. Ford really runs the scale of cinema, con brio and fortissimo."

Perhaps the most interesting review was that of the most interesting critic, James Agee, who put *The Fugitive* on his ten-best list for that year, along with *Monsieur Verdoux, Shoeshine, Great Expectations, Odd Man Out*, and *Beauty and the Beast* (there were giants in those days . . .).

After first explaining that his feelings about the Catholic Church were far more mixed than Ford's, that he disliked allegory and symbolism and romantic photography, all of which *The Fugitive* featured in copious amounts, Agee explained that "I think *The Fugitive* is a bad work of art, tacky, unreal, and pretentious. Yet I think almost as highly of it as of the films mentioned above, because I have seldom seen in a moving picture such grandeur and sobriety of ambition, such continuous intensity of treatment or such frequent achievement of what was obviously worked for, however distasteful or misguided I think it."

The Fugitive is a stillborn curio today just as it was in 1947, a picture that never attains any dramatic momentum, just dissolves from one over-the-top religious tableau to another, abandoning the actors amidst a profusion of picturesque silhouettes and shafts of light.

Ford takes Greene's very specific character, a man awash in the quotidian hunger of alcoholism, and makes him as much of a symbolic abstraction as the setting, an unnamed totalitarian Latin American state where alcohol is banned—possibly Ford's personal idea of hell. The problem with the picture was clearly the impossibility of filming it as written at the time, which was only amplified by Ford's protective attitude toward the Church—an attitude far removed from Graham Greene's more singular brand of Catholicism.

Americans tend to think of religion as something that is chosen, but Ford's religion was more in the European tradition—as part of the rhythm of his life, it chose him, which was one aspect of his problem in coming to grips with Greene's novel. Years later, in 1959, Ford was asked if he would follow the book more closely if he had it to do all over again. He replied that he believed that the weaknesses of Greene's priest were unsuitable material for the screen.

Afflicted with one of the droning Richard Hageman scores for which Ford had a peculiar enthusiasm, *The Fugitive* is less a movie than a series of overly composed stills; it's a violation of Greene's novel, but it's also a violation of every gift Ford had except the visual—left in the Mexican dust is his gift for people, their humanity. Ford had managed to combine all that and visual stylization before, in *The Long Voyage Home*, but here the trick deserted him. Ford had made bad films before and would again, but he seldom made a movie that was boring. *The Fugitive* is boring.

The Fugitive grossed $818,000. Once RKO's distribution fee was deducted, Ford and Cooper were left with slightly more than $500,000 to pay off slightly more than $1 million in debt. If Ford blamed anybody for the debacle, it was the public. "It came out the way I wanted it to—that's why it's one of my favorite pictures," he explained in 1966. "To me it was perfect. It wasn't popular. The critics got at it, and evidently it had no appeal to the public, but I was very proud of my work."

Although he and Dudley Nichols never worked together again, Ford always spoke of him in glowing terms. "We were very close," said Ford in 1964, four years after the writer died. "He loved motion pictures. He never used purple prose. He wrote like people speak, and with a minimum of dialogue. He was a wonderful man. I miss him terribly."

Lindsay Anderson, as forthright in youth as he would be in age, wrote to Ford as he had requested and told him what he thought of the picture, which wasn't much: "a mistaken film, forced in its conception and over-indulgent in its style." Ford didn't reply.

"*The Fugitive*," remembered Don Dewar, "started us off in a hole. In a way, Argosy never recovered. They made some wonderful, moneymaking pictures there, but it was all going to cover the obligations. Plus, we began to see a defensive mechanism on the part of the bankers and RKO: 'How do we know that Ford isn't going to do this again?' You know, you could make any kind of picture at all in that period and make money. Except for *The Fugitive*."

The Fugitive killed any chance that Ford would be able to make *The Quiet Man* at RKO. The banks simply looked the other way when the subject came up, and RKO also thought it was a bad idea. Still, Ford persisted, bringing the subject up several times with Ned Depinet, RKO's head of distribution and an old friend. "You so and so," said Depinet, "you'll make the most beautiful motion picture ever made, but you'll have a bunch of dialogue and nobody will be able to understand one single word. You're in Ireland, and we're in America and I'm not going to pay for that."

Even before *The Fugitive* had been released, Ford and Cooper knew they had to make something commercial for their next Argosy production. Attracted by its persistent overtones of tragedy—and by alcoholism—Jack idly speculated about a film on the life of actress Laurette Taylor. "During the last days of her life she played to an empty house—full of people," he told Hedda Hopper. "Her play [*The Glass Menagerie*] was a great success, but the one guy whom she would have rather have seen it than the rest of the world never came. That was her husband, Hartley Manners, who is dead."

He toyed with an adaptation of Bret Harte's "The Outcasts of Poker Flat," which would combine three other Harte stories—"The Luck of Roaring Camp," "Tennessee's Partner," and "Brown of Calaveras." Ford and Cooper thought about hiring Ernest Haycox, the author of the short story on which Ford and Nichols had based *Stagecoach*, but they ended up commissioning a very good script from Frank Wead for $25,000, with an extra $50,000 if the picture got made. Ford even made some provisional casting decisions—John Wayne as Josh Peabody, Henry Fonda as John Oakhurst, and Victor McLaglen as Stumpy—before the project was put aside.

F ord had met the writer James Warner Bellah in India during the war. The two men became friendly, and Ford took notice of a series of cavalry stories that Bellah began publishing in *The Saturday Evening Post*.

Bellah had been born in New York City and claimed descent from an officer in the Confederate Cavalry. He joined the Royal Canadian Flying Corps during World War I; afterward, he went into advertising and moonlighted by writing his increasingly successful magazine stories.

Argosy bought a batch of Bellah's stories, for prices that usually ran around $4,500 apiece. Stories like "Massacre," which was converted into *Fort Apache*, and "Big Hunt" and "War Party," which were cobbled together to make *She Wore a Yellow Ribbon*, are full of vivid images and specific characters but are hampered by Bellah's arrhythmic prose style and a blatant racism that seriously invoked phrases like "the white man's burden" as late as 1947.

For Bellah, Indians were savages, pure and all too simple. Indians were the "red beast in the night." He informed the readers of *The Saturday Evening Post* that "the smell of an Indian is resinous and salty and rancid. It is the wood smoke of his tepee and the fetidity of his breath that comes of eating body-hot animal entrails. It is his uncured tobacco and the sweat of his unwashed body. It is animal grease in his hair and old leather and fur, tanned with bird lime and handed down unclean from ancestral bodies long since gathered to the Happy Lands."

One does not have to buy into the latter-day sentimental cliché that views the nineteenth-century Indian as a misunderstood child of the soil ravaged by evil white men to find his slant repugnant. "My father was an absolute military snob," said James Warner Bellah Jr. "His politics were just a little right of Attila. He was a fascist, a racist, and a world-class bigot." Bellah surrounded himself with the relics of military tradition—a picture of his mother wearing Douglas MacArthur's campaign hat, regimental flags and banners on the wall, Douglas Southall Freeman on the bookshelves.

Beyond his racism, Bellah's characters have absurd names (MacLerndon Allshard, Toucey Rynders, D'Arcy Topliff, Brome Chadbourne), writing that strains for metaphorical impact ("The sun in August is a molten saber blade . . .") and dialogue tending toward the theatrically ripe: "You have chosen my way of life; I shall see that you attain to it unto its deepest essence or leave your bones to bleach under the prairie moon!" Except for the fact that he was almost completely unsentimental, Bellah was a pulp writer with pretensions, albeit one whose stories had strong narrative spines.

Ford and Bellah were united by one primary belief: the valor and worth of the military. Bellah wrote stories about soldiers, and this would come to occupy an increasing part of Ford's world. The war had stimulated his already strong sense of the community of men, and added a sense of the implicit air of potential tragedy hanging over every moment of a soldier's life.

In adapting Bellah, Ford was able to evade the thick, clotted prose, and completely obliterate the racism, going out of his way to grant Indians a dignity and sense of humanity—for example, the wonderful scene between Nathan Brittles and Pony-That-Walks in *She Wore a Yellow Ribbon*. He would deepen and give shading to the single dimensions of Bellah's stories, including the character of the estranged wife in *Rio Grande*, where Bellah's story only referred to her, adding an element of sexual tension to the main story of a soldier and his son. And when Bellah created something good on his own, like Nathan Brittles's tag line, "Never apologize, Mr. Cohill; it's a mark of weakness," Ford would amplify it as a signature of character.

In Ford's trilogy of films about the cavalry, he made them remarkably benign in terms of waging war. Ford loved the military, but avoided militarism. Colonel Thursday of *Fort Apache* is an arrogant, bitter man who gets himself and a lot of other men needlessly killed by insulting the Apache; the entire plot of *She Wore a Yellow Ribbon* turns on avoiding a battle and bloodshed. (Although *Rio Grande* does involve what could be termed a police action, it is in response to continued attacks.)

For all of his weaknesses, Bellah meshed well with Ford. The director not only adapted Bellah's stories into the cavalry trilogy, he also hired him to co-author the scripts for some of his best late movies—*The Man Who Shot Liberty Valance* and the less important *Sergeant Rutledge*.

Ironically, Bellah didn't particularly respect Ford. "I think my father had great contempt for Ford," said Bellah's son, "not as an artist, but from the social standpoint. He referred to Ford as a shanty Irishman and considered him a tyrant. But my father liked money. He disliked Hollywood; it was full of Jews and crass commoners, but there was money to be made in movie work."

The screenplay for Bellah's "Massacre" was handed to the former film critic for the *New York Times*, Frank Nugent. In turning it into *Fort Apache*, either he or Ford altered the plot, making it clear that the Indians were not villains, but were themselves the victims of government-sanctioned criminals.

Ford had to shoot the picture before the weather in Monument Valley turned cold, so time was of the essence. In mid-June, he traveled back to Maine to pick up an honorary degree from Bowdoin College, and he brought Nugent with him so they wouldn't lose momentum on the script.

A preliminary budget drawn up for *Fort Apache* mandates a sixty-day schedule, and a cost of $2.29 million. Ford was down for $150,000, Merian Cooper for $50,000, with the script costs divided between an uncredited Frank Wead ($25,000) and Nugent ($15,000). Wayne, Fonda, and Shirley Temple got $100,000 apiece, Victor McLaglen received $52,500, and Pedro Armendariz got $20,000. Behind the camera, art director James Basevi got $17,325 for twenty-one weeks of work, while chief cinematographer Archie Stout received $9,600 for twelve weeks' work, and William Clothier got $4,000 for that same twelve weeks as second cameraman. For writing the score, Richard Hageman got $8,000, with another $30,000 allocated for recording. For housing the unit in Monument Valley, Harry and Mike Goulding were to receive $9,750.

Argosy signed for another large note—$1.64 million from Security First National Bank. They then borrowed $360,000 from Leo McCarey's Rainbow Pictures, and prevailed upon McCarey to deposit an additional $220,000 for the Completion Bond. Argosy then went to RKO and got a loan of $610,000 so they could repay McCarey, and pay Ford and Cooper their salaries. Ford and Cooper got John Wayne and Henry Fonda to defer $25,000 apiece from their salaries in exchange for 5 percent of the profits apiece. As security for this morass of debt, Argosy pledged the picture itself. In addition to their distribution fee, RKO's share of the profits was increasing, from 33⅓ percent on *The Fugitive* to 40 percent on *Fort Apache*.

In almost every respect, it was a wretched deal. Before Argosy saw a dime, RKO deducted their distribution fee, the bank got their loan money with interest, and Fonda and Wayne got their deferments with interest. Only then, after everybody else took their cut from the top, would Argosy get 60 percent of whatever remained.

Merian Cooper could feel the noose tightening and wrote Ford accordingly: "I sent you a letter by Ward Bond and told you that we now had firmly in hand $2,300,000 to make the picture and $220,000 reserve so you can spend $2,520,000 without getting us into trouble *but that's all we've got for this picture.* . . . I will depend on your ingenuity to cut off a few days—if possible—from the shooting schedule."

For Argosy to see a dime, *Fort Apache* would have to gross somewhere over $4 million. As a matter of fact, it did, but just barely. For Argosy to have seen any real money, *Fort Apache* would have had to be one of the top five box office attractions in movie history. And, this deal was signed in September 1947, nearly two months before *The Fugitive* sank like a stone, which gives some idea of just how badly the cards were stacked against independent production in Hollywood.

"There were so many things working against independents," recalled Donald Dewar. "There were blocked funds in Europe, but those numbers weren't that great. The real problem was what we knew was happening at RKO. They loaded up everything at the studio and charged it to our pictures. I used to scream my eyes out, because everything but the kitchen sink would be thrown into the overhead of our picture, and it was obvious and arguable. I was constantly over at RKO arguing with Peter Rathvon's financial guy. And they would give up only minor, minor stuff.

"I wanted to hire Price Waterhouse to do an audit, but we didn't have the money, and besides, no [independent producer] had ever done that. It would have cost us $50,000 to run the kind of audit we needed, and we might have come up with a recovery of $10,000 on a speculative basis.

"So we knew they were doing it, and they knew we knew they were doing it. Because that's the way those contracts were written. If you wanted to do business with a major, you lived with it. They felt that they had to protect themselves. They were the ones putting up the second money and the completion money. With *The Fugitive*, Ford had the temerity to go down to Mexico where no one had ever gone before. After that, they were afraid of what he might do. It was hard to argue that they didn't have the right. But they went beyond protecting themselves to stealing after the fact. Every postwar independent producer had the same problem. No independent producer ever got their fair share. And they all went out of business."

Ford's preparation for *Fort Apache* was immaculate. Argosy hired Katherine Spaatz as a researcher, handling specific questions of style and content for Frank Nugent and Katherine Cliffton. Spaatz went to Arizona with Cliffton and interviewed an old cavalry sergeant's widow, as well as talking to her own grandmother, who began her married life in the Seventh Cavalry in Arizona during the 1880s.

Backstories for all the characters were painstakingly constructed. The martinet Owen Thursday "graduated West Point '55 . . . second or third in his class. . . . Remained in Washington until '69 and was sent as Military Observer to Europe. Saw the Prussian-Austrian War. Was present at Sadowa . . . great student of military affairs. A reputation as a brilliant Cavalry Tactician and a very strict soldier. . . .

"He had been forcibly impressed with the Prussians . . . not only by their stern discipline . . . but also their thesis of the power of frontal attack. . . . In politics is a Republican. His greatest weakness as a soldier is that due to his rapid promotion he knows absolutely nothing about supply."

Captain Kirby York was characterized more briefly, as being thirty-eight years old, "the Washington to Thursday's Braddock. He knows the country. He knows the Indians. York has a sense of humor. He loves and is perfectly satisfied with frontier life. He smokes cigars and drinks bourbon. A fair country-style poker player. A great horseman. Better yet, a great horse-trader."

Even the heavy of the piece, Ricker the Indian agent, was sketched in: "Born in New England 50 years before this story opens. He bought his way out of service in the Civil War, made a small pile as a petty subcontractor in Washington, was among the vanguard of the carpet baggers and now is taking his third crack at the dishonest dollar in the Indian service . . . he is probably a secret squaw man, although he does not drink or smoke. He is a thoroughly dishonest and cowardly son of a bitch."

There are notes regarding images: "Suggestion for shot during the charge. A bugler will be sounding the charge. Then the bugle arm will weaken, the bugle start dropping down in the limp hand. The bugler will slowly slide, not fall from his horse. The camera will continue for twelve feet on the riderless horse."

Attention was paid to the Indians; Cochise was said to be "highly intelligent . . . counterpart to Chief Joseph. In our story his name will strike terror and dread into the hearts of men, but when we meet him, he will prove to be an impressive and dignified man, no mere vengeful fighter, but a man who has suffered much at the hands of the whites, and has, in fact, right on his side. He speaks little or no English, but is fluent in Spanish. Unlike Geronimo, who gave and broke his word without compunction, Cochise would not give his word readily unless he meant to keep it.

"In our story, he is presumed to have known Kirby York, and when they meet, will make some special gesture toward him acknowledging this fact." And there are notes about atmosphere and mood—"Vaguely in the background are the families of these men; drab, tired women with tragedy in their eyes and the weary patience of women who spend their lives seeing their men go out to fight, sometimes seeing them return.

"One of the greatest moments of their lives will be the night when Thursday orders the full dress regimental ball and, with mingled eagerness and apprehension, they take from their trunks the dresses they had worn in former days. . . . The company of Fort Bowie will hardly seem impressive at the regimental ball. But next day, on the parade ground, the men will have a dignity they lacked the night before; and the women, as the picture unfolds, will gain stature."

This granting of respectful autonomy to each and every character had always been present in Ford's work, but to specify it beforehand was something different, and bespoke a man who was taking more pains with his work, not just relying on the inspiration of the moment. RKO may have been regarding *Fort Apache* as little more than a make-good for *The Fugitive*, but Ford was taking it far more seriously than that.

Ford's relationship with Frank Nugent was friendly, but Ford never deferred to him, as he would with Dudley Nichols. During a script conference, Ford was thinking out loud about the character of Cochise. "I see him standing straight against the sky line, one hand clutching his pipe and pressed against his chest . . ."

"Wait a minute," protested Nugent. "The Apaches never used pipes. They smoked cigarettes rolled with corn husks at first, then with Mexican corn paper."

Ford paused, then resumed: "I see Cochise, standing straight against the sky line, one hand pressed to his chest . . . that hand may have a flute, it may have an ax, I don't give a damn what he has . . . but he isn't smoking any cigarette!"

"Frank would do what Ford said," recalled Don Dewar. "My impression is that those scripts, whatever they were based on, were Ford. He did a lot of the writing. And that was understood by Frank and he didn't object. Now, when Ford worked with [Laurence] Stallings, that was a different relationship. Ford had a real appreciation of Stallings as a writer on his own level. He appreciated Frank, but Frank was more subservient."

As the script was nearing completion, Ford and Cooper instituted a title contest amongst the Argosy employees. The prize was $100. *Massacre*, the title of Bellah's original story, was considered too intimidating, and *War Party*, the provisional title, wasn't much of an improvement. Ray Harryhausen, on the lot working on *Mighty Joe Young*, suggested *Dragoon*. Otherwise, the suggestions tended toward the generic: *Indian Fighter, Glory, Thursday's Folly, Trumpet Call, Boots and Saddles, Indian Country, Rampage, Valley of Death*, and then descended into the deeply problematic—*The Apache Fight at Dawn, Red, White and Untamed*, followed closely by *Failure Then Defeat*.

Fort Apache had been suggested by Ford himself, but there is no record of whether or not he claimed the $100. The completed script was quickly approved by the Motion Picture Association, but they knew their man and asked that he "Please keep to an *absolute minimum* all scenes of drinking. This is important."

The company arrived in Monument Valley to find the usual primitive conditions. The Gouldings by that time had five special cabins that were reserved for Ford (solo) and the other stars (doubling or tripling up). None of the cabins had a bathroom, and to take a shower you stood under a five-gallon can with holes in the bottom, fed by a hose that carried only cold water.

The floors were hard dirt sloping down to the valley, with a Navajo rug in the middle of the room. There were two small chests of drawers, a chair and a couple of cot-sized beds. In the middle of each cabin was a kerosene heater, which could keep the cabins quite warm. All the other members of the company were housed in tents a mile below the Gouldings', where they had hot water, showers, and good food.

Ford hired Archie Stout as his cameraman. Stout had graduated from shooting five-day Westerns and was closely associated with John Wayne's personal productions. Stout was nearly as obstinate as Ford; as his assistant cameraman, William Clothier—the same cameraman whose sleeping bag Ford had ruined during the war—would remember, "Archie was a guy who argued with directors." Under normal circumstances, Ford might have saved himself the trouble, but Stout's son had been killed while serving in the Field Photographic Unit, and the director felt a sense of obligation to the older man.

As compensation, Ford took Clothier under his wing. Although Clothier was not a young man—he was born in 1903—Ford liked his absolutely straightforward, masculine approach to life and lighting.

"When I was working as an operator for Mr. Ford," Clothier would remember, "on many occasions I would go and squat down by his chair, because he would sit there and study. He would look over at me and say, 'What do you want?' I would never interrupt his thought. I would say, 'Jack, would you come over here and look at the camera? I've got an idea.' He'd get up, come over, and he would either say, 'Yes, that's a good idea,' or he would say, 'No, and I'll tell you why.' And he would have a reason for not wanting to do it. It was that simple; he was that wonderful to work for. . . . This man made no mistakes."

As a means of goosing conventional black and white, Stout suggested that Ford film all the Monument Valley exteriors with infrared film, so that the sky would seem darker than it really was and the clouds would photograph as explosions in the sky. The great James Wong Howe had used infrared the year before for *Pursued,* and Stout thought the mythic look would work well with *Fort Apache.* It was more trouble—exposure was difficult and focusing worse; actors had to wear a special light brown makeup to keep from photographing as if they were coated with chalk— but Ford was always willing to take pains with photography.

Despite Ford's approval of the infrared idea, he and Stout fought throughout the production. "He got into a beef with Ford, a terrible row," remembered William Clothier. "The result was that [Stout] refused to shoot this scene. It was backlit and looked to me like it'd be great. Ford climbed off the parallel, put his arm around my shoulder and said, 'I want you to tell that son of a bitch *never* to tell me that he won't shoot something. If I ask a cameraman to shoot something and it doesn't work, I'll be the first to take it out of the picture.'

" 'Okay, Jack, I'll tell him.' Of course it didn't mean a damn thing to Archie."

Joining the extended filmmaking family was Francis Ford Jr., who had, as he recalled, been "pretty psychopathic" after the war. Frank Jr. had been doing extra work around the studios when his uncle got him into the Directors Guild and made him an assistant.

"There was no favoritism," remembered Frank Jr. "He would ask me to do things he wouldn't ask anybody else to do. One time he asked me to get down on the ground and double for Henry Fonda for a shot of a horse rearing and coming down close to his head. The horse kept coming closer and closer and finally almost stepped on my hand. At that point, he called it off. He wanted to see if I was going to chicken out on him. He was tough, he was hard, but he was absolutely meticulous in making his movies. His great attribute was the ability to see what a scene would look like before he shot it. My father had that, too.

"He gave me a lot of trouble. Well, my father gave him a lot of trouble."

For the first time since 1931, Ford hired George O'Brien. According to O'Brien's wife, the actor had been quietly devastated by their professional estrangement, despite the friendship represented by such things as a Chinese box that Ford gave O'Brien with a note on the bottom: "To George and Marguerite. This box is to be used only for Jack's cigars." As far as Marguerite Churchill O'Brien was concerned, it was good riddance, for she regarded Ford as a bully and a drunk, and habitually referred to him as "that vicious son of a bitch."

Since returning from the war, O'Brien had done little except a small part in a Warners musical entitled *My Wild Irish Rose*. He was still handsome—he would be handsome all his long life—but he was in his late forties, had been off the screen for nearly seven years, and hadn't made an important picture since John Ford stopped using him.

On top of that, O'Brien's marriage was in dicey straits. His wife was still holding a grudge over what she regarded as his abandonment of the family to go off on a glorified boy's adventure called World War II. They were living in a beautiful house in Brentwood, sitting in separate rooms, while O'Brien waited for the phone to ring. But the phone didn't ring.

Finally, Marguerite O'Brien heard Ford was making a Western. She called him and begged him to give his old friend a part.

"I wouldn't do anything for the son of a bitch," Ford said. "He abandoned me in Manila!"

"But you have to, Jack. If you don't give him work and get him out of the house, it'll be the ruin of a good Catholic family!" This was a plea that Ford could not resist.

"Okay, I'll do it, but only on one condition. You have to play his wife."

"You bastard, don't you see? I don't want to play George's wife! That's just the point! We have to separate for a while."

Relenting, Ford took O'Brien back, and even paid a good salary to a man who hadn't made an A picture in fifteen years—$15,000, the third highest actor's salary on the picture. With very little fanfare, O'Brien and Ford picked up right where they left off. Soon, they were seeing each other once a month or so.

"George was worshipful," remembered his son Darcy, "which was the secret to the friendship. It was like father and son, although they weren't far apart in age. My mother thought it was a dependency that was unhealthy, but it remained unchanged from when Ford gave my father his start, and George was totally at home in that relationship and that environment."

The years hadn't changed O'Brien much, and they never would. Gregarious and charming, he was, his son Darcy would say, "very Catholic, very loyal, a great deal like what he played. All of life to my father was like the movies." This tendency would prove devastating to him in just a few years, when his wife divorced him. That had not been in the script.

Ford was in a particularly vile mood during the production, partially because of the ongoing tensions with Stout, partially because of worries about *The Fugitive*. He kept a group of actresses standing in the sun for an hour until Anna Lee fainted. (As Lee came to, the first thing Ford said was, "Anna, you're pregnant again!") He also had yet another brief fistfight with his brother Eddie.

Ford's designated patsy on *Fort Apache* was the young, inexperienced John Agar, newly married to Shirley Temple. Ford didn't like the way Agar talked, walked, or rode. He didn't like the way Agar *breathed*. He called him "Mr. Temple." Stuntman Gil Perkins remembered that Ford just "ate him alive. There was nothing this poor kid could do that was right; he just chewed him up one side and down the other." Finally, Agar began packing to leave the location, leave the movies, leave his wife, when he was stopped by John Wayne, who told him that Ford would soon start bullying him and Henry Fonda, too. Stay calm, keep your head down, and learn, he told the young man.

Fifty years later, time had healed the wounds. "I always thought Mr. Ford was a kidder," said Agar. "I just took it that way, as teasing. I talked to Wayne and Fonda and McLaglen and Dick Foran and they had worked with him for years and they all said, 'We never know when he's kidding and when he's serious.' I think he wanted to have fun, and that to him was fun."

As with John Wayne on *Stagecoach*, the rest of the company did their best to offer Agar some cover. "Wayne and Fonda and Shirley, they were so kind to me and so helpful. It was a family atmosphere."

If it was a family, it was one with a spectacularly irascible father figure. Even Shirley Temple provoked Ford's ire. After Anna Lee delivered her lovely line, "All I can see is the flags," Temple piped up with "I don't think that's good grammar."

"What?" said Ford.

"It should be, 'All I can see *are* the flags.' "

Anna Lee and Irene Rich exchanged worried looks. Not wanting to be damaged by flying adjectives, the cast and crew sidled away. But Ford managed to hold his temper, saying "Where did you go to school, Shirley? And where did you graduate?" The original line stayed in the film.

When he wasn't scourging Agar, he was working over others. Michael Wayne, who accompanied his father on location, remembered seeing tears in Henry Fonda's eyes at one point.

Joining the company for two weeks was Stephen Longstreet, a novelist (*Stallion Road*), screenwriter (*The Jolson Story*), and artist, who had known both Jack and his brother Frank for years. Longstreet found the atmosphere of the company "like living with not-too-bright schoolboys.

Ward Bond was mean; Wayne was easy to take. He believed in dime novel heroics, but only on the screen. The image, big and bold, covered up a very ordinary man."

Longstreet watched the way the stock company kissed up to Ford. The director must have noticed Longstreet wondering, because he explained the transaction to the writer: "It's the game. I'm the fake. I risk much, and they're the band of [authentic] misfits. What the hell; I might be with a shitty professor telling me what I was like."

Longstreet's notes of his conversations with Ford provide an invaluable record of Ford at work and at rest, articulate and corrosive, speaking his mind among friends without a reporter around to make him wary or provoke him into performance.

"John Ford would greet you, if he was in the mood, [with] 'How are they hanging this morning?' " remembered Longstreet. Conversation would often touch on literature—he loved O'Casey and admired Shaw. "He should have been a Catholic," said Ford of Shaw, "a mackerel snapper. He'd have been a great Pope—his red whiskers blowing in the wind as he wound up a Mass . . . and pinching a nun's ass."

But Ford's wounds ran very deep, and Longstreet could see that this secret intellectual's attempt to make himself into a primitive was a transparent failure. "They're all fakes you know," Ford railed. "William S. Hart was a Shakespearean actor back East; Carey was a Broadway ham; Roy Rogers is afraid of his horse. Wayne? I had to teach him to use toilet paper." As for Irish men, "What can you expect of a boy that's lived unmarried until he's thirty or forty? The old biddy up his arse, all the time wasted in the pubs. And the priest's asking him to stop pulling his stiff and come to Mass. Hell, the only bit of fun [is] to run with the IRA and blow up a black Protestant van or a roving Brit army patrol."

Always there was a put-down, a defensiveness camouflaged by a series of preemptive strikes. "Sure, I'm [descended] from a King of Ireland, with shitty underwear, who slept under a bush. Yeats would have showed me the door. Lace curtain Irish? Hell, we used it for a tablecloth."

There was always a point beyond which he would not go—not with women, not with friends—and that point was a serious discussion of his own work. "He never stood naked," observed Longstreet. " 'Shit, it's all there on the screen,' he'd say, 'not in the professors' probing my asshole with their little sticks. I don't know myself where all the nerve ends stick out. My scar tissue is private. I scratch it on my own.' " Intellectuals were to be mocked, in the approved tough-guy manner: "I smell a Phi Beta Kappa. Tell him I no speaka English." And that would lead to a diatribe about what the consciousness of self had wrought in modern civilization.

"That fuck Freud! People say give it a try. No wonder there are no

Hamlets around today; it's too easy. Two couches, no waiting. Tickle your id, polish your libido . . ." Ford sounded like a man well on his way to being an anti-modern reactionary, but the truth was more complicated. He enjoyed a good Picasso, he read Joyce and could quote him from memory, and he would offer an ear to jazz. "The niggers know a thing or two," he grumpily admitted to Longstreet.

Second unit director Cliff Lyons hired Gil Perkins as one of the stunt-men. The strong-minded Perkins hadn't worked for Ford since their blow-up on *The Informer*, and told Lyons it was a bad idea to try again. "If Ford recognizes me, I'll have my little speech all ready, and it'll embarrass you." "Oh, hell, Gil," said Lyons, "that was twelve years ago, don't be ridiculous."

On location at Corriganville, near Chatsworth, Ford walked by Perkins and stopped. "Hey," he said, "I haven't seen you for a long time. How have you been?" He was the soul of cordiality and didn't bother Perkins at all, leading the stuntman to the highly unlikely conclusion that Ford hadn't remembered their argument.

After Monument Valley and two weeks of parade ground exteriors at Corriganville, the company returned from location on August 11 and resumed production two days later on the RKO Pathé lot, best known as the offices of Selznick International. Andrew McLaglen was working as a second assistant director at Republic, and decided to drop in on his father. "They were shooting interiors at the Selznick studio, and we entered the stage. Way down at the end was a little set where my father and John Wayne were working. We tiptoed down to the stage, not making any noise. Then I noticed that all work had stopped.

"Jack had turned around and was watching me approach. Now, you must realize that, for some reason, he never scared me. I had no fear of him. I respected him and that was it.

" 'Hello, Andrew,' he said. 'Wouldn't you expect that if I were coming over to your house I would at least call and tell you I was coming?'

"I just stood there and looked at him. 'Yes, you're right,' I finally said, and he said, 'All right,' and went back to work. I always felt that Ford did these things for effect, to get at you. I got such a kick out of it."

Production wrapped on October 2, after forty-five days of shooting. Ford promptly boarded the *Araner* and sailed for Mazatlán, where Wayne, Bond, and Fonda joined him. "The first four or five days Ford came to town with us," remembered Fonda. "After that he was too drunk to leave his boat." Fonda, Wayne, and Bond proceeded without him, starting their drinking at the Hotel Central, corraling a mariachi band, then moving from "bar to bar, saloon to saloon, whorehouse to whorehouse," according to Fonda. "You went to whorehouses just to sit and drink and listen to the mariachis play. You didn't fuck. You didn't think you should. Those whores looked grungy."

Although there are some similarities between Owen Thursday and George Custer—their ranks are the same, their Civil War records are comparable, and they both achieve the fame they seek by the drastic tactic of being slaughtered in battle—there are also distinct differences. Thursday is a bitter and disappointed man, preoccupied by matters such as proper military dress, while Custer couldn't have cared less about such things. Thursday has no respect for Indians and no experience in Indian warfare.

Fort Apache is one of Ford's most complex creations. Henry Fonda's Lieutenant Colonel Thursday is a churlish, brooding injustice collector, a rigid authoritarian—and not much of a soldier. By comparison, John Wayne's Kirby York is a good-humored man, indicated by his more relaxed body language. *Fort Apache* beautifully depicts the daily routine of life on a distant cavalry outpost, and the rituals that maintain a sense of order in an otherwise savage wilderness—the small points of military courtesy; dress uniforms worn for the (realistically rendered) post dance; new recruits being shown how to ride; the cavalry songs sung while the men march.

The film turns on the difference between Thursday and York; the latter believes Cochise to be an honorable man and makes promises to him, the former can't imagine the term being applied to an Indian, any Indian, and violates the promise. Thursday's vanity and self-righteousness lead him, and most of his company, to destruction.

Thursday is doomed, not so much because he loathes the Apache, but because he doesn't listen, because he arrogantly attempts to impose his version of reality on an intransigent natural world far removed from his Eastern verities. Ford heroes played by Wayne—the Ringo Kid, Tom Doniphon, Nathan Brittles, even the ferocious Ethan Edwards—are never so vain as to attempt to bend the world to their will, preferring either an easy, mutual understanding or a proud exile—a function of Wayne's expansive spirit and humor.

But Henry Fonda's stiff walk sets him against the flow of life around him. In *Young Mr. Lincoln*, *The Grapes of Wrath*, or *My Darling Clementine*, this translates to integrity; in *Fort Apache*, it translates to the tragic inhumanity of a martinet.

The filmmaker Jean-Marie Straub once called Ford the most Brechtian of filmmakers, because he lays bare the contradictions. He never pushed it further than in *Fort Apache*, where the final scene sanctions vain glory and senseless death because it serves the need for a uniting myth.

A reporter gazes at a portrait painting of Colonel Thursday, calls him a great man and a great soldier. Kirby York pauses and reflects. "No man died more gallantly," he says, confirming the legend, even though the legend is a lie.

As Stanley Crouch observed, "Duty was something Ford believed in, even though he knew that it might cost almost more than one could bear or demand more than one would survive."

"It's good for the country," Ford told Peter Bogdanovich. "We've had a lot of people who were supposed to be great heroes, and you know damn well they weren't. But it's good for the country to have heroes to look up to. Like Custer—a great man. Well, he wasn't. Not that he was a stupid man, but he did a stupid job that day."

At most stages of his career, Ford's work embraces deliberate contradictions that defeat any kind of ideological labeling and obliterate those who try to characterize him as a simpleminded embracer of Blarney Stone fantasy. In *Fort Apache*, and in *The Man Who Shot Liberty Valance*, his last great film, Ford creates a factual back story for the agreed-upon American fantasy—politicians are frauds, public heroes are fools, true heroes are punished and die, and America's image of itself is based on lies. If that's all there was, Ford would amount to little more than a perpetual adolescent outraged because life isn't fair. But Ford is a realist as well as a romantic poet. Ford says that the lies are necessary, that the lies are all right, because the most important thing is that the greatest good happens for the greatest number of people.

There are those who think that by showing a commander who causes needless death, and that by having the narrative conceal that fact, Ford is being ironic. But, as Geoffrey O'Brien noted, the ending of *Fort Apache* is more an open acknowledgment of the complexities of command than it is a questioning of the right to command.

Unlike the famous epigraph of *Liberty Valance*, Ford prints both legend *and* fact, because that's where the peculiar strength of America lies—between idealism and pragmatism, between self-sacrifice and self-interest.

All that is truly important is the flow of history, a new world being built on what has come before—on sacrifices made, loves lost, families broken, entire communities disintegrated. And John Ford honors the dead as much as the living, connecting the past and the present in an eternal ribbon of remembrance.

*F*ort Apache was successful with both critics and audiences. After the austere art movies that followed Ford's war service, *Variety* was frankly surprised at the picture's commercial qualities. "He has aimed the picture directly at the average theatregoer, bypassing non-profitable art effects. As a consequence, the film has mass appeal, great excitement and potent box-office outlook." Bosley Crowther of the *New York Times*, with that expansive grasp of cliché that never failed him, wrote that "for the standard movie audience, *Fort Apache* will chiefly provide a handsome and thrilling outdoor drama of 'war' on the American frontier—salty, sizzling visualization of regimental life at a desert fort, of strong masculine personalities and of raging battles beneath the withering sun."

Walter Wanger wrote Merian Cooper, "I think it is a wonderful picture . . . my only regret is that it wasn't in Technicolor and it wasn't made for me. . . . Hope we'll get together soon, and that it won't be long before we're making them together again."

CHAPTER NINETEEN

By February 1948, Merian Cooper was in production on *Mighty Joe Young*, an attempt to replicate the success of *King Kong*. Argosy had taken out another loan, this one for up to $990,000, and once again, Cooper hired the great stop-motion animator Willis O'Brien. Other than 5 percent of the net profits, O'Brien came remarkably cheap: his preproduction salary was $150 a week, while it went up to $400 a week after start of principal photography. O'Brien's assistant Ray Harryhausen, who had been getting all of $2.50 an hour, got a raise to $250 a week after production began.

Mighty Joe Young seems to have cost $1.5 million (there are several different figures to be found in the Argosy files) and should have made some money; it grossed $1.9 million domestic, $1.35 million foreign. As Don Dewar remembered, "It didn't lose money but it was not a money-making machine."

Ford was dismayed by Cooper's involvement with the childish story, and he also seems to have been dismayed by the introductory credit "John Ford and Merian C. Cooper Present." "I had nothing to do with it," he would curtly tell Peter Bogdanovich. According to Don Dewar, Cooper's project contributed to a slight chill in the air around the Argosy offices.

"Ford was very critical of it," said Dewar. "This was not his idea of making a motion picture. His attitude was, 'Why would anybody want to do this?' Slowly, I became aware that I was having more direct contact with Ford than I used to. There would be meetings where I expected Cooper to be there, and he wasn't. This grew to a point where I began to think it could be an untenable situation. Ford was cutting Cooper out.

"It might have had something to do with the fact that Coop was more and more involved with his own activities and interests. Things only went one way; if Cooper wanted to make the same picture Ford wanted to make, fine, but if Cooper wanted to make pictures Ford didn't want to make, well, that was something else entirely."

Ford had a favorite question he would throw around at meetings, often with Cooper present: "What's a producer?" he would ask quietly, often while lighting his pipe. It was a cue for everyone to smile sheepishly and look around the room, because everyone knew that Ford could function quite well as his own producer, that he only needed one to furnish him the necessary tools, primarily money. If Cooper was drifting away into his own projects, it might have been because Ford kept reminding him of how little he really needed him.

With the unrelenting financial pressure, keeping the bankers happy became a job for everyone. Donald Dewar recalled a particularly memorable meeting with George Wallace, the chairman of the board of the Security Bank and one of the most conservative bankers who ever lived. Merian Cooper thought it would be politic to invite Wallace and a few associates to dinner at the Argosy offices. There were five people at a dinner catered by Chasen's, with beautiful crystal and three waiters for every member of the dinner party. George Wallace grew closer to apoplexy with every course, because it was all his money.

Even Ford had to play nice-nice. As part of the loan process, the script for the picture the bank would be financing was sent out for approval. The scripts would often come back with notations penciled in, suggestions from bankers about how to improve the dramatic flow or the dialogue. "Ford would chuckle, but he knew we needed [the bank]," said Dewar, "so he'd call and tell them, 'That's a good idea.' "

Despite the pressures, Dewar noticed few tensions around the office. Ford would come in almost every day around 10:00 to work with writers. Lunch was a big production during which as many as twenty people would gather in his office to devour platters of sandwiches. "Wayne would be there usually," remembered Dewar, "Maureen O'Hara sometimes, Milly Natwick sometimes. But Ward Bond was always there, always wanted to be there. And he took the most atrocious verbal abuse, horrible beatings. And everybody thought it was funny, except me; I thought it was awful. And Bond's reaction would just be, 'Oh, Boss, come on, don't say that . . .' It was like beating a big puppy. Ford loved to take him apart and he did it repeatedly, over anything at all."

The debacle of *The Fugitive* instigated a change in Ford's modus operandi. From now on, he would increasingly rely on Westerns as a means of ensuring a healthy career, as well as a sort of extension of life on board the *Araner*.

"[Making Westerns] gives me a chance to get away from the smog," he would say, "to get away from this town, to get away from people who would like to tell me how to make pictures. You're working with nice people—cowboys, stuntmen, that kind of person. You get up early in the morning and go out on location and work hard all day and then you get home and you go to bed early. It's a great life—just like a paid vacation. I love to make westerns. If I had my choice, that's all I would make."

Since Argosy was still gasping for air, another Western seemed like a good idea. This time it would be *3 Godfathers*, the venerable Peter B. Kyne magazine story published in 1913 that was to launch Dobe Carey on his acting career.

Since MGM had done the last remake of the story, in 1936, and still owned the property, Ford and Cooper would make the picture for Louis B. Mayer. Initially, Argosy planned to finance *3 Godfathers* themselves, and have MGM release the picture. Metro would take 30 percent off the top for distributing the picture worldwide, as well as 25 percent of the profits for contributing the story.

Cooper was clearly leery of MGM's famously homogenizing management style and warned MGM general manager Eddie Mannix that Ford wouldn't stand for approvals by anybody, including Cooper, of story, directing, cutting, etc., up to and including censorship. Although Ford's Catholicism was sincere, it stopped at the studio gate; the deal memo stipulated that Argosy "will not agree that the picture will obtain an 'A' Legion of Decency rating nor are we willing to give [MGM] the right to edit for the Legion of Decency."

None of this would have been a problem; it was money that was the problem. It soon became clear that Argosy was too extended to take out another $1 million production loan. The Bank of America refused to finance the picture, feeling the costs were too high for what seemed to be an ordinary Western.

Cooper regrouped and managed to convince MGM to finance the picture for Argosy to produce. MGM reimbursed Argosy the $43,343 they had spent on the script (Frank Nugent received $1,000 a week, while Laurence Stallings got $2,500) and other preparation costs. Ford would receive $150,000, Cooper $50,000, and MGM would cover all costs for the Technicolor picture up to $1.25 million.

If Ford kept the budget within that figure, MGM would pay Argosy a bonus of $100,000, but if costs rose past $1.25 million, Argosy's $100,000 would be reduced by 50 cents for every dollar they went over budget. If the picture amassed a domestic gross equaling 170 percent of the negative cost, Argosy would receive yet another $100,000. After that, Argosy had no further profit participation. John Wayne was getting his standard

$100,000 and Ward Bond was making the surprisingly large salary of $2,500 a week for ten weeks.

It wasn't going to be an easy shoot. "This budget is based upon a 30-day schedule . . . [and is] purposely tight and Mr. Ford estimates that he will use part or all of the 5% contingency on the other items in the budget," the script estimate reported. The picture was a good deal for both companies, but only marginally better than the deal Ford could have gotten to make the picture without the Argosy monkey on his back.

Ford had hoped to use Gabriel Figueroa as cameraman, but that went by the wayside when the locations were switched from Mexico to America and the cameraman couldn't get into the union on such short notice. Argosy paid Figueroa anyway, $8,112 as per his contract.

As a replacement, Ford added a new weapon to his technical arsenal, the great Technicolor cameraman Winton Hoch. At the time, Hoch was hard at work on *Joan of Arc* for Victor Fleming. When Ward Bond recommended him to Ford, Walter Wanger invited the director to the studio to look at some of Hoch's exemplary footage, by far the best thing in the legendarily dull picture. Hoch's work on *She Wore a Yellow Ribbon*, *The Quiet Man*, and *The Searchers* would constitute highwater marks in the visual aspect of Ford's films.

Ford, Wayne, and Ward Bond went on a location hunt for *3 Godfathers*, and took the home movie camera along. The footage indicates that for the only time, Ford seemed to be using his 16mm camera to try out a few rehearsal shots. Wayne is seen coming over a rise in the sand toward the camera; he takes off his hat, wipes his brow, then keeps moving past the camera. In another shot Wayne is shown on the horizon, trudging from left to right.

February 1, 1948, was Ford's birthday. Just before the company was to leave for location work, Mary threw a small party for her husband. Ollie, Dobe, and Marilyn Carey were there, as were Ward Bond and John Wayne and his wife, Chata. "You're going to hate me when this picture is over," Ford told Dobe more than once that night, "but you're going to give a great performance." And then he told Dobe he wanted him to call him "Uncle Jack."

In Death Valley, the company stayed at the Furnace Creek Inn (singles $4.50, doubles $6). For the second time, Ford brought in Mildred Natwick, his "young Una O'Connor," to do one crucial scene with John Wayne. Natwick was a very gifted actress, and Ford stopped her in mid-take, saying to Wayne, "You look as though you're just watching Millie act; play the scene more."

"I've never forgotten," remembered Natwick, "that Ford seemed pleased with the scene and pleased that I'd done it. I guess because I knew my lines and got through it in [one] morning. . . . I don't know, you get things by osmosis from a wonderful director, I think. His feeling about what the woman was thinking and feeling."

Ford took some pleasure in ruining Pedro Armendariz's day with little things that would throw off the actor's desired image of the dashing bandit. "He'd hang pots and pans and everything all over his horse," chuckled Ben Johnson. "And that would just kill Pete. Pete wanted to have everything like the conquistadores. He'd have three or four things hanging and Ford would go by and say, 'Well, you can take this one off here, we don't need that.' But he'd leave two or three things hanging on him."

That, however, was benevolence personified compared to the hiding Ford gave Harry Carey Jr. Dobe could not recall a single day when Ford was pleasant to him; he was either bearably mean or unbearably mean. "My God, Audie Murphy begged me for this part!" he told Dobe over and over. "Now, for God's sake, try not to screw this up." No action was good enough, no response was correct. Ford responded to a particularly heartfelt scene of Carey's by pantomiming masturbation.

Some days he'd demand that Carey bend over and he'd kick him, hard. When Carey had continuing trouble with a scene, Ford picked up a rock and threw it at Carey's face. The actor ducked, and the rock sailed into Pedro Armendariz's stomach.

After watching Carey's first try at his death scene, Ford responded by saying, "Well, Jesus H. Christ. Now we really are up shit creek! Well, it's too late to get Audie. I mean—what are we going to do with you, kid?" He went on to call the young actor yellow and a coward, and when Carey protested, Ford yelled, "Then lie back down there, goddamn it, and die like a man. Goddamn it, I want to see you die. So die for me, for Chrissakes, and make us all right here believe it." He instructed the entire company to walk back to the shelter of the trucks and left Carey out in the 100 degree sun, without water.

After half an hour, the company returned and Carey, understandably parched, nailed the scene on the next take. Ford took his face in his hands and smiled. "Why didn't you do that the first time? See how easy it was? You done good! It's a wrap!"

Ford's behavior was sadistic and far over the line, although he undoubtedly justified it to himself in several ways: his latent anger at Dobe's father, his continuing love for Dobe—he'd been there when Dobe had been born, had pulled strings and gotten him out of danger during the war—and the fact that the boy was an inexperienced performer without the technique necessary to pull his scenes off to Ford's satisfaction.

But this was the show business equivalent of a fraternity hazing, pure and simple, and Carey would have had to undergo it even if he had been a more experienced actor. The best one can say of it is that it was more honest than cruelty disguised as perfectionism. "The directors of that era were *all* sadistic," insists Sam Goldwyn Jr. "I can remember Wyler on *The Little Foxes* making a guy with a wooden leg [Herbert Marshall] fall twenty times because he hadn't done it right."

Over the years, Carey would see Ford in this mode any number of times, and he noticed that it was preceded by distinct physical manifestations. "You knew you were in trouble when he started rolling his head around, working his neck as if he had a crick in it. It looked like he was some sort of lizard. It was the sadism welling up in his body. And then he'd put the handkerchief in his mouth and let it hang there, and that's when he would begin to let you have it."

But just when the storm clouds looked like they were going to obliterate the landscape, the sun would come blazing through. "The thing that kept him from being really so tough that you couldn't stand him was that he had a wonderful sense of humor. It was Jimmy Stewart who said that John Ford had a quality about him that you wanted to please him; you wanted to be good for him."

With typical generosity, Carey downplayed Ford's spasms of abusiveness toward him and focused instead at the way Ford treated John Wayne. "He would *never* compliment Duke. And it used to kind of annoy me. Like a scene in 3 *Godfathers*. Wayne comes down off that hill after he's found the wagon and the woman having her baby and he was incredible. One take! And [all Ford said was] 'Right!' . . . and then he walked off. They played cards together a lot and Duke had to let him win. A lot of times, Duke used to be home with his family, and Ford wanted to play cards, and off he'd go. That's the way it was. He was *such* an incredible character."

Usually, Ford didn't like distractions while on location, but on the edge of Death Valley something seemed to be called for, so the studio sent new movies, among them George Cukor's *A Double Life*, to keep the cast and crew entertained. When there wasn't a film, there were competitive games of dominoes between Ford, Wayne, Armendariz, and Bond. So long as Ford won, the game was friendly. "The rest of us stood around and listened to them," remembered Hank Worden. "Ford couldn't stand to be topped, so he cheated."

Ford returned from location work to find a full-blown domestic crisis. On July 8, Barbara had married Robert Walker, the talented actor who was still on the rebound from his marriage to and divorce from

Jennifer Jones. Ford didn't like his daughter's taste in men. "What are you doing out with that goddamned sissy son of a bitch?" he demanded.

Walker seems to have sensed Ford's misgivings. In some home movie footage taken on board the *Araner*, Walker looks noticeably glum, as if he'd rather be somewhere, anywhere, else.

By this time, Barbara was, in the words of Andrew McLaglen, "Really a sweet, nice, cute gal." But she was not drop-dead gorgeous. The gap between the woman he had had and the woman he was marrying only increased Walker's feelings of inferiority, which in turn fueled his drinking. John and Mary were not in favor of the marriage, and, after initially planning to host the ceremony, had not been invited.

Ford's instincts were confirmed on August 14, barely five weeks after the marriage, when Walker got drunk and savagely beat Barbara. Mary and Joanne Dru got her out of the house and onto the *Araner*. According to Cecile de Prita, Ward Bond was going to administer a reciprocal beating to Walker, but Ford wouldn't let him do it. "John and Mary Ford have their little girl home with them again," Louella Parsons wrote a few days after the explosion, "but I know they are just as unhappy about the separation as they were when Barbara and Bob married without inviting them to the wedding."

The marriage was over. In later years, Barbara never discussed the subject of Robert Walker. "She iced it out," said her nephew Dan Ford. "She was badly scarred by it."

Completing *3 Godfathers* seemed to calm Ford down. Since Dobe Carey had passed his trial by fire, Jack invited him and his wife, Marilyn, along with Duke Wayne and his wife, to join him on a trip to Catalina. They were all sitting at a bar when Dobe got involved in a conversation with Wayne's wife, Chata. He finally turned around to see his wife dancing with John Wayne, which was unusual because Wayne never danced. Even more unusual was the fact that Wayne was holding Marilyn upside down. Carey told his friend he was going to make Marilyn sick and to turn her around.

The next day, Dobe told Wayne what he had done. Wayne denied that he could ever have done such a thing, no matter how drunk he was. Just to be on the safe side, however, he sent Marilyn an enormous bouquet of flowers. Dobe was now a member in good standing of the Ford stock company.

3 Godfathers emerged as a sweet reverie, the mournful "Streets of Laredo" cuing the moving dedication that comes after the main title: "To the memory of Harry Carey. Bright Star of the early western sky."

It's a loving memory piece, a heartfelt fable of found family. Ward

Bond plays a sheriff with pacifistic overtones: "They ain't payin' me to kill folks," he says after he chases the three badmen who have robbed the bank into the desert. The robbers come across a ruined wagon, with a woman giving birth. The mother dies, and the men resolve to take care of the baby.

The material is sentimental, and Ford is careful never to get too close to realism—the baby almost never cries. After Harry Carey Jr. and Pedro Armendariz die, they come back as ghosts, and just as in *Three Bad Men* (similar title, different story) the dead attend the living, guiding, hectoring, pleading for Wayne's Robert Hightower to keep moving toward the town of New Jerusalem, toward redemption.

The film features some extraordinarily delicate day-for-night work by Winton Hoch, and in some of the daytime shots you can see the waves of heat rising from the ground. Ford costumes Wayne much as in *Stagecoach*—blue jeans with turned-up cuffs, suspenders, and a bandana, making him less ominous and more approachable than most bank robbers.

Although *3 Godfathers* has never had many critical adherents, it remains one of the director's most affecting mid-range films; not overly ambitious, but on its own terms, remarkably effective.

I n one of the most extraordinary documents in his life, on July 15, 1948, Ford wrote James Warner Bellah of his plans for the film that became *She Wore a Yellow Ribbon* (all ellipses not in parentheses are in the original). "Here is what I see . . . vaguely of course and on the screen in color . . . not on paper and without sequence. It is a story of Captain Nathan Brittles who probably joined the Second Dragoons in '36 as a callow rookie . . . from Florida to the West . . . from the West down to Chapultapec [sic] . . . back to the West . . . East to Bull Run . . . Yellow Tavern, finally Appomattox . . . from the ranks to Brevet Colonel and from Brevet Colonel to his permanent grade of Captain (. . .)

"Jim, I think we can make a Remington canvas . . . broad shoulders . . . wide hats . . . narrow hips . . . yellow strips down the pants leg . . . war bonnets and eagle feathers trailing in the dust . . . the brassy sound of bugles in the morning . . . the long reaches of the prairie . . . the buttes and mesas in the distances and the buffalo (. . .)"

Ford, at this point, was planning the picture without stars, somewhat on the model of the later *Wagon Master*; he envisioned Technicolor, and a budget of $600,000.

"I would like to work Custer into it some way . . . not to actually see him on the screen, but to start out a story nine months after the Little Big Horn . . . a group of Cheyenne dog soldiers have broken south and are in the Comanche, Kiowa or Arapahoe country (. . .) I think we should lay out our important scenes, Jim, and between them build some action. I would like to see a scene, for example, with Brittles and Allroyd riding into the hostile camp to argue with the Chief. They have finished the Buffalo Dance and now in mass hysteria are almost into the Ghost or War Dance. As they approach the Chief the Cheyenne dog soldiers whip by screaming and one shoots an arrow between Brittles' feet. Brittles, without stopping, yanks the arrow out, breaks it in two, spits on it, then tosses it over his left shoulder . . . a sharp argument with the Chief and his headman who are old and tired of war . . . but the young bucks who have never been blooded are frantic in their desire to join the Cheyennes . . . and get Henry repeaters . . . scalps . . . coups. It is probably right after this that they raid the pony herd, which I think is a wonderful sequence.

"A nice scene on the distant mesa . . . a small burying ground with a small headstone where Brittles' family lies . . . victims of a smallpox epidemic (. . .) I think the scene of the watch with Brittles trying to voice his thanks and completely fails is truly swell just as it is in [Bellah's original] story (. . .)

"Our story is the fact that Brittles has eight more hours of active duty (. . .) As a matter of fact, we are suffering from the greatest of all boons . . . an overabundance of great material. If we can tie this together simply and in a straight-forward line we've got something (. . .)

"Monument Valley (. . .) has never been photographed in color and (. . .) should be breathtaking. At Monument Valley I have my own personal tribe of Navajo Indians who are great riders, swell actors . . . have long hair and best of all they believe in me. We can braid their long hair in the Cheyenne, Kiowa, Comanche or whatever hairdress we desire . . . choose particularly good costumes . . . have elaborate war bonnets and make them look good. They are tall, sinewy and as the poor bastards never get enough to eat unless I make a picture there, they have no excess fat on them (. . .)

"So I think that with a break in weather we might get something we could be proud of and get a chance to get our investment back . . . plus ten percent (. . .)

"Jim, I'll give you this for what it's worth. Meanwhile I'm going back on the boat and get some rest and do a little fishing and mainly I'll be thinking about the story. I'm delighted at the idea of our working together . . ." Ford closes the letter with a ringing "Up the Rebels!"

It's all here—the texture of legend overlaying creaking leather, a clarity of vision supported by Ford's need for others to trust in him. Ford has not merely dreamed up linchpin scenes—the graveyard, Brittles with the old chief—the entire film is clearly shaped in his mind, needing only the planing of the plot and the finishing touches of dialogue. This is not the shambling Ford of the public image, an aw-shucks working stiff, a shit-kicking, directorial version of Will Rogers. This is the ferociously focused artist the world outside of Hollywood never glimpsed.

For Bellah's "Big Hunt" and "War Party," plus a screenplay, Argosy paid him the bargain rate of $12,000. Bellah turned in a twenty-four page treatment, and a 124-page script, but he didn't work out as a scriptwriter; in September, Ford hired both Frank Nugent (at $1,000 a week) and Laurence Stallings (at $2,500 a week) to work as a team on the script, after first telling Bellah that Nugent and Stallings would be constructing what he called a "banker's script." In fact, Nugent and Stallings would get credit for the script.

Ford did a lot of touch-up work on the script himself. In his hand are notes that he later ignored ("Col. Tim McCoy Technical director"), questions, and script notes: "WINCHESTERS? Could Brittles re-arm his men—with rifles? After leaving fort—trick it someway."

He drafted some dialogue exchanges, such as this between Mildred Natwick's Mrs. Allshard and Brittles: "Why you cantankerous, stubborn, selfish, old—"

"Old! Old! Well, Mr. Capt. Nathan Brittles I'm eleven years younger than you—if you please."

He also wrote down his ideas for the narration, to be recorded by Irving Pichel, who had also contributed the voice-over to *How Green Was My Valley:*

"After the Pony Stampede, a commentary:

" 'So Nathan Brittles rode west into the setting Sun—towards the Sante Fe Trail. Seeking—seeking what—What's there to seek when we're old. Reveries, memories—memories of a job well done . . .'

"Break it suddenly with Ben Johnson riding like hell towards camera—telegraph sequence."

The payroll of the film is instructive. John Wayne got $100,000, Victor McLaglen $35,000, George O'Brien $15,000, Joanne Dru $10,000, Harry Carey Jr., $5,000, and Ben Johnson $5,000. Winton Hoch came on board for $750 a week, and Ford carried his brother Francis at $160 a week for eight weeks even though Francis could have completed his scenes in less than a week and, in any case, the film was only scheduled for a six-week shoot. Hiring two hundred local Navajos in Monument Valley cost $18 a day each for twenty days, or $72,000. Ford paid the Navajos more than he did Mormons, who were also put to work for about $12 a day.

Once again, research provided an immaculate historical background. Although the film opens right after Custer's defeat in June of 1876, Ford specified in the script that the calendar in Brittles's room not have a month, to prevent the viewer from fixing the date. Other events in the film that could be taken as fanciful turn out to be faithful re-creations of events. The final battle, in which Brittles and his men attack an Indian village at night, stampede their horses, and then march the Indians back to the reservation without a single casualty, actually happened several times in the period portrayed in the film.

A check of the film vs. the geographic reality of Monument Valley and Goulding's Trading Post reveals how seamlessly Ford unified what is actually a very disparate group of landmarks, and of how he used the material at hand. The gates of the cavalry post were constructed near the Mittens, twin buttes that are miles away from the buildings that served for the interior of the fort. The soldiers' quarters were actually the original guest cabins built by the Gouldings on the grounds of the trading post. The sutler's place was a Depression-era Civilian Conservation Corps building that became the Gouldings' dining room. The front of the trading post itself was used for cavalry headquarters, while the back of the trading post was pressed into duty as the blacksmith's shop. The personal billet Nathan Brittles comes charging out of every morning was Harry Goulding's potato cellar.

While the settings were picturesque, the fact that almost all the fort scenes could be shot on the grounds of Goulding's meant that Ford could maximize production time; lengthy rides out into the valley were only necessary for action scenes. In this way, Ford knew he could complete the film under schedule in the astonishingly brief time of four weeks, only slightly more than the average television movie of today, and several weeks less than was usual for a Technicolor Western shot on location. There was no downtime; if the weather clouded up so a given scene couldn't be shot, Ben Johnson, a new addition to the stock company, could ride. "He liked to watch me ride a horse," remembered Johnson. "All these guys were better actors than I was but I could beat them all riding a horse."

Johnson was born on an Osage Indian reservation in Oklahoma in 1918, and had been working on a cattle ranch in 1939 when Howard Hughes bought some horses for his film *The Outlaw*. Johnson was making $40 a month at the time, and was hired to accompany the horses to Hollywood. "The first week I was on his payroll," Johnson remembered, "I made $175, as opposed to $40 a month. That's why I stayed in Hollywood."

By 1948, Johnson had doubled for Gary Cooper, Joel McCrea, and most of the Western stars of the time. Johnson was doubling Henry Fonda in *Fort Apache* when a couple of horses ran away with a wagon during a take. Johnson stepped out from behind the camera and stopped the runaway. Moved by the stuntman's unassuming courage, Ford got down off the camera parallel and went over to Johnson. "Ben, you'll be well rewarded for this." Johnson thought that he'd get some more stuntwork out of his good deed, but two weeks later, Ford called him into his office, handed him an envelope, and told him to have his lawyer look at it.

As the envelope wasn't sealed, Johnson pulled out the contents and discovered a personal services contract with Argosy Pictures. "The fifth line down [read] 'to $5,000 a week,' " remembered Johnson. "That's as far as I read. I got a pen off his desk and I signed . . ."

Ford clearly liked the young man a great deal, and saw in him something of Harry Carey's ease and likability. Aside from his natural athletic gifts, Johnson was the token normal person in the Ford stock company. He wasn't a drunk, wasn't given to fits of temper, depression, or grandiosity, but did have a natural authority on screen.

Budgeted at $1.8 million, the picture required Ford to work seven days a week. The first two days of the schedule were given over to selecting locations, then he dove in. The first day, Wednesday, October 27, 1948, he shot action footage of Indians, stagecoaches, and Ben Johnson riding, and covered an astounding eight and a half pages of script. After that, he averaged between five and six pages of script a day (the average for a large-scale studio picture is two to three per day).

She Wore a Yellow Ribbon was the second collaboration between Ford and Winton Hoch, who already understood his director. "What direction do you want to shoot?" Ford asked Hoch one morning early in the production. Hoch wisely wondered why Ford was being so thoughtful, so considerate. It had to be a trap. "Any direction you want is fine with me," he told Ford. "You're the director."

Hoch noticed that Ford would pick a setup by placing his chair where he wanted the camera. His habit of cutting in the camera saved Hoch a great deal of time. " 'I'm only going to carry the scene to this point,' he often said," remembered Hoch. "I didn't have to light for a complete master shot."

Evenings in Monument Valley had a serene, mysterious quality. The women of the production—Mildred Natwick, Joanne Dru, and a visiting Barbara Ford—were all billeted together, and they enjoyed the sounds of the Indians singing and dancing during the night, voices echoing off the buttes. The company was simultaneously playing the West and being the West, and the combination gave the filming a mystical authority.

Some of the days had an otherworldly quality too. Mildred Natwick remembered an Indian named Old Fat who was called over by Ford one day at lunch. "Now this afternoon I want just a few little clouds, not too many, just a few," he told the Indian. Natwick giggled as Old Fat walked away, and Ford silenced her with a sharp look. "And Old Fat went up and sat on the side of a hill working his cloud effects," remembered the actress. "That was Old Fat's serious job . . . to keep the weather right. And my dear, we did have just a few teeny, weeny little clouds that afternoon."

When you weren't working, life in Monument Valley could be a trifle enervating. "On location, on off times, he didn't want everybody around [him]," said John Agar. "He and Duke used to play cards, two-handed bridge, but there really wasn't too much to do up there. I didn't play cards, so I'd just lay back and relax, read, listen to the radio, something like that. All you had to do was work."

This, of course, was the precise point. The conventional way of making a movie on location was and is to house the star in a beautiful suite, slightly lesser accommodations for the second and third leads and so on. The actors and crew mix with nobody but each other, so they remain actors on temporary assignment.

But on a Ford set, the accommodations were liable to be tents. Goulding's dining room wasn't big enough for the cast and crew, so three large tents were set up with long tables. The food was family style—large platters of steaks, eggs, biscuits, and gravy. Ben Johnson remembered that a Ford location shoot always meant a struggle to maintain your waistline.

"We put up tent cities and we mingled with locals," asserted Pat Ford. "If they were Indians, that's what we leashed our horses against . . . [The actors] quickly become the same as the people they are associating with at the time. They're chameleons. Henry Fonda, when he made *Fort Apache*, wasn't Henry Fonda playing a martinet of a colonel, he was there living in a camp [in] tents with the troops and he became the colonel. It makes a difference."

Ford still didn't trust Harry Carey Jr.'s native ability. Since he had wisely concluded that acting lessons for young, scared actors weren't his forte, he assigned Arthur Shields, the brother of Barry Fitzgerald and an Abbey Theatre veteran, to serve as Carey's dramatic coach. Shields developed a viable backstory for Carey's character. "He explained to me that I wasn't the leading man, that I was vying for the girl and I didn't get her. 'Play him like a West Point snob,' he said, 'a rich family snob that doesn't want to be out there in the red dust. Otherwise you won't be noticed. There's nothing worse than a second lead.' It was good advice."

Ford retained his ability to take advantage of happy accidents. During the scene of Victor McLaglen reviewing the troops, one of the Navajo dogs thought it would be a good idea to lie down in the middle of the shot. "Vic," said Ford, "make a comment [on the dog]." "Oh, Jack darling," said McLaglen, "I'll say something." During the next take, Mc-Laglen reached down and petted the ragged mongrel. "Nice dog," he said. "Irish setter."

By this time, McLaglen had mellowed to a surpassing geniality. The result, as Dobe Carey remembered, was that "he'd fall asleep on the set. So you could tell who was not afraid of Jack Ford. We'd be shooting and you'd hear snores, and Vic would be sleeping."

The legendary sequence of the lightning storm, supposedly shot over the objections of Winton Hoch, turns out to be one of the authentic stories about Ford. "The electrical storm came up, and there was lightning crackling all around us," remembered John Agar. "Well, there's metal on bridles and saddles and people were pretty nervous. So [Winton Hoch] yelled out, 'That's a wrap,' as the lightning started striking around us. And Ford said, 'No. We shoot.' So we shot right through the storm. It's a true story; I was in the scene. And the cameraman won the Academy Award, largely for that scene."

Harry Carey Jr.'s version is that the company was moving toward the station wagons when Ford, who had first called a wrap, then called everybody back. He had looked at Hoch and said "Winnie, what do you think?" "It's awfully dark, Jack. But I'll shoot it. I just can't promise anything." "Winnie, open her up [the lens] and let's go for it. If it doesn't come out, I'll take the rap."

Carey's version sounds more authentic, if only because a professional like Hoch is not likely to refuse a director's order. Hoch always denied the story about shooting the scene under protest, but not strenuously, and with a touch of amusement. "Never spoil a good story with a few facts," he told Ford's grandson.

Francis was again playing a drunk for his brother. Some have gone so far as to suggest that Ford's sibling rivalry extended to calling William Wellman and asking him not to use Francis in a major supporting part in *The Ox-Bow Incident*, but that turns out to be false. "Jack Ford called him and thanked him like crazy for doing it," asserted William Wellman Jr. "Dad always said how much Ford appreciated it."

Ford's mood on the set was largely pleasant, and the material was close to his heart, so he felt free to indulge himself with an in-joke: in the cemetery sequences shot back at the studio, where Nathan Brittles makes his regular pilgrimage to his wife's grave, one of the headstones reads "Pvt. B. Devoto," after Bernard Devoto, author of *Across the Wide Missouri* and *The Course of Empire*. There's also a headstone for Douglas Southall Freeman, another of Ford's favorite historians.

During production, Ford gave Wayne a cake with one candle on it. "He never thought of me as an actor," remembered John Wayne, "and then he saw *Red River*, and he wanted to top it, and he did. He gave me that part in *Yellow Ribbon* . . . and I think it's the best thing I've ever done."

What was the candle for?

"Actor. I had finally arrived."

*S*he Wore a Yellow Ribbon is a kind of reverse take on *Fort Apache;* the earlier film is about a military disaster transmuted into glorious heroism by posterity; *Yellow Ribbon* is about a military success in which bloodshed is averted, but it's overweighted with a melancholy air of reverie and grief. The earlier film is about men in the prime of their lives and careers, while the later film is about old men getting ready to retire, and frankly worried about life outside the military. It's among the director's most painterly movies, his way of compensating for the film's extremely loose, ballad-like structure—it's really nothing more than an accumulation of vignettes, some of surpassing loveliness.

In fact, Ford's interest in Frederic Remington extended beyond his palette. Around this time, Merian Cooper asked Lester Ziffren to look into the rights to Remington's life. Ziffren had a talk with the agent for the Remington estate, then went back to Cooper and told him they could make a deal.

"What is your feeling about this agent?" asked Cooper.

"My personal feeling is that I'd keep my hands in my pockets as long as I'm talking to him," said Ziffren. "I don't trust him."

Cooper thought for a moment and sighed. "Lester," he said, "life's too short. Let's forget the whole thing."

A tantalizing possibility submarined, and one of the few extant examples of Cooper not ceding important decisions to his partner.

*W*hile Ford was out in Monument Valley, doing what he loved, Merian Cooper was shuffling Argosy's cards and coming up with diminishing hands. On October 23, he signed an agreement with Security First National Bank cross-collateralizing *She Wore a Yellow Ribbon* and *Fort Apache*. Argosy would not see any money from either of the Westerns until the loan for *The Fugitive* was paid off.

In the latter part of 1948, Ford got the idea of doing a benefit performance of Maxwell Anderson and Laurence Stallings's classic play *What Price Glory* for the Purple Heart Association. The idea seems to have derived from some of the impromptu vaudeville that entertained Ford's cast and crew on locations. Somebody suggested doing a cut-down version of the play, and Ford retorted, "Why cut it down? Let's give it full-length."

The ever-obedient Dobe Carey got a call from Ford. "I'm gonna put you in this play. You live near Gregory Peck, don't you? Tell him to call me." Carey went down the street to Peck's house, and told the excited actor that John Ford wanted to talk to him, only to find out it wasn't for a movie, but a play.

The production was announced to the press on January 13, 1949. Ford and George O'Brien put together a spectacular cast: Ward Bond and Pat O'Brien were Flagg and Quirt, and the supporting cast included John Wayne, Gregory Peck, George O'Brien, Alan Hale Sr., Robert Armstrong, Wallace Ford, Charles Kemper, Henry O'Neill, Jimmy Lydon, Oliver Hardy, Larry Blake, Forrest Tucker, Ed Begley, and, as Charmaine, Maureen O'Hara.

Luis Alberni was the only member of the cast who had been in the original 1924 production, and he encored his performance as Cognac Pete. The studios for whom the various stars worked agreed to coordinate their schedules to the best of their abilities, so the actors would be free to rehearse at night. The rehearsal site was the Masquers Club on Sycamore, a three-story building that had originally been the home of the silent star Antonio Moreno. Except for the hotels where the company would stay on tour, everybody contributed their services; even stage crews worked for free.

Two years earlier, Larry Blake and Alberni had founded the first Alcoholics Anonymous in Hollywood. Thus, Ford's nickname for Blake was "The Captain of AA." Blake's activities on behalf of AA weren't the reasons he was cast; he had been in the Navy, and had earned a Purple Heart.

At first, Ford undertook to direct the show himself. "The kicker," remembered Pat O'Brien, "was that Ford was a lousy stage director. Well, maybe not lousy, but he wasn't very good. He finally called in a fine stage director named Ralph Murphy and told him to clean the show up. 'I just want you to know that you're not going to get any credit,' Jack told him in that crabby way of his. An interesting, interesting man, old Pappy." In fact, Murphy did get a "Staged by" credit.

Rehearsals were what might have been expected. Ford would sit in the theater and ride Ward Bond while Ralph Murphy tried to work. Bond was having trouble memorizing all of his dialogue, and Ford flayed him, without, of course, giving the part to another actor—Ford knew Bond would make a fine Captain Flagg. According to Larry Blake, Ford greatly enjoyed supervising (his credit was "Entire Production Supervised by John Ford") and vicariously scratching what must have been a mild itch to do stage work.

"I played one of the soldiers," remembered Gregory Peck. "I'd been wounded in the leg and had perhaps ten lines. Ford was always around at the rehearsals. He seemed bemused at having all the talent he had on stage."

After rehearsals, everybody except Blake and Alberni would head downstairs to the beautiful wood-carved bar and start drinking. Two full-dress performances were given at the Masquers before an audience that contained many paraplegics.

The night of the dress rehearsal, just before the company left for their week-long road trip, Henry O'Neill got so drunk he fell head-first into some rose bushes, making it to the train station with his face badly scratched.

The production was advertised with large, ugly box ads in the papers—no art, plenty of type: "ONE NIGHT ONLY! IN PERSON! ON STAGE! GREATEST STAR-SPANGLED CAST EVER ASSEMBLED FOR ANY SHOW!" A long list of the actors followed; seats cost between $2.40 and $4.80—average for the time.

Because he was a recovering alcoholic, Larry Blake would occasionally be the target of some good-natured ribbing. On the train to Pasadena, the cast was ensconced in the club car having a fine, wet time when Pat O'Brien introduced Blake to a Jesuit priest as "The president of AA." The priest brightened and said, "Oh? I'm in AA." O'Brien shut up for the rest of the trip.

The production was in a rowdy, crowd-pleasing manner. "When 'What Price Glory' was first presented," said Luis Alberni, "it was done in a quiet way. Ford . . . and Ralph Murphy make the show sing."

The show played February 22 in Long Beach, February 24 in San Jose, February 25 in Oakland, February 27 in San Francisco, and March 1 in Pasadena. The company had been planning the last show to take place at Philharmonic Hall in Los Angeles, which was owned by the Methodist Church, but the church was uncomfortable with the play's famously raucous language, and refused to allow the play on its stage.

This had the unfortunate effect of, first, angering Ford, then, by raising the specter of cultural politics, causing him to lose interest. An interim plan to do it at what is now the El Capitan Theater on Hollywood Boulevard was scrubbed because of the lack of dressing rooms, and they ended up doing it across the street at Grauman's Chinese.

The reviews throughout were respectful, and sometimes more than that. The Pasadena critic wrote that "The play with this cast could move right in on Broadway and become one of the greatest hits in history." The *Los Angeles Times* wrote that "Ward Bond, Pat O'Brien and Maureen O'Hara in the leads acquitted themselves admirably. They could star in the play on any stage."

According to Larry Blake's widow and several cast members, it was a coherent production, but the great fun was the chance to see demigods such as John Wayne and Gregory Peck on stage. When they came on for their few lines, the audience would jump in with applause; during the nightly curtain calls, the audience went wild. Despite all that, at least one of the actors had his doubts. "I don't think it was really very good," said Gregory Peck.

The production of *What Price Glory* was a good deal of work, a great deal of fun, but not wildly profitable. According to accounting statements, the production raised nearly $46,000, but had expenses of $40,439.28. Once the Masquers took their 25 percent of the profits, the balance transferred to the Purple Heart Association was just $4,202.84.

As for Ford's perilous proximity to Alcoholics Anonymous, "My father would have crawled across the desert to help John Ford," said Michael Blake, who became a successful makeup man in the industry. But Ford never made the necessary admission of dependence. Ford and Blake remained cordial acquaintances—Ford hired Blake for "Flashing Spikes," a television episode he directed in 1962—but it would never be possible for him to acknowledge weakness.

At the same time he was "supervising" the production of *What Price Glory*, Ford was preparing the bonus picture he had promised Zanuck in return for lending him Henry Fonda for *The Fugitive*. *Pinky* was the story of a light-skinned black woman passing for white that starred Jeanne Crain and Ethel Waters. While the usual unsourced backchat has always claimed that the picture blew up in Ford's face after one day, he actually shot for a week (March 9–March 17); as always when Ford was unable to finish a picture, his health was suddenly infirm, in this case a "back injury . . . suffered in a tumble last week."

Zanuck called on Elia Kazan for a personal favor, and Kazan said he'd do the picture if he could throw out Ford's footage and go back to New York the day after he finished shooting. Agreed. But when he arrived on the set and began talking to people, he realized that Ford's illness was a sham. "Jack's not sick is he?" Kazan asked Zanuck. "He just wanted out."

"He hated that old nigger woman," replied Zanuck, "and she sure as hell hated him. He scared her next to death." Ford didn't know how to reach Ethel Waters—Kazan would later refer to Waters's truly odd combination of old-time religiosity and free-flowing hatred. Ford couldn't follow his usual tactic and abuse her because he didn't think she'd take it. When he indicated any displeasure with her performance, she reacted with resentment and retreat. Best to walk away and try again with something else. The entire episode was painful for Zanuck, who wrote that, "I fought with John Ford on *Pinky*. He insisted at first that he could not make the picture unless he made it on location. When I finally convinced him to make it at the studio he blew the job."

Philip Dunne, who wrote the script, said that Kazan shot the script word for word. "The stuff [of Ford's] I saw was Ethel Waters sort of moaning spirituals as she hung up the wash. It was pretty much a Stepin Fetchit sort of feeling. . . . [Ford] was far from being a racist. I don't think there was any of that in it, it was just the way he was brought up—we all were."

The question of Ford's racial politics has come to be questioned, and not just in recent years. For the record, he adored Bill and Waverly Ramsey, a black couple who ran the Odin street house for him for years. He trusted the couple with his grandchildren, and broke down completely at Bill Ramsey's funeral. As for Jews, he would occasionally address Harry Wurtzel with anti-Semitic jibes ("Dear Christ-Killer") of the sort that only good friends can get away with. Bea Benjamin, his accountant, once said that "He used to always say, 'Some of my best friends are Jews,' which, you know, is the kiss of death. It means you are anti-Semitic. He used to go to great lengths to prove he wasn't, which probably means he was."

Except for the letters to Harry Wurtzel, Ford's private correspondence is completely free of racial or religious slurs. "Being Jewish and not a big drinker," said Leon Selditz, an editor who worked for Ford, "I always felt uncomfortable with his stock company, which felt reverse discrimination from the Jewish bosses in Hollywood. But Jack was never discriminatory about me or anything. He had a great relationship with every sort of person—with Harry Cohn of Columbia, Woody Strode, the black actor, and the Navajos. He had a penchant for Negroes and Indians—it was his great feeling for liberty."

Lee Marvin, a liberal Democrat who became close to Ford in later years, confirmed Selditz's account, saying, "The real regulars, they were hard-assed boys. And they said things about Jews and blacks. Whether they really meant it or not, they acted it out, because they thought that's what Ford liked, whereas in reality Ford was probably the most liberal man I ever met. Yet he didn't act it."

As for Harry Wurtzel, the occasional target of his jibes, when he died, Ford knelt by the casket for long minutes, praying and crying, completely distraught. For the next few years, Ford continued paying percentages of his income to Harry's estate, even though he didn't have to. The agent had been an inveterate, unsuccessful player in the stock market and hadn't left his wife very well off.

CHAPTER TWENTY

After the debacle of *Pinky*, Ford rummaged around the house for a few weeks, then packed Mary and Barbara on board the *Araner* and sailed for Hawaii. After a month, his mood was considerably lightened, and he arrived back in Hollywood on May 25.

Still miffed with Ford over *Pinky*, Zanuck yanked away a comedy-Western called *A Ticket to Tomahawk* that Ford had wanted to direct. Instead, Ford's make-good picture became *When Willie Comes Marching Home*, a Richard Sale–Mary Loos gloss on Preston Sturges's *Hail the Conquering Hero*.

Ford decided to get even with Sale, who was directing *A Ticket to Tomahawk*, by telling Zanuck, "I want the talented one on my set," meaning Loos. For one of the few times in his career, Ford went out of his way to welcome a writer. The fact that Loos was extremely beautiful might have had something to do with it.

Ford always enjoyed directing comedy, so the film was a pleasant experience, but he seemed a little unsure about leading man Dan Dailey, who got jobs on the picture for a number of his hoofer friends. One day Ford came over and sat on the steps of Dailey's dressing room while Dailey and his friends were entertaining themselves. "You know," Ford finally said as he walked away, "this is a novel experience. It's the first time I've ever tried to make a picture without actors."

In July 1950, Ford and Mary celebrated their thirtieth anniversary. The party was held on the *Araner*, and Ford's 16mm camera memorialized the occasion. The day was at least semiformal; Ford wore a sport coat with his naval decorations prominently displayed. When Ward Bond arrived, he requested permission to come aboard, and received a drink for his troubles. In the afternoon, everyone seems to have taken a nap.

• • •

In the late '40s, Patrick Ford read a book by Stuart Cloete about the Boers' trek to form a land of their own in South Africa. He discussed it with his father, who seemed interested, but the difficulty in making the racist Boers sympathetic killed the story fairly quickly. That evolved into a discussion of an American equivalent—the Mormons' search for a land of their own. That story, Ford thought, had possibilities. Ford put his son and Frank Nugent on the script.

The back-to-back successes of *Fort Apache* and *She Wore a Yellow Ribbon* still hadn't erased the stain of *The Fugitive*. RKO took away the contractual rights of final cut that Ford had long enjoyed at Argosy and even at MGM when he made *3 Godfathers*. Now, Ford's contract stated that "The Corporation may add to, subtract from, arrange, re-arrange, revise and adapt all such material and the Picture in any manner, and the Director hereby waives the 'moral rights' of authors." It was standard contractual boilerplate, but it was the standard contractual boilerplate that had led Ford to form Argosy.

Argosy's money problems continued. The company needed $100,000 for preproduction, and had Jock Whitney guarantee the note. As collateral, they gave Whitney four insurance policies on Ford's life, and a $100,000 note from RKO for monies from *Mighty Joe Young*. The note was paid off within four months, just about the time that Argosy again went to Bankers Trust for a $650,000 loan that provided three fourths of the financing for *Wagon Master*, even though Argosy was only receiving 50 percent of the profits.

While Pat and Nugent worked on the script, Ford got the idea to make the film where the people in the story were headed, north of Mexican Hat, Utah. But that area was inaccessible for equipment and the facilities were too primitive even for Ford. Someone suggested that he think about Moab, a frontier town with plenty of frontier people. Years of carving by the relentless Colorado River on its way to Arizona and California had shaped Moab into a more intimate Monument Valley.

Ford approached the casting with a full measure of his casual confidence. Kathleen O'Malley had worked for Ford as a juvenile on *The Plough and the Stars*, and had gone to school with Barbara. She heard through the grapevine that John Wayne was about to start a picture and asked Ford to put in a word for her with Wayne.

"I don't do that to Duke, and he doesn't do that to me," replied Ford. "It's a pact."

O'Malley made some embarrassed noises and got up to go, when Ford suddenly said, "How'd you like to be in *my* next picture?"

"I'd like that best of all," said O'Malley.

"What have you been doing?"

"Working with the Three Stooges."

"Well," shot back Ford, "that's very good training."

Kathleen O'Malley was cast as the second female lead in *Wagon Master*. The budget was set at $999,370. Script costs were $29,024, and the highest-paid member of the cast was Ward Bond, at $20,000. With such a modest budget, Ford had to shoot the picture in no more than a month, and he made good headway every day, as on Thursday, December 15, when the unit began work at 9:00 A.M., got their first shot at 9:20, and quit at 3:50 P.M. after thirteen camera setups. Some days Ford would get as many as twenty-eight setups and quit early, but the fewest he ever got on a single day was ten.

Ford's instructions to Dobe Carey and Ben Johnson for their introductory scene were typical: "You boys are old friends—probably grew up near each other. You're going to do some horse trading in town, and then go have a few drinks. Just play it relaxed. Have a good time with it. It's a nice scene. Okay kids. Here we go. Ben, you're riding beside Dobe's wagon. Stay back here so you don't turn too far away from the camera. Okay, here we go. This will be picture!" One take, and on to the next shot.

Although Johnson was now a featured player, Ford refused to treat him as such. Johnson had to do his own riding for a sequence in which his character broke a horse. If Johnson had been thrown and hurt, the picture would have had to shut down, but it doesn't seem to have occurred to Ford.

Moab, Harry Carey Jr. remembered, "was a little teeny town. It had a motel up at the head of town and a gas station and a drugstore and we ate in an empty meeting hall with a caterer. The Colorado River didn't run through the town but right behind it, and that's the reason that Jack Ford liked it—because of the river crossings. He loved river crossings. The location was not as rough as Monument Valley because there were good roads."

"[Moab had] the greatest faces in the world," enthused Pat Ford. "I'd snap pictures of people and bring them home and he [would] look at them and say, 'These are what I want. These are the people I want.' Because he was a perfectionist. He wouldn't credit a Hollywood extra if he could do otherwise. He wouldn't use a Hollywood Indian when there was still a real Indian alive. 'I want stone-age faces. I want the faces of men that have seen people die of snake-bite, where babies die at childbirth, women die in childbirth, and guys die from being bucked off horses—just the life of a primitive people.' "

To while away the evenings, the company put on theatricals at the local high school. Rex Allen came up to provide some musical entertainment with the Sons of the Pioneers, followed by a parody production of Robert W. Service's "The Shooting of Dan McGrew," staged and narrated by John Ireland, who was there with his wife, Joanne Dru, *Wagon Master*'s leading lady.

Inspired by the surroundings, the production of *Wagon Master* was one of the most relaxed and enjoyable of Ford's career. He wrote Ollie Carey a note from location: "Dear Goldie, In haste—the Kid is really hitting his stride in this picture—he is really swell. Well, we can stop worrying about him—he's in. Affectionately, Jack."

Ford had heard the music of Stan Jones, a former park ranger who had written "[Ghost] Riders in the Sky," and had fallen hard. Jones was enlisted to write some songs for the picture, so much so that the movie threatened to become a Stan Jones concert with accompanying visuals. The songs sound more like mid–twentieth century Western music than nineteenth-century folk tunes, not that Ford cared. "Ford wasn't interested in things like that," said Harry Carey Jr. "If he fell in love with something he did it."

Besides the impromptu shows at night, there was Danny Borzage, as always serenading the cast and crew with his accordion. Borzage had different songs for different actors. As Ward Bond would arrive on the set, he would be greeted by "Wagons West Are Rolling," while Dobe would get "Streets of Laredo." After *The Grapes of Wrath*, Henry Fonda would always be greeted by "Red River Valley."

Throughout the production, Ford was in a benevolent mood that never seemed to crack. "He was very protective, very considerate, very patient," said Kathleen O'Malley. "I saw him be so kind with Charlie Kemper, who was having trouble with his lines one day. I was standing there watching to learn as much as I could. Mr. Ford looked at the cameraman and said, 'Oh, reloading,' and then walked away, giving Mr. Kemper a couple of minutes. Then he walked up and gave him some direction, then walked away. And Mr. Kemper did the scene immediately."

Another time, a Mormon who was working as an extra came up and introduced himself to Ford, who recognized the name as the same as that on a statue honoring a Moab man who had died in World War II. "Any relation?" asked Ford. "That was my son," said the man, who excused himself and walked away. Ford got up from the table and went and comforted the man. "He was good with anybody who needed to be protected," said Kathleen O'Malley. "Smart-mouths he didn't like. He was a real New Englander: very straight-arrow, no waste of time. Heart of gold."

Once again, Ford utilized stray dogs who hung around on the periphery of the set looking for food scraps. "These two dogs kept fighting and ruining takes," remembered Dobe Carey. "I had to fight a guy named Don Summers, but [Ford] didn't want a John Wayne fistfight, he wanted [us] rolling around in the dirt. So he said, 'Where's those two dogs that fight all the time? When Dobe and Don hit the ground, throw those dogs [at each other].' He wanted the dogs fighting at the same time that we were. So one dog tore the rear end out of Ward Bond's pants and the other dog ran back in the direction of Moab. They wouldn't fight. And that's the only time I ever saw John Ford show his teeth smiling. When Ward's pants got ripped out, he started to laugh. It was one of the funniest days I've ever spent on a movie set."

Wagon Master has the amiable feel of a family folk tale. Ford recalled Alan Mowbray to encore his characterization of an endearing ham from *My Darling Clementine*. One day at breakfast, Mowbray turned to the others at the table and said, "I feel so guilty eating. I feel all these American eyes on me, and they're all saying, 'Lend lease, lend lease, lend lease.' "

It's the only Ford film to start with a scene rather than the credits, a robbery that establishes the cold-blooded capabilities of the marauding Cleggs. And then, as with the Clantons in *My Darling Clementine*, we forget all about them for half the picture as Ford immerses us in the resolute strength of the Mormons and the two amiable horse-traders who are guiding them. It's an easeful picture that takes its lead from the calm leading actors. "Be gentle," says Johnson to his restless horses, and Ford seems to have taken the admonition to heart. Except for the unusually intense spasms of violence in the last third of the film, it's among Ford's most warmhearted movies.

At long last, there was a starring part for Ward Bond, who was more than up to it. Charles Kemper, an occasional social friend of Ford's, is properly chilling as Shiloh Clegg, leader of the family that are the snakes in the wagon train's Eden, and another of Ford's unusually convincing depictions of degenerate patriarchs.

Wagon Master is a lyrical ballad, an affirmation of Ford's folk vision of America, where a dance or a graveside ceremony speaks more for the communally spirited pioneers than all the dramatic battles in the world. The motivation of most Ford heroes is social, not personal; journeys and wanderings, not vengeful quests for retribution—group odysseys.

Ford's Westerns are more about the West itself than they are about Western heroes. Ford's West is a West you can believe in, a West of splintered floors and ragged, resolute people. Westerns were really Ford's vision of an idealized America—a democratic community of equals unified by shared purpose.

The little pony reaching dry land in the last shot of *Wagon Master* affirms the film's place in Ford's gallery of optimistic visions; the satanic

Clegg are vanquished by collective action, and a natural order is restored. It was one of the last times Ford would be able to summon a positive vision of the West. He would increasingly turn to a much darker, even savage outlook; optimism could only be summoned for movies about traditional, settled societies—the Old South in *The Sun Shines Bright*, Ireland in *The Quiet Man*.

For the rest of his life, Ford retained an affection for *Wagon Master*, to such an extent that he would nostalgically reminisce about it. "One night," remembered Pat Ford, "sitting around [on *Mogambo*] we were having a devil of a time, with Ava Gardner and Grace Kelly at each other's throats and playing for position . . . and the subject of *Wagon Master* came up. And I guess he said more about it that night than any other [picture] I remember. How he loved making it, and how he loved the people up there, and loved the scenery. . . . *Wagon Master* was pure of heart, and simple and good, and Frank Nugent and I were pure of heart and simple and good when we wrote it, and maybe John Ford was too."

Fort Apache amassed a world gross of $4.33 million on costs of $2.14 million and stood as RKO's most successful release for the year. *She Wore a Yellow Ribbon* did nearly as well. But it wasn't enough; according to RKO's accounting, neither picture made enough to make much of a dent in the debt from *The Fugitive*.

In March 1949, Merian Cooper began trimming the Argosy staff. In July, Cooper wrote a letter to Louis B. Mayer investigating the possibility of a long-term alliance with MGM. "Quite frankly, the most happy association that I have had since I returned from the war has been with you," wrote Cooper. "I have a definite six-picture offer from another studio but would most surely like to talk to you, because Ford and I want to stick to high quality product . . . and would appreciate your talking to us if you care to, at your earliest convenience." The fairly transparent story about a competing studio failed to fool a wise old fox like Mayer, who preferred in-house production anyway.

In September, Argosy asked RKO for a two-year grace period before they had to repay RKO's $306,000 advance for *The Fugitive*, which, with interest, now stood at $341,074. By late 1949, when Argosy went to the bank to finance *Wagon Master*, all of Argosy's pictures, with the exception of *3 Godfathers*, were cross-collateralized—any money that came in went first to the banks, secondly to RKO, and only then to Argosy. The company was slowly asphyxiating.

After slightly more than three and a half years with Argosy, Don Dewar resigned in August of 1950, and wasn't replaced; his duties were divided between Cooper and secretary-treasurer Lee Van Hoozer. As of October 1950, Argosy owed $332,000 to the bank on *The Fugitive*, and the $341,074 to RKO for the same picture. The bank loans for *Fort Apache* and *She Wore a Yellow Ribbon* were both paid off, but Argosy owed RKO $405,000, plus interest, on the latter picture, and owed the bank $320,000 on *Wagon Master*, and $50,000 on *Mighty Joe Young*. On top of Argosy's indebtedness to the banks and RKO, there was $160,000 in notes issued in 1946 for general corporate overhead and $235,000 owed to Ford and Cooper for unpaid salary.

Casting about for positive spin, Lee Van Hoozer, Argosy's treasurer, noted, "*Fort Apache* became a profit picture only after three years time. After a like period of time, it is possible that both *Yellow Ribbon* and *Wagon Master* will be in a profit position." Actually, it was more than possible, it was certain, but Argosy didn't have three years to wait.

In December 1950, Ford and Cooper both agreed to indefinitely defer their weekly compensation from Argosy ($3,000 for Ford, $1,000 for Cooper) in order to assist the company "through a financial crisis." By March 1951, Lee Van Hoozer was reporting that "some [bank] loans are not only matured, but approach 'outlaw' status."

Part of the problem was the flagrant chicanery that has always been part of the movie business. *She Wore a Yellow Ribbon* had cost $1.85 million, of which Argosy supplied $960,000, borrowed at 5 percent interest. By the early 1950s, the picture's worldwide gross was $4 million. According to RKO's books, Argosy's share of the profits was the minute figure of $13,000.

Likewise, there were problems with *3 Godfathers*. Although the picture had done well, it had not done quite as well as *Fort Apache*. After an equivalent release period, *3 Godfathers* was nearly $100,000 behind *Fort Apache*. To pay off one of their notes, Argosy was waiting for one of their bonus checks for $100,000 that MGM would give them as soon as the picture returned domestic rentals of $1.94 million. Bankers Trust agreed to carry Argosy past the due date. At that point, *3 Godfathers* was $20,383.79 short of the total they needed to get their $100,000.

Argosy might have repaid the loan and waited to be reimbursed by MGM, but they clearly didn't have the $100,000. By the end of June 1950, Bankers Trust was again nudging Argosy about nudging Metro to find a couple of friendly exhibitors to play the picture. "If you could dig up a little specific evidence that MGM was not selling the picture," wrote one banker on June 30, "and would not sell it, I think you could get your money pretty quickly."

The picture was still playing off to the tune of $4,700 a month, so Argosy asked the bank to sit tight. By August 18, the picture had domestic rentals of $1.938 million, but in October the bank still hadn't gotten their money. Finally, on December 20, MGM shipped a check for $100,000 directly to Bankers Trust, along with a hearty wish for a Merry Christmas.

Argosy was living a hand-to-mouth existence. With no better offers on the table, in January 1950, Argosy signed a three-picture deal with Republic. It was, said John Wayne's son Michael, "The last game in town."

Republic was run by an ex-tobacco salesman named Herbert Yates and was considered to be the largest, most stable of the B movie studios, usually generating yearly profits in the vicinity of $600,000 to $700,000. Although modestly successful, it was still a B movie studio; compared to Paramount or MGM, Republic was very thinly capitalized, no more than two consecutive bad years away from bankruptcy. Ford was walking into a cheapjack filmmaking environment very similar to the bad old days at Universal.

Republic's films were divided into four categories: "Jubilee" pictures were cheap seven-day Westerns made for around $50,000 (some of these were being directed by Phil Ford, Frank's son, Jack's nephew); "Anniversary" pictures were shot in fourteen days and had budgets of $200,000; "Deluxe" pictures were shot in twenty-two days and budgeted around $500,000; and then came "Premiere," a recently created category that Yates had designed in order to compete with the major studios in theaters that usually couldn't be bothered with Republic's product. Republic's Premiere pictures were being directed by Orson Welles (*Macbeth*), Allan Dwan (*Sands of Iwo Jima*), Ben Hecht (*Specter of the Rose*), and Lewis Milestone (*The Red Pony*)—A-list talent coming to Republic to make movies they couldn't make anywhere else. Schedules ran around thirty days and the pictures could cost around a million dollars.

The Argosy-Republic contract specified that the pictures were to be made within a two-year period beginning March 6, 1950, that none of the pictures was to exceed $1.25 million in budget or ten thousand feet in length. Republic paid for the production of the pictures, but, except for the odd proviso that the studio would cover the salaries of two secretaries, Argosy had to pay the rest of their expenses themselves. Since Argosy already knew what their production plans were, they decided to cut their losses. The story department was closed, and the company began sending back all story submissions without even bothering to make copies.

There were no provisions for salaries; Ford and Cooper were idealistically committed to the idea that they could survive based on the 50 percent of the profits that Republic would pay Argosy, with Republic advancing Argosy $200,000 per picture against profits.

Republic's distribution fee was set at 25 percent. Either party had the right to cancel the agreement after the first picture. After the humiliating experience of RKO retaining final cut on *Wagon Master*, the Republic deal gave Ford his autonomy back.

Despite final cut, working for Republic was a step down that Ford never would have taken had it not been the only way to get *The Quiet Man* made. The news of the unlikely alliance raised a few eyebrows; Hedda Hopper breathlessly termed it "shattering." For public consumption, Herbert Yates released a statement saying that "This was no sudden decision. We've been thinking about the merger for a long time. This is a great thing for our company."

In August 1950, Cooper wrote to Ned Depinet, sales manager of RKO. "I am very anxious to get our loans paid off. Would it be possible for you to personally push a reissue in the art theaters of *The Fugitive?* I think there might be some real play in it.

"I do hope you are getting behind *Wagon Master, She Wore a Yellow Ribbon* and *Mighty Joe Young* also, and will use your good offices to get as much money unfrozen abroad as possible."

By October 1950, Argosy's debt had been paid down to about $209,000—$169,000 in outstanding loans plus $40,000 interest. As motion pictures went in 1950, this was not an enormous amount. Still, Cooper must have felt that the possibility of retiring it any time in the foreseeable future would be difficult, if not impossible. At Republic, Ford was going to make another cavalry picture to allow him to make *The Quiet Man.* But Cooper was undoubtedly projecting financial returns from *The Quiet Man* that would be equivalent to Ford's other prestige projects—*The Long Voyage Home* and *The Fugitive.* Any profits from the cavalry picture would be eaten up by *The Quiet Man.* He was getting sick of scrounging.

Part of Argosy's problem was blocked funds, whereby movie companies couldn't take all the monies their pictures earned out of the foreign countries where the picture played. For instance, Ford's *Rio Grande* would earn $231,970.49 in England, but $165,576.68 of that stayed there. In Italy, the picture earned $122,000, all of which stayed there.

This practice posed considerable problems for a large motion picture company—MGM set up a British operation largely to make use of the accumulated blocked funds, which is just what the British government had in mind. For an independent concern like Argosy, which was trying to pay off the bank notes for one picture before another picture was launched, this practice was deadly—the difference between profit and loss could be locked in bank vaults between Argentina and Australia.

While all this maneuvering was going on, Ford was in Korea working on *This Is Korea!* a fifty-minute documentary Ford talked Republic into releasing to minimal response. Ford went over with Mark Armistead, but he soon gravitated to Lewis "Chesty" Puller, the most famous Marine of them all.

Armistead noticed once again Ford's gift of instant empathy that could kick in whenever he chose. "His genius was his ability to talk and argue with Koreans, Japanese, black people, Germans—within three minutes, they would talk to him at their level. He never was a linguist, but he always had a few words in any language at that level . . . he knew how the people really thought and felt in their hearts."

By February, Ford and Armistead were in Tokyo, where Ford began drinking, and Armistead and a couple of enlisted men had to devote most of their time to taking care of their commander. By the end of the month, Ford was back at Republic.

"Too many hours in the air catapulting and landing on carriers, helicopters and especially climbing mountains," Ford wrote his new friend Michael Killanin. "I've never climbed so many damned mountains in my life. However, I'm bright eyed and bushy tailed at the moment and working hard."

The time spent making *This Is Korea!* was charged to Ford's military service, and he earned an Air Medal. He promptly retired, thereby advancing one grade. John Ford was now an admiral.

Finally, Ford and Cooper gave up the struggle. Cooper proposed giving RKO ownership of the pictures Argosy had released through them in return for the studio paying off the bank notes. The negotiations took months, largely because of the participation that Leo McCarey's Rainbow Pictures had bought with a loan of $360,000 for *Fort Apache*. While Argosy had paid off the loan with interest, they had failed to get a release of the mortgage. Rainbow, which had been bought by Paramount, was entitled to 7½ percent of the net on the picture. In late April, Paramount offered to sell out their percentage for $40,000, half of it in blocked sterling, but Argosy was in no position to pay even $20,000 to anybody. As a result, RKO looked long and hard at the deal.

Finally, attorney Ole Doering wired Cooper "CLOSING ACCOMPLISHED THIS MORNING." Argosy sold RKO *The Fugitive, Fort Apache, She Wore a Yellow Ribbon, Mighty Joe Young,* and *Wagon Master*. All they received in return was a clean bill of financial health, for RKO agreed to pay off the outstanding bank debt in return for ownership of the pictures (at that point, loans for *The Fugitive* and *Wagon Master* were still outstanding) and accrued interest, less $79,000 that Argosy had already paid.

The pictures were not free and clear: for *The Fugitive*, Henry Fonda owned 7½ percent of the net, because he had done the picture for $50,000 instead of his usual $100,000; on *Fort Apache*, besides Rainbow's percentage, Wayne owned 6 percent, as did Fonda. *Wagon Master* and *She Wore a Yellow Ribbon* had no percentage partners, but *Mighty Joe Young* owed Schoedsack $12,000 in deferments, while his wife, Ruth Rose, had a piece of the net, as did Willis O'Brien.

RKO agreed to all the percentages, although they capped some of them off. With hindsight, Cooper and Ford must have been furious; had they held on for another two or three years, the proceeds from *The Quiet Man* would have paid off all of Argosy's debts and allowed the company to retain ownership of their films, providing Ford and Cooper with a corporate and personal patrimony.

Still, a deal was a deal, and John Ford always tended to look forward to the next picture. "I am very glad, as I know you are, that we have got this behind us," Ole Doering wrote Cooper on May 28, 1951. "Please tell Jack I hope to see him when he comes through New York on his way to Ireland."

CHAPTER TWENTY-ONE

John Ford and Cecil B. DeMille never quite meshed, but then strong-willed patriarchs seldom do. The famous Directors Guild imbroglio between Ford and DeMille in 1950 had its roots in a confrontation over Communism that began nearly three years earlier. It was a doubly ironic set-to, if only because DeMille, according to Edward Dmytryk, had not attended a Guild meeting since his highly publicized fight with the American Federation of Radio Artists (AFRA) over a one-dollar-a-year union surcharge.

Ford's involvement with the Guild had also lessened over the years since he helped found it, but he was still serving on the board of directors during the first wave of hearings held by the House Committee on Un-American Activities. On October 11, 1947, Mabel Walker Willebrandt, counsel to the Guild, dictated a memo to Ford so that he could be up to speed on what was happening in Washington. She gave him a complete list of the people subpoenaed by HUAC, as well as some of the films the committee was objecting to. Among them, wrote Willebrandt, was "*Margie*, which I never heard of, *The Best Years of Our Lives*, if you can believe it (particularly the drug store scene in that film)," *Song of Russia*, *Mission to Moscow*, and *The North Star*.

After outlining her suggestions as to how to handle the situation, Willebrandt told Ford, "One more word of caution—I do not want this memorandum mimeographed or passed around or copied and distributed. Nothing except the list of names are you authorized to use."

On October 20, 1947, the opening day of the hearings, only so-called friendly witnesses were called, among them Sam Wood, archconservative and founder, in 1944, of the Motion Picture Alliance for the Preservation of American Ideals. The Alliance had a strong tilt toward MGM; the president was Sam Wood, and the officers included such Metro stalwarts as Cedric Gibbons, Norman Taurog, Clarence Brown, and James Kevin McGuinness. The first vice president of the Alliance was Walt Disney, and the executive committee included more MGM veterans like Victor Fleming, Arnold Gillespie, King Vidor, and Robert Vogel.

In his testimony on the opening day of the hearings, Sam Wood charged that Communists had infiltrated the Directors Guild. "Among those who tried to steer us into the Red River," Wood testified, "were directors John Cromwell, Frank Tuttle, Irving Pichel and Edward Dmytryk."

The next day Dmytryk, Pichel, Herbert Biberman, Robert Rossen, and Lewis Milestone, in Washington, fired off an outraged telegram to Guild president George Stevens: "We received a copy of your wire to Thomas Committee in which you urged that the Committee give us 'Fair Play.' This is how we got it! Today, one of our attorneys believing with us, and you, that any Citizen has the privilege of cross-examination, attempted to ask [HUAC committee chairman J. Parnell] Thomas for that right, and was forcibly thrown out of the Committee Room. All indications thus far point to the complete domination of the Screen either by the Thomas Committee if they can achieve it, or by their acknowledged fifth column in Hollywood, the Motion Picture Alliance.

"Wood's intent to destroy the Director's Guild is clearly indicated in . . . his testimony. . . . In our opinion, only action which can prevent subjugation of the Guild and the industry to the Thomas Committee or the Motion Picture Alliance is the immediate arrival here of an official delegation from Screen Director's Guild to demand opportunity to refute Wood's perjured testimony."

On October 21, a meeting of the Directors Guild board of directors was held in which a furious William Wyler said that "I think everybody knows that the Director's Guild was never in danger of being taken over by Communism and, in my opinion, the Screen Director's Guild should refute the statement and take Mr. Wood to task for uttering it. He can speak for himself but not for the Guild. I resent it very, very deeply."

Ford, normally a member of the embattled middle, a man who, said Stephen Longstreet, "had no interest in politics unless it was Irish politics," was nudged into action by the foolishness of Wood's testimony, and the feeling among many that the underlying motive behind the Motion Picture Alliance was to return to the days of fifteen years before, when the guilds were nothing but house unions for the studios.

"Of all the pictures made in Hollywood," Ford said waggishly during the board meeting, "there is only one I have seen that smacked of Communism and followed the 'party line'. . . . The little number called *For Whom the Bell Tolls* [directed by Sam Wood]. That followed the Marxist line right on down. I don't know Sam Wood but I read these preposterous statements in the papers. What can we do? . . . This discussion can go on for hours. I would suggest as chairman of the Committee that you write down a simple two line statement just saying Mr. Wood's statement is untrue and send a copy to Parnell Thomas and to Millie [Lewis Milestone]."

It wasn't that easy; there were members of the board who believed Wood was right, among them Lesley Selander: "I've had doubts in my mind regarding three or four Board Members in the past. They're left-handed in my mind."

"Left-handed," said Ford. "You mean Communists?"

"I don't say Communists. They just don't think the way I do, or the way they really should think regarding our Government and our laws."

"But, regarding the Guild itself? . . . Listen, I'm a Roman Catholic and a state of Maine Republican."

". . . [Sam Wood] said this Guild was almost taken over," said Selander. "Can we prove that it wasn't?"

At this point William Wyler spoke up. After pointedly noting that he and Ford were absent—i.e., at war—most of the time John Cromwell was president of the Directors Guild, Wyler asked, "Was John Cromwell a good, reliable, dutiful President of the Guild or was he not?" The response was that Selander and some unnamed others felt that Cromwell had done things he shouldn't have done, sent telegrams that he shouldn't have sent—not as president of the Guild, but as John Cromwell, citizen.

Ford amplified on the tack Wyler was taking. "My objection to this whole thing is that Wood's stand was in bad taste. As a guild member I think like Willie and resent it very, very much. I object to calling names. Right and left and center of the road. There is no such thing if we live up to the context of our Constitution. I mean we're all liberal because it's a liberal Constitution. Thomas Jefferson was possibly the greatest of all liberals and he was considered a leftist at that time."

The meeting grew heated, with the normally mild-mannered Wyler finally saying that while Wood had the right to say that Communists almost took over the Guild, he, Wyler, also had the right to issue a statement saying it was a "goddamned lie." Ford attempted to give each side a piece of the loaf: "I admire Les's stand, and I won't agree to any motion unless it is unanimous and I won't agree unless it is signed by George Stevens. Otherwise I'll have to be a dissenting vote myself."

After more deliberation and argument, the following telegram was sent to Joe Martin, Speaker of the House, and J. Parnell Thomas: "The Board of Directors of the Screen Director's Guild feels called upon to deny the testimony of Mr. Sam Wood regarding communistic activity in the

Screen Director's Guild and it is our considered belief that Mr. Wood's remarks are without foundation."

Sam Wood didn't take this rebuke lightly. On October 23, he fired off an angry letter to George Stevens demanding a retraction. A coolly amused Stevens replied on October 24: "In your letter you do not go on to make clear your reason as to the grounds for such a retraction. If, as appears quite possible from the tone, it is based on the presumption that it is the responsibility of the Guild president to act on your personal orders, I would like to re-acquaint you with the fact that the Guild President is governed by the wishes of a Board, and the Board by the wishes of the membership, a democratic formula which has my compliance and respect. . . ."

It was at this time that Stevens came into open conflict with Cecil B. DeMille. During one meeting, DeMille turned on Stevens and said, "I've been fighting this [Communist] problem here in Los Angeles, what have you done?"

"While you were making your capital gains, I was in Bastogne," replied Stevens. DeMille "went up like a skyrocket," according to Stevens, and that was that.

While Ford, Stevens, and Wyler were winning the skirmish in Los Angeles, the war was being lost in Washington, and that was reflected in the fact that the Screen Directors Guild stopped stenographer's transcripts of meetings of either the general membership or the board of directors, lest the material be subpoenaed.

While Ford was not as liberal in the late 1940s as he had been in the mid-1930s, the rampaging sensibilities of his right-wing friends irritated him. Harry Carey Jr. remembered a time during the shooting of *She Wore a Yellow Ribbon* when much of the stock company was complaining that Roosevelt and Truman were fellow travelers interested only in confiscatory taxation that would hand over all private assets to the state. Ford was passing by and stopped. "I don't know what you guys are talking about," he said. "You all became millionaires off Roosevelt." No one could contradict him. In 1948, Ford voted for Harry Truman.

In 1949, Sam Wood died of a heart attack at least partially brought on by his mania for anti-Communism. By 1950, fear was crippling the industry. Current or onetime members of the Communist Party had been sent to prison, and the blacklist had spread out from there into areas of paranoia and mistaken identity that would have been comic under other circumstances—the director Mark Robson was graylisted because somebody mixed him up with Paul Robeson.

DeMille's conservatism had hardened. He refused to hire Burt Lancaster for the part of a trapeze artist in his new picture, *The Greatest Show on Earth*, simply because someone had told him that Lancaster, besides being an ex–circus acrobat and perfect for the part, was a Communist.

Ford's politics were also in flux, seemingly prone to whoever spoke to him last. A 1950 press release of the Motion Picture Alliance called for the registration of all Communists in the Los Angeles area because "the existence of a shooting war against Communists [in Korea] constitutes the clear and present danger which the United States Supreme Court recognizes as justifying action for the protection of our lives and our institutions."

Listed on the masthead of the organization were John Wayne, Hedda Hopper, Morrie Ryskind, Clarence Brown, Ward Bond, Gary Cooper, Clark Gable, Cedric Gibbons, John Lee Mahin, Leo McCarey, James Kevin McGuinness, Adolphe Menjou, Pat O'Brien, Robert Taylor, Herbert Yates, and, on the executive committee, John Ford.

What brought DeMille and Ford into direct conflict was the matter of a loyalty oath mandated for union officers by the Taft-Hartley Act. Directors Guild president Joseph L. Mankiewicz had signed, but DeMille wanted to go a step further and mandate that every member of the Guild sign an oath as well; he also thought that every director should file a report about the political convictions of the writers and actors on every film he made.

These proposals were defeated by a vote, not of the general membership, but of the board of directors—Seymour Berns, Claude Binyon, Frank Borzage, Clarence Brown, David Butler, Merian Cooper, DeMille, Harvey Dwight, Ford, Tay Garnett, Walter Lang, Frank McDonald, John F. Murphy, Mark Robson, William Seiter, Richard Wallace, and John Waters.

The internal dynamics of the Guild were deeply split. Beneath Mankiewicz were Albert Rogell and Lesley Selander, as, respectively, first and second vice presidents, and Vernon Keays as secretary. All were committed DeMille acolytes. As Robert Wise remembered, "The bottom line was that DeMille was trying to take over the Guild."

While Clarence Brown was certainly a committed conservative— "Chaplin was as red as that tablecloth," he once roared to the author—as was Frank Capra, he seems to have taken no active part in the loyalty oath matter. Nor did any other A-list director. Those who did—Rogell, Selander—were marginal directors of B movies, and it is highly possible that there was an element of careerist toadying in their willingness to serve DeMille.

That summer of 1950, Mankiewicz was in Europe taking a vacation when the board passed a bylaw mandating the compulsory loyalty oath for the entire membership. DeMille's faction then sent the already adopted bylaw for a "courtesy" vote on the part of the membership, on a signed ballot. There was a space for yes, a space for no, and a space for the voter's name. The intimidation factor was obvious. The measure passed, 547 to 14, with 57 abstentions.

Mankiewicz returned from vacation and was enraged to discover what had been pushed through in his absence. When he asked Al Rogell what had been the hurry, Rogell answered that all the guilds and unions in Hollywood were going to institute similar rules, and "we [the board of directors] wanted to lead the way." Mankiewicz nevertheless expressed his outrage to anyone who asked, invoking the term "blacklist."

Mankiewicz wanted to call a meeting in which the entire membership could discuss the loyalty oath and the open ballot. As the DeMille faction wrote in a lawsuit, "Mr. Mankiewicz has . . . pitted himself against the legal governing body of the Guild, its Board of Directors. He repudiates the democratic vote of its membership. . . . He stands with 14 against 547. The issue is whether Mr. Mankiewicz is to rule the Guild." The lawsuit was brought by DeMille, Clarence Brown, David Butler, Frank Capra, Tay Garnett, Henry King, George Marshall, Leo McCarey, Frank McDonald, Albert Rogell, William Seiter, Lesley Selander, Andrew Stone, Richard Wallace, and John Waters.

Simultaneously with the lawsuit, the DeMille faction launched a petition to recall Mankiewicz—which needed a 60 percent affirmative vote to pass. Signing the petition were Al Rogell, John Waters, Jules White, Derwin Abrahams, DeMille, Leo McCarey, Frank Capra, William Seiter, Henry King, and Tay Garnett. Eleven of the fifteen members of the board also signed the recall petition. Ford was not among them.

The DeMille faction sent out telegrams announcing the recall on October 13, explaining that, according to the bylaws, the vice president was empowered to act in the absence of the president, and Mankiewicz had been out of the country when this pressing matter that couldn't be tabled for a few weeks came up.

A quick response was organized, demanding a special meeting of the Guild membership within ten days of receiving the petition. Word of the counterpetition must have reached the DeMille faction because the offices of the Guild were unaccountably closed the next day, Saturday, in a stalling tactic. As Robert Parrish remembered, "The petition had to be signed, notarized and turned in to the executive secretary of the guild before the DeMille recall votes were counted, or all was lost." A quick consultation was held with Martin Gang, the best lawyer in Hollywood. He pointed out that according to the bylaws of the Guild, a member had to sign a loyalty oath to be in good standing and they had to find twenty-five men to sign such a statement. It was a classic catch-22; Mankiewicz couldn't be saved without twenty-five people acquiescing to the very thing to which they were adamantly opposed.

The Mankiewicz faction went out in search of live bodies. "We scoured the fleshpots, the gin mills, the Beverly Hills homes, and the fancy restaurants looking for movie directors who hated the non-Communist oath but were willing to sign it to save Joe Mankiewicz's Guild presidency," wrote Robert Parrish. Walter Reisch, the last signatory, was cornered in a booth at Chasen's. The others were John Huston, H. C. Potter, Edward L. Cahn, Michael Gordon, Andrew Marton, George Seaton, Maxwell Shane, Mark Robson, Richard Brooks, John Sturges, Felix Feist, Robert Wise, Robert Parrish, Otto Lang, Richard Fleischer, Fred Zinnemann, Joseph Losey, William Wyler, Jean Negulesco, Nicholas Ray, Billy Wilder, Don Hartman, Charles Vidor, and John Farrow. (One of the most interesting aspects of this imbroglio is its generational nature; the most conservative members of the Guild tended to be industry pioneers, while the centrists or liberals were twenty and thirty years younger.)

Everyone seems to have known that the resolution would not be through the courts, but through confrontation. The counterpetition was notarized and filed in time; the special meeting of the entire Guild membership was set for Sunday night, October 22, 1950, at 8:00 P.M. in the Crystal Room of the Beverly Hills Hotel.

In keeping with the practice of the Guild for the previous several years, no official transcript was made of the meeting, which meant that, until now, reports of the proceedings were anecdotal, accurate only in the broad, emotional sense. But, as common sense indicated, there was indeed a stenographer present, and the transcript has survived in a private archive. The full story of this historic meeting is now known.

"This meeting," Joe Mankiewicz stated in his opening remarks, "can become very easily the most important in our history. It is entirely up to us whether we shall remember this night with satisfaction and pride or whether it shall be remembered as the night we lost the Guild."

After a thorough and largely impartial recitation of the events that had led up to the meeting, Mankiewicz turned the floor over to Cecil B. DeMille. "Mr. President," began the venerable showman, "I first want to compliment the President on his splendid presentation of events that have led to an unfortunate but not an irreparable situation. . . . I have come before you neither to praise Caesar or to bury him, and I have only one interest at heart in this, and that is the interest of the Guild. There is nothing I want from the Guild. There is nothing the Guild can give me. I do not seek any office, nor would I accept any office . . . my race is nearing its end. It is at the last lap, so that I have nothing to gain but the welfare of this body."

DeMille had quickly taken the temperature of the room and hadn't liked the results. He was rather more conciliatory than was his custom. He called the members who had signed the petition for the meeting, "25 or 30 sensitive, honorable, good Americans who feel there is no necessity to sign such papers . . .

"It has never been the Board's intention to create a black list," he said. "The only purpose of the oath is to give assurance to the men who join this Guild that they are joining a clean organization and to give assurance to the industry and to the country that the men who directed their pictures are not afraid or ashamed to declare their loyalty to the United States. Is that too much to ask? . . . I would be happy to take that oath once a week.

"No one has accused Mr. Mankiewicz of being a Communist. When I nominated him for President of this Guild, I thought he was a good American and I still think he is a good American. As an individual member of this Guild, he has every right to oppose this by-law, and he had every right to refuse to take the oath, but he had no right to use his office as President to obstruct the will of the Guild and to cast forth damaging accusations at its Board of Directors and its members. That and that alone was the reason for the move to recall Mr. Mankiewicz."

So far DeMille was on reasonably solid ground, and was arguing his case cogently and well. And then he made a fatal mistake. "Who are some of these gentlemen [who signed the petition in support of Mankiewicz]? One of them was Chairman of a testimonial dinner for the Hollywood 'ten.' Five of them were on the Committee for the First Amendment. One of them was on the Board of the Actors Lab. Two of them were on the Committee of Arts, Sciences and Professions and another on its predecessor, the Hollywood Democratic Committee. One was a sponsor of the Hollywood League for Democratic Action. The Freedom from Fear Committee was represented. So was the old league of American Writers School. Troubled waters attracted strange specimens sometimes. I am making no accusations against anybody, least of all Mr. Mankiewicz."

It was around this point that DeMille read out the names of the men who had signed the petition to call the meeting, emphasizing, in many cases, their foreign origins—"Villiam Vyler," etc. Although this moment is not preserved in the transcript, everybody still alive who was there says that DeMille did in fact do it, alienating all those in the middle of the argument.

"DeMille didn't have any support among the rank and file," said Richard Fleischer, who had signed the petition demanding the special meeting. "When DeMille took over on the stage, he read the names of the people that had signed the petition to hold the meeting. Myself, Bob Wise, Mark Robson, among others. He read the names, and emphasized their foreignness, the Jewishness of the names, ridiculing them. And then he implied that they were all Communists. It was an outrageous thing to say."

And now, the booing began. DeMille forged ahead. "Is it their object to split this Guild wide open so that the Daily Worker and Pravda can gloat over the spectacle? Do they want to widen the breach between the President and the Board of Directors until members of the Board will resign and leave the door open for these repudiated elements to return to power?"

After throwing around implications of guilt by association, DeMille offered a resolution—that the balloting to recall Mankiewicz be closed and that all the ballots be destroyed without being counted. In effect, he was immediately capitulating, not to the extent of repealing the issue of the loyalty oath, but in letting Mankiewicz stay on. As DeMille ended his speech, Robert Wise was very nervous. As he put it, "DeMille was a very articulate guy." The question of who would carry the day was very much in doubt.

At this point the meeting was thrown open to the membership. For the next four hours, famous men stood up and expressed bafflement, rage, hostility, and sorrow. John Cromwell said that he was "astounded at the acrimonious accusations, the unfounded accusations of Mr. DeMille." Don Hartman said that he resented "paper hat patriots who stand up and holler 'I am an American' and that no one else is." John Huston, openly contemptuous, asked DeMille, "In your tabulation of the 25 [petitioners] how many men were in uniform? How many were in uniform when you were wrapping yourself in the flag?" Delmer Daves stood up and said, "I am a Republican too, Mr. DeMille. My children are fourth-generation Californians, and I resent beyond belief the things that you said as you summarized the 25 men. . . . I think it was disgraceful."

Leo McCarey, a signer of the petition to recall Mankiewicz, stood up and, using a particularly unfortunate metaphor, said "it was a fire, and maybe we used the wrong nozzle."

"As far as using the wrong nozzle is concerned," Joe Mankiewicz retorted, "I am the only one who got wet."

Rouben Mamoulian announced that he was "a little nervous standing up here tonight. . . . It is my accent. I have an accent. The very first accent heard tonight was that of Fritz Lang. I don't remember any time when a fellow director had to get up and before expressing what he had to say he had to declare himself to be an honest, reputable man. He has to mention how far back he goes of any generations to be born in this country. That leaves me hanging in the air, because I was not born in this country. I came here, and I am a naturalized citizen. . . . I feel for me that I have more reason to stand on my being a good American because I chose it. I wanted to be an American, and I would not want anyone challenging my being a good American, so I will forget the embarrassing feeling or being shy about my accent."

George Seaton reminded DeMille of a meeting he witnessed, wherein DeMille walked into studio head Frank Freeman's office to discuss a Guild meeting of the previous day and was told by Freeman that, "C.B., Joe Mankiewicz is no more a Communist than you are."

Freeman's vote of confidence was heartwarming but irrelevant. What was relevant, as Seaton well knew, was DeMille's serving as a conduit to powerful producers, the bête noir of the Directors Guild. Seaton's story prompted William Wellman to stand up and say, "I don't like to go to dinner, the very few times I go to dinner, and hear producers and actors and their wives talk about a subject that concerns the Directors Guild, and they knew a great deal more about it than I did. Where they got it, I don't know. . . . Let Mr. Mankiewicz stay as President. He is a good guy. He is very capable."

George Stevens, a figure of probity respected by left and right alike, and a member of the board of directors, stood up and gave a background briefing about the recall petition. "Mr. Mankiewicz' recall was done in such a manner that no Board member that wasn't part of it could find out anything about it. It was rigged, and it was organized, and it was supposed to work. And, gentlemen, it hasn't."

With DeMille's offer to take back the recall petition still hanging in the air, Don Hartman asked if DeMille would be willing to rescind the charges he had made against the signers of the petition, "which were just as unfounded, which were without any investigation, which were done by insinuation and association, which is the method of rabble rousers."

Having already been pulled through a brier patch, DeMille obstinately refused to let go. "The organizations to which they belong . . . [are] a matter of record in the Capitol. That is not guess-work or hearsay. And the members seem to have admitted membership in these organizations . . . one of those organizations is listed as subversive by the Attorney General of the United States. One is declared to be in the Kenney Report, the Voice of the Communist Party, etc. So these violent attacks that have been going on against me, I don't know whether they are a smoke-screen to cover the issue or not. . . . I am a little astounded that the attack has turned so completely against me, but I have taken attacks before, and I will have to take this one, I presume. I cannot retract it, because my statement is fact."

Don Hartman stood up and asked for DeMille's resignation from the Directors Guild. John Cromwell seconded the motion. William Wyler stood up and said, "I am one of the 25. . . . [According to DeMille] I am a 'Commie' although I tell you that I am not, and I have signed two oaths to that effect. . . . I am sick and tired of having people question my loyalty to my country. The next time I hear somebody do it, I am going to kick the hell out of him. I don't care how old he is or how big.

"I have seen guys that have jobs that are conservative Republicans— good Americans—and they are scared today, because they are not quite as conservative as they are asked to be by the group that is trying to run this Guild. . . . What the Hell is this? Everybody gets up and tries to clear himself. Why? How was this fear spread? Why is it? I think it is absolutely appalling."

Through all of this, Ford sat silently on an aisle, wearing a baseball cap and untied sneakers. "As the waves of emotion rolled over the members," remembered Robert Parrish, "from time to time he would put the pipe away, take out a dirty handkerchief, wipe his glasses with it, and then chew on it for a while. He was an important man in the Guild, and everyone wondered what he thought." As Andre de Toth would note, Ford was universally respected and envied, not just because of his pictures, but because of his authority and assurance—"those things that the weaklings never had."

Finally, at around 1:00 in the morning, Joe Mankiewicz said, "John Ford has to be heard." Ford rose deliberately to his feet and began speaking.

"I am a director of Westerns," he said. "I am one of the founders of this Guild. I must rise to protect the Board of Directors in some of the accusations made here tonight. Before I continue, I would like to state that I have been on Mr. Mankiewicz's side of the fight all through it. . . . I have been sick and tired and ashamed of the whole goddamn thing. . . . If they intend to break up the Guild, goddamn it, they have pretty well done it tonight. . . .

"We organized this Guild to protect ourselves against producers. By producers I don't mean men of the caliber of Zanuck or the late Irving Thalberg or some of the nine men we have as executive producers. I mean the little man that creeps in and says that Russians stink. We organized this Guild to protect ourselves against those people. . . .

"I repeat again that I did not meet in Mr. DeMille's office, as a matter of fact, and I must admit I would be proud to meet there. I think he is a great guy. . . . I don't agree with C. B. DeMille. I admire him. I don't like him, but I admire him. Everything he said tonight he had a right to say . . . you know, when you get the two blackest Republicans I know, Joseph Mankiewicz and C. B. DeMille and they start a fight over Communism, it is getting laughable to me. I know Joe is an ardent Republican. I happen to be a state of Maine Republican.

"I think Joe has been vilified, and I think he needs an apology. . . . I admire C. B.'s guts and courage even if I don't agree with him. [And] if Mr. DeMille is recalled, your Guild is busted up."

Throughout all of this, DeMille stared straight ahead, refusing to look at Ford. At this point, Ford made a brilliant tactical leap to forestall further damage to the Guild. "I believe there is only one alternative, and that is for the [entire] Board of Directors to resign and elect a new Board of Directors. They are under enough fire tonight. It appears they haven't got the support of the men that elected them. I think that there is only one alternative, and that is for us to resign. . . . I don't see any other course."

The motion was quickly voted on and carried. The entire board of directors was deposed, obliterating DeMille's influence and allowing Mankiewicz to continue his stewardship without having to worry about watching his back. After giving the twenty-five signers of the Mankiewicz petition a vote of confidence, the meeting was adjourned at 2:20 in the morning.

Ford had succeeded where the conventional liberals had, if not failed, flailed. Partially because he had more courage, but also because he applied some of his gifts as a director—a sense of drama, superb timing—to a political moment.

George Stevens was jubilant, thrilled by one of the few victories won against right-wing forces in Hollywood. By the time he got to his car in the parking lot, it was 4:00 in the morning, but he drove fifty miles to Ventura, then fifty miles back just to blow off steam and savor the moment. In retrospect, he believed that Ford rallied to his cause so strongly because "it was sort of the white hats and the black hats that night. Ford and Billy Wellman . . . whatever was a thrilling issue, they'd come in along those lines."

There was no question in anyone's mind who had been the deciding factor. "Ford drove the nail into DeMille's coffin," said Vincent Sherman. Robert Wise remembered that "He was the kingpin, and he turned the whole evening around."

A devastated Cecil B. DeMille went home to DeMille Drive. The next day he would tell Henry Wilcoxon, his closest professional associate, that "Nobody is my friend today, Harry. Nobody wants to know me. Last night was one of the worst nights of my entire life." Ford tried to heal the breach by sending DeMille a friendly note soon after the confrontation. DeMille responded with a palpable gratefulness. "Thank you for your friendly expression," he wrote. "Attack I am used to, kindness moves me very deeply."

John Ford went home to Odin Street. "Send the Commie bastard to me," he'd say whenever he heard about someone being blacklisted. "I'll hire him."

While all this was going on, Merian Cooper, undoubtedly motivated by his own experiences fighting the Bolsheviks during and after World War I, was moving even further to the right. Cooper had become an admirer of Douglas MacArthur—"One of the truly great Americans," according to the producer. In October 1952, Cooper made a financial contribution to Senator Joseph McCarthy.

Stephen Longstreet asserted that the only politics that interested Ford were Irish politics, but one wonders. There is a "Dear John" letter from Richard Nixon from March 1953, thanking Ford "for all that you did to make possible our overwhelming victory," and inviting him to drop by anytime he was in Washington. Add to that a letter from the conservative Republican Ohio senator Robert Taft, thanking Ford for his commiseration over the party's nomination of Eisenhower. All this indicates that Ford's enthusiasm for Roosevelt and Harry Truman did not extend to Adlai Stevenson.

While Ford had helped save Mankiewicz and the Directors Guild, he wasn't able to moderate Ward Bond's bull-in-a-china-shop rampage. "Ward had all the gall in the world," said John Wayne. "Ego—unbelievable."

As the influence of the House Committee on Un-American Activities spread, the studios instituted both graylists and blacklists. Hard-core reactionaries, people who genuinely believed that anybody who had voted for Franklin Roosevelt was a Communist or a fool, assumed an importance they had never had within the industry. One word from them could help clear a reputation or restart a stalled career.

When the director Vincent Sherman was graylisted because he had bought a script from the blacklisted writer Ned Young, his agent insisted that he talk, not to a lawyer or a congressman, but to Ward Bond.

"He had the power," remembered Sherman. "He kept me waiting almost an hour. I told him I'd never been a member of the Communist Party. I was a left-leaning Roosevelt Democrat. Perhaps I subscribed to some of the [same] causes [as the Communists] because I thought the cause was right, not because it was Communist. I mean, My God, if you had any interest in what was going on in the world, you had to be. What we saw was a country falling apart; nicely dressed middle-class men selling apples on the corner for a nickel apiece, breadlines, and soup kitchens. You had to wonder what the hell was going on. Someone wasn't running the store.

"Bond listened and said, 'Well, it's not only that. We've got quite a few things against you.'

" 'Well, tell me what they are. I can tell you yes or no as to what I believed.'

" 'One of the members of the Party said you had a lot of influence. While you may not have been a card-carrying Communist, you had a lot of influence in the top echelon.'

"I said that was ridiculous. No, I didn't get to know Bond too well. He didn't behave very nicely."

Ford was now called into service helping people harassed by a reign of terror promoted by some of his best friends. Lester Ziffren, Harry Wurtzel's son-in-law, got into trouble because of his long-ago talk to a group of Hollywood writers after he returned from the Spanish Civil War. "A close friend of mine came to me and told me that Charlie Skouras had told him to stay away from me, that I was suspected of being a Communist.

"I went to Ford. He was working at Republic. He listened to my story and said, 'I'll tell you what. I'll make a few calls and let you know.' A few days later he called me and told me he'd made an appointment for me to see someone down at the FBI. 'Go tell them your story,' he said."

Ziffren trooped down to the FBI. They wanted to know who had attended the writers' meeting; in effect, they wanted Ziffren to name names. "I told them I didn't know any of the writers, that I had just gotten into town at that point and couldn't verify any names. And I didn't hear anything further about it." Shortly after the conversation with the FBI, Ziffren was cleared to take a State Department job and left show business.

Even Frank Capra had un-American aspersions cast on him. When he had trouble getting a security clearance at the end of 1951, more or less because he'd worked with left-wing writers, had donated money to Russian War Relief, and had attempted to forestall congressional investigation into the movie industry, he wrote Ford a panicked letter asking for a testimonial, but not before defensively listing his responses to the charges.

"AM SHOCKED AT LETTER," Ford replied in a telegram. "WHAT WERE WE FIGHTING FOR?" Ford responded with a firm testimonial, which apparently survives only in a roughly typed and hand-corrected draft in Ford's papers.

"I was terribly shocked and worried last week when an Investigating Officer came to me concerning the security risks of my friend Frank Capra," he wrote. "It causes one to think when a man of Capra's attainments as an Officer of the United States Army, a gentleman, and a loyal American Citizen has to be investigated. . . .

"Reference is made to the fact that Frank Capra, or Col. Capra as I prefer to call him, objected to the Congressional Investigation of Hollywood Communists. If so, I never heard him mention it. I don't believe he did. Frankly, I objected to it loudly and vociferously. I'll now go on record as saying I think it was a publicity stunt and the taxpayers would have saved a lot of money in railfares . . . if the investigation had started in Washington.

"I'll close by saying that I think that Col. Capra, Distinguished Service Medal, etc., etc., etc., has always been a shining light and example for good Americans to follow here in Hollywood or elsewhere. In my humble way I think he is a truly great American."

The Un-American Activities Committee and Hollywood's right wing had convinced the studios that resisting their efforts could have a serious economic impact. Vincent Sherman remembered having to sign a loyalty oath when he went over to direct a picture at MGM. "I don't believe in this stuff," Eddie Mannix told Sherman, "but what the hell can we do? We have to have some protection, otherwise we can be picketed by the American Legion."

While Ford had no use for Communism, neither was he favorably disposed toward the intimidation practiced by Bond and his cronies. As for McCarthy personally, Ford would tell his grandson Dan that once Ward Bond had a party for McCarthy. When Ford was invited, he said he "wouldn't meet that guy in a whorehouse," and refused to go.

In February 1950, Ford and Cooper moved onto the Republic lot in Studio City. Their needs were modest: an office apiece for Ford, Cooper, and the accounting department, a storage room for files, space in the vault for their film library—250 cans of nitrate and 150 cans of safety film.

It was understood that Ford's first film for Republic would be a Western, so Ford and Cooper plucked another James Warner Bellah cavalry story from their files. The title was "Mission with No Record," and this time Ford stuck closer to the material than he had with *Fort Apache* and *She Wore a Yellow Ribbon*, where he had added and extrapolated freely. The core story was of a martinet cavalry colonel who is appalled when his only son shows up as a buck private in his outfit, and even more appalled when the boy's mother shows up. Battle proves the boy's mettle, and the colonel and his wife face reconciliation.

Ford made only one major change to the story that ended up as *Rio Grande*, and it was crucial. He changed the name of the character from Mazzarin to Kirby Yorke—the same character that had served with such distinction under the foolish Owen Thursday in *Fort Apache*. Time and chance have weathered Yorke—whose name is spelled without the "e" in the earlier film—so that he's nearly as monomaniacal as Thursday. Still, the name change, as well as the addition of Maureen O'Hara as Yorke's estranged wife to ensure an erotic chemistry, gave the film another dimension.

"He didn't want to make *Rio Grande*, he didn't want any part of it," claimed Patrick Ford. "So then there was the compromise, going back and forth: 'Well, I'll tell you what, if I can have my choice of cast in *Rio Grande*, I'll make it for you. . . .

"And then [Republic's president, Herbert] Yates said, 'Anybody but John Wayne.' Because John Wayne and he had had a fight. And that's exactly who the old man wanted. So the old man went to Duke, and said, 'You have to apologize.' See, Duke wanted to make *The Quiet Man*, too. 'Go apologize to Old Man Yates so he can let you make *Rio Grande*, so I can use you in *The Quiet Man*.' "

Apology made and accepted, Ford set to work, hiring James Kevin McGuinness to write the script. Depending on whose version you believe, McGuinness had been fired or resigned from a lucrative job as story editor at MGM over his archconservative politics—a nearly impossible task at the most conservative studio in town. McGuinness had been making $3,000 a week, and his contract still had several years to run, necessitating a large payoff that *Variety* said "may reach $1,000,000."

A large, handsome, heavy-drinking reactionary, McGuinness's father had been the mayor of Drogheda, Ireland. "In this world," he once told a co-worker, "some people will ride and some will walk. I'm gonna be one who rides." McGuinness had served as the (uncredited) executive producer on *They Were Expendable* only five years before, but his drinking had finished the job his politics (he served as chairman of the executive committee for the Motion Picture Alliance) had started, and Hollywood had not beaten a path to his door. He followed Ford and Cooper to Republic.

McGuinness's script seems to have been a veiled metaphor for the Korea stalemate; just as MacArthur, McGuinness believed, should have been allowed to use any means necessary to wipe out the North Korean Communists, so Sheridan is justified in saying, "I want you to cross the

Rio Grande, hit the Apache and burn them out; I'm tired of hit and run, I'm sick of diplomatic hide and seek." But McGuinness had fallen in love with the sound of his own dialogue, writing long, long speeches. "We rewrote the thing at night," said Pat Ford, "and rehearsed it at night, you know, just before we shot, and it was kind of an impromptu thing."

Yates extracted his pound of flesh from Wayne, making him give up a percentage on *Rio Grande* and work for a flat salary of $100,000. Victor McLaglen received $25,000, and Maureen O'Hara was borrowed from Fox for $50,000. The budget was set at $1.2 million; working quickly, Ford would be through with O'Hara in a bare five weeks (June 15–July 21) on location in Moab, Utah.

For the critical part of Wayne's son, Ford chose Claude Jarman Jr., who had just left MGM five years after his debut in Clarence Brown's *The Yearling*. Jarman was living in Nashville at the time, working in movies on his summer vacations from school. During his first encounter with Ford, Jarman remembered that, "Ford was interested in my athletic skills; whether or not I could ride a horse. I'd already made several Westerns and that seemed to be more important to him than anything else. I was already pretty good on a horse."

The weather in Moab that summer was broiling; Ford had a huge pit excavated, and placed a wet tarpaulin over it. Cots were placed in the bottom of the pit, and whenever the actors weren't working, they would descend into the ground, where it was a good ten degrees cooler, and stretch out on the cots.

Ford had worked abruptly before, but never as abruptly as he did on *Rio Grande*. Ford took thirty-two days to make his film, a total of 646 individual camera setups. For those 646 setups, he made only 665 takes.

Harry Carey Jr. remembered *Rio Grande* as one of Ford's "happy-go-lucky pictures. Fun." Three weeks before the beginning of production, Ford called Carey and Ben Johnson into his office and asked, "You boys know how to Roman ride?" "Where you stand on two horses?" Johnson asked. "No, we never done that." Ford told them they had to learn. Johnson began to explain that three weeks might not be enough, that the horses had to be specially broken, and then . . .

"I don't want to hear the story of your life," said Ford. "Just Roman ride in three weeks."

So Johnson and Carey learned to Roman ride, an insanely risky skill in which a man has one leg on each of two horses galloping abreast. "We was young and our legs was in good shape," dryly commented Johnson. "That's the main thing; if you're gonna be a Roman rider, you got to have your legs in shape." "It's sort of like water skiing," explained Dobe Carey, "only you're fifteen hands in the air."

Ford and Dudley Nichols working on the script for
The Long Voyage Home. (BFI Films: Stills, Posters and Designs)

The Commander. Ford on the set of *The Long Voyage Home.* (Lilly Library)

Gregg Toland's experiments with lighting and deep focus in
The Long Voyage Home led directly to *Citizen Kane* a year later.
(BFI Films: Stills, Posters and Designs)

What keeps *The Grapes of Wrath* from dissolving into little-people
sentimentality is the cold, seditious anger of Henry Fonda's Tom Joad.

How Green Was My Valley revealed Ford's art at its highest peak up to that point.
(Museum of Modern Art Film Stills Archives)

Lining up a shot on Richard Day's magnificent set for *How Green Was My Valley*. Leaning over is the great cameraman Arthur Miller. (Museum of Modern Art Film Stills Archives)

The coiled elegance of Henry Fonda provided *My Darling Clementine* with some of its most memorable moments.

The overt, incessant compositions of *The Fugitive* helped strangle the picture's drama. (Lilly Library)

Henry Fonda in front of the Mittens in Monument Valley, Ford's supreme object of geographical contemplation.

Above. John Wayne and Ford telling Santa what they want for Christmas during one of the annual parties at the Field Photo Farm. (Lilly Library)

Facing page, top. After a professional estrangement that lasted more than fifteen years, Ford welcomed George O'Brien back to the fold in the late 1940s. Here, O'Brien appears with Victor McLaglen, Ben Johnson, and John Wayne in *She Wore a Yellow Ribbon.*

Facing page, bottom. Ford was at his cruelest browbeating a performance out of Harry Carey, Jr. (center) during the shooting of *3 Godfathers* on the edge of Death Valley.

Jack and Mary with their grandsons Tim (left) and Dan. (Dan Ford Collection)

Ford and Merian Cooper dancing with their wives circa 1950.

The sense of an abiding, intact community made
Wagon Master one of Ford's most endearing pictures.

Maureen O'Hara gave Ford's films a carnal charge that no other actress did,
especially in the sexual power struggle that is *The Quiet Man*.

Ford and Clark Gable demonstrate one way to make a long,
African location bearable. (Lilly Library)

Ford and the ever-amiable William Powell on location for
Mister Roberts, before things fell apart. (Lilly Library)

Ford showing Jeffrey Hunter how to greet Vera Miles for the
ending of *The Searchers*. (Museum of Modern Art Film Stills Archives)

"Let's go home, Debbie."

The real John Ford (right) and Ward Bond playing
"John Dodge" in *The Wings of Eagles.*

An unusually playful Ford with some extras on *The Rising of the Moon.*

Ford and Spencer Tracy happily collaborating on the
otherwise disappointing *The Last Hurrah*.

The studio wanted *The Man Who Shot Liberty Valance* in color, the cameraman
wanted it in color, but Ford insisted on black and white because he believed
that the shoot-out at the end wouldn't be half as effective in color.

Above. Ford and his stars on *The Man Who Shot Liberty Valance*.

Facing page, top. Although his energy was now a thing of the past, on occasion Ford could rouse himself, as in this convincing love scene between Rod Taylor and Julie Christie in *Young Cassidy*.

Facing page, bottom. The Last Hurrah: struggling to breathe life into *7 Women* with Margaret Leighton and Sue Lyon.

A year and a half before his death, Ford, already ill with cancer, and John Wayne appeared in *The American West of John Ford*, a TV special produced by grandson Dan Ford.

A few months before he died, Ford was spending almost all of his time in bed, with a book and a box of cigars. Among those attending him was maid/nurse Liz Tippins.

Claude Jarman Jr. picked it up in what Dobe Carey remembered as ten minutes, provoking considerable irritation on the part of Ben Johnson. With typical perversity, Ford shot the risky sequence in a long shot, so the audience assumes that stuntmen were doing the riding, not the actors.

"He was very nice to me throughout the picture," said Jarman. "I was a hammer for him to hit everybody else; he would always tell everyone, 'Look at this kid,' when I got up to Roman ride. That was the picture he was after Ben. Ben was his whipping boy. He was always telling him, 'Forget about talking; just walk out and get on the damn horse.' "

Old Ford hands, who had seen him in the full range of his abusiveness, thought he was rather mellow, but a newcomer like Jarman thought that "People were pretty scared. Everybody. You couldn't see behind the glasses and you didn't know what the hell he was thinking. You never knew what he was going to do. He never screamed, it was always muttered, under his breath—'Jesus Christ, can't we do this right?' "

One day in Moab, Ben Johnson snapped back, with predictable results. Johnson and Dobe Carey had been talking about the day's work at dinnertime. "Well, there was a lot of shootin' goin' on today, but not too many Indians bit the dust," said Johnson.

Ford overheard the remark and took it as a criticism of the way he had directed the action. "What did you say?" he snapped, as the other conversation died away.

"I was just talkin' to Dobe, Mr. Ford."

"I know. What did you say?"

"I was just talkin' to Dobe."

"Hey *stupid!* I asked you a question. What did you say?"

Johnson got up from the table, stopped by Ford, told him very quietly what he could do with his picture, then walked out. Ford told Carey to go get Johnson and bring him back. "He knew he'd been wrong," Carey remembered. "He'd made a mistake and let his temper and vanity overcome him." But Johnson wouldn't take what Wayne and Bond would. He refused to come back to the table.

For the rest of the picture, Ford acted as if nothing had happened, even joking with Johnson about his fishing. But the damage had been done. After *Rio Grande*, Johnson didn't work for Ford for thirteen years, but survived nicely nevertheless. He was undoubtedly the only man in the world to have on his mantel both an Academy Award (for *The Last Picture Show*) and a World Championship Rodeo Award.

Evening theatricals resumed. Victor McLaglen polished up the old vaudeville routine of a referee instructing two fighters in all the things he doesn't want to see them do in the ring, thoroughly beating them up in the process. Maureen O'Hara sang Irish songs, Dobe Carey sang Mormon hymns with the Sons of the Pioneers, and even Ford took part in a skit involving stuntman Fred Kennedy. Participants remembered that the highlight of the entertainments was John Wayne braying an old drinking song called "Dear Old Gal." Wayne was backed by the Sons of the Pioneers, but they'd drop out before the climax, which Wayne did with all the shattering brio of Jolson, even though he had drifted far off-key.

Some nights, the Sons of the Pioneers would sing at twilight. "It was that kind of mystic hour," remembered Michael Wayne, "and you'd be sitting there and the Sons of the Pioneers would be singing and maybe there'd be a thunderstorm and lightning would be crashing and just being there was an event. It was romantic, it was dramatic, it was fun."

It was the only way the Sons of the Pioneers could justify their presence, for Yates had foisted them and their salaries on the picture's budget. Ford liked their music, but he didn't like having to use them, if only because they weren't actors, they didn't look like cavalrymen, and he couldn't figure out a way to turn them into cavalrymen. "He thought they cheapened the picture artistically," said Pat Ford. "[Yates] . . . couldn't conceive of a picture without singing cowboys."

Ford always enjoyed the company of stuntmen, a rough-and-ready crew of roustabouts. Frank McGrath, later to achieve a measure of fame as one of the sidekicks on *Wagon Train*, was a regular member of the stunt crew. McGrath was a heavy drinker who owned a four-unit apartment building in the valley where stuntmen played cards, drank, and fought. McGrath and the other stuntmen would make fun of Fred Kennedy's enormous hands until he'd break down and cry.

One new addition to the company was a young, handsome stuntman named Chuck Roberson, who was amazed, impressed, and terrified on the very first day of production when Ford instantly dismissed an electrician who dared to whistle on the set, an omen of bad luck.

Rio Grande was less atmospheric than *Fort Apache*, but research still led Ford to such niceties as using authentic Sibley tents for the cavalry, with Primus stoves sitting outside, articles widely used on the frontier at the time the story takes place. In the interests of realism, Ford liked his cavalry to look dusty, if not dirty, and he gave strict orders that uniforms were not to be washed for the duration of the shoot. Still, they never seemed quite grimy enough, so every morning all the actors and stuntmen playing cavalry had to be dusted down and have their costumes personally adjusted by Ford. At the same time, he would check everybody's breath to see if they had broken his other rigorously maintained rule, the one that forbade drinking on a Ford set.

This was by no means a rule which Ford winked at. Violation could result in instant dismissal or worse. A few years later, while filming *The Searchers*, Frank McGrath was hitting the bottle. Ford wandered into the stuntman's tent, ostensibly to scare up some participants for a card game. McGrath was nowhere around. Inquiring as to which bed was McGrath's, he pulled back the covers, unzipped his trousers and relieved himself all over McGrath's bed. "If the man can drink it, he can lie in it, and if any of you bastards ever tell him who did it . . ." he said on his way out of the tent.

Roberson got a good picture of Ford's attitudes when he managed to lure a local girl into bed one night. She proved wildly enthusiastic, almost too much so; even though Roberson had her out of the tent by 3:00 A.M., by the time the sun came up, "Ford knew. I don't know how, but he knew." (Roberson's confusion is indicative of common sense overwhelmed by lust; he had, after all, made noisy love with a woman in a tent surrounded by other tents.)

"[Ford] took extra minutes, adjusting my kerchief, trying to get a whiff of my breath. He tugged at the kerchief and ground his cigar butt on it and readjusted my hat ten times. I held my breath until I thought I would turn blue. Then, he turned to walk away and said, 'I guess you had an exciting time last night. Next time get a quiet girl. You kept the whole camp awake.' "

After that, Roberson was known as Bad Chuck, both for his way with women and to differentiate him from another stuntman named Chuck Hayward, who perforce became known as Good Chuck. Despite his transgressions, Roberson became a nominal part of the stunt crew on Ford's films, and spent the next twenty years working as John Wayne's stunt double.

Back at the studio, Wayne went on a wildcat strike over some money he believed Yates owed him from *Sands of Iwo Jima*. "He didn't work for a couple of days, and Ford supported him," said Claude Jarman Jr. "Ford told Yates, 'When you finish harassing my hired help, we'll finish the movie.' And Yates gave in, because they couldn't really shoot around him; he was in every scene that needed to be done."

Although *Rio Grande* does not lack for strong thematics—a son trying to earn the love of a forbidding father, a particularly mature portrait of a relationship between a married couple who love each other but can't live together—it lacks the depth of feeling Ford infused into the other two cavalry pictures, possibly because, as Pat Ford insisted, "he didn't really want to make it, and Duke didn't really want to make it. . . . It was a job."

Victor Young's score gives the film an air of plaintive longing that is appropriate for a film about the difficulty of the family bond. Although there's too much music in the film, it's still far from a negligible work, in spite of Ford jumping plot tracks midway—from the interesting family story to the much less interesting Indians-off-the-reservation story.

There's an unspoken passion and devotion between Yorke and his wife that's captured in the contemplative expressions on their faces as they listen to a serenade of "I'll Take You Home Again, Kathleen." At the end, she capitulates to her husband's way of life, waiting for her man to return from patrol, like the other soldiers' wives at the beginning of the film.

Rio Grande is the beginning of a remarkable maturity in dealing with women; the three Ford films in which John Wayne was paired with Maureen O'Hara (*Rio Grande, The Quiet Man, The Wings of Eagles*) are remarkably complex, mature explorations of all phases of adult love, from the strong sexual yearnings of courtship to the uneasy compromises of daily life to the bitter reality of separation and estrangement.

Basically, *Rio Grande* did exactly what it was supposed to—confirm to Herbert Yates that he had done the right thing in hiring Ford. The negative cost was $1.2 million, and, as of June 1952, it had earned $2 million in film rentals, leaving a net profit of $215,634.98. For Ford, it was on to *The Quiet Man.*

In November 1950, Ford and Ward Bond took off for Ireland with Herbert Yates in tow. It was a selling job to convince Yates of the visual splendors of Ireland; Ford was undoubtedly trying to convince Yates to commit to Technicolor; black and white, he insisted, just wouldn't do.

John Wayne had been dabbling in producing at Republic, making *Angel and the Badman, Wake of the Red Witch,* and *The Fighting Kentuckian* for the studio, all buttressed by his presence as star. Herbert Yates had begun paying him 10 percent of the gross—usually. Wayne had also produced a picture he didn't appear in, originally titled *Torero,* changed by Herbert Yates to the unpromising *The Bullfighter and the Lady,* from an original story by Budd Boetticher, the film's director.

Wayne and Boetticher had a contentious relationship; Boetticher had refused the services of Gabriel Figueroa as cameraman because "He was the best black and white cameraman in the world and nobody would have heard a word of dialogue for watching the beautiful pictures."

Boetticher came back to Republic with a picture that ran 124 minutes, longer by far than anything Republic had ever released. "I couldn't get anyone to see the picture," remembered Boetticher. "I was in direct competition with Robert Rossen and *The Brave Bulls.* Rossen was a great director and had as much right to direct a bullfight picture as I had to make a picture about Jesus Christ." Unbeknownst to Boetticher, Wayne asked Ford to work on the picture, explaining that it needed to be no more than ninety minutes.

One day Boetticher's phone rang. "This is John Ford. When in the hell are you gonna let me see your picture?" A dumbstruck Boetticher could only gasp that he didn't know Ford knew about the picture. "You know how much I love Mexico!" snarled Ford. "Now call the studio and arrange for me to see it. I'll get back to you." Ford hung up before Boetticher had a chance to say, "Yes, sir."

Boetticher waited with bated breath for Ford's reaction to the two-hour film. Finally, the call came. "Is it any good?" asked Boetticher. "Nope." Long pause. "It's great! Now get your ass in here and I'll win you an Academy Award."

"I don't have a pass for the lot, Mr. Ford."

"You know where Herb Yates parks his Rolls-Royce? Park it there, take the keys, and come on in."

Boetticher drove over to the Republic lot in Studio City, parked his MG in Yates's parking space, and went in to Ford's office, where he found Ford and Wayne, the latter of whom was full of ideas about how to improve the picture. "Jesus, Duke," said Ford, "if you're going to start to think, I'm in the wrong office." That put an end to Wayne's end of the conversation.

"You know, you really do have a great picture," continued Ford, shoving a piece of paper across the table at Boetticher. "Now sign here."

"So I signed 'Oscar Boetticher Jr.' and I gave him the right to do whatever he wanted to do with the picture," remembered Boetticher. "And now," said Ford, 'I'm gonna win you an Academy Award. You've only got one problem with this picture. You've got forty-two minutes of real chi-chi shit in this thing. This relationship between [Robert] Stack and [Gilbert] Roland. They're a couple of queers. They love each other."

Boetticher replied that men can love each other without being homosexuals.

"That's a lot of bullshit. And these fucking kids, you don't need all these fucking kids in the picture. And the music is shit."

"So," said Budd Boetticher, "he proceeded to cut out all the bullfighters that preceded Gilbert Roland."

Ford cut Boetticher's film to eighty-seven minutes, and persuaded Victor Young to write a new musical score. Republic released Ford's cut, and it did indeed get Boetticher an Academy Award nomination for Best Original Story, which failed to assuage Boetticher's anger at Ford for disemboweling his movie.

Maurice Walsh's "The Quiet Man" first appeared in the February 11, 1933, issue of *The Saturday Evening Post*. It tells the story of Shawn Kelvin, an ex-boxer who returns to his native Kerry at the age of thirty-five, falls in love with and marries Ellen O'Grady, and ends up fighting her harsh, blowhard brother, "a great, raw-boned, sandy-haired man, with the strength of an ox and a heart no bigger than a sour apple," because he refuses to pay Shawn the two-hundred-pound dowry he had promised.

It's a pleasant vignette, with a plain charm: "He had had enough of fighting, and all he wanted now was peace. He quietly went amongst the old and kindly friends and quietly looked about him for the place and peace he wanted; and when the time came, quietly produced the money for a neat, handy, small farm on the first warm shoulder of Knockamore Hill below the rolling curve of heather. . . . And in the nights, before the year turned, with the wind from the plains of the Atlantic keening above the chimney, they would sit at either side of the flaming peat fire, and he would read aloud strange and almost unbelievable things out of the high-colored magazines."

Ford played with the story for years. Maureen O'Hara remembered weekends on the *Araner* just after World War II. "He'd send the kids ashore to swim, then put on his Irish records and chew on his handkerchief, while I took notes in my Pitman shorthand and typed them up later on."

In 1946, Ford and Cooper thought they had a deal to make the picture for Alexander Korda. The director wrote Michael Killanin that Korda would be approaching him to work on the movie. "We will wander around shooting it in colour all over Ireland but with the stress laid on Spiddal." But the Korda deal didn't happen, and without a firm production deal, Argosy didn't feel they could front the money for a final shooting script. Only after the Republic deal was signed did Ford proceed to a final screenplay. In December 1950, Ford hired Richard Llewellyn, author of *How Green Was My Valley*.

After Llewellyn wrote his draft, Ford hired Frank Nugent to do the shooting script. On February 22, 1951, Nugent was shipped the following books for research: *Irish Names and Surnames, Hanrahan's Daughter, English-Irish Dictionary, 1000 Years of Irish Poetry, Family and Community in Ireland,* Liam O'Flaherty's *Land,* and *The Road Around Ireland.*

Walsh's Shawn Kelvin was a "firmly built, small man with the clean face and the lustrous eyes below steadfast brow"—a welterweight, then. But there could be no one for the part but John Wayne, who was no welterweight.

Walsh's story is very small-scale, a three-hander, with the background barely sketched in, and a touch of philosophy: "Women, in the outside world, begin by loving their husbands; and then, if fate is kind, they grow to admire them; and, if fate is not unkind, may descend no lower than liking and enduring." But Ellen O'Grady can't love a man who won't stand up for himself, and, by extension, her. So the marriage founders until Shawn throws his fear aside and stands up, first throwing the dowry into the flames, then fighting and beating his brother-in-law.

Ford added backstory—a tragic death in the ring motivating Sean's refusal to fight. He added rich characters—the priest who narrates the story and Michaeleen, the waggish village matchmaker. And he added a sense of life as it has gone on in the village of Innisfree for centuries—the mores of the town, the courtship ritual that surrounds the archetypes that are Sean Thornton and Mary Kate Danaher. And he let the brother-in-law give as good as he gets and the fight end in a kind of draw. (For Ford, the fighting was always more important than the winning.) He took a vignette and gave it the configuration of timeless myth.

Republic had never made a picture with the kind of location work that *The Quiet Man* needed, so a great deal of the preproduction labor fell on Argosy. Ford hired Charles FitzSimons, the brother of Maureen O'Hara, to work as location liaison, as well as Michael Killanin, who in turn hired a veritable group of Baker Street Irregulars to fan out across the country looking for likely locations and solving all manner of bottlenecks. "Housing of staff and crew has been most difficult," wrote one of the Irish assistants. "Expect to illuminate problem today Stop Lord Killanin and Charles FitzSimons have been a great help."

Much of the company was headquartered in County Mayo at Ashford Castle. Crew members were billeted in houses scattered around the area, bed-and-breakfasts and the like; as assistant cameraman Ernest Day remembered with a chuckle, "Ashford was first class and we were tourist class."

For his primary location, Ford settled on the village of Cong (from the Gaelic "cunga" meaning "isthmus"). Telephone service was impossible during the summer, because of heavy tourist traffic from Ashford Castle. It became necessary to install a second line between Cong and the nearest trunk line in Ballinrobe to make connections to Dublin easier, as well as a direct Ballinrobe–Hollywood line. The production also asked for twenty-four-hour attendance by operators in Cong.

Ashford Castle had been constructed over a thirty-year period by Arthur Edward Guinness, using some of the enormous profits from the family brewery. It's an impressive structure, with a battlemented facade that incorporates the remains of a thirteenth-century Norman castle, and a costumed staff parading in kilts—festive, if non-Irish. The nearby Lough Corrib, dotted with small islands, is an angler's paradise. Whatever veiled imperial traits Ford wished to incarnate could be satisfied at Ashford.

Ford had to call on the considerable political gifts he chose to muffle beneath his crusty patina. On May 2, he wrote to the American ambassador in Ireland, dropping the names of mutual friends (David Bruce, Michael Killanin, Gene Markey), and asked permission to call on him later that month. Ford was covering all the bases; the ambassador's help might not be needed, but could prove invaluable in a crisis.

Because Ford had been carrying the story around in his head for more than ten years, the scripting process was fairly smooth, although some undated script notes do reveal a contemplated subplot about the IRA: "A blacksmith taking off his apron, putting out the fire in his furnace, puts on his cap, and hastily ties up a bundle, in which we can see three rifles, and departs. . . .

"A view of a chapel. Impressionistic.

"Two candles by the side of the altar. Moonlight, backlighting the stained glass. Silhouetted in front of the altar rail a young priest, already established as the curate, is kneeling, his hands in supplication.

"A striking head close-up.

"The boy in agony.

"Forsaking his vows.

"Praying in Irish. (To be inter-cut with the entire montage.)

"He rises, hastily slips off his cassock, disclosing him in labourer's clothes. Laying the cassock over the rail he quickly exits through the sacristy door.

"In the back of the chapel a dark figure approaches the altar and kneels, laying his hand on the clerical robe he raises his head and prays. We recognize him as the old Parish Priest."

Ford even foresaw drawing Sean Thornton into the troubles, as he leaves to join the IRA after the wedding and the unconsummated marriage. This was jettisoned, perhaps because motivating a new arrival into internecine politics would have been a dramatic feat worthy of Shaw.

All this would, of course, have resulted in a film far more grounded in reality than the romantic idyll that finally emerged. Ford's reasons for cutting the subplot are implicit in one of the script notes: "The 'Terror' is used briefly for dramatic purposes . . . (and after) the coming of the Armistice . . . we should again try to get a gay mood into the picture." As well as firmly fixing the story in the time of the Black and Tans (the story takes place around 1920 to 1922), this would have greatly complicated the picture's tone, and Ford wisely decided to skip it.

There was one brief sequence outlined in the script notes that Ford might have retained, following the wedding and the confrontation with Red Will Danaher: "The scene should end with Sean snatching her bodily out of the house, throwing her on his horse and galloping away, like an O'Flaherty of old.

"Play this for pure effect.

"The veil is streaming, the red hair blowing in the wind. Sean is bareheaded.

"Across the fields. One good scramble jump. They reach the . . . cottage . . .

"Bride is strangely quiet when she dismounts.

"Perhaps during the ride she has suddenly fallen madly in love with Sean. Perhaps before she locks the door of her room, she putters—prepares his tea—puts the house to rights—puts away the bridal veil amid aromatic leaves (check Irish way of putting away old lace)."

Another series of notes reveals the care and thought Ford had put into the setting and characters. "The driver of the sidecar is one Michaeleen Joyce. He is an important character in our story. He is bibulous, loquacious, generous, careless, contumacious and Irish—Galway Irish. He is the handy-man of the village to which we are going. He is a busy-body. He knows everybody from his reverence to his Lordship, from the richest to the poorest. He will give you advice when you don't ask for it. You can trust him with your life and even your honour, but not your servant girl. And above all, don't take a tip on the races from him for it won't be worth a damn. Among other things he is an ex-Connacht ranger recently dishonourably discharged for a slight misunderstanding in India. He is recording secretary for the Connacht Rangers Mutineers Association. (To save our writer or writers, who are not up on their Irishry, a good deal of research, Mr. Ford, who hopes to direct the picture and who is from a long line of Connacht Rangers, says that this regiment is the only one in British history that was neither royal nor loyal.)"

Casting was a nightmare of nepotism; besides the presence of Ford's two brothers—Francis and Eddie—Maureen O'Hara's two brothers, Charles and James FitzSimons, were both in the picture, as were Barry Fitzgerald and his brother Arthur Shields. John Wayne's four children made brief appearances, while Webb Overlander, Wayne's makeup man, played the stationmaster. Ford also used two sisters named Fae Smith and Neva Bourne.

For the all-important job of cameraman, Ford hired Winton Hoch. "They didn't come any better than Hoch," remembered Ernest Day, who worked as a camera assistant on the picture and would go on to be Freddie Young's assistant before graduating to be a director of photography himself. "He was very enthusiastic, very fair, and he wanted it done the way he wanted it done. He was *so* knowledgable; he was a physicist."

For the second unit, Ford again hired Archie Stout, last seen giving him a hard time on *Fort Apache*. As his second assistant director, Ford chose Andrew McLaglen, who was determined to make good for his father's old friend. McLaglen had been working as a first assistant for two years, but he took the demotion because it was Ford, and because it was *The Quiet Man*, "a great script," according to McLaglen.

"I had been around Jack since I was thirteen," remembered McLaglen. "I remember driving to the studio to see my father going to Yuma for the locations for *The Lost Patrol*. Ford came over and patted me on the head. As we drove away, he waved at me."

When it came time to go to work for the man he called Uncle Jack, "I was the working-est goddamn assistant director. I was always at his shoulder. He only had to breathe about something and I was on it."

As the production set up shop in Cong, Ford took charge of who was rooming where. "I was there," remembered Andrew McLaglen, "and he just ripped it up [the existing accommodation list] and threw it down and said, 'I'm billeting the rooms.' " Ford's room was adjacent to O'Hara's, which led many in the company to assume an affair. "Ford wanted access [to Maureen O'Hara]," said Andrew McLaglen. "I think it was an affair." Ford's feelings for O'Hara were an open secret among the stock company.

"He would get crushes on women," said Harry Carey Jr., "and he had a crush on Maureen. And to her, he was a Svengali." Yet, as Carey acknowledged, Ford was not sexually aggressive. "If he had an affair, the woman would have had to be the aggressor."

"Ford had respect for women," remembered Michael Wayne, "but he also had a fear of women. He dealt with them like a guy who was afraid, a little distant—except for Maureen. She was very feminine and just illegally beautiful, which she knew, but she never used that as a weapon."

For the rain-drenched love scene between Wayne and O'Hara, Ford demanded an unusually high number of takes, as he told the actors to make their kisses more passionate, their embrace tighter. "Ford just had me do all the things he wanted to do himself," Wayne told his wife. Patrick Wayne, who was also with the company, said that "Ford saw himself as my father. . . . Maureen O'Hara was the perfect mate for John Wayne and so was the perfect mate for John Ford."

Ford instructed Andrew that he wanted everybody in the cast in wardrobe and on the set every day, whether they were scheduled to work or not. "They're being paid, and I want them there," he said. "The one person that the production manager and I figured out he wouldn't use was his brother Francis," remembered McLaglen. "It took a long time to put his beard on, so we didn't bother. But we had everybody else there.

"Ford walks on, sits down, and says, 'The first shot will be over here with Frank.' I sunk right down to my socks and got that beard on in fifteen minutes. He had double-crossed us on purpose." This insistence on the entire cast being on standby was more than Ford's cussedness; Ford knew that his main location obstacle would not be actors or script, but weather. Hours of drizzle could be followed by twenty minutes of sun, followed by hours more of rain. Shots would have to be grabbed whenever possible, so everybody had to be there.

The extras and stand-ins were chosen from the local population. John Wayne's stand-in was a large man named Joe Mellotte, who later owned a pub in the town of Neale, about two miles from Ashford Castle. "Ford was a tough character, always on the ball," remembered Mellotte. In an attempt to make sure the schedule was adhered to, Ford instituted his usual ban on alcohol, but John Wayne had some trouble keeping up his part of the bargain. "I think it lasted for a week!" was the way Mellotte remembered it. Yet, when Wayne fell off the wagon and went out carousing at night, Ford didn't explode, and maintained his own sobriety. *The Quiet Man* was too serious to be threatened by minor matters.

On June 20, 1951, Barbara, working in the cutting room at Republic, wrote her father that "The film is beautiful—we've received five days' work and it looks just like fairy land—They really hit it on the head when they named it the Emerald Isle—I never dreamed any place could be so lovely—

"Pat is leaving Friday. He's certainly thrilled. You were awfully sweet to ask for him—He's a differant [sic] person already."

Despite the beauty of the rushes, Herbert Yates was not happy. "It's all green," Ford remembered him saying. "Don't they have any browns or blacks in Ireland? Why does it have to be all green?" Aside from the aggravation caused by the unsympathetic studio head, production was difficult. Frank Nugent would later estimate that the company had precisely four days of unbroken sun during the entire six weeks of locations. The rest of the time it was drizzling and overcast.

"If the weather was bad, we waited," remembered Ernest Day. "Ford was a Navy man, and the production was *so* disciplined; I just admired him so much. Everyone would be on standby, on our starting blocks. When the weather cleared, off we went. There wasn't a lot of chitchat, although socially he was approachable. He maintained a quiet discipline, through the department heads who were very much in tune with him, the commander in chief.

"I think what set him apart was the discipline that he radiated, without in any way being a bully. He was knowledgeable to such an extent that everyone wanted to be that knowledgeable. He treated everyone the same: firmly, in a nice way. It was a great education."

Day got a crash course in Ford's immense practical skills one afternoon when they were shooting a brief scene inside Cong's Catholic church. The Technicolor film of that period was slow, and the light levels in the church were low. Ford could have had Hoch boost the light, but that would have destroyed the reflective, noir mood he wanted. Ford instructed Hoch to lower the camera speed to about twelve frames a second, allowing more light into each frame, then took John Wayne aside and explained that, as he rose from his pew and exited down the aisle past the camera, he had to move in slow motion. When the film was projected at the standard twenty-four frames a second, he would appear to be moving normally. Wayne nodded obediently, understood perfectly. "I think we got it on the first take," remembered Ernest Day.

Only a director who had worked in silent films, where camera speeds were often adjusted for dramatic effect, would have known of this gambit; only Ford, in concert with an absolute professional like Wayne, could have tossed it off with such a casual, spur-of-the-moment brio.

The painstaking Winton Hoch relied more on his light meter than his eye, so Ford enjoyed tweaking him. "Winnie . . . constantly had problems with the light," remembered Michael Killanin, "and often thought his meter was wrong because the light was so bright. But, of course, the light in Galway is very bright because of the reflections from the Atlantic. Winnie would always have his back to the actors, checking his light and angles, and an infuriated Jack Ford would rasp, 'Never employ a cameraman to direct a film because he never sees what's going on.' "

For John Wayne's four children, spending their summer vacation with their father, it was a magical time. "The first thing I think about [in relation to *The Quiet Man*] is Ireland," recalled Patrick Wayne. "The greenness, the wetness, the coldness. I was eleven years old, it was the first time I traveled out of the country. It was the biggest thing in the world.

"There was a sense of family. We ate meals together and we worked together and we spent time when we weren't working together. You had a sense that you were a part of it, part of a big family. It all made a huge impression on me."

Ford had chosen Cong for the location because of its aura of timelessness, and it wasn't an illusion. That summer of 1951 the village was finally wired for electricity. "It's like that old joke" said Michael Wayne. "The pilot says, 'We're landing in Ireland; everybody set your watches back 200 years.' They got electricity and they had a big party in the street, and people were dancing around the town square and people were very, very happy. Then they found out that they had to pay for this electricity, and they said, 'Why, we don't need it. Get rid of it.' "

The food at Ashford Castle was excellent, but what passed for coffee became a subject of considerable discontent. At one point, Ward Bond got a shipment from America, setting off a huge celebration. The concept of salads seemed equally abstract, so Bond took it upon himself to whip up some for dinner. Since it stayed light until about 10:00 at night, after dinner everybody would go for walks.

Ford had a room with a bath, as did Wayne, but nearly everybody else shared a large bathroom and a large shower. "We learned very fast," said Toni La Cava, Wayne's daughter, "that if you wanted to get up in the morning and take a shower we shouldn't go in there early because it wouldn't do to have the crew waiting for us to get out of the shower room."

Ford was godfather to Pat Wayne, and the handsome boy had a place in his heart that none of the other Wayne children did. Ford used the four Wayne children as extras during the race sequence of *The Quiet Man.* "I think actually what he wanted was Pat," remembered Toni La Cava, "Patrick and Melinda in the cart with Maureen. And then I think he thought, well, you know, these other two poor souls, they need to be in it too, so Michael and I are standing on either side of the cart and Maureen is in the cart with Patrick and Melinda." The children were also used in the background during the fight sequence.

From Ashford Castle, the company ranged in a fifty-mile diameter, shooting a love scene on the cliffs, the horse race on the strand near Killary Bay, and some of the fight at Tuam and Ballynahinch.

Andrew McLaglen watched Ford carefully, saw the way he knew his script, but gave it room to breathe by thinking up bits of business. "He knew the picture he wanted to make [and] he had great imagination. . . . I can remember vividly when Duke was striding across the countryside on his way to the station to get Maureen back, and all of a sudden he saw this beautiful green meadow with a whole pack of seagulls, hundreds of seagulls. He said, 'Quick, get the camera, set it up. Okay Duke, you're ready? Okay, walk in there.' Duke strode in there and all those seagulls went up in the air. It was great. . . . He took advantage [of the moment]."

Ford was determined that the film would have a complete visual honesty that wouldn't detract from the characters and settings. Ford and Charles FitzSimons were standing on a bridge overlooking a train station, when FitzSimons suggested that the bridge would make a good camera location.

Ford turned to the young man and said, "Charlie, when you talk to somebody, do you climb up on a ladder and look down at them? Or do you lie down on the ground and look up at them? Or do you look at them right between the eyes?"

"I look at them right between the eyes," replied FitzSimons.

"That's how I shoot motion pictures," Ford continued. "The camera will be on the platform watching the train come in."

There was only one momentary episode of trouble, about a third of the way through the location shooting, when Ford contracted a bad cold simultaneously with a case of the blues. "He had some personal trouble with [his son] and Maureen and he got a cold and he was really down," remembered John Wayne. "One morning he said, 'Duke, I don't know what to do; I don't know whether I've got a picture.' " Seeking to encourage his "Coach," Wayne began talking about all the delightful scenes they had already shot, all the things that were good in the picture.

Wayne suggested that Ford take a day or two of bed rest while he went out and shot the exteriors for the race. While Wayne was talking to Ford, Andrew McLaglen came downstairs to begin the day's work and found the production manager pacing anxiously in the lobby.

"The old man's not going to work today."

"What do you mean he's not going to go to work?"

"Jack doesn't feel up to going to work. I think Duke is going to go out and shoot a couple of scenes."

McLaglen went in to talk to Ford, who was sitting at the head of a long table in the dining room. "Oh, Andrew, I'm not feeling up to work today," he told McLaglen. "The more he talked it began to sort of hit my funny bone. He said, 'I just can't go to work today. You go out with Duke and get some run-by shots.' You know what I did? I laughed. So help me God, I laughed out loud—right at him."

Ford didn't get angry, or fire back at McLaglen. "We knew why he was under the weather. I think Maureen had turned him down the night before."

The gentle summer went on. Mildred Natwick estimated that she worked around twelve days for the six weeks the company was in Ireland, and spent the rest of her time sightseeing. There were card games—Wayne and his wife, Chata, played gin rummy incessantly—there were billiards, there were old friends. "We would play all the games the adults played," said Toni La Cava. "Liar's poker, word games. They included us, which was . . . very strange now that I think of it."

The film crew had more money than anybody in Cong could imagine; the owner of the general store that was turned into the exterior of Cohan's Bar was paid £600, enough to buy some farmland as well as underwrite a more laissez-faire attitude toward the general store. The Americans only encountered money trouble when some of them offered ten-to-one odds on the Sugar Ray Robinson–Randy Turpin fight in London on July 10, and were vacuumed clean when Turpin eked out a decision.

Victor McLaglen became very popular and would go out with locals for a pint of Guinness. "He was a powerful, big man," remembered a local man named Jack Murphy, "although by 1951 you could see he was beginning to decline physically. He could be a bit forgetful about his lines and he slowed down the film quite a bit at times. . . . I would drive him about after a day's filming and he'd love to go through to Tuam for a steak. He loved a good Irish steak or Irish stew, which he maintained he couldn't get in Cong or even Ashford Castle."

One day John Wayne's daughter Toni and her sister were whiling away time in the billiard room at the castle when McLaglen discovered them. "What are you girls doing?" he asked. The girls explained that they had nothing to do, so McLaglen proceeded to act out a very involved story about a flea. "We were absolutely mesmerized," remembered Toni La Cava. "He was this huge, rough person, and he was telling this little story." McLaglen finished by noting that Toni, who was tall for her age, was stooping so as to downplay her size. "Stand up straight," he told her. "My daughter is six feet tall; you should be very proud to be tall."

F ord was shooting two to three pages of script a day. "If you had an 8:30 call, you were shooting fifteen minutes after you got there," said Andrew McLaglen. The pace was no easy task considering the drizzly weather. Knowing Ford as he did, Andrew was a trifle paranoid. For the sequence in which Wayne drags O'Hara through the Irish countryside, McLaglen worked with the cast and extras to make sure the background action was perfect. "I had it down to a T, and after the first take, he said 'Cut, do it again.' and I piped up 'Everything was perfect in the background.' " Ford looked at him and said, "I know. I just want to do it again." When McLaglen asked Ford if he should clean the sheep dung from the meadow grass, Ford thought about it for a bit, then snapped, "Leave it there." "Ford really dragged Maureen through a lot of it," chortled McLaglen.

For the donnybrook that ends the picture, Ford enlisted most of the population of Cong as onlookers; on several occasions, he put Victor McLaglen's wardrobe on Ward Bond and used Bond as a double.

All who worked on the film recall it through a golden haze. Ford loved the fact that he was finally making his dream picture, and on location in Ireland. Lulled by the circumstances, Ford was in an unusually generous mood. One day he said to McLaglen, "Andrew, get in the car with me. Jump in the front seat," and had them driven to the house of the Episcopal bishop, near Galway. "We went in and had tea with the bishop, because my grandfather had been an Anglican bishop. Ford got a big kick out of introducing one bishop to the grandson of another." McLaglen wondered why Ford took him to meet the bishop rather than his father; he ended up deciding that Ford thought Andrew would appreciate it more. "I think he liked me," McLaglen would say.

As the son of an old friend, McLaglen might have expected to have been the target of some hazing, but it didn't happen. "He never got on me. I worked my fingers to the bone, but I loved every minute of it. Of course, he never said, 'Good job,' either but he wasn't the kind that did. He expected a good job."

Toward the end of the location work, Ford hosted a large ceremonial dinner. He was at the head of a long table, and he rose and made what Andrew McLaglen recalled as "a very soul-searching kind of speech." He was so happy, he told his actors and crew, to be here making this film, with his closest friends in the business. "This, to me," he said, "would be the perfect way for me to end my career." It was an unusual revelation of the vulnerable side of Ford, of the depths of his feelings for his films and his extended family. But any talk of retirement was ridiculous. "He was like Frank Sinatra," said McLaglen. "He quit for five minutes, then he came right back."

The mood shifted back to the norm for a Ford set once the company relocated back to Hollywood for the interiors. When Red Will Danaher sweeps the dowry off the table, Ford decided that McLaglen couldn't play the scene without being manipulated. Andrew McLaglen saw what happened.

"After the first take Ford said 'Cut. Victor, will you please look at Maureen?'

" 'Yes, Jack.' Well, I'd been watching my father during the take and he had been looking at Maureen. 'Okay, again,' said Ford. 'Cut. Victor, are you gonna look at Maureen?'

" 'Yes, Jack.' Now my father is starting to burn. They did it five times and each time Ford stopped the take. 'Goddamnit Jack, I *am* looking at Maureen,' my dad said.

" 'Cut, wrap it up, that's it for the day,' Ford said. I looked at my watch. It was 1:00 in the afternoon! It looked like my father had caused the film to close down for the day. Well, he was absolutely fuming. Livid. He was shaking mad. I followed him out to his dressing room outside. 'That goddamn Jack, what's wrong with him? You know I was looking at Maureen . . .' When he left he was vibrating with anger.

"I walked back on the set with the next day's call sheet. There wasn't a single person left on the set. Ford came out from behind a flat. 'Where's your dad?'

" 'He went home.'

" 'Was he angry?'

" 'He was plenty angry.'

" 'Okay. See you tomorrow.'

"The next day, when my dad did the scene, he almost knocked the table over when he swept the dowry off. And that stuff hit the wall! And that was the take Ford used. He did that to get the best out of his actors. Now, you didn't have to do that to get it out of my father, but if Jack Ford thought he had to . . ."

For a scene after the wedding, where the revelers bring the furniture back to the cottage, McLaglen noticed that Sean McClory, FitzSimons, and Barry Fitzgerald were wearing different clothes than they had in the preceding scene.

McLaglen went over to Ford and said, "Excuse me, but they're coming from the reception and it's daybreak; don't you think they'd be in their reception wardrobe?"

Ford glanced at the actors and pulled a blank piece of paper out of his pocket. "You're right," he exclaimed. "I made a note of it. Change it."

The only mishap on what was otherwise a smooth shoot occurred during a scene between Wayne and O'Hara. "I was so mad at John Wayne," she remembered. "He was nagging me. He and John Ford would love to nag me, because I always took the bait. I thought, 'I'm gonna hit him and break his jaw.' When the time came, I hauled off and he saw it coming. If you look at the film, you'll see that he puts his hand up, and my wrist snapped. The pain! I thought I was going to die. I hid it in the folds of my skirt, and Duke finally came over and said, 'You nearly broke my jaw. Lemme see your hand.'

"By that time, each finger was a balloon. So they sent me over to the hospital. Of course, he and John Ford loved it. They thought it was funny."

Ford tended to shoot his action off the cuff, but for *The Quiet Man* he prepared rough written continuities of the wedding sequence as well as the epic fight between Wayne and McLaglen. He didn't follow it religiously—the fight as shot and edited has considerably more flavor and humor than the fight as written.

Ford's attitude toward *The Quiet Man* didn't alter in post-production. He fired off memos about the music score ("While Duke is looking at White O'Morn from the bridge . . . 'County Down' theme. . . . When the gals go to put their bonnets on the posts at the finishing line, suggest 'Believe Me If All Those Endearing Young Charms' be played by the bagpipers. It is very effective on the pipes"), and he even rewrote some lyrics to a song called "The Low Backed Car" he was thinking of using.

And now the tussles with Herbert Yates began. First there was a fight over the title, with Yates telling Ford that *The Quiet Man* "was not a good title for John Wayne . . . his boxoffice is better when the title indicates it is an action picture." Yates asked for suggestions from his branch managers, who responded with titles like *Uncharted Voyage, The Fabulous Yankee,*

Hearts Across the Sea, The Man Untamed, and *Homeward Bound.* Had the picture been made in 1923, these might have sufficed, but Ford remained adamant.

Then Yates and Republic executive James Grainger started complaining that the film was too long; Grainger believed they had a shot at a booking at Radio City Music Hall, where, because of the accompanying stage show, the maximum length of a movie was 120 minutes. *The Quiet Man* ran 129 minutes, and, to a man of Yates's B movie mentality, that meant that Republic would lose at least one show per day per theater. Ford put that objection to rest by showing the film to Yates and stopping the projection just as the fight began, explaining that simply lopping off the last reel would bring the film in under two hours. Yates gave in.

In August, with *The Quiet Man* only a month from release, Merian Cooper signed a contract with Cinerama to be their general manager. Although it was regarded as a part-time job, which only paid $600 a week, the producer also sold his Argosy stock.

With the exception of *The Searchers, The Quiet Man* has had the longest afterlife of any of Ford's films. Unlike the Western, however, *The Quiet Man* has never had to be rediscovered; each succeeding generation has simply accepted the film for the benevolent masterpiece it is, the audience finding the same joy as the film's hero, as he is, enmeshed in Ireland's warm greens and desire's flaming reds. It's a celebratory, festive film, literally expansive; the entire community shares in Thornton's problems, and of his joy in his reconciliation with his wife.

Innisfree might as well be called Brigadoon, for it is a place apart from the world's cares. There is very little on screen that links it to the twentieth century. Over the years, feminists, misled by the various boorish imitations of the film that were mounted by Wayne and, once by Ford, have falsely accused *The Quiet Man* of being misogynistic—this for a film in which the main female character refuses to acquiesce to the prevailing order, or to her husband, until she gets what is rightfully hers.

The film is very wise about the shifting nature of power in a sexual relationship, which makes it something more than an airy fairy tale— it's a fable about two people who cannot live together until they have learned humility and how to submit to each other. The plot is mostly about the way in which the town exerts social control of sex, but in the film's first scene the people at the railroad station argue about the right way to Innisfree—a place where time stands still. *The Quiet Man* is an exile's dream of a land and people he had never known.

• • •

The Quiet Man was not greeted with open arms in Ireland. As Brian Desmond Hurst noted, "They didn't like the way it showed how Irish marriages were arranged—the question being how many heifers one had. Also, the film showed an Irish cottage with leaded windows and roses up the pathway to the door, an extremely unlikely sight."

"Well, the trouble with you Irish is you all want to be shown living in castles," Ford responded. In October, Ford wrote to Michael Killanin's wife, Sheila, about what the entire experience had represented for him: "I apologize for my abrupt leave-taking at Shannon. I remember Michael going to the plane with me but I was all choked up at leaving our beloved Ireland and was afraid I would burst into tears, which I did on reaching my berth. . . . It seemed like the finish of an epoch in my somewhat troubled life. Maybe it was a beginning. Can I still come back? Don't be surprised if I show up in the very near future. Galway is in my blood and the only place I have found peace. . . . The Quiet Man looks pretty good. I even like it myself. It has a strange humorous quality and the mature romance comes off well."

CHAPTER TWENTY-TWO

In late October of 1951, Darryl Zanuck called Herbert Yates and asked to arrange a loan-out of Ford to direct a remake of the silent classic *What Price Glory?* It would, Zanuck said, only take six or seven weeks. Yates, who seems to have operated in a perpetual state of dudgeon, grudgingly agreed, with the provisos that the termination date of the existing contract between Argosy and Republic be extended, and that Ford not start work on the script for his third picture for the studio (*The Sun Shines Bright*) until he completed the picture for Fox.

"We do not want to be faced with the same problem [as] when he started *The Quiet Man* and went to Korea costing us considerable money as the [Llewellyn] screenplay was unacceptable and the cost involved was a total waste," Yates wrote. "In other words, Ford must be on the job supervising the screenplay from the time the writer is employed until it is completed."

Fox had already cast James Cagney and Dan Dailey for *What Price Glory?*, which was to be written by the husband and wife team of Henry and Phoebe Ephron, who usually wrote light comedies and musicals. The studio was toying with making it a musical, possibly because censorship made the raciness of the 1926 original impossible to reproduce. But that seems to have been an idea that was quashed when Ford came on board. None of the surviving script materials for the film could be considered blueprints for a musical; of the four extant script drafts, none feature any musical numbers or songs except when the soldiers are marching.

Writing from Paris, Zanuck seemed concerned about the project. "When we consider remaking this picture we must realize that almost all the originality has been removed . . . we decided to go ahead and invent a musical treatment which would give a new dimension to the old story . . . this is our only reason and justification for remaking this property. I believe that every time you remake a picture there must be a specific reason why you do that."

Zanuck tried to nudge Ford in the desired direction, but he refused to exercise his executive authority and order the film turned into a musical. Perhaps because of the impossibility of introducing songs into a movie where people get killed, the picture went ahead as a straight comedy with drama, as opposed to the original, which was more of a drama with comedy. The key to the film's eventual problems lies in a Zanuck memo where he states, "I would rather go overboard to get laughs as long as we keep them reasonably legitimate, than have us underplay and not get any laughs."

James Cagney would have been happy to do a straight remake, or, because he was always eager for a chance to dance, a musical version. But he was disappointed with the results, as was everybody else. The original material is a combination of male bonding melded with an antiwar statement. But the script lacked the bawdy vitality of the original play and silent film and, in any case, after his experiences in World War II, Ford could not commit to the original's ambivalence about the military.

The designated patsy in the cast of *What Price Glory?* was Robert Wagner, at the time a green twenty-one-year-old contract player being groomed for stardom. "Ford was a very tough guy," said Wagner, "and he gave me a hard time. At that age, and having a man like that on top of you . . ."

Ford called Wagner "Boob" rather than "Bob," and attempted to give the boy a sense of industry reality. One day Ford gestured at an actor playing a priest and explained to Wagner that he was Barry Norton, who had played the part Wagner was playing in Raoul Walsh's silent version. "He was a big star," said Ford, "but he became king of the queens. That could happen to you." Wagner was startled and bumped into another actor. "That was King Baggot," said Ford. "Do you know who King Baggot was, Boob? He used to make $27,500 a week, had a gold-lined swimming pool. Look at him. You could be with him. You could be doing what he's doing someday."

Shortly afterward, Ford was shooting on the French street originally built for *The Song of Bernadette*. "The camera was at the far end of the street," remembered Wagner. "I came out of this house, this bivouac, with Bill Demarest and Wally Ford and Dan [Dailey], and Ford said 'Cut.' And then, while everybody watched and waited, he walked the length of the street. 'You know, Boob, if you can't see the camera, the camera can't see you. You be clear to the camera.' And then he pushed me and knocked me down. It woke me up real fast."

The young actor struggled to his feet, and said to James Cagney, "My

God!" "Don't worry kid," said Cagney, "he does that. You'll be all right. Just remember your lines, that's all you have to do." Experiencing Ford at his truculent worst helped James Cagney devise his one-word description of the Irish: "Malice." Like his physicalized fury at Dobe Carey on the set of *3 Godfathers*, Ford's ever-simmering discontent turned to rank bullying when confronted with the inexperience of a young actor.

Ford took a little more time with Zanuck's money than he did with his own; *What Price Glory?* went five days over its scheduled thirty-nine-day schedule, with Ford usually doing two or three takes instead of the single shot he had allocated for the actors on *Rio Grande*.

What Price Glory? features a lovely, atmospheric pre-credit sequence, of a misty battlefield with exhausted soldiers straggling home while "The Battle Hymn of the Republic" plays softly on the soundtrack. "Charmaine," the hit theme song of the original movie, is used as background music, but the only other number involves a song by Livingston and Evans for Marisa Pavan and Robert Wagner, and a sort of number for the French bar. Ford blocks a lot of the interiors like the stage production of a few years before, and the air of unreality is emphasized by shooting the battles on stage sets.

Ford gets the camaraderie, and the ritualistic brawling, but ignores the necessary undertones of desperation and death he brought to *They Were Expendable*. Ford was able to have fun with soldiers, but not with war itself. "That was my racket for a while," he would tell Peter Bogdanovich, "and there wasn't anything funny about it. I wonder what s.o.b. will be the first to make a comedy about Vietnam?"

In retrospect, Zanuck decided that "Our picture was a flop because it was neither fish nor fowl. It was not the powerful *What Price Glory?* of World War I that everyone loved and remembered—and it was certainly not a good comedy."

The relationship between Argosy and Republic was fraught from the very beginning, even though the combination of Ford and John Wayne dragooned money from the public in a way that Herbert Yates's cheapjack product never could have. Republic's series Westerns and serials were made to yield individually minor profits, cumulatively amounting to a sizable total at the end of the year. (Among the pictures the studio released at the same time as *The Quiet Man* were *Tropical Heat Wave*, *The WAC from Walla Walla*, and *The Toughest Man in Arizona*.) But Yates couldn't resist treating Cooper and Ford as if they were run-of-the-mill producers.

On July 8, 1952, Lee Van Hoozer, Argosy's treasurer, wrote an outraged letter to Republic about their accounting for *Rio Grande*. The picture had a foreign gross of $735,131.38, but, according to the studio's bookkeeping, Argosy's 50 percent of the film's net equaled a measly $82,425.90. "Our experience tends to indicate we should expect approximately $250,000 to have been yielded by this gross figure," charged Van Hoozer. "Both Mr. Ford and Mr. Cooper are deeply concerned with the financial reports for this picture."

Yates obviously believed the best defense was a good offense. "Your letter . . . is insulting to me and highly objectionable," he huffed. "In all the years I have been in this business I have never had anyone question our honesty and integrity in any of our dealings. I cannot believe that Mr. Ford requested you to write your letter . . . as I see Mr. Ford every day, and if he or Mr. Cooper has any doubt about our method of release and its obvious quality, multiple bookings in conjunction with other pictures and so forth, it seems to me either Mr. Ford or Mr. Cooper would discuss the matter with me. . . . We do not interfere with Argosy in the production of pictures they make for Republic, and we will not permit Argosy to interfere with the distribution of these pictures, which both Mr. Ford and Mr. Cooper can rest assured will be distributed strictly in accordance with our contract, and on a basis of honesty and integrity."

In the long and glorious history of creative accounting, this letter is a classic. Yates was telling Ford that Republic would continue to divert money from Argosy in more or less any amount they decided was appropriate and if Argosy didn't like it they could leave. The result was a lawsuit that would take years to settle.

By February 1953, Argosy had hired Price Waterhouse to audit Republic's foreign costs and distribution fees, and they found that the studio habitually deducted all foreign costs and distribution fees from American receipts, a procedure that virtually guaranteed an absence of net profits.

It was clear that not only Cooper, but all of Argosy's shareholders were anxious to try to break even and get out. Argosy shareholders included such Wall Street worthies as David Bruce, Otto Doering, Robert Ives Goddard, and Mary Donovan, the wife of Wild Bill Donovan. The fifteen holders of series A notes had subscribed a total of $250,000 to provide Argosy with seed money; as of December 1952, $150,000 remained unpaid.

As *The Quiet Man* made its way around the world, it proved the greatest hit in both Ford's and Republic's history, even getting an Oscar nomination for Best Picture. The thought of his little studio in the valley getting a Best Picture Oscar so thrilled Yates that the penurious studio head authorized $25,000 in extra advertising if the picture won. As it turned out, Yates didn't have to spend the money; Cecil B. DeMille's *The Greatest Show on Earth* won out over the two favorites—*The Quiet Man* and *High Noon*. But Ford won yet another Oscar, as did Winton Hoch and Archie Stout, for their amazing job of smoothing out the lighting in continually adverse conditions.

As before, Ford didn't attend the ceremony and pretended to be indifferent about the outcome. "Oscars aren't the end-all of our business," he would growl in 1964. "The award those of us in this profession treasure most highly is the New York Film Critics Award. And those of us in the directing end treasure the Directors Guild of America Award. These are eminently fair. . . .

"But when awards and such things influence public opinion, it's damned unfortunate. . . . Oh, I'm pleased when I'm honored. But I'm not fooled by it. I don't think it's the measure of my success."

As of April 1, 1955, total film rentals for *The Quiet Man* amounted to nearly $5.8 million against a negative cost of $1.44 million. But by the time Republic finished with their bookkeeping, they were carrying the total cost of the picture at $2.8 million, leaving a net profit of only $1.29 million, with Argosy's share amounting to slightly more than $600,000. The dispute over money went on for years, with Argosy finally receiving a sizable settlement, although nowhere near as sizable as they undoubtedly deserved.

P roblems with Republic aside, 1952 was a good year for Ford. He must have been heartened by the marriage of Barbara to the actor and singer Ken Curtis on May 31. Ken was likable, modest, reasonably talented, *solid*—everything that Robert Walker hadn't been. Perhaps this would be the beginning of a life for Barbara that could lead to an independent career and a family.

Pat was another story. His first marriage broke up, which angered his father; divorce was bad enough, but with children it was unthinkable. "Pat was a talented guy," remembers his son Dan, "a great sense of humor, very funny. God, he could do accents—Mexican, British, Yiddish, whatever. He had a great ear. But both my parents got married before they should have; they were young and immature, and they were both very self-centered people.

"After he and my mother split up, he wasn't around a lot. He got involved with a bunch of bullfight aficionados whose idea of a good time was to get boozed up and go to Tijuana for the bullfights. When he was in town, he'd pick Tim and I up on Saturday and we'd go out plinking with a .22 rifle. We were about twelve years old, and we'd have to buy the bullets, then we'd have to buy him his beer, then we'd have to buy his gas, all with money we made on our paper routes. He always seemed to be broke. He was a flake."

The capricious nature and lack of focus of Francis Ford had popped up in his brother's son. Between Pat's absences and his unsettled life, his two sons naturally gravitated to their grandparents. "They were more responsible," says Dan. "They were steady. They took us on weekends. And they had this wonderful black couple that worked for them, Bill and Waverly Ramsey, who were like another set of parents to us. They were the most wonderful people I've ever known. Sometimes we'd go home with them, in the Crenshaw area. They would take us to Angel games, Hollywood Star games, the Globetrotters. And then there was the *Araner*."

The *Araner* became the boys' ongoing summer camp; they learned how to tie knots, how to fix hose clamps, how to varnish her trim. Ford was a fond grandfather, although not physically demonstrative. He would shadowbox with his grandsons, feinting, slapping, never hurting. He only lost his temper with Dan once, when the boy took a pistol off Ford's den wall and played with the gun. "He walloped me, and I deserved to be walloped," remembered Dan.

Ford had been planning *The Sun Shines Bright* since at least 1949, when he had Laurence Stallings prepare a treatment, although the script proper wasn't prepared and polished until June 1952.

As production of *The Sun Shines Bright* got under way on August 18, 1952, it was scheduled for thirty days, although Ford could undoubtedly have shot it in less. The largest salaried actor was Charles Winninger at $12,500. Stepin Fetchit got $750 a week, as did Russell Simpson, while Francis Ford worked for his brother for the last time, playing an amiable old coot named Feeney for $500 a week.

It was another one of Jack's memory plays, not so much a remake of *Judge Priest* as a revision. Billy Priest is a veteran of Forrest's cavalry, and the story takes place in Kentucky in 1896, but Ford again gives the story the patina of a generalized time remembered.

There are at least as many racial stereotypes running around as there were on *Judge Priest*; Ford portrays the black people, along with the prostitutes, as the town's outcasts. Yet Ford, as well as Billy Priest, clearly values the blacks as much as anybody in the film.

Billy Priest is surrounded by ghosts of all kinds. Priest has a picture of Stonewall Jackson on his wall, while the forgotten James Kirkwood, Mary Pickford's old lover and director, shows up to play a crusty old general. Narratively, it's a more ragged film than *Judge Priest*, but Ford tries to tone up the rambling script with visual grace.

Billy Priest is halfway between the stoic rectitude of Wyatt Earp and the gifted Tammany Hall politician of *The Last Hurrah*. He's idealistic and cynical, as circumstances warrant, and he knows that a touch of demagoguery is a necessary part of politics.

Priest apparently ruins his chances for reelection by alienating the voters he needs: he stops a mob from lynching a black man, and upsets self-righteous churchgoers by giving a prostitute an honorable burial. Yet, fate is capricious; the acts that seem to be self-destructive, if courageous, rebound to Priest's benefit. The mob supports Priest because "He saved us from ourselves." Priest ekes out one final reelection and staggers into his house for a drink to "get my heart started," slowly receding through a series of doors, disappearing into history.

The Sun Shines Bright is uncut Ford, the director at both his best and worst, making a film of memory and loss with characters haunted by their shared past. As in *The Quiet Man*, Ford is constructing a poetic, deeply ordered vision where people are content with their place, where justice is fair and there is room for a genial eccentricity.

The film's centerpiece is the whore's funeral that Ford had been trying to fit into a picture for years. Since we don't really know this prodigal daughter who has come home to die, the sequence has more of a poetic punch than an emotional one. Billy Priest believes that everybody, no matter how fallen, deserves an honorable send-off, and follows the hearse so that she can have the funeral she wanted. One after the other, the rest of the town falls in, even the proper matron played by Jane Darwell. The scene is played naturalistically, the camera tracking quietly beside the slowly growing phalanx of mourners, the only sounds footsteps, the tread of the horses, the wagon wheels crunching stones and dirt. When they reach the church, Billy Priest delivers a eulogy that preaches forgiveness. It's probable that Ford made the entire movie for this single sequence, one of his greatest.

The Sun Shines Bright has a perceptibly darker hue than *Judge Priest;* the original film featured Will Rogers, a man in his fifties who could do everything he always could, while Charlie Winninger's Billy Priest is around seventy and beginning to fade, which probably explains why he's running much harder for office than Will Rogers did. The earlier film celebrates the vaunted graciousness of the Old South, while the later film features a much harsher environment. Now, Billy keeps the secrets of his small town, and they need keeping.

There is good dialogue ("More power to your elbow, Judge") and bad ("the profligate seed of a noble line"). Besides the mournful funeral sequence, there's a fight with whips, and the ending. Priest disappearing through the darkened doors is visually beautiful but gloomy rather than triumphant, and a sharp contrast with the Memorial Day parade that ends *Judge Priest.*

The Sun Shines Bright shows a director gradually diverging from his audience. Both it and *The Quiet Man* involve humanity and ultimate reconciliation, qualities that were becoming absent from the commercial mainstream, which was more attuned to the informer's justifications of *On the Waterfront* and the urban brutality of *The Blackboard Jungle*.

The Quiet Man had been front-loaded with great stars, romance, and the seductive texture of Ireland: audiences and critics had both been entranced. *The Sun Shines Bright* was sadder, had no stars, no love story, and no color. The critics were brutal. "It would be hard to imagine a more laborious, pedantic and saccharine entertainment package," was the opinion in the *Times*, while one trade paper called it "so amateurish as to be almost unprofessional," and *Variety* said that it was "a lightweight comedy-drama, poorly plotted and overlength at 90 minutes." *The Sun Shines Bright* disappeared quickly from theaters.

For all the financial chicanery encountered while working with Herbert Yates, Ford's sojourn at Republic resulted in his greatest commercial and critical hit, and two other pictures that were certainly up to his level. Ford would evidently consider the experience worthwhile: "Republic was the studio where I had the most freedom," he told Bertrand Tavernier. "I did everything the way I wanted."

Mogambo, a Technicolor remake of *Red Dust*, was one of the few pictures Ford undertook for purely commercial reasons. The story of a Great White Hunter torn between Good Girl and Good Bad Girl was too surface for his taste, although the month on location in Uganda compelled him to overlook the banality. "I never saw the original picture," Ford remembered, "[but] I liked the script and the story, I liked the set-up and I'd never been to that part of Africa—so I just did it."

The film was designed for Clark Gable, whose charisma was still intact, and for Ava Gardner, but the third leg of the triangle was open to question. The studio preferred Deborah Kerr, but Ford was resistant, and somebody's suggestion of Greer Garson was vetoed by producer Sam Zimbalist.

At the time, Grace Kelly had made only two films, *Fourteen Hours* and *High Noon*, where she played Gary Cooper's drab Quaker wife who ends up shooting a man to save her husband's life. Nobody seemed to think her performance in *High Noon* was, by itself, strong enough to get her the part that Mary Astor had played in the original, a dutiful wife lured into adultery by the primitive sensuality of Africa. Ford, Zimbalist, and studio head Dore Schary gathered to look at a test she had made at Fox in which she struggled with an Irish accent. Schary remained unimpressed, but Ford was entranced.

"To begin with, for Chrissakes, all she did in *High Noon* was shoot a guy in the back. Cooper should'a given her a boot in the pants and sent her back east. Now, then as far as this test—Darryl miscast her. But this dame has breeding, quality, class. I want to make a test of her—in color—I'll bet she'll knock us on our ass." Ford's test of Kelly won her the part.

Ford was determined to make the film as realistic as possible, ordering all the actors to Africa for two weeks before they were actually needed so everybody would have a natural tan. As it turned out, two weeks was too long; the actors got so dark they needed makeup to lighten their skins.

Cast in the thankless role of Grace Kelly's husband was a young English actor named Donald Sinden, who had never heard of John Ford. "He was this tall gangly figure wearing very dark glasses and a sort of safari suit and baseball cap," said Sinden, "chewing on the end of a filthy dirty handkerchief. Not white, not even yellow. Filthy."

"Donald takes his work very seriously," the casting director told Ford.

"Does he?" said Ford, eyeing the actor. "We'll soon knock the hell out of that."

Which, for the next eleven weeks, Ford proceeded to do. As Sinden would remember, "He blamed me personally for all the problems of Ireland from the time of William of Orange."

Location work began on November 17, 1952, in the town of Rumuruti; Ford was shooting in Africa until January 28, although the second unit shot a week longer than that. It was a large-scale picture; there was even a third unit, under the direction of Yakima Canutt, charged with making background plates for rear projection later in the studio, as well as footage of gorillas.

While Ford played his accustomed role of curmudgeon, behind the facade he seemed to be enjoying himself immensely. "Have you ever heard of the lesser Kudu?" he inquired of Barbara and Ken Curtis in a chatty letter from the Mawingo Hotel on the slopes of Mt. Kenya. "Nope? Well anyway there's such an animal.

"Started shooting—Beautiful stuff so far. . . . Got the cutest lil' baby elephant! 3 weeks old, follows like a dog. Am using him in pix, also a tiny rhino—also wart-hog, wildebeest, impalla [sic] etc., etc., etc.

"Clark, who is a terrific guy, really wonderful to work with & Ava now that Frankie has gone is swell—and I like Frankie too. . . .

"Ma is evidently having a swell time. Wrote from Spain & again from Rome. . . . She must be very *busy* seeing the sights or do you suspect a romance? . . . She says because of the Venice awards + such that she is Mrs. V.I.P. Well I'm glad she's having fun."

"How does the 'Sun Shines Bright' look? Meta [Sterne] says Vic [Victor Young] re-scored the vocals—true? *Why* I wonder—I thought them pretty good.

"Give our love to Ken—and lots to you.

"Y'r daddy."

Donald Sinden continued digging himself in ever deeper during a long, difficult day spent in getting Ava Gardner through a scene in which she had to start drunk and get drunker. At the end of her speech, Sinden was to say "I agree with you."

After a dozen takes, Gardner had still not pulled it off, and then she found the scene. As she went through her speech, Sinden could sense that this was the take, and began willing Ava to keep it up. She did, but as she reached the end of her speech, Sinden dried up completely and couldn't get his line out.

"Everybody knew that had been the take," said Sinden. "There was a silence. Nobody said 'Cut,' and the camera just ground on and on in this silence. Then Ford got up and came toward me. 'He's going to hit me,' I thought. And he came up to me, and very quietly said, 'Donald, I could kick your fucking ass.' "

Since none of the cast were Ford veterans, everybody was in a fairly constant state of nervous excitement, which wasn't helped by the shifting sexual alliances on the set, the sort of thing that drove Ford to distraction—not the sex, but that everybody wasn't focused on the picture . . . and on John Ford.

Frank Sinatra was trying to keep his marriage to Ava Gardner intact, and had accompanied her on location, while Grace Kelly was casting longing glances in Clark Gable's direction. "I was rather intimidated," said Sinden in a masterful display of understatement. "You never meet anything like this in the theater. Never. I wondered if this was the way people always behaved in films."

The British governor of Uganda, Sir Andrew Cohen, invited the actors and Ford to spend a weekend at the Governor's House. Gardner, Sinatra, Kelly, Sinden, and Gable boarded the unit airplane to Entebbe, but at the last minute Ford decided he didn't want to take that plane and came in later.

Gable and Sinden had brought dinner jackets, but Ford arrived looking "disgusting," in Sinden's words. "A very baggy pair of flannels, with not a crease in them, an ancient sports jacket, a washed-out blue shirt, and a tie with an egg stain running down it." When the governor said, "Well, let's dress for dinner," Ford said, "This is all I brought," whereupon the formal dinner was replaced by an informal dinner. Ford was once again asserting his position as alpha male.

Ford introduced the governor to Gardner and Sinatra. "Ava," said Ford, "why don't you tell the Governor what you see in this one-hundred-and-twenty-pound runt?"

"Well," she replied, "there's only ten pounds of Frank but there's a hundred and ten pounds of cock!"

Retorts like that meant that Ford grew fond of Gardner. One day she was playing a scene with a baby elephant, when the animal suddenly pushed her into a pool of mud. Gardner screamed, as did the crew, but Ford yelled, "Shut up, keep it turning," and wouldn't let anybody go in to help her. It was a moment of spontaneity in a canned script, and Ford clung to it like driftwood in a hostile sea.

Ford's attitude toward Clark Gable was more ambivalent. Gable was an absolutely competent pro who would greet people in the morning with an enthusiastic "Hello" and say nothing else for the rest of the day. The only time he could be tempted out of his shell was when he was cleaning one of the ten hunting rifles he had brought on location, at which time he would go on at great length on each gun's specific qualities and workmanship.

For a love scene between Gable and Kelly, Ford picked out an idyllic spot on a cliff overlooking the Rift Valley. After an initial take, Ford got up to talk to the actors, when Gable stepped back and disappeared over the precipice, sliding twenty feet down a slope.

Ford wasn't alarmed, and didn't bother to rush to the edge of the cliff. He walked back toward the camera and sat there chewing on a cigar while Gable was hauled up with a rope.

"King," he asked the sweating Gable, "you ready to go again?"

"Uh, well Jack . . ."

"Oh come on, already . . ."

Another time, Gable asked for an additional take in a scene with Gardner, and Ford simply walked away, cutting him dead in front of the entire cast and crew. Gable was furious, walked off the set, and refused to speak to Ford until the production moved to England for the interiors, when Sam Zimbalist made an uneasy peace. "Look, Clark," said Zimbalist, "Ford's a tyrant. He's been used to John Wayne. When you get in there you just say, 'Yes, Coach,' and everything will be okay." Gable ended up admiring Ford, but from a distance—just the way Ford wanted it.

What nobody knew was that Ford was coping with a mounting panic—he was being troubled by blurred vision. He went to doctors while in London and it was found that he had cataracts. It was an ailment perfectly calibrated to strike terror into the most even-tempered of men, a description that had never been applied to Ford.

• • •

While Ford was shooting *Mogambo*, Michael Killanin was setting up a production outfit called Four Provinces to make a slate of four movies in Ireland, some of which would be directed by Ford. Herbert Yates, fresh from shafting Ford and Cooper on the receipts from *The Quiet Man*, was interested in financing the company.

Killanin wrote Ford, telling him that Yates wanted Ford to direct all four pictures. Ford promptly wrote back, "Having acrimonious legal business complications with Monsieur de la Republic. Suing in process. Just won't pay his obligations. So stall, procrastinate and linger. Absolutely impossible for me personally to do business with him."

The imbroglio over the profits from *The Quiet Man* had a profoundly negative effect on Ford's attitudes toward percentage agreements. "Jack's philosophy was that he preferred to be paid cash up front, rather than a percentage," said Michael Killanin. This would in turn have financial consequences later in life. Although Ford had percentages of almost all of his subsequent films, he was predisposed toward selling them off for lump sums, thereby saving his estate from the attendant problems of wealth.

The location photography for *Mogambo* was by Robert Surtees, but when the unit returned to London for the interiors, Surtees was replaced by Freddie Young, still a few years away from greatness with David Lean and *Lawrence of Arabia*. "John was a lovely person, but he had his quirks," remembered Young. "He would never look through the camera, and he would never interfere with the lighting. He would say, 'Shoot it from here,' indicating with his hand, standing on the studio floor looking at the set. He hated panning and tracking, anything like that. He wanted the actors to play to the camera, move within the composition. He thought the moving camera would disconcert the audience and he didn't like it. He hated to move the camera.

"So I would use the lens that I thought was needed—he never suggested lens or lighting to me—and we'd take a part of that scene. As soon as he got what he wanted, he'd cut. Then we'd move a little bit closer and do another [part of the scene]. He was making it impossible for anybody to alter the way he was [constructing] the picture.

"Now, you must understand that in those days, MGM loved a lot of coverage. We'd do a scene in long shot, a medium shot, an over-the-shoulder, and in separate close-ups. Then we'd send the rushes over and the next day they'd want more close-ups, more coverage. Richard Thorpe was always popular [with the studio] because he directed in that boring way, yet always came in under schedule. You could cut [footage shot like that] together a thousand different ways. But the way John worked, there was no extra footage."

Ford tended to get along with cameramen, but one day he and Young "had a slight disagreement." They spent the rest of the day not speaking. The next day, Ford and Young were in the studio limousine heading out to Borehamwood, still not speaking. Suddenly, Ford exclaimed, "Freddie, my eyes are giving me hell!" That broke the ice, and the two men were once again friends.

Ford would occasionally hear the question, "Mr. Ford, how would you like me to play this scene?" The response would invariably be, "You're the actor, act." As a result, Freddie Young would be accosted by insecure actors desperate for feedback. "Freddie, how was I? He never tells me anything . . ."

"He wouldn't overpraise anybody," recalled Young. In the rushes, he'd simply say, 'Great, Freddie,' and walk out. But you'd jolly well know if he didn't like something because he'd tell you."

Lindsay Anderson visited the set at Elstree and watched Ford pace around while things were being lit, gnawing compulsively on his hand-kerchief, patrolling his front line. The restlessness, the nervousness, were palpable.

Toward the tail end of the production, Ford seems to have thought about taking pity on Sinden, perhaps because the actor was suffering through an agonizing attack of colitis, brought on by nerves. One morning, Sinden came to work to find a specially painted sign mounted near his chair: Be Kind to Donald Week. Although the sign seemed to augur a breaking of the ice, as Sinden was to remember it, "His attitude didn't change at all."

Mogambo did exactly what it was supposed to—make money, and quite a bit of it. Produced at a cost of $3.1 million, *Mogambo*'s worldwide gross was $8.2 million. It contains trace elements of its director, but not much more. There are fewer close-ups than comparable MGM pictures, and Ford is secure enough to play scenes out in medium or long shot, but the film runs out of gas in its latter third because of alterations in the plot. The original version took place in the confined quarters of a Malayan rubber plantation, while the remake involves Gable as a catcher of wild animals for zoos (it obviously gave Howard Hawks the idea for *Hatari!*), and roams all over Africa.

The difference between 1932 and 1953 shows up in other, more dam-aging ways; randiness is replaced by a comparatively demure attitude to-ward infidelity in the far courtlier remake.

Ford does coax a relaxed, unexpectedly touching performance out of Ava Gardner, and it's clear that she could have played some of the same parts as Maureen O'Hara, balancing John Wayne with her strength and sensuality.

• • •

On April 2, 1953, Ford sailed for home on board the *Andrea Doria*. His eyes were getting progressively worse, and he spent most of the voyage in a dark stateroom, unable to read. "I know you will keep it confidential," he wrote Michael Killanin. "It is hard for me to say this, but the facts are briefly that I am afraid I am going blind." In late June, he entered Good Samaritan Hospital in Los Angeles to have cataracts removed from both eyes.

Although the operation was a success, Ford's right eye remained sensitive to light for the rest of his life, and, for several weeks of his recovery, Ford had the terrifying experience of being totally blind. "My eyes are still bothering me terribly," he wrote Killanin on July 30. "Just can't stand the light, although the doctor says that is a natural result of the operation and that I must be patient and allow plenty of time."

Unable to work for ten months while his eyes were mending, Ford was at loose ends, always a dangerous state. The news kept getting worse. Frank Ford was discovered to have a massive malignancy, and was only expected to live for a few months. The *Araner* had been driven aground by a storm in Santa Barbara, and an insurance examination revealed bad dry rot; Jack had to spend nearly $100,000 having the ship repaired. And the beloved house on Odin Street was being claimed by the city under eminent domain because the property was needed for parking for the Hollywood Bowl.

The Fords bought a house at 125 Copa de Oro, just inside the gates of Bel Air. The house had been previously owned by William Wyler and Frank Lloyd, and its prestigious ancestry and imposing facade made it all very Hollywood, which the Odin Street house had never been.

Ford visited his family in Maine, but became depressed. He worried about his career, he worried about his country, he even worried about Communism in the form of a man he had stood with during the Directors Guild imbroglio. "Your letter received," he wrote Michael Killanin, "with the discouraging news that the Reds—to wit: one John Huston is seeking refuge in our lovely Ireland. This ain't good. He is not of the Right Wing."

Worried about his eyes, Ford also seemed unsure about what to do with Argosy. The stockholders were willing to take their profits and close up shop, but Ford wasn't so eager to let go of a movable shelter in a Hollywood where the big studios were beginning their death throes.

Merian Cooper wired Ford about the possibility of bringing Leo McCarey into Argosy. It might not have been a terrible idea; McCarey was an Irish Catholic, had a similar aesthetic sensibility, had just gotten the infamously goofy *My Son John* out of his system, and had plenty of working capital, courtesy of *Going My Way* and *The Bells of St. Mary's*.

But McCarey was slowing down; in the seventeen years left to him, he would complete only three more movies, and only one of them (*An Affair to Remember*) would be at all worthy of its creator. By contrast, Ford needed to make as many movies as he possibly could; it was his identity, his justification. The possible partnership came to nothing.

As 1953 drew to a close, Ford signed a petition against admitting Communist China into the United Nations, in which he was joined by conservatives John Dos Passos, W. R. Hearst Jr., and Herbert Hoover, and liberals like Hubert Humphrey and Jacob Javits.

Professionally, Ford remained in demand. As Judy Garland began gearing up for her comeback in *A Star Is Born*, Ford was on the short list of possible directors, along with Michael Curtiz, Henry Koster, Charles Vidor, Daniel Mann, and George Cukor, the man who got the job.

The critics, both mainstream and fringe, recognized his primacy. In New York, he was still the man who had made *The Informer* and *Grapes of Wrath*, although nobody seemed to understand the frequent trips to Monument Valley. Lindsay Anderson wrote Ford in November 1953, and told him that he thought *The Quiet Man* and *The Sun Shines Bright* were Shakespearean—"[in] the end, all harmony and reconciliation . . . exactly like the close of one of those late 'untidy' magical comedies—*Winter's Tale* or *Cymbeline*."

But not all the critics shared Anderson's enthusiasm. The young François Truffaut had something of a temperamental block on the subject of Ford for years. In 1950, he would call *The Lost Patrol* "a joke, dreadfully dated." In later years, he would admit that "I would have to become a director and turn on the TV to find *The Quiet Man* before I could measure my blindness."

Ford was terribly diminished by the death of his brother Frank on September 6, 1953. Rosary was said the next night at St. Ambrose Church, and a Requiem Mass was held at 9:30 the next morning. Frank hadn't worked since *The Sun Shines Bright*; his wife had written John a year earlier, "I am terribly worried about Frank. . . . He walks the floors constantly."

Jack had thrown Frank a profusion of subtly demeaning acting jobs as if they were table scraps, but it wasn't enough. He had even lent him money to open a bar, but business had been bad and Frank locked the doors and drank all the stock. Yet, Frank was a man without bitterness; he had assisted in the birthing of the movies, had had some of the best of the miraculous new art form, as well as some of the worst.

"There was no jealousy on my father's part," said Francis Ford Jr. "He looked at Jack as one of his success stories. He gave him the idea of what a director has to look for, what a director has to be. He was kind of proud of him."

Jack tried to put the best face possible on Frank's death, writing Michael Killanin the doubtful news that "Frank had an easy passing and all his thoughts were about Ireland. His last hours all he could speak was Irish."

For years after the funeral, whenever Ford ran into their old friend Frank Baker, he would ritualistically ask, "We gave Frank a good send-off, didn't we?" as if that could absolve him of his lingering guilt over the way he had treated his older brother when he was alive.

When Harry Carey died, Ford had cried; when Harry Wurtzel died, Ford had cried. But he didn't cry for his brother. "He didn't show what he was feeling," said Francis Ford Jr. "Like most of us, he went off and cried by himself. And if it had been the other way around, if Jack had died first, my father would have done the same thing."

"Francis was a very nice man," said Andrew McLaglen, "a very, very nice man. I won't say, 'unlike his brother,' but he was different than Jack. 'Nice' isn't the word that you would use [about] Jack Ford; that's a word that's kind of tough on anybody. But Francis Ford was a nice man."

John Ford, 1956

PART SIX

A LION IN WINTER

I will arise and go now, and go to Innisfree,
And a small cabin build there, of clay and wattles made;
Nine bean-rows will I have there, a hive for the honey bee,
And live alone in the bee-loud glade.

And I shall have some peace there, for peace comes dropping slow,
Dropping from the veils of the morning to where the cricket
  sings:
There midnight's all a glimmer, and noon a purple glow,
And evening's full of the linnet's wings.

I will arise and go now, for always night and day
I hear lake water lapping with low sounds by the shore;
While I stand on the roadway, or on the pavements gray,
I hear it in my deep heart's core.

"THE LAKE ISLE OF INNISFREE" BY WILLIAM BUTLER YEATS

CHAPTER TWENTY-THREE

At the age of sixty, John Ford was a man in constant motion. He had always favored as much location work as possible, so the postwar taste for less studio artifice and more locations was just fine with him. He estimated that during the next few years he would travel 72,288 miles scouting and making four pictures: 11,600 miles on *Mister Roberts*, 11,688 on *The Long Gray Line*, 38,000 on *Mogambo*, and more than 11,000 on *The Quiet Man*—less than *Mogambo* because he knew the territory.

On March 15, 1954, Ford began production at West Point on *The Long Gray Line*, the true story of Marty Maher, a minor functionary in the athletic department for fifty years. The picture was scheduled for forty-six days, twenty of them on location at West Point. "Harry [Cohn] didn't bother him," remembered Paul Lazarus Jr., marketing head for Columbia. "He trusted Ford."

The Long Gray Line would be Ford's first experience with Cinema-Scope, the vanguard of the new wide-screen processes. He would tinker with variations on the elongated rectangle—*The Searchers* was filmed in VistaVision, *How the West Was Won* in Cinerama, and *7 Women* in Panavision—but Ford was a classicist, which is to say aesthetically conservative, and he could never appreciate such an arbitrary shape. "I hated it," Ford said. "You've never seen a painter use that kind of composition—even in the great murals, it still wasn't this huge tennis court. Your eyes pop back and forth, and it's very difficult to get a close-up."

Joining a Ford cast for the first time were Tyrone Power and a young actress named Betsy Palmer. Ford became fond of both of them. "Ford always had me come and have lunch with him," remembered Palmer. "He always called me Pat. My first name is Patricia, although how he knew that I don't know. Lunch would consist of Ward Bond, Harry Carey Jr., young Pat Wayne, Ty, sometimes Maureen. Ty was the sweetest man. He would take me into his trailer and show me pictures of his home in Cuernavaca, invite me to parties at his house; just a sweet, sweet man.

"Mr. Ford was Mr. Ford; he was Irish and never more so than with Maureen. 'Get your broad ass over here,' he'd say. He was a great psychologist. Every day at 4:00, everything stopped, a table was set up, and we had tea. People would bring in cakes and sandwiches and we'd sit for a half-hour and have a tea break. With that sugar fix, we'd have energy again and work till 6:00 or 6:30."

Ford cast Dobe Carey as the young Dwight Eisenhower. In those days, Dobe was a drinking man, and on a night when he wasn't scheduled to work the next day, Dobe, Philip Carey, and a couple of other actors went out and raised some hell. Ford found out about it and quickly rescheduled the men for an interior scene in a swimming pool. "It was humid," remembered Patrick Wayne, choking with laughter, "it was hot, they were hungover, and it was *awful*."

As spring came to West Point, Ford's mood lightened. One day he looked at Donald Crisp and said, "Donald, you've always wanted to direct." A startled Crisp looked at him and mumbled, "Sure, Jack." Ford knew very well that Crisp had directed such big-budget hits of the silent era as *Don Q, The Black Pirate*, and Buster Keaton's *The Navigator*, not to mention some rather good programmers for DeMille at the end of the silent era.

Ford turned to the cameraman, ordered a second camera and a crew, told the propman to cobble together a bicycle built for two, then called over the wardrobe mistress and told her to put O'Hara in a fluffy bike-riding outfit and Peter Graves in white pants and straw boater.

"Now you are all going off to shoot stuff I need very badly in this picture," he told the impromptu second unit. And for the rest of the day, Crisp shot footage of Graves and O'Hara riding a tandem through the Hudson Valley.

While they were still at West Point, Dobe Carey took a free day to go down to Woodlawn Cemetery in the Bronx to visit his father's grave. "Take some lilacs," Ford told him. "Harry loved lilacs." Later, Carey would tell his mother about Ford's remark. "Harry didn't give a damn about lilacs," she told her astonished son.

Before the company left West Point to go back to Hollywood, Ford organized a screening of *The Quiet Man* for Marty Maher. "Ford loved to wear his naval uniform," remembered Peter Graves, "and showed up wearing it for this screening. But all the generals had come in civilian clothes. Ford was furious; he stomped upstairs and changed back into civilian clothes while the screening was delayed for twenty minutes.

Now, you can't hate a man like that; he was sadistic when he wanted to be, and he was lovable when he wanted to be. Just a marvelous character."

Ford seems to have had only one tussle with the studio, when Harry Cohn suddenly decided to change the title to *Mr. West Point*. Ford fired off a memo saying, "Frankly, Harry, if I saw the title 'Mr. West Point' on billboards, I'd hastily walk by the theatre. To me it's a cheap, pseudo-sophisticated title. What I'd expect it to be is a wise-cracking, gagged up, phony semi-musical type of picture. . . . I think I owe it to you and the company to say I hate the title. . . . My favorite titles are 'Long Gray Line,' 'Pass in Review,' and 'In the Tradition.' "

Ford got his way on the title, but, despite the presence of Tyrone Power and Maureen O'Hara, the picture didn't do very well; as of November 1966, Columbia was still carrying the $1.7 million picture as $847,000 in the red, but, a few years later, Ford's 10 percent was bringing in the occasional modest stipend—$460.80 in February 1971.

It's not a picture even die-hard Fordians make large claims for. Ford was undoubtedly attracted by the story of an Irish immigrant happily lost in the military, even if it was only the Army. But as written and played, the story of Marty Maher is the saga of a genial screwup. Greatness glides by—Omar Bradley, Dwight Eisenhower, Douglas MacArthur—but all Marty can do is chafe at his lowly role in life, his inability to break away for larger things. Everyone but Marty goes off to glory or death, and *The Long Gray Line* gradually becomes an unpalatable cross between *It's a Wonderful Life* and *Goodbye, Mr. Chips*.

Tyrone Power could nail the borderline between charm and menace, but all *The Long Gray Line* gave him to play was earnestness. The picture slogs on for an unconscionable 138 minutes, but is almost redeemed by an eerily beautiful ending as Marty's beloved dead—his father, his wife, some of the young soldiers—gather on the horizon to watch him be honored by the institution he served for a half-century.

While Ford was shooting *The Long Gray Line*, he had several writers wrestling with a script entitled *The Valiant Virginians*. Because Ford tended to have fewer unmade projects than most filmmakers, *The Valiant Virginians* is of some interest. The story might be briefly synopsized as Scarlett and Rhett as teenagers in the Shenandoah Valley.

James Warner Bellah took a whack at a treatment, then, in August 1954, so did Laurence Stallings. Stallings upped the ages of the characters into their twenties, which helped. It was a long (173 pages), sprawling, historical epic that brought in Jeb Stuart and Stonewall Jackson, but had a slight paucity of action until the end, when cadets from the Virginia Military Institute fight in the Battle of New Market.

Ford could have pulled the picture off, but there was some dicey material for a film made in the mid-1950s—an old black man comes forward to a dying Confederate soldier. "Lawdy, Mistah Hadley, whut am I goin' to tell your grandmammy?"

"He knows you," observes a Union soldier. "He ought to," says the dying soldier. "I own him."

Ford originally placed the project at Columbia, then with C. V. "Sonny" Whitney, the cousin of Jock Whitney, who had decided to take a flyer in the movies. Ultimately, both organizations passed; Whitney was willing to spend $2 million to make the picture, but not the $4 million the script required.

In late March of 1954, Ford was hired to direct Henry Fonda in the film version of his great stage success, *Mister Roberts*. Fonda, who had given up hope of making the film because the producers were talking to younger, more au courant types such as Marlon Brando and William Holden, was thrilled when Ford refused to make the picture with anybody else. He wrote a "Dear Pappy" letter to Ford, who was shooting *The Long Gray Line*, expressing his joy at the news and calling it "a dream come true." Fonda promised to hold some seats for Ford when he came to New York, so he could see the play.

Producer Leland Hayward assembled a dream cast, but one that was not so subtly weighted toward old age in order to make Fonda seem younger: James Cagney (over fifty) as the tyrannical captain, and, after some discussion about Spencer Tracy, William Powell (over sixty) as Doc.

For the on-the-make Ensign Pulver, Ford cast a young actor named Jack Lemmon after he saw a famously atrocious screen test Lemmon made for *The Long Gray Line*. Meanwhile, Leland Hayward, after a brief tour of duty with John Patrick on the script, capitulated to Ford and hired Frank Nugent.

From the beginning, there was trouble. Frank Nugent and his new wife, Jean, flew out to Honolulu to begin work on the script. "Almost from the first evening, Jack was smashed," remembered Jean Nugent. "He was just gobbling down the booze and they hadn't written a line. Barbara was there with Ken Curtis and Pilar was with Duke, and Ward Bond was there. At dinner one night, Jack started telling everybody off, and he made a couple of cracks about Frank. I stood up on my Irish high heels and said, 'Mr. Ford, we can afford to pay for our own dinner, so take your nasty mouth and shove it.'

"Well, my husband was just paralyzed. But from that day on, Jack treated me with complete respect. He couldn't have been nicer. It was always 'Love to Jeanie' all the time, and invitations to the house. He adored my little boy; he always insisted we bring Tony, and Tony was fascinated by him. Ford could hit a brass spittoon from any angle, to Tony's delight. We'd come over, and both of them would just spend time with each other; neither of them cared about all the fancy people downstairs. All it took with Jack Ford was one smack in the face."

Ford sailed into production with high spirits. He walked into the Navy's Office of Information to arrange for locations and use of ships and found the former child star Frank "Junior" Coghlan working there. "Admiral Ford tore into my office with the same fervor [he might bring to] storming a beachhead," remembered Coghlan. Ford told him that he was pleased that someone with actual filmmaking know-how was helping him. He told Coghlan he didn't need to see *Mogambo*, as it was nothing but "tits and tigers," and explained to everyone in the office that Coghlan was one of the original Our Gang kids and that he had played a character called Fatima.

Since Coghlan had only done extra work for the Our Gang films, and had never played any character called Fatima, he tried to gently correct him, but Ford wasn't listening. Ford breezed into a meeting with Admiral Robert Carney, the Chief of Naval Operations, a friend since the war, who also got to enjoy the "tits and tigers" line.

Ford got everything he required, even a stand-in for the old cargo scow the USS *Reluctant*—although the Navy no longer had ships like that in their active fleet, they tracked one down they had sold to Mexico and Warner Bros. rented it.

The cast and crew assembled on Midway Island for the beginning of location photography on September 1, 1954, for a shoot that was supposed to last forty-five days. Almost immediately, things began to go wrong. Ford developed a sudden affection for Lemmon and the character of Pulver. The picture, however, was entitled *Mister Roberts*, not *Ensign Pulver*. The situation became obvious to the entire company. "I could feel the tension between Henry and Jack as soon as we started rehearsing," asserted Harry Carey Jr.

"He got carried away with me and my character," recalled Jack Lemmon. "He started ad-libbing, making up shit for Pulver to do with the nurses, gags with tasting soup. On the whole, he was very good to me, very nice, kidded me a lot. I think I was intimidated to an extent. I don't know if intimidated is the word as much as awed. He was dictatorial, and there were his credentials, and I was the kid of the group. He called me 'Piss-ass.' 'Where's that fucking kid?' he'd say.

"I remember one of the bits he came up with was [for me] to fire off the machine gun, say to the girls, 'That's how it's done,' then lean back on the gun, which was hot from being fired, and burn myself. It started to become Abbott and Costello rather than the legit behavior of the character. He was having me do things I thought were ridiculous. And Hank was having a conniption watching from the sidelines."

In truth, there were several factors behind the tensions forming around *Mister Roberts*, one about the filming of the play, another about politics. "The whole gang had gone way to the right," said Peter Fonda, "and my father kept his head on his shoulders. He thought the House Un-American Activities Committee was terribly un-American. He was incensed by it; he walked across the street to shake hands with someone who was blacklisted. He and Ford and Wayne and Bond had open disagreements, and then Bond suggested he was a pinko, and that was that."

Even allowing for the weakened friendship, Fonda would have been inclined to let his old friend do what he wanted with any other property, but the actor had a proprietary interest in *Mister Roberts*. It was a part he had created and played to unceasing acclaim for years; he felt he knew the material and the characters better than anybody else, up to and including Joshua Logan, the play's co-author and director, and he might have been right. While the play is not done much anymore, it was one of those scripts that caught a particular moment in time, showed Americans as they like to think of themselves—tough, humorous, resourceful. Like *The Best Years of Our Lives*, it captured an underlying wistfulness about the costs of a terrible, traumatic war, added raucous humor, and ended on a note of rueful triumph.

When Lemmon told Fonda that he was having trouble with a scene, Fonda retorted, "That's because he's got you playing everything except Pulver." Fonda decided to make his feelings known to Ford. The result was catastrophe.

"We were staying in the Bachelor Officer's Quarters on Midway," recalled Jack Lemmon. "I was down the hall from Ford. One night I woke up and I heard voices down the hall, sounding like they were arguing. I walked down the hall and looked in the room. Ford was swinging at Hank, windmilling, and Hank was holding him off with his long arms, saying, 'Goddammit, Pappy, stop it!' Finally, Fonda just gave him a hard push and threw him back on the bed." Lemmon, realizing he had witnessed something he shouldn't have, tiptoed back to his bed. Fonda's account of the episode always included Ford knocking him down, which indicates Lemmon looked in some time after Ford began swinging.

The fistfight seems to have occurred on Thursday, September 30, for Ford was listed on the daily production report as being in the hospital as of Friday afternoon, and the company did not shoot on Saturday. After that, Ford and Fonda were nothing if not professional; Lemmon was not on call for the next two days, but by the time he got back to the set, there was no sign of the blowup. "It didn't show on the set," Lemmon said. Ford was back to shooting his usual one or two takes per shot.

Nevertheless, Ford's reaction to the questioning of his authority sent him into an unprecedented tailspin. "I don't know what was in his mind," said Henry Fonda, "but I do know he was stricken by what he had done, by hitting me." Ford began drinking on the job, ordering the propmen to have iced beer on the set. Fonda remembered that he could put away as much as two cases a day.

"I only remember once when it was visible on the set," said Jack Lemmon. "It was a scene where natives are coming out to the ship in canoes; I was up next to him on the bridge, and I could tell he was loaded." Word soon spread among the company that Ford had gone to Leland Hayward and told him, "If you want to take me off the picture, that's your prerogative." Stranded with an expensive cast and crew in the middle of the Pacific, Hayward turned him down, but undoubtedly began reconnoitering for likely substitutes in case the situation didn't improve.

Throughout all of this, James Cagney and William Powell stayed on the sidelines. Cagney had gone through the drill with Ford before, on *What Price Glory?*, and knew that when faced with a Fordian storm it was best to keep your head down. A serene, good-humored Irishman, Cagney would later say that "I did it for a lark, and it was one of the easiest pictures I ever made. Everyone else had to jump and holler all the time. I just pulled my cap over my eyes, walked on deck, barked a command or two, and then went home." Cagney would say that Ford saw the captain as "the most pathetic man on the ship, entirely alone, and not knowing how to exert his authority. He was a lonely soul, removed from everybody and everything. I agreed." Except for the part about not knowing how to exert authority, it was a capsule description of John Ford.

The fight with Fonda hovered over the company like a throbbing hangover that wouldn't go away. One day the still photographer shot a picture of Ford at his most intense—handkerchief in his mouth and the vein on the right side of his neck pulsing. Ford got up, grabbed the camera, and threw it over the side of the ship. "I told you in plain English never to do that without asking," he said, then stalked off.

After Midway, the company moved on to Hawaii, where, said actress Betsy Palmer, "Ford was a king. He knew the royal family, he was very much at home there." Ford hosted a party on board the *Araner*, and proved a gracious host, but the mood on the set remained uneasy.

"He was great at tricking actors," said Jack Lemmon. "[At one point] they had me scheduled for the next day, then the next day, but he never actually used me. Then, one day at 11:00 in the morning, the jeep comes up. 'Pappy's waiting.' 'Waiting for what?' 'The scene where you meet the captain.' Well, luckily, Cagney and I had already rehearsed that scene forever because Cagney had said, 'That son of a bitch is gonna pull something on us.' So we did the scene as we'd rehearsed it, and Ford was just amazed. But that scene wasn't scheduled that day.

"Why did he do that? Maintaining control was part of it. And he would do it at the drop of a hat if there was supposed to be uneasiness or nervousness in the character's behavior.

"Ford adored a quality in himself: leadership. He wanted to be and was the admiral, on set and off, and he furthered that every split second, at anybody's expense. Most great directors have that quality, and they inspire a sense of trust. If they ask you to do something, you'll do it to the best of your ability because they'll probably be right."

It was the second consecutive picture that Betsy Palmer had made with Ford, and word spread through the company that Ford had a crush on her. If so, he never acted on it. "I was very naive about all that at the time. I never considered myself attractive. I know Mr. Ford liked me, but he never made a pass. Never. He just liked having me around, probably because I'm a happy person, and he was a dour man. As was Fonda."

The crush and the drinking resulted in wildly out-of-character behavior—a kittenish Ford, cigar clenched between his teeth, climbing to the high board over a swimming pool in Hawaii, doffing a towel, standing there in all his uncircumcised glory, then hurtling stark naked into the pool in order to impress Palmer. Ken Curtis and Dobe Carey had to haul him out before he tried it again and hurt himself.

The company finished the brief Hawaiian location work on October 8 and headed back to Los Angeles. At this point, the picture was on schedule and more than halfway toward completion.

Production resumed at the Warner Bros. lot on October 12, but after only four days of interiors, on Saturday the 16th, the production reports note that "company did not shoot because of illness of director." The tension and his heavy drinking while on location caused Ford's gall bladder to become inflamed, and he had to enter the hospital on October 18 for surgery. Some believed that the gall bladder story was a smoke screen to hide another drinking bout, but the operation was a reality; Betsy Palmer visited him in the hospital, and Ford, sensitive to the stories that were going around town, insisted on showing her the incision.

On Monday the 18th, Mervyn LeRoy took over directing, and the film quickly fell behind schedule. Scheduled to finish around early November, production limped on till December 13, as LeRoy and Joshua Logan diddled with the picture.

On his first day, LeRoy made a short speech to the assembled company. "I'm not going to try to tell you how to play the parts. You're deep into the film; I'm just going to try to make the film Jack Ford would make."

LeRoy was as good as his word. "Mervyn did a good job of directing the rest of the scenes," noted Jack Lemmon, "staging and shooting them the way Ford might have." LeRoy reshot a few scenes that Ford had already done, including the final sequence where Pulver reads the last letter from Roberts. "I was happy about [the retake] because I thought I could do it better. Mervyn was happy to have us try things, let us have a hand in the creative process. More so than Ford.

"Somebody must have told Pappy I was happy about the retake, because when I went to see him after his operation, he said, 'I hear you thought you could do it better?' And I lied like a trouper and said, 'No, no, not at all.' " There was an initial plan to reshoot the sequences of the arrival of the nurses—Fonda and Hayward remained unhappy about Ford's basic approach to all the material—but it was jettisoned because it would have been too expensive.

Joshua Logan also did some retakes, and, with Hayward, edited out some of the extraneous material Ford had devised on location. Although Ford shot for six weeks, it is likely that Winton Hoch's estimate that Ford was responsible for as much as 90 percent of the finished picture is overly generous.

Mister Roberts is the story of the *Reluctant*, a Navy cargo ship ruled by a tyrannical captain. After two years and four months, Lieutenant Doug Roberts wants to get some action before the war's over. Eventually, he does, and gets killed, but his death makes the irrepressible juvenile Ensign Pulver a man.

Most of the film's subsidiary parts are played so broadly you expect everybody to break into a musical number, but the main actors—the jaunty, humane William Powell and the great James Cagney, who never, ever winks at the audience—keep the picture breathing. Cagney plays the captain in a key of vibrating rage, a man immersed in frustration, venality, and thwarted ambition—one of the worst cases of short man's disease ever. Henry Fonda gives a good, straight performance, but neither the film nor Fonda give much hint of why the play ran for years. A series of inane announcements from the ship's loudspeaker was pillaged by *M*A*S*H*, and Ford works in one good in-joke: the ship's movie one night is old friend Hoot Gibson starring in *The Sheriff's Daughter.*

For his part, Henry Fonda ascribed the entire unfortunate mess to what he characterized as Ford's Irish egomania. "Ford [wanted] to do it his way and there was no way he could do it his way, there was only one way to do it and Josh [Logan] had done it."

Although it made a considerable amount of money (a world gross of $9.9 million against a cost of $2.3 million) and earned three Oscar nominations, including one for Best Picture, *Mister Roberts* has failed to sustain a reputation, coming to be regarded as a missed opportunity.

William Powell found the entire experience so traumatic that he never made another movie. "*Mister Roberts* did me in," he told Myrna Loy. "That long location in Hawaii, Jack Ford getting sick, Mervyn LeRoy coming in. Minnie, I wouldn't even groom my mustache again, much less learn a movie role."

Aside from whatever loss of self-respect it cost him, the debacle also cost Ford the friendship of Henry Fonda; the two men never worked together again. Although he would respond with knee-jerk praise whenever Ford was publicly brought up, privately Fonda would usually call him something along the lines of a "son of a bitch who happens to be a genius."

For fifteen years, Fonda and John Wayne had basically divided the responsibilities and glories of starring in Ford's films. Now Wayne would pick up the slack; for the rest of Ford's career, Wayne would star in nearly half of the director's pictures.

Ford was not nearly as oblivious to his increasing reliance on Wayne as he liked to seem. In December 1955, he wrote Wayne about an upcoming project, possibly *The Wings of Eagles*. "God knows I want you for the picture, but you mustn't do it as a sacrifice to yourself. You have been doing that for me for too many years. If you have any chance for a great deal with Danny O'Shea, please be assured that I understand perfectly. After all, nothing ain't never going to break up our friendship."

The emphasis on Wayne affected the reception of Ford's films. Fonda was a liberal as well as a respected actor who returned to the stage frequently. Wayne was regarded as a great movie star, a skilled screen presence, but not really an actor—and a reactionary in the bargain. Because of Ford's increasing reliance on Wayne, culturally snobbish critics and commentators assumed that Ford shared Wayne's politics, which wasn't necessarily the case. But, as the 1950s gave way to the far more turbulently liberal 1960s, that assumption meant both men would come to be regarded as cultural dinosaurs, out of step with the times.

The *Roberts* debacle showed how tenuous Ford's grip on himself really was. John Ford's primary emotional need was control—of his work, of his actors, of his cronies. Jack had not lost his grip while on the *Araner*, the place where he rewarded himself for months of good behavior by achieving alcoholic oblivion, but on a film set, surrounded by people whose respect he demanded and thrived on. If he felt any humiliation and embarrassment—and he almost certainly did—he concealed it behind his continual compulsion to work.

In April 1955, Ford attended the 64th Congress of the Daughters of the American Revolution to accept an award for the best patriotic film of the year for *The Long Gray Line*. His acceptance speech included a complaint about his inability to find financing for a picture about Valley Forge. "There is a Hollywood taboo on the subject of the American Revolution," he said, citing the financial failures of Griffith's *America* and his own *Drums Along the Mohawk*. Nevertheless, he hoped to induce Columbia, who had financed *The Long Gray Line*, to back him on the project. But Columbia wasn't interested, so Ford proceeded with plans to reunite with Merian Cooper and Frank Nugent on another Western. The project was called *The Searchers*.

CHAPTER TWENTY-FOUR

In broad outline, *The Searchers* is a darkened, inverted version of *3 Godfathers*. Both stories involve apparently endless journeys through a hostile no-man's-land, with a child's rescue as motivation. But *3 Godfathers* is a sunny, consoling work with little violence, while *The Searchers* is a savage, disturbing film that projects all manner of psychological and physical hostility. The earlier film is beautifully executed melodrama motivated by selflessness; the latter is epic tragedy motivated by rage.

The primary difference between Alan LeMay's source novel and John Ford's film is the protagonist. LeMay's is Martin Pawley, Ford's is Ethan Edwards. The film version of the character is far darker than the novel's Amos Edwards, who makes the idealistic speech about bringing civilization to the frontier that the film gives to Ollie Carey's Mrs. Jorgenson. Ethan's secondary motivation, after taking revenge for the killing of his brother's family, is to kill Debbie for becoming the squaw of the Indian Scar. This is entirely the invention of Ford and Nugent, as is Martin Pawley's Indian blood, and, for that matter, the sexual relationship between the Indian and the white girl—in the novel, Debbie becomes Scar's adopted daughter. By making his leading character older and far more conflicted, Ford shifts *The Searchers* from a simple story into a far more complex exploration of racial and sexual tensions.

For financing, Cooper rounded up Cornelius Vanderbilt Whitney. Born in 1899, Whitney had vast inherited wealth. He was one of the founders of Pan American World Airways and served as chairman of the board from 1928 to 1941, as the airline grew from a ninety-mile commuter line to the most powerful commercial transport system in the world. Whitney was universally known as "Sonny," deriving from the inability of some childhood friends to pronounce his given name, Cornelius.

While Sonny's cousin Jock also played around with movies and was almost universally admired, there was a distinct division of opinion about Sonny. "Jock was a great, wonderful, generous man," said the pianist Peter Duchin, who knew both men well. "Sonny was a dreadful shit. When his daughter Gail was dying, she asked to see a favorite house of his for one last time, and he turned her down and said there was no room for her to visit. I'm sure that Sonny's attitude to the movies was, 'Why not? Maybe I'll meet a few stars.' Jock was a great man, but Sonny was nothing but a dabbler—mining, racing, whatever."

Sonny had been interested in movies since Jock inveigled him into investing in *Gone With the Wind*. Although Jock, along with David Selznick and most of the other investors, sold out their interest to MGM, Sonny held on to his percentage and, as his widow, Mary Lou, observed, "I still live on *Gone With the Wind*."

Whitney had told Cooper that he would consider backing him in a picture with Argosy (i.e., Ford) or with Leo McCarey. In November 1953, Cooper wrote him that he had a wonderful setup in Spain as well as another project that took place underwater. As with most rich men, Whitney was skilled at dodging requests for money. "LOOK FORWARD TO SEEING YOU IF YOU COME TO NEW YORK, BUT AM NOT FAVORABLY DISPOSED TO GOING INTO PICTURES AT THIS TIME," he wired Cooper.

Cooper was undiscouraged and kept after Whitney. A year later, the seduction was accomplished, and C. V. Whitney Pictures announced its slate: *The Searchers* with Ford, the first of a series Whitney called "The American Series," and a Technicolor remake of *Chang*. Whitney rented office space at 1256 Westwood Boulevard in Los Angeles, and commenced preproduction.

Whitney took an immediate shine to Ford. "My husband just loved his pictures and loved the man," recalled Mary Lou Whitney. "Ford was so totally different than anybody he had been brought up with. For a man who had relatively little education, Ford was unbelievably brilliant. He could read a script and see what could make a character click; he could read the inner soul of the person he was trying to put on the screen. Of course, he could also get you so riled up you were ready to fight."

As casting began, John Agar, his career sagging into the realm of B movies after a rancorous divorce from Shirley Temple, went in to ask about the part of Martin Pawley. "He wasn't mean to me," remembered Agar, "he had just decided that Jeffrey Hunter was going to play the part. I don't know, the divorce might have had something to do with my never working for him again. In this business, you never know what goes through people's minds."

Also trying for the part, despite the brutal treatment he had received on *What Price Glory?*, was Robert Wagner. "Actors are whores," Wagner would sigh by way of explanation.

"You'd like to play the part, wouldn't you?" asked Ford after some preliminaries.

"Yes, Mr. Ford."

"Well, you're not going to."

A stunned Wagner got up and headed for the door.

"Boob?"

Wagner turned.

"You *really* want to play the part?"

"Very much, Mr. Ford."

"Well, you're still not going to."

Ford returned to the work on his desk and a shaken, humiliated Wagner left. "That's the sort of thing that can keep you up nights," he muttered forty years later.

Ford knew *The Searchers* was something special. "We are busy working on the script of The Searchers," he wrote Michael Killanin in March. "It's a tough, arduous job as I want it to be good. I've been longing to do a Western for quite some time. It's good for my health, spirit, and morale and also good for the physical health of my numerous Feeney Peasantry, by whom I am surrounded."

"My husband worked awfully hard on that movie," remembered Jean Nugent. "He loved it, he really did. And Ford needed to have the same people around him all the time, so he told Frank he had to write a part for Dobe Carey, and he had to write a part for Ken Curtis. But he didn't like Ken, so he told Frank, 'Don't make it too good.' "

Ford began production in Monument Valley on June 13, 1955, with eleven setups. From the very beginning, the mood on the set was serious, the tone intense. Wayne was playing somebody beyond anything he had ever attempted, but he had no trouble with the unforgiving obsidian at the core of Ethan Edwards. The character's righteous steel penetrated into Wayne; although he had no interest in or patience with Method acting, his responses during production were very Method indeed.

"When I looked up at Duke during [the first] rehearsal," remembered Harry Carey Jr., "it was into the meanest and coldest eyes I have ever seen. I don't know how he molded that character. Perhaps he'd known someone like Ethan Edwards as a kid. . . . He was even Ethan at dinner time. He didn't kid around on *The Searchers* like he had done on other shows. Ethan was always in his eyes."

They were back in Monument Valley with the Navajos, with Bob Many Mules, Harry Black Horse, Pete Gray Eyes, Billy Yellow, the three Stanley brothers, back with the Fourth of July celebration that Ford threw with food and fireworks and horse race contests for all the Navajos on the reservation.

The Navajo expressed their appreciation for all that Ford had done for them over the years by presenting him with a ceremonial deer hide, complete with ears, tail, and legs.

> *We present this deer hide*
> *to our fellow tribesman*
> Natani Nez
> *As a token of appreciation for the generosity*
> *and friendship he has extended to us in*
> *his many activities in our valley*
>
> *In your travels may there be*
> *beauty behind you*
> *beauty on both sides of you*
> *and beauty ahead of you*
>
> *from your friends the Navajos of Monument Valley*
> *Utah—Arizona*

While on location, Ford was stung by a scorpion. Sonny Whitney was in Monument Valley, keeping an eye on his investment. Understandably worried about the sudden endangering of his director, a nervous Whitney went to John Wayne. "What if we lose him? What are we going to do?" Wayne told Whitney he'd go see what the situation was. A few minutes later he came out. "It's OK," he explained to Whitney. "John's fine, it's the scorpion that died."

Whitney was astonished by Ford's eye. "He could have 2,300 extras in a scene," he said, "and he could spot the one girl who had too much makeup on. He'd turn around and scream at some poor assistant, 'I see a girl out there with lipstick. Get it off!'"

For his part, Ford found Whitney to be a high-maintenance friend. "He had to spend a lot of creative time . . . amusing Whitney," said Patrick Ford. "[Whitney] would trade you the Hudson's Bay for the Gulf Stream. Cape Horn for the Cape of Good Hope. He'd come around, and he'd want certain things done on pictures and Ford would just con him out of it, and resented it. Resented having to do it. So he assigned me to Whitney. . . . So I'd play around with Whitney. . . . That was the worst thing about Whitney and his money. He had to be right in the middle of everything."

While Pat kept Whitney busy by riding horses, Ford could concentrate on the picture, but there were times when all of Pat's creativity in thinking up diversions failed. At the picture's climax, Whitney insisted on being one of the riders who sails into the Indian camp, scattering warriors, in spite of the fact that he wasn't a very good rider. "We were scared to death he was going to break his check-writing arm," Pat Ford remembered with a laugh.

Ward Bond came on board for a few weeks of work, and developed a fixation that Vera Miles was ravenous for him. Bond spent most of his nonworking hours parading around nude in front of open windows, providing what he believed was the proper atmosphere of seductive sensuality.

Even Ollie Carey was there, still one of the few people that could tell Ford he was wrong and be met with a smile. "She'd say, 'Oh, bullshit, Jack,' and he'd say, 'Shut up, Goldie,' " remembered her son. "Only two people could call her Goldie—her husband and Ford."

Entering the world of the stock company for his first full-fledged part was Patrick Wayne, John Wayne's handsome, second-oldest son, who was cast in a small but showy part as a young lieutenant. "He was crazy about me," remembered Patrick Wayne. "Everyone had their day in the barrel, but I was always spared that. Which was good and bad. I wasn't exactly the most popular person on the set. Everyone was getting reamed but me."

As always with an actor who was green, or not completely to be trusted, Ford outlined the scene carefully for Pat. "This is a young kid," he told him. "He's very nervous; he's trying to pretend that he's a grown-up but he's not."

"He handed everything to me," said Wayne. "Remember, he was the only director I'd worked for at that point, and I figured that this was the way pictures were made. And I had my real father standing there watching me in the scene. I wasn't acting scared; I *was* scared."

After the debacle of his uncharacteristically unprofessional behavior on *Mister Roberts*, Ford was rigorously professional, working with the decisiveness that was a characteristic of him at his best, subtracting dialogue, substituting movement, images. Most days he did ten to fifteen setups, sometimes as few as six or as many as twenty-four. Location work wrapped on July 10—some time was lost to bad weather—and resumed at the studio on the 18th. Ford picked up three days during the studio shooting and wrapped the picture on August 13, a week over schedule, at a cost of $2.5 million.

The Searchers is the story of Ethan Edwards, an unreconstructed Confederate warrior who comes to Texas to visit his brother, sister-in-law, and their children. We are given to understand that Ethan and his sister-in-law have an unspoken love—he barely takes his eyes off her, and she lovingly strokes his jacket. When Ethan is called away after a Comanche diversion, the family is murdered by an Indian named Scar, who takes Debbie, the youngest daughter, with him. Ethan, along with Martin Pawley, vows to take his revenge and recover his niece no matter how long it takes. To Edwards's hatred of the Comanche and what he believes they are doing to his niece is added his fury over his error in judgment in leaving his brother's family alone.

In his maturity, Ford's preferred use of the camera was to put it in the right place and leave it there. Camera movement was limited; when he moved it, you noticed. So the rapid track-in to Ethan's face, contorted with hate as he looks at a group of Indian captives, stands as an especially poignant reminder of the same track-in that Ford had used to introduce a boyish, optimistic John Wayne seventeen years before in *Stagecoach*. Same shot, but both actor and director had deepened over the years. The meaning of John Wayne has changed, and Ford has changed it.

Ethan Edwards seethes with bitterness and rage. He mutilates corpses, behaves with the same ferocious cruelty as the Indians he despises. The years drift by, but Ethan just keeps coming. Ford is making use of what David Thomson called "the way in which [Wayne] could carry heroism so close to something terrible and ugly and solitary. Something not fit to come into the house." Ethan gives no quarter; he even mistreats Martin, his companion for the seven or so years that the film encompasses; the boy is part Indian, therefore not an equal.

The script for *The Searchers* does not open or close with doors, and the climax, in which Ethan confronts and transcends his racism and hatred, is also different.

In the script, after Ethan chases down Debbie, he holds a gun to her head. Because she has become the squaw of the man who killed her parents, she must die. "I'm sorry girl . . . shut your eyes," he says. The camera tracks down Ethan's gun arm and moves into a close-up of Debbie's face, "eyes gazing fearlessly, innocently into Ethan's." The gun lowers; Ethan holsters the weapon and walks over to her. "You sure favor your mother," he says, extending his hand. She takes it, and he helps her to her feet.

This is all right, and makes explicit that the reason Ethan cannot kill the girl is her resemblance to her dead mother, whom Ethan loved. But it lacks dynamism. Ford loses the business and changes the dialogue. In a picturesque medium-long shot, Ethan stands over the cowering young woman, poised for murder, when he suddenly reaches down and hoists her over his head in one swooping movement, a gesture that repeats his greeting to the child Debbie in the beginning of the film. He brings her down into a cradle position and quietly murmurs, "Let's go home, Debbie." The murderous Ethan finally feels the tidal pull of family; humanity is affirmed over hate and destruction. In touching Debbie, he feels the human being rather than the abstractions of his racism.

As performed by John Wayne, it's one of the great moments in movies—*balletique*, emotionally true, murder alchemically transmuted into the protective embrace of love, Ford insisting that we can only realize our truest selves when we can accept all of the many forms of humanity we meet.

Ford shot the film's final scene in the late afternoon. Ethan Edwards brings Debbie and Martin home. They dismount and walk through the doorway, leaving Ethan outside. "It just included a dark doorway," remembered John Wayne. "I was outside and they came in [from outside] and [moved past] the camera and turned around. . . . It was emotional, and as they went in the door in the dark and got out of sight, and there was just me in the doorway and the wind blowing, I thought of Harry Carey. He had a stance where he put his left hand on his right arm. He did this incessantly.

"Well, when they took the little girl past the camera and . . . Ollie looked around at me, I just took the pose. The tears poured out of her eyes. It was a lovely dramatic moment in my life and I'm sure in hers."

The door closes, dooming Ethan Edwards to wander "between the winds" for all eternity. Little more can be added to the tragedy of the American hero. Ford's last great film ended.

"That fucking door," snorted Lindsay Anderson. "That's a literary idea. In no other place in Ford's films does something like that appear. Everything else is naturalistically motivated, but the door is a symbol. There's no reason for the door to close other than to exclude John Wayne. Big deal!"

Nobody could be more eloquent in defending Ford than the iconoclastic English director and critic, and few people could be more scathing. His list of objections to the film that has gradually come to be recognized as Ford's ultimate masterpiece was long and incisively expressed, especially in private. "The scene with Natalie Wood and Jeffrey Hunter in the tepee—'Oh, Marty, let's go home.' It's B movie stuff!" For public consumption, the best Anderson would summon was faint praise: "a handsome film . . . self-conscious [and] unconvincing."

Anderson's objections were generational as much as aesthetic. Anderson had responded to the great humanist statement of *The Grapes of Wrath*, the empathy of *Young Mr. Lincoln*, the easy, rollicking humanity of *The Quiet Man*. But a later generation looked at those and saw the venerated textbook classics of their fathers; they had to find their own Ford classics, and did—*She Wore a Yellow Ribbon*, *The Man Who Shot Liberty Valance*, and *The Searchers*.

Anderson, deeply sensitive to matters of tone, felt the occasional coarseness of *The Searchers*—the irritating gaucheness of Ken Curtis, the banality of Vera Miles and Natalie Wood, and Ford's own visual formality, stiffer than the flowing images of *She Wore a Yellow Ribbon* or *The Quiet Man*, closer at times to the studied rhetoric of *The Fugitive*—disqualified the picture from true greatness. Ford's artiness, Anderson felt, was peeking out of the closet—he was forcing his images and themes.

But what Anderson overlooked is that *The Searchers* is Ford's most cogent statement on the conflict between civilization and wilderness, between freedom and responsibility, and most of it is expressed visually, by the juxtaposition of relentless figures in an isolated, tortured landscape. Ethan Edwards is the kind of man who can clear a path for civilization, but is completely unable to live with it. As Stuart Byron would write, "If the movie achieves epic status, it is because it says—with passionate and agonizing conviction—that the beliefs of both conservatives and liberals are equally valid: The American Dream is real and true, and yet America is a country founded on violence."

As with *Fort Apache*, Ethan Edwards embodies more complexity than people are prepared to encounter at the movies. Ethan hates Indians for their savagery *and* takes their scalps for killing his relatives; he despises Martin Pawley's Cherokee blood *and* makes him his heir; he wants to kill his niece for becoming a squaw *and* he embraces her and takes her safely home. Ethan is a monster *and* he is John Wayne. "Do I contradict myself?" asked Walt Whitman. "Very well then I contradict myself, I am large, I contain multitudes." So does Ethan Edwards; so does John Ford.

Ford connects racism with sexual fear; Ethan is outraged by the idea of Debbie's relationship with Scar, so outraged that he believes he has to kill her. Likewise, when Look, Martin's Indian bride, settles down to sleep beside him, he kicks her down a hill. It's a strange, off-putting sequence; Look is an object of ridicule from the beginning—she's fat, comical, sexually unattractive. Ultimately, she sacrifices her life for Martin.

Ford's treatment of Look feels brutal, painful, and unfunny, especially if, as is almost certainly the case, Ford thought of the sequence as comic relief. It's entirely possible that Ford felt he was working too close to the bone with the material of *The Searchers*, that there was too much about racism, too much about miscegenation. The tension may have needed an outlet, but all the comic interludes devised as a release—Look, Ken Curtis's Charlie McCorry—are too coarse by half.

The Searchers is the beginning of the last stage of Ford's career. As

Ford aged, he lost almost all interest in montage, in editing, and his style became increasingly theatrical. Monument Valley becomes a natural proscenium, with buttes on either edge of the screen and riders in deep focus on the horizon. Additionally, Ford began reducing his elements, narrowing the number of characters and sets, the better to concentrate on his themes. This trend culminates in pocket epics such as *The Man Who Shot Liberty Valance* (which works) and *7 Women* (which doesn't).

As he aged, Ford's melancholy came to preoccupy his work and threatened to turn into morbidity. His heroes had often lost battles and wars, but now they died or had their lives shattered. Ford's gift was predominantly lyrical, and the lyric gift rarely survives into old age. Also, like most aging romantics, he was increasingly haunted by the failure of his dreams.

While *The Searchers* was being edited and scored, Ford occupied himself with odds and ends. In October 1955, he spent four days directing John Wayne in a TV show called "Rookie of the Year," an episode of *Screen Directors Playhouse*. Jack and Mary spent the last three weeks of December and all of January in Honolulu. Ford came back tanned and rested.

For audiences of 1956, *The Searchers* was a good John Wayne Western, nothing more. The critics liked it fairly well: "a rip-snorting yarn," said the *New York Times;* "Far above the average picture," said the *Herald Tribune;* although Robert Ardrey, later a pop anthropologist, groused that "the same John Ford who once gave adults *The Informer* must now give children *The Searchers.*"

The Searchers was successful, grossing $5.9 million worldwide by April of 1958, making it the eleventh biggest grossing movie of 1956. Although it didn't earn a single Academy Award nomination, because of the haunted Ethan Edwards and the film's epic canvas and theme, it has come to be revered as one of the great American films, with a resonance that dwarfs the official classics of its year—*Around the World in 80 Days* and *Giant.*

C. V. Whitney geared up for his next production. *The Missouri Traveler* was a far more modestly budgeted picture than *The Searchers. The Missouri Traveler* was produced by Pat Ford under the careful supervision of his father, which meant that Ford was on the set "all the time," according to Mary Lou Whitney. "He scared us to death. Pat was the producer, but when John arrived you had to stand up while the accordion played and sing 'Bringing in the Sheaves,' bow and say 'Good Morning.' He'd walk on the set and yell, 'My God, she's flat. She doesn't have any boobs! Go buy her some boobs!' But I didn't want to look like Marilyn Monroe. Pat had a very difficult time."

Ford encouraged Whitney's infatuation with the young actress, telling him he "couldn't stand that woman you're married to. I'm glad you're getting rid of her." Mary Ford had a slightly pithier reaction. After she met Mary Lou, she told her daughter, "I can understand him marrying her, but I can't understand him meeting her."

"Pat was in charge of Whitney's company," recalled Andrew Mc-Laglen, "and I didn't feel that he did that good a job with it. I didn't feel that his father was all the way behind him, unlike my dad; he was 110 percent behind me. He told me not to go into the business, said it was too tough, and there were too many disappointments. But once I got established, he was so proud; he'd call producers and actors and ask how they liked working with me. Jack wasn't that kind of father."

Ford's relationship with his grandchildren was considerably easier than his relationships with his children. As a boy, Dan had already decided he wanted to be in the movie business, and Ford encouraged the necessary attentiveness, as in a conversation driving along Waikiki Beach.

"You want to be a director," said Ford. "What does that guy walking through the crosswalk do for a living?"

"Gee, I don't know," said Dan, who then guessed he might be in the Navy.

"No," said Ford, "he's too old. Look at him. He's got Navy shoes on, but he's in civilian clothes. He's probably a steward on the [cruise ship] *Lurleen*. He doesn't work on the deck crew because he looks like he's got soft hands." Another time, with Dan's brother, Tim, Ford pointed to a man wearing an Aloha shirt and a lei.

"What does that guy do? A tourist? No. Look at his arms. They're not tanned. Nobody around here wears a lei unless they're a visitor. Now look at his hands; he might be an engineer."

In January 1956, while *The Searchers* was still in post-production, Ford and Cooper dissolved Argosy Productions. If one doesn't count their maiden effort, *The Long Voyage Home*, technically a Walter Wanger production, Argosy had made nine pictures in ten years. Of those, at least four were superb, and that doesn't include *The Searchers*, even though it was an Argosy picture in all but name and responsibility for the bank loan. By any standards except personal aggravation, Argosy had to be considered a success.

When the liquidation was complete, Argosy had even made a little money, in spite of Herbert Yates's best efforts. Argosy's investors earned about a 30 percent return on their investment, due entirely to *The Quiet Man*.

CHAPTER TWENTY-FIVE

In the spring of 1956, Ford went to Ireland to direct an anthology film called *Three Leaves of the Shamrock*, later changed to *The Rising of the Moon*. Ford had been working on the project as early as 1954, and in September of that year had written to Kate Hepburn, who was in Venice shooting *Summertime* for David Lean, offering her a part in the picture, albeit with several caveats: "We can't offer you much salary, Kate. . . . The company ain't got no dough. . . . I'm doing it for free."

Ford managed to hit a restrained note of bathos as he wrote, "If you had a week or ten days free I would love, as my days are drawing to a close, [to] direct you again." The letter is that of two old friends; there is no sense whatever of a past affair, and this was to hold true of the rest of their very occasional correspondence.

Hepburn elected not to be a part of the movie, but, as Ford enlisted Tyrone Power, he had the only star power he needed. In any case, Ford rethought the importance of Power appearing in the playlet "The Rising of the Moon." Power's own schedule precluded him working on the picture until May 1956, when Ford needed to be back in Hollywood working on *The Wings of Eagles*. Ford's suggestion to Michael Killanin was that Brian Desmond Hurst direct Power's segment.

Beyond that, Ford was uncomfortable about Killanin and Mike Frankovich (the production executive on the picture) trying to get Power in the cast at all costs. "By using Ty," wrote Ford to Killanin, "we immediately destroy the native Irish flavor of what we are trying to accomplish . . . willynilly we are using an American star. This means only one thing . . . more money in Frankovich's pocket. . . . I'd like to do the 'Rising' with him, but not if it throws my life out of proportion." In other words, it was a fine idea to use Power as long as Power was available when

Ford wanted him to be available; otherwise, it would compromise the picture's dramatic integrity.

The entire production cost for the the film was only $256,000—Ford inveigled Frank Nugent into writing the script for $1,000—and Ford took no salary whatever, doing the picture as a *beau geste* for Ireland and Michael Killanin. Ford rammed the film through in thirty-five days, ten under schedule.

"It was a very happy time, that," remembered the actress Eileen Crowe. "John Ford was in great form." Locations were in Galway and Dublin, then over near Limerick, then Clare. The Irish actor Donal Donnelly watched as Ford amused himself by baiting the English crew. "Ford was looking back [to the actors] for approval; he thought he was fighting the fight for Ireland." When it came time for a close-up of the gap-toothed Donnelly, Ford took him aside and told him to keep his mouth closed. "Now this is no offense to you, [but] you are a victim of these guys. These are what is known as Famine Teeth."

"So it was like him and me together," Donnelly told Lindsay Anderson, "two Irish oppressed people, and I was the living witness to the sufferings of my nation. 'Famine Teeth!' Amazing bullshit."

There was some thought given to having Ford introduce and narrate the three stories himself in the manner of Cecil B. DeMille, but after stringing along Ty Power, they had to do something with him, so he served as host. Ford left post-production entirely in the hands of Michael Killanin.

The completed picture was run for Jack Warner, his assistant Steve Trilling, and Warner editor-in-chief Rudi Fehr. "The first two episodes were wonderful," recalled Fehr, "but the third was in a heavy Irish brogue and I couldn't understand a word."

Ford called Trilling for his reaction, and Trilling told him that Fehr felt the dialogue of the last episode needed to be rerecorded. "The next day," said Fehr, "we got together with Ford to work out a post-production schedule. 'Mr. Ford, may I talk to you for a minute?' " asked Fehr.

"What did you say?" said Ford. Fehr repeated himself. Ford turned to the editor and said, "I can't understand a word this guy's saying."

There were some plans laid for Four Provinces to make a film version of *Playboy of the Western World* with Ty Power starring and Brian Desmond Hurst directing, but those were laid low by the actor's premature death in 1958. While multipart story films had attained a certain art house cachet ever since *Dead of Night*, there was to be no such success for *The Rising of the Moon*.

The first two stories ("The Majesty of the Law" and "A Minute's

Wait") strike identical notes of prideful Irish obstinance and convoluted protocol, and feature more Celtic obnoxiousness masquerading as humor than should be allowed in a free society. ("A Minute's Wait" does feature an endearing Irish version of a marriage proposal: "How would you like to be buried with my people?")

The third story, "1921," is based on Lady Gregory's "The Rising of the Moon," and involves a couple of women disguised as nuns breaking an IRA leader out of jail, and follows him as he makes his escape by the Spanish Arch, under the nose of the oblivious English. It's the best episode in the film, but it's too little too late. For the third episode, Ford seems to have given cameraman Robert Krasker his head, and he shoots in his neorealist style, complete with the tilted camera that had been so effective in *The Third Man.*

Warner Bros. gave *The Rising of the Moon* only a token release. It ended up amassing a worldwide gross of $48,000, undoubtedly making it the lowest-grossing feature ever by a major director.

J ack Warner must have been impressed by *The Searchers;* in October 1956, he offered Ford a three-picture deal, to be completed within five years. Warner's would finance all the pictures, and, most importantly for Ford's percentage of the takings, the pictures would not be cross-collateralized. Although the contract would not have tied Ford down exclusively to Warners, he seems to have had some doubts; nearly two years later, the contract remained unsigned, and Jack Warner was peeved.

In any case, Ford had all the work he could handle, and money was no problem. He was able to help Anna Lee out when she ran into a temporary financial shortfall in mid-1956, and she wasn't the only one.

After *The Rising of the Moon*, Ford shot *The Wings of Eagles*, a biography of his friend Frank "Spig" Wead, who had died in November 1947. Wead was a legendary character who began his career as a naval aviator. After falling down the stairs and breaking his back, resulting in paralysis that was slightly ameliorated after years of determined physical therapy, he undertook a different line of work—screenwriting.

The Wings of Eagles is an uneasy mixture of—in its first half—uninspired roughhouse in the manner of a silent comedy, and—in its second half—intense domestic drama, with John Wayne giving a very fine performance, even forgoing his toupee in the last third of the picture.

After Wead's accident, he is hospitalized in a face-down position, and Ford doesn't show us Wayne's face for twenty minutes. Wead's sense of constriction and despair is palpable. Stylistically, *The Wings of Eagles* is unremarkable, and Ford's own interest in the film seems to come and go. The picture was almost certainly damaged by the decision, at the request of Wead's children, to remove scenes of Wead's wife (Maureen O'Hara) descending into alcoholism—exactly the kind of punch-pulling compromise that happens when you make a movie about a pal. As Ford told Peter Bogdanovich, "I didn't want to do the picture . . . but I didn't want anyone *else* to make it."

The film does have an odd undercurrent—Frank Wead is a man consumed by his profession, estranged from any domestic life, a virtual stranger to his children, unable to completely give himself to the wife who loves him, truly comfortable only with the less demanding company of men. The result is a perceptible sense of loss and incompletion that increases as he ages. Either Ford and Wead shared a remarkable number of character traits or Ford was lending him a lot of his own.

The Wings of Eagles is mainly notable for a funny turn by Ward Bond as "John Dodge," a gruff Hollywood director with pictures of Harry Carey and Tom Mix on his office wall, and four Oscars on the shelf. Although Bond is costumed and made up to look like Ford, he doesn't attempt the director's distinctively nasal New England accent.

The sequence provides final confirmation, if any were needed, of Ford's interest in his own myth. Of course, being Ford, a man with a professed disinterest in fame or personal publicity, a cagily admiring self-portrait was out of the question, so he had to pretend it had been done against his will. "I didn't intend it that way," he told Peter Bogdanovich with a straight face, "but [Ward Bond] did. I woke up one morning and my good hat was gone, my pipe and everything else; they'd taken all the Academy Awards and put them in the office set."

In December, Ford took off for Hawaii with Mary and Ward Bond. When he returned, he shot a letter off to John Wayne, who was making *Legend of the Lost* with Henry Hathaway. "First, I want to give you your Christmas present," Ford wrote. "From now on Bond is your exclusive property. You can have him. I must admit, though, that he gave a terrific performance in Hawaii. The only trouble was that he kept switching his character. In the morning he would be the lazy, kindly old beachcomber, the ex-professor of literature at Harvard, Oxford, Heidelberg, etc. Then in the afternoon he would be a retired gentleman—the younger son of a noble family in England. In the evening he became just a sloppy, god-damned guttersnipe—big, boisterous—could lick anybody—his fly open, a good rich vocabulary of four-letter words, and an all-around pain in the ass. From now on, he's your shit."

The ostensible reason for the letter was a project entitled *The Judge and His Hangman* that Ford was trying to set up in Germany. Ford asked Wayne what he thought about a cast including Charles Laughton, Louis Jourdan, Erich von Stroheim, and, perhaps, Basil Rathbone. He passed along good words about *The Wings of Eagles*, which had previewed well, although Ford groused that the MGM executives felt it had too many laughs. "How in the hell can a picture have too many laughs, I ask you? Maybe they should take them out and distribute them over the entire MGM program."

Three weeks later, Ford was writing Wayne again, asking about the Hathaway movie. "Is the picture going all right, or is it just like all other pictures? There doesn't seem to be much fun in making them anymore—just a lot of trouble. We used to say in the old days—all you get out of it is a million bucks, but those happy hours are gone forever."

*T*he Last Hurrah had been under discussion since mid-1956. James Cagney had been Ford's first choice for the part of Frank Skeffington, but the actor seems to have shied away from another go-round with Ford after *Mister Roberts*. Ford then gave some thought to John Wayne. At the end of 1956, while Ford was holed up on the *Araner*, at Ala Wai harbor in Honolulu, he was joined by Frank Nugent and the two men began work on the script.

Four months later, it was done, but ongoing uncertainty over the cast forced postponement of the picture. Then *The Judge and His Hangman* fell through, but Ford was in the mood to work. Michael Killanin quickly began setting up a picture in London.

Ford did not lack for opportunities—Burt Lancaster offered him *Run Silent, Run Deep*, and Kirk Douglas wrote, telling Ford how much he wanted to work for him. For a time, Ford contemplated the tantalizing prospect of a Robert Rossen script for Melville's *Billy Budd*. Younger stars wanted Ford, but he didn't want them. The issue of control was paramount; Lancaster and Douglas were widely known as activist, hands-on actors, and had produced some of their own pictures, anathema to Ford. If, as Andrew Sarris noted, he was increasingly regarded by critics as a voice from the past, "an eccentric antique dealer, with a good eye for vintage Americana," that was the way he wanted it.

For some strange reason, he wanted *Gideon's Day*, or as it was known in its American release, *Gideon of Scotland Yard*, a police procedural with Jack Hawkins. The art director for the film was the great Ken Adam, a German national who flew for the RAF during World War II, still a few years away from his apotheosis in *Dr. Strangelove*, the James Bond films, and *Barry Lyndon*.

Adam went to the Connaught Hotel for his first meeting with Ford. He found a tall, lanky, elderly man chewing continuously on his handkerchief. "One thing I want to get straight with you, Ken, is that I'm not one of those airy-fairy, artsy-craftsy directors that you might have worked with before. I don't shoot up an actor's nostrils and I don't put the camera between his legs. I tell a story and I shoot it the way I think that story should be told. Once we understand each other on that level, I'm sure we'll get along just fine."

Very well. Adam strove for the realism and authenticity Ford obviously wanted. For the set of Gideon's office at Scotland Yard, Adam's design called for a window overlooking Westminster Bridge. Ford didn't want back projection, so Adam designed a model bridge in forced perspective, with cars, pedestrians, and buses attached to a canvas belt traveling across and under the model. It looked great both up close and through the lens, but on the first day the miniature was scheduled to be used, something went terribly wrong, and the belt moved in jerks and jolts or not at all.

Adam was dying inside, but Ford carried on with the scene as though everything was fine. Finally he called out "Cut!" and walked over to Adam. "That didn't look too good, did it, Ken?" he inquired solicitously. "Just how long will it take to repair it?"

The problem was that the canvas belt had stretched and was no longer taut enough; it would have to be replaced by a leather belt and it could only be done overnight. Fully expecting to be fired on the spot, Adam told Ford that they wouldn't be able to use the miniature until the next day. "Don't worry, kid, that's fine; I'll point the camera the other way for the rest of the day." And so he did, shooting reverses on all the other actors in the scene with Jack Hawkins. The next day the miniature worked splendidly, and Ford never mentioned the incident again.

Adam remembered him as "kind and professional," although Ford's eyes continued to bother him. "He was always having trouble with his glasses," said Adam. "I wouldn't have thought of him as a person in the prime of life."

Adam believed that in many respects Ford was a simple man—a professional Irishman, a trait that influenced almost everything he said and did, proud of his own legend, which he was not shy about spreading. Adam noted that Ford frequently told the story about a producer admonishing him for being several days over schedule, whereupon Ford tore some pages out of the script and retorted, "Now we're on schedule." (If the story is true, it can safely be assumed that Ford had already decided to cut the offending pages, and had moved whatever plot points they contained to another scene.)

"Gideon was not a great film," said cinematographer Freddie Young with classic understatement. "It was untypical of John. That particular thing was not his cup of tea. I don't know why he did it; he probably just wanted to make a film in England. He didn't show much emotion about it at all. I never saw him intense or excited."

While Ford was shooting *Gideon,* Pat Ford's career with C. V. Whitney came to an abrupt end when Whitney decided to get out of the movie business. Once again, Ford undertook to find work for his son; Pat was sent to scout locations for a film Ford had planned for 1958 called *The Horse Soldiers.*

While he was in London, Ford agreed to a BBC interview conducted by Lindsay Anderson. The younger man thought him slightly diminished since he had seen him during the production of *Mogambo.* "He gave the impression of being not altogether firm on his feet," remembered Anderson.

Ford harassed Anderson about his "Oxford" accent, and refused to acknowledge that any of Anderson's questions had merit. He lied, he contradicted everything he actually believed, and he pretended not to understand a word of what Anderson was saying, completely demoralizing his most ardent admirer.

After the tape equipment had been safely packed away, he guided Anderson into a discussion of English actors and films, which somehow segued to Ford mentioning that he'd never seen Eisenstein's *Ivan the Terrible.* Anderson offered to have the National Film Theatre screen it for him. And when Anderson rather hesitantly mentioned that he'd recently made a film of his own, called *Every Day Except Christmas,* a documentary about Covent Garden Market, Ford thought it would make a fine companion piece for the Eisenstein film.

A few days later, Ford and Anderson watched the movies. Ford peppered Anderson with a barrage of questions during the unreeling of *Every Day Except Christmas,* greatly discomfitting the young director. Did he use lights? What union did the men belong to? What was a busker? When do the fish come in? There was no pat on the head from the father-figure.

During *Ivan the Terrible,* he was quieter: "Eisenstein was a cameraman, wasn't he? . . . a pure cameraman. . . . No use with people. Look at the way they move. Like puppets." Anderson realized that what Ford wanted from people was facts, not opinions.

Jack Hawkins plays Chief Inspector Gideon as a harassed husband and father; driving his kids to school on the way to the office, he first gets a traffic ticket, then can't find a place to park, etc.

The film might have been intended as a belated response to the Louis de Rochemont–Henry Hathaway actuality noirs of the late 1940s. There are some good actors (Cyril Cusack, Anna Massey) in small, trite parts, and the film is structured as a series of vignettes of one long day. It clips along, rather in the manner of modern television, and it has an entertainingly loony resolution—the villain is an artist who does payroll robberies to finance his painting. After arresting him, Gideon staggers home and asks for his slippers.

When Columbia released the film in America in 1959, they struck only black and white prints, although Ford had shot it in Technicolor; there was no sense throwing good money after bad. Ford made it for $453,600, but only took £5,000 in salary. Like *The Rising of the Moon*, it was another little film without an audience. As of late 1960, it had income of $124,138.

While in London, Ford enjoyed himself, seeing a good deal of Brian Desmond Hurst, attending Mass, going to the Tower of London to see the cell of Thomas More. On September 2, he sat down and wrote a birthday letter to his wife. "Mary darling," he began, "Happy Birthday! Sept. 4, you thot [sic] I'd forget it, dincha?" Brian was planning to go to Las Vegas with her, he reported. Then, after a rundown of his activities, he slipped in a sentence that betrayed their age: "My energy is OK—how's yours?"

By November 1957, Ford was back home and writing Wayne another of his nothing-going-on-here-what's-going-on-there? letters typical of those vacant times when he wasn't working. Wayne was in Japan working on *The Barbarian and the Geisha* for John Huston. Ford had become friendly with Akira Kurosawa, and he asked Wayne to let the the great Japanese director visit Huston's set. "He is a terribly, terribly nice guy.

"If you see any beautiful Japanese dolls—not babes—dolls—I wish you'd get a couple for Barbara. I owe her several. The last lot went astray. But never mind any samurai swords.

"Do you enjoy beer? I do. . . .

"P.S. Would you like to do a western sometime?"

At long last, *The Last Hurrah* was ready to go. The schedule was thirty-five days, and the budget was $2.5 million. Spencer Tracy was receiving $200,000 to star, Ford $125,000 plus a percentage for his direction. Production began on February 24, 1958. Ford went eight days over schedule, but still brought the picture in $200,000 under budget.

There may have been a slight hesitation on Tracy's part over involving himself with Ford. There had been some consideration given to hiring Ford to direct *The Old Man and the Sea*, but Spencer had warned Leland Hayward that "only worry is that he'll shoot picture, you, me, and boy."

If Ford had not entirely forgotten his displeasure over Tracy's forced abdication from *The Plough and the Stars*, he managed to put it aside. The two men worked with enthusiasm and pleasure in each other's company. Tracy took to calling a particularly disreputable hat his John Ford hat. Until the end of his life, Ford regarded Tracy as a good friend, and he managed to transcend any jealousy he might have felt over Tracy's relationship with Kate Hepburn.

Ford filled *The Last Hurrah* with so many old-timers that the picture resembled the waxworks scene from *Sunset Boulevard*. There was Ricardo Cortez, Pat O'Brien, John Carradine, Basil Rathbone, Donald Crisp, James Gleason, Wallace Ford, Jane Darwell, and Edmund Lowe. If Tom Mix had been alive, Ford undoubtedly would have figured out a way to shoehorn him in as well.

Pat O'Brien hadn't made a film for Ford since *Air Mail*, hadn't worked for him since the stage production of *What Price Glory?*, and he noted that Ford "got a little prickly over the years. He was always a very rough disciplinarian. I remember on *The Last Hurrah* he'd go nuts about the littlest things, like marks on the floor. But after the storm, he'd be the same old Jack.

"He would never talk the part you were playing, he'd just tell you what he wanted. 'I hope you can get it,' he'd say, chewing on that handkerchief he always had. When you failed, he'd say, 'That wasn't what I wanted. Try to get what I wanted. We're going to take another whack at it and it better be good.' And after you finally got it he'd come over and put his arms around you. 'Why the hell didn't you get it in the first place?' he'd say. Ford was the genius of them all. He was an artist drawing a portrait in oil."

There was one moment of stark terror, when somebody showed up with a case of whiskey to mark St. Patrick's Day. Since there were enough drunks on the picture to populate a good-sized meeting of Alcoholics Anonymous, Ford froze. "Jesus Christ," he barked, "what do you want to do, shut down the picture?" The booze was quickly removed.

Frank Skeffington is introduced as he descends the stairs of his house and places a rose by a portrait of his late wife, making him one with Judge Billy Priest. Skeffington is running for mayor one more time—one time too many—but he plays out his hand with charm and brio. As has been preordained, at the end of the picture he succumbs to a heart attack.

The death of Skeffington symbolizes the death of the old back-pocket politics at which John Feeney (in Ford's life) and Lincoln (in Ford's art) had excelled—men with a knack for people. But *The Last Hurrah* is comparable to a big fat pitch down the middle of the plate that unaccountably gets popped up. It had all the elements for a classic Ford picture—a good story, an omnipresent sense of loss, a strong leading actor, a rogue's gallery of great character actors—but something is missing.

We get a sense of Skeffington's genius for people in the way he flays those who need to be flayed, comforts those who need reassurance. He strongarms bankers into building public housing, attends a funeral and admires the workmanship of the casket, then smoothly segues into comforting the widow and slipping her some money.

But the primary dramatic lines are botched. The young journalist played by Jeffrey Hunter remains unintegrated into the story. Mostly, he stands around and gives Skeffington someone to talk to. And there's no sense whatever of the city—any city.

Most of the blame falls on Ford's reflexive sneering at half of the characters. Skeffington's son, as well as his young rival, played by Charles FitzSimons, are both airheaded idiots, cartoonishly exaggerated, and so overplayed that they rob the film of a good deal of its conviction, not to mention its poignance.

The director's contemptuous lack of sympathy with the modern world is revealed by his inability to treat it seriously; nobody outside of Skeffington's own generation has any dignity at all, and that lack of respect undermines the picture. If Skeffington can be defeated by obvious clowns, how good can he be? He loses, not for any believable reason, but because it says so in the script.

Anna Lee said that Ford was disappointed with the picture, as well he might have been. Rousing the necessary energy was getting harder and harder; he was now in his mid-sixties, hurtling forward on sheer momentum rather than desire: "I don't want to make great sprawling pictures. I want to make films in a kitchen. . . . The old enthusiasm has gone, maybe. But don't quote that—oh, hell, you can quote it."

Audiences of 1958 weren't in the mood for a muted, ineffective character piece about an old Boston pol. Gross receipts as of May 1963 were only $1.2 million; by August 1971, Columbia carried the losses on the picture as $1.8 million.

On June 8, 1958, Ford appeared on a live TV show, *Wide Wide World*, with Dave Garroway. It was a tribute to the Western, and the producers put together an impressive cast—Broncho Billy Anderson, Gabby Hayes, Walter Brennan, Ward Bond, Gene Autry, John Wayne (in costume for Hawks's *Rio Bravo*), Gary Cooper, Jack Warner (who stumbles reading the cue cards), Delmer Daves, and the new generation of television cowboys such as James Garner and Jack Kelly from *Maverick*.

Ford's initial segment began with a shot grabbed without him knowing he was on camera. He's nervously smoothing his hair with his hands, shifting uneasily in his chair. Garroway asks him if *Stagecoach* was his favorite Western, and he replies that "I sort of like my first big Western *The Iron Horse* . . . one of my favorites is *The Searchers*, and I think my real favorite is *She Wore a Yellow Ribbon* featuring old Duke here."

And did he prefer Westerns?

"As a person, yes; as a director, I just love 'em."

A later segment had Ford explaining how horse falls were accomplished. "I have been in pictures forty-three years," he told the audience, "and I can honestly say I have never hurt a horse."

From being in a reactive position, answering questions from an unseen interviewer, Ford is now in control, instructing stuntmen, and the change in his body language is immediately apparent—looser, obviously relaxed and in charge, or, rather, relaxed *because* he's in charge, calling out orders in a loud, piercing voice. As stuntman Chuck Hayward gets up from a picture-perfect horse fall, Ford nods to the camera and says, "Ladies, he's a bachelor." Anecdotes always implied that command agreed with Ford, but this brief segment is stark proof.

Had Ford been more gregarious, or more interested in money, he could have fronted an anthology show on television along the lines of *Death Valley Days*—the Western equivalent of *Alfred Hitchcock Presents.* But that was something he would never have pursued—not enough control. Besides, it would have put him on an equivalent footing with Ward Bond, who was having the greatest success of his life starring in *Wagon Train*, which went on the air in September 1957. Ford was set in his ways and proud of it, and had been making movies too long to change now.

Ford had maintained an incessant activity when he was commercially surefire, and wasn't about to slow down now that his tastes and the audience's were slowly diverging. Even in his mid-sixties, when most directors are slowing down, usually involuntarily, Ford couldn't stop moving, filling in the spaces between pictures with the occasional TV film, or a documentary project for the Navy.

In the fall of 1958, Ford went to Korea with George O'Brien to make a Defense Department film eventually entitled *Korea: Battleground for Liberty.* One of the photographers was a World War II veteran named Joe Longo, who volunteered to work on the film when he heard that Ford was going to direct it. He asked his friend and associate Harry Perry, the great aerial photographer who shot William Wellman's *Wings*, what he could do to impress Ford.

"You're gonna be using Mitchell cameras," grunted Perry. "He likes to scout his own stuff. Stay behind him."

Longo didn't believe it could be that simple, so he called Mark Armistead, Ford's aide de camp. "The old man will go out to scout the location," said Armistead. "He'll walk forward with his entourage behind him. You stay behind them. And if he stops, he'll put up a right hand or his left. If it's his left, he wants coffee or a cigar. If it's his right, he wants a viewfinder. You run up, give it to him, and get away."

Longo knew the experience was going to be unusual when he flew over to Hawaii to pick up Ford on the way to Taiwan and Korea. It was about 6:30 P.M., and the *Araner* was sitting at the dock, silhouetted in the setting sun. While Longo's associates went to fetch Ford, Longo was lounging by the car, enjoying the view. On board the ship, a tall, lean man moved toward the fantail of the *Araner*, where he stopped, opened his pants, and relieved himself into the water. Mr. Longo, meet Mr. Ford.

A couple of days later, the crew had arrived in Korea and Ford was scouting locations, with Longo staying back. "So, we're in a field," remembered Longo, "and he's walking around. Armistead and George O'Brien are in uniform. He's in khakis, with a dirty shit-brown baseball cap, with a little naval insignia on it. And his eyepatch, and he's sucking on a handkerchief.

"He sees a beautiful spot, and looks at his watch, so he could get the same light the next day. He raises his right hand and I give him the Mitchell finder. He looks through it, sets the frame for the lens, and sets the finder on the ground to mark the spot where the camera should be. He didn't say a word to me."

Later, when the unit was back in its quarters, Longo took out a little pennywhistle and began playing "Danny Boy." One of Ford's assistants came and fetched him. He walked into Ford's quarters and found him sitting on the edge of his bed, nursing a drink.

"Where'd you learn to play that?" asked Ford.

"I was in World War II; 13th Air Force."

"But where'd you learn to play that song?"

"My wife is Irish."

"Play it again."

So Joe Longo played "Danny Boy" again.

"What's your name?" asked Ford when Longo was finished.

"Longo."

"How does a guinea learn to play Irish songs?" Ford wondered aloud.

From that point on, Longo served as Ford's Far Eastern version of Danny Borzage, playing "Danny Boy," "Garry Owen," and other perennials on the pennywhistle. Longo noticed that Armistead and O'Brien were completely subservient to their commander. "If you'd have wanted to kick Ford in the ass, they would have had to move their noses. But it wasn't corporate or self-serving, it was complete respect.

"I never had doors opened and red carpet treatment like I did when I was working with Ford. I spent a lot of time around generals, during the war and Korea and the rest, and they didn't intimidate me. I spent a lot of time with James Doolittle, and I was never intimidated by him at all. But Ford intimidated the hell out of me. It wasn't because he was from Hollywood, it was the way he conducted himself. He had an awful lot of clout; he wasn't any one- or two-star general."

When he wasn't being serenaded by Longo's pennywhistle, Ford became embroiled in one of his rare flings. The woman was a Korean actress named Heran Moon. Attractive, in her mid- to late thirties, Moon appeared to be besotted with Ford after a whirlwind three days. When Ford returned to America, Moon commenced a series of ardent love letters during the latter part of 1959 and the early part of 1960.

From Moon's letters, it's clear that Ford was initially responsive, sending her letters and presents. Moon is frank, probably too much so for her own good: "First I would like to say I love you." From there she moves on to tell him of the coverage in various Korean magazines of his presence, and of how in many of the pictures she was there beside him.

A few days later, Moon wrote and complained that she hadn't heard from Ford in two weeks, and signs off with "All my love and life is yours." The fact that Ford saved the letters rather than discarding them indicates that the relationship was more than one way. He alluded to the affair in a letter to Michael Killanin, when he noted "I've had Asiatic Flu again . . . and this time really bad." The "again" implies that Heran Moon wasn't the first, but she was almost certainly the last.

Whatever emotional leverage Moon may have earned was completely dissipated when, on February 2, 1960, she wrote Ford telling him how much she missed him, then asked him to help her get the title role in *The World of Susie Wong*. Ford must have told her in his typically abrupt fashion not to bother him again, for the letters ceased.

Although Ford had made only a few films for Columbia, and was hardly a social intimate of its president, in February 1958 he was asked to be an honorary pallbearer at Harry Cohn's funeral, along with Paul Lazarus Jr. Ford and Lazarus were seated next to each other for the extravaganza, which took place on a soundstage at Columbia, was staged by George Sidney, and entailed Danny Thomas reading the Lord's Prayer and Danny Kaye delivering a eulogy written by Clifford Odets.

"He was a fire that warmed some and burned others," intoned Kaye. Ford turned to Lazarus and asked, "Who's that talking, the new rabbi?" As the casket was being moved for the trip to Hollywood Memorial Cemetery, Kaye came down the aisle to say hello to Lazarus. "Jack, you know Danny Kaye?" asked Lazarus by way of introduction. Ford fixed him with his direst stare. "How would I know a comic?" he snarled, cutting Kaye dead. As he was leaving the funeral, he leaned over to Frank Nugent and explained his presence: "I just wanted to make sure the son of a bitch was dead."

Never at his best in unfamiliar social situations, Ford also distinguished himself by being a bad winner and a poor loser at cards. Even Patrick Wayne, his beloved godson, didn't get away unscathed. "His wit was very acerbic, razor-sharp. Once, I was flying someplace with him and we were playing gin rummy. I'm a pretty good card player, and I decided to go easy on the Old Man. He won the hand, and said, 'After this, play with small children and Ward Bond.' And I thought, 'Oh, wait until I get you at a card table again.' But it didn't happen. Maybe he knew I was going easy on him."

The actual game was less important than the social transaction. Frank Nugent's wife, Jean, remembered that "Frank loved to play bridge, and Jack was nuts about it too. Lots of Sunday afternoons we'd go out to Duke's house. Ward Bond would be there and we'd play. But they'd fight all the time. When the screaming started, Mary and I would go out to the garden and wait for it to blow over."

Ford's attitude toward people tended to remain frozen at the level at which he had first encountered them. Thus, Ward Bond would always be a dumb football player, and John Wayne would always be the graceless but eager propman. Ford's behavior toward Wayne's family varied. Since he was Pat Wayne's godfather, Pat got a pass, but Michael, who closely resembled his father, received the same brusque—at best—treatment as Duke.

"One time he came in and gave Pat and Tony and Melinda a nice hello," Mike told a friend, "and then he turned to me and said, 'What are you doing, numbnuts?' "

*T*he Horse Soldiers was a throwback to *The Plough and the Stars*—a picture cursed by bad decisions and malevolent fate. The script, about a Union raiding party out to destroy Confederate supply lines all the way to Vicksburg, was by Martin Rackin and John Lee Mahin. William Clothier, the cinematographer, remembered going to Ford and enthusiastically proclaiming that it was the best script he'd ever read.

"If you think I'm going to photograph that goddamn script, you're mistaken," the director retorted. Ford took an equally hard line with his producers, saying, "You know where we ought to make this picture?"

"No, where?"

"Lourdes, because it's going to take a miracle to pull it off."

One of Ford's objections seemed to be that the tag of the script was the same one used in William Wellman's superb *Battleground* just eight years before, only with the Civil War instead of World War II—the beat-up soldiers are marching out and pass the fresh troops marching in. The commander calls Attention, the drums start, the flag waves, and the cycle begins all over again. "It brings tears to my eyes just telling you about it," remembered Clothier. "It's a great tag; corny, but a great tag. Ford wouldn't shoot it. 'It's been done. It's a lot of shit.' " Stealing from himself was one thing—Ford did it all the time—but stealing from another director, even one he liked as much as Bill Wellman, was out of the question.

Ford was troubled by the Louisiana location, and the problem that posed for Althea Gibson, attempting to make the transition from tennis to acting. Segregation was still the rule in 1958, and Ford's conscience wouldn't allow him to have Gibson housed in quarters apart from the white actors. All of Gibson's footage was shot in Hollywood, with doubles used for location long shots.

Despite Ford's unhappiness with the script, the locations were fresh and Ford had graced more than one ordinary script with extraordinary visuals. The cast included William Holden, a big star, a good actor, but far too cynical and contemporary a persona to convincingly play in a Ford Western. Wayne, meanwhile, was preoccupied with setting up his own production of *The Alamo*, which he would begin directing in late 1959, and was constantly on the phone regarding a myriad of production details.

Ford dropped some old friends into the cast—Anna Lee and Hoot Gibson. Ford's unhappiness with the script compelled him to ad-lib a sequence of his own, and it turned out to be the best thing in the picture—a scene of adolescent boys, all that's left of the Confederacy, trooping off to battle, all but one doomed to die. That one is grabbed by his desperate mother and dragged home.

Ford threw the big scene to Lee, playing the mother. Her call was for 10:30 and she was sitting in her room waiting when the message came that Mr. Ford wanted her right away.

"I went and he put on one of his acts," she remembered. " 'Boniface, you're late. How dare you keep us waiting?'

" 'Pappy, I . . . ' "

" 'You're late! It's disgraceful . . .' He just lashed into me. And I had to go straightaway into the scene where I run out and get my little son. He wanted it to be a very emotional scene, and I *was* very emotional. I couldn't understand why he was doing this to me. It was the only time I ever had anything but kindness from him."

The character actor Denver Pyle was recommended to Ford by John Lee Mahin, and he and Strother Martin took the same plane down to Louisiana. "Strother was just scared to death [of Ford]. On the way down to the job, I checked our baggage and got on the plane and said, 'Here's your claim check.' 'Don't give it to me, Denver,' Strother said, 'I'll smoke it.' "

Pyle and Martin ran into bad weather on the way to Louisiana and were diverted to Oklahoma City. They finally arrived at 4:00 in the morning, a bare three hours before they were supposed to be on the set. Completely exhausted, they managed to make it to location on time, and found that Ford had been informed about their travails by the production manager. "I understand you boys have been traveling all night?" he said. "I've had two dressing rooms made up; there's beds and hot coffee for you."

Pyle and Martin got some food and sleep while Ford shot around them for a couple of hours, another example of his sympathy for the movie industry's working class. The loyalty felt by so many for Ford would be inexplicable as anything but the Stockholm Syndrome without an understanding of the generosity that often accompanied his harshness. After making an unfortunate investment in a movie, the actor O. Z. Whitehead fell on hard economic times, so Ford began casting him in smallish parts, using him in *The Last Hurrah*, *The Horse Soldiers*, and other pictures. Even though Whitehead's scenes could invariably be shot in no more than a week, Ford would keep him on salary for the entire shoot.

Some actors could be confused by Ford's anomalous style of direction, but Denver Pyle sensed what he wanted. "He wouldn't tell you how to act something. If you had a line and there was one word that was key, he'd walk by and mumble that word. You were supposed to be talented and capable enough to know what he was trying to tell you. He would only discuss a part in the beginning, tell you what he thought the guy was and how it should be done, and that was the end of that. After that, he'd just keep you honed with a word here or there."

A new addition to the company of players was William Wellman Jr., embarking on an acting career. "It had been a very strange audition," recalled Wellman. "It was an audition like my father ran. You'd come in and talk about what you had for breakfast. There was nothing about the lines, or the part. The next thing I knew, I got the job and went down to Louisiana."

Although he was the son of a man for whom he had high regard, Ford basically ignored Wellman, who slowly developed a case of the frights. "I tried to stay away from him. I didn't like the way he treated people, I wasn't getting any special treatment, and I wanted to stay out of his way. I always got the feeling that if I tried to walk up to this guy and talk to him, I'd only get in trouble. You couldn't laugh, and you couldn't whistle. My first day on the set, I whistled, and everybody stopped me. 'Don't whistle or sing unless he starts it,' they told me. You walked on eggshells."

This overall impression was only amplified one day when Ford suddenly whacked Wellman on the head. It wasn't personal, but rather a successful attempt to make Wellman's hat look less neat, more realistic. "He was often whacking hats while they were on heads, or throwing them on the ground and stomping them, then putting them back. And after he did that, you couldn't touch it. And the handkerchief was always in his mouth, and you could never hear what he was saying."

Ford's quality of making others want to please him once more came into play. Pyle and Martin had a scene to play looking out of a barn loft. "I have this big, blank piece of picture from the time you guys look out the hayloft till the time you come out the front door," Ford said. "Could one of you come out of the hayloft and drop down to the ground?"

Technically, this was a stunt, and should have been done by a stuntman, but Pyle volunteered to do it—once—if the picture needed it.

Ford looked at him. "We'll get along," he said.

What Ford wanted were leading men and juveniles with the souls of character actors, but he rarely managed to find that dream hybrid. What for Denver Pyle was a word here and there that kept him "honed" were for others "cockamamie" instructions that you couldn't understand. In a Ford movie, the juveniles stand around and bump into things, looking like they're scared to death. Which, in many cases, is exactly what Ford wanted the juvenile to look like, the better to showcase the easeful strength of Wayne or Fonda.

On this picture, Ford's designated target of abuse was not Wayne, but William Holden, a good man with a bottle who had never worked with Ford and either didn't know or chose to ignore the unshakable rule about drinking on the job. "Holden had a touch of the flu and was hitting the brandy bottle pretty good," remembered Denver Pyle. "One day, Ford said to me, 'Does Mr. Holden seem a little under the weather to you?' 'Well, I dunno, Mr. Ford, I haven't been that close to him.' Actually, he was hungover something terrible."

Amidst one hundred men on horses, Ford called for a ladder and began framing with his hands. "Get me Bill Holden," he barked. "I want him on a horse." Holden gamely mounted up and came over for his instructions. "Bill, start over there across that stream and ride towards me here and into a big close-up."

Holden dutifully followed instructions, moving across the river and into the frame. Then Ford struck. "Your lower lip is shaking, Mr. Holden."

"Well, I've had the flu, and . . ."

"Are we a little hungover, Mr. Holden?"

"No, but I've been having a little brandy for this cold, trying to break it up . . ."

"Well, I can't have you in a close-up with that lower lip. All right, that's a wrap! We'll start here tomorrow, if Mr. Holden feels better." The company was dismissed, the actor chastised for unprofessional behavior.

W hatever good times were to be had on the set of *The Horse Soldiers* were permanently obliterated one day toward the end of location work.

Among the gang of beloved roughnecks that Ford liked to gather around him was the stuntman Fred Kennedy. He was part of the crew of regulars that Ford carried from picture to picture, who never had dialogue but who worked nearly every day.

"Fred hadn't done stunts for some time," remembered William Wellman Jr. "He had broken his neck and been told not to do stunts, but Ford was trying to give Fred some more money. It was the Wednesday before the Thursday Thanksgiving. It was a simple horse fall, but there were a row of cannons where he was to do the fall, and Fred brushed against a cannon and it threw his fall off. He landed wrong.

"What none of us knew was that there was a practical joke in progress. Ford had told Connie Towers, 'When Fred does his fall, I won't say Cut. You sneak over and kiss him, and then I'll say Cut.' So Fred did his fall, Connie went over to kiss him, leaned over, and then she screamed."

The company rushed over and watched Fred Kennedy's face darken as he died of a broken neck.

For Ford, Fred Kennedy's death was devastating. The price he exacted from others was absolute obedience; in return, he charged himself with taking care of the people that depended on him. "One thing about injury on the job," said stuntman "Bad Chuck" Roberson. "It always tended to shake the Old Man up a bit. He got a little more cautious." A man had died on his watch. He had failed.

Years later, talking to his daughter and grandson, Ford would idly boast that "I can say with pride that I've never hurt a horse, I've never lamed a horse, I've never hurt a rider." Barbara unthinkingly mentioned Fred Kennedy, and Ford immediately shut down. "Let's drop it," he said.

There are those who believe that Kennedy's death drained the last ounce of joy Ford found in the filmmaking process. Ford rushed through the rest of the picture. The script featured a big battle scene in the last reel, but producer Martin Rackin estimated that Ford simply didn't shoot twenty pages of location footage.

Screenwriter and co-producer John Lee Mahin panicked and went to Martin Rackin and the Mirisch brothers, the producers of the picture, trying to talk them into shooting the battle. The response was unanimous: "We've got Ford, Holden and Wayne; we'll make a million."

Mahin kept trying. "This picture goes right out the window. It's a little shaky up to there anyway, so let's at least have a finish."

"No, we won't spend the money." And that was that.

The Horse Soldiers continues the growth of an unusually compliant aspect of Ford, as he directs scenes full of expository dialogue that he would have been sure to throw out as recently as five years earlier. With the single exception of the sequence of the child soldiers marching off to war, the theme of valor is unfelt and the history is uninvolving. There is a battle of sorts at the end, cobbled together on the back lot, but one that's insufficient to the buildup; it's more of a stampede, à la *She Wore a Yellow Ribbon*, than a battle. Despite the often lovely photography of William Clothier, *The Horse Soldiers* is a dud, pure and simple.

The death of Fred Kennedy seemed to be the keynote event of a gradual but persistent darkening of Ford's vision—literally and metaphorically. Chuck Roberson said that Ford became much more cautious about stunts, that horsefalls on movies like *Sergeant Rutledge* became practically nonexistent, and that "the Old Man shut down his usual practical jokes and gags. . . . He had always been growly with the rest of us, but now there was an edge of bitterness to him that seemed to dominate his personality."

Ford's commands grew ever more peremptory; when he wanted to play cards, he would call Roberson and say, "Bad Chuck, get your ass over here. We've got a poker game going, and I'm going to beat you out of a few dollars." As Roberson remembered, "When the Old Man called, you came, or he could make life damn uncomfortable next time you saw him. It didn't matter if you were dying of the Bubonic plague or if you had a hot date and were horny as hell. When the Old Man said, 'Play cards,' you played cards."

"People would say he and my father were the same, but they weren't at all," insisted William Wellman Jr. "You could go up and talk to my father; you couldn't do that to Ford. I felt he was playing a part. I don't know the reason. He was such a strange man. I never saw him happy. He always positioned himself away from everybody; he didn't want to have any connections. He was a loner. In some respects, there are some things that parallel my dad, but my dad *loved* family, and I never saw that with Ford. There was something mean about him."

One by-product of *The Horse Soldiers* was the introduction of cameraman William Clothier as a primary contributor to the Ford company. Clothier had been pressed into service as the go-between during the Ford-Stout fights on *Fort Apache*, but in the years since he had become a prominent cinematographer and was under contract to John Wayne's Batjac Productions. Clothier was a man after Ford's own heart:

plainspoken, honest, hardworking, funny, without false modesty or ego. Clothier would photograph four of Ford's last nine pictures, and quickly developed the knack of intuiting Ford's wishes. Once Ford gave Clothier the camera placement, about all he had to say was something like "I want this in a low key," and he could trust Clothier to give him what he wanted. "In all the years I worked for him," remembered Clothier, "he never told me anything as far as [how to light a set]."

CHAPTER TWENTY-SIX

Between pictures, Ford would have his driver take him for visits with friends. Anna Lee was living alone in Sherman Oaks, and her eldest son was in the Navy. Every February 14, Ford would show up at her house with a box of candy, saying, "All sailors' mothers should be given candy on Valentine's Day." Lee would offer him a drink, but he would always turn it down and settle for a cup or two of Twining's Earl Grey tea.

One day, he suddenly asked, "If anything ever happens to Mary, will you marry me?" A thunderstruck Lee said, well, yes, but nothing was going to happen to Mary and Ford shouldn't talk about that kind of thing. It was an admission of the depth of his feelings for Lee, not to mention his horror of being truly alone, i.e., not on his terms. "He was quite serious," remembered an amazed, slightly flattered Anna Lee, "but I think he said it to other people too; he probably said it to Maureen."

One Sunday morning, George O'Brien and his son Darcy approached Ford in the parking lot of St. Martin of Tours in Brentwood. Although the service usually attracted actors such as Pat O'Brien, James Gleason, and Frank Fay, Ford was always unaccompanied and kept to himself. O'Brien had been somewhat shy about the encounter, and had briefed his son extensively—Ford only wore underwear in frigid conditions, he drank, etc. Darcy had been around Ford over the years—one of his favorite childhood memories was falling asleep in his father's arms in front of the fireplace in their Brentwood house, while Ford, Ben Johnson, and Dobe Carey talked, and Stan Jones sang "[Ghost] Riders in the Sky." But Darcy had been a boy then; now he was a young man, soon to be off to Princeton.

O'Brien introduced his son as "Salty, my manager, a helluva first baseman, Jack, and a pretty fair dishwasher too." Ford promptly invited them both up to the house on Copa de Oro for breakfast. They sat in a room adjacent to a fragrant eucalyptus tree; Ford, Mary, and Darcy sipping Bloody Marys, George drinking tomato juice. Breakfast followed, and afterward there was Irish coffee.

George O'Brien was uneasy; he seemed worried that something might be said that would reopen the rift between the two men begun so many years ago in Manila. Ford and Darcy did most of the talking. Ford inquired about the boy's favorite subject in school. When Darcy said, "English," Ford wanted to know his favorite writers.

"Swift," was the reply, which Ford protested. Swift was not English, but Irish, he said, and a Protestant to boot. Did Darcy know *The Drapier's Letters*? He did not. Ford concisely outlined the content, then asked Mary to fetch the book. He read a few of his favorite paragraphs aloud, the book no more than an inch or two away from his good eye. Swift, Johnson, Fielding, and Sterne were the masters of English prose, he informed the boy. Of these, the greatest was Swift, who could write circles around them all.

Firmly launched on a subject that could not have come up often with Ward Bond or John Wayne, Ford discoursed on literature for a full hour, showed young O'Brien the book (*Famine*) that Liam O'Flaherty had dedicated to him. Was he going to make a movie out of *Famine*? No, he replied, he didn't have the strength anymore. He should have, but now he was too old. The Irish famine was the worst event in the history of the West; the English had been worse to the Irish than the Germans had been to the Jews.

"It was all like a quiz," remembered O'Brien. " 'What do you think of so and so?' I was surprised by it, because at that point I hadn't gotten over my snobbery about the movies; I was only beginning to understand reality. It surprised me that here I was talking to someone as literary as any academic I could come across. He treated me as an adult, which I really liked, and he was very intense, and he didn't make fun of me, or overwhelm me. And he and Mary invited me to come over anytime to play tennis; not to knock or call ahead, just come over. And a couple of times, to impress some girls, I did."

It was now midday, and the effects of the Irish coffee seemed to be making Ford drowsy. O'Brien and his son took their leave. As they rode home, Darcy told his father that Ford was an extraordinary man. "He's got a lot of bitterness in him," George O'Brien said. "He's one of these guys, no matter what he does, he always wants something he doesn't think he has."

"He's an artist."

"That's right, Salty."

The only thing Darcy O'Brien found slightly unnerving about the afternoon was how overshadowed his father had been by Ford. "It occurred to me, even though I couldn't have articulated it, that Ford might have been trying to put my father down by showing how he could communicate with me, and how entranced I was. Did he do it intentionally? Probably, but I can't guarantee it. But he had to know we were having the kind of conversation I couldn't have with my own father. I remember feeling a little sorry for my father at that point. I wonder if Ford was aware of it."

Sergeant Rutledge began as an original story by Willis Goldbeck called "Buffalo Soldier," the Indian term for the black soldiers of the Ninth and Tenth Cavalry. Most of the Buffalo Soldiers—the name came from their ability to hide in the snow under buffalo skins—were former slaves. They learned tracking, how to think and act like an Indian, how to fight. Despite all this, the highest rank a buffalo soldier could reach was first sergeant; their leadership was white.

Goldbeck's original script has an odd third act—it ends before the court-martial, as Rutledge proves himself a hero in battle, with the question of his guilt or innocence of rape and murder very much up in the air. Goldbeck took the idea to James Warner Bellah, and the two prepared a treatment and sent it to Ford.

Ford eagerly took the project on, but, according to Bellah, something seemed to be missing. "He had always been a real tyrant in story sessions, needling and picking away at you. It was his way of making you reach in and give your best. But on *Rutledge* he was awfully mild. Whenever an important subject came up he just said, 'Whatever you think is fine,' or 'Just write it as you see fit, and I'll get it on film.' This wasn't the Jack Ford that I knew."

Warner Bros. was interested in the project, but Jack Warner wanted one of the only two black movie stars of the period to headline the cast: Sidney Poitier or Harry Belafonte. Ford retorted that "They aren't tough enough!" He had a better idea, an ex-UCLA football star named Woody Strode who had played on the same team as Jackie Robinson, and whose Hawaiian wife had gone to school with Ford's children. Born in Los Angeles in 1914, the son of a stonemason, Strode had spent time in the Canadian Football League, worked as a professional wrestler, and had done some small acting parts. He claimed to do one thousand sit-ups, one thousand push-ups, and one thousand knee bends every morning, and given his splendid physique, he was probably telling the truth. He had just finished a notable turn as Kirk Douglas's gladiatorial cohort in *Spartacus*. Ford wanted an actor who didn't need a double, and in Strode he certainly got one.

There were only a couple of drawbacks: Strode couldn't ride, and he couldn't really act. What he could be was a riveting physical presence. Riding could be taught, and was. Rafer Johnson, who would go on to win the 1960 Olympic Decathlon gold medal, and who had a small part in the film, remembers Ford coming out to observe the progress the black actors were making in their riding lessons.

But Ford didn't have time to send Strode for acting lessons, so every day he got up in front of the camera and acted out every scene just the way he wanted Strode to play it. "John Ford played Sergeant Rutledge," asserted Strode, describing how Ford would walk through each scene for him. "Sometimes I would be listening to him, but I wouldn't be looking at him. Boy, that would really make him angry. He'd scream at me, 'WHY AREN'T YOU WATCHING ME?' "

When setting a physical matrix for Strode's performance proved insufficient, he would direct Strode during the shot, just as in the days of silent films: "Constance! Don't touch Woody! Woody, unbutton the shirt. Now ease out of it." It was Harry Carey Jr. and *3 Godfathers* all over again, that is to say an experience somewhere between Parris Island and Alcatraz. "He'd stomp on my feet, slug me, throw rocks at me," said Strode. "One time, he said, 'Bend over, you son of a bitch,' and swatted me with the butt end of my rifle."

There was nothing Ford would not do or say to get his results. In a scene where Strode was sneaking through bushes to spy on some Indians, Ford roared, "WOODY, YOU SON OF A BITCH, QUIT NIGGERING UP MY GODDAMNED SCENE!" Strode had been tiptoeing like he was scared, when he was supposed to move with cunning and intelligence.

The picture, scheduled for forty-three days of work, only nine of them on location at Monument Valley, was ahead of schedule by five days at one point, but, as Ford moved on to the courtroom sequence, things slowed up. Instead of shooting his usual one or two takes, Ford would need as many as nine to get what he wanted from Strode. Still, the picture finished ahead of schedule.

Strode's biggest scene occurred at the end, the courtroom climax. The night before, Ford took Strode to Pat Ford's house and got the actor drunk until he passed out. The next morning, as the muddled Strode struggled to pull himself together at the studio, Ford got in the actor's face. "Oh, you've been drinking, have you?" While Strode ran through his lines, Ford stood over him, pretending to rage. "Do you think you can do the courtroom scene now? You'd better say 'em right or you're through!"

Intimidated, angry, ready to lash out, Strode waited for his cue and delivered his lines: ". . . the Ninth Cavalry is my home and my self-respect. If I deserted them, I wouldn't be nothin' but a swamp runnin' nigger.

And I ain't that, I'm a man." As Ford called "Cut," Strode began to weep. "Now, Woody, stop those tears," Ford said. "It's a sign of weakness."

In spite of the mental and physical abuse, Strode called the scene, "the truest moment I ever had on a screen." He became so close to Ford that the director indulged in some hallucinatory miscasting, using Strode as an Indian chief in *Two Rode Together* and a Mongol warrior in *7 Women*. Strode was a lovely man, remembered by Rafer Johnson as "a complete gentleman, really kind to me and everybody." He was also handy as a club with which to beat John Wayne. "There's the real football player," Ford would say, nodding at Strode. Worse, he'd refer to Strode's service in World War II.

For Strode it was all worth it, both as an actor and a black man. "[*Sergeant Rutledge*] was a classic. It had dignity. John Ford put classic words in my mouth. . . . You never seen a Negro come off a mountain like John Wayne before. I had the greatest Glory Hallelujah ride across the Pecos River that any black man ever had on the screen. And I did it all myself. I carried the whole black race across the river."

Budd Boetticher was also shooting on the Warners lot, and, one day at lunchtime, he walked onto Ford's set and saw everybody sitting in a circle. "Good morning," said Boetticher. "Anybody for lunch?" Unwittingly, Boetticher had interrupted the company during a touchy moment. Amidst a deathly quiet set, Ford was sitting there, chewing on his handkerchief. "Who's that?" he barked.

"Budd Boetticher."

"Oh. I didn't know you without your cape," said Ford, referring to Boetticher's passion for bullfighting. Ford rose, called lunch, and began walking out with Boetticher. " 'I didn't know you without your cape.' " mimicked Boetticher. "What the hell was that?"

"Oh, I don't want those fucking actors to know I have any friends," explained Ford.

*S**ergeant Rutledge* has an unusually plotty script for Ford: a teenage girl has been raped and killed on a frontier outpost, and her father, a major, has also been murdered. Braxton Rutledge, a Buffalo Soldier in the Ninth Cavalry, is seen stumbling from the scene wounded, and is presumed guilty until the court-martial reveals the true killer.

Except for the elegant and soulful Juano Hernandez, the acting throughout *Sergeant Rutledge* is declamatory and not very good, and Woody Strode is more totem than man. But the strong story, the compression of the sets, Ford's ennobling exteriors, and the power of the theme carry the picture through.

It's a film of strong juxtapositions—the expressionist light with which he photographs the murdered girl, the enormous, inflammatory close-up of Woody Strode's hand spread over Constance Towers's face. Unlike *Fort Apache*, Ford plays the elaborate etiquette on cavalry outposts for comedy, helped along by the twitterings of Billie Burke and Mae Marsh. Once again, Ford shows his concern over racism; the unspoken devotion between the white lieutenant and his black troops is moving, as is the scene where Constance Towers cradles a wounded Buffalo Soldier in her arms.

Ford is helped by Bert Glennon's very strong photography, hard lines, and the strong blacks of Technicolor. As shot by Glennon, it's as much a noir as it is a Western. As Ford flashes back from courtroom testimony, the lights in the courtroom dim, a spot comes on the speaker, and then Ford makes a direct cut—a pleasing, rather theatrical effect.

Despite the shaky performances, and an overwrought witness stand confession more suited to *Perry Mason*, *Sergeant Rutledge* is a film of considerable formal beauty about the bonds between a black band of brothers. Not surprisingly, it did miserably at the domestic box office, grossing only $784,000. It did considerably better overseas, grossing $1.7 million, but was probably still a marginal financial failure. Ford blamed the box office on Warner Bros.: "Warners sent a couple of boys on bicycles out to sell it." Strode had seemed primed for a major career, but, while there was a small market for black men who could act, there was none for a black action hero. "Woody," said Ford sadly, "I can make a character actor out of you, but I can't make you a star."

After *Sergeant Rutledge* was completed, Rafer Johnson got in the habit of going across the street from UCLA and visiting Ford at his house. "I would talk to him for hours," remembered Johnson. "Sports, the movies. I liked him a lot. He was very knowledgeable about sports; he was very knowledgeable about a lot of things.

"We never spoke specifically about race, but in terms of how he handled that film, and us, John Ford might have been a little ahead of his time in terms of looking at the issue, and the problems that existed between society and people of color. That film, and the Rutledge character, showed what Ford really was—a man who respected our people and was concerned about what was going on in our country. John Ford was speaking through that film."

Ford had plenty of time to talk to the young athlete; between September 1959, when *Sergeant Rutledge* was completed, and June 1960, John Ford had nothing to do. No directing offers from other people, no films of his own in development. Every career has *longueurs* like this, but Ford didn't deal with *longueurs* very well. Instead of kicking back and plowing through books, he became depressed, and spent a lot of time in bed. His grandson Dan reported that he began to ignore his personal hygiene.

Desperate for activity, he flew down to Texas to "help" Duke Wayne with *The Alamo*. "Wayne had been trying to get *The Alamo* off the ground for 12 years," said Richard Widmark, who was playing Jim Bowie. "He talked about it to Ford, who said, 'Go on, make it! You're ready for it.' In fact, he was expecting Wayne to ask him to direct the movie, but Duke didn't. So Ford invited himself on the set and started poking his nose in everywhere."

"We were about a month into the picture," remembered cameraman William Clothier, "when John Ford shows up about one o'clock in the afternoon. He plunked himself down in the director's chair and stopped Duke's scene. 'Jesus Christ, Duke, that's not the way to do it . . .' "

Wayne had barely gotten the rhythm of the production. The picture was being made on an immense scale, which made it all the more difficult for Wayne, who had never directed before. Further confusing the issue, Richard Widmark's part was being rewritten by Burt Kennedy while the picture was shooting.

To have his beloved father figure show up was a nightmarish imposition, and must have set off every Freudian alarm bell in Wayne's psyche, just as Ford knew it would. Yet, Wayne had allowed—asked—Ford to give him advice during preproduction. Among other things, Ford had sat in on some casting sessions and had told Wayne to hire Laurence Harvey to play Travis. "Don't bother telling him about the part, Duke. We haven't got much time. Just sign the bastard up." Note the royal "We." By not erecting a fire wall between Ford and his film, Wayne had opened the door for even more interference.

Wayne was betwixt and between; he had a responsibility to his picture, but he also had a responsibility to Ford. "[The relationship] was more than father-son," said Patrick Wayne. "It was a mentor relationship. He forever gave Ford total credit for his success, giving him the opportunity to be where he was in the business, which may have been less than the case. I think my father would have been a success at whatever he chose. He was driven, and focused and ambitious.

"But the opportunity *was* presented by Ford and continued to be. And it became awkward at times, when [Wayne was directing *The Alamo*] and Ford would show up. [My father] would *never* say, 'I'm directing this, get out of my way,' although he would with other people. On pictures he made for Batjac, he treated the director like he wasn't there. Other directors, [Henry] Hathaway for instance, who was a monster on the set, he treated with respect. But there was no one else he was that submissive with."

A desperate Wayne went to Clothier. "Goddamn! I want to make this picture, and I don't want Ford directing it. What am I gonna do?" Clothier came up with a brainstorm: give Ford a camera crew, an assistant, all the actors Wayne wouldn't be using, and let him run a second unit. "Ford went out and shot stuff that couldn't possibly be used," asserted Clothier. "It didn't have anything to do with the picture we were making. I don't think we used three cuts that the Old Man did. It cost Duke over $250,000 to give Ford that second unit."

Wayne sent Denver Pyle out as Ford's assistant. "He'd shoot scenes of the Mexicans attacking the fort," said Pyle. "There are people, belittlers, who say that Ford directed the picture. He didn't. He directed a second unit, and I don't know that Wayne used that much of it. They used clips of his footage, but that's all."

Whether out of loyalty to Wayne, or foggy memories, such stories obscure the reality of Ford's contribution to the picture, which extended considerably beyond that of second unit director. "For any important stuff, he was there on his chair, sucking on his handkerchief," remembered Frankie Avalon, who was playing the juvenile lead. "He wasn't there all the time, but he was there a lot of the time. He would help Wayne out on his own scenes, where Wayne had to be directed."

Ford also worked on scenes in the church basement, and an early, important scene where Wayne's Davy Crockett meets Linda Cristal, the film's female lead, for the first time. He even directed a couple of complete scenes, notably the one where Avalon brings news of the impending massacre to Richard Boone, playing Sam Houston. "I hate that scene to this day," said Avalon, "because he gave me the line reading. Boone's line was 'You've been riding for days, get some food and water.' And I say, 'No, sir, I gotta get back to the Alamo.' And Ford directed me to say it like a kid, all wide-eyed and innocent. I cringe every time I see it."

Ford directed other scenes, some with Richard Widmark, some with character actors like Hank Worden. Frankie Avalon estimated Ford's contribution as between 10 and 15 percent of the film. The ironic thing was that Avalon found Wayne to be better with the actors than Ford. "Ford wasn't talkative at all," said Avalon, "but Wayne was a very knowledgeable director. He knew exactly what he wanted. He would never give line readings. He would discuss the scene and talk about it. I remember him directing Widmark, taking him off to the side, talking to him, getting him to relax. He was a real good director and a very sensitive man."

Wayne wrote Ford after he left the location, taking valuable time to kiss his ring and explain why he hadn't kissed it while Ford was actually there. "I've had a helluva cold . . . am good for four hours, then start folding. Well, anyway, I can make it until Saturday, then I'll sleep for thirty hours. There's a light and a camera in the window waiting for your return. Sure appreciate having your shoulder to lean on."

Ford's old stuntman nemesis Gil Perkins was working on the picture, and saw firsthand how difficult it was for Wayne to contradict the man he called Coach. "I was playing a Scot, with a tam on my head. Ford was shooting this scene of a fire in a corral, with horses panicking, and he said to me, 'Your tam's on the wrong way.' I told him that Duke had put it on me that way, and we'd already shot some footage and it shouldn't be changed now or it wouldn't match up. Ford said, 'Oh, what the hell does he know about that stuff?' and he changed the tam.

"A bit later, Duke walks over and says, 'Hey, Coach, how's things going?' 'Okay,' says Ford. 'The Scottish tam was on the wrong way. Gil said you told him to wear it that way.' And Wayne looked at me and said, 'I didn't tell you to put it on the wrong way.' All I could do was look at him and walk away."

For Ford, *The Alamo* was merely a footnote, the sort of dabbling he enjoyed doing when he was at loose ends. It also introduced him to Richard Widmark, who would provide the star power for two of Ford's last three Westerns. When *The Alamo* was released in late 1960, he gave his friend an effusive blurb: "The most important picture ever made. It's timeless, it's the greatest picture I have ever seen. It will last forever—run forever—for all peoples, all families—*everywhere!*"

I n the early months of 1960, there was the matter of Heran Moon, as well as a tax audit with the IRS and dry rot on the *Araner*. No wonder Ford agreed to undertake one of his infrequent television jobs. This one was personal, however, as he had agreed to direct an episode of *Wagon Train*, the successful series that genially ripped off *Wagon Master*, and, at long last, had made a star of Ward Bond.

Despite the opportunity of starring in his own series, Bond had been hesitant to undertake the show because of the lesser status of television. "Listen, you dumb Irishman," snarled Ford, "Don't you act for a living? Well, then you'd better act."

Ford would regularly complain to Bond about the quality of the show's scripts, while at the same time claiming never to have seen a TV Western in his life.

Finally, Bond took the bait and challenged Ford: "If you know so much, why don't you do one?" "Of course," said Bond, "he wrote the story and had the script prepared by his writer. Mine aren't good enough for him." Actually, the credited writer is one Tony Puryear, who never worked for Ford, so he probably had Frank Nugent or some other frequent collaborator give the script a polish. After that, he worked on the script himself; his handwritten notes survive, providing tidy but graceful texture—adding "My dear sir," before a speech from a stuffy character, adding moments, tags to scenes, and specifying them with the character's name, not the actor's.

Perhaps as a result of his age and continuous grumbling, Ford was allotted six days to finish his episode instead of five. Actually, with his ability to visualize and precut a film in his head, Ford was particularly well suited to work in television, as soon became obvious.

Shooting during the second week of May, Ford turned in seventy-two minutes of film in six days, and there was some discussion about spending another couple of days and making it a two-part show. But at the last minute the ever cost-conscious Universal decided to keep it a single show, resulting in the excision of fifteen minutes.

"The Colter Craven Story" is a morality tale about a drunken doctor, traumatized by the events he witnessed in the Civil War, who finds his self-respect again when Seth Adams (Bond) tells him the story of his old friend from Galena, Ulysses Simpson Grant. Ford had a nodding acquaintance with stories about drunken doctors, except here he wasn't featuring Thomas Mitchell or Victor Mature, but a hammy actor named Carleton Young, for whom he had developed an inexplicable fondness.

To get away from the backlot feel, Ford used an entire, expansive sequence from *Wagon Master* (the wagons struggling to get over the mountains). The costumes and scenery of the footage from the feature don't come close to matching those used in the TV episode, but Ford correctly figured nobody would notice. He even got John Wayne, billed as Marion Morrison, to appear in one scene, hiding in the shadows and voicing a single line, as William Tecumseh Sherman.

Except for the unaccustomed appearances of John Carradine, Hank Worden, Ken Curtis, and Jack Pennick, which tip off Ford's presence, "The Colter Craven Story" is visually a fairly ordinary episode—except for a few shots, Ford sticks to shooting the story. Narratively, however, it's far less compressed, far more picaresque, than was usual for *Wagon Train*. In most respects, Ford was back directing a six-day Western at Universal, just as he had forty-four years before, which must have pleased him on some level.

By the time Ford's *Wagon Train* episode was broadcast, he had been thrilled by the election of 1960 that put John F. Kennedy in the White House, the first Irish Catholic to be elected President. There had been a request for support from Celebrities for Nixon, but Ford had demurred. "Thank you for your wire," he wrote in September 1960. "However, I am a lifelong and fervent Democrat—so frankly I prefer not to be on your committee."

•••

S ergeant Rutledge had been ambitious in theme and, intermittently, in execution. Ford's next film, *Two Rode Together*, was a toss-off ("The worst piece of crap I've done in 20 years," he called it at one point), a script he shot on the way to something he cared deeply about, a project titled *The Man Who Shot Liberty Valance*.

Thematically, *Two Rode Together* has strong echoes of *The Searchers:* two ill-matched men (James Stewart and Richard Widmark) go after whites captured by Quanah Parker. But the film has a loose, jocular tone that doesn't jibe with its theme; everything seems pitched a little too high—voices are too loud, actors are too broad, lighting is too bright. The film feels physically slack; the images are recessive, the locations are scrubby and uninteresting, there are mismatched cuts and the whole thing lacks any kind of dramatic tension. There could be no doubt now that the director's gift was beginning to recede; the hand that had once been capable of the most finely filigreed detail was now working with a much broader brush.

"You'd see flashes of brilliance," Harry Carey Jr. would say of this period, "but there was no storyline or anything, no grasp. Of course, nobody was going to come along and say, 'Look you're screwing it up here—you haven't got a shot of him coming out of the Courthouse,' or whatever. . . . So he'd miss a lot of stuff, and that's one reason why the pictures were falling off."

Two Rode Together has a few incidental pleasures—there is a wonderful, very funny scene between Stewart and Widmark on a riverbank, and Henry Brandon basically encores his portrayal of Scar from *The Searchers*. Griffith's leading lady Mae Marsh, a startling apparition from the movies' past, pops up unexpectedly as an old Indian captive, and Widmark is addressed as Natani Nez, Ford's own Navajo name.

From the beginning, Ford was unhappy with Frank Nugent's script. "It was being written as we shot," remembered Shirley Jones, certainly the least Fordian of leading ladies. "You got your pages every morning, and I didn't understand that way of working at all. He had a disregard for actors, men and women. Widmark and Stewart were thrilled to be there, but I couldn't understand the way he worked. I was third down the line, and I was a woman—he didn't really like women at all—I didn't get any direction, and I was the last to know what we were doing. He wasn't hateful, he wasn't mean, I was just last in line."

Complicating Ford's relationship with his leading lady was one of his occasional crushes; Harry Carey Jr. saw him mouth "I love you" to her, which seems to have scared her even further.

Stewart and Ford had an immediate rapport. Although he could play dark, obsessive characters, as a man Stewart was cut from the same cloth as Will Rogers—warm, unpretentious, an instinctual actor who could do it without talking about it. Stewart was immediately drawn to Ford's no-nonsense professionalism and the strong paternal guidance most actors desire. Ford told anyone who would listen that both Stewart and Widmark were "real actors"—as opposed, one presumes, to the hulks he was forced to work with the rest of the time.

"A lotta directors," Stewart remembered, "y'know . . . it's a barrel of laughs on the set and ya have fun . . . and then you see the picture and ya say, 'Where is it?' . . . But Ford *gets* it on the screen. And he's a real leader." Stewart would elaborate on that idea when he told Dan Ford that "The set wasn't calm and relaxed. There was tension, always. But it was a good kind of tension. It was just that with the exception of Ford and a couple of assistant people [you] didn't know just exactly what was going to happen next and that's exactly the way he wanted it."

Ford and Stewart immediately made plans to do more pictures together; such was the actor's respect for Ford that he even acted in a TV film ("Flashing Spikes") that Ford directed in 1962. But nothing was ever pure and simple where Ford was concerned. The film's best scene, the extended scene with Stewart and Widmark on a riverbank, was accompanied by Ford scoring points off his stars. Both Stewart and Widmark wore toupees and had hearing problems to which they pretended to be oblivious. While instructing his actors for the scene, Ford began dropping his voice lower and lower. By the time he was finished with his instructions, said Harry Carey Jr., "You could hardly hear him if you were standing right next to him."

But the actors were not about to admit they hadn't caught what Ford was saying, and just kept nodding and nodding. "Finally," continued Harry Carey, "Jack has established his point and he yells for everyone in the crew to gather around him in the water. When everybody's sloshed over to him, he throws up his arms in this great dramatic gesture and goes, 'Fifty years in this goddamn business, and what do I end up doing? Directing two deaf hairpieces!'"

Although they worked together frequently in the last few years of his career, Harry Carey Jr. would say that "I don't think [Ford] was ever as comfortable with [Stewart] as he was with Wayne and Fonda. They had a flippant kind of relationship, lots of humor between them, but I had a feeling that Jimmy made him edgy, had something that Jack knew he could never quite control the way, say, he ran roughshod over Wayne for so long. Maybe it was just Jimmy's talent and Jack's awareness that he had the real stuff in front of him."

Ford's indifference toward the picture turned into something considerably darker when Ward Bond died suddenly of a heart attack while attending a football game in Texas. *Wagon Train* had made Bond a star and he had seized every prerogative there was; rewriting, redirecting, running the show. The effort had worn him down and undoubtedly contributed to his heart attack.

"Ford was gone a couple of days while he went to the funeral," remembered Shirley Jones. "So finally he gets back and the limousine pulls up on the set and Ford gets out. He takes this long, long walk over to Andy Devine and he says, 'Now *you're* the biggest shit I know.' "

The mood was lightened only by Jack's and Ollie Carey's ongoing imitation of the Bickersons, going strong after nearly fifty years. "Goldie, you're the worst goddamn actress I ever directed," Ford yelled at her one day. "Oh, go fuck yourself," she helpfully explained.

Ford completed *Two Rode Together* on December 16 and left for Honolulu five days later, where he started drinking. After several weeks, he checked into Queen's Hospital for alcoholic dehydration.

Casual in conception and execution, *Two Rode Together* didn't pull its commercial weight; as of April 1971, Columbia was carrying it as $975,000 in the red. It's interesting chiefly as one of the bleakest films Ford ever made; as Donald Dewey wrote in his biography of Stewart, "The Comanches are brutal opportunists, the army officers are crude, hypocritical racists, the civilians are a naive conglomerate waiting only to become a rabid mob." The capsule description promises something corrosive, but the film is actually a flaccid, mistimed dud.

The world of movies was changing. The centralized studios were dying just as the great ruthless pirate moguls who had founded them were dying: Cohn and Mayer were gone, soon to be followed by Warner and Goldwyn. Power was shifting to actors, and a new generation of independent producers to whom John Ford was an aging relic; great in his day, of course, but what had he to say to moviegoers who wanted Brando and Beatty and Audrey—not Katharine—Hepburn? The downward progression in producers working with Ford was plain enough. "Beggars can't be choosers," commented Lindsay Anderson. "Who wanted to make Ford pictures? He was well known as very obstinate."

It wasn't just Ford—it was Ford's entire generation that was having trouble. Merian Cooper was trying to set up a biographical film about Claire and Anna Chennault, but couldn't attract the top stars needed to finance the picture. Cooper dangled *A Thousand Springs* before everybody from Rex Harrison to Jennifer Jones, and he offered the directing job to Ford. Ford was noncommittal, because Cooper then sent a "rough but good" treatment.

The treatment must have been more rough than good; Ford wired Cooper that, while "nothing would make me happier," than to get back in harness with his old friend, he wouldn't be free for at least two years.

Ford was beginning to deteriorate physically. At one point, he threw his back out, and when Woody Strode came to visit he was alarmed by his condition. "Ford looked ten years older than the last time I saw him. He couldn't lift himself up to shake my hand."

Strode gave Ford a back massage, which helped, and Ford asked the actor if he could stay for a few days and work on his back. A couple of days turned into a couple of months. For Ford, any kind of inactivity tended to round back to drinking, and before Strode knew what was happening, Ford was downing bottles of wine in fifteen minutes. At first, Strode tried to keep up with him in a companionable way, but he soon found that was impossible. Ford was off on one of his legendary binges. Finally, Strode began watering Ford's beer, and refused his request for gin.

"You cruel son of a bitch," said Ford, "you'll never work in any of my pictures again."

"If you don't like it, why don't you just get out of that bed and try to kick my ass?"

Twenty years before, perhaps even five years before, nobody could have dropped a challenge like that without terrible consequences, but now all Ford could do was glare. So Strode kept Ford company with the only kind of relationship with which he was at ease—the harsh but loving father and an eager-to-learn son-supplicant.

"Ford had become lonely," remembered Strode. "We'd sit together in his green room, read books and talk all day." Ford made Strode read a book a week, although, said Strode, "He'd read three books to my one. . . . He'd lift up that eye patch and speed read."

Once he was back on his feet and surveying the landscape, Ford didn't like what he saw. His old crew members were dying off or signing up for work in television, where they could be guaranteed thirty-nine weeks of work every year, far more than the retrenching studios could offer. "It's very hard to get a good cameraman now," Ford groused in 1964. "It's also hard to get a good gaffer and a good grip. Television latches onto all of the good ones. You have to have people who know how to pick it up and put it down where you want it."

Ford actually tried to pitch a few projects of his own. He went to Madrid to meet Samuel Bronston, who was making an international splash with pictures like *El Cid* and *King of Kings*. With the backing of DuPont funds, which guaranteed his bank notes, Bronston funded his pictures by selling the script and cast to countries all around the world at so much per territory. Advances in hand, he went off to make his picture.

Bronston had provided development money to Frank Capra for a circus picture that ended up being directed by Henry Hathaway. Capra told Ford about the experience, so Ford went and pitched his project.

Ford had several ideas for a picture for Bronston—Arthur Conan Doyle's *The White Company* was a favorite dream project, but Bronston was unimpressed. Then Ford proposed, of all things, an adaptation of *The Wandering Jew*. "He expounded on it at great length," remembered Paul Lazarus Jr., Bronston's head of marketing. "He had no script and no cast, but he said it was his great dream and we were interested. He left, and nothing ever happened. The funny thing was, he was a good salesman. And he had the authority of all the great pictures he had made in the past.

"But he was going downhill. My advice to Bronston was that it would be tough to sell without a script or stars, and then there was the incongruity of the subject matter for a Ford picture. Bronston was shaky at that time, and couldn't afford a gamble."

In 1949, Dorothy Johnson published her short story "The Man Who Shot Liberty Valance." It carries the same theme as the film that Ford made from it, but differs in most other particulars. The dialogue is much flatter—there is no "when the legend becomes fact, print the legend" here—and Bert Barricune (renamed Tom Doniphon for the film) acts as a sort of fairy godfather to tenderfoot Ransom Stoddard, not merely killing Liberty Valance for him, but goading him on to all his other accomplishments as well, so that Hallie, the woman who rejects Barricune for Stoddard, can be happy.

Ford bought Johnson's story for $7,500 in March 1961, then set up a deal for Willis Goldbeck and James Warner Bellah to work as a team on the script. Each man got $30,000, with Goldbeck pulling down an additional $10,000 for whatever nominal producing chores Ford didn't want to bother with.

The days when a Ford Western could be knocked off cheaply were over, largely because of star salaries, which must have galled him no end. For *The Man Who Shot Liberty Valance*, John Wayne was getting $750,000 and James Stewart $300,000, against 7½ percent of the gross apiece. Ford was earning a comparatively minor $150,000, plus 25 percent of the profits. Lee Marvin got $50,000. The total budget was $3.2 million, a great deal for a black and white Western with only a few days of location work.

As far as the industry was concerned, Wayne was worth whatever he cost. The reality was that at this stage in their careers, Ford needed John Wayne more than John Wayne needed Ford. "[Ford] still had life," said producer Howard W. Koch, who took over as production head of Paramount in 1964, "but the Big Cowboy was really the whole thing."

"For a change no locations," wrote Ford to Wayne on July 7, shortly before production got under way. "All to be shot on the lot. . . . Seriously we have a great script in my humble opinion."

Ford still retained his psychological acuity for what would most effectively motivate a given actor. James Stewart's introductory scene called for him to receive a brutal beating from Lee Marvin. Unusually, Stewart had trouble getting his lines out for several takes. Ford stepped forward and whispered to Stewart, "Jimmy, you are not a coward, you are not a coward." Stewart nailed the next take.

Ford once again hired Denver Pyle and Strother Martin, the latter to play one of Liberty Valance's sidekicks. Martin was still scared to death of Ford, because of his reputation, because of the way he acted, because Ford insisted on calling him Stroker instead of Strother. "He was like a God to Strother," said Denver Pyle—undoubtedly the God of the Old Testament.

Ford always had Pyle's chair next to his, to facilitate the morning conversations he enjoyed. "I think Stroker's getting used to me," Ford observed to Pyle one day. "How's that, Mr. Ford?" asked Pyle.

"He doesn't jump as high now when I call him." Whereupon Ford yelled "STROKER MARTIN!" Martin levitated out of his chair to a height of approximately three feet and hurried over. Ford turned to Pyle. "He didn't jump nearly as high as he used to, did he?"

Toward the end of production, Martin confided to Pyle that he had figured out a way he could deal with Ford: the trick was to surreptitiously touch him every morning, which made him real. Pyle promptly told Ford, which brought no reaction whatever. But two days later, Martin began the day by patting Ford on the knee and saying good morning. Ford turned on him and snarled, "Don't touch me! Don't ever touch me!" Martin blanched and managed to stagger away without fainting.

Willis Goldbeck had been around the movie business since he wrote scripts for Rex Ingram in the silent days, and he accurately appraised Ford's personal insecurity. "He came from Maine," Goldbeck told Kevin Brownlow, "the son of a saloon keeper, and he's never forgotten it. . . . He is fascinated by the fact that his wife is a blue-blooded Virginian. These things come out every once in a while: there is that insecurity underneath. It's hard to believe when a man has been so dominant in this business; but it is there, and I think it accounts for a great [many] of the things he says and does, turning on other people . . . slashing away to keep his own position clear, to keep the people around him reduced."

By this time, Ford's deteriorating condition and flagging personal hygiene were obvious to everybody. Hal Nesbitt, a stagehand at Paramount, was aghast when Ford's assistant was delegated to carry around a bucket filled with sand. "He'd go behind a set and use it to go to the bathroom," remembered Nesbitt. "He wouldn't leave the stage."

William Clothier, once again the cameraman, adored Ford as both a man and an artist, although he had come along too late to see him at his best. "Socially, you never [wanted] any part of him. He's just not that pleasant. . . . If you have a drink, it makes him mad. He also likes to play cards, but if he loses, you're a no-good son of a bitch."

Whether or not Ford held a grudge depended on some private calibration of like or dislike; being a member of the alcoholic brotherhood didn't hurt. He adored Lee Marvin immediately. The two men had a great deal in common: periodic alcoholism, a passion for the sea, brave showings in World War II—Marvin had been a Marine and was badly wounded on Saipan—and surprisingly liberal politics. The fact that Marvin was descended from a brother of George Washington didn't hurt either.

Actors or stuntmen who transgressed might be cast into outer darkness for decades, but others could mouth off and be forgiven immediately. William Clothier remembered an alcoholic electrician who accosted Ford one day and began calling him names. Ford simply said, "Get this guy away from me," but the assistant director took that to mean "permanently" and fired him.

The next day Ford walked on the set and noted the absence of "the little electrician who called me a son of a bitch." Told that he had been fired ("For being drunk?"), Ford refused to turn a camera until the electrician was back on the set. A limousine was sent to the electrician's house and brought him back to work.

Although Paramount would undoubtedly have preferred that *The Man Who Shot Liberty Valance* be in color, Ford stood firm against everybody, even William Clothier. "I didn't like the idea [of black and white]," said Clothier. "Color was becoming more and more necessary in the studio's eyes, and I liked working in color. He said, 'Goddamn it, we're going to do it in black and white; it shouldn't be in color.' "

Ford felt the key scene of the film was the gunfight in the street between Ransom Stoddard and Liberty Valance, and he didn't want that in color. Once the scene was edited, Ford said to Clothier, "See, you got a damn good sequence out of that. It wouldn't have been half as good in color."

"He was really a genius," remembered Clothier. "He'd listen, but if you were smart you'd spend a lot of time listening to him. He knew more about photography than any man who ever worked in the movies. He'd force me into situations where I'd have to sit up and take notice."

• • •

*T*he Man Who Shot Liberty Valance is a memory play, from its under-populated sets to the archetypes of its characters. James Stewart's Ransom Stoddard has come back to Shinbone, the place where his political career began, to bury an old friend, Tom Doniphon.

Doniphon had been nothing much to Shinbone, a sorry old man on the fringes, but Ranse Stoddard, three-term governor, two-term senator, ambassador to the Court of St. James, has come to pay him tribute. Deciding to unburden himself of the truth after forty years, Stoddard tells the story of his coming to Shinbone, of how he went up against the mad gunman Liberty Valance, and who really killed him.

In *Liberty Valance* the landscape is almost completely absent, and Ford's eye for composition is muted—visually, it's among the most ordinary of Ford's movies—but the thematic resonance more than compensates for the fact that it's an old man's movie—not the expansive symphony of *Stagecoach* or *The Searchers*, but a muted chamber piece. It's the last Ford film where his declining energies don't get in the way.

James Stewart is fine and Edmond O'Brien does an entertaining turn as a tosspot newspaperman, but it is John Wayne who is the film's core, again making rage and disappointment palpable; he knows that, on some level, when he kills Valance, he is killing himself.

A sweet gallantry had been a keynote quality of Ford's ever since *Straight Shooting*, but *The Man Who Shot Liberty Valance* overwhelms that with sadness. In movies as disparate as *The Grapes of Wrath*, *My Darling Clementine*, and *The Searchers*, Ford had nudged his characters toward a final ascendance to myth; now, in *Liberty Valance*, he begins with myth and methodically dismantles it on the way to a mournful irony, utterly undercutting the newspaperman's aphorism that has become famous.

There is an odd passivity at the heart of the characters. Doniphon lets Stoddard have his woman, his town, his West, while Stoddard is powerless before Valance, and powerless before Doniphon. In *The Man Who Shot Liberty Valance*, the only true agent of power is time itself, and it does terrible things—the gap between the firmly idealistic Stoddard and the bloviating windbag he becomes is heartbreaking. Stoddard, Hallie, and Linc Appleyard are all haunted, and everything is changed, changed utterly, except for the desert. Everybody has gotten what they thought they wanted, but nobody is happy. Welcome to the twentieth century.

The response to this most mournful of Ford movies was divided by an ocean of sensibility. *Variety* thought it could have been shortened by at least twenty minutes, while the incomparably imperceptive Bosley Crowther of the *New York Times* called it a "rather sinister little fable," and regarded it as an example of creeping Hollywood fatigue.

Andrew Sarris's review was more prescient: "When we realize that the man in the coffin is John Wayne, the John Wayne of *Stagecoach, The Long Voyage Home, They Were Expendable, Fort Apache, She Wore A Yellow Ribbon, Rio Grande, 3 Godfathers, The Quiet Man, The Searchers* and *Wings of Eagles*, the one-film-at-a-time reviewer's contention that Wayne is a bit old for an action plot becomes absurdly superficial." Across the Atlantic, the reviewers sided with Sarris. The London *Observer* thought it was "bathed in Ford's talent and affection" and the London *Times* reported that its "violence had an offhand good humor."

If, as Scott Fitzgerald said, the mark of a first-rate intelligence is the ability to hold two contradictory ideas in your head at the same time, then Ford had a first-rate intelligence all his life. For Ford, every triumph carries the embryo of eventual failure. Even in *The Iron Horse*, it is clear that Davey Brandon's motivation is not the overarching goal of a transcontinental railroad, but the daily act of building that railroad. When the process of building is complete, the vision dies.

In *The Searchers*, as well as *Liberty Valance*, the kind of men needed to master the wilderness are the kind of men that can only function in wilderness; they are men who civilization must expel. If society is to benefit from someone's sacrifice, legend must take precedence over truth. Ford may celebrate America's history and values, but he also articulates the contradictions that can easily lead to a mournful pessimism. Ford is too complex an artist to assert that the modern world is a 180-degree betrayal of the past; rather, he believes that history is organic and the present is the logical extension of the past.

Like many Ford films, *Liberty Valance* focuses on the need to subordinate individual will to a collective struggle for a greater good; unlike many Ford films, *Valance* overtly questions whether the sacrifice is justified.

Doniphon is a horse trader, Valance is a stagecoach robber; both are trapped in obsolescent careers, neither seems willing to adapt. Doniphon and Valance are allied in that they are the best and worst that America can produce—a man too busy with his own affairs to want power or to impose his own beliefs on anybody else, up against a man who can do nothing else—the catalytic agents of the frontier.

The true story of Liberty Valance is never printed, for the newspaper editor kills the story. "This is the West, sir. When the legend becomes fact, print the legend." *Liberty Valance* deftly, shrewdly, shows the ragged process by which stories become legends, and legends become history.

In the end, Ranse and his wife, Hallie, are once again on the train. "Look at it. It was once a wilderness; now it's a garden," says Hallie. "Aren't you proud?"

"Hallie," replies Stoddard, "who put the cactus roses on Tom's coffin?"

"I did."

The two sit, lost in contemplation. The train conductor breaks their reverie and speaks the film's last words: "Nothing's too good for the man who shot Liberty Valance."

Shinbone has not only survived, it has thrived, as has Ransom Stoddard, and it has all been based on a lie. Just as Ranse has pretended to be the man who shot Liberty Valance, Hallie has pretended to love her husband more than she loves Tom Doniphon. Each has paid a price we can only imagine. As that train recedes across a landscape, Ford's bleakest film ends with a poignant, mournful dying fall.

The Man Who Shot Liberty Valance has earned a place in the hearts of movie fans the world over. It even made money, the last Ford film to do so.

During the making of *Liberty Valance*, John Wayne was given an award at the Beverly Hilton, and asked Ford to present it to him. When Ford was announced, he got up and failed to negotiate the stairs, going up two stairs, missing a step, and going right back down two stairs. He quickly braced himself, got up on the stage, and made the presentation. Wayne, sensitive to the older man's wounded vanity, got up and made the same stumble, sliding down two stairs until he righted himself. The audience, thinking it was all part of a prearranged jape, roared, but Wayne had successfully covered up his idol's deteriorating eyesight.

Although intimates knew that the old man was having trouble, the news hadn't leaked out into the industry at large. In 1962, Ford was recruited to contribute a segment to MGM's all-star Cinerama epic *How the West Was Won*. Ford earned $50,000 for his sequence, shot in fourteen days in late May and early June 1961. It was a linking sequence, taking George Peppard from callow farm boy through the Civil War, where he encountered John Wayne as William Tecumseh Sherman.

Although little more than a footnote to Ford's career, *How the West Was Won* inadvertently supplied him with his last partner in motion picture production. Bernard Smith had begun his career as a book editor for Alfred A. Knopf in the 1930s. Leaving in 1947, he went to work as story editor for Sam Goldwyn and, later, Paramount. In 1960, Smith produced *Elmer Gantry*, a major hit that won numerous Academy Awards, and he followed that with *How the West Was Won*, also a success. The two men hit it off; in the manner of many successful partnerships, each supplied something the other lacked. Ford gave Smith the cachet of his legend; Smith gave Ford someone tapped into modern Hollywood, someone who could set up projects.

After the Cinerama film, Ford and Wayne teamed for their last effort together, a gentle, undemanding *l'envoi* called *Donovan's Reef.* Ford had grown fond of Lee Marvin during *The Man Who Shot Liberty Valance*, so he offered him the co-starring role opposite John Wayne—in essence, the Victor McLaglen role. He refused to send him a script.

"Don't you want your kids to be as brown as berries?" he asked Marvin. "Don't you want to spend eight weeks in Hawaii this summer? Then do the picture." Marvin was convinced, but the legendary costumer Edith Head strongly objected to Elizabeth Allen, Ford's choice for the female lead. Head tried to get Allen replaced by Vera Miles, but Ford resisted. As was normally the case with Ford, he felt at ease with a solid professional who couldn't be bullied.

"I fell in love with John," remembered Head. "Every day that I wasn't busy and he was not directing, I would have tea with him. He was exactly like the male leads in his movies: strong, virile, passionate. You'd expect him to drink slugs of straight whiskey. Instead he drank tea. Tea was one of his passions. I thought that I knew how to drink it, but he showed me the fine points. I felt like an idiot, but he told me not to feel bad, that most people didn't know how. The trick, he said, was in lifting both the saucer and the cup simultaneously, one with the left hand and one with the right—never just the cup. I have a wonderful memory of husky, burly John Ford showing me how to lift a teacup and saucer properly."

Ford decided he wanted Tim Stafford, Anna Lee's seven-year-old son and his godson, in the picture. Lee explained to her boy that his godfather was a very nice man, but quite Irish. In Ford's office, Ford asked Tim if he'd like anything to drink. Tim promptly asked for Irish coffee. "He'll have a Coke," said his mother.

Lee told him that Tim couldn't go to Hawaii, because she had already started shooting *Whatever Happened to Baby Jane?* "With those two women?" said an appalled Ford. "He was very cross that I couldn't go with him," remembered Lee. "And finally he said, 'Well, the boy needs a guardian. I'm his godfather, I'll be his guardian.' But he deeply resented the fact that I couldn't leave my job to go there." Ford brought Tim's two older brothers along for the ride as well, and put them all up in the room next to his.

So it was that, beginning July 23, 1962, and continuing for more than forty days, Ford created his vision of Hawaii as Paradise Regained. The budget was $3.58 million, and Ford was getting $175,135, plus 10 percent of the gross in excess of $7.5 million. Since the *Araner* had been written into the script, Ford spent $75,000 getting her ready for the film. As Paramount was only paying him $5,000 for the use of the yacht, it was a financially indefensible decision, but Ford wanted to show the old girl off, and, perhaps, have something of a vacation on company time. As far as he was concerned, that net loss of $70,000 was the cost of doing business.

Ford gathered old friends for the cast. Dorothy Lamour, whom he had nicknamed "Toujy," a diminutive of "Toujours l'amour," played a saloon entertainer; Cesar Romero played the island's governor. (In an amusing in-joke, the name of Romero's character was De Lage, but for one letter the name of the forbidding but forgiving governor played by Raymond Massey in *The Hurricane*.)

Other than a brief part in the 1962 *Road to Hong Kong*, Lamour hadn't made a picture in nearly ten years, and was extremely nervous, as well she should have been. "Ford was pretty crotchety and a grouchy old man by this time," said Cesar Romero. "He wasn't much fun to work with, as [he had been on] *Wee Willie Winkie*. . . . You couldn't talk to him, you couldn't . . . discuss a scene. It wasn't too pleasant working with him. John Wayne, however . . . was great with him."

Ford kept a watchful eye on his godson Tim, and the boy performed well. During one scene, Tim had to eat a papaya, then climb into a jeep between Elizabeth Allen and Cesar Romero. The boy began to feel nauseous. Since Allen was the object of a serious crush, he elected to throw up all over Cesar Romero.

Ford thought it was the funniest thing he'd ever seen; it was around 1:00 in the afternoon, and vomiting on an actor was the perfect end to a perfect day; Ford wrapped. Tim was taken to the hospital just to make sure nothing was seriously wrong. Ford came for a visit, and complimented the boy on the great job he had done in the scene.

Stafford and his brothers had permission to rummage in Ford's suite for food and drinks, so one day they went a little overboard and devoured an entire case of chocolate bars. The next day Stafford was shooting a scene involving priests and nuns when Ford cut the scene and called over one of the actors dressed in priest's garb. "Father, is it a mortal sin to steal candy from someone's refrigerator?" he inquired. Stafford and his brothers were horrified; they were good Catholic boys who attended parochial school. Their guilt was partially assuaged when the actor playing the priest let them off the hook with twelve Hail Marys.

Lamour gradually realized that Ford was not on top of his game. One day she was amazed to see Wayne snap at Ford for what must have been the first time in thirty-odd years. Later, Wayne explained to Lamour that Ford's thinking wasn't as sharp as it had been, and he couldn't see very well anymore. Wayne had deputized himself to watch the rushes every day to make sure everything was all right, and was feeling stressed.

Ford outfitted Lamour in some of Mary's own muumuus, but he was too busy to give an aging, insecure actress the support she needed. Then

Lamour made the mistake of complimenting Lee Marvin on a scene, and Ford called her down in front of the entire cast and crew with his usual litany about how he was the director and in charge of deciding what takes were good and what takes were bad.

Lamour exploded and exited. Ford sent Wingate Smith after her, but Lamour insisted on an apology from Ford himself. Realizing he had been out of line, Ford trooped in five minutes later, hugged Lamour, and made it right.

Ford now tended to stick to a plan even after it was obvious that it wouldn't work. The unit had finished all their Hawaiian location work except for one scene, which was going to be shot day for night. Came the morning and it was overcast. William Clothier's heart sank. "There's no way you can shoot night stuff in the daytime on a cloudy day. There's just no way."

The unit waited for the sun till noon, then Ford gave the order to go ahead with the scene. Clothier protested that the scene wouldn't be any good, but Ford was adamant. Clothier used every arc light he had, spent the rest of the afternoon and all of the next day working, but, "It was no damn good and I knew it. After we were finished I asked Jack, 'Jack, are you going to be happy with this crap that we just got through with?'

" 'It'll be all right.' "

After returning to California, Clothier looked at the rushes and the scene was just as bad as he expected it to be. Ford still didn't believe him. Then editor Otho Lovering came on the set and told him that the scene wasn't good. Finally, Clothier girded his loins and confronted the director. "Years ago you said that if you asked a cameraman to shoot something and it wasn't good, you'd be the first one to take it out of the picture." Ford looked at him for a moment. *"Fort Apache?"* he asked. "Yes, *Fort Apache*," said Clothier.

"I need that goddamn sequence like I need a hole in my head," grumbled Ford. "We'll shoot that whole goddamn thing over right here on the stage."

Clothier managed to dodge that bullet, but Ford's willingness to accept work that he instinctively knew was not up to his visual standard was disheartening proof of carelessness.

Like its director, *Donovan's Reef* tends toward the rickety, although it has its compensations. Mae Marsh and Frank Baker appear briefly, as does Dick Foran. The *Araner* looks beautiful and William Clothier's wife, Carmen, plays one of the nuns. And there is a rather lovely Christmas pageant as Ford portrays a celebratory, intact community for the last time. The plot is basic—prissy New England woman comes to primitive Hawaii and is thawed by the sensuality of the tropics and by the dubious pleasures of observing two grown men beating each other senseless, just as they have for the past twenty-two years.

Elizabeth Allen falls down a few times too often, and the structure is so loose as to be nonexistent. *Donovan's Reef* is as much a Wayne film as it is a Ford film, as it focuses on the same line of broad humor that Wayne had been specializing in with films like *North to Alaska*. Yet, Wayne wasn't any too pleased with the film either. "He never should have used me on that picture. He should have picked some young guy. It didn't require much of him. All he had to be was a good-looking young guy, and I wasn't young enough."

Still, if caught in the right, undemanding mood, *Donovan's Reef* can be a mellow, sunlit idyll. Perhaps it's best to take it on the same level that Ford took it—good summer fun. Martin Scorsese's capsule description of the film seems eminently fair: "That film has got some sloppy things in it, and some silly things, but it's enjoyable—and it really is Ford."

During preproduction on *How the West Was Won*, Ford had asked Bernard Smith, "What kind of uniform should Grant be wearing?" Smith responded by saying, "Mr. Ford, don't ask me a question like that. You can answer that question better than I ever could." Deference was the quickest way to Ford's heart, and the two men quickly became friends, as well as partners.

They were an odd couple, at least in some ways; despite his loyalty to the Democratic Party, Ford was now widely perceived as right-wing, and Smith remained a flaming New Deal liberal. "One day I said to him, 'Jack, all the liberals of Hollywood regard you as not only very conservative, but semi-fascist, and I know it's absurd. Because what you actually are is an old-fashioned anarchist.' And he burst into laughter and said, 'It's absolutely true.' Actually, all Irishmen are fundamentally anarchists."

Still, Smith and Ford wisely kept the conversation centering on movies; politics came up rarely, but Smith enjoyed tweaking his partner. "I once made a wisecrack about his religion," recalled Smith. "He loved lying in bed till late in the day and holding script conferences at his bedside. One day I said to him, 'Jack, you're a devout Catholic, aren't you?'

" 'Of course,' he said.

" 'Well, I'm looking at the beads over your bed, pegged to the wall. How come they're so dusty?' And all he could do was break into laughter."

Smith left aesthetic matters up to Ford. "He knew more about movies than anybody I ever met, and I was very friendly with George Stevens. What I wanted above all was to learn; remember, I was a relatively new man in the motion picture world."

Unfortunately, the Ford of the mid-1960s was not the same man with whom Merian Cooper had conspired to make *Fort Apache* and *The Quiet Man*. One sure signal was the fact that, on movies like *Cheyenne Autumn* and *7 Women*, Ford wanted Smith around on the set every day. "Sometimes he was unsure in his mind," remembered Smith, "and he wanted someone to talk to." John Ford, unsure in his mind?

Smith was frankly admiring of Ford's visual acuity. "For a scene in *Cheyenne Autumn*, he told me how he was going to shoot it so that it wouldn't be necessary to have a later scene we'd originally planned. I listened carefully—his visual description of the foreground, of what was happening in the background, and the far distance. I said, 'I have a feeling you've studied medieval and Renaissance painting.' And he looked at me and smiled.

"He didn't want to shoot until he had the picture in his mind. He didn't have the impulse to write; he was a storyteller with a camera. He was very different than a man like Stevens, who was a story man as well as a script man. Stevens would tell a writer what scene to write next and how to write it. But Ford wanted the writer's draft in front of him, then he could read it and criticize, and he was quite gentle with writers."

Ford was still capable of the grand theatrical gesture. Once, when Smith was out of town, his wife opened the door one morning to find a tall, thin man standing there. "I'm John Ford," he announced, "and I wanted to say hello to you, Mrs. Smith. I wish I had known your husband earlier."

"He was a tough guy [to the world]," said Smith, "but a sentimental slob underneath."

Denver Pyle had been added to the roster of people who would receive occasional phone calls for a command performance in the house on Copa de Oro. "His bedroom had all kinds of pictures and memorabilia," remembered Pyle. "He had a couple of Charlie Russells. And there was a picture of him and Duke. They both had their arms over a horse's rear end." The picture had Ford's signature, Wayne's, and under the horse's rear they had put a facsimile signature of Ward Bond.

Ford wanted to know what Pyle thought of the photo, and Pyle said it was a great likeness, complimented Ford on the way he looked, and the stylish gray Stetson he had on.

Three weeks later, Ken Curtis called Pyle. "Listen, Den, I've got this hat down here that we used to wear in the Sons of the Pioneers and I never liked it. I think it might look good on you." It was the gray Stetson Ford had been wearing in the photo; he'd given it to Curtis to give to Pyle with strict instructions not to tell him where it came from.

• • •

Ford had been interested in Mari Sandoz's book *Cheyenne Autumn* when it was first published in 1953, and had gone so far as to do a treatment with Dudley Nichols that drew no interest whatever. But the partnership with Bernard Smith regenerated Ford's passion for the project, and the two men began shopping it around Hollywood.

As Ford's ties to his extended family remained strong, his ties to his blood family continued to weaken. In April 1963, Pat wrote his father asking for a loan of $20,000 to relocate from Hawaii back to California. The $20,000, he explained, would enable him to buy a house and some horse and cattle stock.

Pat's timing left something to be desired, so Ford responded with one of the more personal letters of his life. The day he sat down to answer Pat's request, Barbara had left Ken Curtis and come home to her parents, dogs and suitcases in her wake. Also, Warners decided to pass on *Cheyenne Autumn*—too expensive, not enough stars.

"I'm not working," wrote Ford, "and no prospects in sight." He then proceeded to outline his financial and domestic situations, which, he said, were intertwined. "[Mary] keeps talking about the enormous holdings I have in A.T.&T. Actually, the bank holds the stock for loans—to pay income tax over the years. She has been told repeatedly over & over, but refuses to believe it—or doesn't want to believe it. 'It's a conspiracy!' her community property rights etc. She spends more than our annual income—silly things. I tried to talk her into giving the 'Araner' to the Navy. We simply can't afford it. She screams—hysteria—'Where is the money going? I'm not spending it! You must be keeping another woman' etc. etc. 'Araner' to her is a status symbol. She hates the boat—won't use it, but refuses to give it up."

Ford went on to enumerate all the reasons that money was tight: Mary had spent $7,000 on clothes for Barbara in the previous year; one day between 10:30 and noon she spent $600 on a car for Dan, $60 for a Hertz rental, and $100 for a coat to wear to baseball games. "Of course [it's] a mania, but I'm a strong believer in the marriage vows, so . . . every time I talk about expenses, she talks about 'Separate maintenance' and such crap. Maybe it isn't crap & perhaps I should turn everything over to her & go to Europe on a tax dodge stint. Maybe I could leave a comfortable estate that way (No! I'm not pessimistic—just Irish).

"Of course, she'd piss everything away in a year.

"I'm really leveling with you, Pat. You must believe me. Let's see what gives. I hate to criticize Nana as I love her dearly and I hope you keep this confidential even to [Pat's second wife] Carol, but it's necessary at long last to inform you of our situation." Ford signed off, "As ever, Gramps."

There is some petty poor-mouthing in this curious letter—at the time he wrote it, Ford's assets were in the vicinity of $1 million—but also a perceptible sense of wounding, and disguised impatience with Pat.

On Pat's side, there was a sense of entitlement that stemmed from Ford's decision, in 1950, to open a trust for Barbara that contained five hundred shares of General Motors. He never opened a comparable trust for Pat, although, over the years, he had made the down payment on Pat's house, contributed to the upkeep of his grandsons, and thrown Pat a lot of movie jobs. In Ford's mind, he had been more than equitable; in Pat's mind, Barbara had gotten a trust fund and he hadn't.

"He wanted to come back and buy a ranch in the Santa Ynez Valley," said Dan Ford about his father. "Now, I'm Jack Ford, and I'm thinking, 'What is he going to do in the Santa Ynez Valley? What is he going to do in Santa Rosa? How many times am I going to be able to get you a job on a picture to support your lifestyle? What's wrong with Encino? Why not get a place where you can get a job, because if things don't work out, you're immediately in a financial corner.' It was Pat living his life with unrealistic expectations."

Pat ended up buying twenty-two acres in Santa Ynez, a horse ranch with a Spanish hacienda. He wasn't able to make the payments and Ford had to take over the mortgage until the place could be sold.

"My grandfather thought my father was lazy," says Dan Ford. "The difference between the two men was that my grandfather was an extraordinary man and my father was an ordinary man, and Jack judged him by his own standards and those of his peers—Frank Capra, Duke Wayne. It wasn't fair."

Complicating Ford's situation was the *Araner*, which had turned into a money pit. "The boat had been going downhill since the early 1950s," remembered Dan Ford. "It was always berthed in warm tropical water, and a boat with the *Araner*'s construction is only going to last twenty to twenty-five years. They loved the islands, they loved Hawaii, but they should have bought a house on any beach on any of the islands and bought a small boat and his family would have been a lot better off.

"For years they had talked about retiring aboard the boat. They had some of the best times of their life on the *Araner*, so it was hard to give up. But his cash flow could not really support that boat, especially when he stopped working. But he kept it for three years after that, and it ate him alive. And when it came time to sell, he couldn't sell it because it was too old and nobody wanted it."

Another continuing financial drain was Barbara, who had slowly declined into alcoholism and was always drying out in some lavishly appointed sanitarium, when, her nephew believed, "she really belonged in the county jail. She needed to hit bottom and get into Alcoholics Anonymous and start working her way back. But my grandmother was her enabler who always covered her tracks and bailed her out. They spent a fortune on her."

Things were clearly out of balance and Ford didn't seem to know how to right them. Beleaguered, confused, aware that, at the age of sixty-nine, it wasn't supposed to be like this, Ford returned to trying to get *Cheyenne Autumn* off the ground.

Bernard Smith went back to Jack Warner and helpfully told him that he had committed far too much money to *My Fair Lady*, and that he needed an insurance policy, "a picture that has a guaranteed audience. What better insurance could you have than a John Ford western, particularly a John Ford western in tune with today's social issues?" Since Warner had barely gotten out alive from *Sergeant Rutledge*, another Ford Western supposedly in tune with social issues, Smith must have been mightily convincing.

After Smith's pitch, Jack Warner gave the picture the green light, approving the very sizable budget of $4.2 million, most of which was going to the actors and the production of the film itself, including alloting the film one of the studio's two commitments for Super Panavision 70 (the other film to get the deluxe treatment was *My Fair Lady*). Smith was taking only $100,000, and Ford was taking $200,000, although their company was in for 50 percent of the profits.

Some of Ford's script notes for the film have survived, and their quantity attests that he was clearly engaged by the material, if uneasy about the draft of the script: "Build! Picture—not words—close-up technique." The problems of the film are present at the creation: the Indians are remote totems, victims of injustice, reacting, never acting—a major structural problem at the heart of the film.

Ford cast the picture with a polyglot of Mexican and Italian actors— Sal Mineo, Gilbert Roland, Ricardo Montalban, and old friend Dolores Del Rio—of the sort that had been de rigueur in Hollywood since Griffith used white actors in blackface for *The Birth of a Nation*.

Nevertheless, Ford paid the tribute that one proud, beaten tribe always pays to another. "I like Indians very much. They're . . . a very moral people. They have a literature. Not written. But spoken. They're very kindhearted. They love their children and their animals. And I wanted to show their point of view for a change."

For some incomprehensible reason, both Ford and Smith must have been impressed with James Webb's script for *How the West Was Won*, because they were paying him $100,000 plus 20 percent of the producer's profits for his screenplay.

It was an uncommercial subject, so to justify the budget, Ford called in his markers, casting stars whenever possible—Richard Widmark, Carroll Baker, and James Stewart in a waggish turn as Wyatt Earp, industriously cheating at cards. Ford intended this bizarrely out-of-key sequence to be a kind of comic intermission; he told Stewart that he wanted a break from the dolor of the Indians, but not to the extent of having the audience actually getting up from their seats.

For the small part of Secretary of the Interior Carl Schurz, Ford wanted Spencer Tracy, and, in early correspondence about the picture, his participation seemed to be a fait accompli. However, Tracy ended up backing out, claiming illness. In fact, he didn't like the script. Ford cast his second choice, Edward G. Robinson.

For the last time, Ford headed out to Monument Valley to direct a film; for the last time he was surrounded by the Mittens, the Big Indian, Totem Pole, the Three Sisters; for the last time he set up his cameras on the spot the Indians called Ford's Point.

Ford was now calling the Valley "my favorite location. It has rivers, mountains, plains, desert, everything the land can offer. I feel at peace there. I have been all over the world, but I consider this the most complete, beautiful and peaceful place on earth." Danny Borzage again struck up "Bringing in the Sheaves" as Ford's car pulled up, followed by "My Darling Clementine" and "The Wild Colonial Boy."

The film was supposed to be shot in seventy-nine days, beginning on September 23, 1963, but a month after he started shooting, Ford was five days behind schedule; by November 22, the day John Kennedy was assassinated, he was still five days behind.

George O'Brien joined the cast, and he noticed that it was getting harder for Ford to communicate with the younger generation of actors. One day, Ford gave a couple of actresses a long weekend, and one of them said she was going to try to squeeze in an extra session with her therapist. Ford inquired as to whether psychiatry did her any good, and the actress assured him that it did.

"Mr. O'Brien and I have an analyst," said Ford. "We get it for free. We go to confession."

More importantly, O'Brien noticed that Ford was estranged from himself, as well as the people he employed. "George, it's not fun anymore," Ford said. The days of an impromptu noon ball game, of morning swims, were no more. O'Brien told his son that Ford had lost touch with his own gift, that his attention could no longer be sustained and he had no real interest in making movies, but continued to work because of a lack of any real alternatives.

Dobe Carey was in the cast and watched day after day as Victor Jory,

Dolores Del Rio, and Gilbert Roland marched across Monument Valley, stopping to deliver dialogue, then marched some more. "I never knew what was going on, but I chalked it up to my being just plain dumb. I was to discover, however, that no one else did either. They did what the Old Man told them. Naturally, they trusted him—he was John Ford—so there must be some reason for what they were doing."

The production was joined by a young film critic named Peter Bogdanovich, who wrote his impressions for *Esquire*. He noted Ford's "stern Yankee face, almost mean, a small growth of white stubble on his sunken cheeks. . . . There was an orange scarf tied around his neck, and the laces of his dark blue sneakers were untied. He passed a Navajo and moved his right hand in a kind of half wave, half salute. 'Yat'hey, shi'kis' he said, and the man answered, 'Yat'hey.' "

Dinner was in the adobe structure that had served as the dining room at Goulding's Lodge for years. Attached to the porch was a dinner bell, which was never rung until Ford took his place at the head of the third table from the door. After dinner, Ford would inaugurate a game of 20 Questions. One night Ford led off with something that was animal and vegetable. No one got close to the answer, and Ford finally revealed, with some disgust, that the object in question was Sherlock Holmes's Moroccan slipper that served double duty as a tobacco pouch. "Probably one of the most famous props in literature," he muttered. "It seems that none of you, including [Victor] Jory, have read Sherlock Holmes." After the game was over, Ford would smoke half a cigar, then nudge his son. "I'm going to call Mother," he would say, and the two men would leave together.

"He was very laid back and in total control," Bogdanovich remembered. "The music told you he was there. He didn't have to do much because all eyes were on him. He looked rather frail; Orson said he looked like he could be blown over with a feather. He sat beneath the camera and gave the actors dialogue that wasn't in the script."

George O'Brien's presence inspired an unaccustomed mood of reverie. "George," asked Ford one night, "did you ever see a picture called *Desperate Trails*? Nineteen twenty-one. Harry Carey and Irene Rich were in it. First picture made with actual nighttime photography. It was based on a story by Courtney Riley Cooper called 'Christmas Eve at Pilot Butte.' Like to remake it sometime. A nice story. Pat was born while we were makin' that picture. And so was Dobe. Within about a week of each other." (It was more like within a month of each other.)

Ford's room looked like a landfill. "Clothes lay everywhere," noted Bogdanovich. "On the floor, on tables and chairs, even on the refrigerator. There were also piles of books on every conceivable subject scattered around the room and next to his bed. On it lay a copy of *Gods, Graves and Scholars*. The little night table was covered with cigars, matches, a watch, pills, glasses, a couple of knives and pencils, loose paper, scripts and frayed handkerchiefs."

Saturday nights were for parties in the lodge dining room. Danny Borzage played, and people danced. If he was so inclined, Ford would take a turn with one of the actresses for a polka or "The Tennessee Waltz." As the party wore down, Borzage segued into the sentimental Irish songs that Ford loved so much, then "Auld Lang Syne." With that song slowly receding into the distance, Ford ambled back to Room 19.

If it was business as usual behind the camera, before the cameras things continued to go subtly wrong. "We were running over budget because of time," said Bernard Smith. "Ford wouldn't shoot unless he could make it the way he wanted it." Because of his limited energy, Ford was already working a short day, from 9:00 till 2:30 P.M. Smith told Ford that he wanted the unit to work until 4:00 P.M.

"The next morning," remembered William Clothier, "I'm waiting to get the setup from the Old Man. I can't light anything until I get the setup. So 8:30 comes and the Old Man's not there . . . at 10:30, his limousine pulls up, the music starts, the Old Man gets out, walks up and says, 'The funniest thing happened. I've had the same goddamn chauffeur for twenty-five years and this morning he got lost!' The next day the Old Man came in at 9:00 and quit at 2:30, just like before."

Dolores Del Rio and Richard Widmark knew how to deal with Ford, but intense young Method actors like Sal Mineo were doomed before they began. Mineo, playing a wild young brave, had a scene where he had to mount a horse in anger and ride off. On his first try, he missed his jump, tried again and made it, then whipped the horse and rode off. Ford printed the take, only to have Mineo ask him for another take that wouldn't be as clumsy.

Ford stared at him for a moment, then asked, "Do you wanna do it again with an empty camera, Sol?" The old John Ford would have walked away, leaving a humiliated actor in his wake, but now he demonstrated an unaccustomed courtesy, explaining to Mineo that "You were very angry. And you missed. I like it. *Completely* in character. I don't want it to look perfect, like a circus. But you can do it again with an empty camera, Sol."

Jack's mood declined still further when John Kennedy was assassinated. Jack called the company together in front of Goulding's Lodge and instructed a bugler to blow taps. The flag was lowered to half-staff, then Ford stood up and addressed the company. The nation, he told them, had lost a great leader, but the republic was sound and America would survive. He led the company in a reading of the Lord's Prayer, then Dobe Carey sang "The Battle Hymn of the Republic." Ford dismissed the company; there was no filming in Monument Valley on November 23.

When the production moved to Gunnison, Colorado, Ford turned an ankle and got zoned on codeine pills, so Richard Widmark took over the direction for a day or two. A furious Bill Clothier, who had drawn the job of rousing Ford in the mornings and getting him to the set, emptied the codeine pills down the toilet, then went out to the car. In a few minutes, an enraged Ford came storming toward Clothier.

"Some son of a bitch flushed my pills down the toilet," roared Ford.

"I did," said Clothier.

"What would you do if I flushed all your *lenses* down the toilet?" screamed Ford. On days when Ford couldn't function, Russ Saunders or Pat Ford, who had shot the second unit footage for *The Searchers*, directed some scenes.

Contrary to other reports, however, Karl Malden, who was playing the heavy, never directed any footage on the picture. "He was a biting, peppery guy," remembered Malden. "I'd never want to get in a fight with John Ford, no sir. It was his picture. He brought the bat and ball and you played the game his way. He was directing every day I was there."

As a newcomer, Malden would have been expected to be a target of abuse, and Ford did bait Malden, asking him for ideas in staging his scenes. Malden gave them, always a trigger for a lashing. But instead of calling the company to a halt and excoriating the actor, as he had been doing since the Harry Carey days, Ford would merely say, "How about standing in front of the fireplace with your hands outstretched on the mantel, feet spread so we can see the fire, and we'll shoot you from the back."

When Ford suggested the same pose for a different scene, Malden mentioned that blocking had already been used. "Does it matter?" asked Ford. "No sir, not at all," replied the suddenly prescient Malden.

Afternoon teas were limited to the inner circle of Ford veterans, people Ford liked—Clothier, Widmark, Del Rio, etc. Malden was on the outside looking in until one day Ford asked him, "What's the matter? Don't you like tea?"

"Yes, I like tea."

"Well, how come you don't have tea with us?"

"I thought it was a private party."

"It is, but I'll invite you if that's what you want."

So Malden was accepted into the inner circle, although, as he remembered, "I never felt that I was really a John Ford actor—an actor who didn't need words."

Cheyenne Autumn was not to be a vintage Ford effort; the days when that level of filmmaking was possible were behind him. It was certainly obvious to Bill Clothier: "On *Cheyenne Autumn*, the same thing happened that happened on a number of the Old Man's later films—he'd give up. Just get tired and lose interest." Patrick Ford concurred. "He was sick. . . . and he physically wasn't up to the heavy load he had to do. His eyesight had gone, to a great extent . . . and with it his sense of composition, so you'd have to subtly go over to him and say, 'You know, you told me once that no matter [what], you should always change angles every scene, just to break things up . . .' He hadn't said that, but he thought he had, so then he'd move the camera."

Peter Bogdanovich sent Ford a draft of his *Esquire* story, and got blistered for his troubles. "I think your article is nauseating," wrote Ford. "I dislike immensely your portrait of the senile, illiterate drunken director. I also think you are a very bad reporter. . . . As a practicising [sic] Roman Catholic I object most strongly to the profanity you had me speak every other word.

"However, I believe that everybody should make a living and if the pittance you receive helps you economically, go ahead. . . . To sum it all up I think it is cheap. . . . Otherwise all is well and I hope you and Polly [Platt, Bogdanovich's wife] have a very merry Christmas."

Actually, Ford liked and respected Bogdanovich—he would hardly have allowed him access to do the career interview that became Bogdanovich's book *John Ford* otherwise—but that only became clear when Bogdanovich wasn't around, when Ford would express appreciation for the younger man's "pure love" for making movies.

William Clothier's ongoing problem with Ford's penchant for day-for-night erupted again. For a night scene in which the Indians fold up their tents and steal away, Ford told Clothier, "We're going to shoot in the daytime. I'm not working at night."

"Well, Jack, why don't we just build the set right outside the motel, so you can direct it on your doorstep?" asked the pugnacious Clothier. "I'm not gonna work at night," repeated Ford. "Go out and make some tests; you figure out how to do it."

Clothier spent three days playing with lights, consulting with Technicolor, and finally felt sure he could pull the scene off, only to be called over by Ford, who was suffering from a modest anxiety attack. "I'm worried," said Ford. "Jack," said an angry Clothier, "I told you it should be done at night. You refused to do it. I've worked this out, it's gonna work fine. Just quit worrying about it and let me do it. You'll like it." Ford acquiesced, and the scene did indeed work well.

Occasionally, there were flashes of the old Ford. One day Ford was staging a scene with Richard Widmark and Karl Malden when Ford turned to Clothier and said, "Jesus Christ, I don't know how to play this scene; I guess I'll have to pull a rabbit out of my hat." It was, remembered Clothier, a commonplace saying of Ford's.

What wasn't commonplace was that Clothier noticed that Ford was wearing a different hat, which was obvious because Ford wore the same clothes day after day after day. After what Clothier remembered as a half-hour of moving actors around, trying to get the scene to work, Ford again turned to Clothier and said, "Well, I guess I'll have to pull a rabbit out of my hat." Whereupon he took off his hat and revealed a stuffed rabbit that had been hidden there all morning. "I never would have believed Ford would do something like that," remembered Clothier with a fond smile.

As if observing his father's failing powers wasn't bad enough, Pat Ford became locked in a power struggle with Bernard Smith. The outcome was a foregone conclusion. Ford was weary of Pat's inability to craft a career of his own, and Smith was an Oscar-winning producer who Ford believed was vital to his ability to function in the movie business, which he cared about more than his family, probably more than life itself. Although Pat retained his associate producer credit on *Cheyenne Autumn*, Ford never worked with his son again.

"That situation was sort of like my father and I," said Ben Johnson. "There was always from ten to forty cowboys on this ranch where I grew up. And my dad always gave me the long way around, never gave me the best of anything, because he didn't want all the other cowboys to think that he was being partial to me. . . . I think that was the same attitude that John Ford had against Pat. . . . It was a tough situation for the whole family . . . because they always got the little end of the horn. He never had time for them."

Pat's attitude toward his father became a compound of pride and bitterness. "He was a gentleman," Pat would say. "He went down and voted, he was a good American citizen, he paid his taxes and never cheated on them. In fact, he overpaid them consistently. And he won his Purple Hearts. . . . He was a good American. That he was. He was a lousy father, but he was a good movie director and a good American."

Cheyenne Autumn was beset with all kinds of problems, but the photography wasn't one of them. William Clothier was doing a splendid job, and Ford knew it. On the last day of production, Ford walked up to Clothier and kissed him on the cheek. "This is the best-photographed picture I ever made in my life," he said.

When Ford turned in his final cut to Warner Bros., there was a degree of reflexive enthusiasm followed by much throat clearing. "Even though all present seemed to like the picture, there was a definite feeling of length," reported Warners' chief editor Rudi Fehr on June 24, 1964. Fehr then went on to delineate twenty-seven specific cuts, mostly small trims meant to get to the meat of a scene faster: "The unfolding of the chair for the Senator by Widmark and the preceding attempt of Carroll Baker to open it seems unnecessarily long; if possible start the scene just as Widmark sets up the chair.... After the poker game in reel 12, we dissolve into the street in Dodge City. Nothing seems to be happening there and we should try to get all the wagons and horseback riders out of town in half the time."

But there was at least one instance where Ford's impatience had resulted in a crucial story point being missed. The scene of Sal Mineo's death seemed unmotivated because the nascent relationship between his character and that of Ricardo Montalban's wife had not, in Fehr's words, been "carried through too well ... it would be of great value to the picture if we could find some close-ups of Mineo and Montalban's youngest wife exchanging looks." Besides that, Ford had evidently shot three variant endings.

"You will appreciate the fact that the information contained in this letter should be kept confidential as far as the Ford-Smith group is concerned," wrote Fehr. "Under no circumstances should the editor, Otto [sic] Lovering, be involved in any of these changes." Lovering's assistant was delegated to make the cuts and told to keep his mouth shut.

In retrospect, it seems that the studio was demonstrating considerable restraint; Ford had turned in a sluggish, muffled picture—the gap between the precision of the shooting and cutting of *The Searchers*, and *Cheyenne Autumn* was and is heartbreaking—but, at this point, all Warner and Fehr seemed to be concerned about was material on the margins.

Perhaps they sensed that the problems were not structural but systemic, and, short of expensive reshooting, the picture really wasn't going to get much better. Perhaps it was just a case of not wanting to throw good money after bad; what with the budget overruns, Warners had $7 million tied up in *Cheyenne Autumn*, but they had more than twice that tied up in the far more commercial *My Fair Lady*.

As *Cheyenne Autumn* neared release, Jack Warner decided more drastic action was in order. Just before the film opened in London, the studio made more cuts, specifically in the massacre sequence, and even changed the position of the intermission. The studio seemed bewildered by the Dodge City sequence, as well they might have been. The 1964 Earp cheats at cards, upholds the law as lackadaisically as possible, and generally serves as the Mel Brooks version of Wyatt Earp. The comic relief is overstressed, overplayed, and wildly out of tone with the rest of the film.

Jack Warner had told Bernard Smith that the picture would open its reserved seat engagements as Ford had left it, but it might have to be cut by as much as twenty minutes for general release (the Earp sequence was a prime candidate for the cutting room floor). Smith, playing for time, assented. And then he found out that Warner had in fact made major changes in the reserved seat print.

Warner had told Smith not to tell Ford about what he insisted were very minor trims, but when Smith saw the film just before the London press preview, he was appalled. "SCREENED FILM THIS MORNING TO CHECK PRINT," Smith wired Ford back in Hollywood, "AND SHOCKED DISCOVER WARNER DRASTICALLY RE-CUT SECOND HALF DESTROYING MANY MAJOR VALUES STOP INTERMISSION PUT IN MIDDLE OF DODGE SEQUENCE STOP FORT ROBINSON MASSACRE REDUCED TO ALMOST NOTHING STOP HOSPITAL SCENE WHEN CHILD BROUGHT IN REDUCED BY DISSOLVE IN MIDDLE STOP RE-UNION OF TRIBE AT VICTORY CAVE REDUCED STOP HAVE CABLED WARNER STRONG PROTEST DEMANDING OPENING BE POSTPONED AND OUR CUT RESTORED THREATENING STATEMENT TO CRITICS."

Both men felt that the shortening of the massacre sequence diminished the audience's involvement with the Indians and placed too much emphasis on Karl Malden's character. "I want you to know that there are some things you did in the film that I approve of highly," Smith wrote Jack Warner on October 12, 1964. ". . . This film is the most important thing Ford has ever done and I need hardly say that it means a great deal to me too. . . . I would say at this point that if the position of the intermission is restored and if a few more shots are added to the massacre, you will hear nothing more about all of this from either Ford or myself, and everybody will be calm and happy."

In retrospect, Smith felt that Jack Warner was right; the picture had the scale of an epic, and it had a stifling dignity, but that's about it. The film is full of static shots that all seem to last too long. It's sincere but unfelt; Ford is too tired to summon any energy or emotion, and the way the script is structured, the audience is expected to feel the tragedy of a people they don't even know.

"*Cheyenne Autumn* was a great hit in Europe," remembered Bernard Smith, "but was disappointing here. Ford and I made a joint mistake in [letting] the picture run too long. We could have cut twenty minutes out of that movie. In Europe they were waiting for it; in America it was ahead of its time."

The reviews were appropriately modest. *Cheyenne Autumn* was nominated for only one Oscar, for William Clothier's photography. Clothier was up against Harry Stradling's work in *My Fair Lady*. When Clothier called the Warners publicity department to see what they had planned for *Cheyenne Autumn*, they were at least honest. "We're sorry, Mr. Clothier, but Jack Warner's not the least bit interested in *Cheyenne Autumn*. Warner's only interested in *My Fair Lady*."

Warners carried the negative cost of *Cheyenne Autumn* at $7.37 million. The picture grossed a mild $3.1 million domestically, $6.3 worldwide, and carried a net loss, as of September 1966, of $5.7 million.

I t had been a long time since a John Ford movie had been a hit. *Liberty Valance* had done well, but no more than was expected of a John Wayne Western, and the films Ford had been making without Wayne had been doing only nominal business. Ford was far too sensitive a man not to know that he was marginalized by his age and the audience's changing tastes.

Moreover, the critics weren't being any more responsive than the public. As the swinging 1960s moved into third gear, what Andrew Sarris called Ford's "cinema of reminiscence ... [where] the mourning hero talks more eloquently to the dead than to the living," seemed irredeemably passé. It was a process that had begun after the war, when Ford turned out four remakes (*3 Godfathers, What Price Glory?, The Sun Shines Bright,* and *Mogambo*) in seven years, making movies that ran against the au courant critical tastes that were more appreciative of Kazan than Ford, James Dean more than John Wayne. Ford had been true to his art by making movies like *The Sun Shines Bright, The Quiet Man,* and *The Searchers*, but he had also cut himself off from what contemporary society regarded as reality.

This culminated in 1965, when the *New York Times*'s Bosley Crowther rose at the annual meeting of the New York Film Critics Circle and proposed a special life achievement award to Ford. The motion was promptly tabled by a majority of the members.

It was no surprise that, when he sat down for an interview with *Cosmopolitan*'s Bill Libby, Ford was in full defensive mode. Clothed in khakis, preceded by his dachshunds, armed with a few casual lies about possessing a master's degree, he sounded like a man pretending defiance about the parade passing him by.

"Every time I make a Western, they say, 'There goes senile old John Ford out West again,' but I just don't give a damn," was a typical remark. "When a motion picture is at its best, it is long on action and short on dialogue. When it tells its story and reveals its characters in a series of simple, beautiful, active pictures, and does it with as little talk as possible, then the motion picture medium is being used to its fullest advantage. I don't know any subject on earth better suited to such a presentation than a Western."

Ford went on to enumerate the list of great Americans who loved

Westerns, including Woodrow Wilson, Franklin Roosevelt, and Jack Kennedy. "Yes, that's right, they *were* all Democrats, and I'm a Democrat, too. I don't try to hide that, either." This would be the last time he would publicly identify himself as a Democrat; as Vietnam heated up, as his beloved military was reviled as a collection of mass murderers, Ford found himself incrementally nudged into Nixonian Republicanism.

Ford was still very much the man who had staked his independence on a deep-dish art movie like *The Fugitive*, that is to say he wanted the applause of intellectuals but could never allow himself to be seen hungering for it. "When I go to Japan, I am more readily recognized and treated more as a celebrity than I am in my own country. When I go to England, I am often paid the respect of being asked to lecture, as I have at Oxford and Cambridge, and am often asked to discuss in particular a film such as *Wagon Master*, which is totally forgotten here."

From complaining about the lack of respect accorded Westerns, not to mention himself, Ford moved on to grouse about movies in general. "Now, I'm a Roman Catholic. But I'm Irish, too. I think I'm fairly masculine and I don't think I'm a prude, but I do think there are certain things that don't belong on the screen. I wouldn't take anyone to see some of the pictures that are being put out today. I wouldn't even take them to see the billboards outside of the movie houses. These and other ads, lurid come-ons with half-naked women, are dishonest and cater to our worst instincts. They aren't making Hollywood any friends."

And so forth. The interview was not remarkable for its sentiments, which are more or less normal for a seventy-year-old man in a business whose emphasis has always been on youth. But it was remarkable for the open neediness that Ford usually cloaked with his gruff exterior.

CHAPTER TWENTY-SEVEN

Sean O'Casey's six volumes of autobiography had been optioned in the early 1960s by two young producers named Robert Graff and Robert Emmett Ginna. The men had become friendly with O'Casey when they had made a documentary about him in 1955 for NBC. O'Casey received £4,000 for the movie rights, the largest single sum he had ever earned from his writing.

The initial script was insufficient, so they asked O'Casey, battling failing eyesight, to polish the dialogue and work on six scenes because, as he protested, "several scenes were indeed, not of me, but an exact contrary of what I am." O'Casey's own suggestion for the title was *A Stormy Road to Samarkand*, but the producers stuck with *Young Cassidy*. Their hopes for a star revolved around Richard Harris or Peter O'Toole, but O'Casey plumped for Norman Rodway or Donal Donnelly. For director, there was nobody to be had but John Ford.

For the pivotal part of the young Sean O'Casey, Ford preferred Sean Connery, who had just broken through in *Dr. No*. But, for whatever reason, probably MGM, he cast Rod Taylor, a burly young Australian who was under contract to the studio. Luckily, Ford and Taylor hit it off immediately. Also joining the cast was a young actress named Julie Christie.

For Ford, it was another picture done for love rather than money; he was receiving only $50,000 and, according to Taylor, his original intention was to make the film one of his black and white art pictures à la *The Rising of the Moon*. "I said, 'You're gonna shoot this in black and white, in Ireland, where the colors are magnificent? You're out of your mind, you have to shoot it in color.' I had the impertinence to say that."

Although Ford had looked forward to *Young Cassidy* with high hopes— "It's the first script I've ever read that I can just go over and shoot," he told Peter Bogdanovich—the summer of 1964 proved catastrophic for Ford. The estrangement from Pat was widening, and, on July 23, Ken Curtis and Barbara announced they were divorcing after twelve years of marriage.

For nearly fifty years, John Ford had tabled domestic problems in order to make pictures, and he wasn't about to change now. Anne Coates, the film editor of David Lean's *Lawrence of Arabia*, wanted desperately to work on *Young Cassidy* because she wanted to work with Ford—"a magical opportunity. I met with Ford briefly. He was in bed—it's the only time I was interviewed by a director in bed—and he told me that he shot in such a way that there was only one way to cut the footage." Ford told Coates that he wouldn't see dailies, and he might not even see the rough cut when she finished it. "He laughed when he said that, though, so he might not have been entirely serious."

At that point, he turned to someone else in the room and said, "If she's good enough for David Lean, she's good enough for me." Coates was hired, but stayed in London while the company traveled to Ireland.

As the footage began to drift back, Coates was dismayed. "I thought the footage was okay, but not great. I was expecting something quite extraordinary. I thought the footage was a little old-fashioned, stagey and with not much energy. His direction didn't seem nearly as dynamic as I thought it would be. I think he was getting old."

Actually, he was getting drunk, heading out for the pubs of Dublin every night in a vain attempt to keep up with the energy and drinking capacity of Rod Taylor, nearly thirty-five years younger. "He just got more frail and more frail," remembered Taylor, "until I was carrying him home in a service elevator in Dublin. I thought he was dead. He was gray. He'd passed out in a pub and gone gray and I was crying my eyes out."

In order to regain some of his strength after his nightly consumption of Guinness and Jameson's, Ford would hold longer and longer courts in his bedroom, chewing on his handkerchief. "Sometimes he wouldn't work and we'd pretend we were talking about scenes and it was an excuse to have him in bed and us to gather around and chitchat," remembered Taylor. "He would sit in bed and play with his balls and chew on his handkerchief. He'd have his knee up and his hairy old testicles wobbling around."

Oblivious to all this was a producer's secretary who was always included in the meetings. Her nickname was Lady Jane, a very well educated, highly sophisticated member of the gentry, complete with a Mayfair accent.

This, of course, was a red flag to Ford, and he worked hard at breaking down her royal pose. But Lady Jane wouldn't crumble. Finally, one day, apropos of nothing whatever, Ford turned to her and snapped, "Jane, do you fuck?"

"Quite enthusiastically," she fired back. "Doesn't everyone?" The company roared, but Ford continued to chew his handkerchief, resolutely unamused.

As Ford took a bit too much time shooting the fight in the pub—a tired repetition of a dozen other similar scenes in his work—he dropped behind schedule, and made up the time by tearing pages out of the script. Coates found that Ford's claims of cutting in the camera were exaggerated, that, in fact, he gave her a good deal of coverage. "He would cover all the dialogue on one person, and the other, and maybe in two different sizes. There was always a choice."

Donal Donnelly, a veteran of *The Rising of the Moon* and *Gideon's Day*, joined the cast and was appalled at Ford's condition. "He stepped, or rather stumbled, out of his caravan, in which he had a fridge, with icecold Guinness, which I think is awful anyway. But iced Guinness he was drinking, and his lips were brown with it, and he was unshaved, and his eyes were all watery and I thought 'Oh My God!' It was indescribable the change, really indescribable."

David Lean, desperately looking for an actress to play Lara in *Doctor Zhivago*, saw Julie Christie's brief bit in *Billy Liar* and called Ford in Dublin for his reaction. With a generosity he never displayed to actor's faces, Ford raved. "She's great, the best young actress that has ever come into the business. No one in the past has shown so much talent at such an early age." Lean asked Anne Coates for some footage of Christie. Coates put a sequence together, and shipped it to Lean, who promptly cast her as Lara. All Christie would remember of her experience with Ford was "a very ill man lying in bed."

"He adored Christie!" exclaimed Rod Taylor. "He was like Hitchcock with Tippi Hedren—'Give her more scenes, she's wonderful.' And she was in her Cockney phase and couldn't have given less of a shit. She was totally unresponsive to him, and to me as well. She didn't know shit about John Ford; as far as she was concerned, he was just an old man with an eyepatch."

On those days when he could haul himself onto the set, Ford could still direct a good scene and terrorize an English crew at the same time. As with a focus puller named Tommy Spradling. "In three weeks, John Ford said two words to me," said Spradling. "One day I reached over to rack focus and he said, 'Fuck off.' "

Because Taylor was one of the authentic, two-fisted types that he liked,

Ford gave him little actual direction. "He'd say, 'You know what the fuck you do in this situation. You love this girl. I don't have to tell you anything. Let's see a little bit of you. Let's have a look at it.'

"He knew exactly what he was doing," recalled Taylor. "The hangovers must have been, at his age, monumental. But his mind was clear and creative. He knew what he wanted and if something better happened, he'd print it and go away. His favorite phrase to me was, 'There are no problems, only opportunities.' He didn't give a fuck what happened, something good could come out of it. And if it was hard to get something good to come out of it, then goddamn it, work until you do. And that's what he'd do with shots, scenes, actors who were failing or miscast. No problems, only opportunities. I've kept that slogan ever since I met him."

For the scene of the funeral of Cassidy's mother, shot in the middle of the Dublin slums, Taylor crept up to a hawthorn tree, dragged his nappy cap off his head, sank to his knees, and started to sob. The shot went on and on, and Taylor began to grow uncomfortable. Finally, through his tears, he said, "Jesus Christ, Jack, cut."

Ford rose out of his chair, walked over to Taylor and kicked him in the shins. "You son of a bitch Aussie," he said. "You made me cry. That's a wrap!" Ford didn't shoot for the rest of the day, and he and Taylor went off on another pub crawl.

The producers of the film were inexperienced, the schedule was not generous, and Ford's eccentricities were making them very nervous. One day, shortly after lunch, Ford called to cameraman Ted Scaife. "How's the light?" he inquired. "A little yellow?"

"No, gov'nor," said Scaife, anxiously looking around. "It looks fine."

"It looks yellow."

"No, really, it's fine."

Ford sat there for a minute, then snapped, "Fucking yellow!" and stalked off to his car and was driven away. It was the end of shooting for another day.

Just as Anne Coates was getting ready to take an early assembly of footage to Ireland to show Ford, he left the picture after what both Taylor and Coates remembered as "a bit longer than three weeks [of shooting]." It was announced that Ford was suffering from a strep condition and was "badly debilitated."

"He was pretty glad to go home," said Rod Taylor. "He was feeling tired. There was some Irish bullshit about, 'Look, me darlin', I'll give you my notes and you direct the fucker.' He said this, and I called Bob O'Brien, the head of MGM, and said I could do it. And he said, 'You're going to go up against Flora Robson?'"

After the picture had been shut down for a week, Ford was replaced by the great cameraman Jack Cardiff, who had directed a critically lauded film of D. H. Lawrence's *Sons and Lovers* a few years before. Coates, who knew and liked Cardiff, was nevertheless "frantically disappointed."

Cardiff did a very good job in the always treacherous situation of matching another director's style and intent, and went only two weeks over schedule, but the reviews were ungenerous. "They said all the good stuff was Ford's, and all the bad stuff was Cardiff's," said Anne Coates, "and that was unfair. It was a bad experience for Jack. Actually, I thought the best scene in the film was the riot, and that was mostly shot by Jack [Cardiff] and Alan McCabe, a phenomenal second unit director."

When Taylor arrived back in Hollywood, he showed the completed film to Ford, who managed to restrain whatever enthusiasm he might have felt. "You read my fucking notes; he should have brought you and Christie back [together]," Ford told Taylor.

"It was hard, Jack. I wrote a scene where she's in a doorway after hooking too much, shabby and dirty, and they didn't go for it. What was I gonna do?"

But if Cardiff had violated Ford's intentions, he would have taken his name off the picture, and he didn't. *Young Cassidy* went into release as "A John Ford Production" "Directed by Jack Cardiff."

Although it never feels particularly Fordian, *Young Cassidy* is still the best picture Ford was associated with after *The Man Who Shot Liberty Valance*. Ford's opening sequence has a slightly jagged, stagey quality, and the Easter uprising seems to take place on one street, but the film soon finds its rhythm, helped along by Julie Christie's vivid carnal charge.

The scene of Cassidy having to bargain with the morticians over his mother's corpse nicely captures the meanness of aspects of Irish life, as well as some of O'Casey's contempt for his own people. There are lovely moments from Maggie Smith, and fine vignettes from Edith Evans as Lady Gregory and Michael Redgrave as Yeats. But Ford was right about the ending—it feels rushed, misshapen; the film needed a scene with Christie at the end.

Young Cassidy was another embarrassment brought on by Ford's drinking, and it is hard to imagine any studio except the increasingly moribund MGM entrusting a picture to so manifestly unreliable a director. In addition, as everyone from Gance to Chaplin to Cukor has proven, directing is no job for an old man. Chronologically, Ford was now seventy years old—physically he was at least ten years older.

After recuperating for a couple of weeks in Los Angeles, Ford flew to Honolulu to meet Mary, who was on the *Araner*. He looked terrible—

frail, emaciated, with clouded eyes. He was in a vile temper, browbeating Mary; when she fell on board and twisted her ankle, he accused her of a "martyr act."

Yet the combination of the *Araner* and the islands worked their familiar magic. Soon Ford began to feel better; his appetite came back and he gained weight. Duke Wayne was in Hawaii shooting *In Harm's Way* for Otto Preminger, and the two men got together to play cards, with the actor battling a persistent cough. Soon after returning to Los Angeles, Wayne was diagnosed with lung cancer; the surgery was performed on September 16, 1964, and a shocked Ford immediately returned to sit by Wayne's side in the hospital.

Wayne had not told Ford of the impending surgery, because, according to Wayne's wife, he was "worried about Ford's mental condition." Pilar Wayne hadn't seem him for some time, and she was shocked at his ravaged appearance, his dirty clothes. Ford noticed her reaction and told her that he "was rich enough to dress any way he damn well pleased."

Ford spent days at Good Samaritan Hospital with Pilar Wayne, talking about their good times together, and his pride in Duke and their work. "I love that damn Republican," he told her. "He's like a son to me," he said, his voice breaking, for once verbalizing what everybody had always known.

He tried to encourage Pilar, and himself, by talking about the future, and the films he and Duke would make together. It was all going to be just like the old days, when all of Hollywood competed to finance John Ford–John Wayne movies. Except it wasn't the old days anymore. Ward Bond and Harry Carey were dead, and Duke Wayne, lying in his hospital bed, seemed half-dead. John Ford and John Wayne would never work together again.

Wayne's illness greatly affected Ford. "I was terribly worried about his health," said Rod Taylor. "He looked awful." So when Jack and Mary invited Taylor and his wife to Hawaii, Taylor enthusiastically agreed. Like many, Taylor was entranced by Mary. "The marriage was a standoff. She would take no shit at all from him. Jack shut his mouth around her. She was beautiful in her age, with that lovely long Indian-like hair. And she was tough."

Ford and Taylor were watching *The Hurricane* on TV one night, when Taylor made a comment that Ford took as disparaging. "What the fuck does an Australian like you know about anything?"

"Oh, fuck that, Jack. We've done things together. You know what I meant . . ."

"You don't know shit!"

One thing led to another, and Taylor and his wife left the ship. Ford called him day and night, entreating him to come back to the *Araner*. "It was like I was a runaway and he was a distraught parent. 'Come to where your real home is,' he'd say. Finally I came back and moved my things on board and then he started to be bitchy again. He was like that, totally charming and ingratiating, and then he could cut your legs off. He could be vicious."

The *Araner* made its way to Pearl Harbor, and Ford showed Taylor the monument erected over the sunken battleship *Arizona*, still lying in the harbor where it sank after the Japanese attack. "He was big for God, president, country; he did a bit of screaming about that. He loved the military life. 'Snap to, son' and all that. He loved that shit. The military would have been his career if he hadn't gone into movies."

I n spite of the fact that Ford had been unable to physically finish his last two pictures, he and Bernard Smith had one more project in the pipeline. In November, he moved into offices on the MGM lot to prepare the picture that was, at this point, carrying the apt title of *Chinese Finale*, about the trials and tribulations of five missionaries and a woman doctor imprisoned by a Chinese warlord.

At any time of Ford's life, it would have been a strange project; the film it most resembled was the recent flop *Satan Never Sleeps*, Leo McCarey's last, sad gasp. Bernard Smith believed Ford undertook the project because he "resented the fact that some people thought of him as a director of cowboy pictures. So he decided to remind them of his versatility." But this last attempt to hack out a clearing apart from John Wayne would prove disastrous.

Just before going into production, Ford celebrated what was publicly announced as his seventieth—actually his seventy-first—birthday. "At my age I have little room for cake and sentiment," he grumped.

As Ford's career wound down, the reappraisals of archivists and scholars began to reaffirm his stature in a way that, *Liberty Valance* excepted, his recent films never could have. The archivist Alex Gordon, while working for 20th Century-Fox, began a retrieval program at the behest of producer William Self. "The vaults were in the hands of two little old ladies," remembered William K. Everson. "Whenever Alex would ask about something, they'd say, 'Oh, we don't have that; thrown out years ago.' And Alex would bring them a box of chocolates, or some flowers, and they'd suddenly remember that yes, they might have that title after all." Titles like Murnau's *City Girl* and von Stroheim's *Hello Sister*, long believed lost, were discovered in the vaults hiding in plain sight as later B films that used the same titles.

By the time he was through with his project, Gordon had found prints of Ford's *Just Pals, Kentucky Pride, The Shamrock Handicap, Hangman's House, Riley the Cop, Born Reckless, Up the River, The Seas Beneath, The Brat,* and *Pilgrimage*—all previously considered lost—and a complete print of *Three Bad Men,* until then surviving only in a five-reel version with Czech titles.

It was an immense cache of material; prior to Gordon's ventures into the vault, the only two silent Ford films known to survive in America were *The Iron Horse* and *Four Sons,* and *The Iron Horse* was the only one that was easily accessible. It was, wrote Everson, "rather like knowing Griffith only via *America* and *Way Down East.* . . . Ford's *Pilgrimage*—until then just a title to me—provided the most exhilarating session that I've ever had in any theater since I first saw *Intolerance* [in London in the 1940s] in an original 35mm toned print with a full orchestra accompanying."

When the films were preserved and began to circulate, they deepened the appreciation of Ford among cineastes. At the same time, a new generation of critics such as Peter Bogdanovich and Andrew Sarris were publishing appreciations of Ford that responded to his deeply felt poetry in spite of the political and social trends of the late 1960s.

In Europe, Ford's stock remained high. As Bertrand Tavernier explained, "The politics of the American cinema is not just a matter of left and right as defined by a European point of view . . . politics is not only whether a film is pro-war or anti-war, but something that is more deeply felt. If you draw the lines this way, you can see that Ford is not a reactionary director. . . . Ford is a director obsessed by collectivity and by group, and not by the hero, the individual, against the rest of the world."

As *Chinese Finale* geared up, Bernard Smith supervised the work of the husband-and-wife writing team of Janet Green and John McCormick. Ford wanted the writers to come to the *Araner* to work and wrote Smith trying to convince him:

"I should tell you that I have greatly improved in health, I'm eating like a horse, swimming two or three times a day and sleeping well. This brings up a point. I think we should all meet, the McCormicks, you and I, for a week or ten days for the final polish. I wish it could be here in Honolulu as it is doing me so much good. TWA has a deluxe Trans-Polar flight from Paris to L.A. A couple of days rest while you visit MGM, and then it's a lovely five-hour flight to Honolulu. What do you think, Bernie? Can you stand the gaff? Remember our latest hobby, superstitions? The main cabin of the *Araner* is lucky. Scripts on *The Informer, Stagecoach, The Long Voyage Home, The Grapes of Wrath, How Green Was My Valley,* were written or finalized here. Think it over." It didn't happen. Ford stayed in Honolulu and the McCormicks stayed in Europe.

The initial casting ideas for *Chinese Finale* were Jennifer Jones as the doctor and Kate Hepburn as the head of the mission, but Bernard Smith wanted no part of Hepburn. "I know her every move, every gesture, every intonation. And I think she too has limitations of depth." Smith preferred Geraldine Page, but Ford found everything about her offensive. Then Smith suggested Margaret Leighton and Ford agreed.

But the combination of Leighton and Patricia Neal, who replaced Jennifer Jones, was not exactly box office dynamite. MGM was clearly nervous about the picture, and okayed a ridiculous salary of $150,000 for Sue Lyon, under the illusion that the actress who played the title role in Kubrick's *Lolita* was going to be a star. Lyon, although playing a small part, was the highest-paid cast member; Patricia Neal was only making $125,000, while Ford was pulling down $250,000. Production began on February 10, 1965, and was scheduled for forty days and a budget of $2.1 million.

With actors and a crew that were largely unfamiliar, Ford had to re-assert his personality. It was fine for Ford to tell the occasional joke, but when Eddie Albert countered with another joke, Ford eyed him grimly and said, "You're not taking the picture seriously."

Ford soon began doing with *7 Women* (as *Chinese Finale* was ultimately titled) what he had done on all of his recent pictures—sour on them before he began. "Let's do the goddamn thing," he snapped to Wingate Smith. "It's no good, but let's do it and get the hell out."

Ford was, remembered Anna Lee, "incensed" that the writers of the script remained in Paris and were unavailable for consultation. "He'd come in with a script, with the new pages, the pink pages, and he'd look at them and say, 'Well, how are we going to do this?' Then suddenly he'd take the whole thing and tear it into shreds and throw it around the room and say, 'All right, now let's start.' "

The main set of the mission was built entirely on one of MGM's im-mense soundstages. A young editor named Alex Beaton was working as an assistant to Otho Lovering, and would often accompany Lovering to the set. "I remember thinking, God, this is a quiet set," remembered Bea-ton. "No shouting at all, no 'Toss that light up here' like you have on a normal set. He wanted it quiet, and it *was* quiet and he could talk in a normal tone of voice and be heard."

Ford was cordial to the young man, who noticed that Ford's relation-ship with Lovering had a ritualistic quality. Every day, after Lovering and Beaton looked at the dailies, they'd go down to the set. Ford would im-mediately say, "Oh God, someone close that door and stop letting people in!" He'd then tell Beaton, "You better hook up with somebody who can teach you something, because *this* son of a bitch"—a jerk of a thumb toward Lovering—"doesn't know anything." Then he would ask Lovering if there was anything he needed, if there was a shot that Ford had missed. "It doesn't matter, Jack," Lovering would say. "I can make it work." Beaton got the general impression that Ford was in a diminished state. Still, he was operating professionally.

Eddie Albert noticed that Ford gave direction in physical externals, never in terms of character's emotions. And every afternoon at 4:00, there was the tea break, taken while the cameraman was lighting a setup, so it didn't alter the production schedule. Any subject was open for discussion except the picture.

"Because he was such a strong character, he dominated the tea," remembered Eddie Albert. "He was extremely well read. He would bring up questions, and we were all naturally very obsequious. We kept our mouths shut. He would hold forth and it was always very fascinating, because he was a marvelous raconteur." But, for all his intellectual energy, "he was an old man and he acted like an old man," said Eddie Albert. "He was tired, and now I'm tired too, goddammit."

"He didn't seem as interested as he had been on the Westerns," remembered Anna Lee. "He was less energetic. It was obvious that it wasn't going well. A doctor would come in and give him shots."

Two weeks into the picture, after Patricia Neal had worked four or five days, the actress had a massive stroke. Ford and Smith cast about desperately for a replacement and managed to snag Anne Bancroft for $50,000. As far as Bernard Smith was concerned, "Things started to go wrong with 7 *Women* when Patricia Neal had her stroke. We got the wrong girl, Anne Bancroft, the wrong girl. She was a wonderful actress, but she once described herself as a guinea from Brooklyn, and what we wanted was an austere lady. The story was much more of a tragic leap that way. And Ford shot it carelessly; he lost interest." Ford also was unhappy with Bancroft; "I couldn't get her to expand," he complained.

But the list of things wrong with 7 *Women* doesn't really include Anne Bancroft. The film is conceptually ambitious—a group of nervous, twittery missionaries disrupted by the arrival of a new doctor, a puttee-wearing, riding-crop-wielding, naturally sexy woman who smokes and ends up giving herself to a vicious warlord to save the others, whom she neither likes nor respects.

The theme of the inevitable disasters wrought by knee-jerk religionists with no sense of the real world is typical for Ford, as is a group of small-minded hypocrites hiding behind a delusional dignity. With a better script, the Ford of ten or twenty years earlier might have pulled the picture off.

But not with artificial, atmosphere-free stage-bound sets—a time warp by the mid-1960s—and not with casting Mike Mazurki and Woody Strode as Chinese bandits. And not with bad acting—Betty Field harshly declamatory, Eddie Albert a cartoon of a eunuch. Ford directs without evincing any interest or creativity, but as a job, a throwback to the days of *The Brat* or *Submarine Patrol*, something done to stay busy in the certain knowledge that a better project would be coming along soon.

Once the picture finished production, Ford disappeared, not even bothering to consult with Elmer Bernstein about his music score. A month before *7 Women* opened, MGM canceled what was to have been Ford's next picture, *The Miracle of Merriford*, a light rewrite of John Hersey's *A Bell for Adano*. In this version, a group of American soldiers raise money for the repair of an English church damaged in a bombing during World War II. The script had been written by James Warner Bellah and Willis Goldbeck, and Dan Dailey had been pegged to star. It was another ancient story that needed a younger actor to animate it commercially, and Dan Dailey hardly qualified.

7 Women was a financial and critical failure. In New York, MGM threw it away on a double bill with an ineffectual B movie, Burt Kennedy's *The Money Trap*. The film's worldwide gross was just under $1 million, putting it $2.3 million in the red. Later, French and English critics would attempt favorable reappraisals for fairly obvious reasons—the characteristic Ford themes, as well as a new theme of repressed sexuality. But the ideas are hammered over with a lack of visual and dramatic grace.

Peter Bogdanovich believed that the casting difficulties hurt, as did the necessity of shooting in color rather than black and white. "Kate Hepburn would have made it a totally different movie. The interrelationship between actors and directors cannot be underestimated. Unless you've made a movie or two, or been there, it's hard to know what the process is like, because it's quite intricate, because it depends so much on things that are as often unsaid as they are said.

"And color. . . . You had to use it by then, and color doesn't have the reality quotient that black and white had. A lot of the older directors had movies suffer because of that."

Hepburn would probably have fleshed out the underwritten role of the mission's chief, but black and white would only have emphasized the archaic nature of the material. In any case, the reappraisals came too late to help the film or Ford, who was utterly demoralized by the experience and by the reception. "He wanted to retire," said Bernard Smith. "He felt he was finished. And I think he was finished."

CHAPTER TWENTY-EIGHT

A nd now it was time to sit . . . and stew. Without the disciplines and parameters of moviemaking, Ford gradually became unmoored. Old friends tried to help—Russell Birdwell wrote to Joseph E. Levine trying to scare up a picture for Ford—but it was too late. A lot of friends had died, and some had moved away; John Wayne was living in Newport Beach and was no longer on call to jolly his "Coach" the way he had been in the 1940s and 1950s. Moreover, he had gotten in the habit of working with more compliant directors. "Wayne spent the last part of his career getting even for the tough times that Ford had given him," said Burt Kennedy, who directed two pictures for Batjac Productions.

After nearly fifty years of directing movies, Ford had amassed an estate estimated by his grandson as $1.7 million, with yearly interest income in the vicinity of $100,000. Good, but not great, and not really enough to take care of the Bel Air house, the *Araner*, and Ford's list of dependents.

One day in 1965, Ford's chauffeur Bill Ramsey was grocery shopping in Westwood when he struck up a conversation with a young Navy man recuperating from wounds suffered in Vietnam. Ramsey suggested Robert Stephens come up and meet Ford, because they didn't have a cook at the moment. "Can you make Navy beans?" inquired Ramsey. "Hell, yes," said Stephens. It was the right answer.

He went to meet Ford and stayed for the next eight months. Bill Ramsey told him that Ford—"he makes pictures"—worked all night, and would eat his main meal around 2:00 in the afternoon. He liked filets, medium rare, Navy beans, and lots and lots of coffee.

"It was about 1:00 in the afternoon," remembered Stephens of the initial meeting, "and he was in bed. The bedroom had pictures, a lot of memorabilia, a 30-06 rifle in the corner, bookshelves. He wore a night-shirt and a half-cigar in his mouth, and a patch on his left eye. I hadn't seen a nightshirt since my grandfather. I knocked and said, 'Permission to come aboard, sir? I'm bringing you coffee.'

" 'Granted.' "

After Ford asked Stephens about the ships he had been on, he said that Stephens should just recuperate at his house. "I can't stay here," Stephens said, "I belong to the service."

"Who's in charge?" asked Ford.

"Admiral Johnson."

"Is that Bert?"

Stephens's heart sank. This old man knew the admiral. He was definitely in the wrong house.

Ford promptly placed a call to Admiral Johnson, and Stephens looked around the room, focusing on the autographed pictures on the walls—Chester Nimitz and Bull Halsey. "God, get me out of here," he prayed. "I'm in an admiral's house. I'm in a world of trouble."

"Is that you, Bert?" Ford barked into the phone. "I haven't talked to you in a while. This is Jack Ford. I've got one of your men up here. Name's Stephens. Here's his serial number. I'm gonna keep him. You need him, you call me."

And that was that. When he hung up, Ford turned to Stephens and said, "You stay here until you get well and cook for me. You don't have to worry about checking in. You just stick around."

So Bob Stephens moved into a room over the garage—in which Mary's 1929 Rolls-Royce was up on blocks—and drove Ford's 1959 Thunderbird for him. He wasn't paid a salary, just room and board, but it beat the VA hospital.

Stephens got the impression of isolation, a quiet, hushed atmosphere without a lot of activity. After 7 *Women* was released, the silence was deafening. "Ford's health was okay. He didn't get out a lot. Most of the time he'd stay in bed, with cigar ashes all over him. That patch he had, all that was wrong with his eye was a cataract, but he was afraid [of another] operation. So he'd read: military histories, plays, some Westerns—Zane Grey, Louis L'Amour—and scripts. He'd stay up all night reading, and maybe come down in the middle of the night and eat a quart of vanilla ice cream. He had very few people around him."

Stephens noticed that Mary was quiet and reserved, often keeping to her own bedroom, but was devoted to her husband. Once, Ford told Stephens that Mary might want to get out of the house and go for a ride, but when he asked her, she said she didn't want to go anywhere. "He might need me for something," she said.

Every once in a while, John Wayne would come over and disappear into Ford's room, where the men would kill a large thermos of coffee between them. Occasionally, the phone would ring. Once, it was a call from Woody Strode, working on a picture in Las Vegas, complaining that they were trying to "make a nigger" out of him.

"Well, tell 'em you're as good as they are," said Ford. "And don't call me collect, use your own money."

"I didn't call you collect," said Strode.

"Oh. Well, then talk all you want."

"Once I asked him why he slept during the day and stayed up at night," remembered Stephens. " 'Well, there's scripts to read and things I do at night.' Actually, he just watched TV, read, and he had his bath. He never took showers. He had this pine fragrance he would put in his bath and he'd sit there for an hour. And sometimes, at 6:00 in the morning, he'd go down and jump in the pool, then go back to bed.

"Ford was proud of his grandson Dan. He liked him very much. A mention of Dan, and Ford would say, 'Oh, he's doing good,' he's doing this, he's doing that. Tim, he didn't say too much about, but he thought a lot of Dan.

"He would go to the Motion Picture Home to visit an old grip, a guy named Clint Hurtibise. And he would take a fifth of whiskey and have a sip with old Clint. He didn't drink like he used to; when I knew him, he didn't drink hardly at all."

Ford had Stephens drive him to San Francisco so he could pay a visit to the dying Chester Nimitz. In honor of the man he was meeting, Stephens had his full dress uniform on, but Ford went in his usual clothes.

"There's been a few rough months around here, Jack," Nimitz said.

"We all have them," said Ford gently. "Bob here takes good care of me. He's been in Vietnam, and he's going back pretty soon."

"What do you think of Vietnam?" asked Nimitz.

"Chester, if they'd let MacArthur do what he wanted to do [in Korea], we wouldn't have Vietnam now."

"Yeah, Jack, I guess that's right," said Nimitz.

After about a half-hour, Ford and Stephens left and drove back to Los Angeles.

In 1966, Ford was lured to Paris by a young press attaché named Bertrand Tavernier to promote a reissue of *Fort Apache*. Ford lurched off the plane so completely smashed he was unable to walk. That was bad enough, but Tavernier was appalled at Ford's physical condition. The years of drinking had corroded him inside and out.

Ford intended to stay just as Tavernier found him. The best Tavernier and his cohorts could do was to keep him clear-minded for a few hours a day. Deep in his cups, Ford would construct the alcoholic's skewed, surreal scenarios, begin railing about the captain of the *Araner*, and call to fire him.

An inveterate film buff, later to become a distinguished director—his film *Round Midnight* owed more than a little to the experience with Ford—Tavernier asked Ford questions whenever he could fit them in amidst the interviews and drinking sessions. Ford's favorite presidents were Lincoln, Kennedy, and Roosevelt. ("I loved Kennedy . . . a fantastic man, humorous, intelligent, generous"), his favorite directors Leo McCarey, Frank Capra, Raoul Walsh ("a little like me, except that he is handsomer and more of a ladies' man"), Tay Garnett, and Henry King. "I like Sammy Fuller, too; he puts a little too much violence in his films, but unlike many others he doesn't do it for base commercial reasons—he is an upright, honest guy. I don't like John Huston, he is a phony."

Although Ford still described himself as a liberal Democrat, Tavernier was worried about Ford's interview with the film critic for *L'Humanité*, the Communist paper. The interview went swimmingly until the writer asked Ford about the racist aspects some French intellectuals detected in Ford's work.

"The people who say such things are crazy," Ford said angrily. "I am a Northerner. I hate segregation and I gave jobs to hundreds of Negroes at the same salary the whites were paid. I had production companies hire poverty-stricken Indians and pay them the highest Hollywood salaries for extras. Me, a racist?

"My best friends are black: Woody Strode, and a caretaker [Bill Ramsey] who has worked for me for 30 years. I even made *Sergeant Rutledge*, about a character who was not just a nice black guy but someone nobler than anybody else in the picture. They wouldn't let me make that picture because they said that a movie about a 'nigger' wouldn't make any money and couldn't be exhibited in the South. I got angry and told them they could at least have the decency to say 'Negro' or 'colored man' because most of those 'niggers' were worth more than they were. When I landed at Omaha Beach there were scores of black bodies lying in the sand. Then I realized that it was impossible not to consider them full-fledged American citizens." Ford then brought up the treatment of Jews in the Soviet Union, and Tavernier had a hard time calming him down.

The harried press aide arranged a visit with Guy Mercadet, a friend from the war who lived in Bayeux. The two old war buddies drank, talked about life and the war—all the things that Ford pretended were more important than the movies. But Tavernier couldn't help observing that one of the few times during the visit when Ford seemed completely alive and happy was the day he visited the set of Claude Chabrol's *The Champagne Murders*. "He seemed to live again, he looked five years younger."

Tavernier had never dealt with an alcoholic with the brakes off before, and he seems to have spent the week in a state of perpetual fluster. Yet, Tavernier adored Ford, or, rather, "Jack," as Ford asked him to call him after a few minutes. He was drunk, he was morose and full of self-pity, but nothing could obscure his humor and strange, brusque kindness.

Late one night, after singing several of the songs he used in his films, Ford went to bed, mumbling, "I can do whatever I want now because I'll never make another picture. They won't let me do another picture." He repeated the phrase over and over, trying to inoculate himself with harsh reality. Tavernier attempted to bolster Ford by suggesting that surely "retired" was too strong a word.

"Well, half-retired," Ford said. "I'm waiting for someone to give me the go-ahead. I'm studying an offer from Samuel Goldwyn, Jr."

A few months before the trip to Paris, Sam Goldwyn Jr. had come to Ford with the idea of making *April Morning*, Howard Fast's novel of the Revolutionary War. Although the younger Goldwyn had pointed out that Ford was the only man to make a good movie about the Revolution, Goldwyn Sr. had not been encouraging. "You don't know what you're getting into," he told his son. "He may be old, but you're no match for him."

Ford had been enthusiastic, so much so that he took a copy of the book to Paris with him so he could point to it as a forthcoming project, blithely ignoring the contradiction this posed to his mantra of "They won't let me do another picture."

As it turned out, Ford got along with young Goldwyn better than he ever had with his father. "I had such admiration for him," remembered Goldwyn, "and I learned so much. The reason I wanted to do the film is that one of the things you get from really good people is the opportunity to go to school again. And that was the experience. Basically, he needed someone young to front for him."

Goldwyn found that Ford "was intensely practical, with an incredible eye. It came out of silent pictures. He had a tremendous sense of storytelling. And he didn't live in the past, unlike, say, King Vidor, who did, totally. I tried to get him to talk about how certain pictures were made, about why he shot in Monument Valley. 'Because it's easy to shoot there,' was all he would say. He wanted to get on with it and get the picture done.

"We'd sit up in his room, and he'd talk, and I learned more about how to prepare a picture, the practicalities of doing things, than I did with anybody else. He had complete confidence in what he could do with people who couldn't act. 'It's all pictures,' he'd say, 'People don't want to hear people talk; they get bored. It's all pictures.'

"He didn't see a lot of films. He would ask me about people, ask me if I'd seen such-and-such, and then we'd go back to people he knew. I tried to get him into a projection room to look at actors, and he would dodge it and come back to a guy he knew. He liked people he knew he could manipulate."

Goldwyn was planning on a modest budget for his film, and was nervous about the number of extras. When he asked Ford how many he thought he would need for battle scenes, Ford simply instructed him to call Western Costume and find out how many Revolutionary War costumes they had in stock. "I'll do it with stuntmen," he told Goldwyn.

For the cast, everybody involved wanted John Wayne, and Goldwyn had the interesting idea of casting Henry Fonda and his son Peter. Many in Hollywood believed that Wayne, weary of his debt to Ford, finally had enough and turned the picture down, effectively submarining the project.

But that would have been wildly out of character for Wayne, who placed loyalty above all other virtues. "Look at *Rio Lobo*," snorts Andrew McLaglen, "a terrible picture by an over-the-hill director. But Hawks wanted Duke and Duke did it. Duke would never have turned down Jack Ford."

Out of pride, Ford refused to ask Wayne to do the picture. "Ever watch him walk, on his tippy toes?" he asked Goldwyn. "On every picture with me, I make him walk on his feet, like a man. But I'm not gonna ask him to be in the picture. He'll turn me down. Why don't you call him?"

Goldwyn was considering how to make the approach when his phone rang. "This is John Wayne. I understand you're interested in me for a picture?"

"Yes."

"Did Pappy talk to you about me?"

"No," Goldwyn lied.

Invited to Wayne's home in Newport Beach, an astonished Goldwyn endured a two-hour monologue in which Wayne went through a laundry list of all the abuse Ford had subjected him to over the years. "I know Pappy needs me for this picture so he can get the money, but he's a very cruel man. Did he tell you I walk like a fairy?"

"No," Goldwyn lied.

"Well, he does with most people. But the dirty son of a bitch, I wouldn't be here today if it wasn't for him. I'll do the picture. I'll do anything for him. I wouldn't be anything if it wasn't for Pappy Ford."

Henry Fonda was not nearly as indebted, at least in his own mind. "He was the best director I ever worked with," he told Goldwyn. "If anybody can pull it off, Pappy can." But, after a few months of will-he-won't-he, Fonda opted out.

Still, Goldwyn kept trying. When Ford's birthday rolled around, Goldwyn gave him a George Catlin drawing of an old bull stomping the ground. "Why'd you pick this picture?" Ford asked him. "Because it reminds me of you," replied Goldwyn. "I never came to see him that he didn't refer to it," remembered Goldwyn. "He *loved* being challenged; I'd say to him, 'Are you this difficult with everybody?' "

Ultimately, *April Morning* fell apart. Although Goldwyn had a complete, eminently shootable script—by Michael Wilson—MGM, having gone through the consecutive debacles of *Young Cassidy* and *7 Women*, was understandably gun-shy. Ford's drinking was an additional consideration. Even Goldwyn realized that "He was too far gone physically. I don't think he would have made it through the picture."

If Hollywood, at long last, had no more use for John Ford, there was the younger generation of critics and the government. Peter Bogdanovich's book-length interview was published, and Ford bought two copies, paying $11.23. He had one of the copies bound in leather and sent it to a friend named "Uncle Al" (Wedemeyer?) with this inscription: "Don't read this, but I think it will look nice in your library. Affection, Jack." To anybody that asked, he claimed that the book was "filled with inaccuracies—however! I wasn't consulted about it."

Ford's grandson Dan was serving part of his Army hitch at Fort Irwin, near Barstow, and began bringing a couple of buddies to the house on Copa de Oro for weekends. One of Dan's friends was a Southern boy Ford took a shine to. "Did Sherman get your house on the way to Savannah?" he inquired one day. "No sir, but they got the barn," the young soldier replied.

Barbara was in residence, still tussling with the bottle. Her parents tried private hospitals, then private nurses. Nothing provided more than a temporary drying out. One day she fell off the wagon and Mary began haranguing her, expressing herself in a manner unusual for the genteel woman. "Please, Mother, watch your language," said Barbara. "There are soldiers present."

Ford dealt with Barbara's alcoholism more or less the way Mary had dealt with his—forbearance and pretending. "Jack's response to Barbara's drinking was anger, guilt, move on," said Dan Ford.

Eventually, Barbara got an apartment on Wilshire. One day Ford came to Bob Stephens and told him that Mary hadn't heard from Barbara and was concerned. Stephens was to go over and find out what was going on. The door wasn't locked, but the chain was on, and Stephens could see Barbara, clad only in a nightgown, lying on the bed, semiconscious. She'd been that way for the better part of a week. When Stephens called her name, she roused herself and began swearing. He found a phone and explained the situation to Ford, who told him to come back and get him, after which they both returned to the apartment.

Ford watched while Stephens broke the door down. An enraged Barbara got up and began swinging, first at her father, then at Stephens, who grabbed her by the neck and forced her under a cold shower. Stephens bundled Barbara into the car, Ford sitting in the passenger seat, not saying a word. When they arrived at Copa de Oro, Ford got out and walked directly to his room while Stephens carried Barbara into the house over his shoulder.

Stephens explained to Mary that Barbara was a little under the weather as well as a trifle angry, which she proved when she spit out the soup Stephens had made for her. Finally, Stephens had had enough. "Do that one more time and I'll slap you across the face in front of your mama. You're forty-two years old and you better act it. Now straighten your ass up."

Barbara turned to her mother. "Mama, I like Bob." And she did. Barbara and Stephens and Barry Goldwater Jr. and his girlfriend would go to Dodgers games, using Ford's four season tickets by the dugout. "Sober, she was great," remembered Stephens. "Sometimes, she'd watch her father's old movies. He had *Fort Apache* and some others, and she'd watch them late at night while he was up in his room."

Barbara settled down. Until the next time. "She wanted something from her father he didn't know how to give," remembered Barry Goldwater Jr. "Approval. He didn't understand why she needed it. His generation didn't. 'Stand on your own two feet,' and all that. Barbara could only really function when she was working, and, at this point, she wasn't working very much at all."

"Ford was scared of her when she was drunk," recalled Stephens. "He'd say, 'Barbara's coming over. She's acting a little crazy. Don't let her in my room.' She was a real mean drunk; she'd use her fists, even with me, until I'd backhand her and then she'd stop it. One night I stayed up all night right by his door, at the steps, because he'd told me he was worried about her coming over. He came down about 2:00 or 3:00 in the morning to check.

" 'Is that you, Bob?'

" 'Yes sir, right here.'

" 'Got coffee?'

" 'Yes sir, right here.' " And then John Ford would take a thermos of coffee up to his room, to keep him company during his long, lonely nights.

• • •

Estranged from one child, helpless to ameliorate the other's alcoholism, and without the solace of his work, Ford was in a truly terrible situation. He hated being on the sidelines, hated not making movies. He placed a call to A. C. Lyles, an old Paramount hand—Lyles arrived on the lot in 1928—who was producing a series of B Westerns for the studio. Lyles's pictures were shot in ten days, featured cut-rate talent, and carried titles like *Red Tomahawk* and *Town Tamer.*

Although the two men had never met, Ford congratulated him on a recent award Lyles had been given. Lyles naturally called him Mr. Ford. "What the hell!" responded Ford. "Mr. Ford? I'm Jack!" One of Lyles's Westerns had been edited by Otho Lovering, and it seemed that Ford had asked Lovering about the producer.

Lyles was amazed a few days later when Ford called back. "I'm mad as hell," he said. "Why haven't you asked me to direct one of your Westerns?" Since Lyles's Westerns were usually directed by R. G. Springsteen, not John Ford, he had a sudden sensation of thinning air.

"Jack, your salary would exceed my budget," said Lyles, not knowing what else to say.

"You pay scale?" asked Ford. "You got me."

They tentatively agreed on a script of Lyles's involving a young boy, a plot element that particularly pleased Ford. He volunteered to use one of Lyles's cameramen ("they know your program"), and they outlined a cast consisting of equal parts Ford buddies and Lyles buddies.

Ford came to Lyles's office at Paramount late one night and silently noted the wall of photos of Lyles with various show business and political notables. A few days later, a messenger arrived with a photograph of Ford inscribed "To A.C., with great admiration and affection. Jack Ford."

Lyles explained that he had to have eight and a half minutes of finished film per day. The two men went over the script, with Ford pointing out ways he could fulfill the daily quota. "Well, we can do this in a master shot . . ." Lyles still had a hard time believing he was going to produce a John Ford film. "Do you want to do this under your own name?" he asked. "Hell, yes," replied Ford. "Do you want to tell me my name doesn't mean anything?"

"He was completely accommodating his talents to my program and my schedule," recalled Lyles. The producer felt he could get an extension of the schedule and the budget from Paramount, but Ford refused. " 'That defeats the purpose,' he said. 'This is the kind of picture you make, not the kind of picture I've been making. It's the kind of picture I *used* to make.' "

The purpose, of course, was to prove that Jack Ford could still direct, even a cheap Western. "I was convinced that, 1. He wanted to do it, and, 2. He could have done it with good health," said Lyles. "I mean, *Stagecoach* wasn't all that big a production, really."

But Ford suddenly backed out, claiming his health was bad. Perhaps he thought better of it; perhaps he had a sudden realization of what the town would say about John Ford working for scale. Perhaps he really didn't feel up to directing even a ten-day, back-lot Western. But the fact that he made the call and the suggestion is a poignant revelation of his veiled but frantic desperation to work.

In the latter part of 1968, Ford supervised the production of a film entitled *Vietnam! Vietnam!* for the United States Information Agency. His participation was the idea of Bruce Herschensohn, at the time the head of the USIA. "The original idea," recalled Herschensohn, "was that there were few if any films on our side of the conflict. The only one was *The Green Berets*; we wanted to make a documentary feature, and all the other documentaries were critical."

Herschensohn, accompanied by the actor Don Defore and another friend, presented the project to Ford at his office on Beverly Drive. Ford was wearing a khaki jacket over a bright red shirt. When the men walked in, Ford stood up, not long enough to shake hands or even say hello, just long enough for his visitors to notice that his fly was open. The office was rather spartan; a painting of Monument Valley, another of Ford in his admiral's uniform. A photo inscribed to Ford by John Bulkeley, pictures of Jimmy Cagney and Will Rogers. No Oscars.

Don Defore began explaining the purpose of the USIA, but Ford grew bored after a few sentences and picked up a letter on his desk. Defore stopped talking. Ford threw down the letter in disgust.

"I can't understand this letter. It's written in Irish. I can hardly read English."

"I suppose it's part of the legacy you left behind in Ireland when you made *The Quiet Man* there," said Herschensohn's friend.

It was the opening Ford needed. "Part of the legacy I left behind in Ireland? What the hell do you mean by that?"

The friend began hemming and hawing. Ford moved in for the kill.

"Legacy! Legacy! I just don't understand! Legacy! Huuuuuuuh?"

"I mean you left a lot of friends there and they still remember you."

"Legacy! I don't understand. Legacy! Legacy!"

At this point, the subject of the proposed film was once again raised, only to be interrupted by Ford's exclamation of "Legacy! I just don't understand that. Legacy!"

The friend tried to save the situation and only buried himself deeper. "On *The Quiet Man*, sir. . . . The people in Ireland must still remember it."

"Did I make *The Quiet Man*?"

"Yes, sir."

"Did I? Did I make it in Ireland?"

"Oh yes, sir. It was beautiful. The hills. All the hills. I'll never forget that."

"When I'm done with a picture, I forget it." Ford picked up a cigar from an ashtray and began chewing it. "Go on."

It was another performance of calculated obstinance. Assuming you weren't the victim, it could be rather funny. "It was," remembered Bruce Herschensohn, "as though God had touched John Ford at the beginning of his life and said, 'How would you like to be a very unique man—like no one else. However, you may scare some people.' ... He wouldn't stop being John Ford, even out of courtesy to someone else. It was just too much fun, and if they couldn't take it, too bad. There would be harder lessons in life for them and this wasn't going to hurt them."

Ford asked Herschensohn if he was Jewish. At the affirmative reply, Ford offered the stunning news that he had graduated from Brandeis University. He then called in his secretary to vouch for his attendance.

Growing bored, Ford finally asked, "Well, what do you want?"

"We feel that all the films made so far about the Vietnam conflict have taken a position against the United States," said Herschensohn.

"Check!" said Ford, thumping his fist on the desk.

"We want to make a film that takes the United States position."

"Check!" The fist slammed again.

"We want you to produce it for us."

"Check!" Thump.

"There's very little money involved, sir."

"Check!" Thump.

"Will you do it for us, Mr. Ford?"

"Check! Check!" Thump. Thump.

Everybody stood up, and his visitors tried hard not to look at Ford's open zipper. Herschensohn assigned Tom Duggan to write the script, and Sherman Beck to direct the film under Ford's supervision.

In the latter part of 1968, Ford spent a couple of weeks in Vietnam. "It was a strange mix," said Herschensohn. "We wanted very much to show Vietcong atrocities as they were happening, but it was almost impossible to do that. Making a documentary is not a tightly scripted thing. Sherman was out there a lot of the time, and John was out there in a supervisory position and to get what was there at the time." While Ford was in Vietnam, Herschensohn called the embassy every night to make sure Ford had come through the day safely, then called Mary in Bel Air to assure her Jack was all right.

Ford would claim, in a letter to a friend, that he got shot down ("Typical Feeney luck . . .") and had the opportunity of going into the boondocks and decorating his grandson Dan. Actually, he met Dan in Saigon and didn't decorate him; others did. And he wasn't shot down.

"It was November of 1968," remembered Dan Ford. "I'd been there since June. I was a forward observer in the 25th Division, a first lieutenant. I had just come out of the jungle, on a five-day sweep, and was dressed in muddy clothes, when I got word that Admiral Ford wanted to see me. I got a helicopter back to Cu Chi, where all the tunnels were, about thirty miles north and west of Saigon."

Dan sat surrounded by body bags. By that time, he had been around so many dead people that it almost didn't bother him. He got a civilian cab and went to the Caravelle Hotel, where his grandfather awaited, sipping a beer amidst the familiar smell of cigar smoke. "My first thought was, 'Oh, shit, I hope he isn't going on a drunk.' " He wasn't. He was, however, unsuccessfully battling jet lag.

"In his restrained, emotional way, he was glad to see me. He wasn't that verbal a man to ask a series of questions. He had an emotive way of communicating. He spoke without speaking. Mainly, he said, 'Are you okay? Are you all right? Do you need anything?' I had only received a couple of Bronze Stars at that time, so there was no decorating done."

The next day, Ford and his grandson spent a half-day together, then he was taken on a series of junkets, showing how the Americans were winning the war. "They showed him some of the 'pacified' villages," said Dan Ford. "All that bullshit. He didn't buy it."

As always, Ford had to create the aura of drama. When Herschensohn came to see him after his return, he found Ford lying naked in bed, with Mary standing by his side. "I got malaria out in Vietnam," Ford moaned. "Oh, Jack, why didn't you tell me?" said Herschensohn, whose concern was submarined by the sight of Mary shaking her head in dismay at her husband's prevarications.

"I've been in five wars now," Ford continued. Herschensohn counted them off: "World War I [Ford was never in World War I], World War II, Korea, Vietnam. What was the fifth?"

"I don't remember."

Once the footage had been shot, Herschensohn began editing in Washington, D.C., then took his assemblies to Hollywood, where he'd run them for Ford. "We'd look at them on interlock, in a screening room, or a Moviola. We'd have discussions, then I'd head back to Washington for a week or two."

One day Herschensohn was reading the narration as the film unreeled when on came a shot of Eugene McCarthy. "Goddamn Irishman, right

Bruce?" yelled Ford. "Right, Jack," said Herschensohn, who was thinking of the grease pencil marks going by on the print, if the sound was at the right level, if the narration was in sync with the picture. And then, with a sinking heart, he realized what he had said. "My God," he thought. "He got me. Now what happens?"

After the picture was over, Ford gave Herschensohn another chance. "That goddamn McCarthy," he said. "An Irishman."

"Oh, Jack," replied Herschensohn. "It's not about him being Irish, it's because he believes the other way."

"Oh."

"I never expected the humor," said Herschensohn of the entire experience. "I never expected the constant testing. He was just so damn funny!

"He showed me his room full of awards and Oscars, the Legion of Honor. 'I have two Legion of Honors,' he told me. 'If I got another one, I wouldn't know what to do with it. France could give me the Eiffel Tower and Brigitte Bardot. At least I could do something with the Eiffel Tower. I could paint it.' I could sense very much that he wanted the equivalent honor from his own country."

Vietnam! Vietnam! was tripped up by history, as it should have been. Making a pro–Vietnam War film in 1969 was waving a red flag at an enraged populace, and the bureaucracy within the USIA was no more well disposed toward the film than the public. *Vietnam! Vietnam!* was released in late 1971, at a cost of $252,751, to virtually no interest. The film was officially "retired" in 1975.

The vision of Vietnam presented in the film is reminiscent of a Western—overall, the point of view is not dissimilar to John Wayne's *The Green Berets*, which is more or less a World War II movie that had the misfortune to be about Vietnam.

Dan Ford touched on what went wrong with the project when he noted that "He would make a big thing about me being in the Army, but my military wasn't his military, my war wasn't his war. He wasn't in the real Navy, he was in John Ford's Navy. His war was Washington and Wild Bill Donovan and flying the Hump to China. My war was tedium and boredom and mud. He loved the service; I hated it. I don't think he understood the real service."

Although *Vietnam! Vietnam!* is irretrievably hawkish, and his own politics were turning conservative, Ford was privately ambivalent: "What's the war all about?" he wondered in a letter. "Damned if I know. I haven't the slightest idea what we're doing there."

At the same time he was dabbling in Vietnam, he was dabbling in another make-work project, a documentary on Lieutenant General Lewis (Chesty) Puller, the legendary Marine. Production began in August 1968, and finished on April 8, 1970. The final scene was a segment featuring John Wayne, shot on the set of *Rio Lobo*, the day after Wayne had finally won an Academy Award for *True Grit*. Waiting for Wayne to finish with Hawks so he could do his scene for him, Ford turned to the crew after every shot. "Look at that famous Academy Award winner now. He does it in one take. When he worked for me, it took 50."

Chesty: A Tribute to a Legend was originally an hour long, but it was trimmed to a half-hour in an effort to find a buyer. In April 1970, the completed film was shown at the Los Angeles Film Exposition to a mixture of boos and applause, and was appraised by *Variety* as "a sentimental right-wing fantasy about the military."

F ord had entered that twilight world of the director who is too old to work, a world of tributes, interviews, and making the rounds of film festivals to collect awards. But Ford was not a man who enjoyed that sort of thing. "He wasn't bitter," remembered Burt Kennedy. "He was angry."

Ford contributed a blurb for Abraham Polonsky's *Tell Them Willie Boy Is Here* ("A very fine picture in the best tradition of the American western. Willie Boy shows the American Indian as part of the United States history in a way never seen before"). His dark, antagonistic sense of humor hadn't deserted him; once a year, he would call Samuel Fuller on his birthday, bark "Fuck the Big Red One," then hang up. Once a Navy man, always a Navy man.

Most of Ford's friends were as old as he was, but there was the occasional young acolyte who managed to penetrate the inner circle—Peter Bogdanovich, or Mark Haggard. Haggard was a Ford-struck student who had idolized the director since *Liberty Valance*. After intermittent efforts over the years, Ford finally agreed to see Haggard at his office for a half-hour or so.

Ford's interest in Haggard perked up when he found out that he was a reader at Warner Bros. "You have access to those executives?" he asked. "I want to do *The White Company*. I can get Guinness and Olivier." Haggard sent a note in to the front office, but nothing happened. Then Haggard brought Ford a script he liked, a submarine picture. Ford was immediately enthusiastic. "We can shoot it in CinemaScope, or whatever it's called. Who do you see in this? Who are the stars today?"

Ford was clearly out of touch with modern Hollywood, not to mention out of sympathy. "You never know who the hell reads the scripts any more," he would grouse. "You can't get an OK here in Hollywood for a script—it's got to go back to New York and through a president and a board of directors and bankers and everybody else. What I used to do was try and make a big picture, a smash, and then I could palm off a little one on them. You can't do it any more."

Nothing happened with the submarine picture, but Haggard kept trying. He found a script by Bernard Girard, a Western about a cowboy fleeing from a posse who comes across a group of nurses. The echoes of *3 Godfathers* were obvious, and Ford loved it.

"Who do you see?" he asked Haggard.

"Duke Wayne and Ingrid Bergman," the younger man replied.

"Yeah, yeah."

Haggard brought Girard over for a couple of script conferences at Ford's house in the late afternoon, which was now Ford's best time. Ford never answered the front door, but was to be found in his bedroom upstairs. Haggard noticed that the house was almost exactly like Frank Skeffington's house in *The Last Hurrah*—winding stairs, with a balcony. Ford's bedroom was at the head of the stairs on the left, with a window overlooking a flagpole. He was always in bed, in a nightshirt, smoking cigars and watching television with an empty food tray in front of him, while the two dachshunds chased each other around the room. "He was obviously tired," remembered Haggard. "He would stay up till 5:00 in the morning reading."

Every once in a while, Ford would say, "Excuse me," and go into the bathroom and urinate with his back to Haggard and Girard. Occasionally he would begin to reminisce out of context. "I thought his mind was really sharp," remembered Haggard, "but he had his own methods of thinking, just like he had his own methods of working." Girard wasn't so sure.

"I'd like to do this," Ford told them. "See what you fellows can come up with." It was obvious to both men that Ford either wasn't going to exert himself to set the picture up, or was not in a position to set the picture up.

It was hard just to get him out of the house. One night, USC invited Ford to speak, and Haggard decorated the hall with his collection of Ford movie posters. To try to get Ford in a receptive mood, Haggard recruited a priest to accompany him to Ford's house. When they arrived at the hall, the crowd sang "Happy Birthday" but Ford didn't say a word of acknowledgment, just said, "Anybody got any questions?"

Afterward, Haggard helped Ford to the front door and stood there as the old man laboriously climbed the stairs to his bedroom. "Jack, are you back?" called Mary from her bedroom.

"Yeah."

"How was it?"

"The usual."

• • •

Everywhere Ford looked there was diminishment and loss. The *Araner* was expensive to keep up—Ford's 1966 expenses for the ship were $27,480—and his beloved Field Photo Farm was increasingly disregarded by the survivors of the unit. In 1967, the Farm's cash on hand was a minimal $2,609, and the assets were almost entirely limited to the property itself.

In January 1969, the clubhouse and everything in it was destroyed by fire. Insurance paid out only $13,955, nowhere near enough to rebuild. On March 17, the land and remaining buildings were donated to the Motion Picture and Television Relief Fund. The chapel was moved to the Motion Picture Home, and the land itself was immediately sold by the fund for $276,825. Ford's most remarkable *beau geste* was no more.

After efforts to sell the *Araner* for a higher valuation were unsuccessful, he ended up dumping it for $25,000 and some shares in a Hawaiian resort. Large parts of Ford's life were being sheared away.

Financially, Ford was nowhere near as well off as contemporaries such as Hitchcock, whose commercial instincts had been much surer, and whose profit participations had paid off to a much greater extent. "He didn't care about the money, unfortunately," said Bea Benjamin. "He only cared about the picture."

In 1964, Ford had made $53,457 in dividends from blue-chip stocks such as AT&T, General Electric, General Motors, R. J. Reynolds, and California Edison, but even returns such as those weren't quite enough to cover his considerable overhead now that he wasn't a working director. According to his tax returns, Ford was claiming his brother Pat, his nephew Francis Jr., and his sister Mary as dependents.

Ford continued to consider projects he wouldn't have looked at a few years before. Woody Strode, who had a fair degree of success starring in Italian Westerns, sent him a script that wasn't good. "The only reason I'd come out of retirement is to direct you," Ford wrote him. "Incidentally, how much money do the Italians pay?"

On April 11, 1969, Ford was lured to a gathering of the Hollywood Foreign Press Association at the Academy. There was a good turnout of his peers—Mamoulian, von Sternberg, Renoir, King Vidor. Vidor was deep in conversation with Ford when he noticed the young English film historian Kevin Brownlow staring at them hopefully. Brownlow was fresh from publishing his landmark history of the silent film, *The Parade's Gone By*, but had never met Ford. Ford's dour look and hungover expression might have intimidated a lesser man, but Brownlow hovered nearby, and Vidor helpfully made the introductions.

Hoping that the subject of Harry Carey would be foolproof, Brownlow mentioned that he had just seen *Straight Shooting*, which had been recently rediscovered in Eastern Europe.

"I don't remember it," said Ford.

Every question or comment Brownlow put to him earned the same response, so Brownlow committed the act of a desperate man: he introduced Ford to his beautiful wife, Virginia, who had bright red hair and the typical complexion of an Irish colleen. The old man immediately perked up.

"Do you come from Ireland?" inquired Ford.

"Ardmore, County Waterford."

"Ardmore! I know it well. I prefer it to Youghal. Do you know that little bridge over the Blackwater as you're coming to Youghal. . . ?"

Ford and Virginia Brownlow were soon deep into a discussion of the topography of Ireland. Kevin Brownlow was banished.

After a number of years in Europe, Robert Parrish arrived back in Hollywood, and was surprised by a phone call from Ford. "He invited me to lunch," remembered Parrish, "and invited all the people I knew—Fonda, Bob Wise, Mark Robson, John Sturges, all the people I'd been in the Navy with. It was like we'd been seeing each other every day." Ford had decided that Parrish's blundering speech of more than twenty years before should be forgiven, if not forgotten.

Once again, he was lured into speaking to film students at UCLA, whose campus was right across the street from his house. The Theater Arts students cobbled together a set for his appearance that resembled a Western barroom. Students yelled out their questions while the professor sitting beside Ford repeated them into his ear. Sometimes he told them utter blarney ("I went to school in Ireland for a while"), sometimes he talked sense. One student asked why, in *Liberty Valance*, he had cast O. Z. Whitehead as Denver Pyle's son when Whitehead and Pyle were obviously about the same age.

Ford magisterially ignored the question until several minutes later, when he turned to the offending student and shouted, "O. Z. Whitehead is *older* than Denver Pyle."

As always, he was helpless to articulate theory about what he had spent his life doing instinctually. "You're probably used to these pedagogic, pedantic treatises on how to make a motion picture," he told a seminar. "*Anybody* can direct a picture once they know the fundamentals. Directing is not a mystery, it's not an art. The main thing about motion pictures is: photograph the people's eyes. Photograph their eyes. . . .

"Forget about the camera. Get a good cameraman—he knows more about a camera than you'll *ever* know—and say, 'I want to get so-and-so and so-and-so in, and I want it very close, because I'm not going to shoot any close-ups in here. . . . Get a good cameraman and work with your people. Look at their faces. See their eyes. You can express more with your eyes than you can with anything else. And that's about all."

He never used the terms "movie" or "film." Like Fitzgerald's Monroe Stahr, he was just making pictures, images that told a story, communicated a mood. "They ask me if I believe in the future of motion pictures and I say yes because I do. But not so eloquently as I believe in their past."

In 1970, Anna Lee married Robert Nathan, the author of *Portrait of Jennie*. "You'll need someone to give you away," Ford said. "I'll be like your father." At the ceremony, when it came time to answer the question, "Who gives this woman?" Ford bellowed, "I do, I do," in a theatrical boom. Then, more quietly, "Don't I have any more lines?"

The actor Seymour Cassel was moonlighting as a camera operator, and was hired to shoot an interview with Ford for French television. "It was 3:00 in the afternoon, he was in bed, he had his glasses up on his head, his eyepatch on, a double Corona cut in half which he wasn't supposed to be smoking, and what he said was a glass of tea. My ass—it was a highball.

"I asked him what he thought of the remake of *Stagecoach*. 'They're assholes,' he said. 'It was a great movie when I made it, Duke was great in it, why remake it? With who?' He was wonderful!"

Other interviewers weren't so lucky. Philip Jenkinson, working for the BBC, had to make more than a half-dozen phone calls to set up a meeting, and found Ford in bed, wearing the remnants of a red sweater, surrounded by empty bottles. He asked Ford where they should put the equipment.

"Equipment? What equipment?" asked Ford.

Jenkinson explained that he had a truck full of camera equipment in the driveway, which might have been why Mary was yelling, "Get them off my property!" Ford claimed that he never gave TV interviews, never. Jenkinson could use a tape recorder and that was all. Jenkinson said that he had seen an interview that Ford had done on English television, whereupon Ford claimed he had done that in Paris and had never given them permission to use it anyplace else.

Finally, Ford said he'd do the interview in his den, but then Mary objected, because "that's where I watch television." The butler removed the TV, and the interview finally began, although Jenkinson soon wished it hadn't.

Ford was antagonistic and uncooperative. The BBC managed to hack out about twenty minutes for broadcast, but the uncut interview survives and it's brutal. A long, involved question about Ford's feelings about the West brought forth, "You'll have to rephrase that question." As Jenkinson grows increasingly desperate, the gaps between his questions and Ford's answers grow longer, more dangerous. When Jenkinson asks if Ford thought the destruction of the Indians was a blot on American history, the trap is definitely sprung.

"What do you think of the Black and Tans in Ireland?" retorted Ford. "Would you consider that a blot on England?"

"But I'm talking about the Indians . . ."

"I'm not talking about Indians. I'm talking about the Black and Tans. . . . So long as you won't answer my question about the Black and Tans, I won't answer your question about the Indians."

Ford asks if Jenkinson is from Manchester, then says his question was "a typical Manchester exaggeration." He spitefully mimics Jenkinson's accent, claims not to remember his early films, occasionally answers a question for a sentence or two, then breaks off and looks around. "Is there anybody here who *doesn't* work for the BBC?" Later, he asks the soundman, "Are you growing a mustache?"

Mark Haggard had been attending the annual Memorial Day observances at the chapel for years, and had met members of Ford's circle such as John Bulkeley, Ray Kellogg, and Mark Armistead. It seemed to Haggard that a short film about the ceremony might make a fitting envoi, and he asked Ford's unofficial aide-de-camp Dick Amador about it. "Don't ask him," said Amador, "he'll say no. Just do it."

So Haggard rounded up a film crew from USC and showed up early on Memorial Day 1970. Anna Lee was there, and so were Danny Borzage, Meta Sterne, Ollie and Dobe Carey, Ray Kellogg, Walter Pidgeon, Archie Stout, and Frank Baker. Ford was clearly surprised by the presence of a camera crew. Whenever it seemed that a camera was aimed at him, he looked away.

Although Haggard's presumption could not have endeared him to Ford, he was too old and tired to remonstrate. In any case, the twelve minutes of *John Ford: Memorial Day 1970* are a valuable record of the fierce old tyrant in his public mode—in uniform, with glasses and eyepatch. He thanks the modest crowd for coming to this day of "meditation and prayer . . . the ceremony must be brief because we have a lot of graves to decorate. Thank you from the bottom of my heart for coming. Usually we have the City of Hope choir, but they're a little late today." The faces are all old, terribly old. After the ceremony, there was a coffee hour and then it was time for Ford to drop carefully into the passenger seat of his car, with Mary in the back seat, a shawl of royal blue covering her head and cascading down her back.

• • •

I n 1970, the painter R. J. Kitaj, who shared a friend with Ford, came by to make a sketch. Ford was in bed, wearing what Kitaj thought was a baseball cap but was actually an admiral's bridge cap.

Kitaj thought Ford looked like a dying man. Ford's rebellious, anti-English chat was memorable—although Kitaj couldn't help but notice the copy of *Burke's Peerage* on the bookshelf—as was his admonition to Kitaj's son Lem to avoid film school because it was a waste of time. When Lem took a few snapshots with a little Minox camera, Ford said, "Make sure you let enough light in that camera, boy."

Kitaj's painting, *John Ford on his Deathbed*, wasn't completed until 1983, but it was soon purchased by the Metropolitan Museum in New York. The artist painted a picture above Ford's head that wasn't actually there, an image from *The Sun Shines Bright*, one of Kitaj's favorite Ford films. At the foot of Ford's bed sit Charley Grapewin and Elizabeth Patterson from *Tobacco Road*, while a younger Ford sits in a director's chair with a megaphone instructing them. Looming ghostlike over all is Victor Mc-Laglen in his cavalry dress uniform.

I n June 1970, Ford headed east for the last time, to Washington and New York, to see Kate Hepburn in the Alan Jay Lerner musical *Coco*. Hepburn knew what it must have cost Ford in terms of energy, and wrote him a thank-you note. Addressing him, as always, as "Sean," she told Ford how much his presence had meant to her and to the entire company. Always sensitive to his inner vulnerability, she told him of the immense respect everyone in show business had for him. During their visit, he told her of his impending fiftieth wedding anniversary, and she promised to alert the state of Maine.

Ford quickly replied on July 1, "Dear Kate—You are right in your assumption—I came east: 1st—To see you. 2nd—To see 'Coco.' I repeat—ad nauseum—that it was worth it + you were wonderful. Love, Sean." Five days later, Jack and Mary celebrated their golden wedding anniversary with a nuptial mass at the little chapel at the Motion Picture Home. It was the first time they had been married in the Catholic church.

Ford began receiving letters from Hepburn again, one in September 1970, while she was shooting *The Trojan Women*, another the following month. They, and several more that followed, are friendly, chatty. There is no attempt to rekindle anything. Hepburn is trying to keep a declining geriatric tied to life through the activities of a loved one.

In October 1970, Ford broke his left hip when he tripped over some laundry on the back patio. He was hospitalized for over a month, finally being released on November 17. By this time, Mary was also beginning to decline, from angina and Parkinson's.

There was nothing to turn his critical intelligence to until the new year, when Frank Capra sent him the manuscript of his autobiography, *The Name Above the Title*. Dictating to Barbara, whose spelling was shaky, Jack wrote Capra a long letter, addressing him as "Panchito," telling him he had finished the book with "tears of gladness," that there was "a punch in every line," that he had written the "story of a little dago from Sicily who scrapped, fought, bit, chewed, without comprimise [sic], from the ghetto to become the world's greatest director."

In fact, Ford told his old friend, the book wanted for only one thing—a new last paragraph. With apologies, but in the spirit of "us hardworking, hard nosed directors [who] are all out to help one another," Ford offered a new last, lengthy paragraph:

"I drove in from Fallbrook for a date with Joe Youngerman—our genial, extremly [sic] efficient secretary general of our Guild—what impelled me, I don't know, but I found myself driving toward old Los Angeles. I found myself in Skid Row. I passed by the salon [sic] where I use [sic] to sell newspapers. It was all changed, this maelstrom of misery. I parked my car and walked slowly toward the street, toward the house where we first lived as penniless peasants from Sicily. I passed in front of the house where my Mother, God rest her lovely, courageous soul, had fought to bring us up in this strange unfriendly land. The house was more decreptid [sic] and dilapidated than I remembered. I breathed a prayer half aloud thanking God for letting me bring them out of this pit and ending their days in comfort. I hoped Mamasito and Papasito could hear it. I lit a cigarette and walked slowly back to my car. . . . I drove slowly towards Hollywood and the Guild. At the first stop light I said to myself 'This could only happen in America.' The hooting of horns aroused me from my reverie. I drove toward the next stop light and mumured [sic] another prayer. 'God bless America.' I stopped and thought—and—then said aloud for all the world to hear, 'God Bless Hollywood.' "

Ford had written a good last scene for a Ford movie; Spencer Tracy could have played the hell out of it. Capra took most of Ford's advice, re-writing his suggested ending into a slightly darker version that eschewed "God Bless America" and "God Bless Hollywood."

Except for the triumphalism and the sound of pealing bells that Ford obviously meant for it to have, his ending plays a lot like George Mi-nafer's last walk through his ravaged and darkened city in Welles's *The Magnificent Ambersons*. With a change of scene from L.A.'s Skid Row to the row houses of Portland, it could also serve as Ford's own valedictory image of his life.

• • •

At the end of August 1971, Ford traveled to Venice to receive the Golden Lion and terrorize more English journalists. Shortly afterward, he began to be troubled by abdominal pain. The specialist enlisted the help of Ford's personal physician, Maynard Brandsma, who had retired. Ford, Barbara, and Dan went to the doctor's office to hear the diagnosis. Ford was nervous and began hiccuping.

It was cancer, Brandsma said. There were two treatment options—aggressive surgery or chemotherapy. Without missing a beat, Ford said, "Cut it out. Let's go for it." And then he stopped hiccuping, which led Barbara to tell Brandsma, "You sure know how to cure hiccups!" The operation revealed a large, inoperable malignancy. His condition was terminal, but the family kept up a front.

"He is improving day by day," Mary wrote to Michael Killanin on October 30, "but an operation as serious as his takes time and much rest." Ollie Carey came for a visit, but she was so shocked by his appearance that when she got back to her car all she could do was cry.

Another documentary, *The American West of John Ford*, was co-produced by his grandson Dan and premiered on CBS on December 5, 1971. Ford put up the usual protests about appearing in the program. Jimmy Stewart's narration claimed that, "He made his first [picture] when he was twenty-two years old. That was in 1917. It was a two-reeler called *The Tornado*. He wrote it, directed it, and also worked in it as an actor."

Ford, sitting behind the camera, bellowed, "What's that? I never acted in that picture or any other. Where the hell did you get that misinformation, Jimmy?"

"It's—uh—that's what it says here, Pappy," said Stewart, pointing to the script.

"Then let it go. It's a lie, but let it go." Print the legend.

Peter Bogdanovich wanted to cast Ben Johnson in his breakthrough film *The Last Picture Show*, use him for his aura of relaxed authority, as well as the associations with Ford, but Johnson was put off by the language and nudity of the script and refused. Bogdanovich appealed to Ford for his help, in spite of the fact that Ford couldn't have been any more in sympathy with the script than Johnson. Nevertheless, loyalty and friendship prevailed.

"John Ford called me in Houston," remembered Ben Johnson, "and asked if I'd do him a favor. And I said, 'Yes, sir.' I didn't even ask what it was. So he said he wanted me to do Bogdanovich's picture. 'Do you want to be Duke's sidekick all your life?' he said. So I called my agent and told him to call the studio and tell them that Ben Johnson wanted twice his salary to do the movie. I knew nobody would pay that much money."

Ten minutes later, the reluctant Ben Johnson had the part for which he would win an Academy Award and a lot more money than he was used to making.

Characteristically, Ford said nothing to Bogdanovich about his breakthrough movie. "I don't remember him ever telling me anything about any of my movies," remembered Bogdanovich. "He did come onto the set of *What's Up, Doc?* at the studio, which was a big deal. I was very touched by it, by the gesture. But I don't know that he saw many movies at that point. He watched television and flipped the channels, watching *The Lone Ranger.* I honestly don't know that he saw *The Last Picture Show.*"

B y now, most of Ford's mail consisted of importunings from potential employees he didn't need, or potential biographers he didn't want. "I'm too old and tired," he wrote one bright-eyed acolyte. A desultory project to co-direct a film called *Valley Forge* with Frank Capra, all proceeds to go to the Motion Picture Fund, came to nothing.

The money situation was growing increasingly uncomfortable. Mary's Parkinson's and Jack's increasingly frail condition made the winding stairway of the Copa de Oro house very difficult to navigate. Then there was the fact that the house was expensive to maintain. Something had to give.

Ford had hired a new business manager to replace the retired Bea Benjamin, and the new man got him to confront his money troubles. "He recommended my grandfather sell his house," said Dan Ford. "This is just before the real estate explosion, when the Copa de Oro house would triple in value in two years, but who knew? He wanted him to buy a more modest home someplace, anyplace. He said that Barbara had to go. My grandfather said, 'I can't tell Mary this. It will kill her.' But the business manager stood up to him, saying this is what you have to do or I'm out of here. So he did it. The move wasn't made for health reasons, it was made for financial reasons."

Kate Hepburn and Frances Rich, the daughter of Irene Rich, went on a house hunt for the couple and found them a suitable place. So in December of 1972, Jack, Mary, and Barbara, more or less filling the role of nurse, moved from Bel Air to Palm Desert.

"We loved every inch of [the Copa de Oro house]," Mary said, "but neither of us could go up or down stairs, so we had to get a place on one floor. And so many of our friends had retired and moved out here. . . . He always loved the desert. . . . I'm just glad he didn't move us to Monument Valley!"

Now that he was out of town, and people had to make a special effort to see him, Ford's isolation increased. Except for one brief meeting, Mark Haggard never saw him again. "He was a very kindly man," said Haggard.

"People might hate him, but they didn't dislike him. Malice was only extended to the people he loved. He had the most gentle, vulnerable eyes; that's one of the reasons he wore the dark glasses. And he was totally different with women than he was with men. The inner Ford only came out with women."

Frank Baker would undoubtedly have agreed. Sitting under a tree after the Memorial Day ceremony, he shook his head and told Mark Haggard, "After sixty years, I never did quite understand him."

While Ford and his son had only a semblance of a relationship now, he stayed loyal to his daughter. "He liked Barbara more than Pat," said Lindsay Anderson. "She was subservient to him." But Barbara was still drinking.

"Barbara was totally sick," said Denver Pyle. "They'd put her in clinics but it never worked. Ford would call me and I'd run down there and she'd be in trouble about something. She'd be in the drunk tank, out of it, in the middle of the floor. Every once in a while, out of nowhere, he'd ask, 'Seen Barbara?' And that's all he'd say. You could tell it was very difficult for him."

"Barbara would call me up at 3:00 or 4:00 in the morning, dead drunk," said Andrew McLaglen. "She just wanted to ramble on and talk about the old times—Ward, Lee Marvin—and I had to be up early to make a picture. I know Lee Marvin took a lot of Barbara's calls. He was a drinker, but a good guy. Anyway, after a few of these calls, Duke came up to me. 'Jack's miffed at you.'

" 'Why?'

" 'Because you weren't nice to Barbara.'

"Well, there was no way to treat Barbara properly at that particular point, there just wasn't."

"Dear, sweet Barbara," sighed Pamela Marvin, Lee's wife. "The beautiful eyes, the way she talked. The laughter. Lee and I would talk to her on the phone for hours. She adopted him, because all the others were gone, dead, or moved away. She leaned on Lee for loving support and conversation. It was always 'Daddy' this or 'Daddy' that. She still called her father 'Daddy.' She'd grown up in this very high-powered life surrounded by bigger-than-life men—her father, John Wayne, Ward Bond, Woody Strode. Now, how do you find someone like that for yourself? How do you find a life like that for yourself? You don't. To the day she died Barbara was Daddy's girl."

For a while, Jack and Mary tried a form of tough love on Barbara and refused to support her. As a result, she was broke. Dobe Carey gave her money, and Lee Marvin hired a chauffeur for her. Finally, Ford relented; one day he called up Marilyn Carey and thanked her for being Barbara's only friend.

A few weeks after Ford told John Wayne he was angry at Andrew McLaglen, he showed up on the set of a picture McLaglen was directing. McLaglen was startled by his frail condition. "He dropped his watch, he coughed in the middle of a take, and not on purpose. He seemed to have suddenly become an old man."

As Budd Boetticher was completing *Arruza*, Peter Bogdanovich told him he should visit Ford. "That son of a bitch? He ruined my picture."

"He loves you," said Bogdanovich. "The only reason he cut your picture was that Duke told him it needed to be an hour and a half long if it was going to be released. He really likes you."

Boetticher grudgingly called, and was soon a regular visitor at 74-605 Old Prospector Trail in Palm Desert. "We never talked about the editing of *The Bullfighter and the Lady*. He wasn't allowed to have any beer, so we would take him a case of stout. The servants would see us coming, they would all hide, and we'd put the stout under the bed. Nobody would say anything.

"He'd keep scooting out from under the covers, and he had a nightgown on, and I'd have to keep covering up his balls, because he wouldn't. So, like Lenny talking to George about the rabbits, I'd say, 'Jack tell me about your new picture.' And he'd tell me about this picture he wanted to make about the black Buffalo Soldiers in the Civil War. He never talked about his old movies, just the ones he was going to make."

On one occasion, when Boetticher and Ford were alone, Ford said simply, "This is a lot of horseshit, isn't it?" Boetticher reflexively told Ford he'd be out and about soon.

At one point, Boetticher loaded Ford into the back seat of his station wagon and took him to see *Arruza*. Ford wrote a note telling Boetticher the film "was an example of what the motion picture industry could be." He signed it, "Your pal, Jack."

"With me at that time, he was wonderful, absolutely wonderful. All he did was destroy my picture. He was like a father that had wronged his son and was trying to do right by him."

Occasionally Peter Bogdanovich would drop by to bask in Ford's sarcasm. "Jesus *Christ* Bogdanovich! Can't you ever end a sentence with anything but a question mark? Haven't you heard of the declarative sentence?"

By now, between the interviews for his book and preparing the documentary, Bogdanovich had spent a lot of time with Ford. When all was said and done, the younger man had little more idea of the inner Ford than anybody else.

"When he'd hear an Irish song or something, you could see that warm look in his eye that meant he'd been touched emotionally. That look was rarely directed at me; sometimes, I'd see it after he'd knocked me down in some vicious way. And then he'd look over at you and smile. He was contradictory as hell."

But, compared to Josef von Sternberg, another sensitive, lonely director with a defensive shell you had to blast through, Ford was far more accessible. "Ford was funny. Jo wasn't, particularly; he was dry and cutting. Ford had more of a sense of humor on the top, and he'd talk more. Sternberg had a sadness; he hadn't been allowed to work for years. Ford was not a happy person, but I don't remember sadness or bitterness."

He spent almost all of his time in bed now, watching television, taking his meals off TV trays. He didn't like to watch movies with actors that had died—Gable, Tracy, etc.—which rather limited the menu of older pictures that were suitable for viewing. Once, his grandson Dan watched *The Wizard of Oz* with him and Ford was very moved at the end. "Boy, that was a hell of a picture," he exclaimed.

He concentrated on newer things. The actor Clu Gulager caught his eye, and Ford thought he had an interesting quality. When he found out that Dobe Carey had worked with Gulager, he peppered him with questions about the actor.

He loved *Jeopardy!* and *Hogan's Heroes*, hated *McHale's Navy*; it was okay for the Army to be buffoons, but not the Navy. His grandson Tim remembered watching *The Battle of the Bulge* with him on TV, with the old man grunting "That's bullshit" at every factual or dramatic inaccuracy. Mostly he used TV as a pacifier, something to fill up the time, but occasionally a TV series would use some action footage he had shot for *Stagecoach*, *Fort Apache*, or *Wagon Master* and then he'd get furious.

At long last, his thirst had gone away. He just didn't enjoy drinking anymore. After he was diagnosed with cancer, the doctors told him to try to keep his weight up, so he'd have an occasional pint of Guinness or some of Budd Boetticher's stout, but that was all.

George Cukor would call regularly, for Ford was one of the few directors he truly admired. The two men had a jocular, kidding relationship, and once Cukor sent him a copy of Leo Rosten's *The Joys of Yiddish*. "There are some great artists in the business," Ford said. "I am not one of them. I think Frank Capra is an artist. George Cukor is a great artist. So are George Stevens, George Sidney and William Wellman. No, Wellman isn't an artist. He's just a goddam good director."

• • •

That winter, Ford's grandson Dan came out to the Palm Desert house to tape his grandparents' reminiscences for the biography he would publish in 1979. Mary Ford's gnarled old voice accompanied a lively intelligence; when she got rolling, she could be every bit the raconteur her husband was, and funnier. Although obviously diminished in terms of energy, and laboring with an old man's mushy diction, Ford's Maine accent still came through. "Parlor" was "pahlah," "part" was "paht."

Ford still had the manner of a man accustomed to being obeyed. "Kill it," he would snap as he grew tired, and Dan would shut off the tape recorder. Ford's deafness forced Dan to yell most of the questions. In most ways, he was no more forthcoming with his grandson than he was with a roomful of inquiring strangers, spinning out polished anecdotes—some verifiable, others arrant bullshit—in the same languid, undramatic fashion, adopting the pleasantly archaic vocabulary he used to let people know he wasn't really a shanty Irish roughneck. "I deem it a very fine souvenir," he said, gesturing toward Pardner Jones's rifle. But, just to keep his questioner off-balance, he would salt his elegance with earthiness: "Now I gotta go pee."

He leveled with his grandson to the extent of admitting that he had been a movie-struck kid, that he had not fallen into a career nearly as accidentally as he usually claimed, and he would occasionally give vent to ribaldry: "I'm an old man now and I think I only have three left, but I'm saving one of them for Elizabeth Allen."

Critical appreciation continued to come: the English magazine *Focus on Film* devoted an entire issue to Ford and his work, and on February 27, 1973, the American Film Institute announced that Ford would be the first recipient of their Life Achievement Award, given to filmmakers whose work "has stood the test of time."

Charlton Heston, at the time the chairman of the AFI, remembered that he "appointed six guys and a couple of women to choose. We met in my office, and I said, 'Well, what do you think?'

" 'Jack Ford, I guess.' 'Yeah, yeah, Jack Ford, no one else.' The meeting was over in five minutes." George Stevens Jr., the director of the institute, went into the next room to call Ford and ask him to accept the award. "You bet," he replied.

At the same time, President Richard Nixon announced that Ford would receive the Medal of Freedom. He had been prodded by Bruce Herschensohn, who was now working in the White House and had never forgotten Ford's desire for honor from his own country. Nixon, who genuinely liked *The Quiet Man*, didn't require a lot of convincing.

Now, in what was clearly the old man's last hurrah, Pat's sense of bad timing again asserted itself. Pat had left the movie business, as well as ranching, and had opted for the sensible life; he was working in the Probation Department of Los Angeles County. He wrote his father a letter saying that Ford should not accept the Medal of Freedom from Nixon, that the President was sure to be impeached over Watergate, and that to associate with a criminal-to-be would negate any honor he might bestow.

Ford had watched television coverage of the POWs' homecoming with his grandson Dan, and his eyes had welled up with tears. It was the closest Dan had ever come to seeing him cry. To Ford, Nixon deserved the credit for bringing the soldiers home, Nixon was going to honor him, and here was Pat trying to screw things up.

"He got *really* mad at Pat," recalled Dan Ford. "I remember him sitting at a table and talking, quoting the things that Pat had said, and his anger was deep. He was really pissed."

Up to this point, Jack and his son had a quasi-relationship. Whenever Jack got mad at Pat, he would threaten to cut him out of the will, and Pat would respond by saying he had a county pension anyway. According to Ford's lawyer, three or four wills had been drawn up, and Pat was in or out, depending on the current state of their relationship, but Barbara was always in. The letter about Nixon changed everything.

The Medal of Freedom presentation was set for the same night as the AFI award—March 31, 1973. As Charlton Heston remembered, "He made a huge effort to get down to the Beverly Hilton. He was in a suite, in bed. Ford's mental condition was pretty good, but he was tired and sick. He was very pleased to be the first [winner of the award], very pleased. He kept sending me messages that weekend that he wanted to do a picture with me sometime. But Hank Fonda told me, 'You wouldn't have liked it. He was a mean son of a bitch.' "

The night of March 31 arrived. There was Henry Kissinger with Liv Ullmann; there was Cary Grant and Fred Astaire and Pat O'Brien. Clint Eastwood sat with Rosalind Russell. On the dais were John Wayne, Jimmy Stewart, Maureen O'Hara, and Ronald Reagan. It was, said producer Frank McCarthy, "the biggest star turnout in my twenty-five years in Hollywood." Two thousand people paid $125 a head for cocktails with John and Pilar Wayne, after which the elect proceeded to the Versailles Room to chat with the President and Mrs. Nixon.

While the ballroom was filling up, Ford was upstairs having a meeting with his lawyer and business manager. Dan Ford was there, helping to get him dressed, and he remembers a closed-door meeting that lasted about fifteen minutes. "It was at that point, I believe, that Pat was cut out of the will. It was never changed back."

• • •

"Ladies and Gentlemen, the President of the United States and Mrs. Nixon and John Ford and Mrs. Ford." Ford, a shrunken figure with a patch over his left eye, cigar in hand, was pushed on in his wheelchair. Bringing up the rear was Nixon, who took a chair next to Ford.

In the rear of the ballroom, a seventy-two-man Marine Corps band broke into "The Caissons Go Rolling Along," "Anchors Aweigh," the Marine Corps Hymn, and "The Star-Spangled Banner." Straining, the old man rose from his wheelchair and stood erect through the National Anthem, eyes glistening, hand to forehead in a salute.

Maureen O'Hara sang, which made sense. So did Leslie Uggams ("It's a Long, Long Way to Tipperary" and a bluesy version of "My Man"), which didn't. Danny Kaye, the MC, was sincere and maudlin. President Nixon announced that he had seen "virtually all" of Ford's 140 or so movies. The lights were so hot that the chocolate table mints melted and Irene Dunne fainted.

John Wayne seemed tongue-tied and cut his own speech short with an abrupt, "I love him; I could say more." James Stewart told a long, funny story about jousting with Ford over the selection of his hat for *Two Rode Together* that ended with Ford finally allowing Stewart to wear his favorite hat. "If, by chance, you ever work for me again," said Ford, "I want you to have in your contract a clause that states you have hat approval."

Stewart noted that he did work for Ford again, but in *The Man Who Shot Liberty Valance* Ford didn't allow him to wear a hat. George Stevens Jr. called Ford "the most important director since the late D. W. Griffith."

When it came time to accept the award, Ford summoned his reserves, rose from his wheelchair, and walked to the podium. Shaking his head, continually licking his lips—a tic resulting from his medication— Ford was clearly moved and said he was "overcome with gratitude." He thanked the trustees, thanked Nixon, and said "that's about all I can say before I break down. Thank you."

Nixon proclaimed Ford a full admiral for the evening and awarded him the Presidential Medal of Freedom. The old man stood next to the President of his country and shook his head in wonderment.

"Thank you, sir," Ford said. "As [recently returned POW] Capt. Jeremiah Denton said, 'God Bless America.' I quote his words with feeling." Ford ended his last public appearance by exclaiming, "God bless Richard Nixon."

For Ford, it was an evening to cherish. After the ceremony itself, there was a receiving line. Mark Haggard waited until everybody else had left the ballroom. John Wayne was standing impassively behind Ford, hands on his wheelchair. Haggard came up to Ford and shook his hand. Ford recognized him, and Haggard was amazed to see the old man break into a crinkly, Barry Fitzgeraldish smile. In all the times he'd spent with Ford, he'd never seen him laugh or smile. After that, John Wayne pushed Ford's wheelchair up the ramp and out of the empty ballroom.

For a half-century, John Ford had portrayed the rich tapestry of American life with a compassion, a visual grandeur, and a largeness of spirit that dwarfed his shortcomings as a man and a father. Now, with illness overwhelming him, he could at last acknowledge some of the needs he had ignored for so long.

One day at the Motion Picture Home, Frank Baker found a petty officer at his front door. "Admiral Ford is in the car outside and he would like to see you." Baker invited him in. Ford was in a wheelchair, and asked Baker for a drink. Since Baker didn't drink, he had a sudden sinking feeling, until he remembered a bottle of scotch that had been brought as a gift several months before by an Australian girl named June Long.

Baker got out the scotch, and to kill time told Ford the story of her visit, telling him that he had always been her favorite director. That was the cue, for Ford suddenly went back into the past. "He was dragging up figures that I'd forgotten," Baker told Anthony Slide, "speaking with a terribly deep sentimental feeling about them. And bringing up Frank again, and Frank in an entirely different light."

Came the time to say goodbye, Ford kept staring at the picture of Baker's wife, Helen, whom he'd always adored. "And he wanted to say, 'So long, I won't be seeing you again,' and he didn't know what to say. . . . Suddenly he said, 'Well,' and he's staring right at her. And he wants to give a toast. He wants to include my wife and he wants to include me, but he can't bring himself to. And he suddenly raises that glass, and he's staring right at this picture, 'To . . .' and he's going to say Helen, my wife, and he knew that would shock me, I guess, for he says, 'To June Long.' And we downed the drink, and he went out, never shook hands with me or anything."

"Well, I guess this is it," Ford said as he went through the door. "I'd like you to know that you're one of the very few people I ever respected. You never crawled on your belly to me."

Brian Desmond Hurst flew over from Europe to visit and stayed at George Cukor's house, limiting himself to a week because "George was so house-proud that he would go round picking up . . . matchsticks that weren't there." Ford asked Hurst to sing "The Rose of Tralee."

Burt Kennedy visited and noticed Ford's tennis shoes peeking out from under the bed. "I've been out jogging all morning," he offered by way of explanation. Stephen Longstreet came by. "It was a hard death," remembered Longstreet. "We talked of small things: Civil War camera work, men in battle whose little vanities [led them to] want to make a good death, the human body not being made for battle. . . . No big view; he didn't want to talk deeply."

Lindsay Anderson was in America promoting *O Lucky Man!* and called from the Beverly Hills Hotel. "Hello, Lindsay! What are you doing in L.A.? Yeah. . . . Come on out—it'll be good to see you." Anderson arrived and met Mary Ford, who was moving carefully through the house with the aid of a walker. "It's the big one," Barbara told him as she led him to Ford's small bedroom. "It's only a matter of time."

Ford was propped up in bed, smoking a cigar and sipping brandy while watching TV. He complimented Anderson on *This Sporting Life*. When the younger man asked him if he'd been working on any projects, Ford replied, "Oh, I had a couple of scripts, but I'm beyond that now. This has put a stop to all that. Haven't got the strength for it."

Anderson was struck by the lack of bitterness; Ford was stating facts, nothing else. When Anderson asked him if there was any producer he had enjoyed working with, Ford said, "Oh, Zanuck. He knew the business. When I'd finished a picture I could go off to Catalina on my boat and fish. Didn't have to hang around. I could leave the editing to him. None of the others knew anything."

When it was time to say goodbye, Anderson took Ford's hand and kissed it. "Thanks for coming," Ford said.

"Is there anything you want?" asked Anderson.

"Only your friendship."

"You have that."

The last time Peter Bogdanovich saw him, he brought Howard Hawks. Bogdanovich was appalled by Ford's appearance; the cancer had shrunk him by half. Ford gave them five minutes, and again fenced with Bogdanovich about his incessant inquiries. "Howard, does he ask you all those damn questions too?" Hawks, normally reserved, even taciturn, came out of his shell "like a college boy in front of his favorite professor," wrote Bogdanovich. But the banter couldn't conceal the old man's alarming condition; he was pale and weak and down to ninety-eight pounds.

Ford began asking for painkillers about two weeks before the end. About the same time, Budd Boetticher made it out to Palm Desert for the last time. Once again, he asked Ford to tell him about his new picture. Ford reached out and took Boetticher's hand "as gently as any lady I have ever known." "Budd," he said, "there isn't going to be another picture." George O'Brien came, and spent time holding Mary's hand, proud of being there at the end.

On August 30, John Wayne arrived. "Come for the death watch,

Duke?" the old man asked. "Hell no, Jack. You're the anchor—you'll bury us all." "Oh, well, maybe I'll stick around a while longer then." The next day, Ford was sinking. Woody Strode arrived around noon, and took his usual spot at the foot of the bed. The old man in the bed didn't speak for a long time. The last intelligible sentence John Ford uttered on this earth was "May I please have a cigar?"

He died at 6:35 P.M. on August 31, 1973. Woody Strode, Pat Ford, and Ford's sister draped an American flag over the body, drank a toast to the man and his life with a glass of brandy, then broke the glasses. "I sat there two hours until the undertaker came to haul his body out," said Woody Strode, "and that's when I said sayonara."

The obituaries were generous, but behind the curve. The *New York Times* indicated that Ford's career had ended shortly after World War II. It honored the director of *The Informer, Stagecoach*, and *The Grapes of Wrath*, while *The Sun Shines Bright, The Searchers*, and *The Man Who Shot Liberty Valance* were ignored. It was a death notice that took the man at his own valuation, reporting that his real name was Sean Aloysius O'Fearna.

Pat made all the funeral arrangements, handled hotel reservations, contacted everybody, did everything perfectly. Ford lay in state at a Hollywood mortuary, his closed mahogany coffin covered by the tattered flag from the Battle of Midway. There was a single altar piece of pink and white gladiolas.

The funeral mass was held on September 5, at the Church of the Blessed Sacrament in Hollywood. The service was scheduled to begin at 10:00, but the church began filling up at 9:00. Woody Strode was the first to arrive, and then came Ford's peers—Capra, Wellman, Wyler. Among the four hundred people that attended were John Wayne—with George Cukor, escorting Barbara—Charlton Heston, Walter Pidgeon, Rod Taylor, Cesar Romero, and Pat O'Brien. William Clothier and Winton Hoch came, as did Anna Lee and Hank Worden and Dobe and Marilyn Carey. Frank Capra was there, and Loretta Young and James Stewart, Iron Eyes Cody—in full tribal regalia—Ricardo Montalban, Gilbert Roland. And Henry Fonda. Wingate Smith moved from group to group, acting as unofficial host.

A little past noon, the coffin was lifted by John Wayne and a group of stuntmen for the funeral procession to Culver City. As the coffin left the church for the trip to Holy Cross Cemetery, a soloist sang "The Battle Hymn of the Republic."

At the cemetery, Jack was buried a few feet from his brother Frank. The Feeney boys were finally at peace.

EPILOGUE

"It was the vision that set him apart. The photographic eye. And the total knowledge and love of the people he was working with. He could look at a thing and compose it as well as Cézanne. All great directors can do that, but Stevens and Hitchcock would have had their Cézannes all around them in sketch form. Ford's Cézannes wouldn't be seen until he did it, because it was in his head. Those others were architects. Ford was a wonderfully fluid painter."

ROD TAYLOR

The tributes continued to pour in. Andrew Sarris called Ford "the supreme American film poet of homecomings and leave-takings, of last stands and lost causes." François Truffaut indulged himself with a forgivable sentimentality when he said that "This man, who has always been described as surly and secretly tender, was surely closer to the characters that he had Victor McLaglen play than to the leading parts that John Wayne interpreted."

Perhaps the shrewdest judgment came from someone whose work had little in common with Ford's. "What I like most in John Ford," said Federico Fellini, "is the artist in a state of purity, unaware and raw, deprived of sterile and farfetched cultural intermediations, immune from intellectualistic contamination. I like his strength and his disarming simplicity. When I think of Ford, I sense the smell of barracks, of horses, of gunpowder. I visualize silent and unending flatlands, the unending trips of his heroes. But above all, I feel a man who liked motion pictures, who lived for the cinema, who has made out of motion pictures a fairy tale to be lived by himself, a dwelling in which to live with joyous spontaneity of entertainment and passion."

The tribute that would have meant the most to Ford is the way that his work has maintained its hold on the imagination of the audience. Ford's vision of America became America's vision of itself, and the world's.

In Monument Valley, at Goulding's Trading Post, the guest book is carefully preserved, pored over by Japanese and German tourists drawn to a trading post in the middle of nowhere by the incantatory power of images made decades before.

"Dear Harry and Mike—Don't know why I should sign this anymore. I'm no guest—this is home—Duke."

"I'll be back. Henry Fonda."

"As always Harry and Mike—my sincere thanks. John Ford."
"Harry, you and I both owe these monuments a lot. Duke."

Truffaut would have cause to revise his benign opinion of the man he admired. In Ford's will, signed—as "John A. Feeney"—in a shaky hand on the last day of March 1973, he disinherited his son. The estate was left to Mary and, after her death, was to be divided between Barbara and Pat's sons, Dan and Tim. Tom Joad would never have disinherited his own blood; neither would Sergeant Quincannon. But the fierce, unforgiving Ethan Edwards would have done it in a heartbeat.

For Pat, it was more of a psychological blow than an actual one. Mary was appalled by her husband's decision; her own will would divide the estate evenly between her children. No matter; Pat was angry at his father, jealous of his sons. "There were some years that Pat and I didn't talk," said Dan Ford ruefully.

At the time of his death, Ford owned 250 shares of Reynolds Tobacco, 720 shares of Ford Motors, 180 shares of General Motors. Excluding land, i.e., the house in Palm Desert, the estate was estimated at $500,000, a shockingly small figure for a man who had been a successful movie director for fifty years, and who had never paid alimony or other typical financial drains of the twentieth century. But Ford had never cared for money as such; over and over he traded money for freedom, whether in the kind of films he could make, or the time spent on his beloved *Araner.*

Mary Ford struggled on with the help of Barbara and a few paid nurses. Katharine Hepburn came to visit occasionally, for the two women shared a similar strength of character and a mutual love for Jack.

"To me, he was the greatest man that ever lived," Mary insisted. The binges were forgotten, as were the occasional slips from complete fidelity and the days and weeks of Ford refusing to speak to her. What she remembered now was the Ford who had provided her with an enveloping security, and a gruff devotion.

"Oh, such a life. It was like a dream. We would leave here the 1st of February and go to Mexico with John Wayne and Henry Fonda and a couple of other friends of Jack's, and go on a fishing trip, and hang around Acapulco and Mazatlán for a while on our boat. Then the 1st of July we headed for Honolulu, and sent the kids back to school. They went to school on the island. We'd fly back and forth and leave the boat there. Isn't that wonderful?

"I just thought he was great because he had a wonderful sense of humor; he made me laugh. I'd seen a lot of misery, a lot of unhappiness. I don't know, there was something about him. It certainly wasn't his looks. I just fell in love with him.

"I wouldn't change a day in my life. Each one has been so perfect. Up in my room, I have a large picture of Jack, and people say to me, 'Why do you sit and look at that?' Because every minute of it was a laugh, something worth having. Buddy Rogers was here the other night. He said, 'One more big job I have to do. I have to find you a husband.' I said, 'You mind your own business.' "

Mary Ford died in July 1979 at the age of eighty-six, and was buried next to her husband.

Barbara's alcoholism had failed to respond to any of the cures and treatments, but after her mother died there was nobody to cover for her anymore. It was sink or swim, and Barbara swam, sobering up and going to work for Peter Bogdanovich, editing *Mask*. Barbara died in June 1985 of cancer. Her brother Pat died a year later, of a heart condition.

John Wayne survived Ford by only six years. Until he died, said Harry Carey Jr., "He loved to reminisce. He loved to talk about Ford pictures; 'Remember the time you got in a jam?' 'Remember the time I did that?' He loved to do that. And then he'd say, 'I never see the people I love!' "

Nobody who knew Ford ever managed to expel him from memory, nor did they want to. He saw everything, and, although he pretended not to, felt everything. "I would rather have been in the Ford stock company than be a big star," said Anna Lee. "There was no way to become a star, but you felt good about your craft. He was a wonderful man in every way. I loved him."

George O'Brien's son realized that his father saw his entire life as a John Ford movie—hearty friendship leavened by conflict, resolved by a wary but enduring reconciliation in the end. In 1981, O'Brien was paralyzed by a stroke. He believed that he had been wounded, not by a burst blood vessel in the brain, but in battle, by Japanese artillery.

In the four years left to him, George O'Brien spoke of only three things—his divorced wife, his son, and Jack Ford. As Darcy O'Brien sat with his father and listened to him, he thought of Beckett's *Krapp's Last Tape*, in which an old man thinks of his single experience of love. Darcy came to realize that it is in a man's emotional attachments that he finds the meaning of life. Just before he died, George O'Brien told his son, "When I get out of here, we'll make a picture together. You'll be the hero, and I'll play the heavy. Old Jack will direct."

Of those places that meant the most to Ford, only a few pieces of the foundation of the Odin Street house survive on a hillside by the Hollywood Bowl; the site of the Field Photo Farm is now a housing tract; the chapel from which Harry Carey and Ward Bond were buried, and where Jack and Mary were married within the Catholic Church on their fiftieth anniversary, sits on the grounds of the Motion Picture Home.

Monument Valley remains.

John Ford was a magnificent piece of work, but no simple hero—he was grander, tougher, and sadder than any hero can allow himself to be. He was clever and he was ruthless. It was not his nature to trust, but to test. Ford had a great capacity for kindness and generosity, so long as he could firmly maintain control, and the beneficiary displayed sufficient gratitude. He had a devotion to his own talent, which required that his wife and family tend to their place on the periphery. Beneath the scary surface, he was a mushy sentimentalist, and beneath that was the hard, selfish core of the true artist.

He cared nothing for money, little for politics, cared a great deal about tradition and character. Lindsay Anderson would eloquently call him "a poet of faith in an age of unbelief," and write, "It was Ford's impassioned humanism that won him his golden reputation . . . the warmth and strength of his apparently populist conviction; his sympathy with the humble, the rejected, the dispossessed . . .

"The better one knows Ford, the more powerful seems the influence of his Irish background, his Irish consciousness . . . for the complementary lyricism of the Celtic temperament, the sweetness of it and its underlying melancholy, the consciousness of time and transience, of partings that must sever the closest bonds of family and friendship, of men who march away, loved ones who disappear into distance, the eternal longing of the dispossessed. . . . He was a leader rather than an officer, always a rogue. And rogues, of course, can do a lot of damage, to themselves as well as to others."

John Ford believed in America and he believed in the future, even as he mourned the past. Ethan Edwards leaves his feelings for his brother's wife unstated because it would destroy the family; Tom Doniphon lets Ranse Stoddard have the girl he loves because he's smart enough to know the lawyer can offer her a world Doniphon can only dream about, and wouldn't want anyway. Always, Ford lingered over the man deserted by time and tide because he knew that it happens to everybody—even film directors.

In the more than forty years since his death, appreciation has continued to grow for Ford's work, especially *The Searchers*. In 1979, Stuart Byron wrote a story in *New York* magazine that asserted that "all recent American cinema derives from John Ford's *The Searchers*," quoting John

Milius ("The best American movie"), Martin Scorsese ("The dialogue is like poetry! And the changes of expressions are so subtle, so magnificent! I see it once or twice a year"), and Steven Spielberg ("It is high on my twenty-favorite-films list").

In 1962, not a single critic put *The Searchers* on the prestigious *Sight and Sound* poll of the greatest films of all time. By 1972, it was ranked eighteenth, in 1982 tenth, in 1992 fifth. The audience followed; if *The Searchers* is too forbidding, too austere to be regarded as affectionately as *Casablanca* or *Star Wars*, it is still firmly ensconced as a film that says something about America and never flinches.

If Ford had never made *The Searchers* or any other Western, he would still be a major director, with a particular gift for repose and an astringent wisdom. But, while the Western would still have a history without Ford, it would be nowhere near as glorious. Ford gave the Western a vision and, in Monument Valley, a signature. No other place evokes the West so unambiguously.

Ultimately, John Ford's greatest gift was his ability to combine the epic with the intimate—not just in the same film, but in the same moment, the personal moving side by side with the mythological.

"Ford was a mass of contradictions," said Sam Goldwyn Jr. "Sentimental, brilliant, very sensitive, cruel, sardonic, with a wall of protection around him."

Completely secure as an artist, he was terribly insecure as a man, and devised a personality that would hide his true nature, prevent him from ever being emotionally wounded. "[General Matthew] Ridgway wore hand grenades," observed Winston Miller, "and he was never going to be close enough to an enemy . . . to throw a hand grenade. Patton wore pearl-handled revolvers. MacArthur had his sixty-mission cap. Well, I think Ford created a command personality for himself."

Burt Kennedy believed that it was all an elaborate performance, and quoted an exchange between Sam Peckinpah and Lee Marvin. "I hate actors," Peckinpah said. "All actors do," Marvin replied. "That," said Kennedy, "always summed up Jack Ford to me."

"It was a facade for sure," said Rod Taylor. "He was an unattractive fellow in his youth, with a brother that dominated him. And in the beginning it was a facade but he did it so long and so often and so successfully that it became him. He was a rough old bastard, but the man I knew was a gentle, sentimental, loving elder brother."

Bob Stephens, the Navy man who Ford took in while he recuperated from his wounds, said that "He was a tough, rugged person, but inside he was a pussycat. Inside, he was just as fine as anyone you'd ever want to meet. He gave me a better understanding of what my military life was going to be like, even though I'd already had fifteen years of it. I had 2,500 men working for me when I finished, and Ford taught me how to make sure that the job got done.

"Ford gave me the ins and outs of leadership, how to display it. Mostly, he could be a hard-ass, but if he was hard with you, he knew that you were able to do it, but were lazy. Ford taught me how to handle people, how to motivate them, how to keep them from getting killed. Being with him was the turning point of my life."

Portland, Maine, bristles with statues—of Henry Wadsworth Long-fellow, of sundry military heroes. But there was nothing, not even a plaque, marking it as the hometown of John Ford. All that changed in July of 1998, when a statue of Ford by the gifted sculptor George Kelly, provided by philanthropist Linda Noe Laine, was unveiled at Gorham Corners. The ten-foot-high bronze pictures Ford sitting in his director's chair, pipe in one hand, battered old cavalry hat on his head, gazing im-passively at the vacant lot on which his father's saloon once stood. Sur-rounding him is a semicircle of six granite tablets that describe each of Ford's Oscar-winning films.

People came from all over the world for the unveiling. There was Harry Carey Jr., Claude Jarman Jr., Patrick Wayne, Nunnally Johnson's daughter Roxana, Ford's grandson Dan and his daughters. From Ireland came the Minister of Arts and Heritage, and the film critic of the *Irish Times*; from Washington came the Secretary of the Navy; from Monu-ment Valley came the ninety-six-year-old Billy Yellow with his son and grandson, all paying tribute to a great artist in the town that helped de-fine him. Ford had finally gotten his due in Portland, just as he had in the rest of the world.

"That is exactly the way I remember him," said Billy Yellow as he gazed at the statue. "Relaxed but alert. Always alert."

How do you sum up an intellectual who hated being an intellectual, a romantic black Irishman who looked upon the world with suspi-cion, an artist who preferred to work with his intellectual inferiors? How do you sum up a man whose films have had such an enduring impact on the perceptions of audiences and artists alike all over the world, from the Japanese who flock to Monument Valley, to the tourists who watch *The Quiet Man* when it is shown at Ashford Castle every afternoon at 4:00?

Stephen Longstreet pondered that question and finally said that he always thought of Ford as some unholy combination of Falstaff, Zorro, Bogart, Mark Twain, the Boston Strangler, and Groucho Marx. Michael Wayne was asked the same question and he succinctly replied, "A genius between 'Action' and 'Cut.' Other times, an interesting human being. Tortured—wild and crazy. But when he said 'Action' something magical happened."

"He had an eye for the motion picture miracle," said William Wellman Jr. "He could see the picture in his head. He could see the finished scene. And, once he got the actors on the set, he could see if it looked unrealistic, or staged, or not honest. And he wanted it honest, he wanted it spontaneous. That accounts for the business of the way he treated actors—or, rather, mistreated actors."

Darryl Zanuck believed that Ford was the best director in the history of cinema because he thought of movies in "purely visual terms. . . . Ford could get more drama into an ordinary interior or exterior long shot than any director and his placement of the camera almost had the effect of making even good dialogue unnecessary or secondary. . . . He was an artist. He painted a picture—in movement, in action, in still shots. . . . He was a great, great pictorial artist."

All this is true, yet none of it is enough. The work of this wild colonial boy flared with a moral imagination equal to the melancholy that marked his life. His instinctive knowledge that things usually end in defeat balanced his idealism and sentimentality. Ford gave the world an America that was a lived experience, a history that can be used. John Ford's history became the history of his time, mirroring it, transfiguring it, explaining America to itself.

Faced with the eternal question framed by Yeats ("The intellect of man is forced to choose/Perfection of the life or of the work"), Ford chose the work. He devised a belligerent, deceitful carapace to protect an inner man on the run from insoluble inner tensions, largely revolving around the gap between what he really wanted to be—a naval hero—and what he actually was—a poet. Like Ethan Edwards, he drove all before him with the force of his fierce personality.

John Ford transcended the imprisonment of his anger, insecurity, and disfiguring alcoholism, and cast his imagination outward, transmuting his deep flaws into a profounder form. His films are about the search for a place we can never find, and form an album of America as it was meant to have been, as well as of the place it really is. His films have the power to burn through space to a place inside us, an art about memory that makes our own lives more vivid.

He shaped a vision of America for the twentieth century every bit as majestic and inclusive as the one Jefferson crafted in the eighteenth century. It's made up of soldiers and priests, of drunks and doctors and servants and whores and half-crazed men driven by their need to be alone, even as they journey toward home, toward reconciliation.

Like Tom Joad, he's all around us in the dark.

The Searchers

ACKNOWLEDGMENTS

This book began on a hot summer day in 1972, as I spent an afternoon talking to John Wayne in a dressing room at CBS. That same year I spent several days with William Clothier, John Ford's favorite cameraman in his later years. Over the years, there were more encounters with members of Ford's extended filmmaking family—John Carradine, Pat O'Brien, and George O'Brien, among others.

In spite of my abiding affection for Ford's films, I never harbored a serious intention to write a book about him until a long lunch with Lindsay Anderson in London more than twenty years after my initial encounter with John Wayne. The notoriously waspish director had reviewed several of my books and found them palatable. From that grew an epistolary friendship, which inevitably touched on Ford.

That lunch, and our discussion of Ford and *The Searchers*, was the acorn from which this particular oak grew, and I remain indebted to Lindsay for the greatest gift any man can give another—friendship and trust. That he died as this book was still in the seedling stage was personally devastating, as was the equally incomprehensible passing of Darcy O'Brien, who had so generously shared with me his intimate insights into his father's relationship with Ford, not to mention his father's diaries.

It goes without saying that Dan Ford does not agree with all of my judgments about his grandfather and his films, but he has freely shared letters, home movies, permissions, and memories in a remarkably even-handed display of trust. He also made it possible for me to spend time with his brother, Tim, a delightful man whose memories of his grandparents further deepened my portrait.

Kevin Brownlow, the ultimate film historian, opened his files for me. Kevin, Pat Stanbury, and the late David Gill gave me free access to the interviews gathered over many years by Photoplay Productions.

As he has for four books and more years than either of us cares to contemplate, Jeff Heise was more than my research assistant, he was my Man Friday. Assisting Jeff was Hal Kemp.

The John Ford papers are at the Lilly Library of Indiana University, and Saundra Taylor and her staff made my weeks there a pleasure. Anthony Slide provided me with some invaluable interviews. Old friend Leonard Maltin supported this book from the beginning and backed me up with masses of material from his own interviews and archival searches. Ron Davis of the Southern Methodist University Oral History Program helped considerably. At SMU, Carrie Rampp and Jennifer Ponder did the legwork for me. Robert G. Marshall, archivist at California State University at Northridge, gave me invaluable help by retrieving transcripts from the Directors Guild Archives relating to the Red Scare in Hollywood.

I owe a special debt to Charles Silver, of the Film Study Center at the Museum of Modern Art. Charles arranged many screenings for me, gave me the benefit of his files and his friendship and his own thoughts about Ford. Also considerably enriching my times at MOMA have been the support and interest of Steven Higgins, Ytte Jensen, and Mary Lea Bandy. Assisting with film screenings at UCLA were Robert Gitt and Lou Ellen Kramer.

My friend and Pordenone cohort James D'Arc gave me complete access to the files of Argosy Productions that he has carefully preserved in his amazing collection at Brigham Young University. At the Museum of Television and Radio in Beverly Hills, Jonathan Rosenthal helped when I needed it. At Wesleyan University, Jeanine Basinger gave me access to the Capra archives.

John Andrew Gallagher couldn't have been a better friend, sending me films and transcripts of his own interviews and even delving into the Selznick Archives at the Ransom Center at the University of Texas for me. Frank Thompson lent a hand when I needed it. With absolutely no advance notice, Rusty Casselton zipped out and borrowed some obscure Ford films from the late David Bradley that he insisted I see. Thanks, pal. As he has for years, David Pierce supplied me with financial figures that provided the parameters for Ford's work in a commercial industry.

I owe an enormous debt to James Curtis, who interviewed Priscilla Bonner for me, provided fascinating material from his own archival searches, and offered much good advice. Aside from that, he's a good friend who makes me laugh.

David Shepard, the doyen of preservationists, encouraged me more than he knew, made it possible for me to talk to Jack Hively, and showed me the hilarious, shriveling footage in which Ford taunts Philip Jenkinson. Patrick McGilligan, the Martin Gilbert of film historians, helped as well.

In Portland, Bill Barry of the Historical Society opened up a wealth of documentation about his town and the place of the Irish in it. Don MacWilliams gave me a guided tour of Munjoy Hill, and Peter Gribbin shared Portland High's collection of Fordiana—or, more properly, Feeneyiana.

In Washington, D.C., Elias Savada plunged deep into immigration and census files and came up with gold. John P. McElwee shared the contents of some of his own Ford files. At the University of Maine, Cindy Therrien helped out a stranger.

My gratitude to all who granted me interviews: Ken Adam, John Agar, Eddie Albert, Bob Allen, the late Lindsay Anderson, Frankie Avalon, Lauren Bacall, Mary Ellin Barrett, Alex Beaton, Elmer Bernstein, Michael Blake, Budd Boetticher, Peter Bogdanovich, Tom Capra, Harry Carey Jr., Marilyn Carey, Tom Carey, David Carradine, the late John Carradine, Anne Coates, Mary Corcoran, Ernest Day, Andre de Toth, Donald Dewar, Peter Duchin, John Gregory Dunne, the late William K. Everson, Rudi Fehr, Richard Fleischer, Peter Fonda, Dan Ford, Francis Ford Jr., Tim Ford, the late John Gillett, Barry Goldwater Jr., Samuel Goldwyn Jr., Peter Graves, Pat Grissom, Mark Haggard, Bruce Herschensohn, Charlton Heston, the late Jack Hively, George Hjorth, Joe Hyams, Claude Jarman Jr., Dorris Bowdon Johnson, Rafer Johnson, Shirley Jones, Thomas Keneally, Burt Kennedy, the late Michael Killanin, Sheila Killanin, Howard W. Koch, Robert Lacey, Paul Lazarus Jr., Anna Lee, Jack Lemmon, Joe Longo, Mary Loos, A. C. Lyles, Karl Malden, Pamela (Mrs. Lee) Marvin, the late Roddy McDowall, Andrew McLaglen, Robert Moreno, Jeff Morey, Hal Nesbitt, Jean (Mrs. Frank) Nugent, the late Darcy O'Brien, Kathleen O'Malley, Betsy Palmer, the late Robert Parrish, Gregory Peck, James Pepper, the late Gil Perkins, the late Denver Pyle, Leni Riefenstahl, the late Cesar Romero, the late Lillian Semenov, Vincent Sherman, Donald Sinden, Bernard Smith, Tim Stafford, Elaine Steinbeck, Bob Stephens, George Stevens Jr., Peter Stone, Gloria Stuart, Rod Taylor, David Totheroh, Robert Wagner, the late John Wayne, Michael Wayne, Patrick Wayne, John Weld Jr., William Wellman Jr., Selden West, Mary Lou Whitney, the late O. Z. Whitehead, James Wilkinson, Robert Wise, Fay Wray, Paul Wurtzel, the late Freddie Young, and Lester Ziffren.

Finally, there are the people without whom there would be no book at all: my agent, Fran Collin, steadfast and true; Chuck Adams, my editor at Simon & Schuster, a dear friend and a fearless guide in our forages through every record bin in lower Manhattan. And the amazing Gypsy da Silva, possessor of the best belly laugh in New York, as well as my painstaking copy editor, Fred Chase, my very helpful proofreader, Matt Hannafin, and my hardworking transferer of AAs, Brandy Wilson.

Michael, Linda, and Callie Connelly opened their home in Los Angeles to me, and Dennis, Amy, and Adam Doros did likewise in New York, enabling me to research at leisure, surrounded by loving friends. Amy Doros and Kevin Brownlow gave the manuscript severe but justified criticisms. Jane Scovell kept a weather eye peeled for interesting Fordian tidbits.

Finally, there are the people at the Palm Beach *Post*, my very own extended stock company. The usual gang of idiots: Mark Buzek, Pat Crowley, and especially Larry Aydlette, who not only put up with my absences, but suggested the title I used and about forty I didn't; Eddie Sears and Tom Giuffrida for presiding with benevolence over such turbulent spirits; Tom Blackburn for serving as my historical advisor without portfolio; and, of course, Jan Tuckwood, whose beauty, energy, humor, and—God knows—patience make journalism fun.

And to my wife, Lynn Robin Kalber Eyman, the founder of this feast called our life: Baby, you're the greatest!

Scott Eyman, October 28, 1993–July 4, 1999.

Monument Valley, Moscow, London, Provo, Hollywood, Pordenone,

New York, Portland, Dublin, Palm Beach, Havana, Venice

JOHN FORD FILMOGRAPHY

(Up to 1922, unless noted, all films were released by Universal Film Corporation. From 1922 through 1930 all films were released by Fox Film Corporation. After 1930, each releasing company is listed. All films are directed by Ford except those noted. Up to the release of *Cameo Kirby*, Ford's director credit was under the name Jack Ford. Release dates for films before 1920 are incomplete, so films for which a date is known are chronologically listed, then the remaining films are alphabetically listed.)

Key	2:	Second unit director
	A:	Acted or appeared in
	AD:	Assistant director
	C:	Cinematographer
	E:	Editor
	EX:	Executive producer
	P:	Producer
	W:	Writer

1914
Lucille Love—The Girl of Mystery (production assistant, propman, and some stuntwork)

The Mysterious Rose (A only) 2 reels

1915
The Birth of a Nation (Epoch Film Corp.) (A only: According to Ford, he was a klansman in the finale) 13 reels

Three Bad Men and a Girl (A only) 2 reels

The Hidden City (A only) 2 reels

The Doorway of Destruction (A, AD) 2 reels

The Broken Coin (A, AD; 22-chapter serial)

The Campbells Are Coming (A only)

1916
(All the films this year were 2–3 reels in length)
Lumber Yard Gang (A only)

Strong-Arm Squad (A only)

The Adventures of Peg O' the Ring (A only; 15-chapter serial)

Chicken Hearted Jim (A only)

A Bandit's Wager (A only)

1917
The Tornado (A, W)

Trail of Hate (A)

The Scrapper (A, W)

The Soul Herder

Cheyenne's Pal (W)

Straight Shooting (First feature-length film)

The Secret Man

A Marked Man

Bucking Broadway

The Purple Mask (Ford supposedly acted in this film)

1918
The Phantom Riders

Wild Women

Thieves' Gold

The Scarlet Drop (W)

Hell Bent (W)

A Woman's Fool

Three Mounted Men

1919
Roped

The Fighting Brothers

A Fight for Love

By Indian Post

The Rustlers

Bare Fists

Gun Law

The Gun Packer (W)

Riders of Vengeance (W)

The Last Outlaw

The Outcasts of Poker Flat

Ace of the Saddle

Rider of the Law

A Gun Fightin' Gentleman (W)

Marked Men

1920
The Prince of Avenue A

The Girl in Number 29

Hitchin' Posts

Under Sentence (W only)

Just Pals   Fox

1921
The Big Punch (W)   Fox

The Freeze-out

The Wallop

Desperate Trails

Action

Sure Fire

Jackie   Fox

1922
Nero (2—uncredited)

Little Miss Smiles

Silver Wings (Co-directed with Edwin Carewe)

The Village Blacksmith

1923
The Face on the Barroom Floor

Three Jumps Ahead (W)

Cameo Kirby

North of Hudson Bay

Hoodman Blind

1924
The Iron Horse (P)

Hearts of Oak

1925
Lightnin'

Kentucky Pride

The Fighting Heart

Thank You

1926
The Shamrock Handicap

3 Bad Men (W)

The Blue Eagle

1927
Upstream

7th Heaven (2—uncredited)

What Price Glory (2—uncredited)

1928
Mother Machree

Four Sons

Hangman's House

Napoleon's Barber (First talkie)

Riley the Cop

1929
Strong Boy

The Black Watch (Co-directed with Lumsden Hare)

Salute

Big Time (A only)

1930
Men Without Women (W—original story)

Born Reckless

Up the River (W—uncredited)

1931

Seas Beneath	Fox
The Brat	Fox
Arrowsmith	Goldwyn/United Artists

1932

Air Mail	Universal
Flesh	MGM

1933

Pilgrimage	Fox
Doctor Bull	Fox

1934

The Lost Patrol	RKO Radio
The World Moves On	Fox
Judge Priest	Fox

1935

The Whole Town's Talking	Columbia
The Informer	RKO Radio
Steamboat 'Round the Bend	Fox

1936

The Prisoner of Shark Island	Fox
The Last Outlaw (W only—story)	RKO Radio
Mary of Scotland	RKO Radio
The Plough and the Stars	RKO Radio

1937

Wee Willie Winkie	20th Century-Fox
The Hurricane	Goldwyn/United Artists

1938

The Adventures of Marco Polo (2—uncredited)	Goldwyn/United Artists
Four Men and a Prayer	20th Century-Fox
Submarine Patrol	20th Century-Fox

1939

Stagecoach (P)	Wanger/United Artists
Young Mr. Lincoln	20th Century-Fox
Drums Along the Mohawk	20th Century-Fox

1940

The Grapes of Wrath   20th Century-Fox

The Long Voyage Home   Wanger/United Artists

1941

Tobacco Road   20th Century-Fox

Sex Hygiene   U.S. Army/Audio
                                       Productions

How Green Was My Valley   20th Century-Fox

1942

Torpedo Squadron   U.S. Navy

The Battle of Midway (Co-C,E,P)   U.S. Navy/20th
                                       Century-Fox

1943

December 7th (Co-directed with Gregg Toland) U.S. Navy

We Sail at Midnight   U.S. Navy

1945

They Were Expendable (P)   MGM

1946

My Darling Clementine   20th Century-Fox

1947

The Fugitive   Argosy/RKO Radio

1948

Fort Apache   Argosy/RKO Radio

3 Godfathers   Argosy/MGM

1949

Mighty Joe Young (P only)   Argosy/RKO Radio

She Wore a Yellow Ribbon   Argosy/RKO Radio

1950

When Willie Comes Marching Home   20th Century-Fox

Wagon Master   Argosy/RKO Radio

Rio Grande   Argosy/Republic

1951

This Is Korea!   U.S. Navy/Republic

The Bullfighter and the Lady (Uncredited editor) Republic

1952

What Price Glory	20th Century-Fox
The Quiet Man	Argosy/Republic

1953

The Sun Shines Bright	Argosy/Republic
Mogambo	MGM
Hondo (2—uncredited)	Wayne-Fellows/Warner Bros.

1955

The Long Gray Line	Roth Productions/ Columbia
The Red, White and Blue Line	U.S. Treasury Dept./ Columbia
Mister Roberts (Co-directed with Mervyn Leroy)	Orange/Warner Bros.

1956

The Searchers	C. V. Whitney/Warner Bros.

1957

The Wings of Eagles	MGM
The Growler Story	U.S. Navy
The Rising of the Moon	Four Provinces/Warner Bros.

1958

The Last Hurrah (P)	Columbia

1959

Gideon of Scotland Yard	Columbia
Korea: Battleground for Liberty	Dept. of Defense
The Horse Soldiers	Mirisch/United Artists

1960

Sergeant Rutledge	Ford Productions/ Warner Bros.
The Alamo (2—uncredited)	Batjac/United Artists

1961

Two Rode Together (P)	Columbia

1962

The Man Who Shot Liberty Valance (P)   Paramount

How the West Was Won (The Civil War)   MGM/Cinerama

1963

Donovan's Reef (P)   Paramount

1964

Cheyenne Autumn   Warner Bros.

1965

Young Cassidy (Co-directed with Jack Cardiff)   MGM

1966

7 Women   MGM

1970

Chesty: A Tribute to a Legend   James Ellworth Prod.
(released in 1976)

1971

Vietnam! Vietnam! (EX)   USIA

Directed by John Ford (A only)   AFI

John Ford: Memorial Day 1970 (A only, unreleased)

TV FILMOGRAPHY

1955

"The Bamboo Cross"   Lewman Ltd./Revue

"Rookie of the Year" *(Screen Directors Playhouse)*   Hal Roach Studios

1960

"The Colter Craven Story" *(Wagon Train)*   Revue

1962

"Flashing Spikes"   Avista/Revue

1971

The American West of John Ford (A only)   CBS-TV

1973

The American Film Institute Salute   AFI/CBS-TV
to John Ford (A only)

SOURCES

The Internet Movie Database

The American Film Institute Catalog of Feature Films: 1911–1920 and 1921–1930

The Motion Picture Guide

John Ford (revised edition) by Peter Bogdanovich

John Ford (Biblioteca Española)

SOURCE NOTES

The John Ford papers, the primary archive of Ford material, are at the Lilly Library at Indiana University in Bloomington. Other major archives I have drawn on include the Argosy Corporation files at Brigham Young University (BYU) in Provo, Utah, the Merian Cooper papers at the same institution, the Museum of Modern Art (MOMA) in New York, the Academy of Motion Picture Arts and Sciences (AMPAS) in Los Angeles, the Fox Legal Files at UCLA, as well as the Department of Special Collections at the University of Southern California (USC) and the Southern Methodist University (SMU) Oral History Program.

Whenever possible I have cited specific files, but the Argosy papers have been completely reorganized since I examined them. Likewise, the Ford papers have recently seen the welcome addition of Ford's naval records, which I examined before they were catalogued.

PROLOGUE

1   *On the boat:* John Gillett to S.E.
1   *"Come in, come in":* Derek Malcolm, London *Guardian*, 8-29-97.
1   *The critic soon disposed of:* John Gillett to S.E.
3   *"The first thing":* Winston Miller oral history, SMU.
3   *"I deny it":* George Mitchell, "Ford on Ford," *Films in Review*, June/July 1964, p. 322.
4   *he had worked as a cowboy:* Mark Haggard, "Ford in Person," *Focus on Film*, Spring 1971, p. 37.
4   *"I was born in a pub":* Mary Lou Whitney to S.E.
4   *"He told so many":* Robert Parrish to S.E.
4   *He told screenwriter:* Joel Sayre, "John Ford, 1895–1973," *Washington Post*, 9-23-73.
5   *"Give me the script":* "John Ford Smokes a Thoughtful Pipe," *New York Times*, 10-6-41.
5   *"I've never known":* Robert Parrish to S.E.
5   *"He knows the birthplace":* "John Ford Smokes a Thoughtful Pipe."

6 *"He cried more than he roared"*: John Ireland oral history, SMU.

6 *He regularly employed a wardrobeman*: Harry Carey Jr. to S.E.

7 *"Behind every assertion of God and Motherhood"*: Geoffrey O'Brien, *Village Voice*, 10-21-86, p. 43.

PART ONE: FROM MAINE TO HOLLYWOOD
CHAPTER 1

11 *"His father was a lobsterman"*: Ollie Carey interview, Box 11, Folder 19, Lilly.

13 *in the long aftermath*: Gray, p. 87.

13 *By 1851*: Gray, p. 95.

13 *John Feeney was born*: New England Naturalization Petitions, Microfilm M1299, Soundex Index, National Archives, Washington, D.C.

13 *"would gladly embrace"*: Miller, p. 399.

14 *It was a farewell party*: Miller and Wagner, pp. 85–86.

14 *John Feeney arrived*: Miller, p. 347.

14 *They were laborers*: Miller, p. 352.

14 *Because of the volume*: Miller, p. 355.

15 *Of these children*: Gallagher, p. 3.

15 *eight years after his arrival*: New England Naturalization Petitions, Microfilm M1299, Soundex Index, National Archives, Washington, D.C.

16 *"He would tell about"*: Bogdanovich, pp. 54–55.

16 *There would be a persistent*: Frank Nugent, "Hollywood's Favorite Rebel," *Saturday Evening Post*, 7-23-49, John Ford file, MOMA.

16 *there was a Michael Connolly*: Records of Volunteer Union Soldiers, Record Group 94, National Archives, Washington, D.C.

17 *On the Confederate side*: Records of Confederate Soldiers, Record Group 109, National Archives, as well as Consolidated Index to Compiled Service Records of Confederate Soldiers, Microfilm M253, National Archives, Washington, D.C.

18 *The Gem Theater*: Sargent, p. 75.

18 *In 1880, the year he was naturalized*: 10th census of the United States (1880) for Cumberland County, Maine, Microfilm 479, National Archives, Washington, D.C.

18 *"Mr. Feeney had a barroom"*: Mary Corcoran to S.E.

18 *"They couldn't always read and write"*: Don MacWilliams to S.E.

18 *there was a family legend*: Box 11, Folder 23, Lilly.

19 *The Portland city directories*: Sinclair, p. 6.

CHAPTER 2

20 *As late as World War II*: Don MacWilliams to S.E.

20 *The modest amounts*: Box 11, Folder 29, Lilly.

20 *"Uncle Jack tried to learn it"*: Mary McPhillips to S.E.

21 *The house on 1st Street*: Dan Ford to S.E.

21 *"We grew everything"*: Davis, p. 24. This and all subsequent references from Davis are taken from *John Ford: Hollywood's Old Master*.

21 *He had to lie in bed for months*: Ford's childhood diphtheria is attested to by his Navy physical of 10-10-41, in his files at Lilly.

21 *He would replicate the experience*: Ford, p. 7.

21 *"He seemed about as unintellectual"*: Davis, p. 27.

21   *"Every time you'd see him"*: Davis, p. 27.

22   *"At the school proms"*: Untitled manuscript, Box 1, Folder 52, Lilly.

22   *"When he was growing up"*: Box 11, Folder 29, Lilly.

22   *Intellectually, Ford was stimulated by*: Box 11, Folder 29, Lilly.

22   *His report card*: Box 1, Folder 1, Lilly.

22   *"I was a good student"*: Box 12, Folder 2, Lilly.

22   *The year after that*: Sheridan Street remains proudly working-class even today, with kids on Rollerblades, men working on their cars, dogs sunbathing. John Feeney and his son would recognize their old house and neighborhood immediately.

22   *Jack usually shared a room*: Davis, p. 21.

23   *"I am of the proletariat"*: George Mitchell, "Ford on Ford," *Films in Review*, June/July 1964, p. 323.

23   *"A woman was sitting halfway back"*: Hedda Hopper, "Ford Keeps Ahead of Young Producers," *Los Angeles Times*, 5-8-62, AMPAS.

24   *He was shy of girls*: Box 11, Folder 23, Lilly.

24   *In a 1950 letter*: John Ford to Bud Cornish, 9-29-50, Box 2, Folder 15, Lilly.

24   *he took out an insurance policy*: Box 1, Folder 1, Lilly.

24   *Every night before dinner*: Box 11, Folder 29, Lilly.

24   *She wouldn't allow Jack*: Box 11, Folder 29, Lilly.

25   *"One word from her"*: Davis, p. 21.

25   *Although it has been reported*: In Gallagher, *John Ford*, p. 2.

25   *Joseph McDonnell, a friend*: Quoted in James Wilkinson, "An Introduction to the Career and Films of John Ford."

25   *he soon won the nickname*: Boyle, p. 38.

25   *The diary of a girl*: In the collection of Peter Gribbin, Portland, Maine.

26   *When it came time*: Peter Gribbin to S.E.

26   *He kept moving*: Robert Birchard, "The Adventures of Francis Ford and Grace Cunard," *American Cinematographer*, July 1993, p. 77, Francis Ford file, MOMA.

26   *Frank seems to have been hired*: Steven Higgins, "The Films of Thomas H. Ince," *Griffithiana*, October 1984.

26   *San Antonio papers*: Frank Thompson to S.E.

27   *that the* Moving Picture World: Quoted in George Pratt, "See Mr. Ince," in Deutelbaum, p. 84.

27   *"Ince had a great influence on films"*: Unsourced clipping, Thomas Ince file, MOMA.

28   *Ince preferred the term "choleric"*: Tuska, p. 26.

28   *A trade paper noted*: Unsourced clipping headlined "Life Stories of the Movie Stars," Francis Ford file, MOMA.

28   *In a 1915 article*: Quoted in George Katchmer, "A Prolific Man: Francis Ford," *Classic Images* 109, Francis Ford file, MOMA.

29   *Within a few years*: Unsourced clipping headlined "Francis Ford: A Director with Heart," Francis Ford file, MOMA.

29   *Frank had a yen for far-off places*: Unsourced clippings in Francis Ford file, MOMA.

29   *On the set, Frank worked*: quoted in Katchmer, "A Prolific Man."

30   *There is a slim chance*: S.E. conversation with University of Maine registrar's office, 10-23-98.

31 *"He remembered his family and friends":* Mary Corcoran to S.E.
31 *in the November 1914 issue:* In the collection of Peter Gribben, Portland, Maine.

PART TWO: LEARNING A CRAFT
CHAPTER 3

35 *"I hope I didn't make a mistake":* Tuska, pp. 66–67.
35 *For entertainment, a group:* Grover Jones, "Magic Lantern," *Saturday Evening Post,* 11-14-36, p. 38, AMPAS.
36 *He was promptly expelled:* Cork Millner, *Santa Barbara Celebrities,* p. 117.
36 *"It was hard to get him":* Harry Carey Jr. to S.E.
36 *Toward the end of her life:* Rosenberg and Silverstein, p. 218.
36 *in June of 1916:* Box 1, Folder 1, Lilly.
37 *slightly more than the monthly rent:* Box 1, Folder 1, Lilly.
37 *"He brought a very strange language":* Grover Jones, "Magic Lantern," p. 40.
37 *"Yeah, a sissy:"* Grady Johnson, "John Ford, Maker of Stars," *Coronet,* December 1953.
37 *"a hell of a smart cookie":* Lefty Hough interview, Box 12, Folder 6, Lilly.
37 *"Those were great days":* Untitled manuscript, Box 1, Folder 56, Lilly.
37 *"I had to drive over":* Axel Madsen, "John Ford: American," *Chaplin* 6, 1973, John Ford file, MOMA.
38 *"put him in the hospital":* Lefty Hough to Kevin Brownlow, Brownlow archives.
38 *Backing up stories:* Robert Birchard, "The Adventures of Francis Ford and Grace Cunard," *American Cinematographer,* July 1993, p. 80.
38 *Nearly twenty years later:* Frank Nugent, "Hollywood's Favorite Rebel," *Saturday Evening Post,* 7-23-49, John Ford file, MOMA. There's another anecdote which makes the same point. In the late 1940s, Ford bought a small boat with red leather seats. John Wayne accidentally burned the seats by carelessly handling a cigar. Ford didn't say a word. Years later, Wayne had a new home in Encino and outfitted his projection room with customized furniture. One night he and Ford were watching a movie. When the lights came up, Ford had burned a huge hole in the middle of a new sofa with his cigar. "We're even," he said to Wayne, who immediately realized what he was referring to. (Kennedy, pp. 21–22.)
38 *"all hell broke loose":* Lefty Hough to Kevin Brownlow, Brownlow archives.
38 *From the vantage point:* Quoted in Gallagher, "Brother Feeney," *Film Comment,* November/December 1976, p. 18.
38 *"The showing of those early pictures":* John Ford, "Veteran Producer Muses."
39 *By 1920, he owned his own home:* 14th census of the United States (1920) for Cumberland County, Maine, Microfilm 639, National Archives, Washington, D.C.
39 *"Jack Ford was his brother's":* Bruskin, pp. 45–46.
40 *in September 1916:* Box 1, Folder 1, Lilly.
40 *He preserved a dismissal letter:* Box 1, Folder 2, Lilly.
40 *for that same month:* Box 1, Folder 2, Lilly.
40 *"There wasn't any":* Box 11, Folder 26, Lilly.
41 *Ford improvised some:* George Mitchell, "Ford on Ford," *Films in Review,* June/July 1964, p. 327.

41 *"Harry had done a picture":* Ollie Carey to Kevin Brownlow, Brownlow archives.
41 *But Universal cut back:* Robert Birchard to S.E.
41 *"He had a magnificent":* Ollie Carey to Brownlow.
42 *"Buck the Scrapper":* Fenin and Everson, p. 129.
42 Moving Picture World: Gallagher, p. 17.
43 *"They weren't shoot-em-ups":* Bogdanovich, p. 39.
43 *For a time:* Sinclair, p. 23.
43 *"I learned a great deal from Harry":* Untitled manuscript, Box 1, Folder 52, Lilly.
43 *a very coquettish girl:* Box 1, Folder 3, Lilly.
44 *"Harry Carey taught me how":* Jack Hively to S.E.
44 *He was not completely impervious:* Box 20, Folder 1, Lilly.
44 *"the old crowd seems pretty much":* Ford, p. 15.
45 *A July 16, 1917, memo:* Box 1, Folder 2, Lilly.
45 *rather than invest:* Bogdanovich, p. 40
45 *"Every once in a while":* William Sistrom to Ford, 3-22-19, Box 1, Folder 4, Lilly.
46 *"He was a great cameraman":* Bogdanovich, p. 40.
47 *"If I order a suit of clothes":* Bogdanovich, p. 43.
47 *he kept the August 18:* It should be noted that Ford's professed disinterest in what others said about his films was utterly phony. He had copies of all the major articles written about him, and many of them carry underlining, check marks, and the occasional question mark that clearly show he read them. He was, moreover, touchy about criticism. "Why do you keep harping on how I was criticized for this and for that," he once snapped at his grandson when he was researching his biography. "You're not writing a story of criticism, for Chrissakes."
47 *"Jack Ford again demonstrates":* quoted in Anderson, p. 191.
48 *The* Universal Weekly *wrote:* Quoted in Gallagher, "Brother Feeney," p. 18.

CHAPTER 4
49 *Frank's films for Universal:* Kevin Brownlow letter to S.E., 7-15-96.
49 *an efficiency expert:* Unsourced clipping dated 4-16-16, Francis Ford file, MOMA.
50 *"Francis scattered himself":* Dan Ford to S.E.
50 *the* New York Times *reviewed:* Sarris, *John Ford*, p. 16.
51 *the* Motion Picture News *was writing:* 10-25-19, John Ford file, AMPAS.
51 *the* Moving Picture World *proclaimed:* Clipping dated 5-24-19, John Ford file, AMPAS.
51 *H. Bruce Humberstone would:* Tuska, p. 75.
51 *Hoot Gibson was once:* Tuska, pp. 75–76.
52 *"Are you licked?":* Harry Carey to Ford, 2-28-19, Box 1, Folder 4, Lilly.
53 *One day Carl Laemmle:* Peter Stone to S.E.
53 *"Ford was making":* Dan Ford to S.E.
53 *shared a room with:* Mary Ford to Anthony Slide, Slide archives.
53 *One of her ancestors:* Roper genealogy, Dan Ford collection.
53 *When he died in Paris:* Dan Ford to S.E.
54 *"We met that night":* Mary Ford to Anthony Slide, Slide archives.

54   *"I had never heard about"*: Mary Ford to Slide.

54   *"an extraordinary woman"*: Dan Ford to S.E.

54   *Irving Thalberg and William K. Howard:* Sinclair, p. 29.

55   *"I am sorry to say"*: John Ford to Mary Ford, undated, Box 1, Folder 7, Lilly.

56   *"Jack—My old sweetheart"*: Mary Ford to John Ford, provisionally dated 1921, Box 1, Folder 7, Lilly.

56   *Martin Feeney would assert:* Ford, p. 24.

56   *One of his early biographers:* Sinclair, p. 31.

57   *On board the* Olympic: Mary Ford to John Ford, Box 1, Folder 7, Lilly.

57   *"He said he only married"*: Gallagher, p. 27.

57   *"I sure miss you and Pat"*: John Ford to Mary Ford, 12-21, Box 1, Folder 7, Lilly.

58   *Barbara was attending:* Davis, p. 51.

58   *"They were producing"*: John Weld to S.E. All Weld quotes derive from this interview.

59   *"For all the artifice"*: Anderson, p. 39.

59   *The critics noticed: Motion Picture News,* 11-27-20, John Ford file, AMPAS.

59   *And William Fox noticed:* William Fox to Sol Wurtzel, 1-19-21, Lillian Semenov collection.

60   *Sheehan took a surprisingly personal:* Tuska, pp. 142–43.

60   *"I am enthusiastic and confident"*: Winfield Sheehan to William Fox, 11-15-21, Box 1, Folder 7, Lilly.

61   *Screenwriter Paul Sloane:* Fritz Guttinger, "John Ford's Lost Classic," *Classic Film Collector* 56, Fall 1977, p. 54.

61   *"Tho it starts out very interesting"*: Undated letter, Box 1, Folder 7, Lilly.

61   *"I propose building several"*: John Ford to Winfield Sheehan, 3-3-22, Box 1, Folder 8, Lilly.

CHAPTER 5

64   *George O'Brien was born:* Background from letters and conversations with the late Darcy O'Brien.

65   *"It may be theatrical"*: Leonard Maltin, "George O'Brien," *Film Fan Monthly,* May 1971.

66   *"We spent a week"*: George Schneiderman, "Preparing to Film *The Iron Horse,*" *American Cinematographer,* March 1925, p. 5.

66   *"We went up there prepared"*: Anderson, p. 20.

66   *"I said to George"*: George Mitchell, "Ford on Ford."

66   *"It was winter"*: Winston Miller to John Gallagher, Gallagher collection.

66   *As propman:* Lefty Hough to Kevin Brownlow, Brownlow archives.

67   *In Dodge, the crew:* Schneiderman, "Preparing to Film," pp. 5–6.

67   *"People ask me about"*: Bellamy, p. 58.

67   *"Received first day's work"*: Sol Wurtzel to Ford, 1-11-24, *Iron Horse* file, Lilly.

68   *"Ford heard I had a couple of bottles"*: On April 23, 1923, Ford signed a pledge of abstention written out for him by a priest at the Church of the Blessed Sacrament in Hollywood. (Box 1, Folder 8, Lilly.) That he kept the pledge in his files, so it could remind him of his continuing failure to honor it, is a plaintive indication of Ford's ability to punish himself. Although his friend Emmett Flynn would be destroyed by his addiction, Ford managed the delicate high-wire act of being a periodic alcoholic sufficiently able to control his bouts so that they rarely affected his work.

69 *"This goes back to the days"*: Gallagher, p. 31. There is a lovely, heartless anecdote deriving from screenwriter Joel Sayre that one can only hope is true.
It seems that Ford was overdue for a binge and a producer told Eddie to
keep a weather eye on him. One day a telegram fell out of Jack's pocket.
Eddie picked it up and read that their mother had died. Shocked, Eddie
rushed to Jack, who sorrowfully told him he'd been contemplating how to
tell his brother. The two men knocked off and spent the rest of the day and
night drinking. The next morning, Eddie phoned home to make the funeral
arrangements. His mother answered the phone. (Sayre, "John Ford, 1895–
1973," *Washington Post*, 9-23-73.)

71 *The company newspaper: Fox Folks Junior,* 1-5-24, Lilly.

71 *"We stood watching"*: Davis, p. 55.

72 *"He's Not a Sheik"*: Fenin and Everson, p. 141.

72 *In Los Angeles*: Beardsley, pp. 93–94.

73 *a brutally cynical capitalism:* Men like Collis Huntington and Leland Stanford
first received land grants from the government, then developed and sold the
lands, taking the proceeds for themselves. They formed private corporations
that overbilled the government-financed railroad company and skimmed
money into their own private companies. Because of this scam, the Union
Pacific was essentially broke by the time the railroad was completed in 1869.
They weren't called robber barons for nothing.

74 *Ford auditioned musicians:* Peter Bogdanovich, "The Autumn of John Ford,"
Esquire, April 1964.

75 *In March 1925: Variety*, 3-4-25, p. 27.

76 *Bessie Love, a veteran:* Love, p. 85.

78 *The* Motion Picture News: Undated clipping, John Ford file, AMPAS.

79 *Although Stone always liked:* Peter Stone (John Stone's son) to S.E. Sol Wurtzel was not exactly an adored figure around the studio. Once, a writer named
Edward Lowe was looking at dailies, when Wurtzel made a suggestion. "That
would be redundant," said Lowe. Wurtzel left the screening and went to the
studio barber shop and got a shave, which he did whenever he was annoyed.
When he got back to his office, he called John Stone and asked what "redundant" meant. When Stone told him, Wurtzel said, "Why didn't the son of a
bitch say that? Fire him." Of course, Wurtzel was also Jewish, which rather
negated Stone's vague suspicions of Ford's anti-Semitism. Wurtzel was an
entertaining—from a distance—paradox, an archetypal penny-pinching,
cigar-chomping producer who raised millions for his temple, offered William Fox his life savings when he was pushed out of his studio, and commis-
sioned a mural for his house that depicted his family in medieval dress, with
Wurtzel himself clad in doublet, hose, and big black cigar. (Gehman, p. 58.)

79 *"When John Ford set as his"*: Fox Folks, January 1926, p. 19, Fox studio archives.

80 *a framing device: Three Bad Men* script file, UCLA.

80 *As Roger Greenspun would write:* Greenspun, "Lessons of the Master I," *Soho
Weekly News*, 8-28-75, John Ford file, MOMA.

80 *Even Variety said: Variety*, 8-18-26.

82 *Ford was earning:* Koszarski, pp. 212–13.

82 *"I could see no relationship"*: Clarke, p. 77.

CHAPTER 6

83   *He asserted that:* Variety, "Inside Stuff" column, 4-14-26.

83   *he came in for some:* Vidor, p. 93.

83   *"When we were children":* Pat Ford interview with James D'Arc, BYU.

84   *Another frequent visitor:* Anobile, p. 7.

84   *"I was too young":* Pat Ford interview with D'Arc.

84   *Once he grabbed a megaphone:* Bellamy, p. 58.

85   *"Another wop":* Box 11, Folder 32, Lilly.

85   *Also becoming part:* Unpublished memoirs of Brian Desmond Hurst, Chapter 4, Anthony Slide collection.

85   *A typically plain-spoken:* Frank Baker interview with Anthony Slide and Robert Gitt, 7-30-77, Slide archives.

86   *Once, visiting him:* Box 11, Folder 23, Lilly.

87   *For Christmas 1926:* Box 1, Folder 9, Lilly.

87   *Ford wrote a waggish:* John Ford to Mary Ford, undated, Box 1, Folder 7, Lilly. A more important document was the will Ford signed on February 9, 1927, fancifully asserting that his real name was John Martin St. Augustine Feeney, "sometimes known as Jack or John Ford, picture director. . . ." He left everything to Mary, and enjoined her to tend to the health and happiness of his parents. To the children's godparents, Emmett Flynn and Ford's sister Josie, he instructed them to make sure that Pat and Barbara were brought up as Roman Catholics. As executor he appointed Sol Wurtzel. (Box 1, Folder 10, Lilly.)

87   *"Harry was a very nice fellow":* Lester Ziffren to S.E.

88   *she grew to adore:* Mary Ford interview, Box 11, Folder 35, Lilly.

88   *The big-hearted Mix:* Mary Ford to Anthony Slide.

88   *"We had more fun":* Sinclair, p. 29.

88   *"There really should be":* Mary Ford to Anthony Slide.

88   *Mary had learned:* Dan Ford to S.E.

89   *"He loved me and he":* Mary Ford interview, Box 11, Folder 35, Lilly.

89   *Priscilla Bonner had grown:* Priscilla Bonner to James Curtis.

89   *"Jack would go upstairs":* Mary Ford to Anthony Slide, Slide archives.

90   *"He was not a drunkard":* John Wayne interview, Box 12, Folder 17, Lilly.

90   *"Stars apart":* William K. Everson, *Films in Review*, December 1974, p. 602.

90   *On February 20, 1927:* Box 1, Folder 10, Lilly.

90   *To William Fox:* Eyman, pp. 158–59.

90   *He told the press:* Moving Picture World, 3-3-27, p. 35.

90   *As part of an overall:* Fox Folks, December 1926, p. 20, Fox studio archives.

92   *According to an item:* "Keeping Films from Error," New York Times, 5-20-28.

92   Variety *called Four Sons:* Variety, 2-15-28, p. 26.

93   *Ford enjoyed needling:* Clarke, p. 83.

93   *Astonished and delighted:* Clarke, p. 83.

93   *"Jack kicked me":* Peter Bogdanovich, "The Duke's Gone West," New York, 6-25-79, p. 68.

94   *"I liked Duke's style":* Davis, Duke, p. 35.

94   *"I really had no intention":* Bogdanovich, "The Duke's Gone West," p. 69.

94   *"I am certain that":* Quoted in Slide, pp. 78–79.

95   *In June 1928:* John Ford, "Veteran Producer Muses," New York Times, 6-10-28.

PART THREE: MASTERING AN ART
CHAPTER 7

99 *"I am up to my neck"*: Liam O'Flaherty, 6-28-24, Kelly, p. 95.

101 *"We were lucky"*: Sinclair, p. 42.

101 *Actually, Ford wrote off:* Gallagher, p. 74.

101 *"I don't think"*: Robert Stephens to S.E.

101 *Frank Baker remembered:* Gallagher, pp. 40–41.

102 *"Fox may not make"*: Gehman, p. 1.

104 *"Winfield Sheehan . . . thought"*: Bogdanovich, p. 50.

104 *After the film was finished:* Loy, p. 58.

104 *One evening in Annapolis:* Davis, p. 65.

105 *"What impressed me"*: Swindell, pp. 74–75.

105 *Sitting at an adjacent:* Swindell, p. 76.

105 *"Spence was as"*: Swindell, p. 83.

106 *It would be several:* Bogdanovich, "The Duke's Gone West," p. 69.

108 *"We had a scene"*: Bogdanovich, p. 53.

108 *she had always regarded:* Ford, p. 57.

109 *George was carrying:* Darcy O'Brien collection.

109 *"Worst storm in 3 years"*: George O'Brien's diary courtesy of the late Darcy O'Brien.

109 *"We've had ten days"*: John Ford to Mary Ford, 1-31, Box 1, Folder 13, Lilly.

111 *The two men arrived:* Clippings dated 4-9 and 4-11, 1931, in *Los Angeles Examiner* John Ford clipping file, USC Department of Special Collections.

112 *Just before Thanksgiving:* Pat Ford to his parents, 11-20-31, Box 1, Folder 14, Lilly.

112 *Around this time:* Brian Desmond Hurst, Chapter 4, unpublished autobiography, Anthony Slide archives.

CHAPTER 8

114 *Goldwyn borrowed Ford:* Goldwyn contract, John Ford file, Fox legal files, UCLA.

115 *After a number of takes:* Brian Desmond Hurst, Unpublished Autobiography, Chapter 4, Anthony Slide archives.

115 *"Who's directing this picture"*: Davis, p. 71.

115 *"bruised and battered"*: Hornblow affidavit, John Ford file, Fox legal files, UCLA.

116 *sent Myrna Loy:* Loy, p. 67.

116 *On October 22, 1931:* Sheehan to Ford, John Ford file, Fox legal files, UCLA.

117 *In 1931, Fox lost:* Solomon, p. 13.

117 Arrowsmith *amassed domestic rentals:* Gallagher, p. 498.

117 *Ford had once again:* Harry Wurtzel to Ford, 12-10-31, Box 1, Folder 14, Lilly.

117 *"Can I have two hundred"*: Francis Ford to Ford, 11-24-31, Box 1, Folder 14, Lilly.

118 *Smith left a note:* The suicide was reported in the *Los Angeles Examiner* on January 3, 1932, John Ford file, USC Department of Special Collections.

118 *For five days:* Ford, p. 67.

118 *The children joined them:* Gallagher, p. 44.

118 *"Rain, rain, rain"*: John Ford to Mary Ford, Box 1, Folder 15, Lilly.

119 *"He was dear"*: Gloria Stuart to S.E. Stuart would have been amazed to hear a

fire-breathing speech Ford delivered in 1933 to the Directors Guild. "In the past few weeks . . . there have been more studio people fired than at any other time. Hundreds have been let go at all the studios. Directors and assistants, writers and stock players, craftsmen and officeworkers of every classification. . . . Why are so many people being let out? Stock market is going down. Business is bad. I don't believe it. Your Board of Directors doesn't believe it. President of the United States doesn't believe it. The Attorney-General's Office in Washington doesn't believe it. Their investigator, Mr. Jackson, doesn't believe it. In fact, he boldly states that the banking industry is going on a sit-down strike. Why? To bring about a financial crisis. So that wages and wage-earners can be pushed back to where they were in 1910." (Gallagher, p. 340.)

119 *"John had a handkerchief"*: Gloria Stuart to S.E.
119 *"[Ford] was mad at everybody"*: Karen Morley to S.E.
120 *Winfield Sheehan relented*: Contract dated 5-7-32, John Ford file, Fox legal files, UCLA.
121 *"I knew nothing at all"*: Merian Cooper to C. V. Whitney, 1-21-70, Cooper papers, BYU.
121 *He wrote a book*: Kevin Brownlow to S.E.
122 "There *was a fascinating man*": Fay Wray to S.E.
122 *"RKO was like"*: Jack Hively to S.E.
122 *"a little cheap picture"*: Merian Cooper letter to Lindsay Anderson, 8-25-63, Cooper papers, BYU.
123 *"within an hour"*: Cooper to Anderson.
123 *Cooper's view of America*: Gilbert Seldes, "Man with a Camera," *New Yorker*, 5-30-31.
123 *The agreement with Ford*: Merian Cooper letter to John Wayne, 3-15-71, Cooper papers, BYU.
123 *But Ford took a liking*: Robert Parrish to S.E.
125 *Ford and Hopper would*: Eels, p. 131.
125 *In Hollywood, the Association*: McBride, *Frank Capra*, pp. 284–88.
126 *When Ford checked onto*: Turner, pp. 169–74.
130 *As critic Martin Rubin noted*: In "Mr. Ford and Mr. Rogers," *Film Comment*, January/February 1974, p. 56.
131 *"Paht of the time"*: Yagoda, p. 312.
131 *"Nobody could write"*: Sterling, p. 151.
131 *"He was just"*: Sterling, p. 151.
132 *Rogers liked Ford*: Sterling, p. 149.
132 *he had the ear*: Sterling, p. 133.
132 *He fired off*: Sterling, p. 133.
132 *"We had a terrible time"*: Sinclair, p. 62.
133 *"They were like"*: Bill Libby, "The Old Wrangler Rides Again," *Cosmopolitan*, March 1964.
133 *On September 27*: Ford medical exam, Box 1, Folder 17, Lilly.
133 *"I'd like to forget that"*: Bogdanovich, p. 59.
133 *Twentieth Century, on the other hand*: Custen, p. 194.
133 *A few months after*: Solomon, p. 24.
134 *"Zanuck's whole drive"*: Roddy McDowall to S.E.
134 *Zanuck once told*: Dunne, "No Fence Around Time," in *How Green Was My Valley, the Screenplay*, Santa Teresa Press, 1990, p. 13.

134   *"He was wonderful":* Winston Miller oral history, SMU.

134   *Zanuck would come:* Behlmer, p. 172.

135   *The ship hadn't been:* Ford, p. 75.

135   *Chaplain John Brady:* Brady to Rear Admiral Tarrant, 7-27-34, Lilly.

136   *testimonial from:* Wurtzel letter, 8-29-34, Lilly.

136   *a few years later:* annual Naval Reserve fitness report, 8-10-36, Lilly.

136   *claiming six months:* officer questionnaire, 10-14-38, Lilly.

136   *to his commanding officer:* Ford, p. 76.

136   *a hilarious gag captain's log:* Davis, p. 75.

CHAPTER 9

138   *In April of 1934:* Kelly, p. 279.

138   *"I had to lock myself":* Renoir, *Letters,* p. 379.

138   *Ford had appreciated:* Thomas, *Music,* p. 115.

139   *"What was* Arrowsmith*":* Joel Sayre, "John Ford, 1895–1973," *Washington Post,* 9-23-73.

139   *"That's so wrong":* Andrew McLaglen to S.E. Andrew McLaglen would note that Ford may have been jealous of the elder McLaglen's distinguished military career. He had been a captain in the British army, provost marshal of Baghdad, and spoke perfect Arabic. On March 10, 1909, he went six rounds with Jack Johnson just a few months after the fighter won the heavyweight championship from Tommy Burns. The Johnson-McLaglen fight, which took place in Vancouver, was originally billed as a title fight but it seems to have turned into an exhibition to provide Johnson with some spending money. McLaglen was a last-minute replacement for one Denver Ed Smith, and was promoted as an "Irish soldier" fighting out of Tacoma. Although McLaglen would say that "He never knocked me down, lad, but he sure beat the livin' be-Jesus out of me," he was knocked down once, in the first round. After that, Johnson may have carried him.

139   *"There is an axiom":* Steen, p. 60.

139   *"Mr. Ford and I":* Gil Perkins to S.E.

140   *Once again, Ford was using:* Robert Parrish to S.E.

141   *Ford adored Kerrigan:* Sayre, "John Ford."

141   *"I was excited":* Jack Hively to S.E.

142   *"The crew knew":* Robert Parrish to S.E.

142   *When Margot Grahame:* Parrish, pp. 132–33.

142   *As Patrick Ford:* Patrick Ford to James D'Arc, BYU.

142   *Ford and Nichols:* Anderson, p. 240.

143   *As an example:* Bardeche and Brasillach, p. 316.

143   *"its style was thought":* Sarris, *John Ford,* p. 68.

144   *Max Steiner's score:* Some of that might be because Steiner was in a mad competition with an onrushing release date and didn't have time for subtlety. According to Steiner's wife, a harpist who played in studio orchestras, the hymn that closes the picture was chosen only the night before the scoring session. (Louise Steiner Elian to S.E.)

144   *It also gave him:* Kelly, p. 406.

144   *He wrote him:* Liam O'Flaherty to Ford, 6-3-35, Box 1, Folder 18, Lilly. *Famine* is not a particularly good novel, but, given its subject—the potato famine of 1846—it's not hard to imagine Ford contributing some ideas on structure, as well as some dialogue that echoes that in some of his films: " 'Robbers!' he

cried, as he shook his upraised fist at the convoy. 'Ye are taking the people's harvest out of the country. Ye are stealing our corn and we dying of hunger. We are laid low now but we will rise again. We'll crush the tyrants that suck our blood. The people will rise again.' " O'Flaherty did rather well out of his year-long stay in America; while in California he met Catherine Tailer, the sister of Katharine Hepburn's good friend Laura Harding, and the woman who would serve as his mistress, helpmate, and, eventually, agent for the rest of his life.

145 *His income followed suit:* Gallagher, p. 498.
145 *"There's nothing surprising":* Emanuel Eisenberg, "John Ford: Fighting Irish," *New Theater,* April 1936.
146 *The* Photoplay *interview:* Howard Sharpe, "The Star Creators of Hollywood," *Photoplay,* October 1936.
146 *In 1935: Portland Express,* 1-31-48. This story was not told by Ford, but by Donahue, who swore it was authentic.
147 *"The legend about":* Jack Hively to S.E.
147 *"shot a lot of film":* Rudi Fehr to S.E.
147 *In June of 1938:* Rosten, p. 246.
147 *"Ford was a peculiar man":* John Carradine to S.E.
148 *"It was an absolutely":* Gloria Stuart to S.E.
148 *as Richard Corliss:* Corliss, p. 179.
148 *"Are you threatening me?":* Johnson, p. 64.
149 *After some years:* Thomas Wood, "Sly Device Man," unpublished manuscript, John Ford file, AMPAS.
149 *Gloria Stuart noticed:* Gloria Stuart to S.E.

CHAPTER 10
150 *they elected to spend:* Dan Ford to S.E.
150 *Barbara wrote Ford:* Barbara Ford to Ford, Box 1, Folder 18, Lilly.
150 *Frank Capra told a:* Capra, p. 146.
150 *He became well known:* Ford, p. 109.
151 *One day in the summer:* Roberts and Olson, pp. 117–18.
151 *But when the gatherings:* Ford, p. 116.
151 *"He was very taut":* Lester Ziffren to S.E.
152 *Ford told Hepburn: Motion Picture,* October 1936, p. 62, John Ford file, MOMA.
153 *She always said:* Joan Kramer to S.E.
153 *"That's nonsense":* Quoted in Rush and Molloy column, *New York Daily News,* 4-12-95.
153 *"an intellectual friendship":* Mary McLean MacDonald to Betty Prashker, 3-22-95, Dan Ford collection.
153 *was insistent that:* O. Z. Whitehead letter to S.E.
153 *Hepburn turned mysteriously coy:* Hepburn, p. 235.
154 *"She would have lied":* Selden West to S.E.
154 *"She was too lusty":* Budd Boetticher to S.E.
154 *In later years:* A. Scott Berg to S.E.
154 *Hepburn wrote Ford:* Katharine Hepburn to Ford, 6-22-36 (Box 1, Folder 18), 3-1-37 (Box 1, Folder 19), 4-10-37 (Box 1, Folder 19), 7-38, 8-15-38, and 4-39 (Box 1, Folder 20), Lilly.

155 *There is a jocular letter:* John Ford to Hepburn, 1-16-37, Box 1, Folder 19, Lilly.

156 *"I thought he was":* Hepburn, p. 236.

156 *According to a letter:* Box 1, Folder 20, Lilly.

157 *there had been:* Sinclair, p. 38.

157 *Cecile de Prita:* Box 11, Folder 23, Lilly.

157 *John Wayne would tell his third wife:* Wayne, p. 57.

158 *"They both would have":* Peter Bogdanovich, "The Cowboy Hero and the American West," *Esquire,* December 1983, p. 420, John Ford file, MOMA.

158 *MGM had agreed:* Selden West to S.E.

159 *he wrote a fascinating:* John Ford to O'Casey, 1-27-36, Robert Sisk Collection, USC. I am indebted to Ned Comstock for calling this letter to my attention, and for much else besides.

160 The Plough and the Stars *is a send-up:* Darcy O'Brien letter to S.E.

160 *O'Casey responded:* Krause, vol. 1, pp. 617–18.

161 *In a letter the same day:* Krause, Vol. 1, pp. 618–19.

161 *Bonita Granville:* Granville oral history, SMU.

162 *"They felt the":* Eileen Crowe to Anthony Slide, Slide archives.

162 *Sam Briskin tried:* Quoted in Jewell, *A History of RKO,* p. 388.

162 *As James Agate wrote:* Quoted in Slide, p. 82.

162 *"I could have wept":* Eileen Crowe to Slide.

163 *he would suggest him:* John Ford to O'Neill, 12-12-40, Box 1, Folder 25, Lilly.

164 *Wurtzel's operation:* Peter Stone to S.E.

164 *"I feel the only way":* Custen, p. 213.

165 *The childish coquetry:* Black, p. 171.

165 *The turning point:* Black, p. 175.

165 *"Ford came over":* Black, p. 179.

165 *"Shirley was actually":* Cesar Romero to S.E.

166 *Ford had also:* Berg, p. 294.

167 *"Ford wanted to":* Samuel Goldwyn Jr. to S.E.

167 *Ford strode over:* Lamour, p. 65.

167 *Later, concerned that:* Berg, p. 297.

168 *Ford shot the:* Astor, p. 134.

168 *The boy parroted:* Astor, p. 135.

168 *"I went for six days":* Ford interview, Box 11, Folder 29, Lilly.

169 *In a letter to:* John Ford to Bob Ford, tentatively dated 9-37, Box 1, Folder 19, Lilly. Among his other charities in 1937 and 1938, Ford donated a total of $800 to the American Legion Post on Peaks Island to get them out of a financial hole. "Every time I smell a fish boat . . . it reminds me of Joe Trott's motor boat and my heart goes homeward," he wrote in a note accompanying one of the checks. (Ford to American Legion, 4-23-37, original in possession of Peaks Island American Legion Post.)

170 *"Our office had":* Lester Ziffren to S.E.

170 *Riefenstahl's impression:* Leni Riefenstahl letter to S.E.

171 *Ford's enthusiasm for the left-wing:* Ford's leftward tilt at the time of the Spanish Civil War provoked the usual response from the Federal Bureau of Investigation—they opened a file on him. Ford's FBI file, obtained through the Freedom of Information Act, contains a precis, dated April 1, 1955, that notes that his films, along with those of Charlie Chaplin, had been selected

to be shown at the House of Cinema Workers in Moscow and had also been praised by the Communist Press. Among other suspicious circumstances were laudatory comments about *Young Mr. Lincoln* from Sergei Eisenstein and generally favorable reviews from *The Daily Worker.*

Included on the list of "Communist Party front groups" and other organizations Ford belonged to were the Screen Director's Guild, the War Symphony Committee ("a Communist inspired group"), the John Steinbeck Committee for Agricultural Workers ("a Communist controlled group"), and the Motion Picture Artists Committee, "Which worked to aid the red 'Loyalist Cause in Spain.' "

The FBI was especially interested in Ford's activities organizing the Director's Guild. "This effort was made by a small group of motion picture directors who professed the 'progressive' position . . . in reality the term 'progressive' meant sympathy for the Communist cause. This small group included John Ford." Unsourced, anecdotal reports in the file state that Ford was "long a fellow traveller," and a member of the Communist Party. Among the other, rather random items in the file was a report from 1947 that Ford had converted (name deleted) to Communism.

Likewise, someone at the FBI viewed Ford's documentary work during World War II with alarm. "On 2/7/42 (name deleted) addressed a confidential memorandum to (name deleted) of 'Time' (magazine) dealing with the John Ford re-enactment of Pearl Harbor." The report went on to state that "it was difficult to get information as to his plans or activities" and that "[while] Ford had no equal in making feature films . . . documentary and journalistic films should be left in the homes [*sic*] of the specialists in that field."

Aside from the absurd vagueness of much of the information, there is sloppy reporting. *The Informer* was reported as having been made in 1939 (actually 1935) for Warner Bros. (actually RKO).

A synopsis of Ford's activities dated February 18, 1943, concluded that "the activities of Ford were of a mild nature, and in all probability he is an innocent." The last items in the file are Ford's visa applications for his visits to Europe in 1960, 1964, and 1971.

171   *"I don't even"*: McGilligan, *Backstory,* p. 63.

171   *"Try the script out"*: Zanuck notes dated 12-22-36, *Submarine Patrol* script file, UCLA.

171   *a character named Quincannon:* Ford's recurring use of the name Quincannon for warm, larger-than-life father figures was a silent tribute to an old Portland friend named Tommy Quincannon, whom Ford referred to as a "grand, grand guy and a beloved friend." (John Ford to Bud Cornish, 9-29-50, Box 2, Folder 15, Lilly.)

CHAPTER 11

173   *"aroused the ire"*: Merian Cooper to Wayne, 3-15-71, Cooper archives, BYU.

174   *Ernest Haycox had published:* Buscombe, *Stagecoach,* p. 35.

174   *"You are acquainted"*: Roberts and Olson, p. 149.

175   *"He knew what"*: Zolotow, p. 147.

175   *"I'd see him"*: John Andrew Gallagher, "Claire Trevor," *Films in Review,* November 1983, p. 538.

176   *Selznick's thinking was:* Behlmer, pp. 119–20.

176   *"I didn't learn"*: Merian Cooper to Wayne, 3-15-71.

176 *"He is an excellent man"*: Behlmer, p. 121.

177 *As late as 1941:* David Selznick to O'Shea, 1-14-41, 2-25-41, Ransom Center, U. of Texas at Austin.

177 *Ford and Nichols added:* Ford also added a few things that were not in the Nichols script; the business of Luke Plummer walking back into the bar after the gunfight in the street only to collapse and die from his wounds was a Ford addition, as was the last dialogue exchange about Ringo and Dallas being "spared the blessings of civilization."

177 *"I read the story"*: Bernstein, p. 147.

178 *"I went up to"*: Michael Wayne to Leonard Maltin, Maltin archives.

178 *the script never:* Nichols's final draft helped out Ford, probably at his request, by including diagrams of the characters' placement within the stagecoach at various times in the story.

178 *the trade papers announced: Los Angeles Examiner* clipping dated 6-3-37, John Ford file, USC Department of Special Collections.

179 *The story for* The Vanishing American: Carlos Gaberscek, "The Vanishing American: Monument Valley Before Ford," *Griffithiana*, October 1989.

179 *this story was corroborated:* in videotape *The Goulding Story;* also in DenDooven, p. 35.

179 *From documents in:* Wills, p. 87.

180 *"That went over big"*: Interview in *The Goulding Story.*

181 *"Duke got his walk"*: Harry Carey Jr. to Leonard Maltin, Maltin archives.

181 *"What was different"*: Michael Wayne to Leonard Maltin, Maltin archives.

181 *"He was an expert"*: Toni La Cava to Leonard Maltin, Maltin archives.

181 *"I've seen him"*: Bert Glennon, "Photographing *Rio Grande*," *American Cinematographer*, September 1950, p. 5.

182 *"He often asked"*: Michael Wayne to Leonard Maltin, Maltin archives.

182 *Ford dashed off:* Quoted in James D'Arc, "Howard Hawks and the Great Paper Chase," *Projections* 6, 1996.

182 *Plunkett said he'd:* Bob Thomas, "The Company Remembers *Stagecoach*," *Directors in Action*, p. 168.

182 *"What are you doing"*: Thomas, "The Company Remembers."

182 *Ford shot* Stagecoach: Buscombe, *Stagecoach*, p. 9.

183 *As the film got under way:* Thomas, "The Company Remembers."

183 *Ford rode Wayne:* Gallagher, "Claire Trevor."

184 *"But when I had a"*: Bogdanovich, "The Duke's Gone West."

184 *"Just raise your"*: Roberts and Olson, p. 159.

184 *Of all the actors:* Roberts and Olson, p. 155.

184 *"My mother had"*: Quoted in Nick Clooney, *AMC Magazine*, October 1996, p. 14.

185 *"You have to run"*: Davis, *Duke*, p. 85.

185 *Ford was using:* Canutt, pp. 109–11.

186 *"It was getting late"*: Bogdanovich, pp. 70–72.

186 *At the wrap party:* Canutt, p. 114.

186 *Sound editor Walter Reynolds:* Thomas, "The Company Remembers."

187 *"I cannot tell you"*: Gallagher, "Claire Trevor."

188 *Perhaps the crux:* Roberts and Olson, p. 161.

188 *the film really belongs:* Wills, p. 81.

189 Variety *noted that:* Quoted in Lloyd, p. 27.

189 Stagecoach *added yet another:* Bodie Thoene and Rona Stuck, "Navajo Nation

Meets Hollywood," *American Way*, September/October 1983, John Ford file, MOMA.

190 *"He would analyze every"*: Michael Wayne to S.E.

CHAPTER 12

191 *He wanted to direct:* John Ford to Zanuck, 3-1-38, Box 1, Folder 20, Lilly.

191 *"one of the most magnificent"*: Behlmer, p. 16.

191 *"Naturally, this coming"*: John Ford to Dover, 10-29-38, Box 1, Folder 20, Lilly.

192 Young Mr. Lincoln *had:* Script background drawn from the UCLA script files for the film.

192 *"Who held Lincoln's hat"*: Davis, p. 106.

193 *"He cast actors"*: Henry Fonda interview, Box 11, Folder 28, Lilly.

194 *By early December 1938:* The UCLA script files contain Faulkner's treatment, dated 3-15-37, as well as Zanuck's script notes, dated 12-4-38 and 4-4-39.

195 *A new addition:* Meyer, pp. 85–87.

196 *"It's much easier"*: Bogdanovich, p. 74.

196 *Zanuck's script conference:* Contained in the UCLA script file for *The Grapes of Wrath*; Zanuck's notes are dated 7-19-39.

197 *"Their money practically gone"*: Custen, pp. 234–35.

197 *"I want complete"*: Custen, p. 233.

197 *Steinbeck loved the scene:* Dorris Bowdon Johnson to S.E.

198 *"If I were assured"*: John Ford to Zanuck, 7-13-39, Box 1, Folder 21, Lilly.

198 *"I'd read the book"*: Bogdanovich, p. 76.

198 *Most of the photos:* The research file survives in the Fox archives, the library currently located in an underground hive built as Darryl Zanuck's bomb shelter on the Fox lot. My thanks to Allan Adler for allowing me to examine this material.

199 *"I was only interested"*: George Mitchell, "Ford on Ford," *Films in Review*, June/July 1964, p. 331.

199 *Ford's main source:* Dorris Bowdon Johnson to S.E.

199 *"No matter what part"*: John Carradine to S.E.

200 *"I don't think"*: David Carradine to S.E.

200 *Eddie Quillan:* Interview with Quillan, *Classic Film Collector*, August 1991, John Ford file, MOMA.

200 *Ford caught Frank Darien:* Anderson, p. 220.

201 *"Nunnally was a"*: Dorris Bowdon Johnson to S.E.

204 *"Well, I tell you"*: French, p. 29.

204 *"Ford didn't even"*: Fonda, pp. 129–30.

205 *After forty-three days:* Ford, p. 145.

206 *Even Eleanor Roosevelt:* The *My Day* column is dated 2-23-40, *Grapes of Wrath* file, MOMA.

206 *"If the conditions"*: French, p. 61.

206 *George O'Brien:* Darcy O'Brien to S.E.

207 *"Zanuck has more"*: Custen, p. 231.

207 *"adored the film"*: Elaine Steinbeck to S.E.

207 *"Every image is so moving"*: Quoted in the *New York Times*, 7-1-73, *Grapes of Wrath* file, MOMA.

CHAPTER 13

208   *Cooper's idea:* Bernstein, pp. 170–71.

208   *Wanger was cutting Argosy:* Argosy-Wanger contract, Argosy papers, Box 1, Folder 19, BYU.

208   *Nichols signed his:* Nichols contract, Argosy papers, Box 5, Folder 15, BYU.

209   *"I was still under":* John Wayne to S.E.

209   *Wayne was worried:* Roberts and Olson, p. 183.

209   *"He told me everything":* Mildred Natwick oral history, SMU.

210   *A visitor to the set:* Lewis Jacobs, "Watching Ford Go By," undated *New York Times* clipping, *Long Voyage Home* file, MOMA.

210   *"As an administrator":* John Wayne to S.E.

211   *Dudley Nichols was:* Dudley Nichols to Ford, Box 1, Folder 25, Lilly.

212   *Ford and O'Neill:* Sarris, *You Ain't Heard,* p. 194.

212   *He attempted to:* "The Long Voyage Home as Seen and Painted by Nine American Artists," *American Artist,* September 1946, Dan Ford collection.

212   *"a stark and tough-fibered":* Bosley Crowther review, 10-9-40, *Long Voyage Home* file, MOMA.

213   *Eugene O'Neill was:* O'Neill, p. 508.

213   *A few weeks later:* Carlotta O'Neill to Ford, 7-29-40, Box 1, Folder 23, Lilly. There was a coincidental connection between the two men, in that Mary Ford's brother Wingate had attended Princeton at the same time as O'Neill. "A damned fine guy, as I remember him," wrote O'Neill, "which I must confess is vaguely because Princeton was so long ago, and I never got beyond freshman year, due to a slight argument with the Dean over the liquor problem." (O'Neill to Ford, 12-12-40, Box 1, Folder 25, Lilly.)

213   *"From all I've heard":* O'Neill, p. 522.

213   *a financial flop:* Bernstein, p. 440.

213   *Cooper told Wanger:* Box 1, Folder 19, Argosy papers, BYU.

214   *Ford wrote out:* Box 1, Folder 24, Lilly.

214   *"What do you think":* Lefty Hough interview, Box 12, Folder 6, Lilly.

215   *Ford intervened:* Mix, pp. 40–42.

215   *beautiful infinity of grays:* It should be noted that the currently available transfers of *Tobacco Road* used for cassette and cable showings are pale approximations of the film's visual qualities when seen in an original nitrate print.

215   *"John of course hadn't":* Nunnally Johnson interview, Box 12, Folder 8, Lilly.

215   *"He was much too":* Johnson, p. 113.

217   *"the tailor business":* Behlmer, p. 43.

217   *"I had made films":* Roddy McDowall to S.E.

218   *Shortly afterward, Wyler:* The best background for *How Green* is contained in Philip Dunne's essay "No Fence Around Time," in the *How Green Was My Valley* screenplay, published by Santa Teresa Press in 1990. The script files at UCLA are also instructive.

218   *"It was as nearly":* Untitled manuscript, Box 1, Folder 52, Lilly.

218   *Lee promptly devised:* Anna Lee to S.E.

218   *his multiple eccentricities:* "Whispering anything on the set would set him off," said Lee. "He had the most uncanny sense of hearing. You could be a hundred yards away, and if you said something, he'd turn around and snap, 'Boniface, be quiet.' And you never knew if you were playing a leading part or nothing at all, because you wouldn't see a script until you got to location.

Arthur Shields once turned down a part and never worked for him again."
(Lee to S.E.)

219 *she would characterize:* Maureen O'Hara to S.E.
219 *he lined up the cast:* George Mitchell, *"How Green Was My Valley*, A Verdant
 Classic," *American Cinematographer*, September 1991, p. 37.
219 *"the director I liked":* Higham, *Hollywood*, p. 147.
219 *Ford circled the sentence:* John Ford to Zanuck, 7-18-41, Box 1, Folder 27, Lilly.
220 *One day she complained:* Server, p. 106.
220 *Anna Lee noted that:* Anna Lee oral history, SMU.
221 *"Ford never cut in":* McGilligan, *Backstory*, p. 160.
221 *"There were extraordinary":* Davis, p. 159.
221 *There was one:* Mitchell, *How Green Was My Valley*, p. 38.
221 *"It was the most succinct":* Roddy McDowall to S.E.
222 *"I remember the day":* Roddy McDowall interview, Box 12, Folder 11, Lilly.
222 *"Nonsense. It took me":* Harry Brand, untitled publicity profile on Ford, 9-18-
 41, John Ford file, AMPAS.
223 *"The shining spirit":* Roddy McDowall to S.E.
223 *"had the quality":* Mitchell, *How Green Was My Valley*, p. 40.
223 *"When the postman":* Server, p. 104.
223 *"Willy was* not": Philip Dunne letter to S.E., 5-24-91.
223 *For years Ford:* Anna Lee to S.E.
224 *"Many ornate and official":* Welles and Bogdanovich, *This Is Orson Welles*, p. 27.
224 *"Sentiment is Jack's vice":* Welles and Bogdanovich, *This Is Orson Welles*, p. 27.
224 *"We went to a movie":* Mitchell, *How Green Was My Valley*, p. 34.
224 *"There was something":* Crouch, pp. 270, 288.
225 "Cape San Lucas": John Ford to Captain Zacharias, 12-39 (?), Box 1, Folder
 21, Lilly.
226 *Ford ended up:* Philip Dunne interview, Box 11, Folder 25, Lilly.
226 *Since Renoir's English:* Renoir, *My Life . . .* , p. 193.
226 *On September 9, 1941:* William Donovan to Knox, 9-9-41, Ford Navy file,
 Lilly.
226 *"Colonel Joy has":* Harry Wurtzel to Ford, 9-19-41, Box 1, Folder 27, Lilly.
226 *"Dear Ma":* John Ford to Mary Ford, 9-30-41, Box 1, Folder 27, Lilly.
226 *Ward Bond sent:* Ward Bond to Ford, 11-25-41, Box 1, Folder 29, Lilly.
227 *"Everybody at that table":* Mary Ford to Anthony Slide, Slide archives.
227 *Two weeks after:* Ford naval orders, 12-20-41, Box 1, Folder 29, Lilly.

PART FOUR: AT WAR
CHAPTER 14
231 *"over-age and rich":* Gallagher, p. 202.
231 *Ford wired Merian Cooper:* Cooper papers, Box 4, File 2, BYU.
231 *this wire from Ford:* Cooper papers, Box 4, File 2, BYU.
232 *Ford offered him:* William Clothier to S.E.
232 *Marguerite took this personally:* Darcy O'Brien to S.E.
232 *"He would be of great value":* John Ford to Mittelstadt, 11-20-40, Box 1, Folder
 24, Lilly.
233 *the men in Ford's unit:* William Stull, "Hollywood's Own Film Unit Volunteers to Film the Navy," *American Cinematographer*, October 1941, p. 466.
233 *enrollment was 50 percent:* Ford to Cooper, 3-19-41, Cooper papers, Box 4,
 File 2, BYU.

233   "*he was too old*": Michael Wayne to Leonard Maltin, Maltin archives.

233   "*Such heroism shall not*": Roberts and Olson, p. 211.

233   *Every once in a while*: Roberts and Olson, p. 243.

234   "*He was rather small*": Fitch, p. 83.

235   *West Pointers called*: Fitch, p. 85.

235   "*an exercise in improvisation*": Fitch, p. 97.

235   *She lost a good deal*: Louella Parsons, Los Angeles *Herald Examiner* story dated 6-20-42, John Ford file, USC Department of Special Collections.

235   "*Honey, it was swell hearing*": John Ford to Mary Ford, 10-2-41, Box 1, Folder 28, Lilly.

235   "*Keep Ma happy*": John Ford to Barbara Ford, 10-2-41, Box 1, Folder 28, Lilly.

235   *Helen Hayes came*: Davis, p. 166.

236   "*He didn't sleep at night*": Sinclair, p. 110.

236   " *'My gawd' you'd never recognize it*": John Ford to Mary Ford, Box 1, Folder 31, Lilly.

236   *Ford remembered that*: Untitled manuscript, Box 1, Folder 52, Lilly.

236   "*His enjoyment was crossing*": Armistead interview, Box 11, Folder 15, Lilly.

236   "*I thought I was joining*": Robert Moreno to S.E.

237   *official carte blanche*: William Donovan to Ford, 5-12-42, Box 1, Folder 31, Lilly. As proof of Ford's comprehensive enthusiasm for his overall assignment, in 1942 he directed the governments's official anti–venereal disease training film, *Sex Hygiene*. Ford shot the rather well-lit (the cameraman was George Barnes) framing story, but not, presumably, the actual VD footage, which is, as William K. Everson described it, "hard-core medical . . . there aren't even any strains of 'Red River Valley' over the close-ups of diseased genitals." It's about a crew of clean-cut kids in an Army canteen—Robert Lowery and George "Superman" Reeves among them. One announces he's going into town for some fun. The others, who must have already seen the film, shake their heads and settle down for a nice, clean game of pool. As the bad boy leaves for town, the eight-ball rolls into an ominous close-up. When next we see our renegade friend, he is walking down a stairway and buckling his belt. The action switches to a lecture hall where an instructor shows detailed medical footage that scares the living hell out of the audience, both within the film and without. Propaganda completed, the instructor delivers his final word on the subject: "If you do go out with a girl in occupied territory, be prepared for the fact that she probably has VD"—the shot cuts to an ominously lit close-up—"and in fact almost certainly will have!"

    "I threw up when I saw it," Ford claimed in later years, although his attitude toward any of his films was that of the patriarch of a large, unruly family—it was all right for him to criticize them, but God help anybody else who ventured a negative opinion. Once, at a seminar at UCLA, a professor made some slighting remarks about his reactions when he saw it as a soldier. "Did it help you?" inquired Ford. "Yes," replied the abashed academic. (George Mitchell, "Ford on Ford," *Films in Review*, June/July 1964.)

237   "*My equipment had*": Herman, p. 248.

238   *At one point*: Jack MacKenzie Jr., as told to Alvin Wyckoff, "Fighting Cameraman," *American Cinematographer*, February 1944, p. 44.

238   *Ford was shooting*: "Director Wounded as He Makes His Greatest Pic Aided by Hollywood Boy," *Hollywood Reporter*, 6-18-42.

239   *"It was a merry"*: Mackenzie, "Fighting Cameraman."

239   *Ford made his way:* Medical report, Box 1, Folder 32, Lilly.

239   *"From that historic moment"*: Ambrose, pp. 182–83. I have also utilized Ambrose for the overall background of the Midway battle.

239   *A bulletin marked:* Message to William Donovan, 6-15-42, Box 1, Folder 32, Lilly.

240   *There was, he believed:* Louella Parsons, "John Ford Hit by Shrapnel in Midway Raid," 7-19-42, John Ford file, AMPAS.

240   *"He wouldn't let"*: Robert Parrish to S.E.

241   *"It is not possible"*: A. J. Bolton to Ford, 11-2-42, Lilly.

242   *"Can't I ever"*: Gussow, p. 108.

242   *Between November 16:* Memo from James S. Simmerman, 7-8-43, Lilly.

242   *But by the time:* John Ford to Roosevelt, 3-20-43, Box 1, Folder 35, Lilly.

242   *"We had a beautiful"*: Ford, p. 183. A few months after Mary's letter, Francis Ford quixotically enlisted in the Home Guard. He was over sixty, but, with the help of some hair dye, managed to get past the induction ceremony. He came by to say goodbye to Mary, and apologized that he couldn't flash any World War I medals on his new uniform because "I was too old to get in the service at the time." His ruse was discovered when he tried to cash a pension check for veterans of the Spanish-American War. (Francis Ford Jr. to S.E.)

242   *his letters to Mary:* John Ford to Mary Ford, 1-10-42, Box 1, Folder 30, 6-43 and 7-26-43, Box 1, Folder 36, Lilly.

243   *Ford also took:* John Ford to William Wellman, undated, Box 1, Folder 34, Lilly.

243   *"I ran* The Informer": John Ford to Dudley Nichols, 3-22-43, Box 1, Folder 35, Lilly.

244   *"It started out"*: Mary Ford to Anthony Slide, Slide archives.

244   *"Mary is always"*: A. J. Bolton to Ford, 11-2-42, Lilly.

244   *"Hold your hat"*: Mary Ford to Ford, 1-24-44, Box 1, Folder 40, Lilly.

245   *"a complete motion picture"*: Frank Knox to William Donovan, undated but 1-42, Lilly.

246   *important people:* Quoted in William T. Murphy, "John Ford and the Wartime Documentary," *Film and History*, February 1976.

246   *"The best general"*: James McGuinness to Ford, 3-24-43, Box 1, Folder 35, Lilly.

247   *"Wear them with honor"*: John Ford to Gregg Toland, 9-16-44, Lilly.

247   *"Mr. Goldwyn"*: John Ford to Gregg Toland, 9-29-44, Lilly.

247   *he wrote a letter to:* Ford letter, 12-6-46, Box 1, Folder 52, Lilly.

247   *The* New York Times: quoted in Murphy, "John Ford and the Wartime Documentary."

248   *"The impact is quick"*: quoted in *BFI Index to Films of John Ford.*

CHAPTER 15

249   *From January to August:* Ford, p. 178.

249   *"inspires real devotion"*: William Donovan to Admiral Harold Train, 4-27-43, Lilly.

249   *In early December:* Ford, pp. 188–89.

249   *"We all feel"*: Frank Wead letter, Box 1, Folder 35, Lilly.

250   *"I know the old"*: John Ford to Harry Wurtzel, 6-22-43, Box 1, Folder 36, Lilly.

250   *Ford reacted with:* John Ford to Fred Totman, 8-18-43, Box 1, Folder 38, Lilly.

251   *"everything is awfully":* Fred Totman to Ford, 8-23-43, Box 1, Folder 38, Lilly.

251   *"Katie Hep is at":* John Ford to Meta Sterne, 8-26-43, Box 1, Folder 38, Lilly.

251   *"As for the picture":* John Ford to Bing Crosby, 2-1-44, Box 1, Folder 40, Lilly. The reference is to Hepburn's memorably awful performance in the grotesque *Dragon Seed*.

251   *"This is quite":* John Ford to Mary Ford, 5-42, Box 1, Folder 36, Lilly.

252   *"Please give my":* John Ford to Captain Gendreau, 4-3-43, Box 1, Folder 36, Lilly.

252   *His method of:* Robert Moreno to S.E.

252   *"crusty, but not mean":* George Hjorth to S.E.

252   *"We are stunned":* John Ford to George Meehan, 2-2-44, Box 1, Folder 40, Lilly.

253   *"The Japs are a lot":* John Ford to Frank Wead, 2-11-44, Box 1, Folder 40, Lilly.

253   *"Have been working":* John Ford to Ollie Carey, 9-18-44, Box 1, Folder 39, Lilly.

253   *After a stretch:* Carey, pp. 75–78.

254   *"I told him":* Robert Moreno to S.E.

254   *Mark Armistead had:* Ford, p. 194.

254   *"All Ford told me":* George Hjorth to S.E.

255   *The last thing:* Ford, p. 195.

255   *The two men became:* Ford, p. 197.

255   *never heard any:* Dan Ford to S.E.

255   *Ford wrote Mary:* John Ford to Mary Ford, 6-8-44, Box 1, Folder 42, Lilly.

255   *George Stevens remembered:* George Stevens to Kevin Brownlow, recounted in Brownlow letter to S.E.

255   *he went off on a major:* Robert Moreno to S.E.

256   *a pillar of America's:* Wedemeyer interview, Box 12, Folder 18, Lilly. In June 1964, Wedemeyer wrote Ford a hilariously loopy letter in which he brooded about Robert Taft not getting the 1952 Republican nomination, thus depriving Douglas MacArthur of the vice presidency and, undoubtedly, the presidency. The letter devolves into a manic Strangeloveian rant about the dangers threatening the republic from all sides, among them left-wingers in the State Department, Fabian Socialists, eggheads, and long-haired do-gooders, "the Commies, the internationalists, the Anglophiles, the Francophiles, and the Zionists . . ."

256   *"This was John Ford's":* Mark Armistead interview, Box 11, Folder 15, Lilly.

257   *"I might see you":* John Ford to James Basevi, 9-12-44, Box 1, Folder 43, Lilly. William Goetz, the son-in-law of Louis B. Mayer, was running Fox while Zanuck was away at war. After Zanuck returned and Goetz was unable to accept being a mere producer, he formed International Pictures, which later merged with Universal.

257   *"This picture":* James Forrestal to Cheston, 9-12-44, Box 1, Folder 43, Lilly.

257   *Ford wrote a memo:* John Ford to Chief of Navy Personnel, 9-20-44, Lilly.

258   *"My militaristic ego":* John Ford to General Albert Wedemeyer, 10-30-44, Box 1, Folder 44, Lilly.

259   *he received a cable:* Francis Ford to John Ford, 3-12-45, Box 1, Folder 45, Lilly.

259   *He still delighted:* Donald Curtis oral history, SMU.

259   *But Reed was:* Fultz, pp. 68–69.

259 *Montgomery was seized:* Anderson, p. 226.
260 *Ford was making:* Anderson, p. 228.
261 *He wrote a painfully:* John Ford to "John," 3-23-45, Lilly.
261 *"I have won":* John Ford to Alan Kirk, 9-28-48, Box 2, Folder 8, Lilly.
262 *"Personnel of his":* Officer's Fitness Report, 9-28-45, Lilly.
263 *"It was as if":* Sinclair, p. 127.
263 *When it was all:* Price Waterhouse audit, 4-23-48, Box 2, Folder 6, Lilly.
264 *it was quite rural:* James Wilkinson to S.E.
264 *"The men would stand":* Ford, p. 209.
264 *For the Christmas:* Carey, pp. 82–83.
264 *"In a sense":* Ken Curtis interview, Box 11, Folder 22, Lilly.
265 *"I think you should":* Robert Parrish to S.E.
265 *Ford's home movies:* provided by Dan Ford.
266 *"Ford would come around":* Pat Grissom to S.E.
266 *Under the ten-picture deal:* 11-5-45, John Ford file, Fox legal files, UCLA.
267 *Zanuck then dangled:* Gussow, p. 121.
267 *Ford reported to Zanuck:* Ford to Zanuck, 11-1-45, Box 1, Folder 46, Lilly.

PART FIVE: THE PERILS OF INDEPENDENCE
CHAPTER 16

271 *He was six feet tall:* Physical information from Navy physical dated 10-10-41, Lilly.
271 *He wore blue dress shirts:* Carey, pp. 19, 41.
271 *Ford's manner and style:* There was another ritual enacted after the picture was completed: the actor would go to his office to thank him for the job. Ford, all noblesse oblige, would be very pleasant. Then he would tell the actor to stop by his secretary's desk and pick out a batch of 11 x 14 matte stills featuring that actor. (Carey, p. 71.)
271 *"The first take":* Ruth Clifford to Anthony Slide, Slide archives.
271 *"There was always":* Frank Baker to Anthony Slide and Robert Gitt, Slide archives.
272 *"He would come in":* Andrew McLaglen to S.E.
272 *"He shot all his own":* William Wellman Jr. to S.E.
272 *"If anyone else":* Davis, p. 80.
272 *Ford was a very lonely:* Carey, p. 178.
272 *"He was always very nice":* Well, not always. Primping drove him to distraction, as Loretta Young found out on *Four Men and a Prayer.* She wouldn't come out of her trailer until her hair and makeup were absolutely perfect. After waiting for what Ford regarded as an unconscionable length of time, he finally enlisted the help of a couple of grips and began violently rocking her trailer back and forth until she came out. (John Gallagher, "Claire Trevor," *Films in Review,* November 1983, p. 539.)
273 *"You could be a pretty good":* Zinnemann, p. 110.
273 *"The settings he chose":* *Action,* November/December 1973, AMPAS.
273 *"You can change a cue":* Mitry, in Sarris, *Interviews with Film Directors,* p. 198.
274 *"I think John Ford":* Froug, p. 240.
275 *"He saw things":* Winston Miller oral history, SMU. Ford kept looking until he finally found a place for the scene a half-dozen years later in *The Sun Shines Bright.*
275 *"They were always":* Stephen Longstreet to S.E.

276 *"I like a story"*: Untitled 1946 manuscript, Box 1, Folder 52, Lilly.
276 *being on a streetcar*: Anderson, p. 241.
277 *"Inside, he was one of the most"*: Ruth Clifford to Anthony Slide, Slide archives.
277 *When Ruth Clifford*: Ruth Clifford to Anthony Slide, Slide archives.
278 *in the masculine manner*: Thomas Wood, "Sly Device Man," manuscript in John Ford file, AMPAS.
278 *"Papa was not"*: first part of quote, Davis, p. 199; second part, Davis, p. 224.
278 *Ford loved dogs*: Dan Ford to S.E.
279 *"She had the patience"*: Patrick Wayne to S.E.
279 *"Mary was wonderful"*: Kathleen O'Malley to S.E.
279 *"They genuinely liked"*: Dan Ford to S.E.
280 *"He was a Navy man"*: Robert Stephens to S.E.
280 *For fiction*: Dan Ford to S.E.
280 *Although his good friend*: Brian Desmond Hurst, unpublished autobiography, Chapter 4, Anthony Slide archives.
281 *in 1946*: Dudley Nichols letter, Box 12, Folder 21, Lilly.
281 *His son Tom*: Harry Carey Jr. to S.E.
282 *"He wasn't much"*: Patrick Ford to James D'Arc, BYU.
282 *"I eat, sleep and drink"*: Howard Sharpe, "The Star Creators of Hollywood," *Photoplay*, October 1936.
282 *"He kept to the studio"*: Andre de Toth to S.E.
282 *"Eddie was a mean"*: Wingate Smith interview, Box 12, Folder 15, Lilly.
283 *"He didn't drive"*: Andre de Toth to S.E.
284 *"All these people"*: Andrew McLaglen to S.E.
284 *He stayed in touch*: "Your expression of respect for me moved me deeply," wrote Libby after a New Year's greeting from Ford. "I likewise have great respect for you, John, especially for the lofty standards upheld by you in your cinema productions. I feel that you are accomplishing on a vastly wider scale much the same thing that I have all my life striven, less effectively, to accomplish in the narrow confines of the schoolroom." (Lucien Libby to Ford, 1-18-50, Box 2, Folder 13, Lilly.)
284 *"Mary was very beautiful"*: Mary McPhillips to S.E.
284 *"We exchanged books"*: John Ford interview, Box 11, Folder 29, Lilly.
285 *Capra's son Tom*: Tom Capra to S.E.
285 *"I'd call it"*: William Wellman Jr. to S.E.
285 *"nobody gave a damn"*: Joe Hyams to S.E.
285 *"I remember getting"*: Dan Ford to S.E.
285 *"until he would"*: Davis, p. 80.
286 *"The first time"*: Marilyn Carey to S.E.
286 *Ford and Smith*: Ace Holmes interview, Box 12, Folder 5, Lilly.
286 *Dru and Barbara*: Joanne Dru interview, Box 11, Folder 24, Lilly.
286 *"Mary was a good wife"*: Mary Lou Whitney to S.E.

CHAPTER 17
288 *The cost of the picture*: Deal memo, Argosy papers, Box 14, Folder 57, BYU.
289 *a 1939 film*: Wyatt Earp comes to Tombstone. After being beaten up by a group of tinhorns including John Carradine, Joe Sawyer, and Lon Chaney Jr., he takes the marshal job. He strikes up a friendship with Doc Halliday, "the coldest killer in these parts," as Cesar Romero, for the first and last time in his career, grimly dominates a saloon. Halliday's girlfriend, a pious nurse

named Sarah, tracks him down and convinces him to abandon the sleazy dance hall girl played by Binnie Barnes. "John, isn't it more thrilling to give life than to take it away?" Sarah says. Halliday successfully operates on a wounded child and is considering a return to his medical career when he's mowed down by the bad guys, motivating Earp to wipe them out at the O.K. Corral. Good girl Nancy Kelly stays in town, and bad girl Binnie Barnes leaves town, the stagecoach passing by Halliday's grave on Boot Hill.

290   *"When there'd be"*: James Stewart oral history, SMU.

291   *Zanuck added:* In notes in the script files, *My Darling Clementine*, UCLA.

291   *Among Ford's enthusiasms:* Ford to Zanuck, 1-2-46, Box 1, Folder 48, Lilly.

291   *"Ford was discussing"*: Winston Miller to John Gallagher.

291   *As Miller remembered:* Lyons, p. 143.

292   *Ford and Miller:* Davis, p. 189.

292   *"I am writing"*: Ford to Capra, 3-29-46, Box 1, Folder 50, Lilly.

293   *Grant Withers:* John Ireland oral history, SMU.

293   *"Can't you even"*: Kennedy, p. 60.

293   *The expected patsy:* Roger Fristoe, "The Original Hunk," *Louisville Courier-Journal Sunday Magazine*, 7-29-84.

294   *He cut a lot:* Lyons, p. 9.

294   *"You have in the film"*: Behlmer, pp. 103–5.

295   *"he didn't like"*: Lindsay Anderson to S.E.

295   *"I have this theory"*: Roddy McDowall to S.E.

295   *Bosley Crowther:* quoted in Lyons, p. 153.

CHAPTER 18

297   *"It was sure"*: Merian Cooper to Bagnall, 5-30-46, Argosy papers, Box 3, Folder 78, BYU.

297   *the $143,000 deficit:* Donald Dewar to Ford-Cooper, Argosy papers, Box 3, Folder 78, BYU.

298   *Ford was sitting:* Wills, pp. 117–18.

298   *After the service:* Robert Parrish to S.E.

299   *Argosy bought the rights:* Contract, Argosy papers, Box 1, Folder 11, BYU.

299   *reasonable supply of properties:* The Argosy story files are at BYU.

300   *half his salary:* The details of Nichols's contract are contained in the Argosy papers, Box 1, Folder 14 and Folder 16, BYU.

300   *"In all honesty"*: Dudley Nichols to Ford, 10-31-46, Box 1, Folder 51, Lilly.

300   *"The following photoplay"*: Nichols's script is in the Argosy papers, Box 13, Folder 13, BYU.

302   *The budget was set:* Norman Freeman to Argosy Productions, 7-29-47, Argosy papers, Box 1, Folder 30, BYU.

303   *"the most embarrassing"*: Steen, pp. 35–36.

303   *Ford had to rely:* Virginia Lee Warren, "Movie Pioneering in Mexico," *New York Times*, 2-16-47; Frank Nugent, "Hollywood Invades Mexico," *New York Times*, 3-23-47.

303   *"The point was made to me"*: Donald Dewar to S.E.

304   *Ford received a fan letter:* Anderson, p. 14; Ford's reply is contained on p. 15.

305   *Ford did a radio: Here's Hollywood*, undated, but probably 4-6-48, Box 14, Folder 23, BYU.

305   *Agee explained that:* Quoted in Sarris, *John Ford*, p. 120.

305   *Ford was asked:* Undated, unsourced clipping in *7 Women* file at MOMA.

SOURCE NOTES · 577

306 *it's a violation:* "I have never been able to bring myself to see the film," wrote Graham Greene, "as it was a total travesty of my book, perhaps due to Ford's Irish type of Catholicism. The illegitimate child was given to the police officer instead of to the priest!" (Gallagher, p. 234.)

306 *"It came out":* Bogdanovich, p. 85.

306 *"We were very close":* Mitchell, "Ford on Ford."

306 *"a mistaken film":* Anderson, p. 15.

306 *"started us off":* Donald Dewar to S.E.

307 *they ended up:* Frank Wead contract, Argosy papers, Box 3, Folder 73, BYU.

307 *Bellah had been:* Wills, p. 165.

308 *"My father was":* Davis, p. 204.

309 *"I think my father":* Davis, p. 204.

309 *A preliminary budget:* in the Universal collection, USC.

310 *it was a wretched:* RKO *Fort Apache* contract, 9-17-47, Argosy papers, Box 1, Folder 33, BYU.

310 *"I sent you":* Merian Cooper to Ford, 8-6-47, Box 2, Folder 3, Lilly.

310 *"There were so many":* Donald Dewar to S.E.

311 *Backstories for all the:* "Character Bio Notes," Argosy papers, Box 4, Folder 25, BYU.

311 *Attention was paid:* Although Ford, in an entirely uncharacteristic burst of masochism, would later claim to feelings of guilt for his screen treatment of Indians, it's hard to see those feelings, if they existed, as justified. *Stagecoach* uses Indians only as a deus ex machina, while the Indians of *Fort Apache* and *She Wore a Yellow Ribbon* are honorable men. Scar, the motivating force of *The Searchers,* is a worthy opponent for Ethan Edwards, and is no more savage than his white counterpart.

312 *"I see him standing":* Prater, pp. 26–27.

312 *"Frank would do":* Donald Dewar to S.E.

313 *a title contest amongst:* "Fort Apache Title Contest," Argosy papers, Box 8, Folder 30, BYU.

313 *All the other members:* Carey, p. 57.

313 *"Archie was a guy":* William Clothier to S.E.

313 *"When I was working":* Tim Hunter, "A Man's Cameraman," *On Film* 1.

314 *"He got into a beef":* William Clothier to S.E.

314 *"There was no":* Francis Ford Jr. to S.E.

314 *the actor had been:* Darcy O'Brien to S.E.

315 *"George was worshipful":* Darcy O'Brien to S.E.

316 *another brief fistfight:* George Turner, "Dust and Danger at Fort Apache," *American Cinematographer,* June 1996, pp. 106–10.

316 *"ate him alive":* Gil Perkins to S.E.

316 *"I always thought":* John Agar to S.E.

316 *Michael Wayne:* Roberts and Olson, p. 295.

317 *Longstreet's notes:* Shared with S.E.

318 *"If Ford recognizes me":* Gil Perkins to S.E.

318 *"They were shooting":* Andrew McLaglen to S.E.

318 *"The first four or five days":* Fonda, p. 176.

319 *proper military dress:* While Thursday considers his men to be a motley, sloppily turned out crew, they probably look better in the movie than they did in reality. One observer, Eben Swift, saw the Fifth Cavalry in the field in 1876 and described them as having "untrimmed, scraggly beards, clothes roughly

patched with canvas, gunny sacks, or anything at hand; hats of buffalo skin or none at all; footwear of rags."

There are several, undoubtedly intentional, variations from history in the picture; the soldiers are working with Springfield carbines, a single-shot weapon that was notoriously unreliable in the field. By the time the story takes place, the soldiers would have been working with Spencer carbines or Winchester 73s. Likewise, Ford habitually pictures his soldiers working with uniform head gear and awkward sabers, when in actuality the most likely spot for swords would have been hanging on a wall. These changes were undoubtedly for reasons of dashing style, while Ford's alteration of the Apache penchant for night or early morning attacks was for reasons of movie practicality.

319 *Henry Fonda's stiff walk:* Wills, p. 21.

320 *"Duty was something":* Crouch, p. 271.

320 *"It's good for the country":* Bogdanovich, p. 86.

320 *the ending of* Fort Apache: Geoffrey O'Brien, "John Ford, Superstar," *Village Voice*, 10-21-86, p. 42, John Ford file, MOMA.

321 *"I think it is":* Walter Wanger to Merian Cooper, 3-22-48, Argosy papers, BYU.

CHAPTER 19

322 *Mighty Joe Young:* Financing information can be found in the Argosy papers, Box 7, Folder 2, and Box 14, Folder 28, BYU.

322 *"It didn't lose money":* Donald Dewar to S.E.

324 *"[Making Westerns] gives me":* Burt Kennedy, "Our Way West," *Films and Filming*, October 1969, p. 30.

324 *the deal memo: 3 Godfathers* agreement, Argosy papers, Box 15, Folder 18, BYU.

326 *"He'd hang pots":* Ben Johnson oral history, SMU.

326 *Dobe could not recall a single day:* Carey, pp. 22–23.

326 *"Why didn't you do that":* Carey, pp. 38–40.

327 *"The directors of that era":* Samuel Goldwyn Jr. to S.E.

327 *"You knew you were":* Harry Carey to S.E.

327 *"The rest of us":* Davis, *Duke*, p. 136.

328 *"What are you doing":* Davis, p. 221.

328 *administer a reciprocal:* Cecile de Prita interview, Box 11, Folder 23, Lilly.

328 *"John and Mary Ford":* Louella Parsons, 8-18-48, John Ford file, *Los Angeles Examiner* files, USC Department of Special Collections.

328 *"She iced it out":* Dan Ford to S.E.

328 *He finally turned:* Fagen, p. 42.

329 *"Here is what I see":* James Pepper Collection.

329 *a Remington canvas:* "It was more Charlie Russell than Remington," Ford would say at the end of his life. "Wardrobe, mostly. Faces." Another, usually uncredited influence was the artist Charles Schreyvogel. "My father kept a copy of a collection by Schreyvogel close by his bedside," said Pat Ford. "He pored over it dreaming up action sequences for his films." (Prater, p. 9.)

331 *In his hand:* Undated notes on yellow paper, Argosy papers, Box 5, Folder 19, Lilly.

331 *The payroll: Yellow Ribbon* budget, Box 10, Folder 13, BYU.

332 *"He liked to watch me ride":* Ben Johnson oral history, SMU.

333   *The first two days: Yellow Ribbon* shooting schedule, Argosy papers, Box 10, Folder 22, BYU.

333   *Hoch noticed:* Winton Hoch interview, Box 12, Folder 3, Lilly.

333   *Mildred Natwick remembered:* Mildred Natwick oral history, SMU.

334   *"On location":* John Agar to S.E.

335   *"The electrical storm":* John Agar to S.E.

335   *He had looked:* Carey, p. 67.

335   *"Jack Ford called":* William Wellman Jr. to S.E.

335   *"He never thought":* Bogdanovich, "The Duke's Gone West," *New York*, 6-25-79.

336   *Ziffren had a talk:* Lester Ziffren to S.E.

336   What Price Glory: Much of the background for this section derives from the scrapbooks of Larry Blake, kindly shared by his son Michael.

337   *"The kicker":* Pat O'Brien to S.E.

337   *"I played one":* Gregory Peck to S.E.

338   *rowdy, crowd-pleasing:* "Filmland Stars Do G.I. Benefit," *Los Angeles Times*, 2-27-49.

339   *"I don't think":* Gregory Peck to S.E.

339   *According to accounting:* Statement of proceeds, Box 2, Folder 9, Lilly.

339   *"My father would":* Michael Blake to S.E.

339   *"He hated":* Kazan, p. 374.

339   *"I fought with":* Behlmer, p. 214.

340   *"The stuff":* Philip Dunne interview, Box 11, Folder 25, Lilly.

340   *broke down completely:* Carey, p. 87.

340   *"He used to always say":* Bea Benjamin interview, Box 11, Folder 17, Lilly.

340   *"Being Jewish":* Sinclair, p. 56.

340   *"The real regulars":* Sinclair, p. 56.

340   *when he died:* Paul Wurtzel to S.E.

340   *continued paying percentages:* Lester Ziffren to S.E.

CHAPTER 20

341   *he arrived back: Variety*, 5-26-49.

341   *"I want the talented one":* Mary Loos to S.E.

341   *"this is a novel":* Dan Dailey oral history, SMU.

342   *Ford's contract stated:* Ford contract, 9-23-49, Argosy papers, Box 16, Folder 6, BYU.

342   *Argosy's money problems: Wagon Master* basic agreement, Argosy papers, Box 1, Folder 35, BYU.

342   *"I don't do that":* Kathleen O'Malley to S.E.

343   *"You boys are":* Carey, p. 88.

343   *"the greatest faces":* Pat Ford to James D'Arc, BYU.

344   *"Dear Goldie":* Carey, p. 88.

345   *Ford's westerns are:* I am indebted to Bertrand Tavernier's discussion of these points in Lloyd, pp. 29–33.

346   *"One night":* Pat Ford to James D'Arc, BYU.

346   *"Quite frankly":* Merian Cooper to Mayer, Argosy papers, BYU.

347   *"Fort Apache became":* Lee Van Hoozer to Doering, 5-3-51, Argosy papers, BYU.

348   *"The last game":* Michael Wayne to Leonard Maltin, Maltin archives.

348 *Republic's films:* McCarthy and Flynn, pp. 25–30.

348 *The Argosy-Republic contract:* Contract, Argosy papers, BYU.

349 *the Republic deal:* Argosy contract abstract, J. E. Baker to Herbert Yates, 10-16-51, Leonard Maltin archives.

349 *"I am very anxious":* Merian Cooper to Ned Depinet, Argosy papers, BYU.

349 *Ford's* Rio Grande: Republic Summary of Foreign Income—*Rio Grande*, Leonard Maltin archives.

350 *"His genius was":* Sinclair, p. 162.

350 *Ford began drinking:* Ford, p. 236.

350 *"Too many hours":* Davis, p. 247.

350 *Ole Doering wired:* Argosy papers, BYU. Eighteen months after the sale, RKO reissued *Fort Apache*, undoubtedly earning returns commensurate with the reissues of other major RKO pictures—*Gunga Din* ($455,000) or *Tall in the Saddle* ($279,000)—i.e., coming close to retiring Argosy's debt.

CHAPTER 21

352 *"One more word":* "Un-American Activities Committee, re Congressional Investigation—Correspondence and Memoranda," Mabel Willebrandt to Ford, 10-11-47, DGA Archives, Box 8, California State University at Northridge.

352 *the opening day:* Schwartz.

353 *On October 21:* Board of directors meeting, 10-21-47, DGA Archives, Box 8, Cal-State Northridge.

355 *"I don't know":* Sinclair, p. 157.

355 *the director Mark Robson:* George Stevens to Kevin Brownlow, Brownlow archives.

355 *He refused to hire:* Wilcoxon, p. 199.

356 *A 1950 press release:* Box 2, Folder 16, Lilly.

356 *"The bottom line":* Robert Wise to S.E.

356 *the compulsory loyalty oath:* "I am not a member of the Communist party or affiliated with such a party, and I do not believe in and I am not a member of nor do I support any organization that believes in or teaches the overthrow of the United States Government by force or by any illegal or unconstitutional method."

357 *As the DeMille faction:* "Recall of Joseph L. Mankiewicz—John Huston et al. vs. Screen Director's Guild of America", DGA Archives, Box 8, Cal-State Northridge.

357 *"The petition had to be":* Parrish, p. 206.

358 *"We scoured the fleshpots":* Parrish, p. 207.

359 *"DeMille didn't have any":* Richard Fleischer to S.E.

360 *"DeMille was a very":* Robert Wise to S.E.

362 *"As the waves":* Parrish, pp. 209–10.

362 *"those things that":* Andre de Toth to S.E.

363 *"it was sort of":* George Stevens to Kevin Brownlow, Brownlow archives.

363 *"Ford drove the nail":* Vincent Sherman to S.E.

363 *"He was the kingpin":* Robert Wise to S.E.

364 *"Thank you for":* Davis, p. 246.

364 *"Send the Commie":* Gallagher, p. 340.

364 *"One of the truly":* Cooper papers, Joseph McCarthy correspondence file, BYU.

364 *"for all that you did"*: Richard Nixon to Ford, 3-28-53, Box 2, Folder 32, Lilly.

364 *"Ward had all the gall"*: John Wayne interview, Box 12, Folder 17, Lilly.

364 *"He had the power"*: Vincent Sherman to S.E.

365 *"A close friend"*: Lester Ziffren to S.E.

366 *"I was terribly"*: Frank Capra to Ford, 12-19-51, and Ford's undated response are both in Box 2, Folder 21, Lilly.

366 *"wouldn't meet that guy"*: John Ford interview, Box 11, Folder 14, Lilly.

367 *"In this world"*: Schwartz, p. 63.

368 *"Ford was interested"*: Claude Jarman Jr. to S.E.

370 *"It was that kind"*: Michael Wayne to Leonard Maltin, Maltin archives.

370 *"He thought they"*: Pat Ford to James D'Arc, BYU.

370 *the other stuntmen:* Paul Wurtzel to S.E.

371 *"If the man can"*: Roberson, p. 160.

371 *"[Ford] took extra"*: Roberson, p. 74.

371 *"He didn't work"*: Claude Jarman Jr. to S.E.

372 *The negative cost:* Republic statement of income and costs, Maltin archives.

372 *"He was the best"*: Budd Boetticher to S.E.

373 *"do whatever he wanted"*: The document, dated November 11, 1950, is preserved in the Ford archives. "Dear Mr. Ford," it reads, "I would greatly appreciate it if you would find the time to help Duke, Dick Van Enger and me with the cutting and scoring of *Torero*. I am in perfect accord with you in the belief that I have become too close to the picture." (Box 2, Folder 16, Lilly.)

374 *"He'd send the kids"*: Peter Steen, "He Couldn't Forget My Eyes," *Parade*, 6-2-91, p. 5.

374 *"We will wander"*: McNee, p. 26.

376 *"A blacksmith taking off"*: undated, unsigned script notes, *The Quiet Man* files, Lilly.

377 *"They didn't come"*: Ernest Day to S.E.

378 *"I had been around"*: Andrew McLaglen to S.E.

378 *"Ford wanted access"*: Andrew McLaglen oral history, SMU.

378 *"He would get"*: Harry Carey Jr. to S.E.

378 *"Ford had respect"*: Davis, p. 250.

378 *"Ford saw himself"*: Roberts and Olson, p. 324.

379 *"Ford was a tough"*: Alf McCreary, "The Quiet Man's Ireland," *British Heritage*, August/September 1997.

379 *"If the weather"*: Ernest Day to S.E.

380 *"I think we"*: Ernest Day to S.E.

380 *"constantly had problems"*: McNee, p. 77.

380 *"The first thing I"*: Patrick Wayne to S.E.

380 *"It's like that old joke"*: Michael Wayne to Leonard Maltin, Maltin archives.

381 *"We learned very fast"*: Toni La Cava to Leonard Maltin, Maltin archives.

381 *"He knew the picture"*: Andrew McLaglen oral history, SMU.

381 *Ford turned to the:* Davis, p. 252.

382 *"He had some personal trouble"*: John Wayne interview, Box 12, Folder 17, Lilly.

382 *"The old man's"*: Andrew McLaglen oral history, SMU.

384 *"After the first take"*: Andrew McLaglen to S.E.

385 *"I was so mad"*: Stephanie Mansfield, "The Unretiring Maureen O'Hara," *Washington Post*, 12-17-96.

385 *First, there was a fight:* Box 2, Folder 20, Lilly.

386 *an exile's dream: The Quiet Man*'s simplicity of story and depth of character were even adapted into a Broadway musical. *Donnybrook!* starred Art Lund and Joan Fagen, with Eddie Foy Jr. in the Barry Fitzgerald part, and opened at the 46th Street Theater in New York on May 18, 1961. The music and lyrics were by Johnny Burke, and it was designed by Rouben Ter-Arutenian and directed by the great choreographer Jack Cole. It ran only sixty-eight performances.

387 *"I apologize"*: McNee, p. 119.

CHAPTER 22

388 *"We do not want"*: Herbert Yates to Jack Baker, October 25, 1951, Maltin archives.

388 *Writing from Paris:* Darryl F. Zanuck story memos, 8-22 and 8-23-51, in script files for *What Price Glory,* UCLA.

389 *"I would rather go overboard"*: Zanuck memos.

389 *"Ford was a very tough"*: Robert Wagner to S.E.

389 *"That was King Baggot"*: Davis, p. 256.

389 *"The camera was"*: Robert Wagner to S.E.

390 *Experiencing Ford:* McGilligan, *Cagney,* p. 272.

390 *"That was my racket"*: Bogdanovich, p. 88.

390 *"Our picture was"*: Gussow, p. 162.

391 *"Our experience"*: Lee Van Hoozer to Herbert Yates, 7-8-52, Maltin archives.

391 *"Your letter"*: Herbert Yates to Lee Van Hoozer, 7-21-52, Maltin archives.

391 *Argosy's shareholders:* Argosy–Republic legal correspondence, BYU.

392 *"Oscars aren't the end-all"*: Bill Libby, "The Old Wrangler Rides Again," *Cosmopolitan,* March 1964.

392 *But by the time:* From documents in the Maltin archives.

392 *marriage of Barbara: Los Angeles Herald Examiner* clipping dated 6-1-52, John Ford file, AMPAS.

392 *"Pat was a talented"*: Dan Ford to S.E.

395 *The critics were brutal:* From reviews in *The Sun Shines Bright* file at MOMA.

395 *"I never saw"*: Bogdanovich, p. 141.

396 *"To begin with"*: Schary, p. 260.

396 *"He was this"*: Donald Sinden to S.E.

396 *"Have you ever heard"*: John Ford to Barbara Ford Curtis, undated, Dan Ford collection.

397 *Ford introduced:* Lacey, p. 128.

398 *For a love scene:* Tornabene, p. 342.

399 *"Having acrimonious"*: McNee, p. 133.

399 *"Jack's philosophy"*: McNee, p. 132.

399 *"John was a"*: Freddie Young to S.E.

400 *gnawing compulsively:* Anderson, p. 27.

401 *"I know you will"*: Davis, p. 263.

401 *"My eyes are"*: Davis, p. 263.

401 *The house had been:* Gallagher, p. 346.

401 *"Your letter received"*: Davis, p. 264. The antipathy toward Huston extended through other members of the Ford stock company. John Wayne loathed him, and once told the author that he believed Huston's father, Walter, was more responsible for *The Maltese Falcon* and *The Treasure of the Sierra Madre* than his son.

401 *Merian Cooper wired:* Merian Cooper to Ford, 2-23-52, Box 2, Folder 27, Lilly.
402 *signed a petition:* Box 2, Folder 31, Lilly.
402 *Ford was on the short list:* Shipman, p. 309.
402 *"[in] the end":* Lindsay Anderson to Ford, 11-6-53, Box 2, Folder 31, Lilly.
402 *"a joke":* Truffaut, p. 22.
402 *"I would have":* Insdorf, p. 36.
402 *"There was no jealousy":* Francis Ford Jr. to S.E.
403 *"Frank had an":* McNee, p. 134.
403 *"We gave Frank":* Gallagher, p. 243.

PART SIX: A LION IN WINTER
CHAPTER 23

407 *"Harry [Cohn] didn't bother him":* Paul Lazarus Jr. to S.E.
407 *"I hated it":* Bogdanovich, p. 92.
407 *"Ford always had me":* Betsy Palmer to S.E.
408 *"It was humid":* Patrick Wayne to S.E.
408 *"Take some lilacs":* Carey, p. 139.
408 *"Ford loved to wear":* Peter Graves to S.E.
409 *"Frankly, Harry":* John Ford to Harry Cohn, 1-55, Box 2, Folder 36, Lilly.
410 *"a dream come true":* Henry Fonda to Ford, 4-5-54, Box 2, Folder 33, Lilly.
410 *"Almost from the first evening":* Jean Nugent to S.E.
411 *"Admiral Ford tore":* Coghlan, p. 236.
411 *"He got carried away":* Jack Lemmon to S.E.
412 *"The whole gang":* Peter Fonda to S.E.
412 *"We were staying":* Jack Lemmon to S.E.
413 *one or two takes:* The film's daily production reports are in Box 6, Folder 14, Lilly.
413 *"I don't know":* Fonda, p. 234.
413 *"I only remember":* Jack Lemmon to S.E.
413 *"I did it for a lark":* McGilligan, *Cagney,* p. 225.
413 *"the most pathetic man":* McGilligan, *Cagney,* p. 271.
413 *"I told you":* Carey, p. 148.
413 *"He was great":* Jack Lemmon to S.E.
414 *"I was very naive":* Betsy Palmer to S.E.
414 *uncircumcised:* Dan Ford to S.E.
415 *"Mervyn did a good job":* Jack Lemmon to S.E.
415 *Although Ford shot for six weeks:* I am indebted to Stuart Galbraith IV, curator of the Warner Bros. collection at USC, for investigating the specifics of Ford's contribution to *Mister Roberts.*
416 "Mister Roberts *did me in":* Loy, p. 276.
416 *"son of a bitch":* Charlton Heston to S.E.
416 *"God knows I want":* John Ford to Wayne, 12-7-55, Box 2, Folder 38, Lilly.
417 *"There is a Hollywood taboo":* Ford's need to portray himself as the patron saint of lost causes could lead him into outright fabrications. *Drums Along the Mohawk* cost about $1.4 million and returned $2.2 million in domestic rentals to Fox, making it profitable without even taking any foreign earnings into account. It was the studio's second highest grossing picture of the year, after *The Rains Came.* (Aubrey Solomon, "Twentieth Century Fox: A Corporate and Financial History.")

CHAPTER 24

419   *"Jock was a great"*: Peter Duchin to S.E.

419   *"I still live"*: Mary Lou Whitney to S.E.

419   *"My husband just"*: Mary Lou Whitney to S.E.

419   *"He wasn't mean"*: John Agar to S.E.

420   *"Actors are whores"*: Robert Wagner to S.E.

420   *"We are busy"*: Davis, p. 271.

420   *"My husband worked"*: Jean Nugent to S.E.

420   *"When I looked"*: Carey, p. 170.

421   *While on location:* At the risk of ruining a perfectly good anecdote, it should be noted that neither Pat Wayne nor Harry Carey Jr. remembers anybody being stung by a scorpion.

421   *"He could have"*: Mary Lou Whitney to S.E.

421   *"He had to spend a lot"*: Patrick Ford to James D'Arc, BYU.

422   *"He was crazy"*: Patrick Wayne to S.E.

422   *Ford picked up three:* Merian Cooper, undoubtedly with Ford's acquiescence, hired Max Steiner to do the music, the first score he had done for Ford since *Mary of Scotland*. Although Steiner was virtually the father of film music, he had been having difficulty since leaving Warner Bros. in 1953, getting less money for less prestigious pictures, as both public and private taste turned to a sparer, jazzier style of music exemplified by composers like Alex North and Elmer Bernstein. Steiner used a number of traditional ballads in his score, as well as coping with a title song by Stan Jones. It seems that Ford gave some thought to using more vocals throughout the picture as storytelling devices, as with *High Noon;* additional verses of the title song survive in Steiner's files at BYU, with very specific weather and plot references that would indicate placement later in the picture. Ford must have thought better of the idea, and used the vocals only at the beginning and end. In any case, it seems Ford was not pleased by Steiner's work. Although Ford's taste in film music was not beyond criticism—he persisted in hiring the ordinary Richard Hageman for years—Steiner's music does seem to have been written for a heavier, more standardized film than *The Searchers.* The result was that Ford felt forced into more involvement in post-production dubbing than was usually the case. In a December 1955 letter, C. V. Whitney wrote a placating note to Steiner after what he termed several successful previews. "I am sorry you are not altogether satisfied with the musical score as cut, but I can assure you that the end result is typically American. . . . For my part, I understand your criticisms. I understand, however, that the mood of reality in the picture is furthered by Mr. Ford's cuts. I am very happy with the end result." (C. V. Whitney to Max Steiner, 12-9-55, Steiner Collection, Box 4, Folder 1, BYU.)

423   *"the way in which"*: David Thomson, "Open and Shut," *Film Comment,* June/ July 1997, p. 31.

423   *In the script:* Frank Nugent's script is in the Merian Cooper papers, BYU.

424   *In touching Debbie:* The moment stands in stark contrast to the ending of Hawks's otherwise splendid *Red River,* as Joanne Dru more or less wags her finger at two homicidal men, tells them to stop fighting, and they do. Both films center on the intolerance and rigidity of the characters played by John Wayne, but Ford is a rigorous enough artist to understand that these feelings have to be resolved internally, not externally.

424   *"That fucking door"*: Lindsay Anderson to S.E.

424 *"a handsome film"*: In Anderson's 1993 BBC documentary on Ford.

425 *"Do I contradict myself"*: I'm indebted to Charles Silver's writing for much of this argument.

426 *The critics liked it:* Quoted in Stuart Byron, "The Searchers: Cult Movie of the New Hollywood," *New York*, 3-5-79, John Ford file, MOMA.

427 *"I can understand"*: Box 11, Folder 34, Lilly.

427 *"Pat was in charge"*: Andrew McLaglen to S.E.

CHAPTER 25

428 *"We can't offer"*: John Ford to Katharine Hepburn, 9-54, Box 2, Folder 34, Lilly.

428 *"By using Ty"*: John Ford to Michael Killanin, 2-6-56, Box 2, Folder 39, Lilly.

429 *"It was a very happy"*: Eileen Crowe to Anthony Slide, Slide archives.

429 *"Ford was looking"*: Anderson, p. 229.

429 *"The first two"*: Rudi Fehr to S.E.

430 *a three-picture deal:* Box 2, Folder 41, Lilly.

430 *He was able to help:* Box 2, Folder 40, Lilly.

430 *The picture was:* Davis, *Duke*, p. 209.

431 *"I didn't want"*: Bogdanovich, p. 96.

431 *"I didn't intend it"*: Bogdanovich, p. 96.

431 *"First, I want to"*: John Ford to John Wayne, 12-26-56, Box 2, Folder 42, Lilly.

432 *"Is the picture"*: John Ford to John Wayne, 1-17-57, Box 2, Folder 43, Lilly.

432 *"an eccentric antique"*: Sarris, *You Ain't Heard*, p. 205.

432 *"One thing I want"*: Ken Adam to S.E.

433 "Gideon *was not*": Freddie Young to S.E.

434 *"He gave the impression"*: Anderson, p. 137.

434 *"Eisenstein was"*: Anderson, p. 139.

435 *"Mary darling"*: John Ford to Mary Ford, 9-2-57, Box 2, Folder 46, Lilly.

435 *"He is a terribly"*: John Ford to John Wayne, 11-4-57, Box 2, Folder 46, Lilly.

435 *Spencer had warned:* Selden West to S.E.

436 *"got a little prickly"*: Pat O'Brien to S.E.

437 *Anna Lee said:* Gallagher, p. 367.

437 *"I don't want"*: Gallagher, pp. 367–68.

438 *"You're gonna be using"*: Joe Longo to S.E.

440 *"First I would like"*: Heran Moon to Ford, 6-14-59, Box 3, Folder 6, Lilly.

440 *"All my love"*: Heran Moon to Ford, 6-29-59, Box 3, Folder 6, Lilly.

440 *"I've had Asiatic"*: Davis, p. 295.

440 *"Who's that talking"*: Paul Lazarus Jr. to S.E.

441 *"His wit was"*: Patrick Wayne to S.E.

441 *"If you think"*: William Clothier to S.E.

442 *All of Gibson's:* Mark Haggard to S.E.

442 *"I went and"*: Anna Lee to S.E.

442 *"Strother was just"*: Denver Pyle to S.E.

443 *"It had been a"*: William Wellman Jr. to S.E.

445 *"Fred hadn't done"*: William Wellman Jr. to S.E.

445 *"One thing about"*: Roberson, p. 167.

445 *death drained:* This view is held by Burt Kennedy, among others.

445 *Martin Rackin estimated:* Mark Haggard to S.E.

445 *John Lee Mahin panicked:* McGilligan, *Backstory*, p. 264.

446 *the Old Man:* Roberson, p. 245.

CHAPTER 26

448   *"If anything ever"*: Anna Lee to S.E.

448   *One Sunday morning*: Darcy O'Brien to S.E.

450   *Goldbeck took the idea:* Anderson, pp. 174–75.

450   *"He had always been"*: Ford, p. 284.

450   *"They aren't tough"*: Strode, p. 199.

451   *"John Ford played"*: Ken Mate, "Woody Strode's Odyssey," *L. A. Weekly*, April 30–May 6, 1982, p. 19.

451   *"Sometimes I would"*: Strode, p. 201.

452   *"a complete gentleman"*: Rafer Johnson to S.E.

452   *"was a classic"*: Charlayne Hunter, "Woody Strode? He Wasn't a Star but He Stole the Movie," *New York Times*, 9-19-71, p. D-5.

453   *"I can make"*: Mate, "Woody Strode's Odyssey."

453   *"I would talk"*: Rafer Johnson to S.E.

454   *His grandson Dan:* Ford, p. 286.

454   *"Wayne had been"*: Jean Michel Frodon, "Richard Widmark, Sheep in Wolf's Clothing," *Guardian Weekly*, 7-16-95, p. 13.

454   *Widmark's part was:* Burt Kennedy to S.E.

454   *"It was a mentor"*: Patrick Wayne to S.E.

455   *"Ford went out"*: William Clothier to S.E.

455   *"He'd shoot scenes"*: Denver Pyle to S.E.

455   *"For any important"*: Frankie Avalon to S.E. Also attesting to Ford's extensive contribution to *The Alamo* was Richard Widmark in the Frodon *Guardian* interview.

455   *Wayne wrote Ford:* Davis, *Duke*, p. 228.

456   *"I was playing"*: Gil Perkins to S.E.

456   *"The most important"*: Clark and Andersen, p. 109.

457   *"The Colter Craven Story"*: Broadcast 11-23-60.

458   *"The worst piece"*: Ford, p. 290.

458   *Quanah Parker:* A mark of the film's indifference is that it throws away the story of Quanah Parker, a real-life character Ford would have carefully sketched in years earlier. Parker was the son of a Comanche chief and a white captive named Cynthia Ann Parker. In 1874, in what seems to have been an attempt to start a large-scale uprising, Parker led a mixed band of Comanche and Kiowa in an abortive attack on some buffalo hunters at Adobe Walls. In 1875, he surrendered at Fort Sill, Oklahoma, and lived until 1911 in a comfortable house in southwestern Oklahoma, surrounded by a harem of young Indian girls.

458   *"You'd see flashes"*: Anderson, p. 214.

458   *"It was being written"*: Shirley Jones to S.E.

458   *saw him mouth:* Harry Carey Jr. to S.E.

459   *"A lotta directors"*: Peter Bogdanovich, "The Autumn of John Ford," *Esquire*, April 1968.

459   *"The set wasn't"*: James Stewart interview, Box 12, Folder 16, Lilly.

459   *Flashing Spikes:* Despite the presence in the cast of Stewart, Jack Warden, Pat Wayne, and a walk-on by one "Michael Morrison" as a Marine sergeant, "Flashing Spikes" is as uninteresting as Ford's similar 1955 TV show on a baseball theme, "Rookie of the Year." In "Flashing Spikes," a ballplayer is accused of throwing a game because he's associated with an old player who was banned years before. The theme is reasonably Fordian, as is the cast, but

the writing and much of the acting is flat and tone-deaf, while the physical production, despite the presence of William Clothier behind the camera, is disappointingly drab, indivisible from the standard TV production of the early 1960s.

459   *"You could hardly hear"*: Dewey, p. 411.
459   *"I don't think"*: Dewey, p. 410.
460   *"Ford was gone"*: Shirley Jones to S.E.
460   *"Goldie, you're the"*: Wills, p. 124.
460   *After several weeks:* Ford, pp. 290–91.
460   *"Beggars can't be"*: Lindsay Anderson to S.E.
460   *Cooper dangled:* Merian Cooper to Ford, undated, Cooper papers, Box 22, Folder 73, BYU.
461   *"Ford looked ten years"*: Strode, p. 216.
461   *Ford had become:* Strode, p. 218.
461   *"It's very hard"*: Mitchell, "Ford on Ford."
462   *"He expounded on it"*: Paul Lazarus Jr. to S. E.
462   *Each man got:* Box 3, Folder 11, Lilly.
462   *"[Ford] still had life"*: Howard W. Koch to S.E.
463   *"For a change"*: Davis, *Duke*, p. 240.
463   *"Jimmy, you are"*: Lee Marvin interview, Box 12, Folder 12, Lilly.
463   *"He was like"*: Denver Pyle to S.E.
463   *"He came from"*: Anderson, p. 235.
464   *"He'd go behind"*: Hal Nesbitt to S.E.
464   *"Socially, you never"*: William Clothier to S.E.
464   *"I didn't like"*: William Clothier to S.E.
465   *declining energies:* Pat Ford would discuss his father's increasing disinterest, pointing to a train scene in *Sergeant Rutledge*, where Ford didn't even bother to have a railroad car set mounted on rockers to give a sense of motion, didn't bother to throw any dust around. "He just didn't have the energy," said Dan Ford.
465   *"When we realize"*: Andrew Sarris, "Cactus Rosebud," *Film Culture* 25, Summer 1962, p. 14.
467   *Wayne had successfully:* Fagen, p. 146.
467   *Bernard Smith had:* Bernard Smith to S.E.
468   *Lee told him:* Anna Lee to S.E.
468   *As Paramount was:* Box 3, Folder 15, Lilly.
469   *"Ford was pretty"*: Cesar Romero to S.E.
469   *During one scene:* Tim Stafford to S.E.
469   *One day she:* Lamour, p. 202.
470   *Lamour exploded:* Lamour, p. 202.
470   *"It was no damn good"*: William Clothier to S.E.
471   *"He never should"*: John Wayne to S.E.
471   *"That film has"*: Kelly, p. 280.
471   *"What kind of uniform"*: Bernard Smith to S.E.
471   *"His bedroom had"*: Denver Pyle to S.E.
473   *Pat wrote his father:* Pat Ford to John Ford, 4-24-63, Box 3, Folder 18, Lilly.
473   *"I'm not working"*: John Ford to Pat Ford, April 1963, Box 3, Folder 18, Lilly.
474   *"He wanted to come"*: Dan Ford to S.E.
475   *"a picture that has"*: Ford, p. 297.
475   *Some of Ford's:* Box 7, Folder 26, Lilly.

475   *"I like Indians":* Bogdanovich, "The Autumn of John Ford."

476   *he didn't like the script:* Selden West to S.E.

476   *he noticed that:* George O'Brien interview, Box 12, Folder 13, Lilly.

477   *"I never knew":* Carey, p. 194.

477   *"He was very":* Peter Bogdanovich to S.E.

477   *"Clothes lay everywhere":* Peter Bogdanovich, "The Autumn of John Ford."

478   *"The next morning":* William Clothier to S.E.

478   *Jack's mood declined:* Ford, p. 301.

479   *"Some son of a bitch":* Burt Kennedy to S.E.

479   *"He was a":* Karl Malden to S.E.

480   *"On Cheyenne Autumn":* William Clothier to S.E.

480   *"I think your":* John Ford to Peter Bogdanovich, 12-6-63, Box 3, Folder 19, Lilly.

480   *William Clothier's ongoing:* William Clothier to S.E.

481   *"That situation was":* Ben Johnson oral history, SMU.

481   *"He was a gentleman":* Pat Ford to James D'Arc, BYU.

483   *"Screened film this":* Bernard Smith to John Ford, 10-5-64, Box 3, Folder 22, Lilly.

483   "Cheyenne Autumn *was":* Bernard Smith to S.E.

484   *"cinema of reminiscence":* Sarris, *John Ford,* pp. 158–59.

484   *The motion was promptly:* Sarris, *John Ford,* p. 160.

484   *"Every time I make a Western":* Bill Libby, "The Old Wrangler Rides Again."

CHAPTER 27

486   *the largest single sum:* Krause, Vol. 4, p. 350.

486   *"several scenes were":* Krause, Vol. 4, pp. 338, 341.

486   *"I said":* Rod Taylor to S.E.

487   *"a magical opportunity":* Anne Coates to S.E.

487   *"He just got":* Rod Taylor to S.E.

488   *"He stepped, or rather":* Anderson, p. 232.

488   *"a very ill man":* Julie Christie letter to S.E.

489   *Ford called to cameraman:* Bob Allen, soundman on *Young Cassidy,* to S.E.

490   *"They said all the good":* Anne Coates to S.E. According to Coates and Bob Allen, Ford shot the opening of the picture, the fight in the pub, the very convincing love scene between Rod Taylor and Julie Christie, and the sequences of Cassidy's mother's death and funeral. The scenes with Michael Redgrave as Yeats are Cardiff's.

490   *directing is no job:* In more than one hundred years of cinema, the only exceptions are Buñuel, Huston, and Kurosawa, who all made great films in their seventies.

490   *He looked terrible:* Ford, p. 306.

491   *"I love that":* Davis, *Duke,* p. 259.

491   *"I was terribly worried":* Rod Taylor to S.E.

492   *he "resented the fact":* Bernard Smith to S.E.

492   *"At my age":* Peter Bart, "Ford's Ladies Vehicle," *New York Times,* 1-31-65.

492   *"The vaults were":* William K. Everson to S.E.

493   *"rather like knowing":* Everson, *Films in Review,* December 1974, p. 600.

493   *"The politics of the American":* Patrick McGilligan, "Journey into Light," *Film Comment,* March/April 1992, p. 12.

493   *"I should tell you":* Ford, pp. 308–9.

494 *"I know her every"*: Bernard Smith to Ford, Box 3, Folder 22, Lilly.
494 *"You're not taking"*: Eddie Albert to S.E.
494 *"He'd come in"*: Anna Lee oral history, SMU.
494 *"I remember thinking"*: Alex Beaton to S.E.
495 *"Because he was such"*: Eddie Albert to S.E.
495 *"Things started to go wrong"*: Bernard Smith to S.E.
495 *"I couldn't get her"*: John Ford interview, Box 12, Folder 2, Lilly.
496 *not even bothering:* Elmer Bernstein to S.E.
496 *"Kate Hepburn would"*: Peter Bogdanovich to S.E.
496 *"He wanted to retire"*: Bernard Smith to S.E.

CHAPTER 28

497 *"Wayne spent the last"*: Burt Kennedy to S.E.
497 *Ford had amassed:* Ford, p. 313.
497 *"It was about"*: Bob Stephens to S.E.
499 *Ford lurched off the plane:* Bertrand Tavernier, "Notes of a Press Attaché," *Film Comment*, July/August 1994.
501 *"I had such admiration"*: Samuel Goldwyn Jr. to S.E.
502 *"Look at* Rio Lobo": Andrew McLaglen to S.E.
503 *Ford bought two:* Box 3, Folder 27, Lilly.
503 *"Don't read this"*: James Pepper collection.
503 *"filled with inaccuracies"*: John Ford to Morton, 9-12-69, Box 3, Folder 29, Lilly.
503 *One of Dan's friends:* Dan Ford to S.E.
503 *"Jack's response"*: Dan Ford to S.E.
503 *Ford came to Bob Stephens:* Bob Stephens to S.E.
504 *"She wanted something"*: Barry Goldwater Jr. to S.E.
505 *"He was completely"*: A. C. Lyles to S.E.
506 *"The original idea"*: Bruce Herschensohn to S.E.
507 *"as though God"*: from "A Meeting with John Ford," an unpublished manuscript by Bruce Herschensohn, printed with his permission.
508 *"It was November"*: Dan Ford to S.E.
509 *He showed me:* Bruce Herschensohn to S.E.
509 *"He would make"*: Dan Ford to S.E.
509 *"What's the war"*: John Ford to Johnston, 5-21-69, Box 3, Folder 28, Lilly.
510 *"Look at that"*: James Bacon, "When Ford Directs, He's the Star," *Los Angeles Herald Examiner*, 11-25-71, John Ford file, AMPAS.
510 *"He wasn't bitter"*: Burt Kennedy to S.E.
510 *"once a year"*: Craig Moderno, "Sam Fuller Tribute," *DGA Magazine*, December/January 1997/1998, p. 94.
510 *"You have access"*: Mark Haggard to S.E.
510 *"You never know"*: Bogdanovich, p. 91.
512 *he ended up dumping it:* Gallagher, p. 453.
512 *"He didn't care"*: Bea Benjamin interview, Box 11, Folder 17, Lilly.
512 *Ford had made:* Box 9, Folder 41, Lilly.
512 *"The only reason"*: John Ford to Strode, 5-12-70, Box 3, Folder 30, Lilly.
512 *Vidor was deep:* Kevin Brownlow to S.E.
513 *Ford magisterially ignored:* Around this time, another young acolyte conned his way into Ford's house. Gesturing toward his Remington prints, Ford told the kid "When you understand what makes a great Western painting, you'll

be a great Western director." His parting shot: "And never spend your own money to make a movie. Now get the hell out of here." Good advice, learned from bitter experience, carefully heeded by Steven Spielberg. ("I Want Gross," *Forbes*, 9-26-94, p. 104.)

513 *"You're probably"*: Mark Haggard, "Ford in Person," *Focus on Film*, Spring 1971, p. 36.

514 *"They ask me"*: Larry Swindell, "Yes, John Ford Knew a Thing or Two About Art," *Philadelphia Inquirer*, 9-16-73, John Ford file, MOMA.

514 *"You'll need someone"*: Anna Lee to S.E.

514 *It was 3:00*: Seymour Cassel to Paul Lomartire, courtesy of Lomartire.

514 *Ford was antagonistic*: Kevin Brownlow shared his notes from an interview with Jenkinson, and David Shepard showed me the complete interview at USC.

516 *Ford began receiving letters*: Katharine Hepburn to John Ford, 9-10-70, 10-8-70, 6-24-73, Lilly.

516 *In October*: Dan Ford to S.E.

517 *"I drove in from Fallbrook"*: John Ford to Capra, 1-4-71, Capra archives, Wesleyan University.

518 *Without missing a beat*: Dan Ford to S.E.

518 *"He is improving"*: Davis, p. 337.

518 *"Then let it go"*: Maurice Zolotow, "The American West of John Ford," *TV Guide*, 12-4-71, John Ford file, AMPAS.

518 *"John Ford called me"*: Ben Johnson interview, *Boxoffice*, 8-4-75, Ben Johnson file, AMPAS.

519 *"I don't remember him"*: Peter Bogdanovich to S.E.

519 *"He recommended"*: Dan Ford to S.E.

519 *Jack, Mary, and Barbara*: Ford, p. 315.

519 *"We loved every inch"*: Mary Ford to Anthony Slide, Slide archives.

519 *"He was a very kindly"*: Mark Haggard to S.E.

520 *"He liked Barbara"*: Lindsay Anderson to S.E.

520 *"Barbara was totally sick"*: Denver Pyle to S.E.

520 *"Barbara would call"*: Andrew McLaglen to S.E.

520 *"Dear, sweet Barbara"*: Pamela Marvin to S.E.

521 *"We never talked"*: Budd Boetticher to S.E.

521 *"Jesus Christ"*: Peter Bogdanovich to S.E.

522 *Mostly he used*: Tim Ford to S.E.

522 *"There are some"*: Steen, p. 64.

523 *"I'm an old man"*: John Ford interview, Box 11, Folder 12, Lilly.

523 *"appointed six guys"*: Charlton Heston to S.E.

524 *"He got really mad:"* Dan Ford to S.E.

524 *"He made a huge"*: Charlton Heston to S.E.

524 *"It was at that point"*: Dan Ford to S.E.

525 *The lights were*: Karen Winner, "A Classic Ford," *Women's Wear Daily*, 4-5-73, John Ford file, MOMA.

525 *awarded him the Presidential*: The commendation reads: "In the annals of American film, no name shines more brightly than that of John Ford. Director and filmmaker for more than a half a century, he stands preeminent in his craft—not only as a creator of individual films of surpassing excellence, but as a master among those who transformed the early motion pictures into a compelling new art form that developed in America and swept the world.

As an interpreter of the nation's heritage, he left his personal stamp indelibly printed on the consciousness of whole generations both here and abroad. In his life and in his work, John Ford represents the best in American films and the best in America."

526 *"Admiral Ford is"*: Frank Baker to Anthony Slide, Slide archives.

526 *"George was so"*: Brian Desmond Hurst, unpublished autobiography, Chapter 4, Slide archives.

526 *"It was a hard"*: Stephen Longstreet letter to S.E.

527 *"Hello Lindsay!"*: Anderson, p. 187.

527 *"like a college boy"*: Bogdanovich, p. 110.

527 *Ford began asking*: Dan Ford to S.E.

528 *He died at*: Ford seems never to have legally changed his name; Pat Ford's birth certificate lists his father's name as John Feeney, and Ford's death certificate lists his name as John Ford, aka Feeney.

EPILOGUE

529 *"It was the vision"*: Rod Taylor to S.E.

531 *Andrew Sarris called*: Sarris, *Village Voice*, 9-13-73, John Ford file, MOMA.

531 *"What I like most"*: Fellini, *Action*, 11-12-73, John Ford file, AMPAS.

532 *In Ford's will*: Last Will and Testament of John A. Feeney, dated 3-31-73, Box 3, Folder 31, Lilly.

532 *"There were some years"*: Dan Ford to S.E.

532 *At the time of his death*: Box 3, Folder 36, Lilly.

532 *"To me, he was"*: Mary Ford to Anthony Slide, Slide archives.

533 *In the four years left*: Darcy O'Brien to S.E.

534 *"It was Ford's impassioned"*: This passage combines material from Anderson, pp. 193, 205.

534 *In 1979, Stuart Byron*: Byron, "The Searchers: Cult Movie of the New Hollywood," *New York*, 3-5-79, John Ford file, MOMA.

535 *"Ford was a mass of"*: Samuel Goldwyn Jr. to S.E.

535 *"Ridgway wore hand"*: Winston Miller oral history, SMU.

535 *Burt Kennedy believed*: Burt Kennedy to S.E.

535 *"It was a facade for sure"*: Rod Taylor to S.E.

535 *"He was a tough"*: Bob Stephens to S.E.

536 *"That is exactly"*: Billy Yellow to S.E.

537 *Michael Wayne was asked*: Michael Wayne to Leonard Maltin, Maltin archives.

537 *"He had an eye"*: William Wellman Jr. to S.E.

537 *Darryl Zanuck believed*: Gussow, pp. 163–64.

BIBLIOGRAPHY

Ambrose, Stephen E. *American Heritage New History of World War II*. New York: Viking, 1997.

Anderson, Lindsay. *About John Ford*. New York: McGraw-Hill, 1981.

Anobile, Richard. *John Ford's Stagecoach*. New York: Darien House, 1975.

Astor, Mary. *A Life on Film*. New York: Delacorte Press, 1971.

Autry, Gene (with Mickey Herskowitz). *Back in the Saddle Again*. New York: Doubleday, 1978.

Bardeche, Maurice, and Robert Brasillach. *The History of Motion Pictures*. New York: Norton, 1938.

Baxter, John. *The Cinema of John Ford*. New York: A. S. Barnes, 1971.

Bazin, Andre. *Bazin at Work*. New York: Routledge, 1997.

Beardsley, Charles. *Hollywood's Master Showman*. New York: Cornwall, 1983.

Behlmer, Rudy. *Memo from Darryl F. Zanuck*. New York: Grove Press, 1993.

Bellamy, Madge. *A Darling of the Twenties*. Vestal: Vestal Press, 1989.

Berg, A. Scott. *Goldwyn*. New York: Knopf, 1989.

Bernstein, Matthew. *Walter Wanger*. Berkeley: University of California, 1994.

Black, Shirley Temple. *Child Star*. New York: McGraw-Hill, 1988.

Bogdanovich, Peter. *John Ford* (second edition). Berkeley: University of California Press, 1978.

Bordwell, David. *On the History of Film Style*. Cambridge: Harvard University Press, 1997.

Bourne, Stephen. *Brief Encounters*. London: Cassel, 1977.

Boyle, Harold. *The Best of Boyle*. Portland: Guy Gannett Publishing, 1980.

Bruskin, David N. *Behind the Three Stooges: The White Brothers*. Los Angeles: Directors Guild of America, 1993.

Buscombe, Edward. *Stagecoach*. London: British Film Institute, 1992.

Buscombe, Edward (ed.). *The BFI Companion to the Western*. New York: Atheneum, 1988.

Cagney, James. *Cagney by Cagney*. Garden City: Doubleday, 1976.

Callow, Simon. *Orson Welles: The Road to Xanadu*. New York: Viking, 1996.

Canutt, Yakima (with Oliver Drake). *Stunt Man*. New York: Walker, 1979.

Carey Jr., Harry. *Company of Heroes*. Metuchen: Scarecrow Press, 1994.

Cary, Diana Serra. *Whatever Happened to Baby Peggy?* New York: St. Martin's, 1996.

Clark, Donald, and Christopher Andersen. *John Wayne's The Alamo*. New York: Citadel Press, 1995.

Clarke, Charles G. (edited by Anthony Slide). *Highlights and Shadows: Memoirs of a Hollywood Cameraman*. Metuchen: Scarecrow Press, 1989.

Coghlan Jr., Frank. *They Still Call Me Junior*. Jefferson: McFarland, 1993.

Corliss, Richard. *Talking Pictures*. Woodstock: Overlook Press, 1974.

Crouch, Stanley. *Always in Pursuit*. New York: Pantheon, 1998.

Custen, George F. *Twentieth Century's Fox: Darryl F. Zanuck and the Culture of Hollywood*. New York: Basic Books, 1997.

Darby, William. *John Ford's Westerns*. Jefferson: McFarland, 1996.

Davis, Ronald L. *Duke: The Life and Image of John Wayne*. Norman: University of Oklahoma Press, 1998.

————. *John Ford: Hollywood's Old Master*. Norman: University of Oklahoma Press, 1995.

DeMille, Cecil B. *Autobiography*. Englewood Cliffs: Prentice-Hall, 1959.

DenDooven, K. C. *Monument Valley: The Story Behind the Scenery*. Las Vegas: K.C. Publications, 1992.

de Toth, Andre. *Fragments*. London: Faber and Faber, 1994.

Deutelbaum, Marshall (ed.). *"Image" on the Art and Evolution of the Film*. New York: Dover, 1979.

Dewey, Donald. *James Stewart*. Atlanta: Turner, 1996.

Dmytryk, Edward. *Odd Man Out*. Carbondale: Southern Illinois University Press, 1996.

Dunne, Philip. *How Green Was My Valley: The Screenplay*. Santa Barbara: Santa Teresa Press, 1990.

Durgnat, Raymond, and Scott Simmon. *King Vidor, American*. Berkeley: University of California Press, 1988.

Eels, George. *Hedda and Louella*. New York: Warner Books, 1973.

Eisenschitz, Bernard. *Nicholas Ray: An American Journey*. London: Faber and Faber, 1993.

Elwell, Edward H. *Portland and Vicinity*. Portland: Greater Portland Landmarks, 1975 (facsimile of 1881 edition).

Eyles, Allen. *John Wayne*. South Brunswick: A. S. Barnes, 1979.

Eyman, Scott. *The Speed of Sound*. New York: Simon & Schuster, 1997.

Fagen, Herb. *Duke: We're Glad We Knew You*. Secaucus: Birch Lane Press, 1996.

Fenin, George N., and William K. Everson. *The Western: From Silents to the Seventies*. New York: Grossman, 1973.

Ferguson, Donald Linton. *Munjoy Hill: Portland's Scenic Peninsula* (privately published).

Fitch, Noel Riley. *Appetite for Life: The Biography of Julia Child*. New York: Doubleday, 1997.

Fonda, Henry (with Howard Teichmann). *Fonda: My Life*. New York: New American Library, 1981.

Ford, Dan. *Pappy: The Life of John Ford*. Englewood Cliffs: Prentice-Hall, 1979.

Fraser, George MacDonald. *The Hollywood History of the World*. New York: William Morrow, 1988.

French, Warren. *Filmguide to The Grapes of Wrath*. Bloomington: Indiana University Press, 1973.

Froug, William. *The Screenwriter Looks at the Screenwriter*. New York: Dell, 1974.

Fultz, Jay. *In Search of Donna Reed*. Iowa City: University of Iowa Press, 1998.

Gallagher, Tag. *John Ford: The Man and His Films*. Berkeley: University of California Press, 1986.

Gehman, Geoff. *Down but Not Quite Out in Hollow-Weird*. Lanham: Scarecrow Press, 1998.

Gray, Peter. *The Irish Famine*. New York: Harry N. Abrams, 1995.

Gussow, Mel. *Don't Say Yes Until I Finish Talking*. Garden City: Doubleday, 1971.

Hardy, Phil. *The Encyclopedia of Western Movies*. Minneapolis: Woodbury Press, 1984.

Hepburn, Katharine. *Me: Stories of My Life*. New York: Knopf, 1991.

Herman, Jan. *A Talent for Trouble*. New York: Putnam, 1995.

Higham, Charles. *Charles Laughton*. Garden City: Doubleday, 1976.

————. *Hollywood Cameramen*. Bloomington: Indiana University Press, 1970.

Holden, Anthony. *Behind the Oscar: The Secret History of the Academy Awards*. New York: Simon & Schuster, 1993.

Insdorf, Annette. *François Truffaut*. Cambridge: Cambridge University Press, 1994.

Jewell, Richard. *A History of RKO Radio Pictures, Incorporated* (unpublished doctoral dissertation, 1978).

Jewell, Richard, with Vernon Harbin. *The RKO Story*. New York: Arlington House, 1982.

Johnson, Nora. *Flashback*. Garden City: Doubleday, 1979.

Kazan, Elia. *A Life*. New York: Knopf, 1988.

Kelly, Mary Pat. *Martin Scorsese: A Journey*. New York: Thunder's Mouth, 1991.

Kennedy, Burt. *Hollywood Trail Boss*. New York: Boulevard, 1997.

Klinck, Richard E. *Land of Room Enough and Time Enough*. Albuquerque: University of New Mexico Press, 1953.

Koszarski, Richard. *An Evening's Entertainment*. New York: Scribner's, 1990.

Krause, David (ed.). *The Letters of Sean O'Casey*. Volume 1, 1910–1941. New York: Macmillan, 1975.

————. *The Letters of Sean O'Casey*. Volume 4, 1959–1964. Washington: Catholic University of America Press, 1992.

Lacey, Robert. *Grace*. New York: Putnam, 1994.

Lamour, Dorothy (with Dick McInnes). *My Side of the Road*. Englewood Cliffs: Prentice-Hall, 1980.

Leaming, Barbara. *Bette Davis*. New York: Simon & Schuster, 1992.

————. *Orson Welles*. New York: Viking, 1985.

Lloyd, Ann. *They Went That-A-Way*. London: Orbis, 1982.

Love, Bessie. *From Hollywood, with Love*. London: Elm Tree Books/Hamish Hamilton, 1977.

Loy, Myrna (with James Kotsilibas-Davis). *Being and Becoming*. New York: Knopf, 1987.

Lyons, Robert (ed.). *My Darling Clementine*. New Brunswick: Rutgers University Press, 1984.

Madsen, Axel. *Stanwyck*. New York: HarperCollins, 1994.

Malden, Karl. *When Do I Start?* New York: Simon & Schuster, 1997.

Mast, Gerald. *Howard Hawks, Storyteller*. New York: Oxford University Press, 1982.

McBride, Joseph. *Frank Capra: The Catastrophe of Success*. New York: Simon & Schuster, 1992.

————. *Hawks on Hawks*. Berkeley: University of California Press, 1982.

McBride, Joseph, and Michael Wilmington. *John Ford*. New York: Da Capo, 1975.

McCarthy, Todd, and Charles Flynn. *Kings of the Bs*. New York: Dutton, 1975.

McGilligan, Patrick. *Backstory*. Berkeley: University of California Press, 1986.

————. *Cagney: The Actor as Auteur*. San Diego: A. S. Barnes, 1982.

————. *George Cukor: A Double Life*. New York: St. Martin's, 1991.

McLaughlin, Dennis. *Wild and Wooly: An Encyclopedia of the Old West*. New York: Doubleday, 1975.

McNee, Gerry. *In the Footsteps of The Quiet Man*. Edinburgh: Mainstream Publishing, 1990.

Meyer, William R. *The Making of the Great Westerns*. New Rochelle: Arlington House, 1979.

Miller, Kerby A. *Emigrants and Exiles: Ireland and the Irish Exodus to North America*. New York: Oxford University Press, 1985.

Miller, Kerby, and Paul Wagner. *Out of Ireland*. Washington: Elliott & Clark, 1994.

Mix, Paul E. *The Life and Legend of Tom Mix*. South Brunswick: A. S. Barnes, 1972.

O'Neill, Eugene (eds. Travis Bogard and Jackson Bryer). *Selected Letters of Eugene O'Neill*. New York: Limelight, 1994.

Parrish, Robert. *Growing Up in Hollywood*. New York: Harcourt Brace Jovanovich, 1976.

Place, J. A. *The Non-Western Films of John Ford*. Secaucus: Citadel Press, 1979.

————. *The Western Films of John Ford*. Secaucus: Citadel Press, 1974.

Pratt, George C. *Spellbound in Darkness*. Greenwich: New York Graphic Society, 1973.

Renoir, Jean. *Letters*. London: Faber & Faber, 1994.

————. *My Life and My Films*. New York: Atheneum, 1974.

Rivkin, Allen, and Laura Kerr. *Hello, Hollywood*. New York: Doubleday, 1962.

Roberson, Chuck. *Fall Guy*. Vancouver: Hancock House, 1980.

Roberts, Randy, and James S. Olson. *John Wayne: American*. New York: Free Press, 1995.

Robinson, Edward G. (with Leonard Spigelgass). *All My Yesterdays*. New York: Hawthorn, 1973.

Rosenberg, Bernard, and Harry Silverstein. *The Real Tinsel*. New York: Macmillan, 1970.

Rosten, Leo C. *Hollywood: The Movie Colony, the Movie Makers*. New York: Harcourt Brace, 1941.

Sargent, Ruth S. *The Casco Bay Islands*. Dover: Arcadia Publishing, 1995.

Sarris, Andrew. *The John Ford Movie Mystery*. Bloomington: Indiana University Press, 1975.

————. *You Ain't Heard Nothin' Yet: The American Talking Film*. New York: Oxford University Press, 1998.

Sarris, Andrew (ed.). *Interviews with Film Directors*. New York: Bobbs-Merrill, 1967.

Schary, Dore. *Heyday*. Boston: Little, Brown, 1979.

Schwartz, Nancy Lynn. *The Hollywood Writers War*. New York: Knopf, 1982.

Selznick, David O. (ed. Rudy Behlmer). *Memo from David O. Selznick*. New York: Viking Press, 1972.

Server, Lee. *Screenwriter*. Pittstown: Main Street Press, 1987.

Seydor, Paul. *Peckinpah: The Western Films*. Urbana: University of Illinois, 1997.

Shipman, David. *Judy Garland: The Secret Life of an American Legend*. New York: St. Martin's, 1992.

Silver, Charles. *The Western Film*. New York: Pyramid, 1976.

Simmons, Garner. *Peckinpah: A Portrait in Montage*. Austin: University of Texas Press, 1982.

Sinclair, Andrew. *John Ford*. New York: Dial, 1979.

Slide, Anthony. *The Cinema and Ireland*. Jefferson: McFarland, 1988.

Solomon, Aubrey. *Twentieth Century-Fox: A Corporate and Financial History*. Metuchen: Scarecrow Press, 1988.

Steen, Mike. *Hollywood Speaks: An Oral History*. New York: Putnam, 1974.

Sterling, Bryan B., and Frances Sterling. *Will Rogers in Hollywood*. New York: Crown, 1984.

Strode, Woody (with Sam Young). *Goal Dust*. New York: Madison Books, 1990.

Swindell, Larry. *Spencer Tracy*. New York: New American Library, 1969.

Thomas, Bob (ed.). *Directors in Action*. Indianapolis: Bobbs-Merrill, 1973.

Thomas, Tony. *Music for the Movies*. South Brunswick: A. S. Barnes, 1973.

Thompson, Frank. *Lost Films*. New York: Citadel Press, 1996.

Thomson, David. *Rosebud: The Story of Orson Welles*. New York: Knopf, 1996.

Tornabene, Lyn. *Long Live the King*. New York: Putnam, 1976.

Truffaut, François. *Correspondence*. New York: Farrar, Straus and Giroux, 1990.

Turner, George (ed.). *The Cinema of Adventure, Romance, and Terror*. Hollywood: ASC Press, 1989.

Tuska, Jon. *The Filming of the West*. Garden City: Doubleday, 1976.

Vidor, King (interviewed by Nancy Dowd and David Shepard). *King Vidor*. Metuchen: Scarecrow Press, 1988.

Wager, Walter. *You Must Remember This*. New York: Putnam, 1975.

Walsh, Raoul. *Each Man in His Time*. New York: Farrar, Straus and Giroux, 1974.

Wayne, Pilar (with Alex Thorleifson). *John Wayne: My Life with the Duke*. New York: McGraw-Hill, 1987.

Welles, Orson, and Peter Bogdanovich. *This Is Orson Welles*. New York: HarperCollins, 1994.

Wilcoxen, Henry (with Katherine Orrison). *Lionheart in Hollywood*. Metuchen: Scarecrow Press, 1991.

Wills, Garry. *John Wayne's America*. New York: Simon & Schuster, 1997.

Wray, Fay. *On the Other Hand*. New York: St. Martin's, 1989.

Yagoda, Ben. *Will Rogers*. New York: Knopf, 1993.

Zinnemann, Fred. *A Life in the Movies*. New York: Scribner's, 1992.

Zolotow, Maurice. *Shooting Star*. New York: Simon and Schuster, 1974.

INDEX

Page numbers in *italics* refer to illustrations.

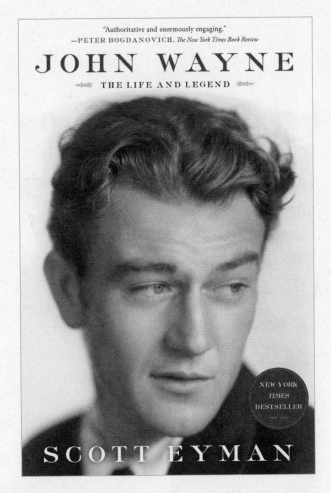